Lecture Notes in Computer Science   9780

Commenced Publication in 1973
Founding and Former Series Editors:
Gerhard Goos, Juris Hartmanis, and Jan van Leeuwen

More information about this series at http://www.springer.com/series/7407

Swarat Chaudhuri · Azadeh Farzan (Eds.)

Computer Aided Verification

28th International Conference, CAV 2016
Toronto, ON, Canada, July 17–23, 2016
Proceedings, Part II

 Springer

Editors
Swarat Chaudhuri
Rice University
Houston, TX
USA

Azadeh Farzan
University of Toronto
Toronto, ON
Canada

ISSN 0302-9743   ISSN 1611-3349 (electronic)
Lecture Notes in Computer Science
ISBN 978-3-319-41539-0   ISBN 978-3-319-41540-6 (eBook)
DOI 10.1007/978-3-319-41540-6

Library of Congress Control Number: 2015943799

LNCS Sublibrary: SL1 – Theoretical Computer Science and General Issues

Printed on acid-free paper

This Springer imprint is published by Springer Nature
The registered company is Springer International Publishing AG Switzerland

Preface

It is our pleasure to welcome you to the proceedings of CAV 2016, the 28th International Conference on Computer-Aided Verification, held in Toronto, Ontario, during July 17–23, 2016.

The CAV conference series is dedicated to the advancement of the theory and practice of computer-aided formal analysis of hardware and software systems. The conference covers the spectrum from theoretical results to concrete applications, with an emphasis on practical verification tools and the algorithms and techniques that are needed for their implementation. CAV considers it vital to continue spurring advances in hardware and software verification while expanding to new domains such as biological systems and computer security.

The CAV 2016 program included four invited keynote talks, four invited tutorials, 58 technical papers (consisting of 46 regular papers and 12 tool papers) accepted out of 195 submissions, and briefings from the SYNTCOMP and SYGUS synthesis competitions. The conference was accompanied by six co-located events: VSTTE (Verified Software: Theories, Tools, and Experiments), NSV (Numerical Software Verification), SYNT (Synthesis), EC^2 (Exploiting Concurrency Efficiently and Correctly), HCCV (High-Consequence Control Verification), and VMW (Verification Mentoring Workshop).

Our invited keynote speakers were Gilles Barthe (IMDEA Software Institute), Gerwin Klein (NICTA and University of New South Wales), and Moshe Vardi (Rice University). Parosh Aziz Abdulla (Uppsala University), Vitaly Chipounov (EPFL), Paulo Tabuada (UCLA), and Martin Vechev (ETH Zurich) gave invited tutorials.

We introduced three significant changes to CAV's review process this year. First, CAV 2016 employed a lightweight double-blind reviewing process. This meant that committee members did not have access to the names and affiliations of the authors as they reviewed a paper, and were able to produce an unbiased initial reivew. However, author names were revealed late in the online discussion process to permit calibration against the authors' prior work. Second, we introduced an External Review Committee, consisting of reviewers committed to producing four to five reviews, and also increased the size of the main Program Committee. These changes significantly reduced the number of papers that a committee had to review. Third, CAV 2016 had a two-phase evaluation process. Each paper received three reviews by the end of the first phase; considering the reviews and accounting for feedback from the reviewers, we solicited up to two additional reviews for papers for which consensus did not exist or further expertise was considered necessary.

Many people worked hard to make CAV 2016 a success. We thank the authors and the invited speakers for providing the excellent technical material, the Program Committee and the External Review Committee for their thorough reviews and the time spent on evaluating all the submissions and discussing them during the online discussion period, and the Steering Committee for their guidance.

We thank Pavol Černý, Sponsorship Chair, for helping to bring much-needed financial support to the conference; Zachary Kincaid, Workshop Chair, and all the organizers of the co-located events for bringing their events to the CAV week; Roopsha Samanta, Publicity Chair, for diligently publicizing the event; and Aws Albarghouthi, Artifact Evaluation Chair, and the Artifact Evaluation Committee for their work on evaluating the artifacts submitted. We gratefully acknowledge NSF for providing financial support for student participants. We sincerely thank the sponsors of CAV 2016 for their generous contributions.

We also thank the University of Toronto and Rice University for their support. Finally, we hope you find the proceedings of CAV 2016 intellectually stimulating and practically valuable.

July 2016   Swarat Chaudhuri
                                                                   Azadeh Farzan

Organization

Program Committee

Rajeev Alur	University of Pennsylvania, USA
Christel Baier	Technische Universität Dresden, Germany
Clark Barrett	New York University, USA
Roderick Bloem	Graz University of Technology, Austria
Pavol Cerny	University of Colorado, Boulder, USA
Adam Chlipala	MIT, USA
Swarat Chaudhuri	Rice University, Houston, USA
Alessandro Cimatti	Fondazione Bruno Kessler, Italy
Loris D'Antoni	University of Wisconsin, Madison, USA
Constantin Enea	University of Paris Diderot (Paris 7), France
Javier Esparza	Technische Universität München, Germany
Kousha Etessami	University of Edinburgh, UK
Azadeh Farzan	University of Toronto, Toronto, Canada
Susanne Graf	VERIMAG, France
Orna Grumberg	Technion, Israel
Franjo Ivancic	Google, USA
Somesh Jha	University of Wisconsin, Madison, USA
Ranjit Jhala	University of California, San Diego, USA
Joost-Pieter Katoen	RWTH Aachen University, Germany
Zachary Kincaid	University of Toronto, Canada
Laura Kovacs	Chalmers University of Technology, Sweden
Viktor Kuncak	EPFL, Switzerland
Marta Kwiatkowska	Oxford University, UK
Shuvendu Lahiri	Microsoft Research, Redmond, USA
Akash Lal	Microsoft Research, Bangalore, India
Pete Manolios	Northeastern University, USA
Kenneth McMillan	Microsoft Research, Redmond, USA
David Monniaux	VERIMAG, France
Kedar Namjoshi	Bell Labs, Alcatel-Lucent, USA
David Parker	University of Birmingham, UK
Corina Pasareanu	Carnegie Mellon Silicon Valley; NASA Ames, USA
Ruzica Piskac	Yale University, USA
Andreas Podelski	University of Freiburg, Germany
Shaz Qadeer	Microsoft Research, Redmond, USA
Andrey Rybalchenko	Microsoft Research, Cambridge, UK
Mooly Sagiv	Tel Aviv University, Israel
Sriram Sankaranarayanan	University of Colorado, Boulder, USA

Sanjit Seshia   University of California, Berkeley, USA
Natasha Sharygina   University of Lugano, Switzerland
Sharon Shoham   Academic College of Tel Aviv-Yaffo, Israel
Fabio Somenzi   University of Colorado, Boulder, USA
Serdar Tasiran   Koç University, Turkey
Mahesh Viswanathan   University of Illinois, Urbana-Champaign, USA
Bow-Yaw Wang   Academia Sinica, Taiwan
Thomas Wies   New York University, USA
Lenore Zuck   University of Illinois, Chicago, USA

External Review Committee

Aws Albarghouthi   University of Wisconsin, Madison, USA
Jade Alglave   Microsoft Research Cambridge; University College
                             London, UK
Sagar Chaki   Software Engineering Institute, Carnegie Mellon
                             University, USA
Hana Chockler   King's College London, UK
Byron Cook   University College London; Amazon, UK
Deepak D'Souza   Indian Institute of Science, India
Thao Dang   CNRS, France
Cezara Dragoi   Inria, France
Pierre Ganty   IMDEA, Spain
Ganesh Gopalakrishnan   University of Utah, USA
Arie Gurfinkel   Software Engineering Institute, Carnegie Mellon
                             University, USA
Jan Hoffmann   Carnegie Mellon University, USA
William Hung   Synopsys, USA
Joxan Jaffer   National University of Singapore
Naoki Kobayashi   University of Tokyo, Japan
Igor Konnov   Vienna University of Technology, Austria
Hillel Kugler   Bar-Ilan University, Israel
Rupak Majumdar   Max Planck Institute for Software Systems, Germany
Sayan Mitra   University of Illinois at Urbana Champaign, USA
Peter Mueller   ETH Zurich, Switzerland
Tim Nelson   Brown University, USA
Jan Otop   University of Wroclaw, Poland
Gennaro Parlato   University of Southampton, UK
Madhusudan Parthasarathy   University of Illinois at Urbana Champaign, USA
Doron Peled   Bar Ilan University, Israel
Pavithra Prabhakar   Kansas State University, USA
Arjun Radhakrishna   University of Pennsylvania, USA
Zvonimir Rakamaric   University of Utah, USA
Nishant Sinha   IBM Research, Bangalore, India
Ana Sokolova   University of Salzburg, Austria
Armando Solar-Lezama   MIT, USA

Viktor Vafeiadis   Max Planck Institute for Software Systems, Germany
Martin Vechev   ETH Zurich, Switzerland
Willem Visser   Stellenbosch University, South Africa
Tomas Vojnar   Brno University of Technology, Czech Republic
Thomas Wahl   Northeastern University, USA
Eran Yahav   Technion, Israel
Karen Yorav   IBM Haifa Research Lab, Israel
Florian Zuleger   Vienna University of Technology, Austria

Additional Reviewers

Houssam Abbas   University of Pennsylvania, USA
Stavros Aronis   Uppsala University, Sweden
Amir Ben-Amram   The Academic College of Tel Aviv-Yaffo, Israel
Dirk Beyer   University of Passau, Germany
Armin Biere   Johannes Kepler University, Austria
David Binkley   Loyola University, USA
James Brotherston   University College London, UK
Domenico Cantone   University of Catania, Italy
Ernie Cohen   Amazon, USA
Sylvain Conchon   LRI, Univesité Paris-Sud 11, France
Chris Hawblitzel   Microsoft Research, Redmond, USA
Jean-François Raskin   Université Libre de Bruxelles, Belgium
Antoine Miné   UPMC University, France
Anders Møller   Aarhus University, Denmark
Andrew Reynolds   Univesity of Iowa, USA
Ulrich Schmid   Vienna University of Technology, Austria
Margus Veanes   Microsoft Research, Redmond, USA

Contents – Part II

Verification in Practice

Model Checking at Scale: Automated Air Traffic Control Design
Space Exploration 3
    Marco Gario, Alessandro Cimatti, Cristian Mattarei, Stefano Tonetta,
    and Kristin Yvonne Rozier

Investigating Safety of a Radiotherapy Machine Using System Models with
Pluggable Checkers 23
    Stuart Pernsteiner, Calvin Loncaric, Emina Torlak, Zachary Tatlock,
    Xi Wang, Michael D. Ernst, and Jonathan Jacky

End-to-End Verification of ARM® Processors with ISA-Formal 42
    Alastair Reid, Rick Chen, Anastasios Deligiannis, David Gilday,
    David Hoyes, Will Keen, Ashan Pathirane, Owen Shepherd,
    Peter Vrabel, and Ali Zaidi

A Practical Verification Framework for Preemptive OS Kernels 59
    Fengwei Xu, Ming Fu, Xinyu Feng, Xiaoran Zhang, Hui Zhang,
    and Zhaohui Li

Probabilistic Automated Language Learning for Configuration Files 80
    Mark Santolucito, Ennan Zhai, and Ruzica Piskac

Concurrency

The Commutativity Problem of the MapReduce Framework:
A Transducer-Based Approach 91
    Yu-Fang Chen, Lei Song, and Zhilin Wu

Liveness of Randomised Parameterised Systems under Arbitrary Schedulers ... 112
    Anthony W. Lin and Philipp Rümmer

Stateless Model Checking for POWER 134
    Parosh Aziz Abdulla, Mohamed Faouzi Atig, Bengt Jonsson,
    and Carl Leonardsson

Hitting Families of Schedules for Asynchronous Programs 157
    Dmitry Chistikov, Rupak Majumdar, and Filip Niksic

ParCoSS: Efficient Parallelized Compiled Symbolic Simulation 177
    Vladimir Herdt, Hoang M. Le, Daniel Große, and Rolf Drechsler

Constraint Solving II

XSat: A Fast Floating-Point Satisfiability Solver................... 187
  Zhoulai Fu and Zhendong Su

Effectively Propositional Interpolants........................... 210
  Samuel Drews and Aws Albarghouthi

Array Folds Logic.. 230
  Przemysław Daca, Thomas A. Henzinger, and Andrey Kupriyanov

Automata and Games

Compositional Synthesis of Reactive Controllers for Multi-agent Systems ... 251
  Rajeev Alur, Salar Moarref, and Ufuk Topcu

Solving Parity Games via Priority Promotion 270
  Massimo Benerecetti, Daniele Dell'Erba, and Fabio Mogavero

A Simple Algorithm for Solving Qualitative Probabilistic Parity Games..... 291
  Ernst Moritz Hahn, Sven Schewe, Andrea Turrini, and Lijun Zhang

Limit-Deterministic Büchi Automata for Linear Temporal Logic.......... 312
  Salomon Sickert, Javier Esparza, Stefan Jaax, and Jan Křetínský

Slugs: Extensible GR(1) Synthesis 333
  Rüdiger Ehlers and Vasumathi Raman

Synthesis II

Synthesis of Fault-Attack Countermeasures for Cryptographic Circuits...... 343
  Hassan Eldib, Meng Wu, and Chao Wang

A SAT-Based Counterexample Guided Method for Unbounded Synthesis ... 364
  Alexander Legg, Nina Narodytska, and Leonid Ryzhyk

QLOSE: Program Repair with Quantitative Objectives 383
  Loris D'Antoni, Roopsha Samanta, and Rishabh Singh

BDD-Based Boolean Functional Synthesis 402
  Dror Fried, Lucas M. Tabajara, and Moshe Y. Vardi

SOUFFLÉ: On Synthesis of Program Analyzers 422
  Herbert Jordan, Bernhard Scholz, and Pavle Subotić

Model Checking II

Property Directed Equivalence via Abstract Simulation   433
  Grigory Fedyukovich, Arie Gurfinkel, and Natasha Sharygina

Combining Model Learning and Model Checking to Analyze
TCP Implementations   454
  Paul Fiterău-Broştean, Ramon Janssen, and Frits Vaandrager

BFS-Based Model Checking of Linear-Time Properties
with an Application on GPUs.   472
  Anton Wijs

BigraphER: Rewriting and Analysis Engine for Bigraphs.   494
  Michele Sevegnani and Muffy Calder

Verification-Aided Debugging: An Interactive Web-Service
for Exploring Error Witnesses.   502
  Dirk Beyer and Matthias Dangl

The KIND 2 Model Checker   510
  Adrien Champion, Alain Mebsout, Christoph Sticksel, and Cesare Tinelli

Author Index   519

Contents – Part I

Probabilistic Systems

Termination Analysis of Probabilistic Programs Through
Positivstellensatz's.   3
   Krishnendu Chatterjee, Hongfei Fu, and Amir Kafshdar Goharshady

Markov Chains and Unambiguous Büchi Automata. 23
   *Christel Baier, Stefan Kiefer, Joachim Klein, Sascha Klüppelholz,
David Müller, and James Worrell*

Synthesizing Probabilistic Invariants via Doob's Decomposition 43
   *Gilles Barthe, Thomas Espitau, Luis María Ferrer Fioriti,
and Justin Hsu*

PSI: Exact Symbolic Inference for Probabilistic Programs 62
   Timon Gehr, Sasa Misailovic, and Martin Vechev

PSCV: A Runtime Verification Tool for Probabilistic SystemC Models 84
   Van Chan Ngo, Axel Legay, and Vania Joloboff

Synthesis I

Structural Synthesis for GXW Specifications 95
   Chih-Hong Cheng, Yassine Hamza, and Harald Ruess

Bounded Cycle Synthesis. 118
   Bernd Finkbeiner and Felix Klein

Fast, Flexible, and Minimal CTL Synthesis via SMT. 136
   Tobias Klenze, Sam Bayless, and Alan J. Hu

Synthesis of Self-Stabilising and Byzantine-Resilient Distributed Systems . . . 157
   Roderick Bloem, Nicolas Braud-Santoni, and Swen Jacobs

Constraint Solving I

A Decision Procedure for Sets, Binary Relations and Partial Functions 179
   Maximiliano Cristiá and Gianfranco Rossi

Precise and Complete Propagation Based Local Search for Satisfiability
Modulo Theories. 199
   Aina Niemetz, Mathias Preiner, and Armin Biere

Progressive Reasoning over Recursively-Defined Strings   218
    Minh-Thai Trinh, Duc-Hiep Chu, and Joxan Jaffar

String Analysis via Automata Manipulation with Logic Circuit
Representation   241
    Hung-En Wang, Tzung-Lin Tsai, Chun-Han Lin, Fang Yu,
    and Jie-Hong R. Jiang

RAHFT: A Tool for Verifying Horn Clauses Using Abstract Interpretation
and Finite Tree Automata.   261
    Bishoksan Kafle, John P. Gallagher, and José F. Morales

Model Checking I

Infinite-State Liveness-to-Safety via Implicit Abstraction
and Well-Founded Relations.   271
    Jakub Daniel, Alessandro Cimatti, Alberto Griggio, Stefano Tonetta,
    and Sergio Mover

Proving Parameterized Systems Safe by Generalizing Clausal Proofs of
Small Instances.   292
    Michael Dooley and Fabio Somenzi

Learning-Based Assume-Guarantee Regression Verification   310
    Fei He, Shu Mao, and Bow-Yaw Wang

Automated Circular Assume-Guarantee Reasoning with N-way
Decomposition and Alphabet Refinement.   329
    Karam Abd Elkader, Orna Grumberg, Corina S. Păsăreanu,
    and Sharon Shoham

JayHorn: A Framework for Verifying Java programs   352
    Temesghen Kahsai, Philipp Rümmer, Huascar Sanchez,
    and Martin Schäf

Program Analysis

Trigger Selection Strategies to Stabilize Program Verifiers   361
    K.R.M. Leino and Clément Pit-Claudel

Satisfiability Modulo Heap-Based Programs   382
    Quang Loc Le, Jun Sun, and Wei-Ngan Chin

Automatic Verification of Iterated Separating Conjunctions Using
Symbolic Execution.   405
    Peter Müller, Malte Schwerhoff, and Alexander J. Summers

From Shape Analysis to Termination Analysis in Linear Time   426
  Roman Manevich, Boris Dogadov, and Noam Rinetzky

RV-Match: Practical Semantics-Based Program Analysis   447
  Dwight Guth, Chris Hathhorn, Manasvi Saxena, and Grigore Roşu

Timed and Hybrid Systems

Under-Approximating Backward Reachable Sets by Polytopes   457
  Bai Xue, Zhikun She, and Arvind Easwaran

Parsimonious, Simulation Based Verification of Linear Systems   477
  Parasara Sridhar Duggirala and Mahesh Viswanathan

Counterexample Guided Abstraction Refinement for Stability Analysis   495
  Pavithra Prabhakar and Miriam García Soto

Symbolic Optimal Reachability in Weighted Timed Automata   513
  Patricia Bouyer, Maximilien Colange, and Nicolas Markey

Automatic Reachability Analysis for Nonlinear Hybrid Models with C2E2. . .   531
  *Chuchu Fan, Bolun Qi, Sayan Mitra, Mahesh Viswanathan,
  and Parasara Sridhar Duggirala*

Author Index   539

Verification in Practice

Model Checking at Scale: Automated Air Traffic Control Design Space Exploration

Marco Gario[1]($\boxtimes$), Alessandro Cimatti[1], Cristian Mattarei[1], Stefano Tonetta[1], and Kristin Yvonne Rozier[2]($\boxtimes$)

[1] Fondazione Bruno Kessler, Trento, Italy
{gario,cimatti,mattarei,tonettas}@fbk.eu
[2] Iowa State University, Ames, IA, USA
kyrozier@iastate.edu

Abstract. Many possible solutions, differing in the assumptions and implementations of the components in use, are usually in competition during early design stages. Deciding which solution to adopt requires considering several trade-offs. Model checking represents a possible way of comparing such designs, however, when the number of designs is large, building and validating so many models may be intractable.

During our collaboration with NASA, we faced the challenge of considering a design space with more than 20,000 designs for the NextGen air traffic control system. To deal with this problem, we introduce a compositional, modular, parameterized approach combining model checking with contract-based design to automatically generate large numbers of models from a possible set of components and their implementations. Our approach is fully automated, enabling the generation and validation of all target designs. The 1,620 designs that were most relevant to NASA were analyzed exhaustively. To deal with the massive amount of data generated, we apply novel data-analysis techniques that enable a rich comparison of the designs, including safety aspects. Our results were validated by NASA system designers, and helped to identify novel as well as known problematic configurations.

1 Introduction

When multiple system design configurations are possible, there is a need to map the design space in order to understand the big picture, and be able to demonstrate the impact of design choices, such as different combinations of potential subcomponents with different features, on the overall functionality and safety of the system. Safety assessment of complex and critical systems can clearly benefit from the use of formal methods techniques [14,15,20,22,24,27–31,34], but a large space of possible designs presents major challenges for model-checking analysis,

---

Thanks to the Flight Trajectory Dynamics and Controls Branch of NASA Ames Research Center, NASA's Functional Allocation Project, and NSF CAREER Award CNS-1552934 for supporting this work. All models and specifications are available at https://es-static.fbk.eu/projects/nasa-aac/.

© Springer International Publishing Switzerland 2016
S. Chaudhuri and A. Farzan (Eds.): CAV 2016, Part II, LNCS 9780, pp. 3–22, 2016.
DOI: 10.1007/978-3-319-41540-6_1

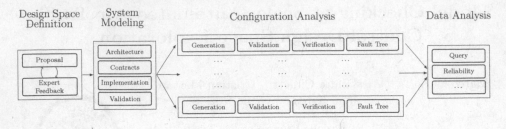

Fig. 1. Process overview

including producing models of each design, cross-design validation, and comparative safety analysis across the large design space. We address these challenges, exemplifying our methodology on NASA's full-scale design space for NextGen air traffic control, in which there are many ways to allocate essential functions such as aircraft separation assurance [26], and competing possible implementations of the same components. The U.S. government made NASA primarily responsible for the design and verification of NextGen air traffic control [2,3]. The new air traffic management system is expected to be in place for decades to come [5] so we must evaluate the design space thoroughly to ensure that we guarantee safety while allowing optimization for important secondary considerations. The importance of early-design stage optimization carries to many classes of critical or long-lived projects, including commercial aircraft and space missions, where the need to change the design later in the system development process would be extremely difficult, and very costly.

In this paper, we discuss the application of model-checking-based techniques to support the exploration of the NextGen design space. This is one of six studies funded within NASA's Functional Allocation Project; it will contribute directly to the final system design. We define a compositional, parameterized modeling framework that can generate more than 20,000 possible designs. In collaboration with NASA Ames and NASA Langley experts, we focus in on the 1,620 that they identified as the most instructive configurations for a comparative analysis. The outcome of this analysis provides significant insights into the features of the various configurations. In order to tackle the huge design space, we develop a new process that relies on multiple tools. The activities, depicted in Fig. 1, can be summarized in four main phases: *Design Space Definition*, *System Modeling*, *Configuration Analysis*, and *Data Analysis*.

Design Space Definition. The stage was set by working with NASA in order to identify precisely (yet informally [26]) the situations of interest, and by defining the modeling dimensions to capture them.

System Modeling. Modeling each solution independently would be too time-consuming (if not outright unfeasible). Plus each model needs to be properly validated to ensure that it upholds the expected properties. Furthermore, independent models would require a lot of maintenance effort to propagate changes and ensure that they are all aligned with NASA's most current designs. We can manage these sources of complexity by combining several ingredients. First, we use an architectural language (i.e., OCRA [17]) to separate the system architecture from the implementation of the single components (obtained as SMV [16] models). This allows us to model each component in isolation, partitioning the effort, and minimizing the time required to validate changes in any component. Additionally, this permits changes to the implementation of a single component without impacting the rest of the system. Second, we use contracts (encoded in OCRA as LTL formulas) to characterize each component. This allows us to properly specify the interactions between components, and decompose the validation properties into more localized subcomponent properties. Third, we use parameters to factor out multiple configurations into a single (although more complex) model. If two configurations require only marginal changes to an implementation, we capture these changes using parameters within the models. These techniques allow us to automatically generate a formal representation for each configuration in the design space, with great confidence in their correctness and alignment.

Configuration Analysis. We verify each model against the properties of interest; in addition, techniques for safety assessment identify which combinations of faults lead to the violation of fundamental properties. The corresponding Fault Trees are automatically computed (using xSAP [10]), thus providing additional information on the reliability of each configuration. We instantiate and analyze each configuration independently, exploiting the typical parallelism of modern computing infrastructures, thus significantly speeding up the analysis.

Data Analysis. Such analysis results in a significant amount of data, and poses the problem of how to analyze it. We combine this data into a symbolically represented dataset, linking each configuration to its satisfied properties and Fault Trees. This dataset is particularly useful in such an exploratory phase, since it describes the whole design space and can be studied offline. For example, by automatically extracting sets of configurations enjoying specific properties (e.g., absence of single points of failure), it is possible to achieve a better understanding of the design space. Our focused analysis of NASA's air traffic control design space confirmed expected results [23, 25] as well as identifying novel ones. In particular, we highlighted the need for additional assumptions when dealing with changes in delegation of separation assurance from an aircraft to the ground, e.g., in case of a request for backup.

The contribution of this paper is twofold. First, we develop a complex and realistic case study of public relevance, and make models, tools, and results publicly available for future investigation (at [4]). This is no ordinary case study, and to be able to handle the massive size, we need to exploit a novel process that is our second contribution. Our process is able to scale to address a large design space exploration problem. The process builds on existing tools and techniques and adds a novel data analysis phase that is necessary to obtain insights from the large amount of generated artifacts. We show that this technology is mature and able to assist designers in formalizing and narrowing down design choices in an early phase of system design.

The rest of the paper is structured according to the process described above (Fig. 1). Sections 2 to 5 illustrate each phase of the process in greater detail. Related works are discussed in Sects. 6 and 7 concludes with possible directions for future work.

2   Design Space Definition

The main objective of an air traffic control system is to avoid aircraft collisions. In air traffic management, a Loss of Separation (LOS) between two aircraft occurs when they are predicted to pass too close to each other. One of the major goals of the next generation of air traffic control is to minimize the number of times that a LOS ever occurs. This task is called *Separation Assurance*. In this case study, we are interested in studying the separation assurance provided by different designs when splitting the functionality between components on-board airplanes and on-ground. In particular, aircraft that always rely on the ground for separation assurance are called Ground Separated (GSEP), while aircraft with on-board separation assurance capabilities are called Self-Separating (SSEP). The main distinction between the two types of aircraft is the ability of SSEP to perform self-separation, without the need for approval from ground control. The goal of distributing the responsibility for separation assurance across different components is to increase efficiency and improve fault tolerance.

Our work started by considering several proposals from NASA's *Flight Dynamics, Trajectory, and Controls* Branch for different solutions regarding Function Allocation for Separation Assurance [26]. These ideas were the result of considering several features and characteristics in a preliminary phase.

Our first step was to identify and formalize the dimensions shared by different proposals, and this allowed us to define the design space. In order to model the airspace and its dynamics, we track each aircraft's intended trajectory through four different time-windows: *Current, Near, Mid,* and *Far.* These indicate increasingly distant points in time. For each window, we encode the intended position of the aircraft. However, since we are only interested in whether two aircraft can potentially be in a conflict, we simplify this information. For a given time-window, we say that two aircraft are in the same *Conflict Area* (CA) *iff* their trajectories are too close to each other and would cause a Loss of Separation. We say that two aircraft are in LOS *iff* they are in the same conflict area in the Current time-window. If two aircraft are in the same CA in another window, we say that they have a *predicted* LOS. These abstractions make it possible to focus on the other modeling dimensions: what information the different agents share, how they behave in case of predicted LOS, and the impacts of the actions of each agent on the overall system. Contrary to previous works (e.g., [28]), we consider more complex interactions between separation agents, components with multiple implementations, and priorities in case of predicted LOS. We derived six modeling dimensions that enable us to capture these different trade-offs:

1. SSEP Separation Agent
2. Aircraft Mix
3. Information Sharing
4. Burdening Rules
5. Communication Steps
6. ACDR (Airborne Conflict Detection and Resolution) Implementations.

SSEP Separation Agent. A key difference between the solutions is who is responsible for performing separation for the SSEPs. We split this task into separation for the Tactical (Near- and Mid-) and Strategic (Far-) windows. For each of these windows we define who is in charge of separating the SSEPs: the ground (*ATC*), the aircraft (*SELF*), or the aircraft with possible delegation to ground (*SATC*). If the ground ATC is in charge of separating the SSEPs, then it computes the resolutions and sends them to the aircraft. If the aircraft is in charge of its own separation, computation of a resolution strategy happens on-board, possibly involving coordination between aircraft. The third case (*SATC*) captures the possibility for an SSEP to delegate its own separation to the ground. This is used to capture different situations such as backup in case of a fault, privileged traffic corridors, and transfer of responsibility in designated airspace regions. In the future, we expect other cases to be studied. For example, resolutions might be computed on-board but require approval from ground.

Aircraft Mix. We consider situations in which all aircraft are of the same type, and also where mixed types coexist. The same design can be analyzed without SSEPs, with an even number of GSEPs and SSEPs, without GSEPs, or any option in-between. Each combination is indicated by the number of GSEPs and SSEPs, i.e., $\langle \#GSEP, \#SSEP \rangle$.

Burdening Rules. A priority must be defined in order to address detected conflicts between aircraft of different types. Burdening rules define who should move when such a conflict occurs: (1) *Undefined*, (2) *GSEP*, (3) *SSEP*. For example, if the burden is on the GSEP, then the conflict should be resolved by changing the trajectory of the GSEP. If the burdening rules are undefined, then each agent will arbitrarily choose a burdened strategy, and consistently apply it to every conflict.

Information Sharing. It is important to consider the minimization of required communications, in order to reduce reaction times and system complexity. Therefore, we need to understand what is the minimum amount of intent that aircraft need to share. We make two main distinctions: information sharing from *GSEPs to SSEPs* and from *SSEPs to ATC*. For each of these two information sharing pipelines, we consider scenarios from sharing no information (*None*) to sharing information concerning just the *Current*-window, up to the *Near*-window, up to the *Mid*-window, or all the windows (*Far*-window).

Communication Steps. In some situations, multiple communication rounds might be needed in order to reach an agreement among the parties. However, delays in

Table 1. Summary of possible and considered design dimensions (difference in size is highlighted in bold)

Name	Possible		Considered	
	Values	Size	Values	Size
SSEP TS SA	ATC, SELF, SATC	3	ATC, SELF, SATC	3
SSEP SS SA	ATC, SELF, SATC	3	ATC, SELF, SATC	3
Aircraft mix	$\langle 4,0 \rangle, \langle 3,1 \rangle, \langle 2,2 \rangle,$ $\langle 1,3 \rangle, \langle 0,4 \rangle$	5	$\langle 4,0 \rangle, \langle 3,1 \rangle, \langle 2,2 \rangle,$ $\langle 1,3 \rangle, \langle 0,4 \rangle$	5
Burdening rules	Undef, GSEP, SSEP	3	Undef, GSEP, SSEP	3
GSEPs to SSEPs info	None, Current, Near, Mid, Far	5	Current, Far	**2**
SSEPs to ATC info	None, Current, Near, Mid, Far	5	Far	**1**
Com steps	1, 2, …	2	1, 2	2
ACDR implementations	Simple, Asymmetric, Non-receptive	3	Simple, Asymmetric, Non-receptive	3
TOTAL		20,250		1,620

communication and availability of the networks make it necessary to minimize the number of communication rounds that need to occur.

ACDR Implementations. We considered different implementations for the Airborne Conflict Detection and Resolution (ACDR) component. The simplest implementation of the ACDR computes a resolution without considering the behavior of the other aircraft ("ACDR Simple"). A more complex implementation instead takes into account how the other SSEPs are going to resolve the conflict, and uses this knowledge to compute a resolution that is guaranteed to solve the current conflict ("ACDR Asymmetric"). Finally, the last implementation (called "ACDR Non-Receptive") is the one in which we declaratively enforce the assumption that conflicts among SSEPs will be resolved without specifying how, thus constraining the environment with a non-receptive specification [6]; this last option is useful to study the system behavior assuming a perfect ACDR.

Table 1 shows the possible dimensions defined during the first analysis, and yields a design space with 20,250 configurations. Though we can scale to automatically generate and analyze this many models, further discussions with NASA domain experts led us to focus our exhaustive analysis on the subset of 1,620 configurations most interesting from the domain point of view. In particular, they decided to fix the information sharing of the SSEPs in order to provide all information (i.e., *Far*) and consider only the two extreme cases for the information shared by the GSEPs: *Current* and *Far*. This reduced the design space to a set of 1,620 configurations (right part of Table 1). These are the configurations analyzed in the rest of the paper.

3 System Modeling

The dimensions described in Table 1 are captured by defining a unified structure including all possible configurations. This structure is equipped with parameters and multiple implementations of the components, making it possible to model the whole system once, and then automatically generate any of the 1,620 possible instances. This reduces the modeling effort that is, in terms of resources, the most expensive part of the process. However, we need to pay particu-

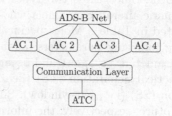

Fig. 2. Model architecture

lar attention to the validation of the instantiated models, in order to make sure that all expected behaviors are properly captured.

The general structure of the model is shown in Fig. 2, and includes four aircraft, the ATC, and two different types of networks: ADS-B and Communication Layer. ADS-B is used only among the aircraft, while the Communication Layer is used between the aircraft and the ATC. This choice makes it simple to provide different characteristics to the two networks: faults, symmetry, amount of information, delays, etc. We always consider up to four aircraft instances. This is sufficient to capture all combinations of conflicts between aircraft of different types: GSEP-to-SSEP, GSEP-to-GSEP, SSEP-to-SSEP. This abstraction only represents how many aircraft can be in a single conflict at the same time, and does not assume anything about the size of the airspace [34].

Figure 3 shows the decomposition of the system into a hierarchy of component types, and this provides an architecture that can be incrementally refined. For example, we break down the definition of the Aircraft and ATC components into subcomponents, and this compositional approach allows us to simplify modeling and validation.

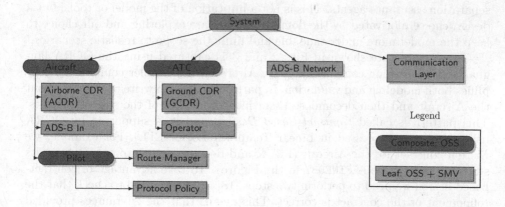

Fig. 3. Hierarchical decomposition

We use the Aircraft component (the most complex component) to exemplify our parametric modeling approach. There are two types of aircraft: SSEP and GSEP. Since these two types differ only in few ways, they are modeled as a generic aircraft component whose behavior is selected via a set of parameters, as listed in Table 2. More specifically, we model the *Aircraft* component as having the following parameters: adsb_in, ts_agent, ss_agent, and burdening. The parameters ts_agent and ss_agent are used to specify who is in charge of the Tactical Separation (TS) (i.e., Near- and Mid-window) and Strategic Separation (SS) (i.e., Far-window). Similarly, the parameters burdening and adsb_in capture, respectively, the information about the burdening rule in use and the availability of the ADS-B receiver. Using this parametric model, we can describe a GSEP as an aircraft that is always separated by the ground controller, and that does not have an ADS-B In component:

```
Aircraft(adsb_in=No, ts_agent=ATC, ss_agent=ATC, burdening=GSEP).
```

The impact of parameter choice is localized to the parameterized subcomponent. For example, the burdening parameter has an impact only on the ACDR component. Having components whose implementations are independent of the model's parameters makes it possible to *re-use* these components for multiple configurations. We also use a similar approach for modeling faults in the communication networks, and we localize all of those faults within the network components: ADS-B Network and Communication Layer. As shown in Fig. 3, there are two different components that are used to capture the ADS-B functionality: the *ADS-B Network* and the *ADS-B In* component. By separating these (conceptually related) components, we are able to model the aircraft independently of the faults, and the number of aircraft connected to the network. Table 2 provides a summary of the input and output information, and of the parameters for the Aircraft component. In each configuration, we enforce that all GSEPs must have the same parameters, and this applies also for the SSEPs. Therefore, in the same configuration there cannot be two SSEPs with, e.g., two different separation assurance agents. This is not a limitation of the model or tools, but a design choice motivated by the domain that we are exploring and our choice to keep the model more understandable and limit the scope to realistic scenarios.

The architecture shown in Figs. 2 and 3 is captured using the OCRA language [17]. Breaking components (e.g., Aircraft) into simpler components simplifies both modeling and validation. In particular, we can write properties about the Aircraft and then decompose them into properties of the subcomponents. This pattern is called *Contract-Based Design*, and it is supported by OCRA using contracts expressed in Linear Temporal Logic (LTL). For example, we write a contract for the Aircraft (Fig. 4) and decompose it into contracts on its subcomponents (see REFINEDBY in the Figure). To take advantage of contract-based design we need to perform two steps [18]. First, we need to check that the refinement of the contract is correct. This means that the guarantees provided by the subcomponents in the refinement are sufficient to prove the guarantee of the supercomponent. After performing this step, we know that independently of the choice of parameters, if the implementations of the ACDR and Pilot satisfy

Table 2. Parameters, Inputs and Outputs of the Aircraft model

Type	Name	Domain
Parameter	id	[1..4]
	adsb_in	Boolean
	ts_sa_agent	{ATC, SELF, SATC}
	ss_sa_agent	{ATC, SELF, SATC}
	burdening	{Undefined, GSEP, SSEP}
Input	suggestion_{near,mid,far}_ground	Conflict area [0..4]
	communication_phase	Boolean
	ac_{1,2,3,4}_intention_{current,near,mid,far}	Conflict area [0..4]
	ac_{1,2,3,4}_{ts,sa}_agent	{ATC, SELF, SATC}
Output	intention_{current,near,mid,far}	Conflict area [0..4]
	predicted_conflict_{near,mid,far}	Boolean
	request_{ts,ss}_sa_ground	Boolean

their contracts, then also the Aircraft satisfies its contract. As a second step, we verify that the implementations of each component satisfy their contracts. This operation is done locally on the component in isolation and, since most components are relatively small, it can be performed efficiently. Every time we modify a basic component, we only need to validate it against its contracts, and we are guaranteed that the composite components will still satisfy their contracts. This way of using contracts significantly speeds up the design loop. To draw a parallel with software engineering, the contracts that we write are comparable to unit tests in which we focus on the correctness of the component in isolation.

```
CONTRACT AC_maintain_intention_ts_self
-- If self-separating, during communication phase if no conflict
-- is predicted, the intention will not change.
-- Tactical Separation Case.
assume: TRUE;
guarantee: always ((communication_phase and ts_sa_agent = SA_SELF) implies
    ((not predicted_conflict_near implies
        next(intention_near) = intention_near) and
    (not predicted_conflict_mid implies
        next(intention_mid) = intention_mid)));
CONTRACT AC_maintain_intention_ts_self
REFINEDBY cdr.ACDR_no_conflict_means_maintain_near,
        cdr.ACDR_no_conflict_means_maintain_mid,
        pilot.Pilot_apply_ts_self,
        pilot.Pilot_intention_is_not_nop;
```

Fig. 4. Example of a contract on the Aircraft component

An added benefit of this process of contract decomposition is that it requires a rigorous understanding of the relationships between the components.

This raises interesting questions about how to define the components, how to divide responsibilities, and what behavior can be expected by every component in nominal situations. In fact, we are forced to define requirements that all component implementations must satisfy. In our case, this investigation was supported by a close collaboration with NASA, which resulted for example, in the definition of multiple possible ACDR implementations, and the definition of more than 130 contracts.

4   Configuration Analysis

Once the unified model is complete, we proceed to analyze each possible configuration in isolation. For each configuration we break the analysis into the following steps:

1. Instance Generation
2. Airspace, Nominal, and Extended Validation
3. Nominal and Extended Verification
4. Fault Tree and Reliability Analysis.

Automation of this phase is very important. Each step is run automatically, from the definition of the instance to the generation of all verification and Fault Tree artifacts. This ensures that the process is reproducible and scalable.

Instance Generation. Each leaf component in our hierarchical architecture is associated with an implementation (a behavioral model defined as an SMV file) by defining a *map* file. The OCRA tool uses this mapping to generate a single monolithic SMV file of the instance. This makes it extremely easy to instantiate the system with multiple functional implementations of the components, and also to create instances with and without faults. We pass parameters through the OCRA architecture using pre-processing instructions to define constants. In this way, the variability of the model is limited to the OCRA architecture and map files used during the generation phase. The outcomes of this phase are three models: *airspace*, *nominal*, and *extended*. These are standard SMV files, without parameters, that can be analyzed by any out-of-the-box technique.

Airspace, Nominal, and Extended Validation. The models for the configuration are generated automatically, therefore, before proceeding to the verification step, we need to gain confidence in the quality of the generated models. For this reason, we perform these additional validation steps.

The *airspace* model captures the system without separation assurance agents. This is the first validation check: the model must allow the occurrence and resolution of LOS. We generated this model by mapping the separation agents to implementations that have no constraints, while using nominal implementations for the aircraft and networks. To certify that the components work correctly together, we verify 18 CTL properties encoding the possibilities of bad and good behaviors, and 24 LTL properties derived from contracts.

The *nominal* model uses a nominal implementation for every component, including separation agents. Unlike the extended model, in this case we do not allow components to fail. We validate this model with 29 LTL properties derived from the contracts of the components.

Finally, the *extended* model uses an implementation for every component that includes faults (95 faults in total, as described in [28]). The validation of the extended model checks that all faults are possible (through 137 CTL possibility properties), and that they respect their dynamics, i.e., permanent or transient, with 29 LTL properties.

Overall, the validation of the 3 models requires a combination of different techniques in order to be effective and be carried out in a limited time. The CTL verification requires a fixpoint-based approach, using BDDs, while for the LTL properties, we use the IC3-based algorithms implemented in nuXmv [16]. Every property is checked against a known result that, if violated, causes the analysis to stop for further investigation.

Nominal and Extended Verification. In this step, we characterize different configurations by verifying additional properties. The most important is whether LOS can always be avoided (NO-LOS), followed by stronger versions: NO-LOS-Near, -Mid, -Far. Other properties provide additional information on the quality of the configuration, e.g., *Detect-Near* "Every conflict in the Near-window (Mid-, Far- respectively) is detected by at least one Agent." This property is satisfied if the ATC (which is an Agent, in this context) detects a conflict between two aircraft, without either of the aircraft detecting it. It is clear that we can devise stronger versions of this property, and apply them to different time-windows (e.g., Detect-Mid, -Far). This provides a simple way of ranking configurations according to how many and which properties they satisfy. During extended verification, we check instead whether these properties are still satisfied in the presence of faults. For most properties this will not be the case. However, if some property is satisfied even with faults, it means that the property and the faults have no relationship in the given configuration. In this step, we verify 24 LTL and 30 invariant properties on both the nominal and extended models.

Fault Tree and Reliability Analysis. We compute the Fault Tree associated with each safety property in order to understand the resilience of each configuration in the presence of faults. Fault Trees are a standard in safety-critical domains [7, 8, 32]. More specifically, we compute the set of minimal cutsets, i.e., all possible faults configurations (called cutsets) that can cause the violation of the given property. These cutsets are minimal because they only include the faults that are necessary to violate the property. Minimal cutsets are computed automatically from the formal model, using the IC3-based technique described in [11] and implemented in xSAP [10]. For each Fault Tree, we also generate a *reliability* function [12]. This function relates the probability of violating the property to the probability of occurrence of each basic fault.

5   Data Analysis

Each configuration can be analyzed independently. We exploit this fact and run the analysis on a cluster with 12 Intel Xeon X5650 processors (72 cores). The average size of the models was 10^{107} states, and each model was checked against 346 properties. The two most difficult steps were those of model validation, due to the need for BDD-based reasoning, and minimal cutset computation, since it requires solving a parameter synthesis problem. These two steps were completed within an hour for most configurations, but for roughly 10 % of the models, they required several hours to complete. Verification of the LTL properties was performed using the nuXmv [16] IC3 implementation, requiring roughly 5 min per model.

Once all results are available, we can perform the last step of the process: *Data Analysis*. Each configuration provides us with a set of verification results and a set of Fault Trees. Therefore, we face the challenge of how to intuitively represent the information provided by more than 1,600 Fault Trees and verification results. We approached the problem by collecting these artifacts into relations. The first, $V \subseteq C \times \mathbb{B}^n$, relates each configuration (i.e., a set of values for the parameters) to the satisfaction of the verification properties. The second, $FT \subseteq C \times \mathbb{N} \times 2^{MCS}$ instead relates each configuration and property index to the set of minimal cutsets (MCS) associated with it. This data can be queried and manipulated offline, by the domain experts, in order to obtain more insights into the design space.

5.1   Summary of Results

Most of the configurations (Table 3) satisfy the key property of avoiding Loss of Separation (NO-LOS). The fact that NO-LOS-Far is satisfied by some SSEP-Only configurations is due to the non-receptive implementation of the ACDR, which assumes that trajectories are computed in a way that avoids potential conflicts in the Far-window. However, not all configurations using the SSEP-Only ACDR are immune to LOS. For example, when including burdening rules, GSEPs (that do not use the ACDR) can interfere with the SSEPs and lead to a LOS.

Table 3. Models satisfying NO-LOS for different windows

	GSEP-Only 4-0	Mixed 3-1	Mixed 2-2	Mixed 1-3	SSEP-Only 0-4	Total
NO-LOS	324	244	212	213	258	1251
NO-LOS-Near	324	244	209	210	252	1239
NO-LOS-Mid	324	192	138	141	198	993
NO-LOS-Far	0	0	0	18	84	102

Prime Implicants. To extract interesting facts from the verification results, we synthesize the region of parameters that satisfy a property of interest. To compute the region of parameters that satisfy a property, we fix the property value and quantify away the other properties in the relation V. E.g., for NO-LOS we define:

$$NO\_LOS(C) = \exists P_1, \cdots, P_n. \ V(C, P_1, \cdots, P_n) \wedge P_{NO\_LOS}$$

where P_i is a Boolean variable associated with the verification result for property i, and C is the set of configuration variables (i.e., parameters). In this way, we can compute the region of parameters associated with the satisfaction of each property. Very few of these regions have a compact representation. To extract interesting facts from these regions, we compute the *prime implicants* of the region, i.e., the set of minimal elements that are sufficient to enforce the satisfaction of the property. For cardinality 1, we obtain the following implicant for NO-LOS:

$$(MIX = \langle 4, 0 \rangle) \vee (SSEP\_TS\_SA = ATC) \vee (SSEP\_SS\_SA = ATC)$$

This tells us that there are three ways to guarantee NO-LOS: (i) having only GSEP airplanes, or having the ATC in control of the (ii) Strategic or (iii) Tactical separation of any SSEP.

By checking that NO-LOS-Far is achieved only by configurations using non-receptive ACDR, we verified the corresponding claim from Table 3. Moreover, we verified that not all configurations using non-receptive ACDR can satisfy NO-LOS-Far, thus discovering a necessary but not sufficient condition. These analyses were performed using pySMT [21] in order to represent the data using BDDs [13] for efficient querying.

Reliability Functions. Analyzing the reliability functions obtained from the Fault Trees, we can synthesize the region of configurations that have a probability of violating a property below a given threshold. This result provides us different sets of candidates that are able to guarantee a high reliability. In addition to that, we want also to analyze the impact of a variation in the probability of failure of different groups of components. In Fig. 5 we demonstrate this last analysis by proceeding as follows. First, we partition the faults into three groups: the ones related to the *Communication Layer*, the *ADS-B*, and all the others. For each configuration and each value of the probability of the faults of the Communication Network (y axis) and of the ADS-B Network (x axis), we compute the probability of reaching a LOS, by considering all other faults to have a fixed probability of 10^{-8} (Basic Probability). In Fig. 5, we summarize this information by plotting how many configurations have a probability of leading to a LOS that is below the threshold of 10^{-4} for the given probability of the faults. Interestingly, we see that reducing the reliability of the Communication Layer has a bigger impact than reducing the reliability of the ADS-B network. We see this because when the probability of faults in the ADS-B is high (x axis close to -2), but the probability of fault of the communication layer is low (y axis close to -8), the probability of reaching a LOS is

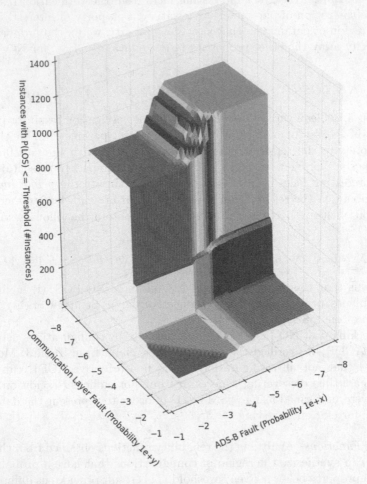

Fig. 5. Impact of the communication faults on LOS probability.

below the threshold of 10^{-4} for more than 800 configurations. If we look at the opposite situation, instead, we see that less than 100 configurations have a probability of reaching LOS that is below the threshold. The insight that we gain from this is that many of the analyzed configurations are robust with respect to failures of the ADS-B.

A different analysis is presented in Fig. 6 in which we analyze how many configurations share the same top N single points of failure. A *single point of failure* is a single fault that is sufficient to (in our case) cause a LOS, and corresponds to a minimal cutset of cardinality one. There are roughly 10 single points of failure that are shared by more than a thousand configurations. However, we also notice that most faults are single points of failure for a limited number of configurations; recall that there are 95 faults in total. If the probability of those

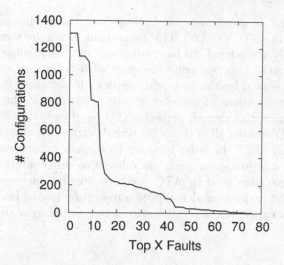

Fig. 6. Configurations impacted by the top N single points of failure.

10 faults is very high, then we can significantly prune the design space, and focus only on the configurations that are not affected by those faults.

5.2 Interesting Executions

A selection of the most relevant results was discussed with the domain experts. In particular, we were able to independently reproduce two known issues, *side-walk* [25,33] and *coincidental* conflicts [23], and discover a new one.

Side-walk Conflict. Side-walk conflicts occur whenever we use the "simple" implementation of the ACDR, in which conflicts between SSEPs are resolved by choosing a free conflict area. The problem occurs when more than one SSEP decides to move to the same conflict area. Due to the symmetry of the resolution algorithm, this strategy is not guaranteed to resolve the conflict. To break this symmetry, we developed the asymmetric version of the ACDR.

Coincidental Conflict. The asymmetric ACDR is not able to resolve conflicts early. In particular, we would like to always satisfy NO-LOS-Mid, i.e., avoid predicted LOS in the Mid-window. This is not possible if we allow only one communication step. In fact, if four aircraft are in two different conflicts that are resolved correctly, they might still end up in a new conflict. Consider the two conflict sets {AC1, AC2} and {AC3, AC4}. AC1 and AC3 decide to move to solve their respective conflicts. However, they choose to move to the same conflict area. An additional round of communication is needed in order to resolve this conflict, and this generalizes to needing at most $log(n)$ communication steps when considering n aircraft.

Backup From Ground. The novel problematic configuration that we identified stems from limited requirements on the behavior of the backup operation, i.e., when an SSEP is able to request backup from the ground and it delegates its separation to the ATC (SATC). This turned out to require more assumptions than were initially considered. In fact, when enabling this behavior, all configurations violate NO-LOS, excluding the ones with non-receptive ACDR. This is motivated (as shown by the counterexamples) by a lack of information and a mismatch of expectations in the airspace. In particular, in the design used in this project, whenever an aircraft requests ATC assistance, the other aircraft are not aware of it. Therefore, all of the other SSEPs expect the aircraft to maintain its behavior as an SSEP. In order to solve this issue, we propose two options. First, requests for ground-assistance are relayed to other aircraft. Second, the algorithm for separation used by ATC needs to take into account that the aircraft was an SSEP, and therefore compute a resolution taking into account what the other SSEPs expect the aircraft to do. These extensions are left as future work.

6   Related Work

Before NASA turned to the question of what designs were best for automated air traffic control, it was necessary to explore what designs were *possible*. To that end, NASA launched several initiatives to formally reason about a *single* such system; two of these works, using symbolic model checking [34] and probabilistic model checking [35] techniques led to the decision to use the former for the problem of broader design space exploration. However, neither technique proved sufficiently scalable to capture all of the relevant details of a single design at the same time.

This paper presents a large advancement along the same line of research of [28], in which a modeling abstraction for the problem was proposed, by designing and verifying a monolithic model. This modeling abstraction proved to be suitable for capturing the problem, however, it could not be scaled to cover the entire design space. Therefore, in this work we devise a tailored process that allows us to model, validate, verify, and compare the full design space (i.e., 20,000 designs and beyond) with exhaustive analysis of the more than 1,600 most likely candidate designs. This was made possible by breaking down the modeling and using a compositional approach based on contract-based design (as opposed to the monolithic approach of [28]). The size of the design space not only created challenges for running the analysis, but also for analyzing the results: we had to consider new ways of looking at the considerable amount of data produced in order to extract interesting information rather than providing NASA with a firehose of data. Thanks to the extensive coverage of the design space enabled by the process described in this paper, we managed to identify some configurations that were of interest for NASA. The examples that we highlight show that this approach pinpointed implicit assumptions and critical points in the design process.

The term *design space exploration* is commonly used to describe the study of a design space (mostly combinatorial) by avoiding the computation of all solutions and optimizing with respect to some cost function. For example, Airbus [9] uses automated techniques to evaluate design spaces, in which multiple solutions are compared and sorted with respect to their weight. It is important to notice, however, that we are dealing with a sequential problem while works such as [9] deal with combinational ones. Moreover, the existence of a cost function allows the optimization engine to prune "bad" configurations, thus reducing the actual number of configurations that will be eventually checked. In our case, there is no cost function defined; we are instead interested in a better understanding of the design space, and thus want to be able to thoroughly analyze every possible design. Therefore, we analyze all of the realistic configurations and collect the data in a form suitable for subsequent comparison.

When we move from combinational to sequential problems, we find works related to product lines, e.g., Software Product Lines [19], that deal with a similar problem of verification of a parametric system. In [19] the authors propose an extension to NuSMV that is able to perform symbolic model checking of an extended version of CTL (feature-oriented CTL). The differences with our work are several. From a process point of view, we focus not only on the verification but also on the validation of the generated models and on safety assessment; the outcome of our process is more informative since it relates the set of configurations with the properties that are satisfied (i.e., parameter synthesis). Finally, we integrate the modeling phase with a compositional approach that helps to save significant modeling effort. In principle, we could try to combine multiple configurations in order to analyze them together in a symbolic way. However, this was not needed and, on the contrary, the ability to work on each configuration independently made it possible to exploit high levels of parallelism provided by modern computing infrastructures.

7   Conclusions and Future Work

In this paper, we presented and released a complex real-world case study demonstrating the application of formal methods to the analysis of the big design space associated with the NextGen Automated Air Traffic Control System under study at NASA. Our approach resulted in a wealth of interesting data that supported the re-discovery of known results, and also the identification of new insights. When we started, NASA engineers had many possible design ideas, all described informally. We helped them to formalize and clarify these ideas, and to make hidden assumptions explicit. To the best of our knowledge, this is the first time that a design space of this scale has been mapped out by considering every possible solution in such depth.

The task of analyzing all the 1,620 designs would have been unfeasible without the novel process that we introduce. Our process combines and builds upon existing techniques and tools to perform model generation, validation, verification, and safety assessment. The process relies on a compositional, parametric, and contract-based approach in order to maximize reuse, and to ensure great confidence in the models by means of aggressive model validation. Overall, our study shows that this technology is mature and able to assist designers in formalizing and narrowing down design choices in an early phase of system design.

We extracted meaningful information from this data, and we expect that even more will be extracted in the future, working in collaboration with the NASA domain experts. In the future, we plan to extend the model by identifying additional modeling dimensions of interest, e.g., the fact that ADS-B information might not propagate equally to all aircraft, or the presence of multiple ATCs. Finally, we plan to leverage more the contract-based infrastructure defined in this work, in order to identify properties that can be proved by pure compositional reasoning. We believe that this process can be applied to other design exploration situations in which the size of the design space stems from the local variability of the components. For example, we have started working with the World Bank through Data Science for Social Good [1] to use an adaptation of the framework presented in this paper to help them root out corruption, collusion, and fraud by comparatively analyzing the temporal behaviors of their large network of suppliers.

References

1. Eric & Wendy Schmidt Data Science for Social Good, University of Chicago. http://dssg.uchicago.edu/
2. NASA airspace operations and safety program. http://www.aeronautics.nasa.gov/programs-aosp.htm
3. Nasa nextgen-airspace. http://www.hq.nasa.gov/office/aero/asp/airspace/
4. Project webpage: Formal methods for automated airspace concepts. https://es-static.fbk.eu/projects/nasa-aac
5. NextGen, May 2016. https://www.faa.gov/nextgen/
6. Abadi, M., Lamport, L.: Composing specifications. ACM Trans. Program. Lang. Syst. **15**(1), 73–132 (1993)
7. ARP4754A guidelines for development of civil aircraft and systems. In: SAE, December 2010
8. ARP4761 guidelines and methods for conducting the safety assessment process on civil airborne systems and equipment. In: SAE, December 1996
9. Bauer, C., Lagadec, K., Bès, C., Mongeau, M.: Flight control system architecture optimization for fly-by-wire airliners. J. Guidance Control Dyn. **30**(4), 1023–1029 (2007)
10. Bittner, B., Bozzano, M., Cavada, R., Cimatti, A., Gario, M., Griggio, A., Mattarei, C., Micheli, A., Zampedri, G.: The xSAP safety analysis platform. In: Chechik, M., Raskin, J.-F. (eds.) TACAS 2016. LNCS, vol. 9636, pp. 533–539. Springer, Heidelberg (2016)
11. Bozzano, M., Cimatti, A., Griggio, A., Mattarei, C.: Efficient anytime techniques for model-based safety analysis. In: Kroening, D., Păsăreanu, C.S. (eds.) CAV 2015. LNCS, vol. 9206, pp. 603–621. Springer, Heidelberg (2015)
12. Bozzano, M., Cimatti, A., Mattarei, C.: Automated analysis of reliability architectures. In: 18th International Conference on Engineering of Complex Computer Systems (ICECCS), pp. 198–207. IEEE, July 2013
13. Bryant, R.E.: Graph-based algorithms for Boolean function manipulation. IEEE Trans. Comput. **100**(8), 677–691 (1986)

14. Butler, R.W., Hagen, G., Maddalon, J.M.: The Chorus conflict and loss of separation resolution algorithms. Technical report, Technical Memorandum NASA/TM-2013-218030, NASA, Langley Research Center, Hampton VA 23681–2199, USA (2013)

15. Can, A.B., Bultan, T., Lindvall, M., Lux, B., Topp, S.: Eliminating synchronization faults in air traffic control software via design for verification with concurrency controllers. Autom. Softw. Eng. **14**(2), 129–178 (2007)

16. Cavada, R., Cimatti, A., Dorigatti, M., Griggio, A., Mariotti, A., Micheli, A., Mover, S., Roveri, M., Tonetta, S.: The NUXMV symbolic model checker. In: Biere, A., Bloem, R. (eds.) CAV 2014. LNCS, vol. 8559, pp. 334–342. Springer, Heidelberg (2014)

17. Cimatti, A., Dorigatti, M., Tonetta, S.: OCRA: a tool for checking the refinement of temporal contracts. In: ASE, pp. 702–705. IEEE (2013)

18. Cimatti, A., Tonetta, S.: Contracts-refinement proof system for component-based embedded systems. Sci. Comput. Program. **97**, 333–348 (2015)

19. Classen, A., Heymans, P., Schobbens, P.Y., Legay, A.: Symbolic model checking of software product lines. In: Proceedings of the 33rd International Conference on Software Engineering, pp. 321–330. ACM (2011)

20. von Essen, C., Giannakopoulou, D.: Analyzing the next generation airborne collision avoidance system. In: Ábrahám, E., Havelund, K. (eds.) TACAS 2014 (ETAPS). LNCS, vol. 8413, pp. 620–635. Springer, Heidelberg (2014)

21. Gario, M., Micheli, A.: pySMT: a solver-agnostic library for fast prototyping of SMT-based algorithms. In: SMT-Workshop (2015)

22. Hagen, G., Butler, R., Maddalon, J.: Stratway: a modular approach to strategic conflict resolution. In: Proceedings of 11th AIAA Aviation Technology, Integration, and Operations (ATIO) Conference, Virgina Beach, VA (2011)

23. Idris, H.R., Shen, N., Wing, D.J.: Improving separation assurance stability through trajectory flexibility preservation. In: 10th AIAA Aviation Technology, Integration, and Operations (ATIO) Conference, p. 9011 (2010)

24. Jeannin, J.-B., Ghorbal, K., Kouskoulas, Y., Gardner, R., Schmidt, A., Zawadzki, E., Platzer, A.: A formally verified hybrid system for the next-generation airborne collision avoidance system. In: Baier, C., Tinelli, C. (eds.) TACAS 2015. LNCS, vol. 9035, pp. 21–36. Springer, Heidelberg (2015)

25. Karr, D.A., Vivona, R.A., Roscoe, D.A., DePascale, S.M., Wing, D.J.: Autonomous operations planner: a flexible platform for research in flight-deck support for airborne self-separation. In: 12th AIAA Aviation Technology, Integration, and Operations (ATIO) Conference and 14th AIAA/ISSMO Multidisciplinary Analysis and Optimization Conference, p. 5417 (2012)

26. Lauderdale, T., Lewis, T., Prevot, T., Ballin, M., Aweiss, A., Guerreiro, N.: Function allocation for separation assurance: research plan, NASA HQ Project Overview, August 2014

27. Loos, S.M., Renshaw, D., Platzer, A.: Formal verification of distributed aircraft controllers. In: Proceedings of the 16th International Conference on Hybrid Systems: Computation and Control, HSCC 2013, pp. 125–130. ACM, New York (2013). http://doi.acm.org/10.1145/2461328.2461350

28. Mattarei, C., Cimatti, A., Gario, M., Tonetta, S., Kristin Yvonne, R.: Comparing different functional allocations in automated air traffic control design. In: Formal Methods in Computer-Aided Design (FMCAD15) (2015)

29. Mehlitz, P.: Trust your model-verifying aerospace system models with Java PathFinder. In: IEEE/Aero (2008)

30. Muñoz, C., Carreño, V.A., Dowek, G.: Formal analysis of the operational concept for the small aircraft transportation system. In: Butler, M., Jones, C.B., Romanovsky, A., Troubitsyna, E. (eds.) Rigorous Development of Complex Fault-Tolerant Systems. LNCS, vol. 4157, pp. 306–325. Springer, Heidelberg (2006)

31. Muñoz, C., Siminiceanu, R., Carreño, V., Dowek, G.: KB3D Reference Manual-Version 1. NASA (2005)

32. Vesely, W., Goldberg, F., Roberts, N., Haasl, D.: Fault Tree Handbook. Technical report NUREG-0492, Systems and Reliability Research Office of Nuclear Regulatory Research U.S. (1981)

33. Wing, D.J., Ballin, M.G., Krishnamurthy, K.: Pilot in command: a feasibility assessment of autonomous flight management operations. In: 24th International Congress of the Aeronautical Sciences (2004)

34. Zhao, Y., Rozier, K.Y.: Formal specification and verification of a coordination protocol for an automated air traffic control system. Sci. Comput. Program. J. **96**(3), 337–353 (2014)

35. Zhao, Y., Rozier, K.Y.: Probabilistic model checking for comparative analysis of automated air traffic control systems. In: Proceedings of the 33rd IEEE/ACM International Conference On Computer-Aided Design (ICCAD 2014), pp. 690–695. IEEE/ACM, San Jose, November 2014

Investigating Safety of a Radiotherapy Machine Using System Models with Pluggable Checkers

Stuart Pernsteiner[1(✉)], Calvin Loncaric[1], Emina Torlak[1], Zachary Tatlock[1], Xi Wang[1], Michael D. Ernst[1], and Jonathan Jacky[2]

[1] Department of Computer Science, University of Washington, Seattle, USA
{spernste,loncaric,emina,ztatlock,xi,mernst}@cs.washington.edu
[2] Department of Radiation Oncology, University of Washington, Seattle, USA
jon@uw.edu

Abstract. Formal techniques for guaranteeing software correctness have made tremendous progress in recent decades. However, applying these techniques to real-world safety-critical systems remains challenging in practice. Inspired by goals set out in prior work, we report on a large-scale case study that applies modern verification techniques to check safety properties of a radiotherapy system in current clinical use. Because of the diversity and complexity of the system's components (software, hardware, and physical), no single tool was suitable for both checking critical component properties and ensuring that their composition implies critical system properties. This paper describes how we used state-of-the-art approaches to develop specialized tools for verifying safety properties of individual components, as well as an extensible tool for composing those properties to check the safety of the system as a whole. We describe the key design decisions that diverged from previous approaches and that enabled us to practically apply our approach to provide machine-checked guarantees. Our case study uncovered subtle safety-critical flaws in a pre-release of the latest version of the radiotherapy system's control software.

Keywords: Case study · Safety-critical systems · SMT-based verification · Lightweight formal methods

1 Introduction

Formal techniques for guaranteeing software correctness have made tremendous progress in recent decades. However, applying these techniques to real-world safety-critical systems remains challenging for three reasons. First, using general-purpose tools to formally prove deep properties of a system component (e.g., functional correctness of a cryptographic primitive [6]) requires substantial expertise and manual effort. Second, many real systems contain components for which effective formal analysis is still an active research topic (e.g., formally guaranteeing liveness for a consensus protocol within a distributed system [22]),

© Springer International Publishing Switzerland 2016
S. Chaudhuri and A. Farzan (Eds.): CAV 2016, Part II, LNCS 9780, pp. 23–41, 2016.
DOI: 10.1007/978-3-319-41540-6_2

and thus in practice, these components can only be analyzed by weaker techniques such as testing or expert review. Third, even when deep properties can be established for individual system components, their composition may not add up to overall system safety, leading to catastrophic failures [25].

This paper reports on a large-scale case study in applying modern verification techniques to check the safety of a radiotherapy system in current clinical use: the Clinical Neutron Therapy System (CNTS) at the University of Washington Medical Center. We describe how to practically address the above challenges with a combination of techniques that reason at the system and component levels, and that provide guarantees of varying strength, from automatic proof to manual review. To check system-level properties (such as "the beam shuts off if physical settings of the machine do not match the prescription"), we developed and analyzed a formal model of CNTS in Alloy [1,26]. Using this model, we obtained partial specifications of critical component-level properties (such as "the therapy control software sends a shut-down message if it receives an out-of-tolerance sensor reading"). To check the resulting component properties, we built a suite of custom tools, ranging from an SMT-based verifier for properties of the control software to a manual review processor for properties of the physical components. These custom tools plug into our *safety case checker* (SCC), which combines the system model with the results of the component checks into a mechanized argument—a form of a *safety case* [28,48]—that CNTS satisfies its critical safety properties.

To the best of our knowledge, this case study presents the *first formal, machine-checked safety case for a real system*. A typical safety case takes the form of a structured argument, expressed in natural language or graphical notation [14,37], that a system satisfies a desired critical property. This argument decomposes the system property into a set of component properties, each of which is justified with concrete *evidence* (e.g., the results of verification, manual review, or testing). As massive informal artifacts, however, typical safety arguments suffer from logical fallacies [21] and are difficult to audit for the presence and sufficiency of evidence. For these reasons, prior work [42,43] has called for mechanization of safety case checking. Our work shows, for the first time, that such mechanization is not only possible, but that it is both practical and useful. Building on existing verification frameworks [1,46], our safety case (including the system model and the component checkers) consists of just 2700 lines of code, yet its checks uncovered safety-critical flaws in pre-release versions of the CNTS control software.

Our work differs from prior efforts [10] at safety case mechanization in that *the safety argument is embedded into a formal model of the system*. In prior work, properties of system components are abstracted by uninterpreted predicates, and a mechanized tool ensures that the logical structure of the argument is sound. With this approach, missing properties or assumptions about the environment are discovered through manual auditing. We take a different approach, which enables us to both check the logical soundness of the argument and mechanically discover (some kinds of) missing properties. In particular, our safety argument takes the form $S \Rightarrow P$, where S is a model of the system and P is the desired safety property. The model S specifies the behavior of the system in terms of the properties $s_1, \ldots, s_n$ of individual components and their interactions. When expressed in Alloy, such a model enables both bounded simulation and checking of abstract executions of the system. Bounded simulation helps ensure that the model S includes all desirable treatment scenarios (thus guarding against vacuous fulfillment of the safety argument $S \Rightarrow P$). The checking, on the other hand, helps detect missing component properties (e.g., "the Ethernet network does not drop messages") that are necessary to establish the safety property P.

A component property s_i serves as a (partial) specification for the implementation of the component c_i in the underlying system. Ideally, each component c_i would be mechanically verified to satisfy s_i, but such verification is currently infeasible for many properties (e.g., the reliability of an Ethernet network). Our safety case therefore employs a pragmatic approach that allows weaker evidence to be used for these properties. In particular, each property s_i is guarded by an uninterpreted predicate, written as $evidence(tool, args) \Rightarrow s_i$, which states that the given external tool establishes the property s_i for the component c_i. When checking a safety case, SCC invokes the specified external tools to determine the truth of these predicates, but it does not reason about the strength of the evidence provided by the tool: the *sufficiency* of evidence is subject to manual auditing. Our safety case aids this manual part of the process by making explicit, and precise, all links from a safety argument to evidence.

The rest of this paper is organized as follows. Section 2 provides an overview of the CNTS system. Section 3 describes our machine-checked safety case for CNTS. Section 4 presents SCC and other tools we built as part of the case study. Section 5 discusses the flaws that these tools helped us find and correct. Section 6 surveys related work, and Sect. 7 concludes the paper.

2   Overview of CNTS

The Clinical Neutron Therapy System (CNTS) is a radiotherapy machine that uses neutron radiation to treat tumors resistant to conventional radiotherapy. Due to the high installation and maintenance costs of neutron-based systems, CNTS has been in service for over 30 years, and it is one of only three systems of this kind in the United States. As such, it depends heavily on custom software developed by CNTS engineers, who have achieved a remarkable safety record, with no serious misadministrations due to machine or control system problems.

CNTS engineers have re-implemented its therapy control software twice since 1984 [30, 35]. The latest controller [31] is implemented in a subset of the EPICS (Experimental Physics and Industrial Control System) dataflow language [17], which is widely used for controlling scientific instruments. This development effort aims to support new therapies, integrate new software and hardware, and adapt to changes in the hospital's systems—with continued safety as the foremost concern.

CNTS as a whole is designed [34] to enforce a number of critical safety properties, including *prescription safety*, which is the focus of our work:

Prescription Safety Property (P_{rx}). *During treatment, the beam will turn off if any physical machine setting moves outside the tolerances specified by the prescription and the operator has not issued the manual override command.*[1]

This property is enforced by a *control subsystem*, consisting of hardware and software components, that monitors and drives the system's physical components. Our safety case for P_{rx} (Sect. 3) spans the control subsystem of CNTS, as well as the physical components involved in a treatment prescription.

Physical Components. The key physical components of CNTS include the cyclotron, the leaf collimator, the gantry, and the treatment couch. The cyclotron generates a broad beam of particles, which passes through the leaf collimator in the gantry head on its way to the patient. The collimator consists of forty steel leaves that control the shape of the beam. The gantry head also contains a set of wedges and filters that can be inserted to further adjust the beam's shape and intensity. The gantry rotates 360 degrees around the treatment couch so that the beam can enter the patient from any angle. The couch itself has five degrees of motion freedom. A treatment prescription specifies settings for all of these components, and the CNTS control subsystem ensures that each setting remains within prescribed tolerances during treatment.

Control Subsystem. The CNTS control subsystem is a collection of hardware and software components, which communicate by exchanging messages through a private Ethernet network. The components relevant to our safety case include:

Embedded Single-Board Computers interface with motors and sensors for controlling the physical components of the system. For example, the Treatment Motion Controller (TMC) monitors the orientation of the couch and the gantry. Separate computers exist for shaping the neutron beam and for monitoring the patient's radiation exposure. These embedded computers were installed by the original system vendor and are treated as black boxes by CNTS engineers

Therapy Control (TC) Software displays the user interface on the operator console, accepts commands from the operator, coordinates the activity of the embedded computers, and helps enforce CNTS safety properties (such as P_{rx}). The TC, now re-implemented in EPICS, runs on a general-purpose Linux computer.

Programmable Logic Controller (PLC) serves as an interface between the networked components and the cyclotron control hardware. The PLC is electrically connected to the Hardwired Safety Interlock System (HSIS), which consists of a series of mechanical relays. These relays carry power to the radio frequency

---

[1] The manual override exists to enable treatment to continue if a sensor for a machine setting generates a false alarm.

amplifiers that accelerate particles in the cyclotron. If any relay is opened, the cyclotron stops receiving power and the neutron beam shuts off. For example, if a machine setting moves out of the prescribed tolerances, the TC sends a signal to the PLC to open an HSIS relay, thus shutting off the beam. The PLC functionality is implemented using ladder logic [36], and the CNTS staff modifies and maintains this implementation in addition to the TC.

3   Building a Case for Prescription Safety

This section describes our approach to building a formal, machine-checkable safety case for a key property of CNTS—prescription safety (P_{rx}). The presentation focuses on the aspects of case design that enabled us to practically and effectively check a deep property of a complex system. The tools we developed, and the results we obtained, are discussed in the following sections. All artifacts comprising the case can be found on the project's web page [3].

3.1   Structuring the Case: A System Model with Pluggable Checkers

Our safety case for P_{rx} consists of two parts: (1) a system model S that specifies partial properties of the components spanned by P_{rx} (Sect. 2), and (2) a set of custom tools for checking if those components satisfy the specified properties. The tools indicate either success or failure, depending on whether a given property can be established (through some means) for a given component. Our safety case checker (SCC) connects the model and the tools through uninterpreted predicates of the form $evidence(tool, args)$, which guard component properties specified by S (see, e.g., Fig. 2). These predicates tell SCC which tools to invoke, and how, to establish a given property. The SCC collects pass/fail results of running the tools and uses an off-the-shelf counterexample finder [1] to check that, assuming the obtained results, $S \Rightarrow P_{rx}$. A safety case constructed in this way provides a high-level safety argument (i.e., the system model S, the system property P_{rx}, and the predicates describing how the evidence is obtained), which aids manual auditing, as well as a formal artifact, which enables automatic checking for (some classes of) safety-critical regressions as the system evolves.

3.2   Making the Case: Diagrams, Models, and Tools

We developed the safety case for P_{rx} in three steps. First, we worked with CNTS engineers to identify the system components and interactions that are relevant to P_{rx}, producing an informal, diagrammatic model of the system. This step was crucial for determining the level of detail at which to model the system, and to understand the engineers' concerns—specifically, which properties mattered most and where to focus our analysis effort. Next, we formalized and refined the system model in Alloy [1,26], a widely-used specification language that extends first-order logic with transitive closure and relational algebra. Throughout the formalization process, we relied heavily on Alloy's counterexample finder

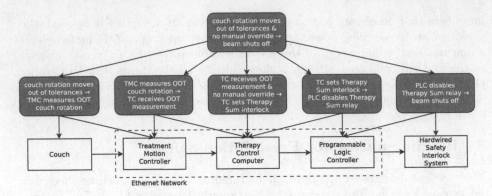

Fig. 1. A fragment of the property-part diagram for a part of the P_{rx} property. Boxes represent system components, and rounded boxes represent properties. Edges originating from a property indicate that the property depends on the target components or properties for its fulfillment. Edges originating from a component indicate interaction via messages. Components within the dashed box are connected via Ethernet.

to detect errors in logical reasoning, as well as component properties that were missing from our informal diagrams. Finally, we used the resulting Alloy model—and feedback from CNTS engineers—to determine where and how to focus our tool-building effort. We describe each of these steps in more detail below.

Drafting an Iinformal Case. To build a safety case for P_{rx}, we first drafted an informal safety argument, expressed as a property-part diagram [27]. This kind of diagram shows how components—or parts—of the system relate to each other and how their individual properties collectively satisfy the desired system property. Figure 1 shows a fragment of the property-part diagram for P_{rx} that covers the rotation angle of the treatment couch. The diagram shows how the top-level property and its sub-properties are established by a combination of other properties and components. For example, the Programmable Logic Controller (PLC) and the Hardwired Safety Interlock System (HSIS) jointly ensure that the beam is turned off when the Therapy Sum relay is opened (disabled). The informal case for P_{rx} includes similar diagrams for other machine parameters that are specified by a treatment prescription.

Formalizing the Case. To formalize the P_{rx} case, we developed an Alloy model of the major components of CNTS. These include the therapy control (TC) software, the Treatment Motion Controller (TMC), the Programmable Logic Controller (PLC), the Hardwired Safety Interlock System (HSIS), the beam, and the machine settings involved in a prescription. Our model specifies the internal states of the components (e.g., whether a given HSIS relay is open or closed) and their external interactions (e.g., the messages exchanged between the TC and the embedded computers) in sufficient detail to capture the key behaviors of the system, such as the beam shutting off when a machine setting enters an out-of-tolerance state, or the beam staying on due to manual override. The lead CNTS engineer audited the model to ensure that it accurately describes the partial properties of the system relevant to the argument.

Figure 2 shows a snippet of our formalization. Lines 7–13 specify a property of the PLC that is relevant to the case. We model the changes in the state of the PLC relays and coils as events ordered by the next relation. Relays can be either open or closed, and coils can be either energized or de-energized. Relay 2754 of the PLC corresponds to the Therapy Sum Interlock relay in Fig. 1. Whenever this relay is in the open state (line 7), PLC coil 1623 enters a de-energized state, which, in turn, electrically signals an HSIS relay to open and cause the beam to shut off (lines 8–13). Other parts of the system are modeled at a similar level of detail.

```
1   evidence[PLC_Analysis,
2           "--mode" -> "all-paths-to-coil-contain-relay" +
3           "--network-file" -> "plc-code/cyclotron/mod1.stu" +
4           "--coil" -> "%M1623" +
5           "--relay" -> "%M2754",
6           Proof] =>
7   all relayOpen: Relay2754.state & RelayOpen |
8     some coilState: Coil1623.state & CoilDeenergized,
9          coilChangeSignal : PLC.sentMsgs & CoilChange |
10    coilState in relayOpen.next and
11    coilChangeSignal in coilState.next and
12    coilChangeSignal.coil = Coil1623 and
13    coilChangeSignal.state = coilState
```

Fig. 2. A property of the PLC, guarded by an evidence predicate. The property states that PLC coil 1623 is de-energized when relay 2754 is open. Coil 1623 controls the neutron beam and relay 2754 is written to by the Therapy Controller (TC)—this is the mechanism by which the TC shuts off the beam when a machine setting is out of its prescribed tolerance. The property (lines 7–13) is a formula in the Alloy language [1,26]. The evidence predicate (lines 1–6) states that the external PLC_Analysis tool (Sect. 4) must be called to establish that the PLC satisfies this property.

```
1   check PrescriptionSafetyCase {
2     all ms: MachineState |
3     (properties and
4     some badSetting[ms] and
5     not badSettingOverriden[ms]) =>
6     some off: Beam.state & BeamOff |
7       happensBefore[ms, off]
8   }
9   for 3 but 10 Event, 2 int
```

Fig. 3. The Alloy formulation of the P_{rx} property. For all machine states, if all component properties (e.g., Fig. 2) hold, a machine setting is out of prescribed tolerances in that state, and the manual override has not been enabled for that machine setting, then a "beam off" event must occur after the given state.

While formalizing the case, we relied heavily on the Alloy Analyzer [1] to discover soundness and vacuity errors in our argument. Checking that the model is sound (permits no behavior that violates P_{rx}) let us detect missing component properties (e.g., the Ethernet network does not drop messages), and checking that the model is not vacuous (permits some behaviors that satisfy P_{rx}) let us detect accidental contradictions in the formalization. To check for soundness errors, we asked the Analyzer to verify that our model of CNTS implies P_{rx} for all event sequences of length up to ten, as shown in Fig. 3. The bound of ten encompasses all known treatment scenarios and is thus large enough to prevent P_{rx} from being vacuously fulfilled. To check this, we asked the Analyzer to verify that a bound of ten events is sufficient to simulate treatment scenarios in which (1) the beam remains on because the machine settings remain within tolerance; (2) a setting goes out of tolerance, but the beam shut off is manually overridden; and (3) the beam shuts off due to an out-of-tolerance setting and the absence of manual override. All of these checks explore massive potential state spaces (on the order of 2^{2800} states), and all pass in seconds.

Building Tools. Having formalized the case, we used it to decide what tools to build in order to establish the specified component properties. In particular, we determined the tool interfaces by going through the model and systematically annotating all component properties with *evidence* predicates, as shown in Fig. 2. An evidence predicate evaluates to true if and only if the specified tool indicates success when invoked with the given arguments. For example, lines 1–6 in Fig. 2 state that the evidence (a proof) for the PLC property is produced by the PLC analysis tool (Sect. 4), invoked with the specified parameters. We determined what kind of evidence was practically sufficient for each component (e.g., a proof, passing tests, or manual review) based on the feedback from CNTS engineers. This process of connecting properties with evidence was crucial in focusing our analysis effort (Sect. 5): building a tool that proves a narrow class of properties is much easier than building a general-purpose verifier. Our safety case both articulated these properties and helped guide the construction of tools for checking them.

4   Tools and Analyses

This section surveys the tools that we built to produce and check evidence for the P_{rx} safety case described in Sect. 3. We focused the analysis effort on the components that are directly modified by the CNTS engineers: the Therapy Control (TC) software and the Programmable Logic Controller (PLC). In particular, we built a linter and an SMT-based verifier for the subset of EPICS in which TC is written, a static analyzer for (a narrow class of) properties of PLC ladder logic code, and a static analyzer for the EPICS-PLC interface code. We relied on expert approval and manual review of documentation to establish the relevant properties of the embedded computers, the Hardwired Safety Interlock System (HSIS), the Ethernet network, and the physical components. The presence of this expert evidence was checked using a simple text-processing tool. We also built a safety case checker (SCC) to connect our formal model of CNTS (Sect. 3) with the results produced by the tools. We describe each of these tools in more detail below, highlighting how the safety case guided our choice of analyses, their construction, and their application.

Safety Case Checker (SCC). Our safety case checker (SCC) automates the integration of external evidence-generating tools into a formal safety argument, expressed with respect to a model of the system. We chose the Alloy language and the Alloy Analyzer as our toolset for system-level reasoning. However, a similar checker could also be created for other formal frameworks (e.g., [9,40,41]).

```
1  procedure SCCCheck(S, P, universe_size):
2    I[evidence] ← {} // partial interpretation
3    for evidence[tool, args, kind] in FindEvidencePredicates(S):
4      result ← InvokePluggableChecker(tool, args)
5      if result = true:
6        I[evidence] ← I[evidence] ∪ {⟨ tool, args, kind ⟩}
7    return AlloyCheckSAT(S ∧ ¬ P, I, universe_size)
```

Fig. 4. Overview of the algorithm used by our safety case checker.

The SCC consists of two parts: (1) an extension to the Alloy language, and (2) a checker for this language extension that is based on the Alloy Analyzer. The language is extended with a small library that provides the uninterpreted evidence predicate. In particular, the formula evidence[tool, args, kind] represents the presence (or absence) of the given kind of evidence, produced by invoking the specified tool on the provided arguments. The checker, as shown in Fig. 4, provides an interpretation for each evidence predicate in a safety case by performing the specified tool invocation and recording the result in Alloy. This invocation is performed through a simple plug-in interface, designed for easy addition of new tools to the checker. The resulting interpretation I gives meaning only to the evidence predicates, and, as such, it is a *partial interpretation* [44,47] for the safety case $S \Rightarrow P$, which includes additional relations (e.g., the next relation in Fig. 2). The checker passes I and $S \land \neg P$ to the Alloy Analyzer, which checks that I cannot be extended into a finite counterexample to the safety case—i.e., an interpretation $I' \supseteq I$ that satisfies $S \land \neg P$ in a finite universe of discourse. The results of SCC verification are sound up to the bound on the universe size, modulo any bugs in the implementation of SCC and the pluggable checkers.

EPICS Verifier. We focused our most advanced analysis, a fully automated verifier for a subset of the EPICS language, on the newest component of the system, the Therapy Control (TC) software. This tool uses an SMT solver to verify safety properties of programs written in a subset of EPICS that includes all code from CNTS. Because the Therapy Control software is finite-state, with bounded execution length and memory consumption, our EPICS verifier is both sound (it does not miss defects) and complete (it does not report false positives) for CNTS. The P_{rx} case uses the verifier to prove that the therapy control software initiates beam shut-off whenever it receives an out-of-tolerance reading from a sensor (see, e.g., Fig. 5).

The verifier builds on Rosette [45], a language for constructing verification and synthesis tools based on SMT solvers. It takes as input an EPICS dataflow program and a safety property, symbolically interprets the program on an arbitrary state and input event, and then invokes the Z3 solver [11] to check that the property holds in the resulting state. The output is either a guarantee that the property holds, or a concrete state and input event (a counterexample) that causes the program to violate the property.

An EPICS dataflow program is a graph consisting of edges, called *links*, and nodes, called *records*, along with configuration settings and initial values for each record. At run time, the EPICS interpreter behaves as a reactive system, responding to *events* (such as arrival of input from external devices or expiration of a timer) by updating the state of the graph and possibly sending output to external devices. In contrast to traditional dataflow systems, which automatically update all dependent values when an input value changes, the EPICS language gives the programmer explicit control over all data flow and control flow in the program. Moreover, EPICS code can modify the structure of the dataflow graph at run time, adding or removing edges, as well as modifying record configurations, such as the expression evaluated in a record. These dynamic features make it challenging to verify general EPICS code.

Unlike general EPICS programs, however, CNTS code is amenable to verification because it does not use the dynamic features of EPICS. Since EPICS forbids dynamic memory allocation and guarantees termination of event handlers, all EPICS programs with no dynamic features are finite-state, and their executions have bounded length. As a result, our verifier can automatically prove deep properties of CNTS code, without requiring loop invariants or imposing artificial bounds on heap size and execution length. Our verifier uncovered a safety-critical bug in a production version of the CNTS therapy control software, in addition to a subtle dependence of a pre-release version of the software on a bug in the EPICS runtime, as described in Sect. 5.1.

```
1  (define (couch-wrong-implies-beam-off)
2    (process_IsoGantryCouchTurntableActual)
3    (assert (=>
4      (and
5        (> (abs (- prescribed actual)) tolerance)
6        (= couch-override 0)
7        (= mode 0))
8      (= beam-interlock 0))))
```

Fig. 5. A property of the CNTS therapy control software verified with the EPICS verifier. It states that, after a couch turntable angle reading is processed (line 2), the beam interlock is triggered ("beam off") if the couch turntable's actual rotation differs from the prescription by more than the tolerance, the manual override is disabled, and the machine is in therapy mode.

EPICS Linter. The EPICS linter establishes a basic well-formedness property assumed by our verifier: all record links (i.e., dataflow edges) in a program refer to valid records. EPICS does not otherwise report broken links, instead assuming that missing records will be provided by other EPICS instances on the same local network. Ensuring that all links are valid implies that a given EPICS program contains all code relevant to the analysis. Our linter uncovered several issues in the therapy control code, described in Sect. 5.1.

EPICS-PLC Interface Checker. The EPICS-PLC interface checker ensures that a given EPICS record is connected to a particular PLC relay. This requires analyzing both the EPICS program and a separate startup script that initializes communication with the PLC. The P_{rx} safety case, for example, uses the interface checker to ensure that the EPICS Therapy Sum Interlock record is properly connected to the PLC Therapy Sum Interlock relay.

PLC Checker. The PLC checker analyzes the graph of connections between coils, relays, and the power source in a ladder logic program. This checker provides two analyses that are useful for the P_{rx} case. First, it can check that a named relay's state is not updated by any other element within the PLC. Second, it can check that all paths from the power source to a named coil pass through a named relay, thus guaranteeing that the coil is energized only when the relay is closed. In the P_{rx} safety case, these checks establish that the Therapy Sum Interlock relay in the PLC is modified only as a result of messages from the therapy control software, and that opening the Therapy Sum Interlock relay must de-energize the PLC coil connected to the Hardwired Safety Interlock System (HSIS).

Expert Evidence. The expert evidence tool allows an expert to assert that a component property holds based on manual inspection of some part of the system. After examining the property in question, the expert creates a text document explaining in prose the nature of the inspection and the evidence that supports the property, along with the expert's name and the current date to support future auditing. For example, the configuration of the CNTS HSIS is defined by a non-machine-readable circuit diagram, so the P_{rx} safety case relies on expert inspection to establish properties of the HSIS. In general, our case relies on expert evidence only for claims that would be impractical to support otherwise.

5 Results and Discussion

This section presents the results of developing a mechanically-checkable safety case for P_{rx}, and the lessons learned from our experience. Developing the case uncovered several issues in the new therapy control software for CNTS, including two safety-critical defects. We also found that structuring the case as a system model with pluggable checkers focused our analysis effort, enabling us to perform deep checks of a complex system, while writing only 2700 lines of code.

5.1   Issues Uncovered

Through the construction of the P_{rx} case, we found several previously unknown issues in a pre-release version of the CNTS therapy control software, and we rediscovered an issue that the CNTS engineers found during a production test run. We discuss these issues first, and conclude by briefly describing a problem that we found in the system model itself.

Array Semantics. While developing the part of the case related to the setting of the couch rotation angle, we discovered a serious issue in the therapy control code and in a major component of the EPICS runtime. The issue concerns array calculations, which are performed using EPICS records of type `acalcout`. An `acalcout` record performs calculations over arrays of a statically specified length. All intermediate values in the computation are truncated or padded with zeros to match this length.

The affected calculation in the therapy control software uses an "in-place slice" operator that retains elements between two given indices and zeroes the rest. In the documentation [16], the bounds on this operator are both inclusive, but in the version of `acalcout` used in CNTS, the upper bound is erroneously treated as exclusive. The therapy control software behaves correctly under the exclusive semantics, but upgrading to a version of `acalcout` that correctly implements the inclusive semantics would introduce subtle errors into several calculations in the therapy control software. Our EPICS verifier, initially implemented using the inclusive semantics, detected one such error in the computation of a flag sent to the PLC to control the neutron beam, for which *sending the wrong value may cause the beam to fail to turn off when a sensor reading is out of prescribed tolerances*. Due to this issue, the CNTS engineers cannot safely upgrade this essential library—correct behavior of the software depends upon the library bug. The CNTS engineers were unaware of this problem until our EPICS verifier revealed it.

Gantry Rotation. Early in the first production run of the new therapy control software, the CNTS engineers identified a safety-critical flaw in the checking of the gantry rotation angle. The gantry angle measurement ranges from $-0.5°$ to $+360.5°$, and the intent when developing the gantry rotation checks was to treat pairs of angles separated by $360°$ as equivalent, so that a rotation measurement of $360°$ would satisfy a prescription for $0°$. However, an error in the arithmetic used in the check caused the system to treat as equivalent any pair of angles equally distant from $180°$; for example, a measurement of $200°$ would satisfy a prescription for $160°$. *This error could have allowed the beam to turn on and remain on with the gantry rotation set to an incorrect angle.*

Before we had completed the relevant portion of the P_{rx} case, the CNTS engineers notified us that the code contained a bug involving the gantry rotation angle, but provided no other details. When we completed the case, SCC detected an error: the EPICS verifier, when asked to prove that the therapy control software triggered the Therapy Sum Interlock upon receiving an out-of-tolerance gantry rotation measurement, instead produced a counterexample containing a rotation measurement and prescription value that erroneously failed to trigger the interlock. We investigated the relevant EPICS code to identify the root cause of the bug and confirmed the details with the EPICS engineers. After applying their fix to the CNTS EPICS code, SCC processed the P_{rx} safety case without errors.

Broken Links. Our EPICS linter uncovered a total of 59 references to nonexistent records in the therapy control software. Three of these represented serious problems: they were caused by a misspelled record name, which would *prevent the operator from being informed of certain error conditions.* The CNTS engineers fixed these issues promptly. Another three turned out to be harmless remnants from an earlier code removal. The remaining 53 links refer to records that should have been annotated as nonlocal, since they exist in a separate EPICS installation that is accessed transparently over the network at runtime. The CNTS engineers are investigating how to annotate these nonlocal links.

Case Error. Our initial formalization of the P_{rx} case contained an error, arising from a misunderstanding about the design of the system: the case claimed that an invalid couch rotation would cause the therapy control software to open the PLC's Gantry/Couch Subsystem Interlock relay, and the PLC would then internally open its Therapy Sum Interlock relay. But while trying to formulate the corresponding `evidence` invocation, we were unable to find the PLC relay number for the Gantry/Couch Subsystem Interlock. In fact, no such relay exists. The therapy software, not the PLC, combines Gantry/Couch Subsystem and other interlocks to compute the Therapy Sum, and it sends the combined Therapy Sum Interlock state to the PLC. Our strategy of connecting every component property to concrete evidence directly led to our discovery of this modeling error.

5.2   Performance

As shown in Fig. 6, end-to-end checking of our safety case takes less than an hour. The figure also shows the sizes of the codebases processed by our analysis tools. The PLC software is developed in a non-textual representation, so we report its size in terms of nodes (relays, coils, and other logic elements) and edges (wires) in the ladder logic graph. The size of the therapy control codebase includes both the EPICS dataflow graph definitions and the startup script used to load the graph and initialize communication between the therapy software and external hardware. The system model for the P_{rx} case is specified in Alloy, extended with the SCC `evidence` library. The EPICS tools (the linter, verifier, and connection checker) share a common codebase, so they are reported together. Most of the common codebase is related to parsing; only 57 lines are specific to the linter, 441 are specific to the EPICS verifier, and 61 are specific to the EPICS-PLC interface checker. The case, in total, consists of 2700 lines of code.

5.3   Lessons Learned

Developing our safety case for CNTS led to three primary insights.

Analysis	Time (s)	Codebase	Size
EPICS verifier	3183.9	PLC	5222 nodes, 10870 edges
EPICS linter	0.9	TC	5448 lines
EPICS-PLC interface checker	0.4	P_{rx} case	645 lines
PLC ladder logic checker	0.4	SCC library	85 lines
Alloy Analyzer	4.1	EPICS tools	1666 lines
Total (including overhead)	3190.0	PLC checker	298 lines

Fig. 6. Total analysis time for the P_{rx} case (left), sizes of the CNTS software components analyzed as part of the case (right, above the line), and sizes of the system model and tools that make up the case (right, below the line). The performance data was collected on a Debian 8 laptop with an Intel Core i7-4900MQ CPU running at 2.80 GHz with 16 GB RAM.

1. System Model as Safety Case. Our decision to base the case on a detailed system model rather than a propositional formula (with component properties represented by uninterpreted predicates) enabled us to detect errors in the case with minimal auditing effort. A missing property in an Alloy model results in a concrete counterexample (an execution of the system that violates the safety property), whereas a missing premise in a propositional argument can be detected only through manual auditing. For example, our safety case for P_{rx} initially failed to specify that the ethernet network does not drop any packets. The Alloy Analyzer produced a counterexample, showing a scenario in which a dropped packet led to a violation of P_{rx}. Using a detailed Alloy model helped us not only ensure that relevant component properties are stated, but also that our argument is not vacuous (because the system model has no executions).

2. Simple Safety Case Checking. The decision to implement our safety case checker (SCC) on top of Alloy significantly eased the development burden while providing us with ready-made automated analysis and visualization facilities. Initially, we had planned to implement SCC using a custom language to handle reasoning about the model and external evidence, as proposed in previous work [10,12,18,19]. However, as part of the development of SCC, we chose to first prototype it directly in Alloy. From this prototype, the general design pattern for evidence predicates emerged, allowing us to easily connect additional external checkers to SCC, leading to a suite of lightweight but effective tools for the P_{rx} case.

3. Deep and Narrow Custom Tools. We found case-guided tool development to be highly effective since it focused our efforts on the important properties of each component. With only 1964 lines of code, we built four custom tools for CNTS that check a narrow class of properties each, as specified by our system model. The integration of these tools into SCC was eased by its simple plug-in architecture. To add a new tool, the tool developer simply registers a plugin, consisting of a small Python script that can invoke the tool and interpret its output to determine success or failure. In particular, the need for the

EPICS-PLC connectivity checker became apparent only late in the development of the P_{rx} case, but because we had already implemented the plug-in architecture for SCC, we were able to both develop and integrate this checker in less than a day.

6   Related Work

There is a large body of literature on ensuring safety of critical systems (see, e.g., [28,38] for a survey). This section surveys the most closely related work, focusing on previous safety efforts at CNTS, methodologies for ensuring safety of complex systems, languages for expressing safety cases, and symbolic techniques for checking properties of software components.

CNTS Safety. The CNTS engineering staff has, over the years, produced a large collection of heterogeneous evidence [29] in support of CNTS safety properties, including P_{rx}. This includes a 200-page document detailing system requirements, developed in consultation with physicists and clinicians; a 2,100 line Z specification [30] of the Therapy Control software; a 16,000 LOC reference implementation of the Z specification in C (in use until July 2015); a 240-page reference manual [33]; a 43-page therapist guide [32]; and an extensive set of end-to-end testing protocols that are executed on a daily, weekly, monthly, and yearly basis. However, none of these prior efforts produced an explicit, mechanically checked safety argument. Our P_{rx} safety case is the first such argument to be created for CNTS, and its creation has already led to improvements in the new CNTS software.

Approaches to Safety. Traditional approaches to system safety are *process-based*. Systems like CNTS or the Mars rover [24] are developed according to strict best practices, by highly skilled engineers. At the system level, these practices involve detailed requirements, documentation, hazard analysis, and formalization of key parts of the system design. At the code level, they include adherence to stringent coding conventions (see, e.g., [23]), manual code reviews, use of static analysis, and extensive testing. Process-based approaches are highly effective at producing low-defect code. However, they provide no explicit argument that the system as a whole satisfies critical properties.

Our work builds on *case-based* approaches to safety (e.g., [25,28,37,39]). These approaches aim to produce an explicit argument [25] that links claims about component behavior to concrete evidence in the form of tests, proofs, manual reviews, etc. Our approach to developing the P_{rx} case is most closely related to that of Near et al. [39]. We also used property-part diagrams [27] to first develop an informal case, which we then formalized in Alloy [1,26]. But Near et al. do not connect their system-level argument to evidence; instead they use an interactive analysis to produce evidence obligations only for the software component of their target system. Our approach, in contrast, uses SCC to connect the system model to evidence generated by a variety of tools, including a fully automatic code verifier. To our knowledge, our case study is also the first to analyze low-level Programmable Logic Controllers as well as the system's software.

Languages for Expressing Safety Cases. Existing languages and tools for developing dependability cases (e.g., [13,37]) focus on managing the structure of a case. In these languages, a safety case takes the form of a semi-formal argument expressed in a graphical notation [37], with safety claims linked to evidence from heterogeneous sources. SCC, in contrast, focuses on expressing the safety argument with respect to a detailed formal model of the system, linked to tool-generated evidence. This approach enables automated reasoning about the logical correctness and non-vacuity of the safety argument.

In terms of automation, SCC is most closely related to the Evidential Tool Bus (ETB) [10]. The ETB is a general-purpose framework for tool integration, for scripting distributed workflows, and for connecting claims with supporting evidence. Its input language is a variant of Datalog. SCC shares with the ETB the idea of a semantics-neutral connection between claims and evidence, using uninterpreted predicates. In contrast to the ETB, however, SCC provides a more expressive formal language (with quantifiers and transitive closure), suitable for system modeling. SCC also provides, via Alloy, automatic soundness and vacuity checking, as well as facilities for counterexample visualization. We made heavy use of these features while developing the P_{rx} safety case.

Software Verification. There is a wide variety of verification tools (e.g., [2,4,5,7, 8,15,20,49]) for general-purpose programming languages. These tools are hard to build, requiring significant effort and expertise. As a result, they are rarely created for more specialized languages, such as EPICS. Our EPICS verifier is, to our knowledge, the first of its kind. Its implementation leverages Rosette [45,46], a language designed for easy creation of domain-specific verification and synthesis tools based on SMT. Our verifier scales to real EPICS programs and is capable of finding subtle flaws that cannot be found without symbolic reasoning.

7   Conclusion

This paper reported on a case study in applying modern verification techniques to construct the first mechanically-checked safety case for a real safety-critical system, the Clinical Neutron Therapy System (CNTS). Our safety case includes a detailed formal model of CNTS and a set of tools for establishing component properties specified by the model. Leveraging existing formal tools, Alloy and Rosette, we built the entire case by writing just 2700 lines of code. The construction of the case revealed serious flaws in the CNTS therapy control software and in the implementation of the EPICS language, which we reported to the CNTS staff. Our results demonstrate that formal, checkable safety cases can provide significant practical benefits by focusing analysis effort on deep properties of system components that matter for the safety of the system as a whole.

Acknowledgments. This material is based on research sponsored by DARPA under agreement numbers FA8750-12-2-0107, FA8750-15-C-0010, and FA8750-16-2-0032. The U.S. Government is authorized to reproduce and distribute reprints for Governmental purposes notwithstanding any copyright notation thereon.

References

1. Alloy: a language and tool for relational models (2014). http://alloy.mit.edu/alloy/
2. Java PathFinder (2015). http://babelfish.arc.nasa.gov/trac/jpf
3. Safety case for CNTS prescription safety, August 2015. http://neutrons.uwplse.org
4. Babic, D., Hu, A.J.: Calysto: scalable and precise extended static checking. In: ICSE (2008)
5. Barnett, M., Rustan, M., Leino, K., Schulte, W.: The Spec# programming system: an overview. In: Barthe, G., Burdy, L., Huisman, M., Lanet, J.-L., Muntean, T. (eds.) CASSIS 2004. LNCS, vol. 3362, pp. 49–69. Springer, Heidelberg (2005)
6. Beringer, L., Petcher, A., Ye, K.Q., Appel, A.W.: Verified correctness and security of openSSL HMAC. In: 24th USENIX Security Symposium (USENIX Security 2015), Washington, D.C., pp. 207–221 (2015). USENIX Association. https://www.usenix.org/conference/usenixsecurity15/technical-sessions/presentation/beringer. ISBN:978-1-931971-232
7. Cadar, C., Dunbar, D., Engler, D.: KLEE: unassisted and automatic generation of high-coverage tests for complex systems programs. In: Proceedings of the 8th Symposium on Operating Systems Designand Implementation (OSDI), San Diego, CA, pp. 209–224, December 2008
8. Clarke, E., Kroning, D., Lerda, F.: A tool for checking ANSI-C programs. In: Jensen, K., Podelski, A. (eds.) TACAS 2004. LNCS, vol. 2988, pp. 168–176. Springer, Heidelberg (2004)
9. Coq development team. Coq Reference Manual, Version 8.4pl5. INRIA, Octobor 2014. http://coq.inria.fr/distrib/current/refman/
10. Cruanes, S., Hamon, G., Owre, S., Shankar, N.: Tool integration with the evidential tool bus. In: Giacobazzi, R., Berdine, J., Mastroeni, I. (eds.) VMCAI 2013. LNCS, vol. 7737, pp. 275–294. Springer, Heidelberg (2013)
11. de Moura, L., Bjørner, N.S.: Z3: an efficient SMT solver. In: Ramakrishnan, C.R., Rehof, J. (eds.) TACAS 2008. LNCS, vol. 4963, pp. 337–340. Springer, Heidelberg (2008)
12. Denney, E., Pai, G.: Evidence arguments for using formal methods in software certification. In: 2013 IEEE International Symposium on Software Reliability Engineering Workshops (ISSREW), pp. 375–380, November 2013. doi:10.1109/ISSREW.2013.6688924
13. Denney, E., Pai, G., Pohl, J.: AdvoCATE: an assurance case automation toolset. In: Ortmeier, F., Daniel, P. (eds.) SAFECOMP Workshops 2012. LNCS, vol. 7613, pp. 8–21. Springer, Heidelberg (2012). doi:10.1007/978-3-642-33675-1_2
14. Dependability Research Group. Safety cases repository, February 2006. http://dependability.cs.virginia.edu/info/Safety_Cases:Repository
15. Dolby, J., Vaziri, M., Tip, F.: Finding bugs efficiently with a SAT solver. In: FSE (2007)
16. EPICS. CalcOut Release Notes. http://www.aps.anl.gov/bcda/synApps/calc/calcReleaseNotes.html
17. EPICS. http://www.aps.anl.gov/epics/

18. Ernst, M.D., Grossman, D., Jacky, J., Loncaric, C., Pernsteiner, S., Tatlock, Z., Torlak, E., Wang, X.: Toward a dependability case language and workflow for a radiation therapy system. In: Summit on Advances in Programming Languages (SNAPL) (2015)
19. Gacek, A., Backes, J., Cofer, D.D., Slind, K., Whalen, M.: Resolute: an assurance case language for architecture models (2014). CoRR, abs/1409.4629. http://arxiv.org/abs/1409.4629
20. Galeotti, J.P.: Software verification using alloy. Ph.D. thesis, University of Buenos Aires (2010)
21. Greenwell, W.S., Knight, J.C., Holloway, C.M., Pease, J.J.: A taxonomy of fallacies in system safety arguments. In: International System Safety Conference (2006)
22. Hawblitzel, C., Howell, J., Kapritsos, M., Lorch, J.R., Parno, B., Roberts, M.L., Setty, S., Zill, B.: Ironfleet: proving practical distributed systems correct. In: Proceedings of the 25th Symposium on Operating Systems Principles, SOSP 2015, pp. 1–17. ACM, New York (2015). doi:10.1145/2815400.2815428, ISBN:978-1-4503-3834-9
23. Holzmann, G.J.: The power of 10: rules for developing safety-critical code. Computer **39**(6), 95–97 (2006). doi:10.1109/MC.2006.212. ISSN:0018-9162
24. Holzmann, G.J.: Mars code. Commun. ACM **57**(2), 64–73 (2014). doi:10.1145/2560217.2560218. ISSN:0001-0782
25. Jackson, D.: A direct path to dependable software. Commun. ACM **52**(4), 78–88 (2009)
26. Jackson, D.: Software Abstractions: Logic, Language, and Analysis. MIT Press, Cambridge (2012)
27. Jackson, D., Kang, E.: Property-part diagrams: a dependence notation for software systems. Technical report, Massachusetts Institute of Technology (2009). http://hdl.handle.net/1721.1/61343
28. Jackson, D., Thomas, M.: Software for Dependable Systems: Sufficient Evidence?. National Academy Press, Washington, D.C. (2007). ISBN:0309103940, 9780309103947
29. Jacky, J.: The Clinical Neutron Therapy System. http://staff.washington.edu/jon/cnts/index.html
30. Jacky, J.: Formal safety analysis of the control program for a radiation therapy machine. In: Schlegel, W., Bortfeld, T. (eds.) The Use of Computers in Radiation Therapy, pp. 68–70. Springer, Heidelberg (2000)
31. Jacky, J.: EPICS-based control system for a radiation therapy machine. In: International Conference on Accelerator and Large Experimental Physics Control Systems (ICALEPCS) (2013)
32. Jacky, J., Risler, R.: Clinical neutron therapy system therapist's guide. Technical report 99–07-01, University of Washington, Department of Radiation Oncology (2002)
33. Jacky, J., Risler, R.: Clinical neutron therapy system reference manual. Technical report 99–10-01, University of Washington, Department of Radiation Oncology (2002)
34. Jacky, J., Risler, R., Kalet, I., Wootton, P.: Clinical neutron therapy system control system specification part I. Technical report 90–12-01, University of Washington, Department of Radiation Oncology (1990)
35. Jacky, J., Risler, R., Reid, D., Emery, R., Unger, J., Patrick, M.: A control system for a radiation therapy machine. Technical report 2001–05-01, University of Washington, Department of Radiation Oncology (2001)

36. John, K.H., Tiegelkamp, M.: IEC 61131–3: Programming Industrial Automation Systems: Concepts and Programming Languages, Requirements for Programming Systems Decision-Making Aids, 2nd edn. Springer Publishing Company, Incorporated, New York (2010). ISBN:3642120148, 9783642120145

37. Kelly, T., Weaver, R.: The goal structuring notation - a safety argument notation. In: Proceedings of the Dependable Systems and Networks 2004 Workshop on Assurance Cases, July 2004

38. Lyu, M.R. (ed.): Handbook of Software Reliability Engineering. McGraw-Hill Inc., Hightstown (1996)

39. Near, J.P., Milicevic, A., Kang, E., Jackson, D.: A lightweight code analysis and its role in evaluation of a dependability case. In: Proceedings of the 33rd International Conference of Computer Safety, Reliability and Security, Waikiki, Honolulu, HI, pp. 31–40, May 2011

40. Nipkow, T., Paulson, L.C., Wenzel, M.: Isabelle/HOL – A Proof Assistant for Higher-Order Logic. LNCS, vol. 2283. Springer, Heidelberg (2002)

41. Owre, S., Rushby, J.M., Shankar, N.: PVS: a prototype verification system. In: Kapur, D. (ed.) CADE 1992. LNCS(LNAI), vol. 607, pp. 748–752. Springer, Heidelberg (1992)

42. Rushby, J.: Formalism in safety cases. In: Safety-Critical Systems Symposium (2010)

43. Rushby, J.: Mechanized support for assurance case argumentation. In: Nakano, Y., Satoh, K., Bekki, D. (eds.) JSAI-isAI 2013. LNCS, vol. 8417, pp. 304–318. Springer, Heidelberg (2014). doi:10.1007/978-3-319-10061-6_20

44. Torlak, E.: Constraint solver for software engineering: finding models and cores of large relational specifications. Ph.D. thesis, Massachusetts Institute of Technology, Cambridge (2009). AAI0821754

45. Torlak, E., Bodik, R.: Growing solver-aided languages with Rosette. In: Proceedings of the 2013 ACM International Symposium on New Ideas, New Paradigms, and Reflections on Programming & Software, Onward! 2013, Indianapolis, IN, pp. 135–152 (2013)

46. Torlak, E., Bodik, R.: A lightweight symbolic virtual machine for solver-aided host languages. In: Proceedings of the 2014 ACM SIGPLAN Conference on Programming Language Design and Implementation (PLDI), Edinburgh, UK, pp. 530–541, June 2014

47. Torlak, E., Jackson, D.: Kodkod: a relational model finder. In: Grumberg, O., Huth, M. (eds.) TACAS 2007. LNCS, vol. 4424, pp. 632–647. Springer, Heidelberg (2007)

48. Weinstock, C., Goodenough, J., Hudak, J.: Dependability cases. Technical report CMU/SEI-2004-TN-016, Software Engineering Institute, Carnegie Mellon University, Pittsburgh (2004)

49. Xie, Y., Aiken, A.: Saturn: a scalable framework for error detection using Boolean satisfiability. ACM Trans. Program. Lang. Syst. (2007)

End-to-End Verification of ARM® Processors with ISA-Formal

Alastair Reid[✉], Rick Chen, Anastasios Deligiannis, David Gilday,
David Hoyes, Will Keen, Ashan Pathirane, Owen Shepherd, Peter Vrabel,
and Ali Zaidi

ARM Limited, 110 Fulbourn Road, Cambridge, UK
{alastair.reid,rick.chen,anastasios.deligiannis,david.gilday,david.hoyes,
will.keen,ashan.pathirane,owen.shepherd,peter.vrabel,ali.zaidi}@arm.com

Abstract. Despite 20+ years of research on processor verification, it remains hard to use formal verification techniques in commercial processor development. There are two significant factors: scaling issues and return on investment. The *scaling issues* include the size of modern processor specifications, the size/complexity of processor designs, the size of design/verification teams and the (non)availability of enough formal verification experts. The *return on investment* issues include the need to start catching bugs early in development, the need to continue catching bugs throughout development, and the need to be able to reuse verification IP, tools and techniques across a wide range of design styles.

This paper describes how ARM has overcome these issues in our Instruction Set Architecture Formal Verification framework "ISA-Formal." This is an end-to-end framework to detect bugs in the datapath, pipeline control and forwarding/stall logic of processors. A key part of making the approach scale is use of a mechanical translation of ARM's Architecture Reference Manuals to Verilog allowing the use of commercial model-checkers. ISA-Formal has proven especially effective at finding micro-architecture specific bugs involving complex sequences of instructions.

An essential feature of our work is that it is able to scale all the way from simple 3-stage microcontrollers, through superscalar in-order processors up to out-of-order processors. We have applied this method to 8 different ARM processors spanning all stages of development up to release. In all processors, this has found bugs that would have been hard for conventional simulation-based verification to find and ISA-Formal is now a key part of ARM's formal verification strategy.

To the best of our knowledge, this is the most broadly applicable formal verification technique for verifying processor pipeline control in mainstream commercial use.

1 Introduction

Modern microprocessor designs apply many optimizations to improve performance: pipelining, forwarding, issuing multiple instructions per cycle, multiple

© Springer International Publishing Switzerland 2016
S. Chaudhuri and A. Farzan (Eds.): CAV 2016, Part II, LNCS 9780, pp. 42–58, 2016.
DOI: 10.1007/978-3-319-41540-6_3

independent pipelines, out-of-order instruction completion, out-of-order instruction issue, etc. All of these optimizations are supposed to be invisible to the programmer in a uniprocessor context: the overall effect should be the same as executing instructions one at a time in program order. But each of these optimizations introduces corner cases that potentially change the behaviour and the different optimizations interact with each other in complex ways.

For example, in a pre-release version of one of ARM's dual-issue processors, there was a defect in the inter-pipeline forwarding control logic that resulted in an instruction reading its input value from the wrong place if the instruction was preceded by a conditional instruction whose condition did not hold (and whose results should therefore not be used as inputs). The shortest instruction sequence which could demonstrate this defect was 5 instructions long. The particular set of instructions that could trigger the defect was fairly narrow because it was necessary that the instructions used particular parts of the pipeline, and the instruction sequence had to be aligned such that the first of these instructions executed in pipeline 0.

For traditional simulation-based verification to detect this defect you would need a detailed understanding of the micro-architecture of that particular processor, of the corner cases caused by the forwarding paths and of the kinds of errors one is likely to make in implementing forwarding control logic. Creating such tests is not only hard and unreliable, but it is also expensive because the tests would be specific to the particular micro-architectural choices in a processor and different tests must be created for each processor.

This paper describes the "ISA-Formal" verification technique that we have developed at ARM for verifying that processors correctly implement the Instruction Set Architecture (ISA) part of the architecture specification. Our method uses bounded model checking to explore different sequences of instructions and was able to detect the above defect prior to release of the RTL to manufacturers.

The *effectiveness* of ISA-Formal is important to its adoption within ARM but it is not the most important requirement we had to satisfy in order to make formal verification a useful part of ARM's processor development flow. Before ISA-Formal could be deployed widely within ARM, we had make it work within the constraints of commercial processor development:

(1) Processor development takes a long time (2 years or more) and it is important to be able to be able to detect bugs at all stages of processor development. We have applied ISA-Formal all the way from incomplete designs that still contain bugs through to complete, heavily tested designs.

(2) Verifying a processor takes longer than design: the long tail of processor development is developing new tests for the processor and fixing any bugs. It is important that useful results can be obtained even in the early stages of verification — before the complete test infrastructure has been developed. ISA-Formal is able to find bugs involving instructions for which we do not have a specification; all we need is a specification of any instruction whose result could be affected by the bug.

(3) Verification teams work in parallel with design teams so it is important that verification teams are able to continue searching for new bugs even when there are multiple outstanding bugs waiting to be fixed. Some bugs can take months to be fixed if they are not critical to immediate project milestones. ISA-Formal is able to work round known bugs in the processor.

(4) Any verification technique requires significant investment so reusability not only of the technique but also of the infrastructure is critical. We are able to reuse the tools across ARM v8-A/R (Application/Real-time) class and across v8-M (Microcontroller) class processors. The only part that needs to be customized for each processor is the Verilog abstraction function that extracts the effective architectural state from the micro-architectural state of a processor. This portability has been a great benefit while developing the technique because it allowed several processor teams to pool resources: one team worked on how to verify floating point instructions while another worked on branches and another worked on load-store instructions.

(5) Modern processor architectures and modern processors are large: the ARM v8-A ISA specification is over 2500 pages long, the v7-M ISA specification is over 600 pages long (almost half the length of the entire specification). It is important that verification techniques scale both in terms of human effort and computing resources. We have written a tool to automatically translate the source of the ARM Architecture Specifications to Verilog; and we split the verification task into thousands of small properties allowing effective use of large compute clusters.

We demonstrated these properties in three small-scale trials on different processors and have since refined and applied the technique on five further ARM processors: checking almost the complete instruction set architecture of these processors ranging from simple 3-stage microcontrollers up to sophisticated 64-bit out-of-order processors. ISA-Formal is now a key part of ARM's formal verification strategy.

We characterise our approach as "end-to-end verification" because it focusses on directly verifying the path from instruction decode through to instruction retire against the architectural specification in contrast to hierarchical or block-level verification which focusses on verifying individual blocks against micro-architectural specifications and then verifying that the composition of those blocks meets the overall specification.

ISA-Formal is strongly based on techniques developed in the academic community; our contribution is a description of the techniques needed to make it scale and of the challenges and solutions in creating a portable approach which can be applied in a commercial setting to a wide range of processor micro-architectures.

The remainder of this paper is structured as follows: Sect. 2 discusses related work; Sect. 3 illustrates the basic idea, demonstrating how ISA-Formal can be applied manually, to a single instruction and discusses the kinds of bugs it was able to discover in real processors; Sect. 4 describes how we scaled this idea up to handle full ISA specifications; Sect. 5 describes adaptations to handle a variety of different micro-architectural features; Sect. 6 reports on the results of applying this method to multiple processors; Sect. 7 concludes.

2 Related Work

Our work builds heavily on the pioneering work from the '90's such as Burch-Dill's automatic verification based on flushing refinements [5] and Srinivasan's verification based on completion refinements [19]. These and many other works used different notions of correctness of which Aagard et al. [1,2] give a useful taxonomy and establish conditions under which different notions of correctness are equivalent.

Our approach focusses on verifying RTL (Verilog) in contrast to work which verifies a high-level model of the microarchitecture design against a specification. For example, Lahiri et al. [14] verified the microarchitecture of the M*-core processor core (an early RISC-style architecture) and [13] verified the microarchitecture for an out-of-order processor through a series of successive refinements but neither verified against the RTL of an actual processor. In our experience, most errors are introduced while translating the microarchitecture design into RTL and during subsequent optimisation so verifying before RTL misses a lot of bugs. The challenge of verifying actual RTL is that it makes it hard to use abstraction techniques such as using uninterpreted functions because the actual RTL of an efficient processor tends not to have convenient blocks which match directly with parts of the original specification.

Many approaches to verifying pipeline control logic have used theorem proving techniques to tackle the difficult problems of handling pipeline forwarding and hazards in in-order processors [12,21] and, later, for out-of-order processors [7–9,16]. Theorem proving techniques are powerful and tend to suffer less machine-scaling issues than more automated techniques but their reliance on verification experts leads to severe human-scaling issues: it is hard to hire enough experts. We prefer to ride Moore's law and use more CPU-intensive but more automatable approaches.

There has been considerable commercial interest recently in formal verification of floating point units such as Kaivola et al. [10], KiranKumar [11] and Slobodova et. al [18]. This is impressive and important work but essentially orthogonal to our own: while it tackles the scaling issues that occur when verifying commercial processors, it focusses on individual blocks processing a single instruction with relatively simple input-output signals while our approach focusses on the entire pipeline and especially the control logic to handle interactions between instructions. We describe how we deal with verification of pipelines containing floating point units in Sect. 5.1.

3 Illustration: Hand-Written Properties

The basic approach to verification that we use in ISA-Formal is based on the above prior work. We start with the processor in a simple, well-defined state

$uArch_0$ with no instructions in the pipeline. We then execute for a number of cycles where each cycle may issue an instruction. This serves to put the processor into a more complex state where hazards, forwarding, etc. can occur. And finally, we execute an instruction I_n and test whether the instruction executes correctly. This is done by applying an abstraction function abs which extracts the architectural state of the processor immediately before I_n executes and immediately after I_n executes. We do not flush the pipe before or after I_n.

$$uArch_0 \xrightarrow{\ I_1\ } uArch_1 \dashrightarrow uArch_{n-1} \xrightarrow{\ I_n\ } uArch_n$$
$$\downarrow abs \qquad\qquad\qquad \downarrow abs$$
$$Arch_{n-1} \xrightarrow{\ I_n\ } Arch_n$$

A key part of making this scalable is that, instead of allowing the formal verification tool to choose any instruction for I_n, we enumerate all the instruction classes supported by the architecture and perform a separate check for each instruction class. Proving these simpler results is helpful early in processor development by making it easy to focus on checking the currently implemented instructions. Later in development, the pattern of failing instructions is a useful guide in localizing the fault: if all branch instructions are failing, there is no need to worry about bugs in the ALU. And as the size of the verification task scales up, splitting the verification task into many small properties lets us make more effective use of our verification cluster which is optimized for running many independent processes across hundreds of machines.

To make this more concrete, consider the task of checking an addition instruction in the classic 5-stage pipeline illustrated in Fig. 1. This consists of 5 pipeline stages responsible for instruction fetch (IF), decode (ID), execute (EX), memory access (MEM) and writeback of results (WB). Values are read from the register file at the ID/EX boundary and results are written to the register file at the MEM/WB boundary. Forwarding paths (aka bypass logic) are used to reduce the number of stalls by allowing the result of one instruction to be used as an input to the ALU if required by the next instruction. Conventionally, most of the control signals from decode and those that control the pipeline and forwarding paths are not shown — although that is where many of the most difficult bugs lie. We use this simple microarchitecture to explain the technique, Sect. 5 discusses how we adapt the approach to handle more realistic microarchitectures including dual issue, out-of-order retire and register renaming.

Our first challenge is to implement the abstraction function abs which is responsible for converting the micro-architectural state of the processor into an architectural state. To verify an addition instruction, the function abs must extract the current values of the integer registers.

Many simple processors commit their results in order in a single pipeline stage. This means that, at the beginning of the cycle where the add instruction commits, the micro-architectural register file should contain the same values as the architectural register file *before* the add executes and, at the end of the cycle, the micro-architectural register file should contain the same values as the

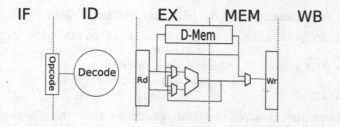

Fig. 1. A 5-stage processor pipeline, with forwarding paths, omitting I-Fetch

architectural register file *after* the add executes. We can therefore obtain the state *before* by reading the state at the end of the writeback stage and the state *after* by reading from the end of the Mem stage.

The other part of the input state of the processor that we require is the opcode of the current instruction. The opcode is normally discarded shortly after instruction decode and is not available at the point where an instruction commits. We therefore need to implement a "pipeline follower" which copies the opcode from one stage to the next and implements the same pipeline stall/flush logic as the datapath. This is similar to the introduction of "ghost state" in Lahiri et al. [13]. The followers and abstraction logic for the pre/post-states are illustrated in Fig. 2

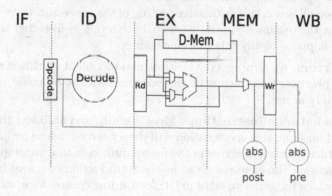

Fig. 2. A 5-stage processor pipeline with state abstraction and follower

Of course, modern ARM processors are considerably more challenging than a simple 5-stage pipeline: Sect. 5 describes the variations on the above approach required to apply ISA-Formal in practice.

Our second challenge is to create a specification of the addition instruction. For any individual instruction, the specification can often be written as a short piece of purely combinational logic. For example, ARM's 16-bit encoding of the instruction "ADD Rd, Rn, Rm" has opcode 0b0001100 | Rm << 6 | Rn << 3 | Rd and adds the contents of registers Rn and Rm and writes the result to register Rd.

This can be implemented by the following System-Verilog.

```
assign ADD_retiring = (pre.opcode & 16'b1111_1110_0000_0000)
                      == 16'b0001_1000_0000_0000;
assign ADD_result   = pre.R[pre.opcode[8:6]]
                      + pre.R[pre.opcode[5:3]];
assign ADD_Rd       = pre.opcode[2:0];
```

To complete the example, we add assertions that the abstracted result matches the result of the specification when retiring an add instruction.

```
assert property (@(posedge clk) disable iff (~reset_n)
    ADD_retiring |-> (ADD_result == post.R[ADD_Rd]));
```

The above specification is remarkably simple so it is worth examining what kinds of defect this specification could catch.

Decode Errors. Most obviously, this specification would detect any error in instruction decoding. But many decode errors are also caught by other verification methods such as directed or random testing so, at first sight, this does not seem especially useful. However, the instruction decoder is responsible not just for determining how to execute the current instruction but also for setting signals that determine whether it is safe to apply optimizations involving later instructions. A property like the above found a decoder bug involving one such signal that determined whether two adjacent instructions could be fused into a single micro-op: the signal was being incorrectly set for one instruction. This defect had been missed despite extensive testing of the processor: there were tests to ensure that the optimization did happen but testing is ill-suited to checking that it never happens in any other circumstance.

Datapath Errors. An error in a datapath would be caught by this kind of check although, in practice, many errors of this kind are caught by other verification methods already in use.

Interactions between Instructions. Most usefully, and unlike methods based on Burch-Dill flushing, this specification will detect errors caused by interactions between instructions such as errors in the forwarding logic that can supply inputs to this instruction. The example given in the introduction of a sequence of five instructions which triggered an error in the forwarding control logic was detected by a hand-written property like the above. Bugs like this are significantly more important to catch because the forwarding paths vary from one processor to another, the control logic is difficult to get right and the errors are hard to catch by conventional tests.

We currently use bounded model checking which verifies that a sequence of n instructions does not go wrong but to show that any sequence does not go wrong, we would need to find invariants about the processor and use those to get unbounded proofs. Going further, in order to complete ISA verification, we would need to verify that instructions are not lost, duplicated or reordered (we have done this for some processors) and, to complete verification of the core, we would need to verify exception taking mechanisms, the instruction fetch unit and the memory management unit.

4   Generating Verification IP with Architecture Explorer

The main challenge in applying the above approach to a full processor is one of scaling. The ARM v8-M architecture has 384 instruction encodings and the instruction set part of the architecture specification is over 600 pages long [4]; and the ARM v8-A/R architecture has 1280 instruction encodings and is over 2500 pages long [3]. Some of the encodings explicitly disallow using certain registers as sources or destinations to the instructions, many of the instructions are conditional and there are a variety of other complications and corner cases. In addition, changes are regularly added to the architecture specification. All these reasons make the prospect of writing, testing and maintaining a Verilog specification like that shown above unattractive.

Over the last 5 years we have developed tools which transform ARM's official Architecture Reference Manuals into executable specifications of the v8-A/R and v8-M architectures [17]. A key part of making this specification useful was to test it thoroughly before using the specification to verify anything else. In many ways, this is like Fox and Myreen's testing of their ARM ISA specification [6] except that we were able to use ARM's internal architecture conformance testsuite (that is normally used to test processors) to test the specifications with billions of instructions that probe each instruction's corner cases.

The core of this specification is ARM's Architecture Specification Language (ASL) that grew out of the pseudocode used in earlier versions of the architecture reference manuals. At a high level, ASL is an indentation-sensitive, imperative, strongly typed, first-order language with type inference, exceptions, enumerations, arrays, records, and no pointers. All integers in ASL are unbounded and there is direct support for N-bit bitstrings and functions are allowed to be polymorphic in the width of a bitstring. For example, memory read returns a value of type bits(8*size) where size is constrained to be 1, 2, 4 or 8.

The task of scaling the ISA-Formal approach up to handle the full instruction sets with all their complexities is therefore one of translating the rich, expressive ASL language to combinational System-Verilog using the synthesizable subset of Verilog that is accepted by commercial Verilog model checkers. The challenge in doing this is that synthesizable Verilog is intended to describe hardware and imposes several limitations upon us; (1) Verilog integers are finite and the bitwidth is a part of the type; (2) Combinational Verilog is normally written in a declarative style with no assignments or control flow and few function calls; (3) Synthesizable Verilog does not support unbounded for-loops or while-loops; (4) Synthesizable Verilog does not support exceptions; (5) The width of bitstrings in Verilog must always be a manifest constant and there is no form of polymorphism over bitwidths of functions.

We were able to overcome the first four issues using relatively conventional compiler techniques. (1) We use a global flow-insensitive value range analysis to compute the required width of most integer variables and use a large, but safe bound for any integers with unknown range. (2) Verilog includes a rarely used procedural subset which most of the language can be translated into. (3) User-supplied bounds on loops can be used to unroll all loops. (4) A whole-program transformation which adds additional flags and control flow to make exception and return-related control flow explicit.

The most challenging problem was dealing with bitstring polymorphism. Virtually all polymorphism was caused by instructions which could operate on data of different widths such as 8, 16, 32 or 64-bit load instructions. This observation enabled us to eliminate almost all polymorphism by automatically specializing such instruction encodings to create a separate instruction for each data width and then to use alternate passes of constant propagatation and a "monomorphization" pass which identifies calls to polymorphic functions where the bitwidth is a manifest constant and replaces the call with a call to a monomorphic instance of the polymorphic function. The remaining polymorphism is handled by a set of ad-hoc transforms in the Verilog backend.

5   Applying ISA-Formal to CPUs

In practice, few processors are as simple as the 5-stage pipeline sketched in Fig. 1 and we have had to develop a number of techniques in writing abstraction functions to deal with complex functional units, out-of-order retire, dual issue pipelines, instruction fusion, and register renaming.

5.1   Complex Functional Units

For the most part, our end-to-end approach to verification works: commercial model checkers are able to handle the complexity of most components without assistance. However, for complex functional units such as floating point and the memory system we choose to use other more scalable verification techniques such as the end-to-end memory-system verification technique described by Stewart et al. [20]. This modular approach lets ISA-Formal verification focus on control logic and forwarding paths that controls, feeds and is fed by these complex units.

In order to make ISA-Formal modular, we partition the specification on function call boundaries into different parts "Instruction Set Architecture (ISA)," "Floating Point," "Exception," "Address Translation," etc. and only generate Verilog for the "ISA" part. Any functions on the interfaces to other partitions are written by hand and many are just a few lines long: returning some component of the result of the pre-state or changing some component of the post-state.

On the interfaces, we adopt a variety of approaches to filling the resulting gaps in the generated Verilog using interface properties, subset behaviour checking and abstract functions. In general, these approaches will prevent us from detecting bugs in some parts of the processor using ISA-Formal. We tackle this by tracking which parts of the processor are not being checked by ISA-Formal and ensuring that an alternative verification technique is used on those parts.

Interface Properties. For some components such as the memory system, we were already creating interface specifications which were sufficiently strong that we could use the interface specification instead of the memory system. This only required us to convert the architectural view of the memory system to the micro-architectural view by translating requests/responses between representations.

Subset Behaviour Checking. For components such as floating point units, a specification of the full behaviour would still be too complex to use in verification but is quite simple if we restrict ourselves to a subset of the full behaviour. For example, if we restrict the inputs to $\pm\{0, 1, \infty, S\text{-}NaN, Q\text{-}NaN\}$ then it is easy to create specifications of all the FP instructions for this subset and perform some verification. Obviously, this would not be sufficient to detect errors in the floating point unit itself, but this subset gives enough different values that errors in the control and forwarding logic can be detected.

We could use SystemVerilog assumptions to restrict inputs to the chosen set of inputs, but this would restrict all of the checks that ISA-Formal performs on instructions: whether the instruction sets condition flags, raises an exception, accesses memory, which registers are written, etc. Instead, we add an additional signal indicating whether the inputs are in the supported subset and use that signal only to restrict checks of the values written to floating point registers.

Abstract Functions. The final option is to use the processor as an oracle. That is, we add logic to track the inputs and outputs from some functional unit and then use the output value if the inputs of a function in the architectural specification match the actual inputs of a functional unit in the processor. Since we are choosing to trust the behaviour of that unit, this cannot detect errors in the unit but it can detect errors in the surrounding control and forwarding logic.

5.2 Out of Order Completion

In an in-order core, all instructions retire strictly in-order, but some slower instructions may complete out of order. Retiring a load (say) after the memory protection check but before the data returns from the memory system allows independent instructions to continue without waiting for the access to complete. Such optimizations are important to verify because they introduce difficult corner cases in the design such as ensuring that the result of the load is written back even if the processor takes an exception.

The difficulty in verifying out-of-order completing instructions is that it is hard to construct the post-state: by the time that the load instruction completes, some of the instructions issued *after* load will also have completed. This is further complicated because some load instructions may be split into multiple micro-ops which complete independently.

Our solution to this is to take a snapshot of the pre-state when the load instruction *retires*. As each micro-op for the instruction under test completes, the snapshot is updated with the change. Finally, when the last micro-op completes, the final post-state is available and the instruction can be checked against the architecture specification.

5.3   Dual Issue Pipelines

Dual issue pipelines decode and execute two consecutive instructions in parallel. To handle dual issue pipelines, we add a further abstraction function to extract the intermediate state between execution of the two instructions. Our initial approach to checking these was to create two copies of the combinational logic implementing the specification: one copy for each pipeline. This worked but consumed a lot of memory and would scale badly for 3 or more-issue processors so, instead, we use a single copy of the specification and insert multiplexors to select which pre/post state is used with the specification.

The most serious problem encountered occurs if the second instruction can suppress part of the behaviour of the first instruction. For example, if both instructions modify the carry flag, then the final value written will be the result of the second instruction. In this case, the carry flag value from the first instruction may not be available at the writeback stage and we need to identify the correct signal to use and add a pipeline follower to propagate the value down to the point of serialization. Any error in choice of signal is detected when that signal is used as part of the pre-state of the second instruction.

5.4   Instruction Fusion

A high-performance processor might wish to fuse commonly occuring pairs of consecutive instructions into a single instruction. For example Malik et al. [15] describes a processor that detects sequences of dependent ALU instructions such as

```
SUB R4, R1, R2    ; R4 := R1 - R2
ADD R4, R4, R3    ; R4 := R4 + R3
```

and fuses them into a single macro-operation that reads three inputs from the register file and performs two add/subtract operations.

Optimizations of this kind raise a potential problem in sequences where the results of the first instruction are overwritten by the second instruction because the processor may not calculate the post-state of the first instruction or the pre-state of the second instruction.

Our solution is to add additional verification logic to calculate the missing intermediate state. The correctness of this logic is verified when checking that all uses of the SUB instruction (i.e., the first instruction of the pair) is correct and that justifies use of the result when checking that the SUB/ADD fused pair (i.e., the first/second instruction pair) gives the correct overall result.

5.5   Register Renaming

Processors with out-of-order instruction issue differ significantly from processors with in-order issue because they speculatively execute instructions past branch instructions. To allow them to recover from mis-speculation, they use a register rename table that maps architectural registers such as "X0" to one of a large pool of physical registers. As instructions are decoded, source registers are "renamed" using this table; free physical registers are allocated and the rename table is updated with mappings from destination register names to these physical registers. Instructions typically execute as soon as their input dependencies are satisfied but, to preserve the illusion that instructions execute in program order, a reorder buffer (ROB) only commits instructions in program order.

Despite the added complexity of speculative execution, register renaming and reorder buffers, it is actually simpler to apply ISA-Formal to out-of-order processors because they have a single clearly identified point of serialization implemented in the reorder buffer. In contrast, in-order processors have a variety of different mechanisms to support a limited degree of out-of-order execution such as varying pipeline length or supporting out-of-order completion of slow instructions and these different mechanisms are scattered across the processor.

5.6 Debugging Abstraction Functions

From the above, it should be apparent that creating the abstraction code remains a difficult task and involves a lot of work with the CPU designers to get right. While debugging these abstraction functions, we have found that it is useful to start by using hand-written properties like those described in Sect. 3 for instructions that touch the major parts of the processor. For example, a data-processing instruction, a load, a store, a floating point move, etc.

It is significantly easier to debug the abstraction function using hand-written specifications than using a mechanical translation from the specification. Once we have debugged the abstraction functions, we switch to using the machine-generated specifications exclusively, and rarely look at the generated code.

5.7 Handling Known Problems

One of the major difficulties we experienced before developing ISA-Formal was that formal verification tools would report variations on the same defect over and over again. This was a problem early in development when we might know that part of the processor was missing or incomplete; and it is a problem at any stage that once the bug report has been filed, the verification team wants to focus on finding other problems until the bug has been dealt with.

A critical technique for handling known problems is to maintain a list of assumptions corresponding to each individual bug or feature. As each bug is fixed, we remove the corresponding assumption and confirm that the bug has been fixed. Using assumptions is a simple technique but it greatly increases our ability to use formal verification to detect errors early in development and it very effectively decouples processor design from verification allowing the tasks to proceed in parallel.

6 Results

This section describes the results of applying ISA-Formal in three small-scale trials and five full-scale uses. These eight trials and uses cover the full lifetime of

ARM processor developments; they cover both application processor targetted at mobile phones, etc. and microcontrollers targetted at embedded uses; and they cover micro-architectures ranging from 3-stage, in-order pipelines through dual-issue, in-order pipelines to out-of-order pipelines.

6.1 ARM's Development Phases

ARM's development process involves four stages of roughly equal length: Develop and Test (D&T), Alpha, Beta and Access. The goal of each stage is to create a basic pipeline design in D&T; make it feature complete by the end of Alpha; improve power, performance and area through Beta; and to improve confidence in the design through the access period where the design is made available to the lead partners for that processor for evaluation and feedback. Testing steadily increases throughout this process and each stage applies roughly an order of magnitude more testing than the previous stage.

6.2 Small-Scale Trials

We carried out three small-scale trials on processors that were already in the access phase to demonstrate the ability of ISA-Formal to detect defects that were hard to detect by other means. These trials consisted of developing hand-written properties like those described in Sect. 3 and demonstrated the ability to detect defects that had been found by other means as well as new defects.

The defect described in the introduction is an example of a bug we detected during this trial process. The trigger sequence of the defect is conditional execution of instructions executing in two pipeline stages with a combination of taken and not-taken instructions. In a 2-pipeline design, the size of the smallest trigger sequence is 5 instructions: one to set up the condition, two (one per pipe) to generate values that might be forwarded, and two (one per pipe) to consume forwarded values. (There are several variations on that basic pattern.) Using traditional simulation-based verification, patterns like this would have to be tested on all combinations of instructions that have forwarding paths between them in that particular micro-architecture and each processor will have a different set of forwarding paths. There are many, many sequences of instructions like this to be tested so defects of this form are typically only found during soaktesting during the Access phase. Using ISA-Formal, we created hand-written properties for one or two instructions corresponding to each major unit in the datapath (the ALU, shifter, multiplier, etc.), we created abstraction functions for each of the two pipelines, and, since we left the opcode received from the fetch unit unconstrained, the commercial bounded-model-checker explored sequences of instructions up to some bound. We ran about a dozen properties through the model checker and after two minutes proof time detected the failing trigger sequence.

The same experience was repeated on all three processors: bugs were found with relatively little effort with the bulk of the work being done by junior engineers supervised by formal experts and with input from the microarchitects.

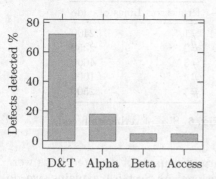

Fig. 3. Defect detection by phase   **Fig. 4.** Defect detection by time

The consistent combination of low human effort and low machine effort was an important part of demonstrating that ISA-Formal could detect difficult defects that, at best, would have been caught only during the Access phase.

6.3 Production Usage

Based on the success of the small-scale trials, ARM decided to adopt ISA-Formal as part of the formal verification strategy on five processors that were in earlier stages in their development: three in D&T, one in Alpha and one in Access. This work used the tool described in Sect. 4 to generate Verilog for all instructions directly from ARM's official Architecture Reference Manuals allowing engineers to focus on developing abstraction functions and testing the processor.

Defects have been found in all five processors with the distribution roughly in proportion to the effort invested in that processor. The small-scale trials had demonstrated that ISA-Formal can detect difficult to detect defects late in processor development; the production usage demonstrated that ISA-Formal is effective at detecting defects in earlier phases of development. Figures 3 and 4 show the distribution of confirmed, distinct defects detected using ISA-Formal by phase and by time. Figure 3 shows that ISA-Formal is capable of catching many defects early in development (overcoming the problem of being able to find many distinct defects in parallel with development) and that it is capable of finding defects late in development even after extensive testing by other methods. Figure 4 shows that ISA-Formal is able to start detecting defects in just a few weeks work and continues to find bugs as processors are developed.

We also found that ISA-Formal was able to detect issues affecting all areas of the instruction set: FP/SIMD, Memory, Branches, Integer, Exceptions and System instructions (e.g., memory fence instructions). Figure 5 shows the distribution of bugs found by ISA-Formal by the area of the processor affected (combining results for all processors). (The "Integer" category includes both integer datapath instructions and basic pipeline control issues — it is often hard to separate the two since integer instructions are so fundamental to a processor.)

FP/SIMD	25%
Memory	21%
Branch	21%
Integer	18%
Exception	8%
System	7%

Processor	Lines of code
#1	2400
#2	2250
#3	4600
#4	1000
#5	2500

Fig. 5. Defect detection by area   **Fig. 6.** Size of verification code

It is encouraging to note that the two largest sources of detected bugs were FP/SIMD instructions and memory instructions. As Sect. 5.1 explains, we do not test the FPU or the memory subsystem but, despite this, we are still able to test and find defects in the forwarding, pipeline control and register logic connected to these units.

The effort of creating, testing and debugging the machine-readable specification and a tool to translate it to Verilog is considerable but can be shared across multiple processors and can be used for other purposes within the company (e.g., documentation, testing of architecture extensions, etc.). The primary cost of implementing ISA-Formal on a new processor is the effort required to implement the pipeline follower and abstraction function on each processor. As a rough indication of the effort required, Fig. 6 shows the number of lines of code required for each (anonymized) processor. Most processors need around 2,500 lines of support code: a fairly modest cost. The outliers are processor #4 which has not yet added a follower for floating point registers and processor #3 which is a more complex processor than the other four.

Beyond the bug numbers, we found that applying ISA-Formal early in the development was capable of finding bugs that would not normally be caught until much later. For example, very early in development of an out-of-order processor, ISA-Formal found a bug that occurred when all the free registers in the physical register pool were in use. This was found before the processor could even execute load-store instructions so we would not normally be catching such bugs that early.

7   Conclusions

Two barriers to widespread industry adoption of formal verification techniques to check processors are scaling and return on investment issues. The end-to-end approach to verification that we adopt tackles both issues: it allows machine-generation of verification IP from the architecture specification, it allows engineers to detect bugs that affect actual instruction sequences very early in deployment, and it encourages creation of reusable tools, techniques and IP that can be used across an unusually wide range of micro-architectural styles.

This paper describes the steps needed to turn the basic idea into a scalable, reusable technique: automation, dealing with a range of different micro-architectural design techniques, and initial bringup issues. We have applied this method to 8 different ARM processors spanning all stages of development up to release. In all processors, this has found bugs that would have been hard for conventional simulation-based methods to find and ISA-Formal is now a key part of ARM's formal verification strategy.

To the best of our knowledge, this is the most broadly applicable formal verification technique for verifying processor pipeline control in mainstream commercial use.

References

1. Aagaard, M.D., Cook, B., Day, N.A., Jones, R.B.: A framework for microprocessor correctness statements. In: Margaria, T., Melham, T.F. (eds.) CHARME 2001. LNCS, vol. 2144, pp. 433–448. Springer, Heidelberg (2001). http://dl.acm.org/citation.cfm?id=646705.702043
2. Aagaard, M.D., Jones, R.B., Melham, T.F., O'Leary, J.W., Seger, C.-J.H.: A methodology for large-scale hardware verification. In: Johnson, S.D., Hunt Jr., W.A. (eds.) FMCAD 2000. LNCS, vol. 1954, pp. 300–319. Springer, Heidelberg (2000)
3. ARM Ltd: ARM Architecture Reference Manual (ARMv8, for ARMv8-A architecture profile). ARM Ltd (2013)
4. ARM Ltd: (In Preparation) ARM Architecture Reference Manual (ARMv8, for ARMv8-M architecture profile). ARM Ltd (2016)
5. Burch, J.R., Dill, D.L.: Automatic verification of pipelined microprocessor control. In: Dill, D.L. (ed.) CAV 1994. LNCS, vol. 818, pp. 68–80. Springer, Heidelberg (1994). http://dl.acm.org/citation.cfm?id=647763.735662
6. Fox, A., Myreen, M.O.: A trustworthy monadic formalization of the ARMv7 instruction set architecture. In: Kaufmann, M., Paulson, L.C. (eds.) ITP 2010. LNCS, vol. 6172, pp. 243–258. Springer, Heidelberg (2010). doi:10.1007/978-3-642-14052-5_18
7. Higgins, J.T., Aagaard, M.D.: Simplifying design and verification for structural hazards and datapaths in pipelined circuits. In: Ninth IEEE International Proceedings of the High-Level Design Validation and Test Workshop, HLDVT 2004, pp. 31–36 (2004). http://dx.doi.org/10.1109/HLDVT.2004.1431229
8. Hunt Jr., W.A., Sawada, J.: Verifying the FM9801 microarchitecture. IEEE Micro 19(3), 47–55 (1999). doi:10.1109/40.768503
9. Jhalal, R., McMillan, K.L.: Microarchitecture verification by compositional model checking. In: Berry, G., Comon, H., Finkel, A. (eds.) CAV 2001. LNCS, vol. 2102, p. 396. Springer, Heidelberg (2001). doi:10.1007/3-540-44585-4_40
10. Kaivola, R., et al.: Replacing testing with formal verification in Intel® Core™ i7 processor execution engine validation. In: Bouajjani, A., Maler, O. (eds.) CAV 2009. LNCS, vol. 5643, pp. 414–429. Springer, Heidelberg (2009). http://dx.doi.org/10.1007/978-3-642-02658-4_32
11. KiranKumar, V., Gupta, A., Ghughal, R.: Symbolic trajectory evaluation: the primary validation vehicle for next generation Intel processor graphics FPU. In: Formal Methods in Computer-Aided Design (FMCAD), pp. 149–156. IEEE (2012)
12. Kroening, D., Paul, W., Mueller, S.: Proving the correctness of pipelined micro-architectures. In: Waldschmidt, K., Grimm, C. (eds.) Proceedings of ITG/GI/GMM-Workshop "Methoden und Beschreibungssprachen zur Modellierung und Verifikation von Schaltungen und Systemen", pp. 89–98. VDE Verlag (2000)

13. Lahiri, S.K., Bryant, R.E.: Deductive verification of advanced out-of-order micro-processors. In: Hunt Jr., W.A., Somenzi, F. (eds.) CAV 2003. LNCS, vol. 2725, pp. 341–354. Springer, Heidelberg (2003). doi:10.1007/978-3-540-45069-6_33

14. Lahiri, S.K., Pixley, C., Albin, K.: Experience with term level modeling and verification of the M*CORE^{TM} microprocessor core. In: Proceedings of the Sixth IEEE International High-Level Design Validation and Test Workshop 2001, Monterey, California, USA, 7–9 November 2001, pp. 109–114 (2001). http://dx.doi.org/10.1109/HLDVT.2001.972816

15. Malik, N., Eickemeyer, R.J., Vassiliadis, S.: Interlock collapsing ALU for increased instruction-level parallelism. In: Proceedings of the 25th Annual International Symposium on Microarchitecture, pp. 149–157. MICRO 25, CA (1992). http://dl.acm.org/citation.cfm?id=144953.145794

16. McMillan, K.L.: Verification of an implementation of Tomasulo's algorithm by compositional model checking. In: Vardi, M.Y. (ed.) CAV 1998. LNCS, vol. 1427, pp. 110–121. Springer, Heidelberg (1998). http://dl.acm.org/citation.cfm?id=647767.733764

17. Reid, A.: Creating trustworthy specifications of ARM v8-A and v8-M system level architecture. In: preparation (2016)

18. Slobodová, A., Davis, J., Swords, S., Hunt Jr., W.: A flexible formal verification framework for industrial scale validation. In: 2011 9th IEEE/ACM International Conference on Formal Methods and Models for Codesign (MEMOCODE), pp. 89–97. IEEE (2011)

19. Srinivasan, S.K.: Automatic refinement checking of pipelines with out-of-order execution. IEEE Trans. Comput. **59**(8), 1138–1144 (2010)

20. Stewart, D., Gilday, D., Nevill, D., Roberts, T.: Processor memory system verification using DOGReL: a language for specifying end-to-end properties. In: International Workshop on Design and Implementation of Formal Tools and Systems, DIFTS 2014 (2014)

21. Windley, P.J.: Formal modeling and verification of microprocessors. IEEE Trans. Comput. **44**(1), 54–72 (1995)

A Practical Verification Framework
for Preemptive OS Kernels

Fengwei Xu[1,2], Ming Fu[1,2](✉), Xinyu Feng[1,2], Xiaoran Zhang[1,2], Hui Zhang[1,2],
and Zhaohui Li[1,2]

[1] School of Computer Science and Technology,
University of Science and Technology of China,
Hefei, China
fuming@ustc.edu.cn
[2] Suzhou Institute for Advanced Study,
University of Science and Technology of China,
Suzhou, China

Abstract. We propose a practical verification framework for preemptive
OS kernels. The framework models the correctness of API implementations in OS kernels as contextual refinement of their abstract specifications. It provides a specification language for defining the high-level
abstract model of OS kernels, a program logic for refinement verification of concurrent kernel code with multi-level hardware interrupts, and
automated tactics for developing mechanized proofs. The whole framework is developed for a practical subset of the C language. We have
successfully applied it to verify key modules of a commercial preemptive
OS μC/OS-II [2], including the scheduler, interrupt handlers, message
queues, and mutexes *etc*. We also verify the priority-inversion-freedom
(PIF) in μC/OS-II. All the proofs are mechanized in Coq. To our knowledge, our work is the first to verify the functional correctness of a practical *preemptive* OS kernel with machine-checkable proofs.

1 Introduction

Verifying OS kernels has long been recognized as an important but also extremely
challenging task. There have been exciting efforts for OS kernel verification
[4,13,16,27] in recent years, but most of them have no or limited support of
kernel-level preemption, which allows tasks to be preempted even in kernel mode.
This limitation restricts their applicability to real-time systems, where preemptive multitasking is indispensable to achieve real-time guarantees.

Preemptive kernels require explicit invocation of schedulers inside interrupt
handlers and careful interrupt management in the kernel code, which make the
kernel highly concurrent and complex. In this paper we propose a verification
framework for preemptive OS kernels, and show its application in verifying key
modules of μC/OS-II [2], a commercial preemptive real-time multitasking kernel
for microprocessors and microcontrollers. The verification is fully mechanized

This work is supported in part by grants from National Natural Science Foundation
of China (NSFC) under Grant Nos. 61103023, 61229201, 61379039 and 91318301.

S. Chaudhuri and A. Farzan (Eds.): CAV 2016, Part II, LNCS 9780, pp. 59–79, 2016.
DOI: 10.1007/978-3-319-41540-6_4

in Coq [1]. To our knowledge, it is the first verification of (key modules of) a *preemptive* OS kernel with machine-checkable proofs. The key contribution of the work is to adapt existing theories on interrupt verification [11] and contextual refinement of concurrent programs [17,19,24,25], and integrate them into a framework for real-world preemptive OS kernel verification. Specifically, our work makes the following new contributions:

First, we formulate and verify the correctness of the APIs of OS kernels as *contextual refinement* between their implementations and specifications. Although refinement approaches have been applied in earlier work on OS kernel verification [4,13,16], we believe our work is the first to explicitly specify and prove contextual refinement for APIs of a preemptive OS kernel, following recent progress on refinement verification of *concurrent* programs [17,19,24,25]. As we explain in Sect. 2.2, contextual refinement not only serves as a very strong notion of functional correctness of system APIs, but also allows us to prove properties based on the more abstract API specifications and then carry it down to the level of concrete implementations, which makes the verification much simpler than doing proofs directly at the concrete level.

Second, we provide a simple modeling language for specifying kernel primitives. The language strives for balance between abstraction and expressiveness for scheduling. On the one hand, we want the specification to abstract away implementation details. On the other hand, it should provide enough details so that many important properties can be specified at the abstract specification level. Our modeling language provides an abstract **sched** command, allowing us to specify explicitly when the scheduler is invoked in synchronization primitives or interrupt handlers. Semantics of **sched** is parameterized over abstract scheduling policies (*e.g.*, priority-based or round-robin). Expressiveness about these details are necessary to specify system-wide scheduling properties.

Third, we propose a program logic for refinement verification of concurrent kernel programs. The logic supports multi-level nested hardware interrupts and configurable schedulers. It extends concurrent separation logic [21] (CSL) with relational assertions that relate program states at the implementation and the specification levels, as in Liang *et al.* [17,19]. It also assigns ownership-transfer semantics to interrupt management operations and verify multi-level hardware interrupts in a realistic setting. Different from traditional Hoare-style program logics, whose soundness ensures the semantic interpretation of Hoare-triples, our logic explicitly establishes contextual refinement, which is more useful for establishing abstractions for system APIs, as explained above.

Fourth, our framework is developed for a practical subset of C. It has been successfully applied to verify key APIs of μC/OS-II [2], including the timer interrupt handler (and a pseudo interrupt handler to demonstrate the support of multi-level interrupts), the scheduler, the time management; and four synchronization mechanisms: message queues, mail boxes, semaphores, and mutexes. It is worth noting that, unlike existing works [4,13,16,27] that are focused on kernels newly developed with verification in mind, we take a *commercial system developed by an independent third-party* and verify the code with minimum modification, which demonstrates the generality and applicability of our framework.

Fifth, we also specify and verify priority inversion freedom (PIF) of μC/OS-II. PIF is a crucial property for real-time systems and is worth verifying in its own right. Moreover, since the specification and verification are done at the level of the abstract model (*i.e.*, specifications) of the kernel, they also help validate our model of system APIs. As we explain above, many important properties cannot be specified if the model is too weak or overly abstract.

Coq proofs and a companion technical report are available at http://staff.ustc.edu.cn/~fuming/research/certiucos.

2 Background and Overview of Our Work

2.1 Preemptive OS Kernels and Interrupts

In a preemptive OS kernel, execution of a task inside the kernel can be interrupted at any program point (unless interrupts are disabled). Then the control is switched to the interrupt handler. When the handler finishes, it may invoke the scheduler and switch the execution context to a different task, instead of returning to the original interrupted task. For instance, with priority-based scheduling, the interrupt handler always switches to the highest priority task at its end.

The x86 Interrupt Mechanism. Interrupt handling and management are indispensable in preemptive OS kernels. We give an overview of the interrupt mechanism in x86 systems (based on the Intel 8259 A interrupt controller).

The CPU has a flag bit IF indicating whether interrupts are enabled or not. The **cli/sti** instruction clears/sets the bit to disable/enable interrupts. In 8259 A there is a register isr, each bit of which corresponds to a hardware interrupt and records if the interrupt is being served or not. Different priority levels are assigned to different sources of interrupts, with level-0 being the highest. When an interrupt request comes, we check IF and isr. If the interrupts are enabled and there is currently no interrupt with higher or the same priority being served, the request will be served. The corresponding bit in isr is set to 1 and the control jumps to the corresponding interrupt handler.

On the invocations of an interrupt handler, the CPU flags (including IF) are saved on the stack, and interrupts are disabled automatically. If interrupts are enabled again inside the handler, the handler could be further interrupted by requests with higher priorities, causing nested interrupts.

The handler returns to the program being interrupted using the **iret** instruction, which also restores the flags (including IF). Before the handler returns, it needs to execute **eoi** to send an "end of interrupt" signal to the interrupt controller, which clears the corresponding bit in isr. Note that after **eoi** but before **iret**, if interrupts are enabled (IF = 1), the handler could be interrupted by interrupts at a lower or the same level.

Overview of μC/OS-II. μC/OS-II is a commercial preemptive real-time multitasking OS kernel developed by Micrium [2]. The kernel has 6000+ lines of C code and 300+ lines of assembly. It allows a fixed number of tasks, multi-level interrupts, and preemptive priority-based scheduling. The system APIs include *"semaphores; event flags; mutual-exclusion semaphores that eliminate unbounded priority inversions; mailboxes; message queues; task, time and timer management; and fixed sized memory block management"* [2]. μC/OS-II is developed for microprocessors and microcontrollers, and it does not support virtual memory. It has been deployed in many real-world safety critical applications, including avionics (*e.g.*, the Mars Curiosity Rover) and medical equipments.

2.2 Overview of the Verification Framework

An OS kernel hides details of the underlying hardware and provides an abstract programming model for application-level programmers. The implementation of the kernel must ensure that behaviors of user applications in the real machine are consistent with their behaviors under the abstract model [14]. Thus the OS verification can be reduced to verifying refinement between the concrete and abstract programming models.

Contextual Refinement as Correctness. We consider three entities, the application A, the abstract specifications of the system APIs and interrupt handlers $\mathbb{O}$, and their concrete implementations O. When system calls are made or interrupts are handled, routines in O are invoked in the real execution, while in the programmers' mind those in $\mathbb{O}$ are invoked instead at the abstract level. Then the correctness of OS kernels requires O refines $\mathbb{O}$ under *all contexts* A:

$$\forall A. [\![A[O]]\!] \subseteq [\![A[\mathbb{O}]]\!]$$

where $[\![\_]\!]$ maps a program P to the set of its observable behaviors. It says that, for all applications, executing the concrete code O does not have more observable behaviors than executing the abstract version $\mathbb{O}$. In this paper, observable behaviors are defined as finite prefixes of execution traces consisting of observable events, following Liang *et al.* [17].

Contextual refinement is a very strong notion of functional correctness of system APIs since it quantifies over *all* applications. Moreover, it makes verification of system-wide properties simpler. For instance, if we want to verify certain property Φ about a whole system $A[O]$, *i.e.*, Φ holds over every trace in $[\![A[O]]\!]$, we could prove that it holds over every trace in the superset $[\![A[\mathbb{O}]]\!]$ instead. Proofs at the abstract level could be much simpler than the concrete level.

The Whole Verification Framework. Figure 1 shows the structure of our verification framework. To model OS kernels and applications, we introduce two languages (in block A), the low-level language for the concrete code implementation and the high-level language for the abstract specification. Above them we have a program logic (in block B) that allows us to prove the low-level kernel implementation contextually refines the high-level specifications. The framework also provides a set of Coq tactics (in block C) to automatically generate and prove verification conditions. The μC/OS-II modules certified in this framework are shown in block D. Below we give details of some of the building blocks.

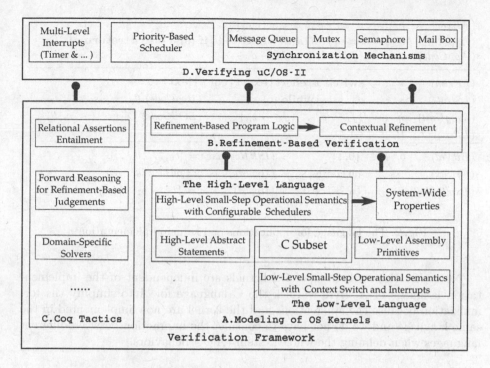

Fig. 1. Structure of the verification framework and μC/OS-II verification

3   Modeling of OS Kernels

As explained above, the correctness of OS kernels is formalized based on three
entities — user applications A, the concrete implementation O, and the abstract
specification $\mathbb{O}$. In this section we introduce the programming (or modeling)
languages for the three entities (see block A in Fig. 1). Due to space limit, we
only show the main language features with simplifications for clear presentation.
The details are available at TR and the Coq code [26].

3.1   The Low-Level Language

The low-level language consists of two parts for implementations of user applications and OS kernels, respectively.

Application Language. The application language is shown at the top of Fig. 2.
It is a subset of the C language consisting of function calls, pointer operations
(except pointer arithmetics), arrays, structs, bit operations, *etc.* The application
code A maps function names to their function bodies. The command $f(\bar{e})$ calls
the function f, which could be either an application function in A or an OS API
(in O at the low-level or in $\mathbb{O}$ at the high-level, as we explain below).

$$
\begin{array}{llll}
(AExpr) & e & ::= & n\,|\,x\,|\,*e\,|\,\&e\,|\,e.id\,|\,e[e]\,|\,\ldots \\
(AppStmts) & d & ::= & e=e\,|\,f(\bar{e})\,|\,d;d\,|\,\textbf{while }(e)\ d\,|\,\textbf{if }(e)\ d\ \textbf{else}\ d\,|\,\textbf{return}\ e\,|\,\ldots \\
(AppCode) & A & ::= & \{f_1 \rightsquigarrow d_1, \ldots, f_n \rightsquigarrow d_n\}
\end{array}
$$

$$
\begin{array}{llll}
(LPrim) & \iota & ::= & \textbf{switch }x\,|\,\textbf{encrt}\,|\,\textbf{excrt}\,|\,\textbf{eoi}\ k\,|\,\textbf{iext}\,|\,\ldots \\
(LStmts) & s & ::= & d\,|\,\iota\,|\,s;s\,|\,\textbf{while }(e)\ s\,|\,\ldots \qquad (ItrpCode)\ \theta\ ::=\ [s_0, \ldots, s_{N-1}] \\
(ProgUnit) & \eta & ::= & \{f_1 \rightsquigarrow s_1, \ldots, f_n \rightsquigarrow s_n\} \qquad\quad (LOSCode)\ O\ ::=\ (\eta_a, \eta_i, \theta) \\
(LProg) & P & ::= & (A, O)
\end{array}
$$

$$
\begin{array}{llll}
(BitVal) & b, ie \in \{0,1\} & (ISRReg)\ isr ::= [b_0, \ldots, b_{N-1}] \\
(CrtStk) & cs ::= \textsf{nil}\,|\,ie :: cs & (ItrpStk)\ is ::= \textsf{nil}\,|\,k :: is \\
(ItrpTaskSt) & \delta ::= (ie, is, cs) & (ItrpSt)\ \pi ::= \{t_1 \rightsquigarrow \delta_1, \ldots, t_n \rightsquigarrow \delta_n\}
\end{array}
$$

Fig. 2. The language for applications and kernel implementation

Note that the correctness of OS kernels are independent of the implementation language of A. Here we pick the C language for A to simplify the formalization because the applications and the kernel are now implemented in the same language and we do not have to consider the interaction between different languages when defining the whole system ($A[O]$) behaviors.

Low-Level Language for OS Kernels. The middle of Fig. 2 shows the low-level language for the concrete implementation of OS kernels. Usually the kernels are implemented in C with inline assembly. However, giving semantics directly to C with inline assembly requires us to expose stacks and registers, which make the semantics overly complex. To avoid this problem, we extend the C statements with assembly primitives ι to encapsulate the assembly code. Semantics of these primitives will be given below.

switch x switches to the target task x. **encrt** enters a critical region by disabling interrupts. It also saves the old IF onto the stack to allow nested critical regions. Note we use ie to model the IF flag and abstract away other bits in the hardware EFLAGS register. **excrt** exits the current critical region by popping the stack to recover ie. Since we hide stacks in our state model, we use an abstract stack cs to save the historical ie bits (see Fig. 2, which is explained below). **eoi** k clears the k-th bit in isr, indicating that the k-th interrupt is no longer in service. **iext** enables interrupts and returns to the interrupted program.

The kernel implementation O consists of the system API implementation η_a, the internal functions η_i and the interrupt handlers θ. The internal functions are called only by code in η_a or θ. θ is a sequence of N interrupt handlers, where N is the maximum number of interrupts we support. The handler with the lower identifier has the higher priority. Then a complete low-level program P is defined as a pair of the application code A and the kernel code O.

Operational Semantics. The language is concurrent, with multiple continuations (*i.e.*, control stacks) in the state, each corresponding to a task. All tasks share memory, but each has its own local variables and local interrupt states (see δ in Fig. 2, which is explained below). We also separate the program state (including memory and variables) into two disjoint parts, one for the application code A and the other for the kernel code O. The only way for A to access kernel states is to call system APIs in O, and O cannot access application states.

We give small-step operational semantics to the language. For each step, the processor picks the continuation of the current task and executes its current command or expression. To model concurrency and interrupts, both commands and *expressions* could be executed in multiple steps, where each step corresponds to the granularity of a single machine instruction (as in CompCertTSO [22], but we use the sequential consistent model instead of the x86-TSO memory model).

The assembly implementation of the context switch routine is abstracted into the primitive **switch** x. It switches the execution from the current task to the target task x, where x stores the task identifier.

The other assembly primitives ι are all related to interrupts management and handling. To model their semantics, we introduce interrupt states in the state model, as shown at the bottom of Fig. 2. The *global* register *isr* is shared by all tasks. It models the *isr* register in the 8259 A interrupt controller, as explained in Sect. 2.1. In addition, there are *local* interrupt states δ for each task. It contains a local copy *ie* of the IF flag in the EFLAGS register (see Sect. 2.1) recording whether interrupts are enabled, a stack *cs* consisting of the historical values of *ie* to support nested critical regions, and another stack *is* recording the sequence of interrupts that interrupt the execution of *the task*. The stack *is* is auxiliary data introduced mainly for verification purposes. π records the δ of each task.

encrt enters a critical region by disabling interrupts (*i.e.*, clearing the *ie* bit using **cli**). It also saves the old *ie* onto the *cs* stack. **excrt** exits the critical region by popping off the top value on *cs* and using it to restore *ie* (executing **sti** if the value is 1).

Interrupt requests may arrive non-deterministically after each step if $ie = 1$. A level-k request is served only if there is no request at higher or the same level being served (*i.e.*, $\forall k'.k' \leq k \rightarrow isr(k') = 0$). Then the processor clears *ie*, sets $isr(k)$ to 1, pushes the number k onto the logical stack *is*, saves the execution context and the local variables onto the abstract control stack (*i.e.*, the continuation), and finally jumps to the interrupt handler $\theta(k)$.

eoi k clears the k-th bit in *isr*, indicating that the k-th interrupt is no longer in service. **iext** is an abstraction of the **iret** instruction. It resets the *ie* bit to 1 to enable interrupts, pops out the topmost interrupt number on the *is* stack, and returns to the interrupted program.

3.2 The High-Level Specification Language

Viewing from the aspect of application programmers, we model the OS kernel as an extended C language with multi-tasking and system calls. As explained above, the C language is used to implement user applications A, and the system calls invoke an abstract version of system routines in $\mathbb{O}$, which are implemented using a simple specification language. Correspondingly, the low-level concrete

$$
\begin{array}{lll}
(HStmts) & \mathrm{s} ::= \mathbf{sched} \,|\, \gamma(\bar{v}) \,|\, \mathbf{assert}\ \mathrm{b} \,|\, \mathbf{end} \,|\, \mathrm{s}_1; \mathrm{s}_2 \,|\, \mathrm{s}_1 + \mathrm{s}_2 \\
(HAPISet) & \varphi ::= \{f_1 \rightsquigarrow \mathrm{s}_1, \ldots, f_n \rightsquigarrow \mathrm{s}_n\} & (HEvtSet)\ \varepsilon ::= [\mathrm{s}_0, \ldots, \mathrm{s}_{N-1}] \\
(HSched) & \chi \in HAbsSt \rightarrow TaskId \rightarrow Prop & (TaskId)\ \ t \in Nat \\
(HOSCode) & \mathbb{O} ::= (\varphi, \varepsilon, \chi) & (HProg)\ \ \mathbb{P} ::= (A, \mathbb{O}) \\
\hline
(HAbsSt) & \Sigma ::= \{\mathrm{a}_1 \rightsquigarrow \Omega_1, \ldots, \mathrm{a}_n \rightsquigarrow \Omega_n\} & (HDataNm)\ \mathrm{a} ::= \mathsf{tcbls} \,|\, \mathsf{ctid} \,|\, \ldots \\
(HData) & \Omega ::= \alpha \,|\, t \,|\, \ldots & (HStatus)\ \ ts ::= \mathsf{rdy} \,|\, \ldots \\
(HTCBLs) & \alpha ::= \{t_1 \rightsquigarrow (pr_1, ts_1, \ldots), \ldots, t_n \rightsquigarrow (pr_n, ts_n, \ldots)\}
\end{array}
$$

Fig. 3. High-level spec. language and abstract states

representation of kernel states is modeled as algebraic abstract states at the high level. This section presents the high-level language and its semantics.

As shown in Fig. 3, the whole high-level program $\mathbb{P}$ consists of the application code A and the abstract specification of the kernel $\mathbb{O}$. The application code A is the same as in the low-level language (see Fig. 2). $\mathbb{O}$ contains the specifications φ for kernel APIs, ε for interrupt handlers, and χ for the scheduler.

Programmers at this level have *no* control over interrupts (*e.g.*, enabling or disabling interrupts). Always enabled, interrupts are modeled implicitly as abstract external events that may occur non-deterministically at any program points. At the high level an incoming level-k event is always handled by executing $\varepsilon(k)$, *i.e.* the k-th handler specified in ε.

The system APIs and interrupt handlers are specified as an abstract statement s, which forms a simple but expressive specification language. **sched** does scheduling. Its semantics is determined by the abstract scheduler specification χ. As defined in Fig. 3, χ is a binary relation between abstract states and task identifiers. That is, given an abstract state Σ (defined at the bottom of Fig. 3), χ finds a related task identifier as the next task to execute. Note that χ is a relation instead of a function, therefore the abstract scheduler could be non-deterministic. Since χ is provided as part of the kernel specification, the semantics of **sched** in our language is configurable. Specifying details of the scheduling policies (instead of using a more abstract non-deterministic scheduler that may pick *any* task) allows us to specify and verify scheduling properties such as PIF at the high level.

$\gamma(\bar{v})$ is a meta-level relation (defined in Coq) that takes $\bar{v}$ as arguments and maps an abstract state to another. It can be instantiated to specify any *atomic* transitions over abstract states. **assert** b asserts that the predicate b holds over the current abstract state. **end** represents the end of abstract APIs or interrupt handlers. $\mathrm{s}_1; \mathrm{s}_2$ and $\mathrm{s}_1 + \mathrm{s}_2$ are statements for sequential composition and non-deterministic choices respectively.

Abstract States. The kernel state is represented as the abstract state Σ at the high level. As defined at the bottom of Fig. 3, Σ is a mapping from names a to the abstract data Ω. Here tcbls is the name for the high-level abstract TCB list α, which maps task identifiers to abstract tasks, including the priority *pr* (a natural number), the task status (ready, waiting, *etc.*) and so on, depending on the low-level implementations. ctid is the name for the current task identifier t.

Example of High-Level Specifications. We use $\mathbb{s}_{\text{dly}} \overset{\text{def}}{=} (\gamma_{\text{err}}(\text{ticks}) + (\gamma_{\text{dly}}(\text{ticks}); \mathbf{sched}))$ to specify the system API "void OSTimeDly(Int16u ticks)", which delays the current task for the specified number of system ticks. The atomic operation $\gamma_{\text{err}}(\text{ticks})$ specifies the error case when ticks $= 0$. $\gamma_{\text{dly}}(\text{ticks})$ defines the atomic behavior of updating the status of the current task from "ready" to "waiting" with the duration set to ticks when ticks > 0, and the following **sched** switches to another ready task, following the scheduling policy specified by the abstract scheduler χ. Note that the exclusive conditions over ticks in $\gamma_{\text{err}}(\text{ticks})$ and $\gamma_{\text{dly}}(\text{ticks})$ make the non-deterministic choice statement deterministic. We omit the definitions of $\gamma_{\text{err}}(\text{ticks})$ and $\gamma_{\text{dly}}(\text{ticks})$ here.

As another example, below we show the abstract scheduler specification $\chi_{\mu\text{C}/\text{OS-II}}$ for μC/OS-II. It requires that the selected task be ready and have the highest priority among all the ready tasks.

$$\chi_{\mu\text{C}/\text{OS-II}} \overset{\text{def}}{=} \lambda \Sigma, t.\exists \alpha, pr. \Sigma(\text{tcbls}) = \alpha \wedge \alpha(t) = (pr, \text{rdy}) \wedge$$
$$\forall t', pr'. (t \neq t' \wedge \alpha(t') = (pr', \text{rdy})) \rightarrow pr' \prec pr$$

3.3 OS Correctness

As we explain in Sect. 2.2, the correctness of OS kernels can be defined in terms of contextual refinement. Below we give its formal definition.

Definition 3.1 (OS Correctness). $O \sqsubseteq_\psi \mathbb{O}$ iff
$\forall A, W, \mathbb{W}. \text{Match}(\psi, W, \mathbb{W}) \Longrightarrow ((A, O), W) \preccurlyeq ((A, \mathbb{O}), \mathbb{W})$
where $\psi \in LOSFullSt \rightarrow HAbsSt \rightarrow Prop$ and
$\quad \text{Match}(\psi, (T, \Delta, \Lambda, t), (T, \Delta, \Sigma)) \overset{\text{def}}{=}$
$\quad\quad (t \in dom(T)) \wedge (\psi \, \Lambda \, \Sigma) \wedge (t = \Sigma(\text{ctid})) \wedge (dom(T) = dom(\Sigma(\text{tcbls})))$

The low-level kernel code O refines its high-level abstract specifications $\mathbb{O}$ with constraints ψ over initial kernel states, denoted as $O \sqsubseteq_\psi \mathbb{O}$, if and only if for any client code A, *low-level state* W and *high-level state* $\mathbb{W}$, if W and $\mathbb{W}$ satisfy certain consistency constraint (w.r.t. ψ), then the set of observable behaviors of the low-level configuration $((A, O), W)$ is a subset of $((A, \mathbb{O}), \mathbb{W})$ (*i.e.*, $(P, W) \preccurlyeq (\mathbb{P}, \mathbb{W})$, following the event trace refinement in [17]).

Due to space limit, we elide the definitions of W and $\mathbb{W}$ in Sects. 3.1 and 3.2. The low-level whole program state W is in the form of (T, Δ, Λ, t), where the *task pool* T maps task identifiers to their continuations, Δ is the client state, Λ is the low-level kernel state, and t is the identifier of the current task. The high-level program state $\mathbb{W}$ is in the form of (T, Δ, Σ), where Σ is an abstraction of the low-level kernel state Λ and the current task id t.

The constraint Match requires that: (1) initially W and $\mathbb{W}$ have the same task pool T and client state Δ; (2) the current task t is in T; (3) the low-level

```
inc(){
  int done=0, tmp;
  while(!done){
    tmp=cnt;
    done=cas(&cnt,tmp,tmp+1) }
}
```

(a) Implementation of inc	(b) Wrong spec.	(c) Weak spec.	(d) Refinement spec.

(b) $\{\texttt{cnt} = N\}$ $\texttt{inc()};$ $\{\texttt{cnt} = N+1\}$

(c) $\{\exists N.\, \texttt{cnt} = N\}$ $\texttt{inc()};$ $\{\exists N.\, \texttt{cnt} = N\}$

(d) $\{\texttt{cnt} = \texttt{CNT} \wedge [|\langle\texttt{CNT++}\rangle|]\}$ $\texttt{inc()};$ $\{\texttt{cnt} = \texttt{CNT} \wedge [|\mathbf{end}|]\}$

Fig. 4. Specification of concurrent programs

kernel state Λ and the high-level abstract state satisfy ψ; (4) the *current* task at the low level and the high level are the same; and (5) the set of tasks in the abstract TCB list should be the same as those in the low-level task pool.

4   Relational Program Logic for Refinement Verification

In this section, we present a CSL-style *relational* program logic for refinement verification. The logic uses relational assertions to prove refinement between an implementation and its specification. It also follows the ownership-transfer semantics in CSL to reason about multi-level hardware interrupts.

Refinement of Concurrent Programs, and Relational Reasoning. For concurrent programs, refinement establishes stronger functional correctness than traditional Hoare triples. As an example, the function inc shown in Fig. 4(a) increments the counter cnt. It may be called simultaneously by concurrent tasks. Figure 4(b) gives pre-/post-conditions to specify inc, which would be valid in a sequential setting and is sufficient to describe the functionality. However, they cannot be used in a concurrent setting because they are not stable with respect to concurrent behaviors of other tasks. To make them stable, we may need the specifications in Fig. 4(c), which is too weak to capture the functionality.

Figure 4(d) gives a relational specifications to show that inc refines an abstract operation $\langle\texttt{CNT++}\rangle$ [19], where $\langle C \rangle$ represents an *atomic* operation C. The relational assertions specify three important entities, the concrete state (cnt), the abstract state (CNT) and the abstract operation ($\langle\texttt{CNT++}\rangle$) that the program refines (which could be non-atomic in general [19]). The precondition requires that initially cnt has the consistent value with its abstract counterpart CNT, and the abstract operation that inc needs to refine is $\langle\texttt{CNT++}\rangle$. The postcondition ensures cnt and CNT remain consistent and the remaining abstract operation that needs to be refined is **end** (*i.e.*, $\langle\texttt{CNT++}\rangle$ has been accomplished).

Our refinement proofs for OS kernels follow the same kind of relational reasoning, where the assertions now relate the concrete kernel state, the abstract kernel state (Σ) and the abstract statement (s).

Assertions. Below is the assertion language, and its semantics is given in Fig. 5.

$$(Asrt)\ p, q, r ::= \mathsf{emp} \mid \mathsf{empE} \mid x \mapsto v \mid \mathsf{ISR}(isr) \mid \mathsf{IE}(ie) \mid \mathsf{IS}(is) \mid \mathsf{CS}(cs) \mid \llcorner k \lrcorner \mid \chi \triangleright t$$
$$\mid \mathsf{a} \rightarrowtail \Omega \mid [|\mathsf{s}|] \mid p * p \mid p \wedge p \mid \ldots$$
$$(Inv)\qquad I\ ::= [p_0, \ldots, p_N]$$

$(RelState)\ \Theta ::= (\sigma, \Sigma, \mathbb{s})\quad (LTaskCfg)\ \sigma ::= (m, isr, \delta)\quad (LTaskSt)\ m\ ::=\ (G, E, M)$

$(\sigma, \Sigma, \mathbb{s}) \models \mathsf{emp}$ iff $\sigma.m.M = \emptyset \wedge \Sigma = \emptyset$

$(\sigma, \Sigma, \mathbb{s}) \models \mathsf{empE}$ iff $\sigma.m.E = \emptyset \wedge (\sigma, \Sigma, \mathbb{s}) \models \mathsf{emp}$

$(\sigma, \Sigma, \mathbb{s}) \models x \mapsto v$ iff $\exists a.(\sigma.m.G)(x) = a \wedge \sigma.m.M = \{a \rightsquigarrow v\} \wedge \Sigma = \emptyset$

$(\sigma, \Sigma, \mathbb{s}) \models \mathsf{ISR}(isr')$ iff $\sigma.isr = isr' \wedge (\sigma, \Sigma, \mathbb{s}) \models \mathsf{emp}$

$(\sigma, \Sigma, \mathbb{s}) \models \llcorner k \lrcorner$ iff $((k = N \wedge is = \mathsf{nil}) \vee \exists is'.(\sigma.\delta.is = k :: is')) \wedge (\sigma, \Sigma, \mathbb{s}) \models \mathsf{emp}$

$(\sigma, \Sigma, \mathbb{s}) \models \chi \triangleright t$ iff $\chi\ \Sigma\ t$

$(\sigma, \Sigma, \mathbb{s}) \models [\![\mathbb{s}']\!]$ iff $\mathbb{s} = \mathbb{s}' \wedge (\sigma, \Sigma, \mathbb{s}) \models \mathsf{emp}$

$(\sigma, \Sigma, \mathbb{s}) \models \mathbb{a} \rightarrowtail \Omega$ iff $\Sigma = \{\mathbb{a} \rightsquigarrow \Omega\} \wedge \sigma.m.M = \emptyset$

$f \perp g \overset{\text{def}}{=} dom(f) \cap dom(g) = \emptyset$ $\Sigma_1 \uplus \Sigma_2 \overset{\text{def}}{=} \begin{cases} \Sigma_1 \cup \Sigma_2 \text{ iff } \Sigma_1 \perp \Sigma_2 \\ undef \qquad\quad \text{otherwise} \end{cases}$

$\sigma_1 \uplus \sigma_2 \overset{\text{def}}{=} \begin{cases} ((G, E, M_1 \cup M_2), isr, \delta) & \text{iff } M_1 \perp M_2 \wedge \sigma_1 = ((G, E, M_1), isr, \delta) \\ & \wedge \sigma_2 = ((G, E, M_2), isr, \delta) \\ undef & \text{otherwise} \end{cases}$

$\Theta_1 \uplus \Theta_2 \overset{\text{def}}{=} (\sigma_1 \uplus \sigma_2, \Sigma_1 \uplus \Sigma_2, \mathbb{s})$ where $\Theta_1 = (\sigma_1, \Sigma_1, \mathbb{s}) \wedge \Theta_2 = (\sigma_2, \Sigma_2, \mathbb{s})$

$\Theta \models p_1 * p_2$ iff $\exists \Theta_1, \Theta_2.\Theta = \Theta_1 \uplus \Theta_2 \wedge \Theta_1 \models p_1 \wedge \Theta_2 \models p_2$

Fig. 5. Semantics of relational assertions

As explained above, the assertions are interpreted over relational states Θ, which consist of the low-level task-local states σ, the high-level abstract states Σ, and the abstract statements $\mathbb{s}$ that the low-level code needs to refine. Σ and $\mathbb{s}$ are defined in Fig. 3. σ, as shown in Fig. 5, consists of a task-local view m of program variables and memory, and also the global isr register and the task-local interrupt states δ (see Fig. 2). Here m contains the global and local variables (G and E respectively) and the memory M, whose definitions are omitted.

Assertion emp says the low-level memory and the high-level abstract state are both empty. empE further requires that the local variable environment be empty too. $x \mapsto v$ specifies a singleton memory cell with v stored in the global program variable x. $\mathsf{ISR}(isr)$, $\mathsf{IS}(is)$, $\mathsf{IE}(ie)$ and $\mathsf{CS}(cs)$ specify the value of the corresponding interrupt status (see Fig. 2). $\llcorner k \lrcorner$ means that the currently running interrupt handler is at level k (or $k = N$, meaning no running handlers).

$\chi \triangleright t$ says that, based on the high-level abstract state, the abstract scheduler χ picks t as the target task. $\mathbb{a} \longmapsto \Omega$ specifies a singleton high-level abstract state mapping the data name $\mathbb{a}$ to the abstract data Ω. $[\![\mathbb{s}]\!]$ means the current abstract statement remaining to be refined is $\mathbb{s}$. The separating conjunction $p_1 * p_2$ means p_1 and p_2 hold over disjoint parts of a relational state.

Ownership-Transfer Semantics for Multi-level Interrupts. CSL [21] prevents data races by enforcing disjoint ownership of resources among tasks. Synchronization is modeled in terms of ownership

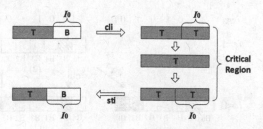

Fig. 6. Memory partition for handler and non-handler (Figure taken from [11])

transfer. Feng *et al.* [11] extend CSL and assign ownership-transfer semantics to interrupt operations. The idea is demonstrated in Fig. 6, which shows the *logical* memory model when there are only one task and single-level interrupt. Since the interrupt handler can preempt the task, we let the handler to reserve its required memory first (represented as block B). B must remain publicly available if the interrupt is enabled. Then the task can only access the remaining part (block T). We use grey boxes to represent *local* resources of the task. Disabling interrupts (**cli**) by the task essentially transfers the ownership of B from public to task-local. Correspondingly, **sti** converts the block from task-local to public, therefore the task *cannot* access it anymore. Similarly, invocation of the interrupt handler (not shown in the figure) automatically transfers B from public to the local resource of the handler, while **iret** transfers it back to public.

Since block B is shared between the interrupt handler and the task, it must be well-formed when it is public. We use the resource invariant I_0 to specify the well-formedness. Then the above ownership transfer semantics of **cli** and **sti** can be formalized in the following (simplified) program logic rules:

$$\overline{I_0 \vdash \{p_t\} \textbf{cli} \{p_t * I_0\}} \qquad\qquad \overline{I_0 \vdash \{p_t * I_0\} \textbf{sti} \{p_t\}}$$

Note that the partition between B and T is enforced *logically* using the separating conjunction in separation logic (see Fig. 5). It does not require physical separation in the program state model.

In this paper we extend this idea to support multi-level nested interrupts, where the ownership transfer of interrupt primitives is determined not only by the *ie* flag, but also by the *isr* register. Figure 7 shows the memory model (where the number N of interrupts is set to 6). Interrupt handlers at levels 0 to $N-1$ are assigned with resource blocks $B_0, \ldots, B_{N-1}$ respectively. B_N represents the resource shared only among tasks, *i.e.*, the non-handler code. We omit task-local resources, therefore there are *no* counterparts to block T in Fig. 6. Handlers' priorities to reserve their required resources are consistent with their interrupt priority levels. That is, B_0 satisfies all the need of the level-0 (highest priority) handler, while the level-k handler may need to access $B_0, \cdots, B_{k-1}$, in addition to B_k. The non-handler has the lowest priority. Each block B_k is specified by the resource invariant $I(k)$, where I is defined as a sequence of $N+1$ assertions (see the assertion syntax defined above).

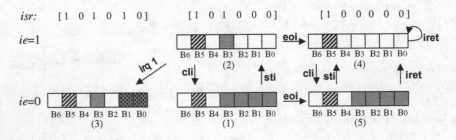

Fig. 7. Ownership-transfer for multi-level interrupts

Figure 7 demonstrates the ownership transfer of resource caused by interrupt operations under different conditions. The grey or dotted blocks represent resources exclusively owned in interrupt handlers, different textures for different interrupts. The white ones represent resources *available* for share. Suppose initially we are at state (1), where the level-3 handler is being executed, as the value of *isr* indicates. Since interrupts are disabled, the handler owns $B_0 - B_3$, knowing *no* requests of levels 0 to 3 could be served. Enabling interrupts (**sti**) loses $B_0 - B_2$, as shown by state (2), but B_3 is remained because $isr(3) = 1$ and requests of the same (or lower) level are not handled. However, if $isr(3) = 0$ instead (as in state (5)), executing **sti** loses B_3 as well. Ownership transfer by **cli** is the dual of **sti**.

Executing **eoi** at state (1) leads to state (5), but it causes no ownership transfer because interrupts are disabled anyway. If interrupts are enabled instead, as in state (2), **eoi** loses the ownership of B_3 because another level-3 request may be handled in state (4). **iret** can be executed only after **eoi**. If interrupts are disabled (as in state (5)), it transfers $B_0 - B_3$ from local resources to shared resources. Otherwise (as in state (4)) there is no ownership transfer because the handler has lost the ownership of $B_0 - B_3$ already.

At state (2), interrupts with higher priority can be served. The "**irq** 1" step sets the bit $isr(1)$, disables interrupts, and transfers B_0 and B_1 from shared resources to local resources of the level-1 handler, as in state (3).

The Top Rule. We show some selected program logic rules in Fig. 8. The TOPRULE establishes the judgment $\vdash_\psi O : \mathbb{O}$, ensuring the correctness of O w.r.t. $\mathbb{O}$ if the initial concrete and abstract kernel states satisfy ψ (explained in Sect. 3.3).

To verify the kernel, we need to come up with a specification Γ for the internal functions η_i in the low-level code, and a sequence of invariants I for kernel states. Γ assigns a pair of pre-/post-conditions to each internal function. We omit the formal definition here.

Then we prove that the internal functions, the API implementations and the interrupt handlers in the low-level kernel satisfy their specifications, respectively (the last three premises in the first line of the TOPRULE rule). The proof of each component carries the abstract scheduler specification χ and the invariant I.

The rule also requires that ψ ensures the initial states satisfy the invariant $I[0, N]$, the interrupt-related states are properly initialized, and the initial local variable environment is empty. $I[n, m]$ defined in Fig. 8 is the separating conjunction of invariants from level n to m. $OS[isr, ie, is, cs]$ specifies the status of interrupts, and requires that the currently executing handler (on top of *is*) have the highest priority among those in service (as recorded in *isr*). $\lfloor \psi \rfloor$ lifts ψ to relational assertions (definition omitted). We also omit some more detailed side conditions about the initial states in the rule.

Verifying Interrupt Handlers. We omit the rules of proving $\chi; I \vdash \eta_i : \Gamma$ and $\Gamma; \chi; I \vdash \eta_a : \varphi$ for internal functions and APIs respectively, which are similar to the rules for interrupt handlers. The ITRP rule proves the correctness of

$$O = (\eta_a, \eta_i, \theta) \quad \mathbb{O} = (\varphi, \varepsilon, \chi) \quad \chi; I \vdash \eta_i : \Gamma \quad \Gamma; \chi; I \vdash \eta_a : \varphi \quad \Gamma; \chi; I \vdash \theta : \varepsilon$$
$$\frac{\lfloor \psi \rfloor \Rightarrow I[0, N] * \mathsf{OS}[\bar{0}, 1, \mathsf{nil}, \mathsf{nil}] * \mathsf{empE} \qquad \text{other side conditions}}{\vdash_\psi O : \mathbb{O}} \text{ (TopRule)}$$

$$p = \mathsf{BldItrpPre}(k, \varepsilon, isr, is, I) \quad p_i = \mathsf{BldItrpRet}(k, isr, is, I)$$
$$\frac{dom(\theta) = dom(\varepsilon) \quad \Gamma; \chi; I; \mathsf{false}; p_i \vdash \{ p \} \, \theta(k) \, \{ \mathsf{false} \} \quad \text{for all } k \in \{0, \dots, N-1\}}{\Gamma; \chi; I \vdash \theta : \varepsilon} \text{ (ITRP)}$$

$$\frac{}{\Gamma; \chi; I; r; p_i \vdash \{ \mathsf{OS}[isr, 1, is, cs] * \llcorner k \lrcorner * [\![s]\!] \} \, \mathbf{encrt} \, \{ \mathsf{OS}[isr, 0, is, 1 :: cs] * \mathsf{INV}(I, k) * I[0, k-1] * [\![s]\!] \}} \text{ (ENCRT)}$$

$$\frac{}{\Gamma; \chi; I; r; p_i \vdash \{ \mathsf{OS}[isr, 0, is, cs] * [\![s]\!] \} \, \mathbf{encrt} \, \{ \mathsf{OS}[isr, 0, is, 0 :: cs] * [\![s]\!] \}} \text{ (ENCRT-0)}$$

$$\frac{}{\Gamma; \chi; I; r; p_i \vdash \{ \mathsf{OS}[isr, 0, is, 1 :: cs] * \llcorner k \lrcorner * \mathsf{INV}(I, k) * I[0, k-1] * [\![s]\!] \} \, \mathbf{excrt} \, \{ \mathsf{OS}[isr, 1, is, cs] * [\![s]\!] \}} \text{ (EXCRT)}$$

$$\frac{}{\Gamma; \chi; I; r; p_i \vdash \{ \mathsf{OS}[isr, 1, k :: is, cs] * I(k) * [\![s]\!] \} \, \mathbf{eoi} \, k \, \{ \mathsf{OS}[isr\{k \rightsquigarrow 0\}, 1, k :: is, cs] * [\![s]\!] \}} \text{ (EOI)}$$

$$\frac{p \Leftrightarrow \mathsf{SWINV}(I) * \mathsf{IS}(is) * \mathsf{CS}(cs)}{\Gamma; \chi; I; r; p_i \vdash \{ (p * [\![\mathbf{sched}; s]\!]) \wedge \chi \triangleright x \} \, \mathbf{switch} \, x \, \{ p * [\![s]\!] \}} \text{ (SWITCH)}$$

$$\frac{p \Rightarrow p_i}{\Gamma; \chi; I; \mathsf{false}; p_i \vdash \{ p \} \, \mathbf{iext} \, \{ \mathsf{false} \}} \text{ (IEXT)} \qquad \frac{p \Rightarrow p' \quad \Gamma; \chi; I; r; p_i \vdash \{ p' \} \, s \, \{ q' \} \quad q' \Rightarrow q}{\Gamma; \chi; I; r; p_i \vdash \{ p \} \, s \, \{ q \}} \text{ (ABSCSQ)}$$

$$I[n, m] \overset{\text{def}}{=} \begin{cases} I(n) * I(n+1) * \dots * I(m) & \text{if } 0 \le n \le m \le N \\ \mathsf{emp} & \text{otherwise} \end{cases}$$

$$\mathsf{OS}[isr, ie, is, cs] \overset{\text{def}}{=} \exists k. \, \mathsf{ISR}(isr) * \mathsf{IE}(ie) * \mathsf{IS}(is) * \mathsf{CS}(cs) * \llcorner k \lrcorner * (\forall k'. \, 0 \le k' < k \to isr(k') = 0)$$

$$\mathsf{INV}(I, k) \overset{\text{def}}{=} \exists isr. \, \mathsf{ISR}(isr) * ((isr(k) = 1 \wedge \mathsf{emp}) \vee ((isr(k) = 0 \vee k = N) \wedge I(k)))$$

$$\mathsf{SWINV}(I) \overset{\text{def}}{=} \mathsf{ISR}(\bar{0}) * \mathsf{IE}(0) * (\exists \, k. \, \llcorner k \lrcorner * I[0, k])$$

$$\mathsf{BldItrpPre}(k, \varepsilon, isr, is, I) \overset{\text{def}}{=} \mathsf{OS}[isr\{k \rightsquigarrow 1\}, 0, k :: is, \mathsf{nil}] * I[0, k] * [\![\varepsilon(k)]\!] * \mathsf{empE}$$

$$\mathsf{BldItrpRet}(k, isr, is, I) \overset{\text{def}}{=} \exists ie. \, \mathsf{OS}[isr\{k \rightsquigarrow 0\}, ie, k :: is, \mathsf{nil}] * ((ie = 1 \wedge \mathsf{emp}) \vee (ie = 0 \wedge I[0, k])) * [\![\mathbf{end}]\!]$$

Fig. 8. Selected inference rules

interrupt handlers. It requires that each individual interrupt handler is correct with respect to its specification. The judgment for statements is in the form of $\Gamma; \chi; I; r; p_i \vdash \{ p \} \, s \, \{ q \}$. We follow the CSL-style reasoning, where I specifies shared resource blocks, and the pre-/post-conditions specify *local* resources that are accessed exclusively by the current task. The precondition is p, while q, r and p_i are all post-conditions for different exits, *i.e.*, sequential composition, return from functions, and return from interrupts, respectively. For the whole body of interrupt handlers, we disable the other two exits by setting r and q to false.

We build the pre-/post-conditions of handlers with the auxiliary definitions BldItrpPre and BldItrpRet given in Fig. 8. The precondition says that, when entering the level-k handler, $isr(k)$ is set to 1, the interrupt is disabled and k is pushed onto the interrupt stack is (therefore $\mathsf{OS}[isr\{k \rightsquigarrow 1\}, 0, k::is, \mathsf{nil}]$). Since there is no handler of higher-priority in service, the handler has exclusive access to the resource $I[0, k]$ (see Fig. 7). It also needs to refine the high-level specification code $\varepsilon(k)$. empE requires there are no local variables at the beginning.

The built post-condition requires that: (1) the corresponding isr bit has been cleared; (2) if interrupts are enabled ($ie = 1$), the handler has no access to the shared resources; otherwise it needs to ensure that its owned resources are well formed w.r.t. $I[0, k]$ (see the two **iret** steps in Fig. 7); and (3) there is no high-level specification code remaining to be refined (*i.e.*, the abstract specification code $\varepsilon(k)$ specified in the precondition has been fulfilled).

Rules for Commands. The IEXT rule simply requires that the post-condition p_i holds when we reach the end of the interrupt handler. The ENCRT rule shows the ownership transfer when interrupts are disabled. Suppose we are at the level-k handler ($k = N$ means we are executing the non-handler code). Disabling interrupts prevents interrupt requests from level 0 to $k-1$, therefore the current task gains the ownership of $I[0, k-1]$. The transfer of the k-th block is specified by $\mathsf{INV}(I, k)$ in Fig. 8. If the bit $isr(k)$ is 0 (or $k = N$), the task also gains the ownership of $I(k)$, otherwise it already owns the k-th block and there is no extra ownership transfer. The two scenarios are also demonstrated by the two **cli** steps in Fig. 7. If interrupts are already disabled when **encrt** is executed, there is no ownership transfer, as shown by the ENCRT-0 rule.

The EXCRT rule is the dual of the ENCRT rule (see the two **sti** steps in Fig. 7). Correspondingly there is a EXCRT-0 rule, which is omitted here. The EOI rule says, if interrupts are enabled, the task loses the ownership of $I(k)$ after **eoi** k. Otherwise there is no ownership transfer and the corresponding rule is omitted (see the two **eoi** steps in Fig. 7).

The SWITCH rule requires that the invariant $\mathsf{SWINV}(I)$ holds before switching away and it is preserved after switching back. $\mathsf{SWINV}(I)$, defined in Fig. 8, says that interrupts must be disabled, and all the bits of isr are 0 (*i.e.*, either we are running non-handler code or we are in the outmost layer of nested invocation of interrupt handlers and have already executed **eoi**). Also if we are running level-k code (either handler or non-handler if $k = N$), the resource blocks 0 to k acquired before should satisfy $I[0, k]$, so that the target task could access them. The rule also says that the task-local states is and cs are not changed by **switch**.

To establish refinement, the precondition also requires that the high-level abstract scheduler χ picks the same task with the one in x, and **switch** x at the low level correspond to the **sched** step at the high level. Therefore in the post-condition **sched** is no longer in the remaining abstract operations.

Following [19], the ABSCSQ rule looks like a regular consequence rule but allows us to *execute* the abstract code. The implication $p \Rightarrow p'$ is defined below.

$$\forall \sigma, \Sigma, \mathsf{s}. ((\sigma, \Sigma, \mathsf{s}) \models p) \Longrightarrow \exists \Sigma', \mathsf{s}'. \left((\mathsf{s}, \Sigma) \bullet\!\!-_H\!\!\overset{*}{\to} (\mathsf{s}', \Sigma')\right) \wedge ((\sigma, \Sigma', \mathsf{s}') \models p')$$

That is, given a related state $(\sigma, \Sigma, \mathsf{s})$ satisfying p, the abstract code s could execute zero or multiple steps starting from Σ and reach (Σ', s'), so that the resulting related state $(\sigma, \Sigma', \mathsf{s}')$ satisfies p'. This rule allows us to establish simulation between the concrete and the abstract code, which then ensures refinement.

We can look at Fig. 4 to see the use of this rule. Suppose we want to verify `inc()` using the specification in Fig. 4(d). When we reach the **cas** command (see Fig. 4(a)), we have the precondition $(\mathtt{tmp} = \mathtt{cnt} \wedge \mathtt{cnt} = \mathtt{CNT} \wedge [|\mathtt{<CNT++>}|] \vee \ldots)$ (the case for $\mathtt{tmp} \neq \mathtt{cnt}$ omitted). Right after **cas**, we have $(\mathtt{done} \wedge \mathtt{cnt} = \mathtt{CNT}{+}1 \wedge [|\mathtt{<CNT++>}|] \vee \neg\mathtt{done} \wedge \ldots)$. We have $\mathtt{cnt} = \mathtt{CNT}{+}1$ because $\mathtt{cnt}$ increments if **cas** succeeds. To establish the simulation, we apply the ABSCSQ rule to execute the abstract code, because $(\mathtt{cnt} = \mathtt{CNT}{+}1 \wedge [|\mathtt{<CNT++>}|]) \Rightarrow (\mathtt{cnt} = \mathtt{CNT} \wedge [|\mathtt{end}|])$, following the above definition of $p \Rightarrow p'$.

Theorem 4.1 gives the soundness of the framework. The proofs are based on a compositional simulation following [18], and have been formalized in Coq. More details about the logic can be seen in TR [26].

Theorem 4.1 (Soundness). $\vdash_\psi O : \mathbb{O} \Longrightarrow O \sqsubseteq_\psi \mathbb{O}$.

5   Proving Priority-Inversion-Freedom

Formalization of PIF. Earlier work [6] defines priority inversions in terms of whether there is a higher priority task waiting directly or indirectly for a lower priority task. Since the definition refers to the *current* priority of tasks, its meaning is affected by algorithms that dynamically change the priority of tasks, such as the classic priority ceiling and priority inheritance algorithms [23]. We give a new formalization of PIF, which is based on the *original* priorities assigned by the programmers, reflecting the actual degree of urgency.

Definition 5.1 (Priority Inversion Freedom). PIF(Σ) holds, iff for any t, t_c, pr and pr_c, if $t \neq t_c$, $t_c = \mathsf{CurTask}(\Sigma)$, $pr = \mathsf{OrgPr}(t, \Sigma)$, $pr_c = \mathsf{OrgPr}(t_c, \Sigma)$, $\mathsf{IsWait}(t, \Sigma)$ and $\neg\mathsf{IsOwner}(t_c, \Sigma)$, then $pr \preceq pr_c$.

It says, if the *current* task t_c does not own any shared resources, then its *original* priority should be higher than (or equal to) any other waiting tasks t. Here $\mathsf{OrgPr}(t, \Sigma)$ represents t's original priority assigned by programmers. $\mathsf{IsWait}(t, \Sigma)$ means that t is blocked, waiting for certain shared resource, and $\neg\mathsf{IsOwner}(t_c, \Sigma)$ means that the task t_c does not own any shared resource (*e.g.*, mutexes).

If each task eventually releases its shared resource (*i.e.*, there is no deadlock), the definition ensures that the waiting task with higher priority will be eventually released and executed. Therefore it prevents unbounded priority inversion [23].

PIF of μC/OS-II. The mutex of μC/OS-II is implemented with a simplified priority ceiling protocol [23]. When proving it satisfies PIF, we find a counterexample (given in TR [26]) showing that PIF cannot be guaranteed unless there is no nested use of mutexes. By adding the assumption of no nested mutexes, we prove that the mutex in μC/OS-II ensures our PIF definition.

Theorem 5.2 (PIF without Nested Use of Mutexes).
If $\mathsf{Init}(\Sigma)$, $(A, \mathbb{O}_{\mu C/OS\text{-}II}) \vdash (T, \Delta, \Sigma) =_H\Rightarrow^* (T', \Delta', \Sigma')$, $\mathsf{NoNCR}(A, \Sigma, T, \Delta)$, *and* $\mathsf{SchedProp}(\Sigma')$, *then* $PIF(\Sigma')$.

It says, for any application code A, task pool T, client state Δ and abstract kernel state Σ, if initially there are no tasks waiting for mutexes ($\mathsf{Init}(\Sigma)$), and there is no nested use of mutexes ($\mathsf{NoNCR}(A, \Sigma, T, \Delta)$), then for any T', Δ' and Σ' generated during the execution, if Σ' is consistent with the priority-based scheduling (*i.e.*, the currently running task always has the highest priority among all the ready tasks, represented as $\mathsf{SchedProp}(\Sigma')$), then it must satisfy PIF. Here we use a simplified $\mathbb{O}_{\mu C/OS\text{-}II}$ that contains the PIF mutex as the only APIs. The proof is formalized in Coq.

6 Verifying µC/OS-II

We have applied our framework to verify key modules (around 1300 lines of C code without counting comments and empty lines) of µC/OS-II V2.52, including the scheduler, the timer interrupt handler, mutexes, message queues, mail boxes, semaphores, and the time management. These 1300 lines of C code verified in our framework correspond to around 3250 lines of code in their original format (with comments and empty lines) in the source files of µC/OS-II, including "ucos_ii.h", "os_q.c", "os_sem.c", "os_mbox.c", "os_mutex.c", "os_time.c", "os_core.c" and "os_cpu_a.c". The verified modules cover 63 % of the frequently used APIs and internal functions [2]. We ignore some synchronization APIs which have similar functionality as the verified ones. Verification of task creation/deletion is still ongoing work based on the presented framework.

Modifications to the Original Code. Our verification is based on the original code with some minor modifications. For instance, the API OSQPend(S) is used to receive a message from a queue, and its original code does not check if the input pointer S points to a valid event control block, because it assumes that the client code always gets S by calling OSQCreate() (thus S should already be valid). We drop this assumption about the client code. Correspondingly we insert code that checks whether S is a valid pointer. If S is invalid a new error code is returned. Similar modifications are made to some other modules too. The reason for doing above modifications is that the contextual refinement proved in our verification framework assumes arbitrary client code, while kernels are usually implemented with assumptions over client code for efficiency.

Table 1. The Verification Package

Framework	Coq lines	Verified Modules	lines of C	Coq lines
Basic Libraries	32061	Global Declarations	187	-
Machine & Logic	23095			
Automated Tactics	21050	Message Queue	240	4537
Total	76206	Semaphore	166	2441
Certified µC/OS-II	**Coq lines**	Mailbox	171	3326
C Code Definitions	1824	Mutex	301	17331
Specifications	6012	Time Management	39	861
Priority Inversion Freedom	9570	Timer Interrupt	17	443
Libraries for µC/OS-II	62085	Internal Functions	195	5447
Auto. Generated Code	25357	Final Theorems	-	501
Total	104848	Total	1316	34887

Proof Efforts. The Coq implementation consists of around 216,000 lines of code and proofs in Coq8.4pl6. Table 1 gives a break down of the number of lines for various components. Compiling the entire Coq package takes around 16 h on a machine with 3.6 GHz cpu and 32G memory. The work takes us around 5.5 person years in total, including 4 person years for the framework and 1 person year for verifying the first μC/OS-II module (Message Queue). With the facilities (tactics, libraries and invariants *etc.*) being stabilized, verifying the remaining modules (around 900 lines of C code) only takes us around 6 person months.

The most challenging part is to verify the timer interrupt handler, which traverses the entire TCB list and updates task status in each TCB block. It needs to access all the shared data structures in μC/OS-II. Several different updates to shared data structures make the loop invariant quite complicated.

Also verifying an existing OS kernel is more difficult than verifying a new one written for verification purpose. When verifying μC/OS-II the major difficulty comes from the gap between the low-level concrete data structure and the high-level abstract representation. For instance, μC/OS-II uses a smart bitmap algorithm to record whether a task is in the waiting queue. The implementation requires us to establish a subtle consistency relation between the low-level bitmap and the high-level abstract waiting queue. The verification would have been much simpler if the waiting queue is simply implemented as a linked list.

Coq Tactics. Proof automation is essential to improve the productivity. We develop tactics for automatically proving relational separation logic assertions and generating verification conditions based on existing techniques [5,7,20]. They do forward reasoning for statements, including function calls and primitives entering and exiting critical regions, *etc.* Also some domain-specific tactics are implemented for individual data structures used in μC/OS-II, including ones for the arithmetic properties of *Int32* and bitmaps. Thanks to these tactics, the ratio of Coq proof scripts to the verified C code is around 26:1. Another advantage of the tactics is that they can extract lemmas independent of program contexts for verifying functionality of code. Users can verify code using the tactics without knowing much about the underlying framework.

7   Related Work and Conclusion

There have been a number of OS verification projects, including seL4 [15,16], Verisoft [4], VCC/VeriSoftXT [3,9], Verve [27], and CertiKOS [8,13]. Most of them have no or limited support of preemption and multi-level interrupts.

seL4 [15,16] is one of the milestone OS kernel verification projects. The verification is fully mechanized in Isabelle/HOL. The kernel of seL4 does not support general preemption. Instead, tasks are preemptible only at specific points. Therefore the code verified is mostly sequential. On the other hand, the seL4 project has verified rich features and properties such as virtual memory, real-time properties and security properties, which are not done in our work.

The Verisoft project also verifies OS microkernels [4] in Isabelle/HOL, but the CVM model used there does not permit interrupts inside the kernel. Its successor project, Verisoft XT [3], uses VCC [9] to verify the commercial Hyper-V hypervisor. VCC supports verification of concurrent C code by inserting auxiliary code and ghost states. The proofs have a refinement flavor, but VCC does not establish contextual refinement as what we do. Also it is unclear how VCC is applied to verify multi-level nested interrupts in hypervisors.

Verve [27] combines a type-safe kernel with a minimal hardware abstraction layer. The kernel is concurrent, but the properties verified are mostly about type safety, much weaker than our contextual refinement property. Also Verve simply squashes multiple interrupt levels into a single level and does not really handle multi-level interrupts. VCC/VerisoftXT and Verve use the Z3 SMT solver [10] for better automation, while we use Coq which generates machine-checkable proofs. Also the soundness of our program logic is proved in Coq. Therefore the trusted computing base (TCB) of our approach is smaller.

Gu *et al.* [13] verify the mCertiKOS hypervisor. Their kernel is sequential. Recently, Chen *et al.* [8] propose a framework for building certified interruptible OS kernels (based on mCertiKOS) with device drivers. Their framework does not support preemptive concurrency as ours, and it requires that interrupt handlers for device drivers and non-handler kernel code should not share any state.

Gotsman and Yang [12] developed a program logic based on CSL, which decomposes the verification of preemptive kernels into verifying the scheduler and the tasks. Their proofs are on-paper only and not mechanized. The machine model does not support multi-level interrupts, also their program logic is used to prove partial correctness, not contextual refinement as we do.

Conclusion. We have developed a practical verification framework for general verification purpose of preemptive OS kernels with multi-level interrupts. Correctness of the OS kernel is formalized as a contextual refinement between the low-level concrete implementations and the high-level specifications. As far as we know, our work is the first to establish contextual refinement for system APIs of a preemptive OS kernel. We have applied the framework to verify key modules and PIF of μC/OS-II, a commercial embedded real-time OS.

It is worth noting that although our verification framework is developed to verify μC/OS-II, it is a general verification framework and most of its building blocks can be reused to verify other OS kernels. As shown in Fig. 1, the small-step semantics for the C subset, the program logic and the tactics are all general and mostly independent of the μC/OS-II verification project. A potential limitation is that the interrupt mechanism in our operational semantics is modeled specifically based on the Intel 8259 A interrupt controller, and the program logic rules for interrupts are designed accordingly. However, the logic rules follow the general ownership transfer idea from CSL. With a different processor and interrupt mechanism, even though we may need to change the current inference rules for interrupt primitives, we can apply the same ownership transfer idea, and the required change should be superficial. Another limitation is that our C subset is chosen based on the μC/OS-II code. In particular, it does not allow function pointers, which requires the support of higher-order functions in the logic.

References

1. The coq development team: The Coq proof assistant. http://coq.inria.fr
2. The real-time kernel: μC/OS-II. http://micrium.com/rtos/ucosii/overview
3. The Verisoft XT Project (2007). http://www.verisoftxt.de
4. Alkassar, E., Paul, W.J., Starostin, A., Tsyban, A.: Pervasive verification of an OS microkernel. In: Leavens, G.T., O'Hearn, P., Rajamani, S.K. (eds.) VSTTE 2010. LNCS, vol. 6217, pp. 71–85. Springer, Heidelberg (2010)
5. Appel, A.W.: Tactics for separation logic (2006). http://www.cs.princeton.edu/~appel/papers/septacs.pdf
6. Babaoglu, O., Marzullo, K., Schneider, F.B.: A formalization of priority inversion. Real-Time Syst. **5**, 285–303 (1993)
7. Cao, J., Fu, M., Feng, X.: Practical tactics for verifying C programs in coq. In: CPP, pp. 97–108 (2015)
8. Chen, H., Wu, N., Shao, Z., Lockerman, J., Gu, R.: Toward compositional verification of interruptible os kernels and device drivers. In: PLDI (2016, to appear)
9. Cohen, E., Dahlweid, M., Hillebrand, M., Leinenbach, D., Moskal, M., Santen, T., Schulte, W., Tobies, S.: VCC: a practical system for verifying concurrent C. In: Berghofer, S., Nipkow, T., Urban, C., Wenzel, M. (eds.) TPHOLs 2009. LNCS, vol. 5674, pp. 23–42. Springer, Heidelberg (2009)
10. de Moura, L., Bjørner, N.S.: Z3: an efficient SMT solver. In: Ramakrishnan, C.R., Rehof, J. (eds.) TACAS 2008. LNCS, vol. 4963, pp. 337–340. Springer, Heidelberg (2008)
11. Feng, X., Shao, Z., Dong, Y., Guo, Y.: Certifying low-level programs with hardware interrupts and preemptive threads. In: PLDI, pp. 170–182 (2008)
12. Gotsman, A., Yang, H.: Modular verification of preemptive OS kernels. J. Funct. Program. **23**(4), 452–514 (2013)
13. Gu, R., Koenig, J., Ramananandro, T., Shao, Z., Wu, X.N., Weng, S.-C., Zhang, H., Guo, Y.: Deep specifications and certified abstraction layers. In: POPL, pp. 595–608 (2015)
14. Klein, G., Andronick, J., Elphinstone, K., Heiser, G., Cock, D., Derrin, P., Elkaduwe, D., Engelhardt, K., Kolanski, R., Norrish, M., Sewell, T., Tuch, H., Winwood, S.: seL4: Formal verification of an operating-system kernel. Commun. ACM **53**(6), 107–115 (2010)
15. Klein, G., Andronick, J., Elphinstone, K., Murray, T.C., Sewell, T., Kolanski, R., Heiser, G.: Comprehensive formal verification of an OS microkernel. ACM Trans. Comput. Syst. **32**(1), 2 (2014)
16. Klein, G., Elphinstone, K., Heiser, G., Andronick, J., Cock, D., Derrin, P., Elkaduwe, D., Engelhardt, K., Kolanski, R., Norrish, M., Sewell, T., Tuch, H., Winwood, S.: sel4: Formal verification of an os kernel. In: SOSP, pp. 207–220 (2009)
17. Liang, H., Feng, X.: Modular verification of linearizability with non-fixed linearization points. In: PLDI, pp. 459–470 (2013)
18. Liang, H., Feng, X., Fu, M.: A rely-guarantee-based simulation for verifying concurrent program transformations. In: POPL, pp. 455–468 (2012)
19. Liang, H., Feng, X., Shao, Z.: Compositional verification of termination-preserving refinement of concurrent programs. In: CSL-LICS, pp. 65: 1–65: 10 (2014)
20. McCreight, A.: Practical tactics for separation logic. In: Berghofer, S., Nipkow, T., Urban, C., Wenzel, M. (eds.) TPHOLs 2009. LNCS, vol. 5674, pp. 343–358. Springer, Heidelberg (2009)

21. O'Hearn, P.W.: Resources, concurrency and local reasoning. In: Gardner, P., Yoshida, N. (eds.) CONCUR 2004. LNCS, vol. 3170, pp. 49–67. Springer, Heidelberg (2004)
22. Sevcík, J., Vafeiadis, V., Nardelli, F.Z., Jagannathan, S., Sewell, P.: Compcerttso: a verified compiler for relaxed-memory concurrency. J. ACM **60**(3), 22 (2013)
23. Sha, L., Rajkumar, R., Lehoczky, J.P.: Priority inheritance protocols: an approach to real-time synchronization. IEEE Trans. Comput. **39**, 1175–1185 (1990)
24. Turon, A., Dreyer, D., Birkedal, L.: Unifying refinement and hoare-style reasoning in a logic for higher-order concurrency. In: ICFP, pp. 377–390 (2013)
25. Turon, A., Thamsborg, J., Ahmed, A., Birkedal, L., Dreyer, D.: Logical relations for fine-grained concurrency. In: POPL, pp. 343–356 (2013)
26. Xu, F., Fu, M., Feng, X., Zhang, X., Zhang, H., Li, Z.: A practical verification framework for preemptive OS kernels (technical report and coq implementations), May 2016. http://staff.ustc.edu.cn/~fuming/research/certiucos
27. Yang, J., Hawblitzel, C.: Safe to the last instruction: automated verification of a type-safe operating system. In: PLDI, pp. 99–110 (2010)

Probabilistic Automated Language Learning for Configuration Files

Mark Santolucito, Ennan Zhai, and Ruzica Piskac[✉]

Yale University, New Haven, USA
ruzica.piskac@yale.edu

Abstract. Software failures resulting from configuration errors have
become commonplace as modern software systems grow increasingly
large and more complex. The lack of language constructs in configuration files, such as types and grammars, has directed the focus of a
configuration file verification towards building post-failure error diagnosis tools. In addition, the existing tools are generally language specific,
requiring the user to define at least a grammar for the language models and explicit rules to check. In this paper, we propose a framework
which analyzes datasets of correct configuration files and derives rules
for building a language model from the given dataset. The resulting
language model can be used to verify new configuration files and detect
errors in them. Our proposed framework is highly modular, does not rely
on the system source code, and can be applied to any new configuration
file type with minimal user input. Our tool, named ConfigC, relies on
an abstract representation of language rules to allow for this modular-
ity. ConfigC supports learning of various rules, such as orderings, value
relations, type errors, or user defined rules by using a probabilistic type
inference strategy and defining a small interface for the rule type.

1 Introduction and System Overview

Configuration errors are one of the most important root-causes of modern software system failures [10,11]. In practice, misconfiguration problems may result
in security vulnerabilities, application crashes, severe disruptions in software
functionality, and incorrect program executions [9,10,12,13]. Although several
tools have been proposed to automate configuration error diagnosis after failures
occur [3,5–7], these tools rely on a manual approach to understand and detect
the failure symptoms. The main reasons for this are: (1) entries in configuration
files are untyped assignments, (2) there is no explicit structure policy for the
entries in configuration files, and (3) there are surprisingly few rules specifying
the entries' constraints.

We propose an approach to the verification of configuration files which is based
on learning rules about the language model for configuration files. There is no universal definition of a "configuration file". In general, most configuration files tend

© Springer International Publishing Switzerland 2016
S. Chaudhuri and A. Farzan (Eds.): CAV 2016, Part II, LNCS 9780, pp. 80–87, 2016.
DOI: 10.1007/978-3-319-41540-6_5

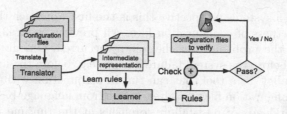

Fig. 1. ConfigC's workflow. The green boxes represent configuration files, including both correct general configuration files and users' input configuration files. The purple boxes are the components within ConfigC. The yellow boxes are results generated by ConfigC's components.

to be a series of assignment to system variables. Configuration files generally do not have more complicated language constructs, lest they become a setup script.

Figure 1 describes an overview of our system. We start with the assumption that we are given a number of correct configuration files belonging to the same category (for instance, MySQL or Apache). Such files follow similar patterns, which we exploit in a learning algorithm to build rules that describe a language model for the files. Since the "language" of configuration types is untyped and unstructured, we first parse the files and translate them into a more structured, intermediary representation. When running type inference on a configuration file, the type of a variable cannot always be fully determined from a single value. We address this problem by introducing so called *probabilistic types*. Rather than giving a variable a single type, we assign several types with their probability distributions. We can then use these more structured files as a training set to learn the rules. The learning algorithm is template-based to be easily extensible. We provide an initial set of templates and the learner learns some concrete instances from the training set. These rules are used for detecting errors violating the learned constraints in the files given by the user.

As an illustration of a simple rule that we can learn, consider a template $X_1 \leq X_2$, where X_1 and X_2 are integer variables. The learner might derive the rule stating that `mysql.max_persistent` $\leq$ `max_connections`. There is a classification and taxonomy of configuration errors in the existing work on automated configuration troubleshooting [1,11]. We provide templates for every class that ConfigC can handle: we consider integer constraints, ordering constraints, typing constraints, and constraints about correlated entries (such as "if X is present, Y has to appear as well"). Unfortunately, we cannot handle the class of errors that rely on the analysis of the whole operating system. Our language-based approach can only learn on sets of text files, not the system environment.

From a practical perspective ConfigC introduces no additional burden to the users: they can simply use ConfigC to check for errors in their configuration files. However, they can also easily extend the framework themselves. The system is designed to be highly modular. If there is a class of rules that ConfigC is not currently learning, the user can develop their own templates and learners for that class. The new learner can be added to ConfigC and this way it can check additionally a new set of errors.

Finally, from a systems perspective this is the first approach that *proactively* checks the correctness of configuration files. All previous work [3,5–7,10,12,13] tries to identify the problem after the failure occurred. Our approach isolates potential errors before the system failure occurs, e.g. before the installation. We can also see ConfigC as a tool that can run in conjunction with existing tools. Pre-analyzed configuration files are already free from language-based errors, and this way the workloads of post-failure forensics at the runtime is significantly reduced, thus making these tools truly practical.

To summarize, this tool paper makes the following contributions. First, we designed and implemented a tool, ConfigC, that can learn a language model from an example set of correct configuration files, and we use the model to verify new configuration files. Second, we use probabilistic types to assign a confidence distribution over a set of types to a value. Finally, in ConfigC we define an interface for describing a verification attribute in a learning context, making it easy to add new rules to the system.

2   Motivating Examples

When writing configuration files, users usually take already existing files and modify the files, with little knowledge of the system. The non-expert user can then easily introduce in errors. Even worse, the original file may already corrupted and the errors are propagated further. Below we show some real worlds examples of the errors commonly found in configuration files. All these examples are extracted from real-world reports [8,11]. The deep, domain specific knowledge needed to identify these error manually is strong motivation for a tool such as ConfigC.

Example 1: Ordering Errors. When configuring PHP to run with the Apache HTTP Server, the user writes, among others, the following lines:

```
extension = mysql.so
...
extension = recode.so
```

This file caused the Apache server to fail to start due to a segmentation fault error. When using PHP in Apache, the extension "mysql.so" depends on "recode.so" and the relative ordering of two of them is crucial. ConfigC would inform the user that "recode.so" should appear before "mysql.so", and return the error:

```
ORDERING ERROR: Expected "extension" recode.so"
BEFORE "extension" "mysql.so"
```

Example 2: Entry Missing Errors. If the user wants to use OpenLDAP to enable her directory access protocol, she needs to use the password policy overlay. This is usually done through the following entries in the OpenLDAP configuration file:

```
include schema/ppolicy.schema
overlay ppolicy
```

When using the password policy overlay in OpenLDAP, we have to first include the related schema. Leaving out the "include" statement will cause the failure of this LDAP. Running ConfigC on such a misconfiguration file would return:

```
MISSING KEYWORD ERROR: Expected "overlay" "ppolicy"
in the same file as:"include" "schema/ppolicy.schema"
```

Example 3: Type Errors. If the user tries to install MySQL, she first needs to initiate the path for the log information generated by MySQL. A user may put the following code in the MySQL configuration file:

```
general_log = /var/log/mysql/mysql.log
```

However, the entry "general_log" should be an integer, not a string. In MySQL, there is another entry named "general_log_file" which is used to specify the log path. After ConfigC analyzes this configuration file, it correctly identifies the error:

```
TYPE ERROR: Expected a Int with P=1.0 for
"general_log[mysqld]"
```

Example 4: Value Correlation Errors. When configuring PHP on MySQL, the user may write the following lines of entries in both the PHP and MySQL configuration files:

```
mysql's config
max_connections = 300
...
php's config
mysql.max_persistent = 400
```

This could cause MySQL to abort with the error information: "too many connections". In this case, the "mysql.max persistent" in PHP should be no larger than the "max_connections" in MySQL configuration file. Another rule we have implemented is learning inequality relations between integers. Running ConfigC on this combined configuration file would return:

```
INTEGER RELATION ERROR:
Expected "max_connections">="mysql.max_persistent"
```

3 Learning the Rules

To learn rules, we first translate to the intermediate representation where each line of a configuration file is reduced to a keyword-value pair (k, v). Parsing is language dependent and users may provide extra help to the translator for their specific language, such as specifying a comment character. We must assign types to the keywords to guide the learning modules. With typed keyword-value pairs, we can run each learning module independent of each other. We learn a set of rules over every file, then merge them.

Introducing the Types. Based only on a single example value of v we cannot fully determine the type of k. Consider for instance the following example:

```
foo = 300
bar = 300.txt
```

Most likely `foo` is an integer and we learn an equality rule, but it could also be a string. In this case we want to learn the rule `foo` ∈ substrings(`bar`). We therefore assign a distribution of types to a value, an idea closely related to existentially quantified types [4]. We introduce *probabilistic types* to address this issue.

Let $\mathcal{T}$ be a set of basic types. In ConfigC set $\mathcal{T}$ contains strings, integers, file paths, sizes and IP addresses. A probabilistic type built from $\mathcal{T}$ is a list of pairs $[(\tau_1, p_1), \ldots, (\tau_n, p_n)]$ such that $\tau_i \in \mathcal{T}$, $0 \leq p_i \leq 1$ and $\Sigma p_i = 1$. These probabilities are updated each time a new example value for a keyword is encountered.

When a value has a probabilistic type, we generate rules for all its types. This means that by assigning `foo` a probabilistic type (e.g. $(foo, 300, [(Int, 90\,\%), (String, 10\,\%)])$) we now generate rules for both strings and integers. Once the type inference can uniquely determine the type, the probability of all other types is set to zero, and the associated rules are withdrawn.

Note that typing is also a system module than can be easily extended to support more types. In that case the user will need to provide rules for type inference and probability distributions for values where type inference is ambiguous.

Rule Learning. With every type we associate a set of templates, specific to this type. Once the input files are fully type-annotated, we generate rules that are instances of these templates. We always learn the largest set of rules that all correct configuration files satisfy. This way ConfigC can guarantee that, over the set of rules we consider, there will be no false negatives that could have been caught with the given learning set. The only case of a false negative can be when there was no evidence of such a rule in the learning set - we cannot generate rules from nothing.

4   Implementation and Evaluation

Implementation. ConfigC is implemented in Haskell and takes full advantage of its polymorphism to make the system more modular. In particular, rules are represented as a type, where the type must support a particular interface (called a typeclass in Haskell) to be compatible with our system. By using language extensions (FlexibleInstances and MultiParamTypeClasses), this typeclass can be made polymorphic over the data structure as denoted by `Foldable t =>`. The user can then choose a data structure that is most natural to the rule they are implementing. For example, in our implementation, Missing Entries were easier to manipulate in lists, while Type Errors fit more naturally into a hashmap. This typeclass defines the three functions that each set of rules must implement to work with our system. The core learning algorithm is simply a fold using `merge` over the derived rules from running `learn` on each file in the learning set.

Typeclasses and other features of Haskell means that our system consists of only 267 lines of code, with another 233 for the rule modules. With an average size of 58 lines of code for each rule module, this is evidence of how simple it is to extend ConfigC with new rules.

```
class Foldable t => RuleSet t a where
  learn :: IRConfigFile -> t a
  merge :: t a -> t a -> t a
  check :: t a -> IRConfigFile -> Error
```

Since we learn a set of rules on each file in isolation from the other, we have a pleasingly parallel situation. Haskell allows us to easily take advantage of this by using the parallel mapping library [2], both for translation to the intermediate representation, and for learning the rules on each file. The merge stage could also easily be parallelized, using a divide and conquer approach, but ConfigC runs fast enough over our learning set (28 files, 961 lines of code) that this has not been necessary.

The integer relation rule has an unusual implementation that uses function as first-class objects in Haskell. Rather than associated keywords with SMT formula, we directly associate them with a function of type (Int->Int->Bool). Since we need to compare rules over equality, we must have a way to compare functions. This limits the types of functions we use to (==),(>=),(<=). Although this is sufficient for most cases, more fine-grained relations could be encoded with SMT formulas then passed to a solver.

The tool is available for download at http://marksantolucito.com/cavae.html.

Evaluation. To evaluate our tool, we take a subset of 20 benchmarks from an existing dataset of configuration errors [1,8,11] which are supported by our tool. Table 1 contains an evaluation summary. We do not report the running times, since they are negligible: even when running in the interpreter mode, files are analyzed instantaneously. We spent approximately 30 s on learning the rules. When we run the compiled version, we need for learning and verification combined less than 5 s. Our focus is usefulness of the tool: its ability to detect configuration errors and the number of false positives. For every benchmark class we took five examples. The middle column represents the number of detected errors, while the right column represents the number of returned false positives per each benchmark.

A benchmark passes a test if it reports an error on the source of the misconfiguration (it is not a false negative). We call false positives any reported error that was unrelated to the value of interest. It is worth noting that this is in fact a conservative estimate. Since these benchmarks are taken from online forums, there is no guarantee the files contain only a single error. Indeed, on some benchmarks, ConfigC found errors in the file that were similar to rules broken by other benchmarks.

We fail one benchmark in Value Relations because we do not yet support relations between file sizes of different units (Mb to Kb). In one Keyword Ordering benchmark, ConfigC reports a type error on the value of interest instead of an ordering error. This is a result of our context embedding in the translation to the intermediate representation - reordering the value puts it in a new context where the type is now also incorrect.

Table 1. Benchmarks for misconfiguration detection

Error type	Passing tests	False positives
Missing Entry	5/5	1, 0, 0, 0, 4
Type Error	5/5	0, 0, 0, 0, 0
Keyword Ordering	5/5	0, 2, 1, 0, 6
Value Relations	4/5	0, 0, 0, 1, 0

All but one false positive reports were integer relations. They are the result of overfitting on rules. ConfigC can learn overapproximating rules when the learning set does not show the full spectrum of possible values. Since integer relations have a larger space of relation than ordering relations for instance, ConfigC needs a larger learning set in order to eliminate false positives.

The false positive for the Value Relation was a Missing Entry error. This is a result of the fact that we cannot learn rules that are disjunctions. In this case, no socket is provided to [mysqld], failing a rule we had learned over the dataset. In fact, this is not a misconfiguration because a socket only needs to be provided to one (or both) [mysqld] or [wampsqld]. We reported an error since none of the files in the learning set had no socket associated with [mysqld]. In fact, since we do not support disjunctive rules, we could not have even learned such a rule - though in practice these seem to be uncommon.

5   Conclusions

In this paper, we introduce ConfigC, a highly-modular framework that allows verification of configuration files, even without a language model of the file. New verification properties require only a small amount of code and are not language specific, all indicating that ConfigC could be widely adopted by system administrators. Such a verification tool that scales in both performance and expressivity can revolutionize configuration file checking, reducing the cost of system maintenance and failure dramatically.

The field of verification must guarantee the reliability of entire systems, and 31 % of all system failures are caused by misconfiguration, while only 20 % are caused by program bugs [9]. We hope ConfigC can be a catalyst to spark interest in the potential impact of verification for configuration files.

Acknowledgements. We thank the anonymous reviewers for their insightful comments. We also thank Tianyin Xu for his valuable feedback on earlier version of this work. This research was supported by the NSF under grant CCF-1302327.

References

1. Misconfiguration dataset. https://github.com/tianyin/configuration_datasets
2. parallel-3.2.1.0: Parallel programming library. https://hackage.haskell.org/package/parallel-3.2.1.0/docs/Control-Parallel-Strategies.html
3. Attariyan, M., Flinn, J.: Automating configuration troubleshooting with dynamic information flow analysis. In: 9th USENIX Symposium on Operating Systems Design and Implementation (OSDI), October 2010
4. Launchbury, J., Jones, S.L.P.: Lazy functional state threads. In: Programming Language Design and Implementation (PLDI), pp. 24–35. ACM Press (1993)
5. Su, Y., Attariyan, M., Flinn, J.: AutoBash: improving configuration management with operating systems. In: 21st ACM Symposium on Operating Systems Principles (SOSP), October 2007
6. Wang, H.J., Platt, J.C., Chen, Y., Zhang, R., Wang, Y.: Automatic misconfiguration troubleshooting with PeerPressure. In: 6th USENIX Symposium on Operating Systems Design and Implementation (OSDI), December 2004
7. Whitaker, A., Cox, R.S., Gribble, S.D.: Configuration debugging as search: finding the needle in the haystack. In: 6th USENIX Symposium on Operating Systems Design and Implementation (OSDI), December 2004
8. Xu, T., Jin, L., Fan, X., Zhou, Y., Pasupathy, S., Talwadker, R.: Key, you have given me too many knobs!: Understanding and dealing with over-designed configuration in system software. In: 10th Joint Meeting on Foundations of Software Engineering (ESEC/FSE), August 2015
9. Xu, T., Zhang, J., Huang, P., Zheng, J., Sheng, T., Yuan, D., Zhou, Y., Pasupathy, S.: Do not blame users for misconfigurations. In: 24th ACM Symposium on Operating Systems Principles (SOSP), November 2013
10. Xu, T., Zhou, Y.: Systems approaches to tackling configuration errors: a survey. ACM Comput. Surv. **47**(4), 70 (2015)
11. Yin, Z., Ma, X., Zheng, J., Zhou, Y., Bairavasundaram, L.N., Pasupathy, S.: An empirical study on configuration errors in commercial and open source systems. In: 23rd ACM Symposium on Operating Systems Principles (SOSP), October 2011
12. Yuan, D., Xie, Y., Panigrahy, R., Yang, J., Verbowski, C., Kumar, A.: Context-based online configuration-error detection. In: USENIX ATCUSENIX Annual Technical Conference (USENIX ATC), June 2011
13. Zhang, J., Renganarayana, L., Zhang, X., Ge, N., Bala, V., Xu, T., Zhou, Y.: Encore: exploiting system environment and correlation information for misconfiguration detection. In: Architectural Support for Programming Languages and Operating Systems (ASPLOS), March 2014

Concurrency

The Commutativity Problem of the MapReduce Framework: A Transducer-Based Approach

Yu-Fang Chen[1(⊠)], Lei Song[2], and Zhilin Wu[2]

[1] Institute of Information Science, Academia Sinica, Taipei, Taiwan
yfc@iis.sinica.edu.tw
[2] State Key Laboratory of Computer Science, Institute of Software,
Chinese Academy of Sciences, Beijing, China

Abstract. MapReduce is a popular programming model for data parallel computation. In MapReduce, the *reducer* produces an output from a list of inputs. Due to the scheduling policy of the platform, the inputs may arrive at the reducers in different order. The *commutativity problem* of reducers asks if the output of a reducer is independent of the order of its inputs. Although the problem is undecidable in general, the MapReduce programs in practice are usually used for data analytics and thus require very simple control flow. By exploiting the simplicity, we propose a programming language for reducers where the commutativity problem is decidable. The main idea of the reducer language is to separate the control and data flow of programs and disallow arithmetic operations in the control flow. The decision procedure for the commutativity problem is obtained through a reduction to the equivalence problem of *streaming numerical transducers* (SNTs), a novel automata model over infinite alphabets introduced in this paper. The design of SNTs is inspired by streaming transducers (Alur and Cerny, POPL 2011). Nevertheless, the two models are intrinsically different since the outputs of SNTs are integers while those of streaming transducers are data words. The decidability of the equivalence of SNTs is achieved with an involved combinatorial analysis of the evolvement of the values of the integer variables during the runs of SNTs.

1 Introduction

MapReduce is a popular framework for data parallel computation. It has been adopted in various cloud computing platforms including Hadoop [8] and Spark [16]. In a typical MapReduce program, a *mapper* reads from data sources and outputs a list of key-value pairs. The scheduler of the MapReduce framework reorganizes the pairs $(k, v_1), (k, v_2) \ldots (k, v_n)$ with the same key k to a pair (k, l), where l is a list of values $v_1, v_2, \ldots, v_n$, and sends (k, l) to a *reducer*. The reducer then iterates through the list and outputs a key-value pair[1]. More specifically, taking the "word-counting" program as an example. It counts the occurrences

---

[1] We focus on the Hadoop style reducer in this work.

© Springer International Publishing Switzerland 2016
S. Chaudhuri and A. Farzan (Eds.): CAV 2016, Part II, LNCS 9780, pp. 91–111, 2016.
DOI: 10.1007/978-3-319-41540-6_6

of each word in a set of documents. The mappers read the documents and output for each document a list in the form of $(word_1, count_1)$, $(word_2, count_2)$, ..., $(word_n, count_n)$, where $count_k$ is the number of occurrences of $word_k$ in the document being processed. These lists will be reorganized into the form of $(word_1, list_1), (word_2, list_2), \ldots, (word_n, list_n)$ and sent to the reducers, where $list_k$ is a list of integers recording the number of occurrences of $word_k$. Note that the *order* of the integers in the lists can differ in different executions due to the scheduling policy. This results in the *commutativity problem*.

A reducer is said to be *commutative* if its output is independent of the order of its inputs. The commutativity problem asks if a reducer is commutative. A study from Microsoft [18] reports that 58 % of the 507 reducers submitted to their MapReduce platform are non-commutative, which may lead to very tricky and hard-to-find bugs. As an evidence, those reducers already went through serious code review, testing, and experiments with real data for months. Still, among them 5 reducers containing very subtle bugs caused by non-commutativity (confirmed by the programmers).

The reducer commutativity problem in general is undecidable. However, in practice, MapReduce programs are usually used for data analytics and have very simple control structures. Many of them just iterate through the input list and compute the output with very simple operations. We want to study if the commutativity problem of real-world reducers is decidable. It has been shown in [3] that even with a simple programming language where the only loop structure allowed is to go over the input list once, the commutativity problem is already undecidable. Under scrutiny, we found that the language is still too expressive for typical data analytics programs. For example, it allows arbitrary multiplications of variables, which is a key element in the undecidability proof.

Contributions. By observing the behavioral patterns of reducer programs for data analytics, we first design a programming language for reducers to characterize the essential features of them. We found that the commutativity problem becomes decidable if we partition variables into *control variables* and *data variables*. Control variables can occur in transition guards, but can only store values directly from the input list (e.g., it is not allowed to store the sum of two input values in a control variable). On the other hand, data variables are used to aggregate some information for outputs (e.g. sum of the values from the input list), but cannot be used in transition guards. This distinction is inspired by the streaming transducer model [1], which, we believe, provides good insights for reducer programming language design in the MapReduce framework. Moreover, we assume that there are no nested loops in the language for reducers, which is a typical situation for MapReduce programs in practice.

We then introduce a formalism called *streaming numerical transducers (SNT)* and obtain a decision procedure for the commutativity problem of the aforementioned language for reducers. Similar to the language for reducers, SNTs distinguish between control variables and data variables. Although conceptually SNTs are similar to streaming transducers over data words introduced in [1], they are intrinsically different in the following sense: The outputs of SNTs are integers and the integer variables therein are manipulated by linear arithmetic operations. On the other hand, the outputs of streaming transducers are data words, and the data word variables are manipulated by concatenation operations. SNTs in this paper are assumed to be *generalized flat*, which generalizes the "flat" automata (c.f. [11]) in the sense that each nontrivial strongly connected component (SCC) of the transition graph is a collection of cycles, instead of one single cycle. Generalized flat transition graphs are sufficient to capture the transition structures of the programs in the aforementioned language for reducers.

The decision procedure for the commutativity problem is obtained by reducing to the equivalence problem of SNTs, which is further reduced to the non-zero output problem. The non-zero output problem asks whether given an SNT, there exists some input data word w and initial valuation of variables such that the output of the SNT on w is defined and non-zero. For the non-zero output problem of SNTs, we apply a nontrivial combinatorial analysis of the evolvement of the integer variables during the runs of SNTs (Sect. 5.1). The key idea of the decision procedure is that, generally speaking, if only the non-zero output problem is concerned, the different cycles in the SCCs can be dealt with *independently* (Sects. 5.2 and 5.3). As a further evidence of the usefulness of SNTs for MapReduce programs, we demonstrate that SNTs can be composed to model and analyze the reducer programs that read the input list multiple times (Sect. 6).

As a novel formalism over infinite alphabets, the model of SNTs is interesting in its own right: On the one hand, SNTs are expressive in the sense that they include linear arithmetic operations on integer variables, while at the same time admit rather general transition graphs, that is, generalized flat transition graphs. On the other hand, despite this strong expressibility, it turns out that the commutativity problem, the equivalence problem, and the non-zero output problem of SNTs are still decidable.

Related Work. SNTs can be seen as generalizations of register automata [10,14] where registers correspond to the control variables in our terminology. Although register automata can have very general transition graphs beyond the generalized flat ones, they do not allow arithmetic operations on the variables. There have been many automata models that contain arithmetic operations. Counter automata contain counters whose values can be updated by arithmetic operations (see [5–7,9,11], to cite a few) in each transition. Intuitively, the major difference between SNTs and counter automata is that SNTs work on data words and can apply arithmetic operations to an unbounded number of independent integer values, whereas counter automata contain a bounded number of counters which involve only a bounded number of integer values in one configuration. Cost register automata (CRA) [2] also contain arithmetic operations, where the costs are stored into registers for which arithmetic operations can be applied. The equivalence of CRAs with the addition operation is decidable. SNTs are different from CRAs since the inputs of CRAs are words on finite alphabets, while those of SNTs are data words. Moreover, SNTs allow guards over variables ranging over an infinite domain but CRAs do not. There have been several transducer models on data words: Streaming transducers [1] mentioned before and symbolic transducers [17]. Symbolic transducers have data words as both inputs and outputs. They can put guards on the input value in one position of data words, but are incapable of comparing and aggregating multiple input values in different positions. In [13], the authors considered a model for reducers in the MapReduce framework where the only comparison that can be performed between data values are equalities, and the reducers are essentially register automata/transducers. Their model can describe a system with multiple layers of mappers and reducers.

The rest of the paper is organized as follows. Section 2 defines the notations used in this paper. Section 3 describes our design of the programming language for reducers. Section 4 defines SNTs. Section 5 describes the decision procedure of SNTs. Section 6 discusses how to use our approach to analyze the commutativity property of more challenging data analytics programs. We conclude this work in Sect. 7. The missing technical details and proofs can be found in the full version of this paper [4].

2   Preliminaries

Let $\mathbb{Z}$, $\mathbb{Z}^{\neq 0}$ be the set of integers, non-zero integers, respectively. We assume that all variables range over $\mathbb{Z}$. For a function f, let $\mathsf{dom}(f)$ and $\mathsf{rng}(f)$ denote the *domain* and *range* of f, respectively.

An *expression* e over the set of variables Z is defined by the following rules, $e ::= c \mid cz \mid (e + e) \mid (e - e)$, where $z \in Z$ and $c \in \mathbb{Z}$. As a result of the commutativity and associativity of $+$, without loss of generality, we assume that all expressions e in this paper are of the form $c_0 + c_1 z_1 + \cdots + c_n z_n$, where $c_0, c_1, \ldots, c_n \in \mathbb{Z}$ and $z_1, \ldots, z_n \in Z$. For an expression $e = c_0 + c_1 z_1 + \cdots + c_n z_n$, let $\mathsf{vars}(e)$ denote the set of variables z_i such that $c_i \neq 0$. Let $\mathcal{E}_Z$ denote the set of all expressions over the set of variables Z. In this paper, it is assumed that all the constants in the expressions are encoded in binary.

A *valuation* ρ of Z is a function from Z to $\mathbb{Z}$. A *symbolic valuation* Ω of Z is a function that maps a variable in Z to an expression (possibly over a different set of variables). The value of e under a valuation ρ (resp. symbolic valuation Ω), denoted by $[\![e]\!]_\rho$ (resp. $[\![e]\!]_\Omega$), is defined recursively in the standard way. For example, let Ω be a symbolic valuation the maps z_1 to $z_1 + z_2$ and z_2 to $3z_2$, then $[\![2z_1 + z_2]\!]_\Omega = 2[\![z_1]\!]_\Omega + [\![z_2]\!]_\Omega = 2(z_1 + z_2) + 3z_2 = 2z_1 + 5z_2$. For a valuation ρ, a variable z, and $c \in \mathbb{Z}$, define the valuation $\rho[c/z]$ such that $\rho[c/z](z) = c$ and $\rho[c/z](z') = \rho(z')$ for $z' \neq z$.

In this paper, we use X and Y to denote the sets of *control variables* and *data variables*, respectively. We use the variable $\mathsf{cur} \notin X \cup Y$ to store the data value that is currently being processed in the input list and use X^+ to denote the set $X \cup \{\mathsf{cur}\}$. A *guard* is a formula either of type 1 defined by the rules $g ::= \mathsf{true} \mid \mathsf{cur} \leq x \mid \mathsf{cur} > x \mid g \wedge g$, or of type 2 defined by the rules $g ::= \mathsf{true} \mid \mathsf{cur} \geq x \mid \mathsf{cur} < x \mid g \wedge g$, where $x \in X$, and $c \in \mathbb{Z}$. Note that the guards defined here are *equality-free* in the sense that for each guard g, no equalities between the variables in X^+ can be inferred from g. Let ρ be a valuation of X^+ and g be a guard. Then ρ satisfies g, denoted by $\rho \models g$, iff g is evaluated to true under ρ. Let $[n]$ denote the set $\{1, 2, \ldots, n\}$, and $[a, b]$ denote the set $\{a, a+1, \ldots, b\}$ when $b \geq a$ and $\emptyset$ otherwise. A *permutation* on $[n]$ is a bijection from $[n]$ to $[n]$. The set of permutations on $[n]$ is denoted by S_n.

A *data word* w is a sequence of integer values $d_1 \ldots d_n$ such that $d_i \in \mathbb{Z}$ for each i. We use $\mathsf{hd}(w)$, $\mathsf{tl}(w)$, and $|w|$ to denote the data value d_1, the tail $d_2 \ldots d_n$, and the length n, respectively. We use ϵ to denote an empty data word. As a convention, we let $\mathsf{hd}(\epsilon) = \perp$, $\mathsf{tl}(\epsilon) = \perp$, and $|\epsilon| = 0$. Given two data words w, w', we use $w.w'$ to denote their concatenation. Given $\sigma \in S_n$, we lift σ to data words by defining $\sigma(w) = d_{\sigma(1)} \ldots d_{\sigma(n)}$, for each data word $w = d_1 \ldots d_n$. We call $\sigma(w)$ as a permutation of w.

3   Language for Integer Reducers

We discuss the rationale behind the design of the programming language for reducers such that the commutativity problem is decidable. The language intends to support the following typical behavior pattern of reducers: A reducer program iterates through the input data word once, aggregates intermediate information into variables, and produces an output when it stops. Later in Sect. 6, we will show an extension that allows resetting the iterators so that an input data word can be traversed multiple times.

$$s \in Statements ::= y := e; \mid y \mathrel{+}= e; \mid x := x'; \mid s\ s \mid \mathsf{next}; \mid \mathsf{if}\ (g)\{s\}\ [\mathsf{else}\ \{s\}]$$
$$p \in Programs ::= \mathsf{loop}\{s\ \mathsf{next};\}\mathsf{ret}\ r; \mid s\ \mathsf{next}; p$$

Fig. 1. A simple programming language for reducers. Here $x \in X$ are control variables, $y \in Y$ are data variables, $x' \in X^+$, $e \in \mathcal{E}_{X^+}$ are expressions, and r is an expression in $\mathcal{E}_{X \cup Y}$. The square brackets mean that the else branch is optional.

More concretely, we focus on the programming language in Fig. 1. The language includes the usual features of program languages, variable assignments, sequential compositions, and conditional branchings. It also includes a statement next; which is used to advance the data word iterator. The loops next; statement repeatedly executes the loop body s next; until reaching the end of input data word. The novel feature of the language is that we partition the variables into two sets: *control variables* X and *data variables* Y. The variables from X are used for guiding the control flow and the variables from Y are used for storing aggregated intermediate data values. The variables from X can store only either initial values of variables in X or values occurring in the input data word. They can occur both in guards g or arithmetic expressions e. On the other hand, the variables from Y can aggregate the results obtained from arithmetic expressions e, but cannot occur in guards g or arithmetic expressions e. The initial values of variables can be arbitrary. Given a program p, a data word w, and a valuation

ρ_0, we use $p_{\rho_0}(w)$ to denote the output of p on w, with the initial values of variables given by ρ_0. The formal semantics of the language can be found in the full version [4].

In this paper, we assume that the reducer programs p satisfy that *all the guards between two consecutive* next *statements are mono-typed*, more specifically, for each execution path in the control flow graph of p and each pair of consecutive next statements, either all the guards g of the branching statements between them are of type 1, or all the guards between them are of type 2 (cf. Sect. 2 for the definition of guards). In addition, to simplify the presentation, we assume that the reducer programs p are *transition-enabled* in the following sense, for each execution path in the control flow graph of p, there is an input w and initial valuations of variables ρ_0 so that the run of p over w and ρ_0 follows the execution path.

Note that we do not allow multiplications in the language, so the reduction from the Diophantine equations in [3] no longer works. Even though, if we do not distinguish the control and data variables, we can show easily that commutativity problem for this language is still undecidable, by a reduction from the reachability problem of Petri nets with inhibitor arcs [12,15]. The reachability problem of Petri nets with inhibitor arcs is reduced to the reachability problem of the reducer programs, which is in turn easily reduced to the commutativity problem of reducer programs.

Notice that in the programming language, we only allow additions (+=) or assignments (:=) of a new value computed from an expression over X^+ to data variables. In Fig. 2 we demonstrate a few examples performing data analytics operations. Observe that all of them follow the same behavioral pattern: The program iterates through the input data word and aggregates some intermediate information into some variables. The operations used for the aggregation are usually rather simple: either a new value is added to the variable (e.g. sum and cnt in Fig. 2) storing the aggregated information, or a new value is assigned to the variable (e.g. max and 2nd_largest in Fig. 2). Actually, the similar behavioral pattern occurs in all programs we have investigated. Still, one may argue that allowing only additions and subtractions is too restrictive for data analytics.

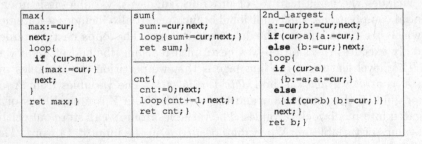

Fig. 2. Examples of reducers performing data analytics operations

In Sect. 6, we will discuss the extensions of the language to support more challenging examples, such as *Mean Absolute Deviation* and *Standard Deviation*.

We focus on the following problems of reducer programs: (1) *Commutativity*: given a program p, decide whether for each data word w and its permutation w', it holds that $p_{\rho_0}(w) = p_{\rho_0}(w')$ for all initial valuations ρ_0. (2) *Equivalence*: given two programs p and p', decide whether for each data word w and each initial valuation ρ_0, it holds that $p_{\rho_0}(w) = p'_{\rho_0}(w)$.

4 Streaming Numerical Transducers

In this section, we introduce *streaming numerical transducers* (SNTs), whose inputs are data words and outputs are integer values. A SNT scans a data word from left to right, records and aggregates information using control and data variables, and outputs an integer value when it finishes reading the data word. We will use SNTs to decide the commutativity and equivalence problem of the reducer programs defined in Sect. 3.

A SNT S is a tuple $(Q, X, Y, \delta, q_0, O)$, where Q is a finite set of states, X is a finite set of control variables to store data values that have been met, Y is a finite set of data variables to aggregate information for the output, δ is the set of transitions, $q_0 \in Q$ is the initial state, O is the output function, which is a partial function from Q to $\mathcal{E}_{X \cup Y}$. The set of transitions δ comprises the tuples (q, g, η, q'), where $q, q' \in Q$, g is a guard over X^+ (defined in Sect. 2), and η is an assignment which is a partial function mapping $X \cup Y$ to $\mathcal{E}_{X \cup Y}$ such that for each $x \in \mathrm{dom}(\eta) \cap X$, $\eta(x) = x'$ for some $x' \in X^+$. We write $q \xrightarrow{(g,\eta)} q'$ to denote $(q, g, \eta, q') \in \delta$ for convenience. We would like to remark that the guards in the transitions can be of both types, that is, of type 1 or type 2.

Moreover, we assume that an SNT S satisfies the following constraints. (1) *Deterministic*: For each pair of distinct transitions originating from q, say (q, g_1, η_1, q_1') and (q, g_2, η_2, q_2'), it holds that $g_1 \wedge g_2$ is unsatisfiable. (2) *Generalized flat*: Each SCC (strongly connected component) of the transition graph of S is either a single state or a set of simple cycles $\{C_1, \ldots, C_n\}$ which contains a state q such that for each $i, j : 1 \le i < j \le n$, q is the *only* state shared by C_i and C_j. (3) *Independently evolving and copyless*: For each $(q, g, \eta, q') \in \delta$ and for each $y \in \mathrm{dom}(\eta) \cap Y$, $\eta(y) = e$ or $\eta(y) = y + e$ for some expression e over X^+.

The semantics of an SNT S is defined as follows. A *configuration* of S is a pair (q, ρ), where $q \in Q$ and ρ is a valuation of $X \cup Y$. An *initial* configuration of S is (q_0, ρ_0), where ρ_0 assigns arbitrary values to the variables from $X \cup Y$. A sequence of configurations $(q_0, \rho_0)(q_1, \rho_1) \ldots (q_n, \rho_n)$ is a *run* of S over a data word $w = d_1 \ldots d_n$ iff there exists a path (sequence of transitions) $P = q_0 \xrightarrow{(g_1, \eta_1)} q_1 \xrightarrow{(g_2, \eta_2)} q_2 \ldots q_{n-1} \xrightarrow{(g_n, \eta_n)} q_n$ such that for each $i \in [n]$, $\rho_{i-1}[d_i/\mathsf{cur}] \models g_i$, and ρ_i is obtained from ρ_{i-1} as follows: (1) For each $x \in X$, if $\eta_i(x) = \mathsf{cur}$ then $\rho_i(x) = d_i$, otherwise, if $\eta_i(x) = x' \in X$ then $\rho_i(x) = \rho_{i-1}(x')$, otherwise $\rho_i(x) = \rho_{i-1}(x)$. (2) For each $y \in Y$, if $y \in \mathrm{dom}(\eta_i)$, then $\rho_i(y) = [\![\eta_i(y)]\!]_{\rho_{i-1}[d_i/\mathsf{cur}]}$, otherwise, $\rho_i(y) = \rho_{i-1}(y)$. We call (q_n, ρ_n) the *final configuration* of the run.

In this case, we also say that the run follows the path P. We say that a path P in $\mathcal{S}$ is *feasible* iff there exists a run of $\mathcal{S}$ following P. An SNT $\mathcal{S}$ is said to be *transition-enabled* if each path in $\mathcal{S}$ is feasible. We assume that all SNTs considered in this paper are transition enabled.

Given a data word $w = d_1 \ldots d_n$ and an initial configuration (q_0, ρ_0), if there is a run of $\mathcal{S}$ over w starting from (q_0, ρ_0) and with the final configuration (q_n, ρ_n), then the output of $\mathcal{S}$ over w w.r.t. ρ_0, denoted by $\mathcal{S}_{\rho_0}(w)$, is $[\![O(q_n)]\!]_{\rho_n}$. Otherwise, $\mathcal{S}_{\rho_0}(w)$ is undefined, denoted by $\perp$.

Example 1 (SNT for Max). The SNT $\mathcal{S}_{\max}$ for computing the maximum value of an input data word is defined as $(\{q_0, q_1\}, \{\mathsf{max}\}, \emptyset, \delta, q_0, O)$, where the set of transitions δ and the output function O are illustrated in Fig. 3 (here $X = \{\mathsf{max}\}$, $Y = \emptyset$, and $\mathsf{max} := \mathsf{cur}$ denotes the assignment of cur to the variable max).

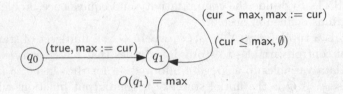

$$O(q_1) = \mathsf{max}$$

Fig. 3. The SNT $\mathcal{S}_{\max}$ for computing the maximum value

Proposition 1. *For each reducer program p, one can construct an equivalent SNT $\mathcal{S}$ where the number of states and the maximum number of simple cycles in an SCC of the transition graph are at most exponential in the number of branching statements in p.*

Intuitively, the exponential blow-up in the construction is due to the following difference between reducer programs p and SNTs $\mathcal{S}$: A reducer program moves to the next value of an input data word only when a next statement is executed, while an SNT advances the iterator in each transition. Therefore, a sequence of statements with k branching points between each pair of consecutive next statements in the control flow of p correspond to at most 2^k transitions of $\mathcal{S}$.

We focus on three decision problems of SNTs: (1) *Commutativity*: Given an SNT $\mathcal{S}$, decide whether $\mathcal{S}$ is commutative, that is, whether for each data word w and each permutation w' of w, $\mathcal{S}_{\rho_0}(w) = \mathcal{S}_{\rho_0}(w')$ for all initial valuations ρ_0. (2) *Equivalence*: Given two SNTs $\mathcal{S}, \mathcal{S}'$, decide whether $\mathcal{S}$ and $\mathcal{S}'$ are equivalent, that is, whether over each data word w, $\mathcal{S}_{\rho_0}(w) = \mathcal{S}'_{\rho_0}(w)$ for all initial valuations ρ_0. (3) *Non-zero output*: Given an SNT $\mathcal{S}$, decide whether $\mathcal{S}$ has a non-zero output, that is, whether there is a data word w and an initial valuation ρ_0 such that $\mathcal{S}_{\rho_0}(w) \notin \{\perp, 0\}$.

We first observe that the commutativity problem can be reduced to the equivalence problem of SNTs, which can be further reduced to the non-zero output problem of SNTs. For analyzing the complexity of the decision procedure in the next section, we state the complexity of the reductions w.r.t. the following factors of SNTs: the number of states, the number of control variables (resp. data variables), and the maximum number of simple cycles in an SCC of the transition graph. We will adopt the convention that if after a reduction, some factor becomes exponential, then this fact will be stated explicitly, and on the other hand, if some factor is still polynomial after the reduction, then this fact will be made implicit and will not be stated explicitly.

Proposition 2. *The commutativity problem of SNTs is reduced to the equivalence problem of SNTs in polynomial time.*

We briefly describe the idea of the reduction in Proposition 2 here. Suppose that $S = (Q, X, Y, \delta, q_0, O)$ is an SNT such that $X = \{x_1, \ldots, x_k\}$ and $Y = \{y_1, \ldots, y_l\}$. Without loss of generality, we assume that the output of S is defined only for data words of length at least two. We will construct two SNTs S_1 and S_2 so that S is commutative iff S is equivalent to both S_1 and S_2.

- Intuitively, over a data word $w = d_1 d_2 d_3 \ldots d_n$ with $n \geq 2$, S_1 simulates the run of S over $d_2 d_1 d_3 \ldots d_n$, that is, the data word obtained from w by swapping the first two data values.
- Intuitively, over a data word $w = d_1 d_2 d_3 \ldots d_n$ with $n > 2$, S_2 simulates the run of S over $d_2 d_3 \ldots d_n d_1$, that is, the data word obtained from w by moving the first data value to the end.

The correctness of this reduction follows from the fact that all the permutations of $d_1 \ldots d_n$ can be generated by composing the two aforementioned permutations corresponding to S_1 and S_2 respectively (cf. Proposition 1 in [3]). The construction of S_1 (resp. S_2) from S is in polynomial time w.r.t. the size of S.

Proposition 3. *From SNTs S_1 and S_2, an SNT S_3 can be constructed in polynomial time such that $(S_1)_{\rho_0}(w) \neq (S_2)_{\rho_0}(w)$ for some data word w and valuation ρ_0 iff $(S_3)_{\rho_0}(w) \notin \{\bot, 0\}$ for some data word w and valuation ρ_0.*

Proposition 3 can be proved by a straightforward product construction.

The lemma below states a property of SNTs, due to the fact that the SNTs are assumed to be transition-enabled and the guards are equality-free (cf. the definition of guards in Sect. 2).

Proposition 4. *Let S be an SNT and P be a path in S. There is a data word w such that (1) there is a run of S over w which follows P; (2) no data values occur twice in w.*

5   Decision Procedure for the Non-zero Output Problem

We prove our main result, Theorem 1, by presenting a decision procedure for the non-zero output problem of SNTs. We fix an SNT $S = (Q, X, Y, \delta, q_0, O)$

such that $X = \{x_1, \ldots, x_k\}$ and $Y = \{y_1, \ldots, y_l\}$. We first define summaries of the computations of $\mathcal{S}$ on paths and cycles in Sect. 5.1, then present a decision procedure for the case that the transition graph of $\mathcal{S}$ is a *generalized lasso* in Sect. 5.2. The transition graph of $\mathcal{S}$ is said to be a generalized lasso if it comprises a handle $H = q_0 \xrightarrow{(g_1, \eta_1)} q_1 \ldots q_{m-1} \xrightarrow{(g_m, \eta_m)} q_m$ and a collection of simple cycles $C_1, \ldots, C_n$ such that q_m is the unique state shared by each pair of distinct cycles from $\{C_1, \ldots, C_n\}$. We extend the procedure to SNTs whose transition graphs are not necessarily generalized lassos in Sect. 5.3.

Theorem 1. *The non-zero output problem of SNTs can be decided in time exponential in the number of data variables and the maximum number of simple cycles in an SCC of transition graphs.*

Corollary 1. *The commutativity problem of reducer programs can be decided in time exponential in the number of data variables, and doubly exponential in the number of branching statements of reducer programs.*

Remark 1. Though the decision procedure for the commutativity problem of reducer programs has a complexity exponential in the number of data variables, and doubly exponential in the number of branching statements, we believe that the decision procedure could still be implemented to automatically analyze the programs in practice, in which these numbers are usually small.

5.1   Summarization of the Computations on Paths and Cycles

Suppose $P = p_0 \xrightarrow{(g_1, \eta_1)} p_1 \ldots p_{n-1} \xrightarrow{(g_n, \eta_n)} p_n$ is a path of $\mathcal{S}$. We assume that the initial values of the control and data variables are represented by a symbolic valuation Ω over $X \cup Y$. We use the variables $\eth_1^{\overline{P}}, \eth_2^{\overline{P}}, \ldots, \eth_{r^{\overline{P}}}^{\overline{P}}$ to denote the data values introduced while traversing P. Notice that according to Proposition 4, one can choose different values for different positions of P. Therefore, for each position of P, a fresh variable is introduced to represent the data value in that position. Thus we have $r^{\overline{P}} = n$. Here we use the superscript $\overline{P}$ to denote the fact that $r^{\overline{P}}$ (resp. $\eth_1^{\overline{P}}, \ldots$) is associated with the path P.

Proposition 5. *Suppose that P is a path and the initial values of $X \cup Y$ are represented by a symbolic valuation Ω. Then the values of $X \cup Y$ after traversing the path P are specified by a symbolic valuation $\Theta^{(P, \Omega)}$ satisfying the following conditions.*

- *The set of indices of X, i.e., $[k]$, is partitioned into $I_{pe}^{\overline{P}}$ and $I_{tr}^{\overline{P}}$, the indices of persistent and transient control variables, respectively. A control variable is persistent if its value has not been changed while traversing P, otherwise, it is transient.*
- *For each $x_j \in X$ such that $j \in I_{pe}^{\overline{P}}$, $\Theta^{(P, \Omega)}(x_j) = \Omega(x_j)$.*
- *For each $x_j \in X$ such that $j \in I_{tr}^{\overline{P}}$, $\Theta^{(P, \Omega)}(x_j) = \eth_{\pi^{\overline{P}}(j)}^{\overline{P}}$, where $\pi^{\overline{P}} : I_{tr}^{\overline{P}} \to [r^{\overline{P}}]$ is a mapping from the index of a transient control variable to the index of the data value assigned to it.*

- *For each $y_j \in Y$, $\Theta^{(P,\Omega)}(y_j) = \varepsilon_j^{\overline{P}} + \lambda_j^{\overline{P}}\Omega(y_j) + \sum_{j' \in [k]} \alpha_{j,j'}^{\overline{P}}\Omega(x_{j'}) +$*

  $\sum_{j'' \in [r^{\overline{P}}]} \beta_{j,j''}^{\overline{P}}\eth_{j''}^{\overline{P}}$, *where $\varepsilon_j^{\overline{P}}, \lambda_j^{\overline{P}}, \alpha_{j,1}^{\overline{P}}, \ldots, \alpha_{j,k}^{\overline{P}}, \beta_{j,1}^{\overline{P}}, \ldots, \beta_{j,r^{\overline{P}}}^{\overline{P}}$ are integer con-*

  stants such that $\lambda_j^{\overline{P}} \in \{0,1\}$ (as a result of the "independently evolving and copyless" constraint). It can happen that $\lambda_j^{\overline{P}} = 0$, which means that $\Omega(y_j)$ is irrelevant to $\Theta^{(P,\Omega)}(y_j)$. Similarly for $\alpha_{j,1}^{\overline{P}} = 0$, and so on.

In Proposition 5, the sets $I_{pe}^{\overline{P}}$, $I_{tr}^{\overline{P}}$, the mapping $\pi^{\overline{P}}$, and the constants $\varepsilon_j^{\overline{P}}$, $\lambda_j^{\overline{P}}, \ldots, \beta_{j,r^{\overline{P}}}^{\overline{P}}$ only depend on P and are independent of Ω. In addition, they can be computed in polynomial time from (the transitions in) P. We define $(\pi^{\overline{P}})^{-1}$ as the inverse function of $\pi^{\overline{P}}$, that is, for each $j' \in [r^{\overline{P}}]$, $(\pi^{\overline{P}})^{-1}(j') = \{j \in I_{tr}^{\overline{P}} \mid \pi^{\overline{P}}(j) = j'\}$.

As a corollary of Proposition 5, the following result demonstrates how to summarize the computations of S on the composition of two paths.

Corollary 2. *Suppose that P_1 and P_2 are two paths in S such that the last state of P_1 is the first state of P_2. Moreover, let $\Theta^{(P_1,\Omega)}$ (resp. $\Theta^{(P_2,\Omega)}$) be the symbolic valuation summarizing the computation of S on P_1 (resp. P_2). Then the symbolic valuation summarizing the computation of S on P_1P_2 is $\Theta^{(P_2,\ \Theta^{(P_1,\Omega)})}$.*

In order to get a better understanding of the relation between $\Theta^{(P_2,\ \Theta^{(P_1,\Omega)})}$ and $(\Theta^{(P_1,\Omega)}, \Theta^{(P_2,\Omega)})$, in the following, for each $y_j \in Y$, we obtain a more explicit form of the expression $\Theta^{(P_2,\ \Theta^{(P_1,\Omega)})}(y_j)$, by unfolding therein the expression $\Theta^{(P_1,\Omega)}$.

$$\Theta^{(P_2,\ \Theta^{(P_1,\Omega)})}(y_j) = \left(\varepsilon_j^{\overline{P_2}} + \lambda_j^{\overline{P_2}}\varepsilon_j^{\overline{P_1}}\right) + \left(\lambda_j^{\overline{P_2}}\lambda_j^{\overline{P_1}}\right)\Omega(y_j) + \sum_{j' \in I_{pe}^{\overline{P_1}}}\left(\alpha_{j,j'}^{\overline{P_2}} + \lambda_j^{\overline{P_2}}\alpha_{j,j'}^{\overline{P_1}}\right)\Omega(x_{j'}) +$$

$$\sum_{j' \in I_{tr}^{\overline{P_1}}}\left(\lambda_j^{\overline{P_2}}\alpha_{j,j'}^{\overline{P_1}}\right)\Omega(x_{j'}) + \sum_{j' \in \text{rng}(\pi^{\overline{P_1}})}\left(\lambda_j^{\overline{P_2}}\beta_{j,j'}^{\overline{P_1}} + \sum_{j'' \in (\pi^{\overline{P_1}})^{-1}(j')}\alpha_{j,j''}^{\overline{P_2}}\right)\eth_{j'}^{\overline{P_1}} +$$

$$\sum_{j' \in [r^{\overline{P_1}}]\setminus\text{rng}(\pi^{\overline{P_1}})}\left(\lambda_j^{\overline{P_2}}\beta_{j,j'}^{\overline{P_1}}\right)\eth_{j'}^{\overline{P_1}} + \sum_{j' \in [r^{\overline{P_2}}]}\beta_{j,j'}^{\overline{P_2}}\eth_{j'}^{\overline{P_2}}.$$

In the equation, $j' \in I_{pe}^{\overline{P_1}}$ implies that $x_{j'}$ remains unchanged when traversing P_1, which means the initial value of $x_{j'}$ before traversing P_2 is still $\Omega(x_{j'})$ and therefore we have the item $(\alpha_{j,j'}^{\overline{P_2}})\Omega(x_{j'})$. When $j' \in \text{rng}(\pi^{\overline{P_1}})$, the initial value of $x_{j''}$ for each $j'' \in (\pi^{\overline{P_1}})^{-1}(j')$ before traversing P_2 is $\eth_{j'}^{\overline{P_1}}$ and therefore we have the item $\left(\sum_{j'' \in (\pi^{\overline{P_1}})^{-1}(j')}\alpha_{j,j''}^{\overline{P_2}}\right)\eth_{j'}^{\overline{P_1}}$. For all $j' \in [k] = I_{pe}^{\overline{P_1}} \cup I_{tr}^{\overline{P_1}}$, we have the item $(\lambda_j^{\overline{P_2}}\alpha_{j,j'}^{\overline{P_1}})\Omega(x_{j'})$, i.e. the coefficient of $\Omega(x_{j'})$ in $\Theta^{(P_1,\Omega)}$ multiplied by $\lambda_j^{\overline{P_2}}$. Moreover, for all $j' \in [r^{\overline{P_1}}] = \text{rng}(\pi^{\overline{P_1}}) \cup ([r^{\overline{P_1}}]\setminus\text{rng}(\pi^{\overline{P_1}}))$, we have the item $(\lambda_j^{\overline{P_2}}\beta_{j,j'}^{\overline{P_1}})\eth_{j'}^{\overline{P_1}}$, i.e. the coefficient of $\eth_{j'}^{\overline{P_1}}$ in $\Theta^{(P_1,\Omega)}$ multiplied by $\lambda_j^{\overline{P_2}}$.

In the following, by utilizing Proposition 5 and Corollary 2, for each path C^ℓ which is obtained by iterating a cycle C for ℓ times, we illustrate how $\Theta^{(C^\ell,\Omega)}$ is related to $\Theta^{(C,\Omega)}$ and ℓ. For convenience, we call ℓ a *cycle counter variable*.

Proposition 6. *Suppose that C is a cycle and $P = C^\ell$ such that $\ell \geq 2$. Then the symbolic valuation $\Theta^{(C^\ell,\Omega)}$ to summarize the computation of S on P is as follows,*

$$
\begin{aligned}
\Theta^{(C^\ell,\Omega)}(y_j) = {}& \left(1 + \lambda_j^{\overline{C}} + \cdots + (\lambda_j^{\overline{C}})^{\ell-1}\right) \varepsilon_j^{\overline{C}} + (\lambda_j^{\overline{C}})^\ell \Omega(y_j) + \\
& \sum_{j' \in I_{pe}^{\overline{C}}} \left(1 + \lambda_j^{\overline{C}} + \cdots + (\lambda_j^{\overline{C}})^{\ell-1}\right) \alpha_{j,j'}^{\overline{C}} \Omega(x_{j'}) + \sum_{j' \in I_{tr}^{\overline{C}}} (\lambda_j^{\overline{C}})^{\ell-1} \alpha_{j,j'}^{\overline{C}} \Omega(x_{j'}) + \\
& \sum_{j' \in \mathrm{rng}(\pi^{\overline{C}})} \sum_{s \in [\ell-1]} \left(\lambda_j^{\overline{C}} \beta_{j,j'}^{\overline{C}} + \sum_{j'' \in (\pi^{\overline{C}})^{-1}(j')} \alpha_{j,j''}^{\overline{C}}\right) (\lambda_j^{\overline{C}})^{\ell-s-1} \mathfrak{d}_{j'}^{\overline{C},s} + \\
& \sum_{j' \in [r^{\overline{C}}] \backslash \mathrm{rng}(\pi^{\overline{C}})} \sum_{s \in [\ell-1]} \left((\lambda_j^{\overline{C}})^{\ell-s} \beta_{j,j'}^{\overline{C}}\right) \mathfrak{d}_{j'}^{\overline{C},s} + \sum_{j' \in [r^{\overline{C}}]} \beta_{j,j'}^{\overline{C}} \mathfrak{d}_{j'}^{\overline{C},\ell},
\end{aligned}
$$

where the variables $\mathfrak{d}_1^{\overline{C},s}, \ldots, \mathfrak{d}_{r^{\overline{C}}}^{\overline{C},s}$ for $s \in [\ell]$ represent the data values introduced when traversing C for the s-th time.

From Proposition 6 and the fact that $\lambda_j \in \{0,1\}$, we have the following observation.

– If $\lambda_j^{\overline{C}} = 0$, then

$$
\begin{aligned}
\Theta^{(C^\ell,\Omega)}(y_j) = {}& \varepsilon_j^{\overline{C}} + \sum_{j' \in I_{pe}^{\overline{C}}} \alpha_{j,j'}^{\overline{C}} \Omega(x_{j'}) + \sum_{j' \in \mathrm{rng}(\pi^{\overline{C}})} \left(\sum_{j'' \in (\pi^{\overline{C}})^{-1}(j')} \alpha_{j,j''}^{\overline{C}}\right) \mathfrak{d}_{j'}^{\overline{C},\ell-1} + \\
& \sum_{j' \in [r^{\overline{C}}]} \beta_{j,j'}^{\overline{C}} \mathfrak{d}_{j'}^{\overline{C},\ell}.
\end{aligned}
$$

– If $\lambda_j^{\overline{C}} = 1$, then

$$
\begin{aligned}
\Theta^{(C^\ell,\Omega)}(y_j) = {}& \ell \varepsilon_j^{\overline{C}} + \Omega(y_j) + \sum_{j' \in I_{pe}^{\overline{C}}} \ell \alpha_{j,j'}^{\overline{C}} \Omega(x_{j'}) + \sum_{j' \in I_{tr}^{\overline{C}}} \alpha_{j,j'}^{\overline{C}} \Omega(x_{j'}) + \\
& \sum_{j' \in \mathrm{rng}(\pi^{\overline{C}})} \sum_{s \in [\ell-1]} \left(\beta_{j,j'}^{\overline{C}} + \sum_{j'' \in (\pi^{\overline{C}})^{-1}(j')} \alpha_{j,j''}^{\overline{C}}\right) \mathfrak{d}_{j'}^{\overline{C},s} + \\
& \sum_{j' \in [r^{\overline{C}}] \backslash \mathrm{rng}(\pi^{\overline{C}})} \sum_{s \in [\ell-1]} \beta_{j,j'}^{\overline{C}} \mathfrak{d}_{j'}^{\overline{C},s} + \sum_{j' \in [r^{\overline{C}}]} \beta_{j,j'}^{\overline{C}} \mathfrak{d}_{j'}^{\overline{C},\ell}.
\end{aligned}
$$

5.2   Decision Procedure for Generalized Lassos

In this section, we present a decision procedure for SNTs whose transition graphs are generalized lassos. From Proposition 6, we know that the coefficients containing the cycle counter variable ℓ in $\Theta^{(C^\ell,\Omega)}(y_j)$ can be non-zero when $\lambda_j^{\overline{C}} = 1$. The non-zero coefficients may propagate to the output expression. In such a case, because the SNTs are "transition-enabled" (i.e. for any sequence of transitions, a corresponding run exists), intuitively, one can pick a run corresponding to a very large ℓ so that it dominates the value of the output expression and makes the output non-zero. In the decision procedure we are going to present, we first check if the handle of the generalized lasso produces a non-zero output in Step I. We then check in Step II the coefficients containing ℓ in the output expression is non-zero. If this does not happen, then we show in Step III that the non-zero output problem of SNT can be reduced to a finite state reachability problem and thus can be easily decided.

Before presenting the decision procedure, we introduce some notations. Let e be an expression consisting of symbolic values $\Omega(z)$ for $z \in X \cup Y$ and variables $\eth_1, \ldots, \eth_s$ corresponding to the values of the input data word. More specifically, let $e := \mu_0 + \mu_1 \Omega(z_1) + \cdots + \mu_{k+l} \Omega(z_{k+l}) + \xi_1 \eth_1 + \cdots + \xi_s \eth_s$, such that $\mu_0, \mu_1, \ldots, \mu_{k+l}, \xi_1, \ldots, \xi_s$ are expressions containing only constants and cycle counter variables. Then we call μ_0 the *constant atom*, $\mu_i \Omega(z_i)$ the $\Omega(z_i)$-atom for $i \in [k + l]$, and $\xi_j \eth_j$ the $\eth_j$-atom for $j \in [s]$ of the expression e. Moreover, $\mu_1, \ldots, \mu_{k+l}, \xi_1, \ldots, \xi_s$ are called the *coefficients* and $\Omega(z_1), \ldots, \Omega(z_{k+l}), \eth_1, \ldots, \eth_s$ the *subjects* of these atoms. A non-constant atom is said to be *nontrivial* if its coefficient is *not* identical to zero.

In the rest of this subsection, we assume that the transition graph of S comprises a handle $H = q_0 \xrightarrow{(g_1, \eta_1)} q_1 \ldots q_{m-1} \xrightarrow{(g_m, \eta_m)} q_m$ and a collection of simple cycles $C_1, \ldots, C_n$ such that q_m is the unique state shared by each pair of distinct cycles from $\{C_1, \ldots, C_n\}$. Moreover, without loss of generality, we assume that $O(q_m) = a_0 + a_1 x_1 + \cdots + a_k x_k + b_1 y_1 + \cdots + b_l y_l$, and $O(q)$ is undefined for all the other states q.

A *cycle scheme* $\mathfrak{s}$ is a path $C_{i_1}^{\ell_1} C_{i_2}^{\ell_2} \ldots C_{i_t}^{\ell_t}$ such that $i_1, \ldots, i_t \in [n], \ell_1, \ldots, \ell_t > 1$, and for each $j \in [t-1]$, $i_j \neq i_{j+1}$. Intuitively, $\mathfrak{s}$ is a path obtained by first iterating C_{i_1} for ℓ_1 times, then C_{i_2} for ℓ_2 times, and so on. From Proposition 6 and Corollary 2, a symbolic valuation $\Theta^{(\mathfrak{s}, \Omega)}$ can be constructed to summarize the computation of S on $\mathfrak{s}$.

Lemma 1. *Suppose* $\mathfrak{s} = C_{i_1}^{\ell_1} C_{i_2}^{\ell_2} \ldots C_{i_t}^{\ell_t}$ *is a cycle scheme, and* Ω *is a symbolic valuation representing the initial values of the control and data variables. For all* $j' \in I_{pe}^{\overline{C_{i_1}}}$, *let* $r_{j'}$ *be the largest number* $r \in [t]$ *such that* $j' \in \bigcap_{s \in [r]} I_{pe}^{\overline{C_{i_s}}}$, *i.e.,* $x_{j'}$ *remains persistent when traversing* $C_{i_1}^{\ell_1} C_{i_2}^{\ell_2} \ldots C_{i_{r_{j'}}}^{\ell_{r_{j'}}}$. *Then for each* $j \in [l]$ *and* $j' \in I_{pe}^{\overline{C_{i_1}}}$, *the coefficient of the* $\Omega(x_{j'})$-atom in $\Theta^{(\mathfrak{s}, \Omega)}(y_j)$ is

$$e + \sum_{s_1 \in [r_{j'}]} \left(1 + \lambda_j^{\overline{C_{i_{s_1}}}} + \cdots + (\lambda_j^{\overline{C_{i_{s_1}}}})^{\ell_{s_1} - 1} \right) \alpha_{j,j'}^{\overline{C_{i_{s_1}}}} \prod_{s_2 \in [s_1+1,t]} \left(\lambda_j^{\overline{C_{i_{s_2}}}} \right)^{\ell_{s_2}},$$

where (1) $e = 0$ *when* $r_{j'} = t$ *and (2)* $e = (\lambda_j^{\overline{C_{i_s}}})^{\ell_s - 1} \alpha_{j,j'}^{\overline{C_{i_s}}} \prod_{s' \in [s+1,t]} \left(\lambda_j^{\overline{C_{i_{s'}}}} \right)^{\ell_{s'}}$ *with* $s = r_{j'} + 1$ *when* $r_{j'} < t$.

The constant atom of $\Theta^{(\mathfrak{s},\Omega)}(y_j)$ is

$$\sum_{s_1\in[t]}\left(1+\lambda_j^{\overline{C_{is_1}}}+\cdots+(\lambda_j^{\overline{C_{is_1}}})^{\ell_{s_1}-1}\right)\varepsilon_j^{\overline{C_{is_1}}}\prod_{s_2\in[s_1+1,t]}\left(\lambda_j^{\overline{C_{is_2}}}\right)^{\ell_{s_2}}$$

Moreover, for all $j\in[l]$, in $\Theta^{(\mathfrak{s},\Omega)}(y_j)$, only the constant atom and the coefficients of the $\Omega(x_{j'})$-atoms with $j'\in I_{pe}^{\overline{C_{i1}}}$ contain a subexpression of the form $\mu_\mathfrak{s}\ell_1$ for some $\mu_\mathfrak{s}\in\mathbb{Z}$.

Notice that above, $\lambda_j^{\overline{C_{is_1}}}\in\{0,1\}$ for $j\in[l]$ and $s_1\in[t]$. Hence the value of $(1+\lambda_j^{\overline{C_{is_1}}}+\cdots+(\lambda_j^{\overline{C_{is_1}}})^{\ell_{s_1}-1})$ can only be 1 or ℓ_{s_1} and $\left(\lambda_j^{\overline{C_{is_2}}}\right)^{\ell_{s_2}}\in\{0,1\}$. Therefore, both the constant atom and the coefficient of the $\Omega(x_{j'})$-atom with $j'\in I_{pe}^{\overline{C_{i1}}}$ can be rewritten to the form of $c_0+c_1\ell_1+c_2\ell_2+\cdots+c_t\ell_t$ for $c_0\ldots c_t\in\mathbb{Z}$. Note that some of $c_0\ldots c_t$ might be zero.

Step I: We are ready to present the decision procedure. At first, we observe that after traversing H with the initial values of the variables given by some valuation Ω_0, for each $j'\in I_{tr}^{\overline{H}}$, the value of the control variable $x_{j'}$ becomes $\mathfrak{d}_{\pi^H(j')}^{\overline{H}}$, more formally, $\Theta^{(H,\Omega_0)}(x_{j'})=\mathfrak{d}_{\pi^H(j')}^{\overline{H}}$.

In Step I, we check if $[\![O(q_m)]\!]_{\Theta^{(H,\Omega_0)}}$ is not identical to zero. This can be done by checking if the constant-atom or the coefficient of some non-constant atom of the output expression $[\![O(q_m)]\!]_{\Theta^{(H,\Omega_0)}}$ is not identical to zero.

> **Step I.** Decide whether $[\![O(q_m)]\!]_{\Theta^{(H,\Omega_0)}}$ is not identical to zero. If the answer is yes, then the decision procedure terminates and returns the answer true. Otherwise, go to Step II.

Complexity Analysis of Step I. Since $\Theta^{(H,\Omega_0)}$ can be computed in polynomial time from H, it follows that Step I can be done in polynomial time.

Step II: The goal of Step II is either showing that in $f=[\![O(q_m)]\!]_{\Theta^{(\mathfrak{s},\Theta^{(H,\Omega_0)})}}$, all subexpressions containing the cycle counter variables are identical to zero and hence can be ignored or showing that f is not identical to zero. Let $\mathfrak{s}=C_{i_1}^{\ell_1}C_{i_2}^{\ell_2}\ldots C_{i_t}^{\ell_t}$ be a cycle scheme. From Lemma 1, for each $j'\in I_{pe}^{\overline{C_{i1}}}$ and symbolic valuation Ω, the only subexpression containing ℓ_1 in the coefficient of $\Omega(x_{j'})$-atom of $[\![O(q_m)]\!]_{\Theta^{(\mathfrak{s},\Omega)}}$ is

$$\sum_{1\leq j\leq l}b_j\left((\lambda_j^{\overline{C_{i2}}})^{\ell_2}\ldots(\lambda_j^{\overline{C_{it}}})^{\ell_t}\right)\left(1+\lambda_j^{\overline{C_{i1}}}+\cdots+(\lambda_j^{\overline{C_{i1}}})^{\ell_1-1}\right)\alpha_{j,j'}^{\overline{C_{i1}}}. \qquad (*)$$

Since $\lambda_j^{\overline{C_{i_1}}}, \lambda_j^{\overline{C_{i_2}}}, \ldots, \lambda_j^{\overline{C_{i_t}}} \in \{0,1\}$, the expression $(*)$ can be rewritten as $\mu_{\mathfrak{s},(i_1,j')}\ell_1 + \nu_{\mathfrak{s},(i_1,j')}$ for some integer constants $\mu_{\mathfrak{s},(i_1,j')}$ and $\nu_{\mathfrak{s},(i_1,j')}$.

The only subexpression containing ℓ_1 in the constant atom of $[\![O(q_m)]\!]_{\Theta(s,\Omega)}$ is

$$\sum_{1 \le j \le l} b_j \left((\lambda_j^{\overline{C_{i_2}}})^{\ell_2} \ldots (\lambda_j^{\overline{C_{i_t}}})^{\ell_t} \right) \left(1 + \lambda_j^{\overline{C_{i_1}}} + \cdots + (\lambda_j^{\overline{C_{i_1}}})^{\ell_1 - 1} \right) \varepsilon_j^{\overline{C_{i_1}}}. \quad (**)$$

The expression $(**)$ can be rewritten as $\mu_{\mathfrak{s},(i_1,0)}\ell_1 + \nu_{\mathfrak{s},(i_1,0)}$ for some integer constants $\mu_{\mathfrak{s},(i_1,0)}$ and $\nu_{\mathfrak{s},(i_1,0)}$. If $\mu_{\mathfrak{s},(i_1,0)} = 0$ and $\mu_{\mathfrak{s},(i_1,j')} = 0$ for all $j' \in I_{pe}^{\overline{C_{i_1}}}$, then we can ignore all subexpressions containing the cycle counter variable ℓ_1 in $[\![O(q_m)]\!]_{\Theta(s,\Omega)}$, i.e., the subexpressions $\mu_{\mathfrak{s},(i_1,0)}\ell_1$ and $\mu_{\mathfrak{s},(i_1,j')}\ell_1$ for all $j' \in I_{pe}^{\overline{C_{i_1}}}$.

Step II. For each $i_1 \in [n]$, check all cycle scheme $\mathfrak{s} = C_{i_1}^{\ell_1} C_{i_2} \ldots C_{i_t}$ such that $i_2, \ldots, i_t$ are mutually distinct. There are only finitely many this kind of cycle schemes. If one of the following constraints is satisfied, then return true.

(1) There is $j' \in I_{pe}^{\overline{C_{i_1}}}$ such that $\mu_{\mathfrak{s},(i_1,j')} \ne 0$. (2) $\mu_{\mathfrak{s},(i_1,0)} \ne 0$.

If the decision procedure has not returned yet, then go to Step III.

Complexity analysis of Step II. Since $i_1, \ldots, i_t$ are mutually distinct, the number of cycle schemes $\mathfrak{s} = C_{i_1}^{\ell_1} C_{i_2} \ldots C_{i_t}$ in Step II is exponential in the number of cycles in the generalized lasso. Once the cycle scheme is fixed, the two constraints in Step II can be decided in polynomial time. Therefore, the complexity of Step II is exponential in the number of cycles in the generalized lasso.

If there exists $j' \in I_{pe}^{\overline{C_{i_1}}}$ such that $\mu_{\mathfrak{s},(i_1,j')} \ne 0$, then $[\![O(q_m)]\!]_{\Theta(s,\Theta(H,\Omega_0))}$ contains some nontrivial non-constant atom for $\mathfrak{s} = C_{i_1}^{\ell_1} C_{i_2} \ldots C_{i_t}$ and some $\ell_1 = s$. The guards in the path $C_{i_1}^s C_{i_2} \ldots C_{i_t}$ enforce a preorder over the subjects of those nontrivial non-constant atoms. Pick one of the nontrivial non-constant atoms with a maximal subject w.r.t. the preorder. Since the subject is maximal, it can be assigned an arbitrarily large number so that the corresponding atom dominates $[\![O(q_m)]\!]_{\Theta(s,\Theta(H,\Omega_0))}$. This is sufficient to make $[\![O(q_m)]\!]_{\Theta(s,\Theta(H,\Omega_0))}$ non-zero. Otherwise, if $[\![O(q_m)]\!]_{\Theta(s,\Theta(H,\Omega_0))}$ contains some other nontrivial non-constant atoms, then we can apply a similar argument as above and conclude that $[\![O(q_m)]\!]_{\Theta(s,\Theta(H,\Omega_0))}$ can be made non-zero. On the other hand, if $[\![O(q_m)]\!]_{\Theta(s,\Theta(H,\Omega_0))}$ contains no nontrivial non-constant atoms, but $\mu_{\mathfrak{s},(i_1,0)} \ne 0$, then we can let ℓ_1 arbitrarily large to make the expression $[\![O(q_m)]\!]_{\Theta(s,\Theta(H,\Omega_0))}$ non-zero. Therefore, when there is $j' \in I_{pe}^{\overline{C_{i_1}}}$ such that $\mu_{\mathfrak{s},(i_1,j')} \ne 0$, or $\mu_{\mathfrak{s},(i_1,0)} \ne 0$, we are able to conclude that there *must be* an input to make $[\![O(q_m)]\!]_{\Theta(s,\Theta(H,\Omega_0))}$ non-zero. Similar arguments can be applied to $\ell_2 \ldots \ell_n$.

If Step II does not return true, we show below that for all cycle schemes $\mathfrak{s}_1 = C_{i_1}^{\ell_1} C_{i_2}^{\ell_2} \ldots C_{i_{s_1}}^{\ell_{s_1}}$ with $i_1, i_2, \ldots, i_{s_1} \in [n]$, all subexpressions containing cycle counter variables in $[\![O(q_m)]\!]_{\Theta^{(\mathfrak{s},\Omega)}}$ are identical to zero and hence can be removed. Let $i'_2 \ldots i'_{s_2}$ be the sequence obtained from $i_2 \ldots i_{s_1}$ by keeping just one copy for each duplicated index therein. In Step II we already checked a cycle scheme $\mathfrak{s}_2 = C^{\ell_1}_{i_1} C_{i'_2} \ldots C_{i'_{s_2}}$. Step II guarantees that all subexpressions containing ℓ_1 in $[\![O(q_m)]\!]_{\Theta^{(\mathfrak{s}_2,\Omega)}}$ are identical to zero and hence can be removed. Because for all $j \in [l]$, $\lambda_j^{\overline{C_1}}, \ldots, \lambda_j^{\overline{C_n}} \in \{0,1\}$, $(\lambda_j^{\overline{C_{i_2}}})^{\ell_2} \ldots (\lambda_j^{\overline{C_{i_{s_1}}}})^{\ell_{s_1}} = \lambda_j^{\overline{C_{i'_2}}} \ldots \lambda_j^{\overline{C_{i'_{s_2}}}}$. We proved that the $(*)$ and $(**)$ style expressions are equivalent in both $\mathfrak{s}_1$ and $\mathfrak{s}_2$. Hence we can also remove all subexpressions containing ℓ_1 from $[\![O(q_m)]\!]_{\Theta^{(\mathfrak{s}_1,\Omega)}}$, without affecting its value. Those subexpressions containing ℓ_2 can also be removed by considering the cycle scheme $\mathfrak{s}_3 = C^{\ell_2}_{i_2} C_{i''_3} \ldots C_{i''_{s_3}}$ and applying a similar reasoning, where the sequence $i''_3 \ldots i''_{s_3}$ is obtained from $i_3 \ldots i_{s_1}$, similarly to the construction of $i'_2 \ldots i'_{s_2}$ from $i_2 \ldots i_{s1}$. The same applies to all other cycle counter variables $\ell_3, \ldots, \ell_{s_1}$. We use the notation $\Theta^{(\mathfrak{s},\Omega)^-}(y_j)$ to denote the expression obtained by removing from the constant atom and coefficients of the non-constant atoms of $\Theta^{(\mathfrak{s},\Omega)}(y_j)$ all subexpressions containing the cycle counter variables, for all $y_j \in Y$.

Lemma 2. *Suppose that the decision procedure has not returned* true *after Step II. For each cycle scheme $\mathfrak{s}$, let $f = [\![O(q_m)]\!]_{\Theta^{(\mathfrak{s},\Theta^{(H,\Omega_0)})}}$ and $f' = [\![O(q_m)]\!]_{\Theta^{(\mathfrak{s},\Theta^{(H,\Omega_0)})^-}}$. For all valuations ρ, $[\![f]\!]_\rho \neq 0$ iff $[\![f']\!]_\rho \neq 0$.*

Step III: For each cycle scheme $\mathfrak{s}$, let

$$\Theta^{(\mathfrak{s},\Theta^{(H,\Omega_0)})^-}(y_j)$$

$$= \quad \varepsilon_j^{(\overline{\mathfrak{s}})^-} + \lambda_j^{\overline{\mathfrak{s}}}\Theta^{(H,\Omega_0)}(y_j) + \sum_{j' \in [k]} \alpha_{j,j'}^{(\overline{\mathfrak{s}})^-}\Theta^{(H,\Omega_0)}(x_{j'}) + \sum_{j' \in [r^{\overline{\mathfrak{s}}}]} \beta_{j,j'}^{\overline{\mathfrak{s}}}\mathfrak{d}_{j'}^{\overline{\mathfrak{s}}}$$

$$= \quad \left(\varepsilon_j^{(\overline{\mathfrak{s}})^-} + \lambda_j^{\overline{\mathfrak{s}}}\varepsilon_j^{\overline{H}}\right) + \left(\lambda_j^{\overline{\mathfrak{s}}}\lambda_j^{\overline{H}}\right)\Omega_0(y_j) + \sum_{j' \in I_{pe}^H} \left(\alpha_{j,j'}^{(\overline{\mathfrak{s}})^-} + \lambda_j^{\overline{\mathfrak{s}}}\alpha_{j,j'}^{\overline{H}}\right)\Omega_0(x_{j'})$$

$$+ \sum_{j' \in I_{tr}^H} \left(\lambda_j^{\overline{\mathfrak{s}}}\alpha_{j,j'}^{\overline{H}}\right)\Omega_0(x_{j'}) + \sum_{j' \in \mathrm{rng}(\pi^H)} \left(\lambda_j^{\overline{\mathfrak{s}}}\beta_{j,j'}^{\overline{H}} + \sum_{j'' \in (\pi^H)^{-1}(j')} \alpha_{j,j''}^{(\overline{\mathfrak{s}})^-}\right)\mathfrak{d}_{j'}^{\overline{H}}$$

$$+ \sum_{j' \in [r^H]\setminus\mathrm{rng}(\pi^H)} \left(\lambda_j^{\overline{\mathfrak{s}}}\beta_{j,j'}^{\overline{H}}\right)\mathfrak{d}_{j'}^{\overline{H}} + \sum_{j' \in [r^{\overline{\mathfrak{s}}}]} \beta_{j,j'}^{\overline{\mathfrak{s}}}\mathfrak{d}_{j'}^{\overline{\mathfrak{s}}}.$$

Note that the coefficients of the $\mathfrak{d}_1^{\overline{\mathfrak{s}}}$-atom, $\ldots$, and $\mathfrak{d}_{r^{\overline{\mathfrak{s}}}}^{\overline{\mathfrak{s}}}$-atom in $\Theta^{(\mathfrak{s},\Theta^{(H,\Omega_0)})^-}(y_j)$ are the same as those in $\Theta^{(\mathfrak{s},\Theta^{(H,\Omega_0)})}(y_j)$.

We first observe that the coefficients of the atoms in $\Theta^{(\mathfrak{s},\Theta^{(H,\Omega_0)})^-}(y_j)$ are from a bounded set.

Lemma 3. *Suppose that the decision procedure has not returned yet after Step II. For all cycle scheme $\mathfrak{s}$ and $y_j \in Y$, the constant atom and the coefficients of all non-constant atoms in $\Theta^{(\mathfrak{s},\Theta^{(H,\Omega_0)})^-}(y_j)$ are from a finite set $U \subset \mathbb{Z}$ comprising*

(1) the constant atom and the coefficients of the non-constant atoms in the expression $\Theta^{(C_i^{\ell_i}, \Theta^{(H, \Omega_0)})^-}(y_j)$ for $i \in [n]$ and $\ell_i \in \{1, 2\}$,

(2) the numbers $\alpha_{j,j'}^{\overline{C_{s_2}}} + \beta_{j, \pi^{\overline{C_{s_1}}}(j')}^{\overline{C_{s_1}}}$ and $\alpha_{j,j''}^{\overline{C_{s_1}}} + \alpha_{j,j''}^{\overline{C_{s_2}}}$, where $s_1, s_2 \in [n]$, $j \in [l]$, $j' \in \overline{I_{tr}^{C_{s_1}}} \cap \overline{I_{tr}^{C_{s_2}}}$, $j'' \in [k]$.

We define the abstraction of $\Theta^{(\mathfrak{s}, \Theta^{(H, \Omega_0)})^-}$, denoted by $\mathsf{Abs}(\mathfrak{s})$, as the union of the following three sets of tuples:

- the tuple for the constant atom: $\left\{\left(0, \left(\varepsilon_1^{(\overline{\mathfrak{s}})^-} + \lambda_1^{\overline{\mathfrak{s}}} \varepsilon_1^{\overline{H}}, \ldots, \varepsilon_1^{(\overline{\mathfrak{s}})^-} + \lambda_1^{\overline{\mathfrak{s}}} \varepsilon_1^{\overline{H}}\right)\right)\right\}$,
- tuples for the control variable atoms: $\{(j', (c_{j',1}, \ldots, c_{j',l})) \mid j' \in [k]\}$, where $c_{j',j}$ is the coefficient of the $\Theta^{(\mathfrak{s}, \Theta^{(H, \Omega_0)})^-}(x_{j'})$-atom in $\Theta^{(\mathfrak{s}, \Theta^{(H, \Omega_0)})^-}(y_j)$ for $j \in [l]$,
- tuples for the other atoms: $\{(k+1, (c_1, \ldots, c_l))\}$, where $(c_1, \ldots, c_l) \in U^l$ is the vector of coefficients of the $\mathfrak{d}'$-atom in $(\Theta^{(\mathfrak{s}, \Theta^{(H, \Omega_0)})^-}(y_j)$ for all $j \in [l]$ and $\mathfrak{d}' \notin \{\Theta^{(\mathfrak{s}, \Theta^{(H, \Omega_0)})^-}(x_{j'}) \mid x_{j'} \in X\}$.

Let $\mathscr{A} = \bigcup\{\mathsf{Abs}(\mathfrak{s}) \mid \mathfrak{s} \text{ a cycle scheme}\}$. Then $\mathscr{A}$ can be constructed as follows: We first compute $\mathsf{Abs}(HC_1), \ldots \mathsf{Abs}(HC_n)$, put them into $\mathscr{A}$, then compute from them the abstractions $\mathsf{Abs}(HC_1 C_1), \ldots, \mathsf{Abs}(HC_1 C_n), \mathsf{Abs}(HC_2 C_1), \ldots$ by appending $C_1, \ldots, C_n$, put them into $\mathscr{A}$, and so on, until reaching a fixed point.

Step III. We first construct the set $\mathscr{A}$ and then.

1. Check whether there is $(0, (c_{0,1}, \ldots, c_{0,l})) \in \mathscr{A}$ such that $a_0 + b_1 c_{0,1} + \cdots + b_l c_{0,l} \neq 0$. If the answer is yes, then return true.
2. Check whether there are $j' \in [k]$ and $(j', (c_{j',1}, \ldots, c_{j',l})) \in \mathscr{A}$ such that $a_{j'} + b_1 c_{j',1} + \cdots + b_l c_{j',l} \neq 0$. If the answer is yes, then return true.
3. Check whether there is $(k+1, (c_1, \ldots, c_l)) \in \mathscr{A}$ such that $b_1 c_1 + \cdots + b_l c_l \neq 0$. If the answer is yes, then return true.

If the decision procedure has not returned yet, return false.

Complexity Analysis of Step III. The size of the set U is polynomial over the size of the generalized lasso (i.e. the size of the transitions in the generalized lasso). The size of $\mathscr{A}$ is exponential over l, the number of data variables. The three conditions in Step III can be checked in time polynomial over the size of $\mathscr{A}$. In summary, the complexity of Step III is exponential over the number of data variables.

5.3   Decision Procedure for SNTs

We generalize the decision procedure to the case that the transition graphs of SNTs are generalized lassos to the full class of SNTs. We first define a *generalized multi-lasso* as a sequence $\mathfrak{m} = H_1(C_{1,1}, \ldots, C_{1,n_1}) H_2(C_{2,1}, \ldots,$ $C_{2,n_2}) \ldots H_r(C_{r,1}, \ldots, C_{r,n_r})$ s.t. (1) for each $s \in [r]$, $H_s = q_{s,1} \xrightarrow{(g_2,\eta_2)}$ $q_{s,2} \cdots q_{s,m_s-1} \xrightarrow{(g_{m_s},\eta_{m_s})} q_{s,m_s}$ is a generalized lasso, (2) for $1 \leq s < s' \leq r$, $H_s(C_{s,1}, \ldots, C_{s,n_s})$ and $H_{s'}(C_{s',1}, \ldots, C_{s',n_{s'}})$ are state-disjoint, except the case that when $s' = s+1$, $q_{s,m_s} = q_{s',1}$, and (3) $q_{1,1} = q_0$.

Since the transition graph of $\mathcal{S}$ can be seen as a finite collection of generalized multi-lassos, in the following, we shall present the decision procedure by showing how to decide the non-zero output problem for generalized multi-lassos.

We fix a generalized multi-lasso below and assume without loss of generality that $O(q_{r,m_r}) = a_0 + a_1 x_1 + \cdots + a_k x_k + b_1 y_1 + \cdots + b_l y_l$ and $O(q')$ is undefined for every other state q' in $\mathfrak{m}$.

$$\mathfrak{m} = H_1(C_{1,1}, \ldots, C_{1,n_1}) H_2(C_{2,1}, \ldots, C_{2,n_2}) \ldots H_r(C_{r,1}, \ldots, C_{r,n_r}).$$

Step I′: We do the same analysis as in Step I for the path $H_1 \ldots H_r$.

Step II′: Let $s \in [1, r-1]$. In order to analyze the set of cycles $\mathcal{C} = \{C_{s,1}, \ldots, C_{s,n_s}\}$, next we show how to summarize the effect of the path $H_{s+1} \ldots H_r$ on the values of the variables in the state q_{s,m_s} by extending the output function and defining $O(q_{s,m_s})$ (note that q_{s,m_s} is the unique state shared by all those cycles in $\mathcal{C}$). Suppose that $[\![O(q_{r,m_r})]\!]_{\Theta^{(H_{s+1}\cdots H_r,\Omega)}} = a_0 + a_1\Omega(x_1) + \cdots + a_k\Omega(x_k) + b_1\Omega(y_1) + \cdots + b_l\Omega(y_l) + e$, where $\Omega(x_1) \ldots \Omega(x_k)$ and $\Omega(y_1) \ldots \Omega(y_l)$ represent the values of $x_1 \ldots x_k$ and $y_1 \ldots y_l$ in the state q_{s,m_s}, and e is a linear combination of the variables that represent the data values introduced when traversing $H_{s+1} \ldots H_r$. Then we let $O(q_{s,m_s}) := a_0 + a_1 x_1 + \cdots + a_k x_k + b_1 y_1 + \cdots + b_l y_l$.

Step II′. For each $s \in [r]$, $s' \in [n_s]$, and each cycle scheme $\mathfrak{s} = C_{s,s'}^{\ell_1} C_{i_2} \ldots C_{i_t}$ such that $C_{i_2} \ldots C_{i_t} \in \{C_{s,1}, \ldots, C_{s,n_s}, \ldots, C_{r,1}, \ldots, C_{r,n_r}\}$ and $C_{i_2} \ldots C_{i_t}$ are mutually distinct, we perform an analysis of the expression $[\![O(q_{s,m_s})]\!]_{\Theta(\mathfrak{s},\Theta^{(H_1 \ldots H_s, \Omega_0)})}$, in a way similar to Step II. If the decision procedure does not return during the analysis, then go to Step III′.

Intuitively, in Step II′, during the analysis of the cycle scheme $\mathfrak{s} = C_{s,s'}^{\ell_1} C_{i_2} \ldots C_{i_t}$, the effect of the paths $H_{s+1}, \ldots, H_r$ and the cycles $C_{i_2}, \ldots, C_{i_t}$ on the atom coefficients which contain the cycle counter variable ℓ_1, is described by the expressions $\lambda_j^{\overline{H_{s+1}}} \ldots \lambda_j^{\overline{H_r}} \lambda_j^{\overline{C_{i_2}}} \ldots \lambda_j^{\overline{C_{i_t}}}$ for $j \in [l]$. Since the output expression $O(q_{s,m_s})$ defined above has already taken into consideration the expressions $\lambda_j^{\overline{H_{s+1}}} \ldots \lambda_j^{\overline{H_r}}$ for $j \in [l]$, in Step II′, we can do the analysis for the cycles in $\mathcal{C}$ as if we have a generalized lasso where the handle is $H_1 \ldots H_s$, the collection of cycles is $\{C_{s,1}, \ldots, C_{s,n_s}, \ldots, C_{r,1}, \ldots, C_{r,n_r}\}$, and the output state is q_{s,m_s}, with the output expression $O(q_{s,m_s})$.

Step III′: After Step II′, if the decision procedure has not returned yet, then similar to Lemma 3, the following hold.

- For each $s \in [r]$ and each path $\mathfrak{s} = H_1\mathfrak{s}_1 H_2 \ldots H_s\mathfrak{s}_s$ such that for each $s' \in [s]$, $\mathfrak{s}_{s'}$ is a cycle scheme over the collection of cycles $\{C_{s',1}, \ldots, C_{s',n_{s'}}\}$, it holds that the constant atom and all the coefficients of the non-constant atoms in $\Theta^{(\mathfrak{s},\Omega_0)^-}(y_j)$ are from a bounded domain U.
- Moreover, an abstraction of $\mathfrak{s}$, denoted by $\mathsf{Abs}(\mathfrak{s})$, can be defined, so that $\mathscr{A}$, which contains the set of $\mathsf{Abs}(\mathfrak{s})$ for the paths $\mathfrak{s} = H_1\mathfrak{s}_1 H_2 \ldots H_s\mathfrak{s}_s$ (where $s \in [r]$), can be computed effectively from $H_1, C_{1,1}, \ldots, C_{1,n_1}, H_2, \ldots, H_r, C_{r,1}, \ldots, C_{r,n_r}$.

Step III′. We apply the same analysis to $\mathscr{A}$ as in Step III. If the procedure does not return during the analysis, then return false.

Complexity Analysis of Step I′–III′. The complexity of Step I′ is polynomial in the maximum length of generalized multi-lassos in $\mathcal{S}$. The complexity of Step II″ is exponential in the maximum number of simple cycles in a generalized multi-lasso. The complexity of Step III′ is exponential in the number of data variables in $\mathcal{S}$.

```int avg() { sum:=cur; cnt:=0;next; loop{ sum!=cur; cnt+=1; next;} ret sum/cnt;}```	```int MAD() { sum:=cur;cnt:=0;next; loop{sum+=cur;cnt+=1;next;} avg:= sum/cnt;mad:=0;init; loop{ if(cur<avg){mad!=avg-cur,} else{mad+=cur-avg;}next;} ret mad/cnt;}```	```int SD() { sum:=cur;cnt:=0;next; loop{sum+=cur;cnt+=1;next;} avg:= sum/cnt;sd:=0;init; loop{ sd+=(cur-avg)*(cur-avg);next; } ret SQRT(sd/cnt);}```

Fig. 4. More challenging examples of reducers performing data analytics operations

6   Extensions

In this section, we discuss some extensions of our approach to deal with the more challenging examples. For cases with multiplication, division, or other more complicated functions at the return point, e.g., the avg program, we can model them as an *uninterpreted k-ary function* and verify that all k parameters of the uninterpreted functions remain the same no matter how the input is permuted, e.g., the avg program always produces the same sum and cnt for all permutation of the same input data word. This is a *sound* but *incomplete* procedure for verifying programs of this type. Nevertheless, it is not often that a practical program for data analytics produces, e.g., $2q/2r$ from some input and q/r for its permutation. Hence this procedure is often enough for proving commutativity for real world programs (Fig. 4).

The MAD (Mean Absolute Deviation) program is a bit more involved. Beside the division operator / that also occurs in the avg example, it uses a new iterator operation init, which resets cur to the head of the input data word. The strategy to verify this program is to divide the task into two parts: (1) ensure that the value of avg is independent of the order of the input, (2) treat avg as a control variable whose value is never updated and then check if the 2nd half of the program (c.f., Fig. 5) is commutative.

We handle the division at the end of the program in Fig. 5 in the same way as we did for the avg program. The guarantee we obtain after the corresponding SNT is checked to be commutative is that the program outputs the same value for any value of avg and any permutation of the input data word.

```
int MAD2() {
  avg:= cur;next;
  loop{
    if(cur<avg){mad+=avg-cur;}
    else{mad+=cur-avg;}
    next;}
  ret mad/cnt;}
```

Fig. 5. The 2nd half of MAD

The SD (Standard Deviation) program is even more challenging. The main difficulty comes from the use of multiplication in the middle of the program (instead of at the return point). In order to have a sound procedure to verify this kind of programs, we can extend the transitions of SNTs to include uninterpreted k-ary functions. However, this is not a trivial extension and we leave it as future work.

7   Conclusion

The contribution of the paper is twofold. We propose a verifiable programming language for reducers. Although it is still far away from a practical programming language, we believe that some ideas behind our language (e.g., the separation of control variables and data variables) would be valuable for the design of a practical reducer language. On the other hand, we propose the model of streaming numerical transducers, a transducer model over infinite alphabets. To our best knowledge, this is the first decidable automata model over infinite alphabets that allows linear arithmetics over the input values and the integer variables. Although we required that the transition graphs of SNTs are generalized flat, SNTs with such kind of transition graphs turn out to be quite powerful, since they are capable of simulating reducer programs without nested loops, which is a typical scenario of reducer programs in practice. At last, we would like to mention that although we assumed the integer data domain, all the results obtained in this paper are still valid when a dense data domain, e.g. the set of rational numbers, is assumed.

Acknowledgements. Yu-Fang Chen is partially supported by the MOST project No. 103-2221-E-001-019-MY3. Zhilin Wu is partially supported by the NSFC grants No. 61100062, 61272135, 61472474, and 61572478.

References

1. Alur, R., Cerny, P.: Streaming transducers for algorithmic verification of single-pass list-processing programs. In: POPL, pp. 599–610. ACM (2011)
2. Alur, R., Antoni, L.D, Deshmukh, J., Raghothaman, M., Yuan, Y.: Regular functions and cost register automata. In: LICS, pp. 13–22 (2013)
3. Chen, Y.F., Hong, C.D., Sinha, N., Wang, B.Y.: Commutativity of reducers. In: Baier, C., Tinelli, C. (eds.) TACAS 2015. LNCS, vol. 9035, pp. 131–146. Springer, Heidelberg (2015)
4. Chen, Y., Lei, S., Wu, Z.: The commutativity problem of the mapreduce framework: a transducer-based approach. CoRR, abs/1605.01497 (2016)
5. Comon, H., Jurski, Y.: Multiple counters automata, safety analysis and presburger arithmetic. In: Hu, A.J., Vardi, M.Y. (eds.) CAV 1998. LNCS, vol. 1427, pp. 268–279. Springer, Heidelberg (1998)
6. Finkel, A., Göller, S., Haase, C.: Reachability in register machines with polynomial updates. In: Chatterjee, K., Sgall, J. (eds.) MFCS 2013. LNCS, vol. 8087, pp. 409–420. Springer, Heidelberg (2013)
7. Haase, C., Halfon, S.: Integer vector addition systems with states. In: Ouaknine, J., Potapov, I., Worrell, J. (eds.) RP 2014. LNCS, vol. 8762, pp. 112–124. Springer, Heidelberg (2014)
8. Hadoop. https://hadoop.apache.org
9. Ibarra, O.H.: Reversal-bounded multicounter machines and their decision problems. J. ACM 25(1), 116–133 (1978)
10. Kaminski, M., Francez, N.: Finite-memory automata. Theor. Comput. Sci. 134(2), 329–363 (1994)
11. Leroux, J., Sutre, G.: Flat counter automata almost everywhere! In: Software Verification: Infinite-State Model Checking and Static Program Analysis. Dagstuhl Seminar Proceedings, vol. 6081 (2006)
12. Minsky, M.L.: Computation: Finite and Infinite Machines Prentice-Hall, Englewood Cliffs (1971)
13. Neven, F., Schweikardt, N., Servais, F., Tan, T.: Distributed streaming with finite memory. In: ICDT, pp. 324–341 (2015)
14. Neven, F., Schwentick, T., Vianu, V.: Finite state machines for strings over infinite alphabets. ACM Trans. Comput. Logic 5(3), 403–435 (2004)
15. Reinhardt, K.: Reachability in petri nets with inhibitor arcs. Electron. Notes Theor. Comput. Sci. 223, 239–264 (2008). RP
16. Spark. http://spark.apache.org
17. Veanes, M., Hooimeijer, P., Livshits, B., Molnar, D., Bjorner, N.: Symbolic finite state transducers: algorithms and applications. ACM SIGPLAN Not. 47(1), 137–150 (2012)
18. Xiao, T., Zhang, J., Zhou, H., Guo, Z., McDirmid, S., Lin, W., Chen, W., Zhou, L.: Nondeterminism in mapreduce considered harmful? An empirical study on non-commutative aggregators in mapreduce programs. In: ICSE, pp. 44–53 (2014)

Liveness of Randomised Parameterised Systems under Arbitrary Schedulers

Anthony W. Lin[1](✉) and Philipp Rümmer[2](✉)

[1] Yale-NUS College, Singapore, Singapore
anthony.w.lin@yale-nus.edu.sg
[2] Uppsala University, Uppsala, Sweden
philipp.ruemmer@it.uu.se

Abstract. We consider the problem of verifying liveness for systems with a finite, but unbounded, number of processes, commonly known as *parameterised systems*. Typical examples of such systems include distributed protocols (e.g. for the dining philosopher problem). Unlike the case of verifying safety, proving liveness is still considered extremely challenging, especially in the presence of randomness in the system. In this paper we consider liveness under arbitrary (including unfair) schedulers, which is often considered a desirable property in the literature of self-stabilising systems. We introduce an automatic method of proving liveness for randomised parameterised systems under arbitrary schedulers. Viewing liveness as a two-player reachability game (between Scheduler and Process), our method is a CEGAR approach that synthesises a progress relation for Process that can be symbolically represented as a finite-state automaton. The method is incremental and exploits both Angluin-style L*-learning and SAT-solvers. Our experiments show that our algorithm is able to prove liveness automatically for well-known randomised distributed protocols, including Lehmann-Rabin Randomised Dining Philosopher Protocol and randomised self-stabilising protocols (such as the Israeli-Jalfon Protocol). To the best of our knowledge, this is the first fully-automatic method that can prove liveness for randomised protocols.

1 Introduction

Verification of parameterised systems is one of the most extensively studied problems in computer-aided verification. Parameterised systems are infinite families of finite-state systems that are described in some finite behavioral description language. Distributed protocols (e.g. for the dining philosopher problem) are typical examples of parameterised systems since they can represent any finite (but unbounded) number of processes. Verifying a parameterised system, then, amounts to verifying *every instance* of the infinite family. In the case of a dining philosopher protocol, this amounts to verifying the protocol with any number of philosophers. Although the problem was long known to be undecidable [11], a lot of progress has been made to tackle the problem resulting in such techniques as network invariants (including cutoff techniques), symbolic model checking (including regular model checking), and finite-range abstractions, to name a few.

© Springer International Publishing Switzerland 2016
S. Chaudhuri and A. Farzan (Eds.): CAV 2016, Part II, LNCS 9780, pp. 112–133, 2016.
DOI: 10.1007/978-3-319-41540-6_7

The reader is referred to the following excellent surveys [2,7,17,77,79] covering these different approaches to solving the problem.

Nowadays there are highly effective automatic methods that can successfully verify *safety* for many parameterised systems derived from real-world concurrent/distributed algorithms (e.g. see [2–7,10,13,20–23,36,43,44,49,54,56,63, 75,77,78]). In contrast, there has been much less progress in automatic techniques for proving *liveness* for parameterised systems. In fact, this difficulty has also been widely observed (e.g. see [8,48,67,77]). Proving liveness amounts to proving that, under a class of adversarial schedulers (a.k.a. *adversaries* or just *schedulers*), something "good" will eventually happen. The problem is known to be reducible to finding an infinite path satisfying a Büchi condition (e.g. see [7,24,65,67,72–74,77]). The latter problem (a.k.a. repeated reachability) in general requires reasoning about the transitive closure relations, which are generally observed to be rather difficult to compute automatically.

Randomised parameterised systems are infinite families of finite-state systems that allow both nondeterministic and probabilistic transitions (a.k.a. Markov Decision Processes [52]). This paper concerns the problem of verifying liveness for randomised parameterised systems, with an eye towards a fully-automatic verification algorithm for well-known *randomised distributed protocols* that commonly feature in finite-state probabilistic model checkers (e.g. PRISM [51]), but have so far resisted fully-automatic parameterised verification. Such protocols include Lehmann-Rabin's Randomised Dining Philosopher Protocol [55] and randomised self-stabilising protocols (e.g. Israeli-Jalfon's Protocol [47] and Herman's Protocol [46]), to name a few. Randomised protocols generalise deterministic protocols by allowing each process to make probabilistic transitions, i.e., not just a transition with probability 1. Randomisation is well-known to be useful in the design of distributed protocols, e.g., to break symmetry and simplifies distributed algorithms (e.g. see [39,58]). Despite the benefits of randomisation in protocol design, the use of randomisation makes proving liveness substantially more challenging (e.g. see [58,59,69]). Proving liveness for probabilistic distributed protocols amounts to proving that, under a class of adversaries, something "good" will eventually happen *with probability 1* (e.g. see [12,29,35,52,53,58,76]). Unlike the case of deterministic protocols, proving liveness for probabilistic protocols requires reasoning about *games* between an adversary and a stochastic process player (a.k.a. $1\frac{1}{2}$-player game), which makes the problem computationally more difficult even in the finite-state case (e.g. see [53]). To the best of our knowledge, there is presently no fully-automatic technique which can prove liveness for such randomised distributed protocols as Lehmann-Rabin's Randomised Distributed Protocols [55], and self-stabilising randomised protocols including Israeli-Jalfon's Protocol [47] and Herman's Protocol [46].

Contribution: The main contribution of the paper is a fully-automatic method for proving liveness over randomised parameterised systems over various network topologies (e.g. lines, rings, stars, and cliques) under arbitrary (including unfair) schedulers. Liveness under arbitrary schedulers is a desirable property in the literature of self-stabilising algorithms since an unfair scheduler (a.k.a.

daemon) enables a *worst-case* analysis of an algorithm and covers the situation when some process is "frozen" due to conditions that are external to the process (e.g. see [14,33,41,50]). There are numerous examples of self-stabilising protocols that satisfy liveness even under unfair schedulers (e.g. see [14,31,39,47,50]). Similar examples are also available in the literature of mutual exclusion protocols (e.g. [34,70]), and consensus/broadcast protocols (e.g. [25,39]). Our algorithm can successfully verify liveness under arbitrary schedulers for a fragment of FireWire's symmetry breaking protocol [35,60], Israeli-Jalfon's Protocol [47], Herman's Protocol [46] considered over a linear array, and Lehmann-Rabin Dining Philosopher Protocol [34,55].

It is well-known that for proving liveness for a finite-state Markov Decision Process (MDP) only the topology of the system matters, not the actual probability values (e.g. see [29,30,45,76]). Hence, the same is true for randomised parameterised systems since each instance is a finite MDP. In this paper, we follow this approach and view the problem of proving liveness under arbitrary schedulers as a 2-player reachability game between Scheduler (Player 1) and Process (Player 2) over non-stochastic parameterised systems, obtained by simply ignoring the actual probability values of transitions with non-zero probabilities (transitions with zero probability are removed). This simple reduction allows us to adopt any symbolic representation of non-stochastic parameterised systems. In this paper, we represent parameterised systems as finite-state letter-to-letter transducers, as is standard in *regular model checking* [2,7,23,65,77]. In this framework, configurations of parameterised systems are represented as words over a finite alphabet Σ (usually encoding a finite set of control states for each local process). Many distributed protocols that arise in practice can be naturally modelled as transducers.

To automatically verify liveness of parameterised systems in this representation, we develop a counterexample-guided method for synthesising Player 2 strategies. The core step of the approach is the computation of *well-founded relations* guiding Player 2 towards winning configurations (and the system towards "good" states). In the spirit of regular model checking, such well-founded relations are represented as letter-to-letter transducers; however, unlike most regular model checking algorithms, we use learning and SAT-based methods to compute the relations, in line with some of the recent research on the application of learning for program analysis (e.g. [40,62–64]). This gives rise to a counterexample-guided algorithm for computing winning strategies for Player 2. We then introduce a number of refinements of the base method, which turn out to be essential for analysing challenging systems like the Lehmann-Rabin protocol: strategies for Player 2 can be constructed *incrementally*, reducing the size of automata that have to be considered in each inference step; symmetries of games (e.g., rotation symmetry in case of protocols with ring topology) can be exploited for acceleration; and inductive over-approximations of the set of reachable configurations can be pre-computed with the help of learning. To the best of our knowledge, the last refinement also represents the first successful application of Angluin's L*-algorithm [9] for learning DFAs representing inductive invariants in the regular model checking context.

We have implemented our method as a proof of concept. Besides the four aforementioned probabilistic protocols that we have successfully verified against liveness (under all schedulers), we also show that our tool is competitive with existing tools (e.g. [8,65]) for proving liveness for deterministic parameterised systems (Szymanski's mutual exclusion protocol [70], Left-Right Dining Philosopher Protocol [58], Lamport's Bakery Algorithm [15,39], and Resource-Allocator Protocol [32]). Finally, we report that our tool can also automatically solve classic examples from combinatorial game theory on infinite graphs (take-away game and Nim [38]). To the best of our knowledge, our tool is the first verification tool that can automatically solve these games.

Related Work: There are currently only a handful of fully-automatic techniques for proving liveness for randomised parameterised systems. We mention the works [27,35,61] on proving almost-sure termination of sequential probabilistic programs. Strictly speaking, these works are not directly comparable to our work since their tools/techniques handle only programs with variables over integer/real domains, and cannot naturally model the protocol examples over line/ring topology that we consider in this paper. Based on the work of Arons *et al.* [12], the approach of Esparza *et al.* [35] aims to guess a terminating pattern by constructing a nondeterministic program from a given probabilistic program and a terminating pattern candidate. This allows them to exploit model checkers and termination provers for nondeterministic programs. The approach is sound and complete for "weakly-finite" programs, which include parameterised programs, i.e., programs with parameters that can be initialised to arbitrary large values, but are finite-state for every valuation of the parameters. The approach of [27] is a constraint-based method to synthesise ranking functions for probabilistic programs based on martingales and may be able to prove almost sure termination for probabilistic programs that are not weakly finite. Monniaux [61] proposed a method for proving almost sure termination for probabilistic programs using abstract interpretation, though without tool support.

As previously mentioned, there is a lot of work on liveness for non-probabilistic parameterised systems (e.g. see [8,24,37,65,67,68,72–74]). We assess our technique in this context by using several typical benchmarking examples that satisfy liveness (more precisely, deadlock-freedom) under arbitrary schedulers including Szymanski's Protocol, Bakery Protocol, and Deterministic Dining Philosopher with Left-Right Strategy.

Two-player reachability games on automatic graphs (i.e. regular model checking with non-length preserving transducers) have been considered by Neider [62], who proposed an L*-based learning algorithm for constructing the set of winning regions enriched with "distance" information, which is a number that can be represented in binary or unary. [Embedding distance information in a reachability set was first done in regular model checking by Vardhan *et al.* [75]] Augmenting winning regions or reachability sets with distance information, however, often makes regular sets no longer regular [63]. In this paper, we do not consider non-length preserving transducers and our algorithm is based on constructing progress relations for Player 2. In particular, part of our algorithm employs an L*-based algorithm for synthesising an inductive invariant which, however, differs from [62,75] since membership tests (i.e. reachability of a single configuration) are decidable. Recently Neider and Topcu [64] proposed a learning algorithm for solving safety games over rational graphs (an extension of automatic graphs), which are *dual* to reachability games.

2   Preliminaries

General notations: For any two given real numbers $i \leq j$, we use a standard notation (with an extra subscript) to denote real intervals, e.g., $[i,j]_{\mathbb{R}} = \{k \in \mathbb{R} : i \leq k \leq j\}$ and $(i,j]\{k \in \mathbb{R} : i < k \leq j\}$. We will denote intervals over integers by removing the subscript, e.g., $[i,j] := [i,j]_{\mathbb{R}} \cap \mathbb{Z}$. Given a set S, we use S^* to denote the set of all finite sequences of elements from S. The set S^* always includes the empty sequence which we denote by ϵ. Given two sets of words S_1, S_2, we use $S_1 \cdot S_2$ to denote the set $\{v \cdot w : v \in S_1, w \in S_2\}$ of words formed by concatenating words from S_1 with words from S_2. Given two relations $R_1, R_2 \subseteq S \times S$, we define their composition as $R_1 \circ R_2 = \{(s_1, s_3) : (\exists s_2)((s_1, s_2) \in R_1 \wedge (s_2, s_3) \in R_2)\}$.

Transition systems: Let ACT be a finite set of *action symbols*. A *transition system* over ACT is a tuple $\mathfrak{S} = \langle S; \{\rightarrow_a\}_{a \in \mathsf{ACT}}, \{U_b\}_{b \in \mathsf{AP}} \rangle$, where S is a set of *configurations*, $\rightarrow_a \subseteq S \times S$ is a binary relation over S, and $U_b \subseteq S$ is a unary relation on S. In the sequel, we will often consider transition systems where $\mathsf{AP} = \emptyset$ and $|\mathsf{ACT}| = 1$, in which case $\langle S; \{\rightarrow_a\}_{a \in \mathsf{ACT}}, \{U_b\}_{b \in \mathsf{AP}} \rangle$ will be denoted as $\langle S; \rightarrow \rangle$. If $|\mathsf{ACT}| > 1$, we use $\rightarrow$ to denote the relation $\left(\bigcup_{a \in \mathsf{ACT}} \rightarrow_a \right)$. The notation $\rightarrow^+$ (resp. $\rightarrow^*$) is used to denote the transitive (resp. transitive-reflexive) closure of $\rightarrow$. We say that a sequence $s_1 \rightarrow \cdots \rightarrow s_n$ is a *path* (or *run*) in $\mathfrak{S}$ (or in $\rightarrow$). Given two paths $\pi_1 : s_1 \rightarrow^* s_2$ and $\pi_2 : s_2 \rightarrow^* s_3$ in $\rightarrow$, we may concatenate them to obtain $\pi_1 \odot \pi_2$ (by gluing together s_2). We call π_1 a *prefix* of $\pi_1 \odot \pi_2$. For each $S' \subseteq S$, we use the notations $pre_{\rightarrow}(S')$ and $post_{\rightarrow}(S')$ to denote the pre/post image of S' under $\rightarrow$. That is, $pre_{\rightarrow}(S') := \{p \in S : \exists q \in S'(p \rightarrow q)\}$ and $post_{\rightarrow}(S') := \{q \in S : \exists p \in S'(p \rightarrow q)\}$.

Words and automata: We assume basic familiarity with word automata. Fix a finite alphabet Σ. For each finite word $w = w_1 \ldots w_n \in \Sigma^*$, we write $w[i,j]$, where $1 \leq i \leq j \leq n$, to denote the segment $w_i \ldots w_j$. Given an automaton $\mathcal{A} = (\Sigma, Q, \delta, q_0, F)$, a run of $\mathcal{A}$ on w is a function $\rho : \{0, \ldots, n\} \rightarrow Q$ with $\rho(0) = q_0$ that obeys the transition relation δ. We may also denote the run ρ by the word $\rho(0) \cdots \rho(n)$ over the alphabet Q. The run ρ is said to be *accepting* if $\rho(n) \in F$, in which case we say that the word w is *accepted* by $\mathcal{A}$. The language $L(\mathcal{A})$ of $\mathcal{A}$ is the set of words in Σ^* accepted by $\mathcal{A}$.

Reachability games: We recall some basic concepts on 2-player reachability games (e.g. see [42, Chapter 2] on games with 1-accepting conditions). An *arena* is a transition system $\mathfrak{S} = \langle S; \rightarrow_1, \rightarrow_2 \rangle$, where S (i.e. the set of "game configurations") is partitioned into two disjoint sets V_1 and V_2 such that $pre_{\rightarrow_i}(S) \subseteq V_i$ for each $i = 1, 2$. The transition relation $\rightarrow_i$ denotes the actions of Player i. Similarly, for each $i = 1, 2$, the configurations V_i are controlled by Player i. In the sequel, Player 1 will also be called "Scheduler", and Player 2 "Process". Given a set $I_0 \subseteq S$ of initial states and a set $F \subseteq S$ of final (a.k.a. target) states, the goal of Player 2 is to reach F from I_0, while the goal of Player 1 is to avoid it. More formally, a *strategy* for Player i is a partial function $f : S^*V_i \to S$ such that, for each $v \in S^*$ and $p \in V_i$, if vp is a path in $\mathfrak{S}$ and that p is not a dead end (i.e. $p \to_i q$ for some q), then $f(vp)$ is defined in such a way that $p \to_i f(vp)$. Given a strategy f_i for Player $i = 1, 2$ and an initial state $s_0 \in S$, we can define a unique (finite or infinite) path in $\mathfrak{S}$ $\pi : s_0 \to_{j_1} s_1 \to_{j_2} \cdots$ such that $s_{j_{k+1}} = f_i(s_0 s_1 \ldots s_{j_k})$ where $i \in \{1, 2\}$ is the (unique) number such that $s_{j_k} \in V_i$. Player 2 *wins* iff some state in F appears in π, or if the path is finite and the last configuration belongs to Player 1. Player 1 *wins* iff Player 2 does not win (i.e. *loses*). A strategy f for Player i is *winning* from I_0, for each strategy g for Player $i + 1 \pmod 2$, the unique path in $\mathfrak{S}$ from each $s_0 \in I_0$ witnesses a win for Player i. Such games (a.k.a. *reachability games*) are *determined* (e.g. see [42, Proposition 2.21]), i.e., either Player 1 has a winning strategy or Player 2 has a winning strategy.

Convention 1. *For simplicity's sake, we make the following assumptions on our reachability games. They suffice for the purpose of proving liveness for parameterised systems. The techniques can be easily adapted when these assumptions are lifted.*

(A0) *Arenas are strictly alternating, i.e., a move made by a player does not take the game back to her configuration (i.e. $post_{\to_i}(S) \cap A_i = \emptyset$, for each $i \in \{1, 2\}$).*

(A1) *Initial and final configurations belong to Player 1, i.e., $I_0, F \subseteq V_1$.*

(A2) *Non-final configurations are no dead ends, i.e., $\forall x \in S \setminus F, \exists y : x \to_1 y \lor x \to_2 y$.*

3   The Formal Framework

Parameterised systems are an infinite family $\mathcal{F} = \{\mathfrak{S}_i\}_{i \in \mathbb{N}}$ of finite-state transition systems. Similarly, *randomised parameterised systems* are an infinite family $\mathcal{F} = \{\mathfrak{S}_i\}_{i \in \mathbb{N}}$ of *Markov Decision Processes* [52], which are finite-state transition systems $\mathfrak{S} = \langle S; \to_1, \to_2 \rangle$ that have both "nondeterministic" transitions $\to_1$ and "probabilistic" transitions $\to_2$.

We first informally illustrate the concept of randomised parameterised systems by means of Israeli-Jalfon Randomised Self-Stabilising Protocol [47] (also see [66]). The protocol has a ring topology and each process either holds a token (denoted by $\top$) or does not hold a token (denoted by $\bot$). At any given step, the Scheduler chooses a process P that holds a token. The process P can then pass the token to its left or right neighbour each with probability 0.5. In doing so, two tokens that are held by a process are merged into one token (held by the same process). It can be proven that under arbitrary schedulers, starting from any configuration with *at least* one token, the protocol will converge to a configuration with *exactly* one token with probability 1. This is an example of liveness under arbitrary schedulers.

It is well-known that the liveness problem for finite MDPs $\mathfrak{S}$ depends on the topology of the graph $\mathfrak{S}$, not on the actual probability values in $\mathfrak{S}$ (e.g. [29,30,45,76]). In fact, this result easily transfers to randomised parameterised systems since *every* instance in the infinite family is a finite MDP. Following this approach, we may view the problem of proving (almost-sure) liveness for randomised parameterised systems under arbitrary schedulers as a 2-player eachability game between Scheduler (Player 1 with moves $\rightarrow_1$) and Process (Player 2 with moves $\rightarrow_2$) over the arena $\mathfrak{S} = \langle S; \rightarrow_1, \rightarrow_2 \rangle$ obtained by simply *ignoring* the actual probability values of transitions in $\rightarrow_2$ (with non-zero probabilities). This simple reduction allows us to view randomised parameterised systems as an *infinite family of finite arenas* and adopt standard symbolic representations of non-stochastic parameterised systems (many of which are known). Our formal framework uses the standard symbolic representation using letter-to-letter transducers. To simplify our presentation, *we will directly define liveness for randomised parameterised systems in terms of non-stochastic two player games and relegate this standard reduction in the full version for interested readers.*

3.1   Liveness as Games

Given a randomised parameterised system $\mathcal{F} = \{\mathfrak{S}_i\}_{i \in \mathbb{N}}$, a set $I_0 \subseteq V_1$ of initial states, and a set $F \subseteq V_1$ of final states, we say that a randomised parameterised system *satisfies liveness under arbitrary schedulers with probability 1 (a.k.a. almost surely terminates)* if from *each* configuration $s_0 \in post_{\rightarrow^*}(I_0)$, Player 2 has a winning strategy reaching F in $\mathcal{F}$ (viewed as an arena). The justification of this definition is in the full version.

3.2   Representing Infinite Arenas

Our formal framework uses the standard symbolic representation of parameterised systems from regular model checking [7,23,65,77], i.e., transducers. Many distributed protocols that arise in practice can be naturally modelled as transducers. *Transducers* are *letter-to-letter automata* that accept k-ary relations over words (cf. [19]). In this paper, we are only interested in binary *length-preserving relations* [7], i.e., a relation $R \subseteq \Sigma^* \times \Sigma^*$ such that each $(v, w) \in R$ implies that $|v| = |w|$. For this reason, we will only define length-preserving transducers and only for the binary case. Given two words $w = w_1 \ldots w_n$ and $w' = w'_1 \ldots w'_n$ over the alphabet Σ, we define a word $w \otimes w'$ over the alphabet $\Sigma \times \Sigma$ as $(w_1, w'_1) \cdots (w_n, w'_n)$. A letter-to-letter transducer is simply an automaton over $\Sigma \times \Sigma$, and a binary relation R over Σ^* is *regular* if the set $\{w \otimes w' : (w, w') \in R\}$ is accepted by a letter-to-letter automaton $\mathcal{R}$. Notice that the resulting relation R only relate words that are of the same length. In the sequel, to avoid notational clutter, we will use R to mean both a transducer and the binary relation that it recognises.

Definition 1 (Automatic systems). *A system* $\mathfrak{S} = \langle S; \{\rightarrow_a\}_{a \in ACT}, \{U_b\}_{b \in AP}\rangle$ *is said to be automatic if S and U_b (for each $b \in AP$) are regular sets over some non-empty finite alphabet Σ, and each relation $\rightarrow_a$ (for each $a \in ACT$) is given by a transducer over Σ.*

We warn the reader that the most general notion of automatic transition systems [19], which allow non-length preserving transducers, are not needed in this paper. When the meaning is understood, we shall confuse the notation $\rightarrow_a$ for the transition relation of $\mathfrak{S}$ and the transducer that recognises it.

Example 1. We shall now model Israeli-Jalfon Protocol as an automatic transition system $\mathfrak{S} = \langle S; \rightarrow_1, \rightarrow_2\rangle$, where Scheduler's actions are labeled by 1 and Process's actions are labeled by 2. In general, configurations of Israeli-Jalfon protocol are circular structures, but they can easily be turned into a word over a certain finite alphabet by linearising them. More precisely, the domain S of $\mathfrak{S}$ is the set of words over $\Sigma = \{\bot, \top, \hat{\top}\}$ of the form $(\bot + \top)^* \top (\bot + \top)^*$, or $(\bot + \top)^* \hat{\top} (\bot + \top)^*$.

For example, the configuration $\top\bot\top\bot$ denotes the configuration where the 1st and the 3rd (resp. 2nd and 4th) processes are (resp. are not) holding a token. The letter $\hat{\top}$ is used to denote that Scheduler chooses a specific process that holds a token. Note that the intersection of languages generated by these two regular expressions is empty. The transition relation $\rightarrow_1$ is given by the regular expression $I^*(\top, \hat{\top})I^*$ where $I := \{(\top, \top), (\bot, \bot)\}$. The transition relation $\top_2$ is given by a union of the following regular expressions:

- $I^*(\hat{\top}, \bot)((\bot, \top) + (\top, \top)) I^*$ $-\ ((\bot, \top) + (\top, \top)) I^*(\hat{\top}, \bot)$
- $I^*((\bot, \top) + (\top, \top))(\hat{\top}, \bot)I^*$ $-\ (\hat{\top}, \bot)I^*((\bot, \top) + (\top, \top))$

Note that the right column represents transitions that handle the circular case. Also, note that if $I_0 = (\bot + \top)^* \top (\bot + \top)^*$ and $F = \bot^* \top \bot^*$, Player 2 can always win the game from any reachable configuration (note: $post_{\rightarrow^*}(I_0) = I_0$) by simply minimising the distance between the leftmost token and the rightmost token in the configuration. $\square$

3.3   Algorithm for Liveness (an Overview)

Our discussion thus far has led to a reformulation of liveness for probabilistic parameterised systems as the following decision problem: given an automatic arena $\mathfrak{S} = \langle S; \rightarrow_1, \rightarrow_2\rangle$, a regular set $I_0 \subseteq S$ of initial configurations, and a regular set F of final configurations, decide if Player 2 can force the game to reach F in $\mathfrak{S}$ starting from each configuration in $post_{\rightarrow^*}(I_0)$. In the sequel, we will call $\langle \mathfrak{S}, I_0, F\rangle$ a *game instance*. Note that the aforementioned problem is undecidable even when $\rightarrow_2$ is restricted to identity relations, which amounts to the undecidable problem of safety [7]. We will show now that decidability can be retained if "advice bits" are provided in the input.

Advice bits are a pair $\langle A, \prec\rangle$, where $A \subseteq S$ is a set of game configurations and $\prec \subseteq S \times S$ is a binary relation over the game configurations. Intuitively, A is an inductive invariant, whereas $\prec$ is a well-founded relation that guides Player 2 to win. More precisely, the advice bits $\langle A, \prec \rangle$ are said to *conform* to the game instance $\langle \mathfrak{S}, I_0, F \rangle$ if:

(L1) $I_0 \subseteq A$,
(L2) A is $\rightarrow$-inductive, i.e., $\forall x, y : x \in A \wedge (x \rightarrow y) \Rightarrow y \in A$,
(L3) $\prec$ is a *strict preorder*[1] on S,
(L4) Player 2 can progress from A by following $\prec$:

$$\forall x \in A \setminus F, y \in S \setminus F : \big((x \rightarrow_1 y) \ \Rightarrow \ (\exists z \in A : (y \rightarrow_2 z) \wedge x \succ z) \big).$$

Conditions **(L1)** and **(L2)** ensure that $post_{\rightarrow^*}(I_0) \subseteq A$, while conditions **(L3)**–**(L4)** ensure that Player 2 has a winning strategy from each configuration in $post_{\rightarrow^*}(I_0)$. Note that **(L3)** implies well-foundedness of $\prec$, provided that $\prec$ only relates words of the same length (which is always sufficient for advice bits, and will later follow from the use of length-preserving transducers to represent $\prec$).

Theorem 1. *Let* $\mathfrak{S} = \langle S; \rightarrow_1, \rightarrow_2 \rangle$ *be a* $\rightarrow^*$*-image-finite arena, i.e.,* $post_{\rightarrow^*}(s)$ *is finite, for each* $s \in S$. *Given a set* $I_0 \subseteq V_1$ *of initial configurations, and a set* $F \subseteq V_1$ *of final configurations, the following are equivalent:*

1. *Player 2 has a winning strategy reaching* F *in* $\mathfrak{S}$ *starting from each configuration in* $post_{\rightarrow^*}(I_0) \cap V_1$.
2. *There exist advice bits* $\langle A, \prec \rangle$ *conforming to the input* $\langle \mathfrak{S}, I_0, F \rangle$.

Advice bits $\langle A, \prec \rangle$ are said to be *regular* if A (resp. $\prec$) is given as a regular set (resp. relation). With the help of regular advice bits, the problem of deciding a winning strategy for Player 2 becomes decidable:

Lemma 1. *Given an automatic arena* $\mathfrak{S} = \langle S; \rightarrow_1, \rightarrow_2 \rangle$, *a regular set* $I_0 \subseteq S$ *of initial configurations, a regular set* F *of final configurations, and regular advice bits* $T = \langle A, \prec \rangle$, *we can effectively decide whether* T *conforms to the game instance* $\langle \mathfrak{S}, I_0, F \rangle$.

Lemma 1 follows from the fact that each of the conditions **(L1)**–**(L4)** is expressible in first-order logic interpreted over the given game instance extended with the advice bits, i.e., the transition systems $\langle S; \{\rightarrow_1, \rightarrow_2, \prec\}, \{I_0, F, A\} \rangle$. Decidability then follows since model checking first-order logic formulas over automatic transition systems is decidable (e.g. see [18, 19] and see [71] for a detailed complexity analysis), the proof of which is done by standard automata methods.

To decide whether Player 2 has a winning strategy for the reachability game, Lemma 1 tells us that one can systematically enumerate all possible regular advice bits and check whether they conform to the input game instance $\langle \mathfrak{S}, I_0, F \rangle$. A naive enumeration would simply go through each $k = 1, 2, \ldots$ and all advice bits $\langle A, \prec \rangle$ where each of the two automata have at most k states. This would be extremely slow.

---

[1] A binary relation $\prec$ on a set A is said to be a *strict preorder* if it is irreflexive (i.e. for each $s \in A$, $s \not\prec s$) and transitive (for each $s, s', s'' \in A$, $s \prec s'$ and $s' \prec s''$ implies that $s \prec s''$).

4   Automatic Liveness Proofs

We now describe how regular advice bits $\langle A, \prec \rangle$ for (regular) game instances $\langle \mathfrak{S}, I_0, F \rangle$ can be computed automatically, thus proving that Player 2 can win from every reachable configuration, which (as we saw in the previous section) establishes liveness for randomised parameterised systems. We define a constraint-based method that derives $\langle A, \prec \rangle$ as the solution of a set of Boolean formulas representing the conditions **(L1)**–**(L4)** from Sect. 3.3. Since a full Boolean encoding of **(L1)**–**(L4)** would be exponential in the size of the automata representing the advice bits, our algorithm starts with a relaxed version of **(L1)**–**(L4)** and gradually refines the encoding with the help of counterexamples; in this sense, our approach is an instance of CEGAR [28], and has similarities with recent learning-based methods for computing inductive invariants [63].

Throughout the section we assume that an alphabet Σ and game instance $\langle \mathfrak{S}, I_0, F \rangle$ has been fixed. We will represent the well-founded relation $\prec$ using a transducer $\mathcal{T}_\prec = (\Sigma \times \Sigma, Q_\prec, \delta_\prec, q^0_\prec, F_\prec)$, and the set A as automaton $\mathcal{A}_A = (\Sigma, Q_A, \delta_A, q^0_A, F_A)$. Our overall approach for computing the automata makes use of two main components, which are invoked iteratively within a refinement loop:

Synthesise Candidate automata $(\mathcal{A}_A, \mathcal{T}_\prec)$ with n_A and $n_\prec$ states, respectively, are computed simultaneously with the help of a SAT-solver, enforcing a relaxed set of conditions encoded as a Boolean constraint ψ. The transducer $\mathcal{T}_\prec$ is length-preserving and irreflexive by construction; this implies that the relation $\prec$ is a well-founded preorder iff it is transitive.

Verify It is checked whether the automata $(\mathcal{A}_A, \mathcal{T}_\prec)$ satisfy conditions **(L1)**–**(L4)** from Sect. 3.3. If this is not the case, ψ is strengthened to eliminate counterexamples, and Synthesise is again invoked; otherwise, $(\mathcal{A}_A, \mathcal{T}_\prec)$ represent a winning strategy for Player 2 by Theorem 1.

This refinement loop is enclosed by an outer loop that increments the parameters n_A, and $n_\prec$ (initially set to some small number) when Synthesise determines that no automata satisfying ψ exist anymore. Initially, the formula ψ approximates **(L1)**–**(L4)**, by capturing aspects that can be enforced by a Boolean formula of polynomial size. The next sections described Synthesise and Verify in detail.

4.1   Verify: Checking (L1)–(L4) Precisely

Suppose that automata $(\mathcal{A}_A, \mathcal{T}_\prec)$ have been computed. In the Verify stage, it is determined whether the automata indeed satisfy the conditions **(L1)**–**(L4)**, which can effectively be done due to Lemma 1. The check will have one of the following outcomes:

1. $(\mathcal{A}_A, \mathcal{T}_\prec)$ represent correct advice bits.
2. **(L1)** is violated: some word $x \in I_0$ is not accepted by $\mathcal{A}_A$.

3. **(L2)** is violated: there are words $x \in A$ and y with $x \to y$, but $y \notin A$.
4. **(L3)** is violated: $\mathcal{T}_\prec$ does not represent a transitive relation (recall that $\mathcal{T}_\prec$ is length-preserving and irreflexive by construction).
5. **(L4)** is violated: there are words $x \in A \setminus F$ and $y \in S \setminus F$ such that $x \to_1 y$, but no word $z \in A$ exists with $y \to_2 z$ and $x \succ z$.

In cases 2–5, the computed words are counterexamples that are fed back to the SYNTHESISE stage; details for this are given in Sect. 4.3.

The required checks on $(\mathcal{A}_A, \mathcal{T}_\prec)$ can be encoded as validity of first-order formulas, and finally carried out using automata methods (e.g. see [71]). In **(L3)** and **(L4)**, it is in addition necessary to eliminate the quantifier $\exists z$ by means of projection. Note that all free variables in the formulas are implicitly universally quantified.

(L1) $I_0(x) \Rightarrow A(x)$
(L2) $A(x) \wedge (x \to_1 y \vee x \to_2 y) \Rightarrow A(y)$
(L3) $x \prec y \wedge y \prec z \Rightarrow x \prec z$
(L4) $A(x) \wedge \neg F(x) \wedge \neg F(y) \wedge (x \to_1 y) \Rightarrow \exists z.\, \big(A(z) \wedge (y \to_2 z) \wedge x \succ z\big)$

4.2   SYNTHESISE: Computation of Candidate Automata

We now present the Boolean encoding used to search for (deterministic) automata $(\mathcal{A}_A, \mathcal{T}_\prec)$, and to this end make the simplifying assumption that the states of the transducer $\mathcal{T}_\prec$ are $Q_\prec = \{1, \dots, n_\prec\}$, states of the automaton $\mathcal{A}_A$ are $Q_A = \{1, \dots, n_A\}$, and that $q_\prec^0 = q_A^0 = 1$ are the initial states. The following Boolean variables are used to represent automata: a variable $x_t^\prec$ for each tuple $t = (q, a, b, q') \in Q_\prec \times \Sigma \times \Sigma \times Q_\prec$; a variable x_t^A for each tuple $t = (q, a, q') \in Q_A \times \Sigma \times Q_A$; and a variable z_q^M for each $q \in Q_M$ and $M \in \{\prec, A\}$. The assignment $x_t^M = 1$ is interpreted as the existence of the transition t in the automaton for M; likewise, we use $z_q^M = 1$ to represent that q is an accepting state (in DFAs it is in general necessary to have more than one accepting state).

The set of considered automata in step SYNTHESISE is restricted by imposing a number of conditions. Most importantly, only deterministic automata are considered, which is important for refinement: to eliminate counterexamples, it will be necessary to construct Boolean formulas that state *non-acceptance* of certain words, which can only be done succinctly in the case of languages represented by DFAs:

(C1) The automata $\mathcal{A}_A$ and $\mathcal{T}_\prec$ are deterministic.
    The second condition encodes irreflexivity of the relation $\prec$:
(C2) Every accepting path in $\mathcal{T}_\prec$ contains a label (a, b) with $a \neq b$.

The third group of conditions captures minimality properties: automata that can (obviously) be represented with a smaller number of states are excluded:

(C3) Every state of the automata $\mathcal{A}_A$ and $\mathcal{T}_\prec$ is reachable from the initial state.
(C4) From every state in the automata $\mathcal{A}_A$ and $\mathcal{T}_\prec$ an accepting state can be reached.

Finally, we can observe that the states of the constructed automata can be reordered almost arbitrarily, which increases the search space that a SAT solver has to cover. The performance of SYNTHESISE can be improved by adding *symmetry breaking* constraints. Symmetries can be removed by asserting that automata states are sorted according to some structural properties extracted from the automaton; suitable properties include whether a state is accepting, or which self-transitions a state has:

(C5) The states $\{2, \ldots, n_M\}$ (for $M \in \{\prec, A\}$) are sorted according to the integer value of the bit-vector $\langle z_q^M, x_{(q,l_1,q)}^M, \ldots, x_{(q,l_k,q)}^M \rangle$ where $q \in \{2, \ldots, n_M\}$ and $l_1, \ldots, l_k$ is some fixed order of the transition labels in M.

Encoding as formulas. The encoding of **(C1)** and **(C5)** as a Boolean constraint is straightforward. For **(C2)**, we assume additional Boolean variables r_q (for each $q \in Q_\prec$) to identify states that can be reached via paths with only (a, a) labels. **(C2)** is ensured by the following constraints, which are instantiated for each $q \in Q_\prec$:

$$(q \neq q_0^\prec) \vee r_q, \qquad \neg z_q^\prec \vee \neg r_q, \qquad \neg r_q \vee \bigwedge_{a \in \Sigma, q' \in Q_\prec} (\neg x_{(q,a,a,q')}^\prec \vee r_{q'}).$$

The first constraint ensures that r_q holds for the initial state, the second constraint excludes r_q for all final states. The third constraint expresses preservation of the r_q flags under (a, a) transitions.

We outline further how **(C3)** can be encoded for $\mathcal{A}_A$ (the other parts of **(C3)** and **(C4)** are similar). We assume additional variables y_q (for each $q \in Q_A$) ranging over the interval $[0, n_A - 1]$, to encode the distance of a state from the initial state, these integer variables can further be encoded in binary as a vector of Boolean variables. The following formulas, instantiated for each $q \in Q_A$, define the value of the variables, and imply that every state is only finitely many transitions away from the initial state:

$$y_1 = 0, \qquad (q = 1) \vee \bigvee_{a \in \Sigma, q' \in Q_A} (x_{(q',a,q)}^A \wedge y_q = y_{q'} + 1).$$

4.3   Counterexample Elimination

If the VERIFY step discovers that $(\mathcal{A}_A, \mathcal{T}_\prec)$ violate some of the required conditions **(L1)**–**(L4)**, one of four possible kinds of counterexample will be derived, corresponding to outcomes #2–#5 described in Sect. 4.1. The counterexamples are mapped to constraints CE_i (for $i = 1, \ldots, 4$) to be added to ψ in SYNTHESISE as a conjunct:

- A configuration x from I_0 has to be included in A: $CE_1 = A(x)$
- A configuration y has to be included in A, under the assumption that x is included: $CE_2 = \neg A(x) \vee A(y)$
- Configurations x, z have to be related by $\prec$, under the assumption that x, y and y, z are related: $CE_3 = x \not\prec y \vee y \not\prec z \vee x \prec z$

– Player 2 has to be able to make a $\prec$-decreasing step from y, assuming $x \to_1 y$ and x is included in A: $CE_4 = \neg A(x) \vee \exists z. \big(A(z) \wedge (y \to_2 z) \wedge x \succ z\big)$

Each of the formulas can be directly translated to a Boolean constraint over the vocabulary introduced in Sect. 4.2, augmented with additional auxiliary variables; the most intricate case is CE_4, due to the quantifier $\exists z$. More details are given in the full version.

5   Optimisations and Incremental Liveness Proofs

The monolithic approach introduced so far is quite fast when compact advice bits exist (as shown in Sect. 6), but tends to be limited in scalability for more complex systems, because the search space grows rapidly when increasing the size of the considered automata. To address this issue, we introduce a range of optimisations of the basic method, in particular an *incremental* algorithm for synthesising advice bits, computing the set A and the relation $\prec$ by repeatedly constructing small automata.

5.1   Incremental Liveness Proofs

We first introduce a disjunctive version of the advice bits used to witness liveness:

Definition 2. *Let $(J, <)$ be a non-empty well-ordered index set.[2] A disjunctive advice bit is a tuple $\langle A, (B_j, \prec_j)_{j \in J} \rangle$, where $A, B_j \subseteq S$ are sets of game configurations, and each $\prec_j \subseteq S \times S$ is a binary relation over the game configurations, such that:*

(D1) $I_0 \subseteq A$;
(D2) A *is $\to$-inductive, i.e.,* $\forall x, y : x \in A \setminus F \wedge (x \to y) \Rightarrow y \in A$;
(D3) A *is covered by the B_j sets and F, i.e.,* $A \subseteq F \cup \bigcup_{j \in J} B_j$;
(D4) *for each $j \in J$, the relation $\prec_j$ is a strict preorder on S;*
(D5) *for each $j \in J$, player 2 can progress from B_j by following $\prec_j$:*

$$\forall x \in A \cap B_j \setminus (F \cup \bigcup_{i < j} B_i), y \in S \setminus F : \begin{pmatrix} (x \to_1 y) \Rightarrow \\ \exists z \in B_j : (y \to_2 z) \wedge z \prec_j x \end{pmatrix}.$$

The difference to monolithic advice bits (as defined in Sect. 3.3) is that the global preorder $\prec$ is replaced by a set of preorders $\prec_j$. Player 2 progresses to sets B_i with smaller index $i < j$ by following $\prec_j$, and this way eventually reaches F. A monolithic order $\prec$ can be reconstructed by defining

$$x \prec y \quad \Leftrightarrow \quad \begin{cases} idx(x) < idx(y) & \text{if } idx(x) \neq idx(y) \\ x \prec_j y & \text{if } idx(x) = idx(y) = j \end{cases}$$

---

[2] This means, $<$ is a strict total well-founded order on J.

Algorithm 1. Incremental liveness checker

---

1 $A \leftarrow S$;   // *Over-approximation of reachable configurations*
2 $W \leftarrow F$;   // *Under-approximation of winning configurations*

3 **while** $A \not\subseteq W$ **do**
4   choose a word $u \in A \setminus W$;
5   **if** u *is reachable* **then**
6          $W \leftarrow W \cup win(u, A, W)$;   // *Widen set of winning configurations*
7   **else**
8          $A \leftarrow A \cap invariant(u, A)$;   // *Tighten set of reachable configurations*

9 **return** *"Player 2 can win from every reachable configuration!"*

---

where $idx(x) = \min\{j \in J \mid x \in B_j\}$, and $idx(x) = \min J$ in case these is no $j \in J$ with $x \in B_j$. From this, it immediately follows that Theorem 1 also holds for disjunctive advice bits. We can further note that if J is finite and all sets in $(A, (B_j, <_j)_{j \in J})$ are regular, then the disjunctive advice bits correspond to regular monolithic advice bits; in general this is not the case for infinite J.

Algorithm 1 outlines the incremental liveness checker, defined with the help of disjunctive advice bits. The algorithm repeatedly refines a set A over-approximating the reachable configurations, and a set F under-approximating the configurations from which player 2 can win, and terminates as soon as all reachable configurations are known to be winning. The algorithm makes use of two sub-routines: in line 8, $invariant(u, A)$ denotes a *relatively inductive* invariant I [26] excluding u, i.e., a set $I \subseteq S$ such that

(RI1) $u \notin I$;
(RI2) $I_0 \subseteq I$,
(RI3) A is $\rightarrow$-inductive relative to A, i.e., $\forall x, y : x \in (I \cap A \setminus F) \wedge (x \rightarrow y) \Rightarrow y \in I$.

If A satisfies conditions **(D1)** and **(D2)**, and I is inductive relative to A, then also $A \cap I$ is an inductive set in the sense of **(D1)** and **(D2)**. We can practically compute automata representing sets I using a SAT-based refinement loop similar to the one in Sect. 4.

The second function $win(u, A, W)$ (line 6) computes a further progress pair $(B, \prec)$ witnessing the ability of Player 2 to win from u, and returns the set B, subject to:

(PP1) $u \in B$;
(PP2) the relation $\prec$ is a strict preorder on S;
(PP3) Player 2 can progress from B by following $\prec$:

$$\forall x \in A \cap B \setminus W, y \in S \setminus F : \big((x \rightarrow_1 y) \Rightarrow \exists z \in B : (y \rightarrow_2 z) \wedge z \prec x\big).$$

Again, a SAT-based refinement loop similar to the one in Sect. 4 can be used to find regular progress pairs $(B, \prec)$ satisfying the conditions. Comparing **(RI1)**–**(RI3)** and **(PP1)**–**(PP3)** with **(D1)**–**(D5)**, it is also clear that disjunctive advice bits can be extracted from every successful run of Algorithm 1, which implies soundness. Algorithm 1 is in addition complete in the following sense: if there exist (monolithic) regular advice bits conforming to a game $\langle \mathfrak{S}, I_0, F \rangle$, if the words u chosen in line 4 are always of minimum length, and if the functions *invariant* and *win* always compute minimum-size automata (representing sets I and $(B, \prec)$) solving the conditions **(RI1)**–**(RI3)** and **(PP1)**–**(PP3)**, then Algorithm 1 terminates. This minimality condition is satisfied for the learning-based algorithms derived in Sect. 4.

5.2   Pre-Computation of Inductive Invariants

Algorithm 1 can be optimised in different regards. First of all, the assignment $A \leftarrow S$ (line 1) initialising the approximation A of reachable states can be replaced with more precise pre-computation of the reachable states, for instance with the help of abstract regular model checking [22]. In fact, any set A satisfying **(D1)** and **(D2)** can be chosen.

We propose an efficient method for initialising A by utilising Angluin's $L*$-learning algorithm [9], which is applicable due to the property of length-preserving arenas that reachability of a given configuration w (a word) from the initial configurations I_0 is *decidable*. Decidability follows from the fact that there are only finitely many configurations up to a certain length, and the words occurring on a derivation $w_0 \rightarrow w_1 \rightarrow \cdots \rightarrow w_n$ all have the same length, so that known (explicit-state or symbolic) model checking methods can be used to decide reachability.

Reachability of configurations enables us to construct an $L*$ teacher (a.k.a. oracle). Membership queries for individual words w are answered by checking reachability of w in the game. Once the learner produces an hypothesis automaton $\mathcal{H}$, the teacher verifies that:

1. $\mathcal{H}$ includes the language I_0, i.e., **(D1)** is satisfied. If this is not the case, the teacher informs the learner about some further word in I_0 that has to be accepted by $\mathcal{H}$.
2. $\mathcal{H}$ is inductive, i.e., satisfies condition **(D2)**, which can be checked by means of automata methods (as in Sect. 4). If **(D2)** is violated, the counterexample pair (x, y) is examined, and it is checked whether the configuration x is reachable. If x is not reachable, the teacher gives a negative answer and demands that x be removed from the language; otherwise, the teacher demands that y is added to the language.
3. $\mathcal{H}$ describes the precise set of reachable configurations, for configuration length up to some fixed n. In other words, whenever $\mathcal{H}$ accepts some word w with $|w| \leq n$, the configuration w has to be reachable; otherwise, the teacher demands that w is eliminated from the language.

If all three tests succeed, the teacher accepts the produced automaton $\mathcal{H}$, which indeed represents a set A satisfying **(D1)** and **(D2)**. Tests 1 and 2 ensure that $\mathcal{H}$ is an inductive invariant, while test 3 is necessary to prevent trivial solutions: without the test, the algorithm could always return an automaton $\mathcal{H}$

recognising the universal language Σ^*. The parameter n determines the precision of synthesised invariants: larger n lead to automata $\mathcal{H}$ that are tighter over-approximations of the precise language of reachable configurations.[3]

This algorithm is guaranteed to terminate if the set of reachable configurations in an arena is regular; but it might only produce some inductive over-approximation of the reachable configurations. In our experiments, the computed languages usually capture reachable configurations very precisely, and the learning process converges quickly.

5.3   Exploitation of Game Symmetries

As a second optimisation, the incremental procedure can be improved to take symmetries of game instances into account, thus reducing the number of iterations needed in the incremental procedure; algorithms to automatically find symmetries in parameterised systems have recently proposed in [57]. This corresponds to replacing line 6 of Algorithm 1 with the assignment $W \leftarrow W \cup \sigma^*(win(u, A, W))$; where σ is an *automorphism* of the game instance $\langle \mathfrak{S}, I_0, F \rangle$, and $\sigma^*(L) = L \cup \sigma(L) \cup \sigma^2(L) \cup \cdots$ represents unbounded application of σ to a language $L \subseteq \Sigma^*$. An automorphism (or *symmetry pattern* [57]) is a length-preserving bijection $\sigma : \Sigma^* \to \Sigma^*$ such that 1. initial and winning configurations are σ-invariant, i.e., $\sigma(I_0) = I_0$ and $\sigma(F) = F$; and 2. σ is a homomorphism of the moves, i.e., $u \to_i v$ if and only if $\sigma(u) \to_i \sigma(v)$ for $i \in \{1, 2\}$.

A symmetry commonly present in systems with ring topology is *rotation*, defined by $\sigma_{\mathrm{rot}}(u_1 u_2 \ldots u_n) = u_2 \ldots u_n u_1$; the Israeli-Jalfon protocol (Example 1) exhibits this symmetry, as do many other examples. In addition, the fixed-point $\sigma_{\mathrm{rot}}^*(L)$ can effectively be constructed for any regular language $L \subseteq \Sigma^*$ using simple automata methods, which is of course important for implementing the optimised incremental algorithm.

In terms of disjunctive advice bits $\langle A, (B_j, \prec_j)_{j \in J} \rangle$, application of a symmetry σ corresponds to including a sequence $(B, \prec), (\sigma(B), \prec^\sigma), (\sigma^2(B), \prec^{\sigma^2}), \ldots$ of progress pairs, defining $(u \prec^\rho v) \Leftrightarrow (\rho^{-1}(u) \prec \rho^{-1}(v))$ for any bijection $\rho : \Sigma^* \to \Sigma^*$. The resulting monolithic progress relation will in general not be regular; in terms of ordinals, this means that a well-order $(J, <)$ greater than ω is chosen.

6   Experiments and Conclusion

All techniques introduced in this paper have been implemented in the liveness checker SLRP [1] for parameterised systems, using the SAT4J [16] solver for Boolean constraints. For evaluation, we consider a range of (randomised and deterministic) parameterised systems, as well as Take-away and Nim games, shown in Table 1. Two of the randomised protocols, Lehmann-Rabin and Israeli-Jalfon are symmetric under rotation. Since Herman's original protocol in a ring

---

[3] In our implementation we currently hard-code n to be 5.

[46] only satisfies liveness under "fair" schedulers, we used the version of the protocol in a line topology, which does satisfy liveness under all schedulers. Firewire is an example taken from [35,60] representing a fragment of Firewire symmetry breaking protocol. For handling combinatorial games, the monolithic method in Sect. 4 was adapted by removing condition (L2); adaptation of the incremental algorithm from Sect. 5.1 to this setting has not been considered yet.

All models could be solved using at least one of the considered CEGAR modes. In most cases, the monolithic approach from Sect. 4 displays good performance, and in case of the deterministic systems is competitive with existing tools (e.g. [8,65]). Monolithic reasoning outperforms the incremental methods (Sect. 5) in particular for Szymanski, which is because Algorithm 1 spends a lot of time computing a good approximation A of reachable states, although liveness can even be shown using $A = \Sigma^*$.

In contrast, the most complex model, the Lehmann-Rabin protocol for Dining Philosophers, can only be solved using the incremental algorithm, and only when accelerating the procedure by exploiting the rotation symmetry of the game (Sect. 5.3). In configuration Incr+Inv+Symm, Algorithm 1 computes an initial set A represented by a DFA with 23 states (Sect. 5.2), calls the

Table 1. Verification results for parameterised systems and games. **Mono** is the monolithic method from Sect. 4, **Incr** the incremental algorithm from Sect. 5.1, and **Inv** and **Symm** the optimisations introduced in Sect. 5.2 and 5.3, respectively. A dash — indicates that a model is not symmetric under rotation, or that the incremental algorithm is not applicable (in case of Take-away and Nim). The numbers in the table give runtime (wall-clock time) for the individual benchmarks and configurations; all experiments were done on an AMD Opteron 6282 32-core machine, Java heap memory limited to 20 GB, timeout 2 h.

	Mono	Incr	Incr+Inv	Incr+Symm	Incr+Inv +Symm
Randomised parameterised systems					
Lehmann-Rabin (DP) [34]	T/O	T/O	T/O	48 min	10 min
Israeli-Jalfon [47]	4.6s	22.7s	21.4s	9.9s	9.7s
Herman [46]	1.5s	1.6s	2.4s	—	—
Firewire [35,60]	1.3s	1.3s	2.0s	—	—
Deterministic parameterised systems					
Szymanski [4,65]	5.7s	27 min	10 min	—	—
DP, left-right strategy	1.9s	6.4s	3.4s	—	—
Bakery [4,65]	1.6s	2.7s	1.9s	—	—
Resource allocator [32]	2.2s	2.2s	2.0s	—	—
Games on infinite graphs					
Take-away [38]	2.8s	—	—	—	—
Nim [38]	5.3s	—	—	—	—

function *win* 25 times to obtain further progress relations (Sect. 5.1), and overall needs 4324 iterations of the refinement procedure of Sect. 4. To the best of our knowledge, this is the first time that liveness under arbitrary schedulers for randomised parameterised systems like Lehmann-Rabin could be shown fully automatically.

Future Work. We conclude with two concrete research questions among many others. The most immediate question is how to embed fairness in our framework of randomised parameterised systems. Another research direction concerns how to extend transducers to deal with data so as to model protocols where tokens may store arbitrary process IDs (examples of which include Dijkstra's Self-Stabilizing Protocol [31]).

Acknowledgment. We thank anonymous referees, Parosh Abdulla, Bengt Jonsson, Ondrej Lengal, Rupak Majumdar, and Ahmed Rezine for their helpful feedback. We thank Truong Khanh Nguyen for contributing with the development of the tool parasymmetry [57], on top of which our current tool (SLRP) builds. Lin is supported by Yale-NUS Grants, Rummer by the Swedish Research Council.

References

1. SLRP website, May 2016. https://github.com/uuverifiers/autosat/tree/master/LivenessProver
2. Abdulla, P.A.: Regular model checking. STTT **14**(2), 109–118 (2012)
3. Abdulla, P.A., Atig, M.F., Cederberg, J.: Analysis of message passing programs using SMT-solvers. In: Van Hung, D., Ogawa, M. (eds.) ATVA 2013. LNCS, vol. 8172, pp. 272–286. Springer, Heidelberg (2013)
4. Abdulla, P.A., Delzanno, G., Ben Henda, N., Rezine, A.: Regular model checking without transducers (on efficient verification of parameterized systems). In: Grumberg, O., Huth, M. (eds.) TACAS 2007. LNCS, vol. 4424, pp. 721–736. Springer, Heidelberg (2007)
5. Abdulla, P.A., Delzanno, G., Rezine, A.: Parameterized verification of infinite-state processes with global conditions. In: Damm, W., Hermanns, H. (eds.) CAV 2007. LNCS, vol. 4590, pp. 145–157. Springer, Heidelberg (2007)
6. Abdulla, P.A., Haziza, F., Holík, L.: All for the price of few. In: Giacobazzi, R., Berdine, J., Mastroeni, I. (eds.) VMCAI 2013. LNCS, vol. 7737, pp. 476–495. Springer, Heidelberg (2013)
7. Abdulla, P.A., Jonsson, B., Nilsson, M., Saksena, M.: A survey of regular model checking. In: Gardner, P., Yoshida, N. (eds.) CONCUR 2004. LNCS, vol. 3170, pp. 35–48. Springer, Heidelberg (2004)
8. Abdulla, P.A., Jonsson, B., Rezine, A., Saksena, M.: Proving liveness by backwards reachability. In: Baier, C., Hermanns, H. (eds.) CONCUR 2006. LNCS, vol. 4137, pp. 95–109. Springer, Heidelberg (2006)
9. Angluin, D.: Learning regular sets from queries and counterexamples. Inf. Comput. **75**(2), 87–106 (1987)
10. Annichini, A., Bouajjani, A., Sighireanu, M.: TREX: a tool for reachability analysis of complex systems. In: Berry, G., Comon, H., Finkel, A. (eds.) CAV 2001. LNCS, vol. 2102, pp. 368–372. Springer, Heidelberg (2001)

11. Apt, K.R., Kozen, D.: Limits for automatic verification of finite-state concurrent systems. Inf. Process. Lett. **22**(6), 307–309 (1986)
12. Arons, T., Pnueli, A., Zuck, L.D.: Parameterized verification by probabilistic abstraction. In: FoSSaCS, pp. 87–102 (2003)
13. Bardin, S., Finkel, A., Leroux, J., Petrucci, L.: FAST: acceleration from theory to practice. STTT **10**(5), 401–424 (2008)
14. Beauquier, J., Gradinariu, M., Johnen, C.: Randomized self-stabilizing and space optimal leader election under arbitrary scheduler on rings. Distrib. Comput. **20**(1), 75–93 (2007)
15. Ben-Ari, M.: Principles of Concurrent and Distributed Programming, 2nd edn. Addison-Wesley, Reading (2006)
16. Berre, D.L., Parrain, A.: The Sat4j library, release 2.2. JSAT **7**(2–3), 59–64 (2010)
17. Bloem, R., Jacobs, S., Khalimov, A., Konnov, I., Rubin, S., Veith, H., Widder, J.: Decidability of Parameterized Verification. Synthesis Lectures on Distributed Computing Theory. Morgan & Claypool Publishers, San Rafael (2015)
18. Blumensath, A.: Automatic structures. Master's thesis, RWTH Aachen (1999)
19. Blumensath, A., Grädel, E.: Finite presentations of infinite structures: automata and interpretations. Theory Comput. Syst. **37**(6), 641–674 (2004)
20. Boigelot, B., Legay, A., Wolper, P.: Iterating transducers in the large. In: Hunt Jr., W.A., Somenzi, F. (eds.) CAV 2003. LNCS, vol. 2725, pp. 223–235. Springer, Heidelberg (2003)
21. Bouajjani, A., Habermehl, P., Rogalewicz, A., Vojnar, T.: Abstract regular (tree) model checking. STTT **14**(2), 167–191 (2012)
22. Bouajjani, A., Habermehl, P., Vojnar, T.: Abstract regular model checking. In: Alur, R., Peled, D.A. (eds.) CAV 2004. LNCS, vol. 3114, pp. 372–386. Springer, Heidelberg (2004)
23. Bouajjani, A., Jonsson, B., Nilsson, M., Touili, T.: Regular model checking. In: Emerson, E.A., Sistla, A.P. (eds.) CAV 2000. LNCS, vol. 1855, pp. 403–418. Springer, Heidelberg (2000)
24. Bouajjani, A., Legay, A., Wolper, P.: Handling liveness properties in (omega-)regular model checking. Electron. Notes Theoret. Comput. Sci. **138**(3), 101–115 (2005)
25. Bracha, G., Toueg, S.: Asynchronous consensus and broadcast protocols. J. ACM **32**(4), 824–840 (1985)
26. Bradley, A.R., Manna, Z.: Property-directed incremental invariant generation. Formal Aspects Comput. **20**(4), 379–405 (2008)
27. Chakarov, A., Sankaranarayanan, S.: Probabilistic program analysis with martingales. In: Sharygina, N., Veith, H. (eds.) CAV 2013. LNCS, vol. 8044, pp. 511–526. Springer, Heidelberg (2013)
28. Emerson, E.A., Sistla, A.P.: Counterexample-guided abstraction refinement. In: Emerson, E.A., Sistla, A.P. (eds.) CAV 2000. LNCS, vol. 1855, pp. 154–169. Springer, Heidelberg (2000)
29. Courcoubetis, C., Yannakakis, M.: The complexity of probabilistic verification. J. ACM **42**(4), 857–907 (1995)
30. de Alfaro, L.: Computing minimum and maximum reachability times in probabilistic systems. In: Baeten, J.C.M., Mauw, S. (eds.) CONCUR 1999. LNCS, vol. 1664, pp. 66–81. Springer, Heidelberg (1999)
31. Dijkstra, E.W.: Self-stabilizing systems in spite of distributed control. Commun. ACM **17**(11), 643–644 (1974)
32. Donaldson, A.F.: Automatic techniques for detecting and exploiting symmetry in model checking. Ph.D. thesis, University of Glasgow (2007)

33. Dubois, S., Tixeuil, S.: A taxonomy of daemons in self-stabilization. CoRR, abs/1110.0334 (2011)
34. Duflot, M., Fribourg, L., Picaronny, C.: Randomized dining philosophers without fairness assumption. Distrib. Comput. **17**(1), 65–76 (2004)
35. Esparza, J., Gaiser, A., Kiefer, S.: Proving termination of probabilistic programs using patterns. In: Madhusudan, P., Seshia, S.A. (eds.) CAV 2012. LNCS, vol. 7358, pp. 123–138. Springer, Heidelberg (2012)
36. Esparza, J., Ganty, P., Poch, T.: Pattern-based verification for multithreaded programs. ACM Trans. Program. Lang. Syst. **36**(3), 9:1–9:29 (2014)
37. Fang, Y., Piterman, N., Pnueli, A., Zuck, L.D.: Liveness with invisible ranking. STTT **8**(3), 261–279 (2006)
38. Ferguson, T.S.: Game Theory, 2nd edn. Online Book (2014)
39. Fokkink, W.: Distributed Algorithms. MIT Press, Cambridge (2013)
40. Garg, P., Löding, C., Madhusudan, P., Neider, D.: Learning universally quantified invariants of linear data structures. In: Sharygina, N., Veith, H. (eds.) CAV 2013. LNCS, vol. 8044, pp. 813–829. Springer, Heidelberg (2013)
41. Goddard, W., Srimani, P.K.: Daemon conversions in distributed self-stabilizing algorithms. In: Ghosh, S.K., Tokuyama, T. (eds.) WALCOM 2013. LNCS, vol. 7748, pp. 146–157. Springer, Heidelberg (2013)
42. Grädel, E., Thomas, W., Wilke, T. (eds.): Automata, Logics, Infinite Games: A Guide to Current Research [outcome of a Dagstuhl seminar, February 2001]. LNCS, vol. 2500. Springer, Heidelberg (2002)
43. Habermehl, P., Holík, L., Rogalewicz, A., Simácek, J., Vojnar, T.: Forest automata for verification of heap manipulation. Formal Methods Syst. Des. **41**(1), 83–106 (2012)
44. Hague, M., Lin, A.W.: Synchronisation- and reversal-bounded analysis of multithreaded programs with counters. In: Madhusudan, P., Seshia, S.A. (eds.) CAV 2012. LNCS, vol. 7358, pp. 260–276. Springer, Heidelberg (2012)
45. Hart, S., Sharir, M., Pnueli, A.: Termination of probabilistic concurrent program. ACM Trans. Program. Lang. Syst. **5**(3), 356–380 (1983)
46. Herman, T.: Probabilistic self-stabilization. Inf. Process. Lett. **35**(2), 63–67 (1990)
47. Israeli, A., Jalfon, M.: Token management schemes and random walks yield self-stabilizing mutual exclusion. In: PODC, pp. 119–131 (1990)
48. Jonsson, B., Saksena, M.: Systematic acceleration in regular model checking. In: Damm, W., Hermanns, H. (eds.) CAV 2007. LNCS, vol. 4590, pp. 131–144. Springer, Heidelberg (2007)
49. Kaiser, A., Kroening, D., Wahl, T.: Dynamic cutoff detection in parameterized concurrent programs. In: Touili, T., Cook, B., Jackson, P. (eds.) CAV 2010. LNCS, vol. 6174, pp. 645–659. Springer, Heidelberg (2010)
50. Kakugawa, H., Yamashita, M.: Uniform and self-stabilizing token rings allowing unfair daemon. IEEE Trans. Parallel Distrib. Syst. **8**(2), 154–163 (1997)
51. Kwiatkowska, M., Norman, G., Parker, D.: PRISM 4.0: verification of probabilistic real-time systems. In: Gopalakrishnan, G., Qadeer, S. (eds.) CAV 2011. LNCS, vol. 6806, pp. 585–591. Springer, Heidelberg (2011)
52. Kwiatkowska, M.Z.: Model checking for probability and time: from theory to practice. In: LICS, p. 351 (2003)
53. Laroussinie, F., Sproston, J.: State explosion in almost-sure probabilistic reachability. Inf. Process. Lett. **102**(6), 236–241 (2007)
54. Legay, A.: T(O)RMC: a tool for (ω)-regular model checking. In: Gupta, A., Malik, S. (eds.) CAV 2008. LNCS, vol. 5123, pp. 548–551. Springer, Heidelberg (2008)

55. Lehmann, D., Rabin, M.: On the advantage of free choice: a symmetric and fully distributed solution to the dining philosophers problem (extended abstract). In: POPL, pp. 133–138 (1981)
56. Lin, A.W.: Accelerating tree-automatic relations. In: FSTTCS, pp. 313–324 (2012)
57. Lin, A.W., Nguyen, T.K., Rümmer, P., Sun, J.: Regular symmetry patterns. In: Jobstmann, B., Leino, K.R.M. (eds.) VMCAI 2016. LNCS, vol. 9583, pp. 455–475. Springer, Heidelberg (2016). doi:10.1007/978-3-662-49122-5_22
58. Lynch, N.: Distributed Algorithms. Morgan Kaufmann, San Francisco (1996)
59. Lynch, N.A., Saias, I., Segala, R.: Proving time bounds for randomized distributed algorithms. In: PODC, pp. 314–323 (1994)
60. McIver, A.K., Morgan, C., Hoang, T.S.: Probabilistic termination in B. In: Waldén, M., Bert, D., Bowen, J.P., King, S. (eds.) ZB 2003. LNCS, vol. 2651, pp. 216–239. Springer, Heidelberg (2003)
61. Monniaux, D.: An abstract analysis of the probabilistic termination of programs. In: Cousot, P. (ed.) SAS 2001. LNCS, vol. 2126, pp. 111–126. Springer, Heidelberg (2001)
62. Neider, D.: Reachability games on automatic graphs. In: Domaratzki, M., Salomaa, K. (eds.) CIAA 2010. LNCS, vol. 6482, pp. 222–230. Springer, Heidelberg (2011)
63. Neider, D., Jansen, N.: Regular model checking using solver technologies and automata learning. In: Brat, G., Rungta, N., Venet, A. (eds.) NFM 2013. LNCS, vol. 7871, pp. 16–31. Springer, Heidelberg (2013)
64. Neider, D., Topcu, U.: An automaton learning approach to solving safety games over infinite graphs. In: Chechik, M., Raskin, J.F. (eds.) TACAS 2016. LNCS, vol. 9636, pp. 204–221. Springer, Heidelberg (2016). doi:10.1007/978-3-662-49674-9_12
65. Nilsson, M.: Regular model checking. Ph.D. thesis, Uppsala Universitet (2005)
66. Norman, G.: Analysing randomized distributed algorithms. In: Baier, C., Haverkort, B.R., Hermanns, H., Katoen, J.P., Siegle, M. (eds.) Validation of Stochastic Systems. LNCS, vol. 2925, pp. 384–418. Springer, Heidelberg (2004)
67. Pnueli, A., Shahar, E.: Liveness and acceleration in parameterized verification. In: Emerson, E.A., Sistla, A.P. (eds.) CAV 2000. LNCS, vol. 1855, pp. 328–343. Springer, Heidelberg (2000)
68. Pnueli, A., Xu, J., Zuck, L.D.: Liveness with $(0, 1, \infty)$-counter abstraction. In: Brinksma, E., Larsen, K.G. (eds.) CAV 2002. LNCS, vol. 2404, pp. 107–122. Springer, Heidelberg (2002)
69. Pnueli, A., Zuck, L.D.: Verification of multiprocess probabilistic protocols. Distrib. Comput. 1(1), 53–72 (1986)
70. Szymanski, B.K.: A simple solution to Lamport's concurrent programming problem with linear wait. In: ICS, pp. 621–626 (1988)
71. To, A.W.: Model checking infinite-state : generic and specific approaches. Ph.D. thesis, LFCS, School of Informatics, University of Edinburgh (2010)
72. To, A.W., Libkin, L.: Recurrent reachability analysis in regular model checking. In: Cervesato, I., Veith, H., Voronkov, A. (eds.) LPAR 2008. LNCS (LNAI), vol. 5330, pp. 198–213. Springer, Heidelberg (2008)
73. To, A.W., Libkin, L.: Algorithmic metatheorems for decidable LTL model checking over infinite systems. In: FoSSaCS, pp. 221–236 (2010)
74. Vardhan, A., Sen, K., Viswanathan, M., Agha, G.: Using language inference to verify omega-regular properties. In: Halbwachs, N., Zuck, L.D. (eds.) TACAS 2005. LNCS, vol. 3440, pp. 45–60. Springer, Heidelberg (2005)
75. Vardhan, A., Viswanathan, M.: LEVER: a tool for learning based verification. In: Ball, T., Jones, R.B. (eds.) CAV 2006. LNCS, vol. 4144, pp. 471–474. Springer, Heidelberg (2006)

76. Vardi, M.Y.: Automatic verification of probabilistic concurrent finite-state programs. In: FOCS, pp. 327–338 (1985)
77. Vojnar, T.: Cut-offs and automata in formal verification of infinite-state systems. Habilitation Thesis, Faculty of Information Technology, Brno University of Technology (2007)
78. Wolper, P., Boigelot, B.: Verifying systems with infinite but regular state spaces. In: Vardi, M.Y. (ed.) CAV 1998. LNCS, vol. 1427, pp. 88–97. Springer, Heidelberg (1998)
79. Zuck, L.D., Pnueli, A.: Model checking and abstraction to the aid of parameterized systems (a survey). Comput. Lang. Syst. Struct. 30(3–4), 139–169 (2004)

Stateless Model Checking for POWER

Parosh Aziz Abdulla, Mohamed Faouzi Atig, Bengt Jonsson,
and Carl Leonardsson[✉]

Department of Information Technology,
Uppsala University, Uppsala, Sweden
carl.leonardsson@it.uu.se

Abstract. We present the first framework for efficient application of
stateless model checking (SMC) to programs running under the relaxed
memory model of POWER. The framework combines several contributions. The first contribution is that we develop a scheme for systematically deriving operational execution models from existing axiomatic
ones. The scheme is such that the derived execution models are well
suited for efficient SMC. We apply our scheme to the axiomatic model
of POWER from [8]. Our main contribution is a technique for efficient
SMC, called *Relaxed Stateless Model Checking* (RSMC), which systematically explores the possible inequivalent executions of a program. RSMC
is suitable for execution models obtained using our scheme. We prove
that RSMC is sound and optimal for the POWER memory model, in
the sense that each complete program behavior is explored exactly once.
We show the feasibility of our technique by providing an implementation
for programs written in C/pthreads.

1 Introduction

Verification and testing of concurrent programs is difficult, since one must consider all the different ways in which parallel threads can interact. To make matters worse, current shared-memory multicore processors, such as Intel's x86,
IBM's POWER, and ARM, [9,28,29,45], achieve higher performance by implementing *relaxed memory models* that allow threads to interact in even subtler
ways than by interleaving of their instructions, as would be the case in the
model of *sequential consistency* (SC) [32]. Under the relaxed memory model of
POWER, loads and stores to different memory locations may be reordered by the
hardware, and the accesses may even be observed in different orders on different
processor cores.

Stateless model checking (SMC) [25] is one successful technique for verifying concurrent programs. It detects violations of correctness by systematically
exploring the set of possible program executions. Given a concurrent program
which is terminating and threadwisely deterministic (e.g., by fixing any input
data to avoid data-nondeterminism), a special runtime scheduler drives the SMC
exploration by controlling decisions that may affect subsequent computations, so
that the exploration covers all possible executions. The technique is automatic,
has no false positives, can be applied directly to the program source code, and

© Springer International Publishing Switzerland 2016
S. Chaudhuri and A. Farzan (Eds.): CAV 2016, Part II, LNCS 9780, pp. 134–156, 2016.
DOI: 10.1007/978-3-319-41540-6_8

can easily reproduce detected bugs. SMC has been successfully implemented in tools, such as VeriSoft [26], CHESS [37], Concuerror [17], rInspect [49], and Nidhugg [1].

However, SMC suffers from the state-space explosion problem, and must therefore be equipped with techniques to reduce the number of explored executions. The most prominent one is *partial order reduction* [18,24,39,47], adapted to SMC as *dynamic partial order reduction* (DPOR) [2,23,40,43]. DPOR addresses state-space explosion caused by the many possible ways to schedule concurrent threads. DPOR retains full behavior coverage, while reducing the number of explored executions by exploiting that two schedules which induce the same order between conflicting instructions will induce equivalent executions. DPOR has been adapted to the memory models TSO and PSO [1,49], by introducing auxiliary threads that induce the reorderings allowed by TSO and PSO, and using DPOR to counteract the resulting increase in thread schedulings.

In spite of impressive progress in SMC techniques for SC, TSO, and PSO, there is so far no effective technique for SMC under more relaxed models, such as POWER. A major reason is that POWER allows more aggressive reorderings of instructions within each thread, as well as looser synchronization between threads, making it significantly more complex than SC, TSO, and PSO. Therefore, existing SMC techniques for SC, TSO, and PSO can not be easily extended to POWER.

In this paper, we present the first SMC algorithm for programs running under the POWER relaxed memory model. The technique is both sound, in the sense that it guarantees to explore each programmer-observable behavior at least once, and optimal, in the sense that it does not explore the same complete behavior twice. Our technique combines solutions to several major challenges.

The first challenge is to design an execution model for POWER that is suitable for SMC. Existing execution models fall into two categories. Operational models, such as [12,21,41,42], define behaviors as resulting from sequences of small steps of an abstract processor. Basing SMC on such a model would induce large numbers of executions with equivalent programmer-observable behavior, and it would be difficult to prevent redundant exploration, even if DPOR techniques are employed. Axiomatic models, such as [7,8,36], avoid such redundancy by being defined in terms of an abstract representation of programmer-observable behavior, due to Shasha and Snir [44], here called *Shasha-Snir traces*. However, being axiomatic, they judge whether an execution is allowed only after it has been completed. Directly basing SMC on such a model would lead to much wasted exploration of unallowed executions. To address this challenge, we have therefore developed a scheme for systematically deriving execution models that are suitable for SMC. Our scheme derives an execution model, in the form of a labeled transition system, from an existing axiomatic model, defined in terms of Shasha-Snir traces. Its states are partially constructed Shasha-Snir traces. Each transition adds ("commits") an instruction to the state, and also equips the instruction with a parameter that determines how it is inserted into the Shasha-Snir trace. The parameter of a load is the store from which it reads its value. The parameter of a store is its position in the coherence order of stores to the same memory location. The order in which instructions are added must respect various dependencies between instructions, such that each instruction makes sense at the time when it is added. For example, when adding a store or a load instruction, earlier instructions that are needed to compute which memory address it accesses must already have been added. Our execution model therefore takes as input a partial order, called *commit-before*, which constrains the order in which instructions can be added. The commit-before order should be tuned to suit the given axiomatic memory model. We define a condition of *validity* for commit-before orders, under which our derived execution model is equivalent to the original axiomatic one, in that they generate the same sets of Shasha-Snir traces. We use our scheme to derive an execution model for POWER, equivalent to the axiomatic model of [8].

Having designed a suitable execution model, we address our main challenge, which is to design an effective SMC algorithm that explores all Shasha-Snir traces that can be generated by the execution model. We address this challenge by a novel exploration technique, called *Relaxed Stateless Model Checking* (RSMC). RSMC is suitable for execution models, in which each instruction can be executed in many ways with different effects on the program state, such as those derived using our execution model scheme. The exploration by RSMC combines two mechanisms: (i) RSMC considers instructions one-by-one, respecting the commit-before order, and explores the effects of each possible way in which the instruction can be executed. (ii) RSMC monitors the generated execution for data races from loads to subsequent stores, and initiates alternative explorations where instructions are reordered. We define the property *deadlock freedom* of execution models, meaning intuitively that no run will block before being complete. We prove that RSMC is sound for deadlock free execution models, and that our execution model for POWER is indeed deadlock free. We also prove that RSMC is optimal for POWER, in the sense that it explores each *complete* Shasha-Snir trace exactly once. Similar to sleep set blocking for classical SMC/DPOR, it may happen for RSMC that superfluous *incomplete* Shasha-Snir traces are explored. Our experiments indicate, however, that this is rare.

To demonstrate the usefulness of our framework, we have implemented RSMC in the stateless model checker Nidhugg [33]. For test cases written in C with pthreads, it explores all Shasha-Snir traces allowed under the POWER memory model, up to some bounded length. We evaluate our implementation on several challenging benchmarks. The results show that RSMC efficiently explores the Shasha-Snir traces of a program, since (i) on most benchmarks, our implementation performs no superfluous exploration (as discussed above), and (ii) the running times correlate to the number of Shasha-Snir traces of the program. We show the competitiveness of our implementation by comparing with an existing state of the art analysis tool for POWER: goto-instrument [5].

Outline. The next section presents our derivation of execution models. Section 3 presents our RSMC algorithm, and Sect. 4 presents our implementation and experiments. Proofs of all theorems, and formal definitions, are provided in our technical report [4]. Our implementation is available at [33].

2   Execution Model for Relaxed Memory Models

POWER — A Brief Glimpse. The programmer-observable behavior of POWER multiprocessors emerges from a combination of many features, including out-of-order and speculative execution, various buffers, and caches. POWER provides significantly weaker ordering guarantees than, e.g., SC and TSO.

We consider programs consisting of a number of threads, each of which runs a deterministic code, built as a sequence of assembly instructions. The grammar of our assumed language is given in Fig. 1. The threads access a shared memory, which is a mapping from addresses to values. A program may start by declaring named global variables with specific initial values. Instructions include register assignments and conditional branches with the usual semantics. A load 'r:=[a]' loads the value from the memory address given by the arithmetic expression a into the register r. A store '[a_0]:=a_1' stores the value of the expression a_1 to the memory location addressed by the evaluation of a_0. For a global variable x, we use x as syntactic sugar for [&x], where &x is the address of x. The instructions sync, lwsync, isync are fences (or memory barriers), which are special instructions preventing some memory ordering relaxations. Each instruction is given a label, which is assumed to be unique.

As an example, consider the program in Fig. 2. It consists of two threads P and Q, and has two zero-initialized memory locations x and y. The thread P loads the value of x, and stores that value plus one to y. The thread Q is similar, but always stores the value 1, regardless of the loaded value. Under the SC or TSO memory models, at least one of the loads L0 and L2 is guaranteed to load the initial value 0 from memory. However, under POWER the order between the load L2 and the store L3 is not maintained. Then it is possible for P to load the value 1 into r_0, and for Q to load 2 into r_1. Inserting a sync between L2 and L3 would prevent such a behavior.

Axiomatic Memory Models. Axiomatic memory models, of the form in [8], operate on an abstract representation of observable program behavior, introduced by Shasha and Snir [44], here called *traces*. A trace is a directed graph,

$$\langle prog \rangle ::= \langle varinit \rangle^* \; \langle thrd \rangle^+$$
$$\langle varinit \rangle ::= \langle var \rangle \; \text{'='} \; \mathbb{Z}$$
$$\langle thrd \rangle := \text{'thread'} \; \langle tid \rangle \; \text{':'} \; \langle linstr \rangle^+$$
$$\langle linstr \rangle ::= \langle label \rangle \; \text{':'} \; \langle instr \rangle \; \text{';'}$$

$$
\begin{aligned}
\langle instr \rangle ::= \; & \langle reg \rangle \; \text{':='} \; \langle expr \rangle \; | && \text{// register assignment} \\
& \text{'if'} \; \langle expr \rangle \; \text{'goto'} \; \langle label \rangle \; | && \text{// conditional branch} \\
& \langle reg \rangle \; \text{':='} \; \text{'['} \; \langle expr \rangle \; \text{']'} \; | && \text{// memory load} \\
& \text{'['} \; \langle expr \rangle \; \text{']'} \; \text{':='} \; \langle expr \rangle \; | && \text{// memory store} \\
& \text{'sync'} \; | \; \text{'lwsync'} \; | \; \text{'isync'} && \text{// fences}
\end{aligned}
$$
$$\langle expr \rangle ::= \text{(arithmetic expression over literals and registers)}$$

Fig. 1. The grammar of concurrent programs

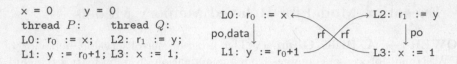

Fig. 2. Left: An example program: LB + data. Right: A trace of the same program.

Event	Parameter	Semantic Meaning
L3: x := 1	0	First in coherence order for x
L0: r_0 := x	L3	Read value 1 from L3
L1: y := r_0+1	0	First in coherence order for y
L2: r_1 := y	L1	Read value 2 from L1

Fig. 3. The run L3[0].L0[L3].L1[0].L2[L1], of the program in Fig. 2 (left), leading to the complete state corresponding to the trace given in Fig. 2 (right). Here we use the labels L0–L3 as shorthands for the corresponding events.

in which vertices are executed instructions (called *events*), and edges capture dependencies between them. More precisely, a *trace* π is a quadruple $(E, \mathsf{po}, \mathsf{co}, \mathsf{rf})$ where E is a set of *events*, and po, co, and rf are relations over E^1. An *event* is a tuple (t, n, l) where t is an identifier for the executing thread, l is the unique label of the instruction, and n is a natural number which disambiguates instructions. Let $\mathbb{E}$ denote the set of all possible events. For an event $e = (\mathsf{t}, n, l)$, let $\mathsf{tid}(e)$ denote t and let $\mathsf{instr}(e)$ denote the instruction labelled l in the program code. The relation po (for "program order") totally orders all events executed by the same thread. The relation co (for "coherence order") totally orders all stores to the same memory location. The relation rf (for "read-from") contains the pairs (e, e') such that e is a store and e' is a load which gets its value from e. For simplicity, we assume that the initial value of each memory address x is assigned by a special *initializer instruction* init_x, which is first in the coherence order for that address. A trace is a *complete trace of the program* $\mathcal{P}$ if the program order over the committed events of each thread makes up a path from the first instruction in the code of the thread, to the last instruction, respecting the evaluation of conditional branches. Figure 2 shows the complete trace corresponding to the behavior described in the beginning of this section, in which each thread loads the value stored by the other thread.

An axiomatic memory model M (following the framework [8]) is defined as a predicate M over traces π, such that $M(\pi)$ holds precisely when π is an allowed trace under the model. Deciding whether $M(\pi)$ holds involves checking (i) that the trace is internally consistent, defined in the natural way (e.g., the relation co relates precisely events that access the same memory location), and (ii) that various combinations of relations that are derived from the trace are acyclic or irreflexive. Which specific relations need to be acyclic depends on the memory model.

---

[1] [8] uses the term "execution" to denote what we call "trace".

We define the *axiomatic semantics under* M as a mapping from programs $\mathcal{P}$ to their denotations $[\![\mathcal{P}]\!]_M^{Ax}$, where $[\![\mathcal{P}]\!]_M^{Ax}$ is the set of complete traces π of $\mathcal{P}$ such that $M(\pi)$ holds. In the following, we assume that the axiomatic memory model for POWER, here denoted M^{POWER}, is defined as in [8]. The interested reader is encouraged to read the details in [8], but the high-level understanding given above should be enough to understand the remainder of this text.

Deriving an Execution Model. Let an axiomatic model M be given, in the style of [8]. We will derive an equivalent execution model in the form of a transition system.

States. States of our execution model are traces, augmented with a set of fetched events. A state σ is a tuple of the form $(\lambda, F, E, \mathsf{po}, \mathsf{co}, \mathsf{rf})$ where $\lambda(\mathsf{t})$ is a label in the code of t for each thread t, $F \subseteq \mathbb{E}$ is a set of events, and $(E, \mathsf{po}|_E, \mathsf{co}, \mathsf{rf})$ is a trace such that $E \subseteq F$. (Here $\mathsf{po}|_E$ is the restriction of po to E.) For a state $\sigma = (\lambda, F, E, \mathsf{po}, \mathsf{co}, \mathsf{rf})$, we let $\mathsf{exec}(\sigma)$ denote the trace $(E, \mathsf{po}|_E, \mathsf{co}, \mathsf{rf})$. Intuitively, F is the set of all currently fetched events and E is the set of events that have been committed. The function λ gives the label of the next instruction to fetch for each thread. The relation po is the program order between all fetched events. The relations co and rf are defined for committed events (i.e., events in E) only. The set of all possible states is denoted $\mathbb{S}$. The initial state $\sigma_0 \in \mathbb{S}$ is defined as $\sigma_0 = (\lambda_0, E_0, E_0, \varnothing, \varnothing, \varnothing)$ where λ_0 is the function providing the initial label of each thread, and E_0 is the set of all initializer events.

Commit-Before. The order in which events can be committed – effectively a linearization of the trace – is restricted by a *commit-before order*. It is a parameter of our execution model which can be tuned to suit the given axiomatic model. Formally, a commit-before order is defined by a *commit-before function* cb, which associates with each state $\sigma = (\lambda, F, E, \mathsf{po}, \mathsf{co}, \mathsf{rf})$, a *commit-before order* $\mathsf{cb}_\sigma \subseteq F \times F$, which is a partial order on the set of fetched events. For each state σ, the commit-before order cb_σ induces a predicate $enabled_\sigma$ over the set of fetched events $e \in F$ such that $enabled_\sigma(e)$ holds if and only if $e \notin E$ and the set $\{e' \in F \mid (e', e) \in \mathsf{cb}_\sigma\}$ is included in E. Intuitively, e can be committed only if all the events it depends on have already been committed. Later in this section, we define requirements on commit-before functions, which are necessary for the execution model and for the RSMC algorithm respectively.

Transitions. The transition relation between states is given by a set of rules, in Fig. 4. The function $\mathsf{val}_\sigma(e, a)$ denotes the value taken by the arithmetic expression a, when evaluated at the event e in the state σ. The value is computed in the natural way, respecting data-flow. (Formal definition in the technical report [4].) For example, in the state σ corresponding to the trace given in Fig. 2, where e is the event corresponding to label L1, we would have $\mathsf{val}_\sigma(e, \mathsf{r_0+1}) = 2$. The function $\mathsf{address}_\sigma(e)$ associates with each load or store event e the memory location accessed. For a label l, let $\lambda_{\mathsf{next}}(l)$ denote the next label following l in the program code. Finally, for a state σ with coherence order co and a store e to some memory location x, we let $extend_\sigma(e)$ denote the set of coherence orders co' which result from inserting e anywhere in the total order of stores to x in co.

$$F_t = \{e'' \in F | \text{tid}(e'') = \text{t}\} \quad e = (\text{t}, |F_t|, \lambda(\text{t}))$$

$$\frac{\nexists e', a, l \, . \, e' \in F \setminus E \wedge \text{tid}(e') = \text{t} \wedge \text{instr}(e') = (\text{if } a \text{ goto } l)}{\sigma \xrightarrow{FLB} (\lambda[\text{t} \hookleftarrow \lambda_{\text{next}}(\lambda(\text{t}))], F \cup \{e\}, E, \text{po} \cup (F_t \times \{e\}), \text{co}, \text{rf})} \text{FETCH}$$

$$\frac{\text{instr}(e) = (\text{if } a \text{ goto } l) \quad \text{t} = \text{tid}(e)}{\text{val}_\sigma(e, a) \in \mathbb{Z} \setminus \{0\} \quad enabled_\sigma(e)}{\sigma \xrightarrow{FLB} (\lambda[\text{t} \hookleftarrow l], F, E \cup \{e\}, \text{po}, \text{co}, \text{rf})} \text{BRT} \qquad \frac{\text{instr}(e) \in \{\text{sync}, \text{lwsync}, \text{isync}, \text{r} \text{:=} a\}}{enabled_\sigma(e)}{\sigma \xrightarrow{FLB} (\lambda, F, E \cup \{e\}, \text{po}, \text{co}, \text{rf})} \text{LOC}$$

$$\frac{\text{instr}(e) = (\text{if } a \text{ goto } l)}{\text{val}_\sigma(e, a) = 0 \quad enabled_\sigma(e)}{\sigma \xrightarrow{FLB} (\lambda, F, E \cup \{e\}, \text{po}, \text{co}, \text{rf})} \text{BRF} \qquad \frac{\text{instr}(e) = ([a] \text{:=} a') \quad enabled_\sigma(e) \quad \text{M}(\text{exec}(\sigma'))}{\sigma' = (\lambda, F, E \cup \{e\}, \text{po}, \text{co}', \text{rf}) \quad \text{co}' \in extend_\sigma(e)}{\sigma \xrightarrow{e[position_{\text{co}'}(e)]} \sigma'} \text{ST}$$

$$\frac{\text{instr}(e) = (\text{r} \text{:=} [a]) \quad enabled_\sigma(e) \quad e_w \in E \quad \text{instr}(e_w) = ([a'] \text{:=} a'')}{\text{address}_\sigma(e_w) = \text{address}_\sigma(e) \quad \sigma' = (\lambda, F, E \cup \{e\}, \text{po}, \text{co}, \text{rf} \cup \{(e_w, e)\}) \quad \text{M}(\text{exec}(\sigma'))}{\sigma \xrightarrow{e[e_w]} \sigma'} \text{LD}$$

Fig. 4. Execution model of programs under the memory model M. Here $\sigma = (\lambda, F, E, \text{po}, \text{co}, \text{rf})$.

For each such order co$'$, we let $position_{\text{co}'}(e)$ denote the position of e in the total order: I.e. $position_{\text{co}'}(e)$ is the number of (non-initializer) events e' which precede e in co$'$.

The intuition behind the rules in Fig. 4 is that events are committed non-deterministically out of order, but respecting the constraints induced by the commit-before order. When a memory access (load or store) is committed, a non-deterministic choice is made about its effect. If the event is a store, it is non-deterministically inserted somewhere in the coherence order. If the event is a load, we non-deterministically pick the store from which to read. Thus, when committed, each memory access event e is parameterized by a choice p: the coherence position for a store, and the source store for a load. We call $e[p]$ a *parameterized event*, and let $\mathbb{P}$ denote the set of all possible parameterized events. A transition committing a memory access is only enabled if the resulting state is allowed by the memory model M. Transitions are labelled with FLB when an event is fetched or a local event is committed, or with $e[p]$ when a memory access event e is committed with parameter p.

We illustrate this intuition for the program in Fig. 2 (left). The trace in Fig. 2 (right) can be produced by committing the instructions (events) in the order L3, L0, L1, L2. For the load L0, we can then choose the already performed L3 as the store from which it reads, and for the load L2, we can choose to read from the store L1. Each of the two stores L3 and L1 can only be inserted at one place in their respective coherence orders, since the program has only one store to each memory location. We show the resulting sequence of committed events in Fig. 3:

the first column shows the sequence of events in the order they are committed, the second column is the parameter assigned to the event, and the third column explains the parameter. Note that other traces can be obtained by choosing different values of parameters. For instance, the load L2 can also read from the initial value, which would generate a different trace.

Next we explain each of the rules: The rule FETCH allows to fetch the next instruction according to the control flow of the program code. The first two requirements identify the next instruction. To fetch an event, all preceding branch events must already be committed. Therefore events are never fetched along a control flow path that is not taken. We point out that this restriction does not prevent our execution model from capturing the observable effects of speculative execution (formally ensured by Theorem 1).

The rules LOC, BRT and BRF describe how to commit non-memory access events.

When a store event is committed by the ST rule, it is inserted non-deterministically at some position $n = position_{co'}(e)$ in the coherence order. The guard $M(exec(\sigma'))$ ensures that the resulting state is allowed by the axiomatic memory model.

The rule LD describes how to commit a load event e. It is similar to the ST rule. For a load we non-deterministically choose a source store e_w, from which the value can be read. As before, the guard $M(exec(\sigma'))$ ensures that the resulting state is allowed.

Given two states $\sigma, \sigma' \in \mathbb{S}$, we use $\sigma \xrightarrow{FLB(max)} \sigma'$ to denote that $\sigma \xrightarrow{FLB}^{*} \sigma'$ and there is no state $\sigma'' \in \mathbb{S}$ with $\sigma' \xrightarrow{FLB} \sigma''$. A run τ from some state σ is a sequence of parameterized events $e_1[p_1].e_2[p_2] \cdots e_k[p_k]$ such that $\sigma \xrightarrow{FLB(max)} \upsilon_1 \xrightarrow{e_1[p_1]} \sigma'_1 \xrightarrow{FLD(max)} \cdots \xrightarrow{e_k[p_k]} \sigma'_k \xrightarrow{FLB(max)} \sigma_{k+1}$ for some states $\sigma_1, \sigma'_1, \ldots, \sigma'_k, \sigma_{k+1} \in \mathbb{S}$. We write $e[p] \in \tau$ to denote that the parameterized event $e[p]$ appears in τ. Observe that the sequence τ leads to a uniquely determined state σ_{k+1}, which we denote $\tau(\sigma)$. A run τ, from the initial state σ_0, is *complete* iff the reached trace $exec\tau(\sigma_0)$ is complete. Figure 3 shows an example complete run of the program in Fig. 2 (left).

In summary, our execution model represents a program $\mathcal{P}$ as a labeled transition system $TS^{\mathcal{P}}_{M,cb} = (\mathbb{S}, \sigma_0, \longrightarrow)$, where $\mathbb{S}$ is the set of states, σ_0 is the initial state, and $\longrightarrow \subseteq \mathbb{S} \times (\mathbb{P} \cup \{FLB\}) \times \mathbb{S}$ is the transition relation. We define the *execution semantics under* M *and* cb as a mapping, which maps each program $\mathcal{P}$ to its denotation $[\![\mathcal{P}]\!]^{Ex}_{M,cb}$, which is the set of complete runs τ induced by $TS^{\mathcal{P}}_{M,cb}$.

Validity and Deadlock Freedom. Here, we define validity and deadlock freedom for memory models and commit-before functions. Validity is necessary for the correct operation of our execution model (Theorem 1). Deadlock freedom is necessary for soundness of the RSMC algorithm (Theorem 4). First, we introduce some auxiliary notions.

We say that a state $\sigma' = (\lambda', F', E', po', co', rf')$ is a *cb-extension* of a state $\sigma = (\lambda, F, E, po, co, rf)$, denoted $\sigma \leq_{cb} \sigma'$, if σ' can be obtained from σ by fetching in program order or committing events in cb order. Formally $\sigma \leq_{cb} \sigma'$ if $po = po'|_F$, $co = co'|_E$, $rf = rf'|_E$, F is a po'-closed subset of F', and E is a $cb_{\sigma'}$-closed subset of E'. More precisely, the condition on F means that for any events $e, e' \in F'$, we have $[e' \in F \wedge (e, e') \in po'] \Rightarrow e \in F$. The condition on E is analogous.

We say that cb is *monotonic* w.r.t. M if whenever $\sigma \leq_{cb} \sigma'$, then (i) $M(exec(\sigma')) \Rightarrow M(exec(\sigma))$, (ii) $cb_\sigma \subseteq cb_{\sigma'}$, and (iii) for all $e \in F$ such that either $e \in E$ or $(enabled_\sigma(e) \wedge e \notin E')$, we have $(e', e) \in cb_\sigma \Leftrightarrow (e', e) \in cb_{\sigma'}$ for all $e' \in F'$. Conditions (i) and (ii) are natural monotonicity requirements on M and cb. Condition (iii) says that while an event is committed or enabled, its cb-predecessors do not change.

A state σ induces a number of relations over its fetched (possibly committed) events. Following [8], we let $addr_\sigma$, $data_\sigma$, $ctrl_\sigma$, denote respectively address dependency, data dependency and control dependency. Similarly, $po\text{-}loc_\sigma$ is the subset of po that relates memory accesses to the same memory location. Lastly, $sync_\sigma$ and $lwsync_\sigma$ relate events that are separated in program order by respectively a sync or lwsync. The formal definitions can be found in [8], and in our technical report [4]. We can now define a weakest reasonable commit-before function cb^0, capturing natural dependencies:

$$cb_\sigma^0 = (addr_\sigma \cup data_\sigma \cup ctrl_\sigma \cup rf)^+,$$

where R^+ denotes the transitive (but not reflexive) closure of R.

We say that a commit-before function cb is *valid* w.r.t. a memory model M if cb is monotonic w.r.t. M, and for all states σ such that $M(exec(\sigma))$ we have that cb_σ is acyclic and $cb_\sigma^0 \subseteq cb_\sigma$.

Theorem 1 (Equivalence with Axiomatic Model). Let cb be a commit-before function valid w.r.t. a memory model M. Then $[\![\mathcal{P}]\!]_M^{Ax} = \{exec(\tau(\sigma_0)) \mid \tau \in [\![\mathcal{P}]\!]_{M,cb}^{Ex}\}$.   □

Program		Blocked run τ	Blocked state σ
x = 0	y = 0	L3[0]	L0: r_0:=y $\leftarrow$ $\rightarrow$ L3: x:=3
thread P:	thread Q:	L5[0]	data↓ ↓sync
L0: r_0:=y;	L3: x:=3;	L0[L5]	L1 x:=r_0 co /\ rf L4: sync
L1: x:=r_0;	L4: sync;	L2[0]	po-loc↓ ↓sync
L2: x:=2;	L5: y:=1;	(L1 blocked)	L2: x:=2 $\diagup$ $\diagdown$ L5: y:=1

Fig. 5. If the weak commit-before function cb^0 is used, the POWER semantics may deadlock. When the program above (left) is executed according to the run τ (center) we reach a state σ (right) where L0, L2, L3–L5 are successfully committed. However, any attempt to commit L1 will close a cycle in the relation $co; sync_\sigma; rf; data_\sigma; po\text{-}loc_\sigma$, which is forbidden under POWER. This blocking behavior is prevented when the stronger commit-before function cb^{power} is used, since it requires L1 and L2 to be committed in program order.

The commit-before function cb^0 is valid w.r.t. M^{POWER}, implying (by Theorem 1) that $[\![\mathcal{P}]\!]^{Ex}_{M^{POWER},cb^0}$ is a faithful execution model for POWER. However, cb^0 is not strong enough to prevent blocking runs in the execution model for POWER. I.e., it is possible, with cb^0, to create an incomplete run, which cannot be completed. Any such blocking is undesirable for SMC, since it corresponds to wasted exploration. Figure 5 shows an example of how the POWER semantics may deadlock when based on cb^0.

We say that a memory model M and a commit before function cb are *deadlock free* if for all runs τ from σ_0 and memory access events e such that $enabled_{\tau(\sigma_0)}(e)$ there exists a parameter p such that $\tau.e[p]$ is a run from σ_0. I.e., it is impossible to reach a state where some event is enabled, but has no parameter with which it can be committed.

Commit-Before Order for POWER. We will now define a stronger commit before function for POWER, which is both valid and deadlock free:

$$cb^{power}_\sigma = (cb^0_\sigma \cup (addr_\sigma; po) \cup \text{po-loc}_\sigma \cup sync_\sigma \cup lwsync_\sigma)^+$$

Theorem 2. cb^{power} is valid w.r.t. M^{POWER}.

Theorem 3. M^{POWER} and cb^{power} are deadlock free.

3   The RSMC Algorithm

Having derived an execution model, we address the challenge of defining an SMC algorithm, which explores all allowed traces of a program in an efficient manner. Since each trace can be generated by many equivalent runs, we must, just as in standard SMC for SC, develop techniques for reducing the number of explored runs, while still guaranteeing coverage of all traces. Our RSMC algorithm is designed to do this in the context of semantics like the one defined above, in which instructions can be committed with several different parameters, each yielding different results.

Our exploration technique basically combines two mechanisms:

(i) In each state, RSMC considers an instruction e, whose cb-predecessors have already been committed. For each possible parameter value p of e in the current state, RSMC extends the state by $e[p]$ and continues the exploration recursively.

(ii) RSMC monitors generated runs to detect read-write conflicts (or "races"), i.e., the occurrence of a load and a subsequent store to the same memory location, such that the load would be able to read from the store if they were committed in the reverse order. For each such conflict, RSMC starts an alternative exploration, in which the load is preceded by the store, so that the load can read from the store.

Mechanism (ii) is analogous to the detection and reversal of races in conventional DPOR, with the difference that RSMC need only detect conflicts in which a load is followed by a store. A race where a load follows a store does not induce reordering by mechanism (ii). This is because our execution model allows the load to read from any of the already committed stores to the same memory location, without any reordering.

Instruction	Parameter	Semantic Meaning
L0: r_0 := x	$init_x$	(read initial value)
L1: y := r_0+1	0	(first in coherence of y)
L2: r_1 := y	$init_y$	(read initial value)
L3: x := 1	0	(first in coherence of x)

Fig. 6. The first explored run of the program in Fig. 2

We illustrate the basic idea of RSMC on the program in Fig. 2 (left). As usual in SMC, we start by running the program under an arbitrary schedule, subject to the constraints imposed by the commit-before order cb. For each instruction, we explore the effects of each parameter value which is allowed by the memory model. Let us assume that we initially explore the instructions in the order L0, L1, L2, L3. For this schedule, there is only one possible parameter for L0, L1, and L3, whereas L2 can read either from the initial value or from L1. Let us assume that it reads the initial value. This gives us the first run, shown in Fig. 6. The second run is produced by changing the parameter for L2, and let it read the value 1 written by L1.

During the exploration of the first two runs, the RSMC algorithm also detects a race between the load L0 and the store L3. An important observation is that L3 is not ordered after L0 by the commit-before order, implying that their order can be reversed. Reversing the order between L0 and L3 would allow L0 to read from L3. Therefore, RSMC initiates an exploration where the load L0 is preceded by L3 and reads from it. (If L3 would have been preceded by other events that enable L3, these would be executed before L3.) After the sequence L3[0].L0[L3], RSMC is free to choose the order in which the remaining instructions are considered. Assume that the order L1, L2 is chosen. In this case, the load L2 can read from either the initial value or from L1. In the latter case, we obtain the run in Fig. 3, corresponding to the trace in Fig. 2 (right).

After this, there are no more unexplored parameter choices, and so the RSMC algorithm terminates, having explored four runs corresponding to the four possible traces.

In the following section, we will provide a more detailed look at the RSMC algorithm, and see formally how this exploration is carried out.

3.1 Algorithm Description

In this section, we present our algorithm, RSMC, for SMC under POWER. We prove soundness of RSMC, and optimality w.r.t. explored *complete* traces.

The RSMC algorithm is shown in Fig. 7. It uses the recursive procedure **Explore**, which takes parameters τ and σ such that $\sigma = \tau(\sigma_0)$. **Explore** will explore all states that can be reached by complete runs extending τ.

First, on line 1, we fetch instructions and commit all local instructions as far as possible from σ. The order of these operations makes no difference. Then we turn to memory accesses. If the run is not yet terminated, we select an enabled event e on line 2.

```
// P[e] holds a run
// preceding the load event e.
global P = λe.⟨⟩
// Q[e] holds a set of continuations
// leading to the execution of the
// load event e after P[e].
global Q = λe.∅

Explore(τ, σ)
      // Fetch & commit local greedily.
 1: while(∃σ'.σ ──FLB──> σ'){σ := σ';}
      // Find committable memory access e.
 2: if(∃e.enabled_σ(e)){
 3:   if(e is a store){
        // Explore all ways to execute e.
 4:     S := {(n,σ')|σ ──e[n]──> σ'};
 5:     for((n,σ') ∈ S){
 6:       Explore(τ.e[n], σ');
 7:     }
 8:     DetectRace(τ, σ, e);
 9:   }else{ // e is a load
10:     P[e] := τ;
        // Explore all ways to execute e
11:     S := {(e_w,σ')|σ ──e[e_w]──> σ'};
12:     for((e_w,σ') ∈ S){
13:       Explore(τ.e[e_w], σ');
14:     }
        // Handle R -> W races.
15:     explored = ∅;
16:     while(∃τ' ∈ Q[e]\explored){
17:       explored := explored∪{τ'};
18:       Traverse(τ, σ, τ');
19:     }
20:   }
21: }
```

```
DetectRace(τ, σ, e)
 1: for⎛ e_r[e_w] ∈ τ s.t.                        ⎞{
       ⎜ e_r is a load ∧ (e_r,e) ∉ cb_σ           ⎟
       ⎝ ∧ address_σ(e_r) = address_σ(e)          ⎠
      // Compute postfix after P[e_r].
 2:   τ' := the τ' s.t. τ = P[e_r].τ';
      // Remove events not cb-before e.
 3:   τ'' := normalize(cut(τ',e,σ),cb_σ);
      // Construct new continuation.
 4:   τ''' := τ''.e[*].e_r[e];
      // Add to Q, to explore later.
 5:   Q[e_r] := Q[e_r]∪{τ'''};
 6: }

Traverse(τ, σ, τ')
 1: if(τ' = ⟨⟩){
 2:   Explore(τ, σ);
 3: }else{
      // Fetch & commit local greedily.
 4:   while(∃σ'.σ ──FLB──> σ'){σ := σ';}
 5:   e[p].τ'' := τ'; // Get first event.
 6:   if(p = *){
        // Explore all ways to execute e
 7:     S := {(n,σ')|σ ──e[n]──> σ'};
 8:     for((n,σ') ∈ S){
 9:       Traverse(τ.e[n], σ', τ'');
10:     }
11:   }else if(∃σ'.σ ──e[p]──> σ'){
12:     Traverse(τ.e[p], σ', τ'');
13:   }else{
        // Only happens when the final
        // load in τ' does not accept its
        // parameter. Stop exploring.
14:   }
15: }
```

Fig. 7. An algorithm to explore all traces of a given program. The initial call is **Explore**$(\langle\rangle, \sigma_0)$.

If the chosen event e is a store (lines 3–8), we first collect, on line 4, all parameters for e which are allowed by the memory model. For each of them, we recursively explore all of its continuations on line 6. I.e., for each coherence position n that is allowed for e by the memory model, we explore the continuation of τ obtained by committing $e[n]$. Finally, we call **DetectRace**. We will return shortly to a discourse of that mechanism.

If e is a load (lines 9–20), we proceed in a similar manner. Line 10 is related to **DetectRace**, and discussed later. On line 11 we compute all allowed parameters for the load e. They are (some of the) stores in τ which access the same address as e. On line 13, we make one recursive call to **Explore** per allowed parameter. The structure of this exploration is illustrated in the two branches from σ_1 to σ_2 and σ_5 in Fig. 8(a).

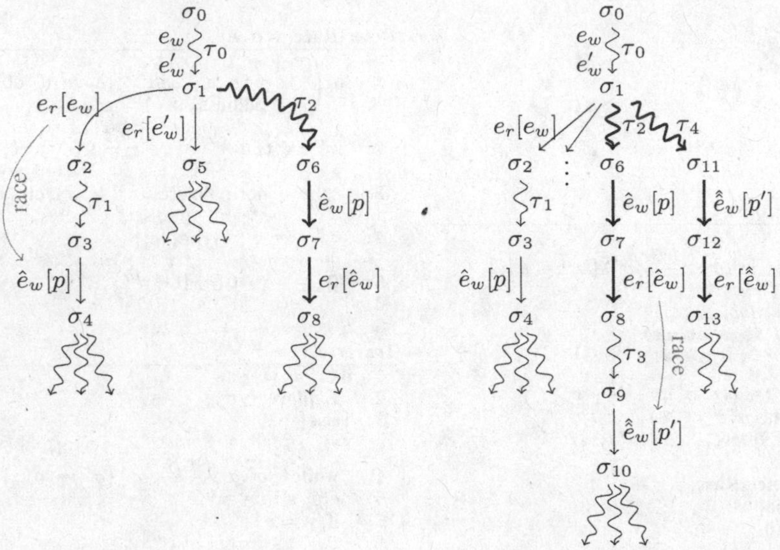

(a) A new branch $\tau_2.\hat{e}_w[*].e_r[\hat{e}_w]$ is added to $\mathbf{Q}[e_r]$ and later explored, starting from σ_1. τ_2 is a restriction of τ_1, containing only events that are cb_{σ_4}-before $\hat{e}_w$.

(b) Another read-write race is detected, starting from the leaf of a branch explored by **Traverse**. The new branch $\tau_4.\hat{\hat{e}}_w[*].e_r[\hat{\hat{e}}_w]$ is added at σ_1, not at σ_7.

Fig. 8. How **Explore** applies event parameters, and introduces new branches. Thin arrows indicate exploration performed directly by **Explore**. Bold arrows indicate traversal by **Traverse**.

Notice in the above that both for stores and loads, the available parameters are determined entirely by τ, i.e. by the events that precede e in the run. In the case of stores, the parameters are coherence positions between the earlier stores occurring in τ. In the case of loads, the parameters are the earlier stores occurring in τ. For stores, this way of exploring is sufficient. But for loads it is necessary to also consider parameters which appear later than the load in a run. Consider the example in Fig. 8(a). During the recursive exploration of a run from σ_0 to σ_4 we encounter a new store $\hat{e}_w$, which is in a race with e_r. If the load e_r and the store $\hat{e}_w$ access the same memory location, and e_r does not precede $\hat{e}_w$ in the cb-order, they could appear in the opposite order in a run (with $\hat{e}_w$ preceding e_r), and $\hat{e}_w$ could be an allowed parameter for the load e_r.

This read-write race is detected on line 1 in the function **DetectRace**, when it is called from line 8 in **Explore** when the store $\hat{e}_w$ is being explored. We must then ensure that some run is explored where $\hat{e}_w$ is committed before e_r so that $\hat{e}_w$ can be considered as a parameter for e_r. Such a run must include all events that are before $\hat{e}_w$ in cb-order, so that $\hat{e}_w$ can be committed. We construct τ_2, which is a template for a new run, including precisely the events in τ_1 which are cb-before the store $\hat{e}_w$. The run template τ_2 can be explored from the state σ_1 (the state where e_r was previously committed) and will then lead to a state where $\hat{e}_w$ can be committed. The run template τ_2 is computed from the complete run in **DetectRace** on lines 2 and 3. This is done by first removing (at line 2) the prefix τ_0 which precedes e_r (stored in P[e_r] on line 10 in **Explore**). Thereafter (at line 3) events that are not cb-before $\hat{e}_w$ are removed using the function cut (here, $\text{cut}(\tau, e, \sigma)$ restricts τ to the events which are cb_σ-before e), and the resulting run is normalized. The function normalize normalizes a run by imposing a predefined order on the events which are not ordered by cb. This is done to avoid unnecessarily exploring two equivalent run templates. The run template $\tau_2.\hat{e}_w[*].e_r[\hat{e}_w]$ is then stored on line 5 in the set Q[e_r], to ensure that it is explored later. Here we use the special pseudo-parameter $*$ to indicate that every allowed parameter for $\hat{e}_w$ should be explored (See lines 6–10 in **Traverse**).

All of the run templates collected in Q[e_r] are explored from the same call to **Explore**(τ_0, σ_1) where e_r was originally committed. This is done on lines 15–19. The new branch is shown in Fig. 8(a) in the run from σ_0 to σ_8. Notice on line 18 that the new branch is explored by the function **Traverse**, rather than by **Explore** itself. This has the effect that τ_2 is traversed, with each event using the parameter given in τ_2, until $e_r[\hat{e}_w]$ is committed. The traversal by **Traverse** is marked with bold arrows in Fig. 8. If the memory model does not allow e_r to be committed with the parameter $\hat{e}_w$, then the exploration of this branch terminates on line 13 in **Traverse**. Otherwise, the exploration continues using **Explore**, as soon as e_r has been committed (line 2 in **Traverse**).

Let us now consider the situation in Fig. 8(b) in the run from σ_0 to σ_{10}. Here $\tau_2.\hat{e}_w[*].e_r[\hat{e}_w]$, is explored as described above. Then **Explore** continues the exploration, and a read-write race is discovered from e_r to $\hat{\hat{e}}_w$. From earlier DPOR algorithms such as e.g. [23], one might expect that this case is handled by exploring a new branch of the form $\tau_2.\hat{e}_w[p].\tau_3'.\hat{\hat{e}}_w[p'].e_r[\hat{\hat{e}}_w]$, where e_r is simply delayed after σ_7 until $\hat{\hat{e}}_w$ has been committed. Our algorithm handles the case differently, as shown in the run from σ_0 to σ_{13}. Notice that P[e_r] can be used to identify the position in the run where e_r was last committed by **Explore** (as opposed to by **Traverse**), i.e., σ_1 in Fig. 8(b). We start the new branch from that position (σ_1), rather than from the position where e_r was committed when the race was detected (i.e., σ_7). The new branch τ_4 is constructed when the race is detected on lines 2 and 3 in **DetectRace**, by restricting the sub-run $\tau_2.\hat{e}_w[p].e_r[\hat{e}_w].\tau_3$ to events that cb-precede the store $\hat{\hat{e}}_w$.

The reason for returning all the way up to σ_1, rather than starting the new branch at σ_7, is to avoid exploring multiple runs corresponding to the same trace. This could otherwise happen when the same race is detected in multiple runs. To see this happen, let us consider the program given in Fig. 9. A part of its exploration tree is given in Fig. 10. In the interest of brevity, when describing the exploration of the program runs, we will ignore some runs which would be explored by the algorithm, but which have no impact on the point of the example. Throughout this example, we will use the labels L0, L1, and L2 to identify the events corresponding to the labelled instructions. We assume that in the first run to be explored (the path from σ_0 to σ_3 in Fig. 10), the load at L0 is committed first (loading the initial value of x), then the stores at L1 and L2. There are two read-write races in this run, from L0 to L1 and to L2. When the races are detected, the branches L1[*].L0[L1] and L2[*].L0[L2] will be added to Q[L0]. These branches are later explored, and appear in Fig. 10 as the paths from σ_0 to σ_6 and from σ_0 to σ_9 respectively. In the run ending in σ_9, we discover the race from L0 to L1 again. This indicates that a run should be explored where L0 reads from L1. If we were to continue exploration from σ_7 by delaying L0 until L1 has been committed, we would follow the path from σ_7 to σ_{11} in Fig. 10. In σ_{11}, we have successfully reversed the race between L0 and L1. However, the trace of σ_{11} turns out to be identical to the one we already explored in σ_6. Hence, by exploring in this manner, we would end up exploring redundant runs. The **Explore** algorithm avoids this redundancy by exploring in the different manner described above: When the race from L0 to L1 is discovered at σ_9, we consider the entire sub-run L2[0].L0[L2].L1[1] from σ_0, and construct the new sub-run L1[*].L0[L1] by removing all events that are not cb-before L1, generalizing the parameter to L1, and by appending L0[L1] to the result. The new branch L1[*].L2[L1] is added to Q[L0]. But Q[L0] already contains the branch L1[*].L2[L1] which was added at the beginning of the exploration. And since it has already been explored (it has already been added to the set explored at line 17) we avoid exploring it again.

```
thread P:    thread Q:    thread R:
L0: r := x   L1: x := 1   L2: x := 2
```

Fig. 9. A small program where one thread P loads from x, and two threads Q and R store to x.

Soundness and Optimality. We first establish soundness of the RSMC algorithm in Fig. 7 for the POWER memory model, in the sense that it guarantees to explore all Shasha-Snir traces of a program. We thereafter establish that RSMC is optimal, in the sense that it will never explore the same complete trace twice.

Theorem 4 (Soundness). Assume that cb is valid w.r.t. M, and that M and cb are deadlock free. Then, for each $\pi \in [\![\mathcal{P}]\!]_M^{Ax}$, the evaluation of a call to **Explore**($\langle\rangle, \sigma_0$) will contain a recursive call to **Explore**(τ, σ) for some τ, σ such that exec(σ) = π.   □

Corollary 1. RSMC is sound for POWER using M^{POWER} and cb^{power}.

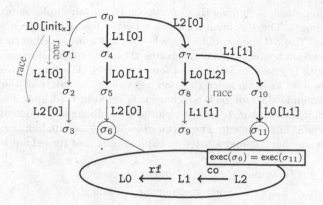

Fig. 10. Part of a faulty exploration tree for the program above, containing redundant branches. The branches ending in σ_6 and σ_{11} correspond to the same trace. The RSMC algorithm avoids this redundancy by the mechanism where all branches for read-write races from the same load e_r are collected in one set $\mathbb{Q}[e_r]$.

The proof of Theorem 4 involves showing that if an allowed trace exists, then the races detected in previously explored runs are sufficient to trigger the later exploration of a run corresponding to that trace.

Theorem 5 (Optimality for POWER). Assume that $M = M^{POWER}$ and $cb = cb^{power}$. Let $\pi \in [\![\mathcal{P}]\!]_M^{Ax}$. Then during the evaluation of a call to **Explore**$(\langle\rangle, \sigma_0)$, there will be exactly one call **Explore**(τ, σ) such that $exec(\sigma) = \pi$. ⊓

While the RSMC algorithm is optimal in the sense that it explores precisely one complete run per Shasha-Snir trace, it may initiate explorations that block before reaching a complete trace (similarly to sleep set blocking in classical DPOR). Such blocking may arise when the RSMC algorithm detects a read-write race and adds a branch to $\mathbb{Q}$, which upon traversal turns out to be not allowed under the memory model. Our experiments in Sect. 4 indicate that the effect of such blocking is almost negligible, without any blocking in most benchmarks, and otherwise at most 10 % of explored runs.

4 Experimental Results

In order to evaluate the efficiency of our approach, we have implemented it as a part of the open source tool Nidhugg [33], for stateless model checking of C/pthreads programs under the relaxed memory. It operates under the restrictions that (i) all executions are bounded by loop unrolling, and (ii) the analysis runs on a given compilation of the target C code. The implementation uses RSMC to explore all allowed program behaviors under POWER, and detects any assertion violation that can occur. We validated our implementation by successfully running all 8070 relevant litmus tests published with [8].

Table 1. A comparison of running times (in seconds) for our implementation Nidhugg and goto-instrument. The F column indicates whether fences have been inserted code to regain safety. The LB column indicates whether the tools were instructed to unroll loops up to a certain bound. A t/o entry means that the tool failed to complete within 900 s. An asterisk (*) means that the tool found a safety violation. A struck out entry means that the tool gave the wrong answer regarding the safety of the benchmark. The superior running time for each benchmark is given in bold font. The SS column indicates the number of complete traces explored by Nidhugg before detecting an error, exploring all traces, or timing out. The B (for "blocking") column indicates the number of incomplete runs that Nidhugg started to explore, but that turned out to be invalid.

Tool running time (s), and trace count						
	goto-instrument			Nidhugg		
	F	LB	Time	Time	SS	B
dcl_singleton		7	*0.40	*0.13	3	0
dcl_singleton	y	7	5.05	**0.19**	7	0
dekker		10	*229.39	*0.11	5	0
dekker	y	10	t/o	**0.76**	246	0
fib_false			*1.86	t/o	109171	0
fib_false_join			*0.84	*35.46	11938	0
fib_true			7.05	t/o	109122	0
fib_true_join			8.92	57.67	19404	0
indexer		5	68.16	**1.57**	19	0
lamport		8	*635.45	*0.12	3	0
lamport	y	8	t/o	**0.20**	50	2
parker		5	~~1.20~~	*0.13	5	0
parker	y	5	**1.24**	7.44	1126	0
peterson			*0.24	*0.11	3	0
peterson	y		0.19	**0.11**	10	1
pgsql		8	*161.05	*0.11	2	0
pgsql	y	8	t/o	**0.58**	16	0
pgsql_bnd			t/o	*0.11	2	0
pgsql_bnd	y		t/o	t/o	36211	0
stack_safe			**13.84**	73.86	1005	0
stack_unsafe			*1.03	*3.32	20	0
szymanski			*1.02	*0.11	17	0
szymanski	y		304.87	**0.31**	226	0

The main goals of our experimental evaluation are (i) to show the feasibility and competitiveness of our approach, in particular to show for which programs it performs well, (ii) to compare with goto-instrument, which to our knowledge is

the only other tool analyzing C/pthreads programs under POWER[2], and (iii) to
show the effectiveness of our approach in terms of wasted exploration effort.

Table 1 shows running times for Nidhugg and goto-instrument for several
benchmarks in C/pthreads. All benchmarks were run on an 3.07 GHz Intel Core
i7 CPU with 6 GB RAM. We use goto-instrument version 5.1 with cbmc version
5.1 as backend.

We note here that the comparison of running time is mainly relevant for the
benchmarks where *no* error is detected (errors are indicated with a * in Table 1).
This is because when an error is detected, a tool may terminate its analysis
without searching the remaining part of the search space (i.e., the remaining
runs in our case). Therefore the time consumption in such cases, is determined
by whether the search strategy was lucky or not. This also explains why in
e.g. the dekker benchmark, fewer Shasha-Snir traces are explored in the version
without fences, than in the version *with* fences.

Comparison with goto-instrument. goto-instrument employs code-to-code transformation in order to allow verification tools for SC to work for more relaxed
memory models such as TSO, PSO and POWER [5]. The results in Table 1
show that our technique is competitive. In many cases Nidhugg significantly
outperforms goto-instrument. The benchmarks for which goto-instrument performs better than Nidhugg, have in common that goto-instrument reports that
no trace may contain a cycle which indicates non-SC behavior. This allows goto-
instrument to avoid expensive program instrumentation to capture the extra
program behaviors caused by memory consistency relaxation. While this treatment is very beneficial in some cases (e.g. for stack_* which is data race free and
hence has no non-SC executions), it also leads to false negatives in cases like
parker, when goto-instrument fails to detect Shasha Snir-cycles that cause safety
violations. In contrast, our technique is precise, and will never miss any behaviors caused by the memory consistency violation within the execution length
bound.

We remark that our approach is restricted to thread-wisely deterministic
programs with fixed input data, whereas the bounded model-checking used as
a backend (CBMC) for goto-instrument can handle both concurrency and data
nondeterminism.

Efficiency of Our Approach. While our RSMC algorithm explores precisely one
complete run per Shasha-Snir trace, it may additionally start to explore runs
that then turn out to block before completing, as described in Sect. 3. The SS
and B columns of Table 1 indicate that the effect of such blocking is almost
negligible, with no blocking in most benchmarks, and at most 10 % of the runs.

A costly aspect of our approach is that every time a new event is committed
in a trace, Nidhugg will check which of its possible parameters are allowed by the
axiomatic memory model. This check is implemented as a search for particular

---

[2] The cbmc tool previously supported POWER [6], but has withdrawn support in
later versions.

cycles in a graph over the committed events. The cost is alleviated by the fact that RSMC is optimal, and avoids exploring unnecessary traces.

To illustrate this tradeoff, we present the small program in Fig. 11. The first three lines of each thread implement the classical Dekker idiom. It is impossible for both threads to read the value 0 in the same execution. This property is used to implement a critical section, containing the lines L4–L13 and M4–M13. However, if the fences at L1 and M1 are removed, the mutual exclusion property can be violated, and the critical sections may execute in an interleaved manner. The program *with* fences has only three allowed Shasha-Snir traces, corresponding to the different observable orderings of the first three instructions of both threads. *Without* the fences, the number rises to 184759, due to the many possible interleavings of the repeated stores to z. The running time of Nidhugg is 0.01 s with fences and 161.36 s without fences.

```
x = 0    y = 0    z = 0

thread P:          thread Q:
L0:  x := 1;       M0:  y := 1;
L1:  sync;         M1:  sync;
L2:  r0 := y;      M2:  r1 := x;
L3:  if r0 = 1     M3:  if r1 = 1
        goto L14;         goto M14;
L4:  z := 1;       M4:  z := 1;
L5:  z := 1;       M5:  z := 1;
L6:  z := 1;       M6:  z := 1;
L7:  z := 1;       M7:  z := 1;
L8:  z := 1;       M8:  z := 1;
L9:  z := 1;       M9:  z := 1;
L10: z := 1;       M10: z := 1;
L11: z := 1;       M11: z := 1;
L12: z := 1;       M12: z := 1;
L13: z := 1;       M13: z := 1;
L14: r0 := 0;      M14: r1 := 0;
```

Fig. 11. SB+10W+syncs: A litmus test based on the idiom known as "Dekker" or "SB". It has 3 allowed Shasha-Snir traces under POWER. If the sync fences at lines L1 and M1 are removed, then it has 184759 allowed Shasha-Snir traces. This test is designed to have a large difference between the *total* number of coherent Shasha-Snir traces and the number of *allowed* Shasha-Snir traces.

We compare this with the results of the litmus test checking tool herd [8], which operates by generating all possible Shasha-Snir traces, and then checking which are allowed by the memory model. The running time of herd on SB+10W+syncs is 925.95 s with fences and 78.09 s without fences. Thus herd performs better than Nidhugg on the litmus test without fences. This is because a large proportion of the possible Shasha-Snir traces are allowed by the memory model. For each of them herd needs to check the trace only once. On the other hand, when the fences are added, the performance of herd deteriorates. This is because herd still checks every Shasha-Snir trace against the memory model, and each check becomes more expensive, since the fences introduce many new dependency edges into the traces.

We conclude that our approach is particularly superior for application style programs with control structures, mutual exclusion primitives etc., where relaxed memory effects are significant, but where most potential Shasha-Snir traces are forbidden.

5   Conclusions

We present the first framework for efficient SMC for programs running under POWER. It combines solutions to several challenges. We developed a scheme for systematically deriving execution models that are suitable for SMC, from axiomatic ones. We present RSMC, a novel algorithm for exploring all relaxed-memory traces of a program, based on our derived execution model. We show that RSMC is sound for POWER, meaning that it explores all Shasha-Snir traces of a program, and optimal in the sense that it explores the same complete trace exactly once. RSMC can in some situations waste effort by exploring blocked runs, but our experimental results shows that this is rare in practice. Our implementation shows that the RSMC approach is competitive relative to an existing state-of-the-art implementation. We expect that RSMC will be sound also for other similar memory models with suitably defined commit-before functions.

Related Work. Several SMC techniques have been recently developed for programs running under the memory models TSO and PSO [1,20,49]. In this work we propose a novel and efficient SMC technique for programs running under POWER.

In [8], a similar execution model was suggested, also based on the axiomatic semantics. However, compared to our semantics, it will lead many spurious executions that will be blocked by the semantics as they are found to be disallowed. This would cause superfluous runs to be explored, if used as a basis for stateless model checking.

Beyond SMC techniques for relaxed memory models, there have been many works related to the verification of programs running under relaxed memory models (e.g., [3,11,13–15,19,30,31,35,48]). Some of these works propose precise analysis techniques for finite-state programs under relaxed memory models (e.g., [3,11,21]). Others propose algorithms and tools for monitoring and testing programs running under relaxed memory models (e.g., [14–16,22,35]). Different techniques based on explicit state-space exploration for the verification of programs running under relaxed memory models have also been developed during the last years (e.g., [27,30,31,34,38]). There are also a number of efforts to design bounded model checking techniques for programs under relaxed memory models (e.g., [6,13,46,48]) which encode the verification problem in SAT/SMT. Finally, there are code-to-code transformation techniques (e.g., [5,10,11]) which reduce verification of a program under relaxed memory models to verification of a transformed program under SC. Most of these works do not handle POWER. In [21], the robustness problem for POWER has been shown to be PSPACE-complete.

The closest works to ours were presented in [5,6,8]. The work [5] extends cbmc to work with relaxed memory models (such as TSO, PSO and POWER) using a code-to-code transformation. The work in [6] develops a bounded model checking technique that can be applied to different memory models (e.g., TSO, PSO, and POWER). The cbmc tool previously supported POWER [6], but has withdrawn support in its later versions. The tool herd [8] operates by generating all possible Shasha-Snir traces, and then for each one of them checking whether it is allowed by the memory model. In Sect. 4, we experimentally compare RSMC with the tools of [5,8].

References

1. Abdulla, P.A., Aronis, S., Atig, M.F., Jonsson, B., Leonardsson, C., Sagonas, K.: Stateless model checking for TSO and PSO. In: Baier, C., Tinelli, C. (eds.) TACAS 2015. LNCS, vol. 9035, pp. 353–367. Springer, Heidelberg (2015)
2. Abdulla, P.A., Aronis, S., Jonsson, B., Sagonas, K.F.: Optimal dynamic partial order reduction. In: POPL, pp. 373–384. ACM (2014)
3. Abdulla, P.A., Atig, M.F., Chen, Y.-F., Leonardsson, C., Rezine, A.: Counter-example guided fence insertion under TSO. In: Flanagan, C., König, B. (eds.) TACAS 2012. LNCS, vol. 7214, pp. 204–219. Springer, Heidelberg (2012)
4. Abdulla, P.A., Atig, M.F., Jonsson, B., Leonardsson, C.: Stateless model checking for POWER (to appear)
5. Alglave, J., Kroening, D., Nimal, V., Tautschnig, M.: Software verification for weak memory via program transformation. In: Felleisen, M., Gardner, P. (eds.) ESOP 2013. LNCS, vol. 7792, pp. 512–532. Springer, Heidelberg (2013)
6. Alglave, J., Kroening, D., Tautschnig, M.: Partial orders for efficient bounded model checking of concurrent software. In: Sharygina, N., Veith, H. (eds.) CAV 2013. LNCS, vol. 8044, pp. 141–157. Springer, Heidelberg (2013)
7. Alglave, J., Maranget, L.: Stability in weak memory models. In: Gopalakrishnan, G., Qadeer, S. (eds.) CAV 2011. LNCS, vol. 6806, pp. 50–66. Springer, Heidelberg (2011)
8. Alglave, J., Maranget, L., Tautschnig, M.: Herding cats: modelling, simulation, testing, and data mining for weak memory. ACM Trans. Program. Lang. Syst. **36**(2), 7:1–7:74 (2014)
9. ARM: ARM Architecture Reference Manual, ARMv7-A and ARMv7-R edition (2014)
10. Atig, M.F., Bouajjani, A., Parlato, G.: Getting rid of store-buffers in TSO analysis. In: Gopalakrishnan, G., Qadeer, S. (eds.) CAV 2011. LNCS, vol. 6806, pp. 99–115. Springer, Heidelberg (2011)
11. Bouajjani, A., Derevenetc, E., Meyer, R.: Checking and enforcing robustness against TSO. In: Felleisen, M., Gardner, P. (eds.) ESOP 2013. LNCS, vol. 7792, pp. 533–553. Springer, Heidelberg (2013)
12. Boudol, G., Petri, G., Serpette, B.P.: Relaxed operational semantics of concurrent programming languages. In: EXPRESS/SOS 2012. EPTCS, vol. 89, pp. 19–33 (2012)
13. Burckhardt, S., Alur, R., Martin, M.M.K.: CheckFence: checking consistency of concurrent data types on relaxed memory models. In: PLDI, pp. 12–21. ACM (2007)
14. Burckhardt, S., Musuvathi, M.: Effective program verification for relaxed memory models. In: Gupta, A., Malik, S. (eds.) CAV 2008. LNCS, vol. 5123, pp. 107–120. Springer, Heidelberg (2008)
15. Burnim, J., Sen, K., Stergiou, C.: Sound and complete monitoring of sequential consistency for relaxed memory models. In: Abdulla, P.A., Leino, K.R.M. (eds.) TACAS 2011. LNCS, vol. 6605, pp. 11–25. Springer, Heidelberg (2011)
16. Burnim, J., Sen, K., Stergiou, C.: Testing concurrent programs on relaxed memory models. In: ISSTA, pp. 122–132. ACM (2011)
17. Christakis, M., Gotovos, A., Sagonas, K.F.: Systematic testing for detecting concurrency errors in erlang programs. In: ICST, pp. 154–163. IEEE Computer Society (2013)

18. Clarke, E.M., Grumberg, O., Minea, M., Peled, D.A.: State space reduction using partial order techniques. STTT **2**(3), 279–287 (1999)
19. Dan, A.M., Meshman, Y., Vechev, M., Yahav, E.: Predicate abstraction for relaxed memory models. In: Logozzo, F., Fähndrich, M. (eds.) Static Analysis. LNCS, vol. 7935, pp. 84–104. Springer, Heidelberg (2013)
20. Demsky, B., Lam, P.: SATCheck: SAT-directed stateless model checking for SC and TSO. In: OOPSLA 2015, pp. 20–36. ACM (2015)
21. Derevenetc, E., Meyer, R.: Robustness against power is PSpace-complete. In: Esparza, J., Fraigniaud, P., Husfeldt, T., Koutsoupias, E. (eds.) ICALP 2014, Part II. LNCS, vol. 8573, pp. 158–170. Springer, Heidelberg (2014)
22. Flanagan, C., Freund, S.N.: Adversarial memory for detecting destructive races. In: PLDI, pp. 244–254. ACM (2010)
23. Flanagan, C., Godefroid, P.: Dynamic partial-order reduction for model checking software. In: POPL, pp. 110–121. ACM (2005)
24. Godefroid, P. (ed.): Partial-Order Methods for the Verification of Concurrent Systems. LNCS, vol. 1032. Springer, Heidelberg (1996)
25. Godefroid, P.: Model checking for programming languages using verisoft. In: POPL, pp. 174–186. ACM Press (1997)
26. Godefroid, P.: Software model checking: the VeriSoft approach. Form. Methods Syst. Des. **26**(2), 77–101 (2005)
27. Huynh, T.Q., Roychoudhury, A.: Memory model sensitive bytecode verification. Form. Methods Syst. Des. **31**(3), 281–305 (2007)
28. IBM: Power ISA, Version 2.07 (2013)
29. Intel Corporation: Intel 64 and IA-32 Architectures Software Developers Manual (2012)
30. Kuperstein, M., Vechev, M.T., Yahav, E.: Automatic inference of memory fences. In: FMCAD, pp. 111–119. IEEE (2010)
31. Kuperstein, M., Vechev, M.T., Yahav, E.: Partial-coherence abstractions for relaxed memory models. In: PLDI, pp. 187–198. ACM (2011)
32. Lamport, L.: How to make a multiprocessor that correctly executes multiprocess programs. IEEE Trans. Comput. **28**(9), 690–691 (1979)
33. Leonardsson, C.: Nidhugg. https://github.com/nidhugg/nidhugg
34. Linden, A., Wolper, P.: A verification-based approach to memory fence insertion in PSO memory systems. In: Piterman, N., Smolka, S.A. (eds.) TACAS 2013 (ETAPS 2013). LNCS, vol. 7795, pp. 339–353. Springer, Heidelberg (2013)
35. Liu, F., Nedev, N., Prisadnikov, N., Vechev, M.T., Yahav, E.: Dynamic synthesis for relaxed memory models. In: PLDI, pp. 429–440. ACM (2012)
36. Mador-Haim, S., et al.: An axiomatic memory model for POWER multiprocessors. In: Madhusudan, P., Seshia, S.A. (eds.) CAV 2012. LNCS, vol. 7358, pp. 495–512. Springer, Heidelberg (2012)
37. Musuvathi, M., Qadeer, S., Ball, T., Basler, G., Nainar, P.A., Neamtiu, I.: Finding and reproducing Heisenbugs in concurrent programs. In: OSDI, pp. 267–280. USENIX (2008)
38. Park, S., Dill, D.L.: An executable specification and verifier for relaxed memory order. IEEE Trans. Comput. **48**(2), 227–235 (1999)
39. Peled, D.A.: All from one, one for all: on model checking using representatives. In: Courcoubetis, C. (ed.) CAV 1993. LNCS, vol. 697, pp. 403–423. Springer, Heidelberg (1993)
40. Saarikivi, O., Kähkönen, K., Heljanko, K.: Improving dynamic partial order reductions for concolic testing. In: ACSD, pp. 132–141. IEEE Computer Society (2012)

41. Sarkar, S., Memarian, K., Owens, S., Batty, M., Sewell, P., Maranget, L., Alglave, J., Williams, D.: Synchronising C/C++ and POWER. In: PLDI, pp. 311–322. ACM (2012)

42. Sarkar, S., Sewell, P., Alglave, J., Maranget, L., Williams, D.: Understanding POWER multiprocessors. In: PLDI, pp. 175–186. ACM (2011)

43. Sen, K., Agha, G.: A race-detection and flipping algorithm for automated testing of multi-threaded programs. In: Bin, E., Ziv, A., Ur, S. (eds.) HVC 2006. LNCS, vol. 4383, pp. 166–182. Springer, Heidelberg (2007)

44. Shasha, D., Snir, M.: Efficient and correct execution of parallel programs that share memory. ACM Trans. Program. Lang. Syst. **10**(2), 282–312 (1988)

45. SPARC International Inc.: The SPARC Architecture Manual Version 9 (1994)

46. Torlak, E., Vaziri, M., Dolby, J.: MemSAT: checking axiomatic specifications of memory models. In: PLDI, pp. 341–350. ACM (2010)

47. Valmari, A.: Stubborn sets for reduced state space generation. In: Rozenberg, G. (ed.) Advances in Petri Nets 1990. LNCS, vol. 483, pp. 491–515. Springer, Heidelberg (1991)

48. Yang, Y., Gopalakrishnan, G., Lindstrom, G., Slind, K.: Nemos: a framework for axiomatic and executable specifications of memory consistency models. In: IPDPS. IEEE (2004)

49. Zhang, N., Kusano, M., Wang, C.: Dynamic partial order reduction for relaxed memory models. In: PLDI, pp. 250–259. ACM (2015)

Hitting Families of Schedules
for Asynchronous Programs

Dmitry Chistikov[1,2P], Rupak Majumdar[1(✉)], and Filip Niksic[1]

[1] Max Planck Institute for Software Systems (MPI-SWS),
Kaiserslautern and Saarbrücken, Germany
{dch,rupak,fniksic}@mpi-sws.org
[2] Department of Computer Science, University of Oxford, Oxford, UK

Abstract. We consider the following basic task in the testing of concurrent systems. The input to the task is a partial order of events, which models actions performed on or by the system and specifies ordering constraints between them. The task is to determine if some scheduling of these events can result in a bug. The number of schedules to be explored can, in general, be exponential.

Empirically, many bugs in concurrent programs have been observed to have small bug depth; that is, these bugs are exposed by every schedule that orders d specific events in a particular way, irrespective of how the other events are ordered, and d is small compared to the total number of events. To find all bugs of depth d, one needs to only test a *d-hitting family* of schedules: we call a set of schedules a d-hitting family if for each set of d events, and for each allowed ordering of these events, there is some schedule in the family that executes these events in this ordering. The size of a d-hitting family may be much smaller than the number of all possible schedules, and a natural question is whether one can find d-hitting families of schedules that have small size.

In general, finding the size of optimal d-hitting families is hard, even for $d = 2$. We show, however, that when the partial order is a tree, one can explicitly construct d-hitting families of schedules of small size. When the tree is balanced, our constructions are polylogarithmic in the number of events.

1 Introduction

Consider the following basic task in systematic testing of programs. We are given n events $a_1, a_2, \ldots, a_n$, and we ask if the execution of some ordering of these events can cause the program to exhibit a bug. In the worst case, one needs to run $n!$ tests, one corresponding to each ordering of events. Empirically, though, many bugs in programs depend on the precise ordering of a small number of events [3,13,16]. That is, for many bugs, there is some constant d (called the *bug depth*, small in comparison to n) and a subset $a_{i_1}, \ldots, a_{i_d}$ of events such that some ordering of these d events already exposes the bug no matter how

This research was funded in part by the ERC Synergy award (IMPACT).

S. Chaudhuri and A. Farzan (Eds.): CAV 2016, Part II, LNCS 9780, pp. 157–176, 2016.
DOI: 10.1007/978-3-319-41540-6_9

all other events are ordered. This empirical observation is the basis for many different systematic testing approaches such as context-bounded testing [14], delay-bounded testing [6], and PCT [3]. Can we do better than $n!$ tests if we only want to uncover all bugs of depth up to d, for fixed d? An obvious upper bound on the number of tests is given by

$$\binom{n}{d} \cdot d! \le n^d,$$

which picks a test for each choice of d events and each ordering of these events. In this paper, we show that one can do significantly better—in this as well as in more general settings.

Hitting Families of Schedules. We consider a more general instance of the problem, where there is a partial ordering between the n events. A *schedule* is a linearization (a linear extension) of the partial order of events. A dependency between two events a and b in the partial order means that in any test, the event a must execute before b. For example, a may be an action to open a file and b an action that reads from the file, or a may be a callback that enables the callback b.

The *depth* of a bug is the minimum number of events that must be ordered in a specific way for the bug to be exposed by a schedule. For example, consider some two events a and b in the partial order of an execution. If a bug manifests itself only when a occurs before b, the bug depth is 2. If there are three events that must occur in a certain order for a bug to appear, the depth is 3, and so on. For example, an order violation involving two operations is precisely a bug of depth 2: say, event a writes, event b reads, or vice versa (race condition). Basic atomicity violation bugs are of depth 3: event a establishes an invariant, b breaks it, c assumes the invariant established by a; bugs of larger depth correspond to more involved scenarios and capture more complex race conditions. A schedule is said to *hit* a bug if the events that expose the bug occur in the schedule in the required order. The question we study in this paper is whether it is possible to find a family of schedules that hits all potential bugs of depth d, for a fixed $d \ge 2$ —we call such a family a *d-hitting family* of schedules.

For a general partial order, finding an optimal d-hitting family is NP-hard, even when $d = 2$ [24]; in fact, even approximating the optimal size is hard [4,9]. Thus, we focus on a special case: when the Hasse diagram of the partial order is a tree. Our choice is motivated by several concurrent programming models, such as asynchronous programs [8,11,20] and JavaScript events [17], whose execution dependencies can be approximated as trees.

Constructing Hitting Families for Trees. For trees and $d = 2$, it turns out that two schedules are enough, independent of the number of events in the tree. These two schedules correspond to leftmost and rightmost DFS (depth-first) traversals of the tree, respectively.

For $d > 2$ and an execution tree of n events, we have already mentioned the upper bound of n^d for the size of an optimal d-hitting family (cf. delay-bounded scheduling [6]). Our main technical results show that this family can be exponentially sub-optimal. For $d = 3$ and a balanced tree on n nodes, we show an explicit construction of a 3-hitting family of size $O(\log n)$, which is optimal up to a constant factor. (Our construction works on a more general partial order, which we call a *double tree*.) For each $d > 3$, we show an explicit construction of a d-hitting family of size $f(d) \cdot (\log n)^{d-1}$, which is optimal up to a polynomial. Here $f(d)$ is an exponential function depending only on d. As a corollary, the two constructions give explicit d-hitting families of size $O(\log n)$ (for $d = 3$) and $O((\log n)^{d-1})$ (for $d > 3$) for antichains, i.e., for the partial order that has no dependencies between the n events. We also show a lower bound on the size of d-hitting families in terms of the height of the tree; in a dual way, for an antichain of n events, the size of any d-hitting family is at least $g(d) \cdot \log n$ for each $d > 2$.

For a testing scenario where the *height* of the tree (the size of the maximum chain of dependencies) is exponentially smaller than its *size* (the number of events), our constructions give explicit test suites that are exponentially smaller than the size—in contrast to previous techniques for systematic testing.

Related Work. Our notion of bug depth is similar to bug depth for shared-memory multi-threaded programs introduced in [3]. The quantity in [3] is defined as the minimal number of additional constraints that guarantee an occurrence of the bug. Depending on the bug, this can be between half our d and one less than our d. Burckhardt et al. [3] show an $O(mn^{d'-1})$ family for m threads with n instructions in total (d' denotes bug depth according to their definition). Since multi-threaded programs can generate arbitrary partial orders, it is difficult to prove optimality of hitting families in this case.

Our notion of d-hitting families is closely related to the notion of *order dimension* for a partial order, defined as the smallest number of linearizations, the intersection of which gives rise to the partial order [5, 19, 23]. Specifically, the size of an optimal 2-hitting family is the order dimension of a partial order, and the size of an optimal d-hitting family is a natural generalization. To the best of our knowledge, general d-hitting families have not been studied before for general partial orders. A version of the dimension ($d = 2$) called fractional dimension is known to be of use for approximation of some problems in scheduling theory [2]. Other generalizations of the dimension are also known (see, e.g., [22]), but, to the best of our knowledge, none of them is equivalent to ours.

Summary. The contribution of this paper is as follows:

- We introduce d-hitting families as a common framework for systematic testing (Sect. 2). The size of optimal d-hitting families generalizes the order dimension for partial orders, and the families themselves are natural combinatorial objects of independent interest.

– We provide explicit constructions of d-hitting families for trees that are close to optimal: up to a small constant factor for $d = 3$ and up to a polynomial for $d > 3$ (Sects. 3–5). Our families of schedules can be exponentially smaller than the size of the partial order.

We outline some challenges in going from our theoretical constructions to building practical and automated test generation tools in Sect. 6.

2   Hitting Families of Schedules

In this section, we first recall the standard terminology of partial orders, and then proceed to define schedules (linearizations of these partial orders) and hitting families of schedules.

Preliminaries: Partial Orders. A *partial order* (also known as a partially ordered set, or a poset) is a pair $(\mathcal{P}, \leq)$ where $\mathcal{P}$ is a set and $\leq$ is a binary relation on $\mathcal{P}$ that is:

(1) reflexive: $x \leq x$ for all $x \in \mathcal{P}$,
(2) antisymmetric: $x \leq y$ and $y \leq x$ imply $x = y$ for all $x, y \in \mathcal{P}$,
(3) transitive: $x \leq y$ and $y \leq z$ imply $x \leq z$ for all $x, y, z \in \mathcal{P}$.

One typically uses $\mathcal{P}$ to refer to $(\mathcal{P}, \leq)$. We will refer to elements of partial orders as *events*; the *size* of $\mathcal{P}$ is the number of events in it, $|\mathcal{P}|$.

The relation $x \leq y$ is also written as $x \leq_\mathcal{P} y$ and as $y \geq x$; the event x is a *predecessor* of y, and y is a *successor* of x. One writes $x < y$ iff $x \leq y$ and $x \neq y$. Furthermore, x is an *immediate predecessor* of y (and y is an *immediate successor* of x) if $x < y$ but there is no $z \in \mathcal{P}$ such that $x < z < y$. The *Hasse diagram* of a partial order $\mathcal{P}$ is a directed graph where the set of vertices is $\mathcal{P}$ and an edge (x, y) exists if and only if x is an immediate predecessor of y. Partial orders are sometimes identified with their Hasse diagrams.

Events x and y are *comparable* iff $x \leq y$ or $y \leq x$. Otherwise they are *incomparable*, which is written as $x \parallel y$. Partial orders $(\mathcal{P}_1, \leq_1)$ and $(\mathcal{P}_2, \leq_2)$ are *disjoint* if $\mathcal{P}_1 \cap \mathcal{P}_2 = \emptyset$; the *parallel composition* (or *disjoint union*) of such partial orders is the partial order $(\mathcal{P}, \leq)$ where $\mathcal{P} = \mathcal{P}_1 \cup \mathcal{P}_2$ and $x \leq y$ iff $x, y \in \mathcal{P}_k$ for some $k \in \{1, 2\}$ and $x \leq_k y$. In this partial order, which we will denote by $\mathcal{P}_1 \parallel \mathcal{P}_2$, any two events not coming from a single $\mathcal{P}_k$ are incomparable: $x_1 \in \mathcal{P}_1$ and $x_2 \in \mathcal{P}_2$ imply $x_1 \parallel x_2$.

For a partial order $(\mathcal{P}, \leq)$ and a subset $\mathcal{Q} \subseteq \mathcal{P}$, the *restriction* of $(\mathcal{P}, \leq)$ to $\mathcal{Q}$ is the partial order $(\mathcal{Q}, \leq_\mathcal{Q})$ in which, for all $x, y \in \mathcal{Q}$, $x \leq_\mathcal{Q} y$ if and only if $x \leq y$. Instead of $\leq_\mathcal{Q}$ one usually writes $\leq$, thus denoting the restriction by $(\mathcal{Q}, \leq)$. We will also say that the partial order $\mathcal{P}$ *contains* the partial order $\mathcal{Q}$. In general, partial orders $(\mathcal{P}_1, \leq_1)$ and $(\mathcal{P}_2, \leq_2)$ are *isomorphic* iff there exists an isomorphism $f : \mathcal{P}_1 \to \mathcal{P}_2$: a bijective mapping that respects the ordering, i.e., with $x \leq_1 y$ iff $f(x) \leq_2 f(y)$ for all $x, y \in \mathcal{P}_1$. Containment of partial orders is usually understood up to isomorphism.

Schedules and Their Families. A partial order is *linear* (or total) if all its events are pairwise comparable. A linearization (linear extension) of the partial order $(\mathcal{P}, \leq)$ is a partial order of the form $(\mathcal{P}, \leq')$ that is linear and has $\leq'$ which is a superset of $\leq$. We call linearizations (linear extensions) of $\mathcal{P}$ *schedules*. In other words, a schedule α is a permutation of the elements of $\mathcal{P}$ that *respects* $\mathcal{P}$, i.e., *respects* all constraints of the form $x \leq y$ from $\mathcal{P}$: for all pairs $x, y \in \mathcal{P}$, whenever $x \leq_\mathcal{P} y$, it also holds that $x \leq_\alpha y$. We denote the set of all possible schedules by $S(\mathcal{P})$; a *family* of schedules for $\mathcal{P}$ is simply a subset of $S(\mathcal{P})$.

In what follows, we often treat schedules as words and families of schedules as languages. Indeed, let $\mathcal{P}$ have n elements $\{v_1, \ldots, v_n\}$, then any schedule α can be viewed as a word of length n over the alphabet $\{v_1, \ldots, v_n\}$ where each letter occurs exactly once. We say that α *schedules* events in the order of occurrences of letters in the word that represents it.

Suppose α_1 and α_2 are schedules for disjoint partial orders $\mathcal{P}_1$ and $\mathcal{P}_2$; then $\alpha_1 \cdot \alpha_2$ is a schedule for the partial order $\mathcal{P}_1 \parallel \mathcal{P}_2$ that first schedules all events from $\mathcal{P}_1$ according to α_1 and then all events from $\mathcal{P}_2$ according to α_2. Note that we will use the $\cdot$ to concatenate schedules (as well as individual events); since some of our partially ordered sets will contain strings, concatenation "inside" an event will be denoted simply by juxtaposition.

Admissible Tuples and d-Hitting Families. Fix a partial order $\mathcal{P}$ and let $\boldsymbol{a} = (a_1, \ldots, a_d)$ be a tuple of $d \geq 2$ distinct elements of $\mathcal{P}$; we call such tuples *d-tuples.* Suppose α is a schedule for $\mathcal{P}$; then the schedule α *hits* the tuple $\boldsymbol{a}$ if the restriction of α to the set $\{a_1, \ldots, a_d\}$ is the sequence $a_1 \cdot \ldots \cdot a_d$.

Note that for a tuple $\boldsymbol{a}$ to have a schedule that hits $\boldsymbol{a}$ it is necessary and sufficient that α respect $\mathcal{P}$; this condition is equivalent to the condition that $a_i \leq a_j$ or $a_i \parallel a_j$ whenever $1 \leq i \leq j \leq d$. We call d-tuples satisfying this condition *admissible*.

Definition 1 (d-hitting family). A family of schedules F for $\mathcal{P}$ is *d-hitting* if for every admissible d-tuple $\boldsymbol{a}$ there is a schedule $\alpha \in F$ that hits $\boldsymbol{a}$.

It is straightforward that every $\mathcal{P}$ with $|\mathcal{P}| = n$ has a d-hitting family of size at most $\binom{n}{d} \cdot d! \leq n^d$: just take any hitting schedule for each admissible d-tuple, of which there are at most $\binom{n}{d} \cdot d!$. For $d = 2$, the size of the smallest 2-hitting family is known as the dimension of the partial order [5, 23]. Computing and even approximating the dimension for general partial orders is known to be a hard problem [4, 9, 24]. In the remainder of the paper, we focus on d-hitting families for specific partial orders, most importantly trees (which can, for instance, approximate happens-before relations of asynchronous programs). We first consider two simple examples.

Example 2 (chain). Consider a chain of n events (a linear order): $\mathcal{C}_n = \{1, \ldots, n\}$ with $1 < 2 < \ldots < n$. This partial order has a unique schedule: $\alpha = 1 \cdot 2 \cdot \ldots \cdot n$; a d-tuple $\boldsymbol{a} = (a_1, \ldots, a_d)$ is admissible iff $a_1 < \ldots < a_d$, and α hits all such d-tuples. Thus, for any d, the family $F = \{\alpha\}$ is a d-hitting family for $\mathcal{C}_n$.

Example 3 (chain with independent event). Consider $C_n \parallel \{\dagger\}$, the disjoint union of C_n from Example 2 and a singleton $\{\dagger\}$. There are $n + 1$ possible schedules, depending on how $\dagger$ is positioned with respect to the chain: $\alpha_0 = \dagger \cdot 1 \cdot 2 \cdot \ldots \cdot n$, $\alpha_1 = 1 \cdot \dagger \cdot 2 \cdot \ldots \cdot n$, ..., $\alpha_n = 1 \cdot 2 \cdot \ldots \cdot n \cdot \dagger$. For $d = 2$, admissible pairs are of the form (i, j) with $i < j$, $(\dagger, i)$, and $(i, \dagger)$ for all $1 \leq i \leq n$; the family $F_2 = \{\alpha_0, \alpha_n\}$ is the smallest 2-hitting family. Now consider $d = 3$. Note that all triples $(i, \dagger, i + 1)$ with $1 \leq i \leq n - 1$, as well as $(\dagger, 1, 2)$ and $(n - 1, n, \dagger)$, are admissible, and each of them is hit by a unique schedule. Therefore, the smallest 3-hitting family of schedules consists of all $n + 1$ schedules: $F_3 = \{\alpha_0, \ldots, \alpha_n\}$. For $d \geq 4$, it remains to observe that every d-hitting family is necessarily d'-hitting for $2 \leq d' \leq d$, hence F_3 is optimal for all $d \geq 3$.

An important **corollary** of this example is that, for any $d \geq 3$ and any partial order $\mathcal{P}$, every d-hitting family must contain at least $m + 1$ schedules, where m denotes the maximum number n such that $\mathcal{P}$ contains $C_n \parallel \{\dagger\}$. This m is upper-bounded (and this upper bound is tight) by the *height* of the partial order $\mathcal{P}$, sometimes called *length*: the maximal cardinality of a chain (a set of pairwise comparable events) in $\mathcal{P}$.

3   Hitting Families of Schedules for Trees

3.1   Definitions and Overview

Consider a complete binary tree of height h with edges directed from the root. This tree is the Hasse diagram of a partial order $\mathcal{T}^h$, unique up to isomorphism; we will apply tree terminology to $\mathcal{T}^h$ itself. The root of $\mathcal{T}^h$ forms the 0th *layer*, its children the 1st layer and so on. The maximum k such that $\mathcal{T}^h$ has an element in the kth layer is the height of the tree $\mathcal{T}^h$. We will assume that elements of $\mathcal{T}^h$ are strings: $\mathcal{T}^h = \{0, 1\}^{\leq h}$ with $x \leq y$ for $x, y \in \mathcal{T}^h$ iff x is a prefix of y. The kth layer of $\mathcal{T}^h$ is $\{0, 1\}^k$, and nodes of the hth layer are *leaves*. Unless $x \in \mathcal{T}^h$ is a leaf, nodes $x\,0$ and $x\,1$ are left- and right-children of x, respectively. (Recall that the juxtaposition here denotes concatenation of strings, with the purpose of distinguishing individual strings and their sequences.) The tree $\mathcal{T}^h$ has $n = 2^{h+1} - 1$ nodes.

The central question that we study in this paper is as follows: How big are optimal d-hitting families of schedules for $\mathcal{T}^h$ with n nodes?

As it turns out, for $\mathcal{T}^h$ very efficient constructions of d-hitting families exist. It is, in fact, possible to find such families that have size *exponentially smaller* than n, the number of events. More specifically, we prove the following results (h is the height of the partial order—the size of the longest chain):

1. For arbitrary $d \geq 3$, there is a simple d-hitting family of size $O(n^{d-2})$ (Claim 5 in the following Subsect. 3.2).
2. For $d = 3$, there is a 3-hitting family of size $O(h)$ (Theorem 7 in Sect. 4).
3. For arbitrary $d \geq 3$, there is a d-hitting family of size $O(h^{d-1})$ (Theorem 10 in Sect. 5).

Our main technical results are Theorems 7 and 10, shown in the next sections—where they are stated for complete binary trees, with $h = \log(n+1) - 1$. (Arbitrary trees are, of course, contained in these complete trees, and our constructions extend in a natural way.) The remainder of this section is structured as follows. In Subsect. 3.2, we prove, as a warm-up, Claim 5. After this, in Subsect. 3.3, we show that the problem of finding families of schedules with size smaller than n turns out to be tricky even when there are no dependencies between events at all. This problem arises as a sub-problem when considering trees (as, indeed, there are no dependencies between the leaves in a tree), and thus our main constructions in Sects. 4 and 5 must be at least as agile.

3.2   Warm-Up: d-Hitting Families of Size $O(n^{d-2})$

Claim 4. The smallest 2-hitting family of schedules for T^h has size 2.

The construction is as follows. Take $F_{\mathsf{dfs}} = \{\lambda, \rho\}$ where λ and ρ are left-to-right and right-to-left DFS (depth-first) traversals of T^h, respectively. More formally, these schedules are defined as follows: for $x, y \in T^h$, $x \leq_\lambda y$ if either $x \leq y$ (i.e., x is a prefix of y) or $x = u\,0\,x'$ and $y = u\,1\,y'$ for some strings $u, x', y' \in \{0,1\}^*$; $x \leq_\rho y$ if either $x \leq y$ or $x = u\,1\,x'$ and $y = u\,0\,y'$. For instance, T^2 has $\lambda = \varepsilon \cdot 0 \cdot 00 \cdot 01 \cdot 1 \cdot 10 \cdot 11$ and $\rho = \varepsilon \cdot 1 \cdot 11 \cdot 10 \cdot 0 \cdot 01 \cdot 00$. The family F_{dfs} is 2-hitting: all admissible pairs (x, y) satisfy either $x \leq y$, in which case they are hit by any possible schedule, or $x \parallel y$, in which case neither is a prefix of the other, $x = u\,a\,x'$ and $y = u\,\bar{a}\,y'$ with $\{a, \bar{a}\} = \{0, 1\}$, so λ and ρ schedule them in reverse orders. Since it is clear that a family of size 1 cannot be 2-hitting for T^h with $h \geq 1$ (as T^h contains at least one pair of incomparable elements), the family F_{dfs} is optimal.

Based on this construction for $d = 2$, it is possible to find d-hitting families for $d \geq 3$ that have size $o(n^d)$ where $n = 2^{h+1} - 1$ is the number of events in T^h:

Claim 5. For any $d \geq 3$, T^h has a d-hitting family of schedules of size $O(n^{d-2})$.

Indeed, group all admissible d-tuples $a = (a_1, \ldots, a_d)$ into bags agreeing on $a_1, \ldots, a_{d-2}$. For each bag, construct a pair of schedules $\lambda' = \lambda'(a_1, \ldots, a_{d-2})$ and $\rho' = \rho'(a_1, \ldots, a_{d-2})$ as follows. In both λ' and ρ', first *schedule* $a_1, \ldots, a_{d-2}$: that is, start with an empty sequence of events, iterate over $k = 1, \ldots, d-2$, and, for each k, append to the sequence all events $x \in T^h$ such that $x \leq a_k$. The order in which these $x$es are appended is chosen in the unique way that respects the partial order T^h. Events that are predecessors of several a_k are only scheduled once, for the least k. Note that no a_k, $1 \leq k \leq d$, is a predecessor of any a_j for $j < k$, because otherwise the d-tuple $a = (a_1, \ldots, a_d)$ is not admissible. After this, the events of T^h that have not been scheduled yet form a disjoint union of several binary trees. The schedule λ' then schedules all events according to how the left-to-right DFS traversal λ would work on T^h, omitting all events that have already been scheduled, and the schedule ρ' does the same based on ρ. As a result, these two schedules hit all admissible d-tuples that agree on $a_1, \ldots, a_{d-2}$; collecting all such schedules for all possible $a_1, \ldots, a_{d-2}$ makes a d-hitting family for T^h of size at most $2n^{d-2}$.

3.3   Antichains: d-Hitting Families of Size $f(d) \log n$

An *antichain* is a partial order where every two elements are incomparable: $\mathcal{A}_n = \{v_1\} \parallel \{v_2\} \parallel \cdots \parallel \{v_n\}$. The set of all schedules for $\mathcal{A}_n$ is S_n, the set of all permutations, and the set of all admissible d-tuples is the set of all d-arrangements of these n events.

For our problem of finding hitting families of schedules for trees, considering antichains is, in fact, an important subproblem. For example, a complete binary tree with m nodes contains an antichain of size $\lceil m/2 \rceil$: the set of its leaves. Thus, any d-hitting family of sublinear size for the tree must necessarily extend a d-hitting family of sublinear size for the antichain—a problem of independent interest that we study in this section.

Theorem 6. *For any $d \geq 3$, the smallest d-hitting family for $\mathcal{A}_n$ has size between $g(d) \log n - O(1)$ and $f(d) \log n$, where $g(d) \geq d/2 \log(d+1)$ and $f(d) \leq d!\, d$.*

We sketch the proof of Theorem 6 in the remainder of this section. We will show how to obtain the upper bound by two different means: with the probabilistic method and with a greedy approach. From the results of the following Sect. 4 one can extract a derandomization for $d = 3$, also with size $O(\log n)$; and Sect. 5 achieves size $f(d) \cdot (\log n)^{d-1}$ for $d \geq 3$. In the current section we also show a lower bound based on a counting argument; the reasoning above demonstrates that this lower bound for antichains extends to a lower bound for trees (see Corollary 8).

Upper Bound: Probabilistic Method. Consider a family of schedules $F = \{\alpha_1, \ldots, \alpha_k\}$ where each α_i is chosen independently and uniformly at random from S_n; the parameter k will be chosen later. Fix any admissible $\boldsymbol{a} = (a_1, \ldots, a_d)$. What is the probability that a specific α_i does not hit $\boldsymbol{a}$? A random permutation arranges $a_1, \ldots, a_d$ in one of $d!$ possible orders without preference to any of them, so this probability is $1 - 1/d!$. Since all α_i are chosen independently, the probability that none of them hits $\boldsymbol{a}$ is $(1 - 1/d!)^k$. By the union bound, the probability that *at least one* d-tuple $\boldsymbol{a}$ is not hit by any of α_i does not exceed $p = n^d \cdot (1 - 1/d!)^k$.

Now observe that this value of p is exactly the probability that F is not a d-hitting family. If we now choose k in such a way that $p < 1$, then the probability of F being a d-hitting family is non-zero, i.e., a d-hitting family of size k exists. Calculation shows that $k > (d!\, d) \log n / \log e$ suffices.

The probabilistic method, a classic tool in combinatorics, is due to Erdős [1].

Upper Bound: Greedy Approach. We exploit the following connection between d-hitting families and *set covers*. Recall that in a set cover problem one is given a number of sets, $R_1, \ldots, R_s$, and the goal is to find a small number of these sets whose union is equal to $R = R_1 \cup \ldots \cup R_s$. A set R_i covers an element $e \in R$ iff $e \in R_i$, and this covering is essentially the same as hitting in

d-hitting families: elements $e \in R$ are admissible d-tuples $\boldsymbol{a} = (a_1, \ldots, a_d)$, and each schedule α corresponds to a set R_α that contains all d-tuples $\boldsymbol{a}$ that it hits. A d-hitting family of schedules is then the same as a set cover.

A well-known approach to the set cover problem is the greedy algorithm, which in our setting works as follows. Initialize a list of all admissible $\boldsymbol{a} = (a_1, \ldots, a_d)$; on each step, pick some schedule α that hits the largest number of tuples in the list, and cross out all these tuples. Terminate when the list is empty; the set of all picked schedules is a d-hitting family.

While this algorithm can be used for any partial order $\mathcal{P}$, in our case we can estimate the quality of its output. The so-called greedy covering lemma by Sapozhenko [18] or a more widely known Lovász-Stein theorem [12,21] gives an explicit upper bound on the size of the obtained greedy cover in terms of $|R|$ and the density of the instance (the smallest γ such that every $e \in R$ belongs to at least γs out of s sets). In our case, $|R| \leq n^d$, and the density is $1/d!$; the obtained upper bound on the size of the smallest d-hitting family is $d! \, d \cdot \log n / \log e - \Theta(d! \, d \log d)$.

Lower Bound. Consider the case $d = 3$. Take any 3-hitting family $F = \{\alpha_1, \ldots, \alpha_k\}$ and consider the binary matrix $B = (b_{ij})$ of size $k \times (n-1)$ where $b_{ij} = 1$ iff the schedule α_i places event v_j before v_n. We claim that all columns of B are pairwise distinct. Indeed, if for some $j' \neq j''$ and all i it holds that $b_{ij'} = b_{ij''}$, then no schedule from F can place $v_{j'}$ before v_n without also placing $v_{j''}$ before v_n, and vice versa. This means that no schedule from F hits the 3-tuples $\boldsymbol{a}' = (v_{j'}, v_n, v_{j''})$ and $\boldsymbol{a}'' = (v_{j''}, v_n, v_{j'})$, so F cannot be 3-hitting.

Since all columns of B are pairwise distinct and B is a $0/1$-matrix, it follows that the number of columns, $n-1$, cannot be greater than the number of all subsets of its rows, 2^k. From $n - 1 \leq 2^k$ we deduce that $k \geq \log(n-1)$. The construction in the general case $d \geq 3$ is analogous.

As we briefly explained above, the lower bound for an antichain of size n remains valid for any partial order that *contains* an antichain of size n (as defined in Sect. 2). We invoke this argument in Theorem 7 and Corollary 8 in the following section.

4   3-Hitting Families of Size $O(\log n)$

The goal of this section is to construct 3-hitting families of schedules for trees. In fact, the construction that we develop is naturally stated for slightly more involved partial orders, which we call double trees. These double trees are extensions of trees (see Fig. 1). We construct explicit 3-hitting families of schedules of logarithmic size for double trees, so that restriction of these 3-hitting families to appropriate subsets of events gives explicit 3-hitting families for trees and for antichains, also of logarithmic size.

The *(binary) double tree* of half-height $h \geq 1$ is the partial order $\mathcal{D}$ defined as follows. Intuitively, each $\mathcal{D}^h$ is a parallel composition (disjoint union) of two copies of $\mathcal{D}^{h-1}$, with additional top and bottom (largest and smallest) events;

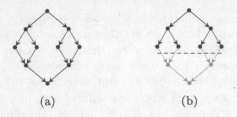

Fig. 1. (a) A double tree ($h = 2$); (b) A tree embedded into a double tree

and the induction basis is that $\mathcal{D}^0$ consists of a single event. Figure 1 depicts $\mathcal{D}^2$, the double tree of half-height 2.

More precisely, (the Hasse diagram of) $\mathcal{D}$ consists of two complete binary trees of height h that share their set of 2^h leaves; in the first tree, the edges are directed from the root to the leaves, and in the second tree, from the leaves to the root. Formally, $\mathcal{D}^h = \{-1, +1\} \times \{0, 1\}^{\leq h-1} \cup \{0\} \times \{0, 1\}^h$; note that the cardinality of this set is $3 \cdot 2^h - 2$. Each event $x = (s_x, x') \in \mathcal{D}^h$ either belongs to one of the trees ($s_x \in \{-1, +1\}$) or is a shared leaf ($s_x = 0$). We define the ordering by taking the transitive closure of the following relation: let $x = (s_x, x')$ and $y = (s_y, y')$ be events of $\mathcal{D}^h$; if $\{s_x, s_y\} \subseteq \{-1, 0\}$, then $x \leq y$ whenever x' is a prefix of y'; and if $\{s_x, s_y\} \subseteq \{0, +1\}$, then $x \leq y$ whenever y' is a prefix of x'. (Note that all events x, y with $s_x = s_y = 0$ are pairwise incomparable.)

Theorem 7. *The smallest 3-hitting family for the double tree $\mathcal{D}^h$ with $n = 3 \cdot 2^h - 2$ events has size between $2h = 2\log n - O(1)$ and $4h = 4\log n - O(1)$.*

Recall that a double tree with $3 \cdot 2^h - 2$ events contains a complete binary tree with $2 \cdot 2^h - 1$ nodes, which in turn contains an antichain of size 2^h. As a corollary, $\mathcal{T}^h$, a tree with $n = 2 \cdot 2^h - 1$ nodes, has a 3-hitting family of size $4h = 4\log(n+1) - 4$. Similarly, $\mathcal{A}_n$, an antichain of size $n = 2^h$, has a 3-hitting family of size $4\log n$. Unlike the constructions from Subsect. 3.3, the construction of Theorem 7 is explicit.

Corollary 8. *For an arbitrary (not necessarily balanced) tree of height h, out-degree at most Δ, and with at least 2 children of the root, the smallest 3-hitting family has size between h and $4h\log\Delta$.*

Note that lower bounds proportional to h follow from Example 3. We describe the construction of Theorem 7 below.

Matrix Notation. We use the following notation for families of schedules. Let $\mathcal{P}$ be a partial order, $|\mathcal{P}| = n$. Let F be a family of schedules for $\mathcal{P}$, $|F| = m$. We then write

$$F = \begin{pmatrix} a_{11} & a_{12} & \cdots & a_{1n} \\ a_{21} & a_{22} & \cdots & a_{2n} \\ \vdots & \vdots & \ddots & \vdots \\ a_{m1} & a_{m2} & \cdots & a_{mn} \end{pmatrix}$$

where $F = \{\alpha_1, \ldots, \alpha_m\}$ and $\alpha_i = a_{i1} \cdot a_{i2} \cdot \ldots \cdot a_{in}$ for $1 \le i \le m$. In other words, a family of m schedules for an n-sized partial order is written as an $m \times n$-matrix whose entries are elements of $\mathcal{P}$, with no element appearing more than once in any row. In particular, if α is a schedule for $\mathcal{P}$, then we represent it with a row vector. The union of families naturally corresponds to stacking of matrices: $F_1 \cup F_2 = \begin{pmatrix} F_1 \\ F_2 \end{pmatrix}$, and putting two matrices of the same height m next to each other corresponds to concatenating two families of size m, in order to obtain a family of size m for the union of two partial orders: $(F_1\ F_2)$.

Construction of 3-Hitting Families for Double Trees. We define the families of schedules using induction on h; in matrix notation, the families will be denoted and structured as follows:

$$M_h = \begin{bmatrix} A_h & B_h \\ C_h & D_h \end{bmatrix}$$

where all four blocks are of size $(3 \cdot 2^{h-1} - 1) \times 2h$; in total, M^h will contain $4h$ schedules, each with $3 \cdot 2^h - 2$ events.

Base case, $h = 1$:

$$[A_1|B_1] = [C_1|D_1] = \begin{bmatrix} (-1,\varepsilon)\ (0,0) & (0,1)\ (+1,\varepsilon) \\ (-1,\varepsilon)\ (0,1) & (0,0)\ (+1,\varepsilon) \end{bmatrix}.$$

Note that M_1 specifies both possible schedules two times. However, this redundancy disappears in the inductive step.

Inductive step from $h \ge 1$ to $h + 1$: Note that, for $\ell \in \{0, 1\}$, restricting $\mathcal{D}^{h+1}$ to events of the form (s, x') where $x' = \ell x''$ leads to a partial order isomorphic to $\mathcal{D}^h$; these two partial orders are disjoint, and we denote them by $\mathcal{D}^h(\ell)$, $\ell \in \{0, 1\}$; in fact, $\mathcal{D}^h(0) \cup \mathcal{D}^h(1) \cup \{(-1, \varepsilon), (+1, \varepsilon)\}$ forms a partition of $\mathcal{D}^{h+1}$. We assume that the matrix M_h is known (the inductive hypothesis); for $\ell \in \{0, 1\}$, we denote its image under the (entry-wise) mapping $(s, x') \mapsto (s, \ell x')$ by $M_h(\ell)$. In other words, $M_h(\ell)$ is the matrix that defines our (soon proved to be 3-hitting) family of schedules for $\mathcal{D}^h(\ell)$; we will also apply the same notation to A, B, C, and D.

Finally, we will need two auxiliary schedules for double trees, which we call *left* and *right* traversals. The left traversal λ of $\mathcal{D}^{h+1}$ is defined inductively as follows: it first schedules $(-1, \varepsilon)$, then takes the left traversal of $\mathcal{D}^h(0)$, then the left traversal of $\mathcal{D}^h(1)$, and then schedules $(+1, \varepsilon)$. The right traversal ρ is defined symmetrically. Denote by $\lambda(\ell)$ and $\rho(\ell)$ left and right traversals of $\mathcal{D}^h(\ell)$, respectively (we omit reference to h since this does not create confusion). Then

$$A_{h+1} = \begin{bmatrix} (-1,\varepsilon) & & & \\ \vdots & A_h(0) & A_h(1) \\ (-1,\varepsilon) & & \\ \hline (-1,\varepsilon) & \lambda(0) \\ (-1,\varepsilon) & \lambda(1) \end{bmatrix}, \quad B_{h+1} = \begin{bmatrix} & & & (+1,\varepsilon) \\ B_h(1) & B_h(0) & \vdots \\ & & (+1,\varepsilon) \\ \hline \lambda(1) & (+1,\varepsilon) \\ \lambda(0) & (+1,\varepsilon) \end{bmatrix},$$

$$C_{h+1} = \begin{bmatrix} (-1,\varepsilon) & & & \\ \vdots & C_h(1) & C_h(0) \\ (-1,\varepsilon) & & \\ \hline (-1,\varepsilon) & \rho(0) \\ (-1,\varepsilon) & \rho(1) \end{bmatrix}, \quad D_{h+1} = \begin{bmatrix} & & & (+1,\varepsilon) \\ D_h(0) & D_h(1) & \vdots \\ & & (+1,\varepsilon) \\ \hline \rho(1) & (+1,\varepsilon) \\ \rho(0) & (+1,\varepsilon) \end{bmatrix}.$$

Our result is that, for each h, M_h is a 3-hitting family of schedules for $\mathcal{D}^h$. The key part of the proof relies on the following auxiliary property, which is a stronger form of the 2-hitting condition.

Lemma 9. *For any pair of distinct events $\boldsymbol{a} = (a_1, a_2)$ from $\mathcal{D}^h$, if there is a schedule for $\mathcal{D}^h$ that hits $\boldsymbol{a}$, then each of the matrices $\begin{bmatrix} A_h | B_h \end{bmatrix}$ and $\begin{bmatrix} C_h | D_h \end{bmatrix}$ contains a schedule for $\mathcal{D}^h$ where a_1 is placed in the first half and a_2 is placed in the second half.*

5 d-Hitting Families for $d \geq 3$ of Size $f(d)(\log n)^{d-1}$

Fix some d and let T^h be a complete binary tree of height h, as defined in Subsect. 3.1. In this section we prove the following theorem.

Theorem 10. *For any $d \geq 2$ the complete binary tree of height h has a d-hitting family of schedules of size $\exp(d) \cdot h^{d-1}$.*

Note that in terms of the number of nodes of T^h, which is $n = 2^{h+1} - 1$, Theorem 10 gives a d-hitting family of size polylogarithmic in n. The proof of the theorem is constructive, and we divide it into three steps. The precise meaning to the steps relies on auxiliary notions of a *pattern* and of d-tuples *conforming to* a pattern; we give all necessary definitions below.

Lemma 11. *For each admissible d-tuple $\boldsymbol{a} = (a_1, \ldots, a_d)$ there exists a pattern p such that $\boldsymbol{a}$ conforms to p.*

Lemma 12. *For each pattern p there exists a schedule α_p that hits all d-tuples $\boldsymbol{a}$ that conform to p.*

Lemma 13. *The total number of patterns, up to isomorphism, does not exceed $\exp(d) \cdot h^{d-1}$.*

The statement of Theorem 10 follows easily from these lemmas. The key insight is the definition of the pattern and the construction of Lemma 12.

In the sequel, for partial orders that are trees directed from the root we will use the standard terminology for graphs and trees (relying on Hasse diagrams): node, outdegree, siblings, 0- and 1-principal subtree of a node, isomorphism. We denote the parent of a node u by par u and the *least common ancestor* of nodes u and v by $\text{lca}(u, v)$.

If T is a tree and $X \subseteq T$ is a subset of its nodes, then by $[X]$ we denote the lca-closure of X: the smallest set $Y \subseteq T$ such that, first, $X \subseteq Y$ and, second, for any $y_1, y_2 \in Y$ it holds that $\text{lca}(y_1, y_2) \in Y$. The following claim is a variation of a folklore Lemma 1 in [7].

Claim 14. $\|[X]\| \leq 2|X| - 1$.

Definition 15 (pattern). A *pattern* is a quintuple $p = (D, \preccurlyeq, s, \ell, \pi)$ where:

- $d \leq |D| \leq 2d - 1$,
- $(D, \preccurlyeq)$ is a partial order which is, moreover, a tree directed from the root,
- the number of non-leaf nodes in $(D, \preccurlyeq)$ does not exceed $d - 1$,
- each node of $(D, \preccurlyeq)$ has outdegree at most 2,
- the partial function $s\colon D \rightharpoonup \{0, 1\}$ specifies, for each pair of siblings v_1, v_2 in $(D, \preccurlyeq)$, which is the left and which is the right child of its parent: $s(v_t) = 0$ and $s(v_{3-t}) = 1$ for some $t \in \{1, 2\}$; the value of s is undefined on all other nodes of D,
- the partial function $\ell\colon D \rightharpoonup \{0, 1, \ldots, h - 1\}$ associates a *layer* with each non-leaf node of $(D, \preccurlyeq)$, so that $u \prec v$ implies $\ell(u) < \ell(v)$; the value of ℓ is undefined on all leaves of D, and
- π is a schedule for $(D, \preccurlyeq)$.

We remind the reader that the symbol $\leq$ refers to the same partial order as T^h.

Definition 16 (conformance). Take any pattern $p = (D, \preccurlyeq, s, \ell, \pi)$ and any tuple $\boldsymbol{a} = (a_1, \ldots, a_d)$ of d distinct elements of the partial order T^h. Consider the set $\{a_1, \ldots, a_d\}$: the restriction of $\leq$ to its lca-closure $A = [\{a_1, \ldots, a_d\}]$ is a binary tree, $(A, \leq)$. Suppose that the following conditions are satisfied:

(a) the trees $(D, \preccurlyeq)$ and $(A, \leq)$ are isomorphic: there exists a bijective mapping $i\colon D \to A$ such that $v_1 \preccurlyeq v_2$ in D iff $i(v_1) \leq i(v_2)$ in T^h;
(b) the partial function s correctly indicates left- and right-subtree relations: for any $v \in D$, $s(v) = b \in \{0, 1\}$ if and only if $i(v)$ lies in the b-principal subtree of $i(\text{par}(v))$;
(c) the partial function ℓ correctly specifies the layer inside T^h: for any non-leaf $v \in D$, $\ell(v) = |i(v)|$; recall that elements of T^h are binary strings from $\{0, 1\}^{\leq h}$;
(d) the schedule π for $(D, \preccurlyeq)$ hits the tuple $i^{-1}(\boldsymbol{a}) = (i^{-1}(a_1), \ldots, i^{-1}(a_d))$.

Then we shall say that the tuple $\boldsymbol{a}$ *conforms to* the pattern p.

We now sketch the proof of Lemma 12. Fix any pattern $p = (D, \preccurlyeq, s, \ell, \pi)$. Recall that we need to find a schedule α_p that hits all d-tuples $\boldsymbol{a} = (a_1, \ldots, a_d)$

```
<img src="..." onload="javascript:loaded()"/>
<script>
  function loaded() {
    document.getElementById('p').innerHTML = 'Loaded';
  }
</script>
<p id="p">Waiting...</p>
```

Fig. 2. Example of bugs of depth $d = 2$ and $d = 3$ in a web page

conforming to p. We will pursue the following strategy. We will cut the tree T^h into multiple pieces; this cutting will be entirely determined by the pattern p, independent of any individual a. Each piece in the cutting will be associated with some element $c \in D$, so that each element of D can have several pieces associated with it. In fact, every piece will form a subtree of T^h (although this will be of little importance). The key property is that, for every d-tuple $a = (a_1, \ldots, a_d)$ conforming to p, if i is the isomorphism from Definition 16, then each event a_k, $1 \leq k \leq d$, will belong to a piece associated with $i^{-1}(a_k)$. As a result, the desired schedule α_p can be obtained in the following way: arrange the pieces according to how π schedules elements of D and pick any possible schedule inside each piece. This schedule will be guaranteed to meet the requirements of the lemma.

6   From Hitting Families to Systematic Testing

Hitting families of schedules serve as a theoretical framework for systematically exposing all bugs of small depth. However, bridging the gap from theory to practice poses several open challenges, which we describe in this section.

To make the discussion concrete, we focus on a specific scenario: testing the rendering of web pages in the browser. Web pages exhibit event-driven concurrency: as the browser parses the page, it concurrently executes JavaScript code registered to handle various automatic or user-triggered events. Many bugs occur as a consequence of JavaScript's ability to manipulate the structure of the page while the page is being parsed. Previous work shows such bugs are often of small depth [10,17].

As an example, consider the web page in Fig. 2. In the example, the image (represented by the `<img>` tag) has an on-load event handler that calls the function `loaded()` once the image is loaded. The function, defined in a separate script block, changes the text of the paragraph p to *Loaded*. There are two potential bugs in this example. The first one is of depth $d = 2$, and it occurs if the image is loaded quickly (for example, from the cache), before the browser parses the `<script>` tag. In this case, the on-load handler tries to call an undefined function. The second bug is of depth $d = 3$, and it occurs if the handler is executed after the `<script>` tag is parsed, but before the `<p>` tag is parsed. In this case, the function `loaded()` tries to access a non-existent HTML element.

Next, we identify and discuss three challenges.

```
<img src="..." onload="javascript:loaded()"/>
<script>
  function loaded() {
    var p = document.getElementById('p');
    if (p == null) {
      setTimeout(loaded, 10);
    } else {
      p.innerHTML = 'Loaded';
    }
  }
</script>
<p id="p">Waiting...</p>
```

Fig. 3. Using a timer to fix the bug from Fig. 2 involving a non-existent element

Events and Partial Orders Need Not Be Static. Our theoretical model assumes a static partially-ordered set of events, and allows arbitrary reordering of independent (incomparable) events. For the web page in Fig. 2, there are three parsing events (corresponding to the three HTML tags) and an on-load event. The parsing events are chained in the order their tags appear in the code. The on-load event happens after the `<img>` tag is parsed, but independently of the other parsing events, giving a tree-shaped partial order.

In more complex web pages, the situation is not so simple. Events may be executions of scripts with complex internal control-flow and data dependencies, as well as with effect on the global state. Once a schedule is reordered, new events might appear, and some events might never trigger. An example showing a more realistic situation is given in Fig. 3. In order to fix the bug involving a non-existent HTML element p, the programmer now explicitly checks the result of `getElementById()`. If p does not exist (p == null), the programmer sets a timer to invoke the function `loaded()` again after 10 milliseconds. As a consequence, depending on what happens first—the on-load event or the parsing of `<p>`—we may or may not observe one or more timeout events. Note that the chain of timeout events also depends on parsing the `<script>` tag. If the tag is not parsed, the `loaded()` function does not exist, so no timer is ever set. Moreover, the number of timeout events depends on when exactly the `<p>` tag is parsed.

The example shows that there is a mismatch between the assumption of static partially ordered events and the dynamic nature of events occuring in complex web pages. Ideally, the mismatch should be settled in future work by explicitly modeling this dynamic nature. However, even the current theory of hitting families can be applied as a testing heuristic. While we lose completeness (in the sense of hitting all depth-d bugs), we retain the variety of different event orderings. In the context of web pages, an initial execution of a page gives us an initial partially ordered set of events. We use it to construct a hitting family of schedules, which we optimistically try to execute. The approach is based on the notion of *approximate replay*, which is employed by R^4, a stateless model checker for web pages [10]. We come back to this approach later in the section.

Another approach is to construct hitting families *on the fly*: Such a construction would unravel events and the partial order dynamically during execution, and non-deterministically construct a schedule from a corresponding hitting family. In this way, the issue of reordering events in an infeasible way does not arise, simply because nothing is reordered. This is in line with how PCT [3] and delay-bounded scheduling [6] work. On-the-fly constructions of small hitting families are a topic for future work.

Beyond Trees. Our results on trees are motivated by the existing theoretical models of asynchronous programs [6,8,11], where the partial order induced by event handlers indeed form trees. However, in the context of web pages, events need not necessarily be ordered as nodes of a tree. An example of a feature that introduces additional ordering constraints is deferred scripts. Scripts marked as deferred are executed after the page has been loaded, and they need to be executed in the order in which their corresponding <script> tags were parsed [15]. The tree approximation corresponds to testing the behavior of pages when the deferred scripts are treated as normal scripts and loaded right away. An open question is to generalize our construction to other special cases of partial orders that capture common programming idioms.

Unbalanced Trees. For a tree of height h, constructions from Sects. 4 and 5 give 3-hitting families of size $O(h)$ and $O(h^2)$, respectively. If the tree is balanced, the cardinality of these families are exponentially smaller than the number of events in the tree. However, in the web page setting, trees are not balanced.

In order to inspect the shape of partial orders occurring in web pages, we randomly selected 24 websites of companies listed among the top 100 of Fortune 500 companies. For each website, we used R^4 [10] to record an execution and construct the happens-before relation (the partial order). Table 1 shows the number of events and the height of the happens-before graph for the websites. The results indicate that a typical website has most of the events concentrated in a backbone of very large height, proportional to the total number of events.

The theory shows that going below $\Theta(h)$ is impossible in this case unless $d < 3$; and this can indeed lead to large hitting families: for example, our construction for $h = 1000$ and $d = 4$ corresponds to several million tests. However, not all schedules of the partial ordering induced by the event handlers may be relevant: if two events are independent (commute), one need not consider schedules which only differ in their ordering. Therefore, since hitting families are defined on an *arbitrary* partial order, not only on the happens-before order, we can use additional information, such as (non-)interference of handlers, to reduce the partial ordering first.

For web pages, we apply a simple partial order reduction to reduce the size of the input trees in the following way. We say a pair of events *race* if they both access some memory location or some DOM element, with at least one of them

Table 1. For each website, the table show the number of events in the initial execution, the height of the partial order (happens-before graph), the number of schedules generated for $d = 3$, and the number of schedules for $d = 3$ with pruning based on races.

Website	# Events	Height	$d = 3$	$d = 3$ (pruned)
abc.xyz	337	288	561	0
newscorp.com	1362	875	2689	100
thehartford.com	2018	1547	3913	138
www.allstate.com	4534	3822	9023	106
www.americanexpress.com	2971	2586	5897	340
www.bankofamerica.com	2305	2095	4561	150
www.bestbuy.com	301	248	576	10
www.comcast.com	188	118	337	16
www.conocophillips.com	4184	3478	8286	248
www.costco.com	7331	6390	14614	364
www.deere.com	2286	1902	4516	236
www.generaldynamics.com	2820	2010	5611	272
www.gm.com	2337	1473	4600	94
www.gofurther.com	1117	638	2154	568
www.homedepot.com	3780	2100	7515	1526
www.humana.com	5611	4325	11174	2058
www.johnsoncontrols.com	2953	2395	5881	450
www.jpmorganchase.com	4134	3519	8247	1316
www.libertymutual.com	3885	3500	7735	324
www.lowes.com	6938	4383	13778	3438
www.massmutual.com	3882	3313	7682	1852
www.morganstanley.com	2752	2301	5402	128
www.utc.com	4081	3266	8100	206
www.valero.com	2116	1849	4178	38

writing to this location or the DOM element. Events that do not participate in races commute with all other events, so they need not be reordered if our goal is to expose bugs.

R^4 internally uses a race detection tool (EventRacer [17]) to overapproximate the set of racing events. In order to compute hitting families, we construct a pruned partial order from the original tree of events. As an example, for $d = 3$ and the simple $O(n^{d-2})$ construction, instead of selecting a_1 arbitrarily, we select it from the events that participate in races. We then perform the left-to-right and right-to-left traversals as usual. In total, the number of generated schedules is $2r$, where r is the number of events participating in races. This number can be significantly smaller than $2n$, as can be seen in the fourth ($d = 3$) and fifth ($d = 3$ pruned) columns of Table 1.

7   Conclusions

We have introduced hitting families as the basis for systematic testing of concurrent systems and studied the size of optimal d-hitting families for trees and related partial orders.

We have shown that a range of combinatorial techniques can be used to construct d-hitting families: we use a greedy approach, a randomized approach, and a construction based on DFS traversals; we also develop a direct inductive construction and a construction based on what we call patterns. The number of schedules in the pattern-based construction is polynomial in the height—for balanced trees, this is exponentially smaller than the total number of nodes.

Our development of hitting families was motivated by the testing of asynchronous programs, and we studied the partial ordering induced by the happens-before relationship on event handlers. While this ordering gives a useful testing heuristic in scenarios such as rendering of web pages, the notion of hitting families applies to any partial ordering, and we leave its further uses to future work.

Acknowledgements. We thank Madan Musuvathi for insightful discussions and comments.

References

1. Alon, N., Spencer, J.H.: The Probabilistic Method, 3rd edn. Wiley, New York (2008)
2. Ambühl, C., Mastrolilli, M., Mutsanas, N., Svensson, O.: Precedence constraint scheduling and connections to dimension theory of partial orders. Bull. EATCS **95**, 37–58 (2008)
3. Burckhardt, S., Kothari, P., Musuvathi, M., Nagarakatte, S.: A randomized scheduler with probabilistic guarantees of finding bugs. In: Proceedings of the 15th International Conference on Architectural Support for Programming Languages and Operating Systems, ASPLOS 2010, Pittsburgh, Pennsylvania, USA, March 13–17, 2010, pp. 167–178 (2010)
4. Chalermsook, P., Laekhanukit, B., Nanongkai, D.: Graph products revisited: Tight approximation hardness of induced matching, poset dimension and more. In: Sanjeev Khanna, editor, Proceedings of the Twenty-Fourth Annual ACM-SIAM Symposium on Discrete Algorithms, SODA 2013, New Orleans, Louisiana, USA, January 6–8, 2013, pp. 1557–1576. SIAM (2013)
5. Dushnik, B., Miller, E.W.: Partially ordered sets. Am. J. Math. **63**(3), 600–610 (1941)
6. Emmi, M., Qadeer, S., Rakamaric, Z.: Delay-bounded scheduling. In: Proceedings of the 38th ACM SIGPLAN-SIGACT Symposium on Principles of Programming Languages, POPL 2011, Austin, TX, USA, January 26–28, 2011, pp. 411–422 (2011)

7. Fomin, F.V., Lokshtanov, D., Misra, N., Saurabh, S.: Planar $\mathcal{F}$-deletion: Approximation, kernelization and optimal FPT algorithms. In: 53rd Annual IEEE Symposium on Foundations of Computer Science, FOCS 2012, New Brunswick, NJ, USA, October 20–23, 2012, pp. 470–479. IEEE Computer Society (2012)

8. Ganty, P., Majumdar, R.: Algorithmic verification of asynchronous programs. ACM Trans. Program. Lang. Syst. **34**(1), 6 (2012)

9. Hegde, R., Jain, K.: The hardness of approximating poset dimension. Electron. Notes Discrete Math. **29**, 435–443 (2007)

10. Jensen, C.S., Møller, A., Raychev, V., Dimitrov, D., Vechev, M.T.: Stateless model checking of event-driven applications. In: Proceedings of the 2015 ACM SIGPLAN International Conference on Object-Oriented Programming, Systems, Languages, and Applications, OOPSLA 2015, part of SLASH 2015, Pittsburgh, PA, USA, October 25–30, 2015, pp. 57–73 (2015)

11. Jhala, R., Majumdar, R.: Interprocedural analysis of asynchronous programs. In: POPL 2007: Proceedings 34th ACM SIGACT-SIGPLAN Symposium on Principles of Programming Languages, pp. 339–350. ACM Press (2007)

12. Lovász, L.: On the ratio of optimal integral and fractional covers. Discrete Math. **13**(4), 383–390 (1975)

13. Lu, S., Park, S., Seo, E., Zhou, Y.: Learning from mistakes: a comprehensive study on real world concurrency bug characteristics. In: Proceedings of the 13th International Conference on Architectural Support for Programming Languages and Operating Systems, ASPLOS 2008, Seattle, WA, USA, March 1–5, 2008, pp. 329–339 (2008)

14. Musuvathi, M., Qadeer, S.: CHESS: systematic stress testing of concurrent software. In: Puebla, G. (ed.) LOPSTR 2006. LNCS, vol. 4407, pp. 15 16. Springer, Heidelberg (2007)

15. Petrov, B., Vechev, M.T., Sridharan, M., Dolby, J.: Race detection for web applications. In: ACM SIGPLAN Conference on Programming Language Design and Implementation, PLDI 2012, Beijing, China - June 11–16, 2012, pp. 251–262 (2012)

16. Qadeer, S., Rehof, J.: Context-bounded model checking of concurrent software. In: Halbwachs, N., Zuck, L.D. (eds.) TACAS 2005. LNCS, vol. 3440, pp. 93–107. Springer, Heidelberg (2005)

17. Raychev, V., Vechev, M.T., Sridharan, M.: Effective race detection for event-driven programs. In: Proceedings of the 2013 ACM SIGPLAN International Conference on Object Oriented Programming Systems Languages & Applications, OOPSLA 2013, part of SPLASH 2013, Indianapolis, IN, USA, October 26–31, 2013, pp. 151–166 (2013)

18. Sapozhenko, A.A.: On the complexity of disjunctive normal forms obtained with a gradient algorithm. In: Diskretnyj Analiz (Discrete Analysis), vol. 21, pp. 62–71. Institute for Mathematics in the Siberian Section of the Academy of Sciences, Novosibirsk (1972, In Russian)

19. Schröder, B.S.W.: Ordered Sets: An Introduction. Springer, New York (2003)

20. Sen, K., Viswanathan, M.: Model checking multithreaded programs with asynchronous atomic methods. In: Ball, T., Jones, R.B. (eds.) CAV 2006. LNCS, vol. 4144, pp. 300–314. Springer, Heidelberg (2006)

21. Stein, S.K.: Two combinatorial covering theorems. J. Comb. Theory Ser. A **16**(3), 391–397 (1974)

22. Trotter, W.T.: A generalization of Hiraguchi's: Inequality for posets. J. Comb. Theory Ser. A **20**(1), 114–123 (1976)

23. Trotter, W.T.: Combinatorics and Partially Ordered Sets: Dimension Theory. Johns Hopkins Studies in the Mathematical Sciences. Johns Hopkins University Press, Baltimore (2001)
24. Yannakakis, M.: The complexity of the partial order dimension problem. SIAM J. Algebraic Discrete Methods **3**(3), 351–358 (1982)

ParCoSS: Efficient Parallelized Compiled Symbolic Simulation

Vladimir Herdt[1](✉), Hoang M. Le[1], Daniel Große[1,2], and Rolf Drechsler[1,2]

[1] Group of Computer Architecture, University of Bremen, 28359 Bremen, Germany
{vherdt,hle,grosse,drechsle}@cs.uni-bremen.de
[2] Cyber-Physical Systems, DFKI GmbH, 28359 Bremen, Germany

Abstract. We present the tool ParCoSS for verification of cooperative multithreading programs. Our tool is based on the recently proposed Compiled Symbolic Simulation (CSS) technique. Additionally, we employ parallelization to further speed-up the verification. The potential of our tool is shown by evaluation.

1 Introduction

In this paper we propose our tool *ParCoSS* (Parallelized Compiled Symbolic Simulation) for verification of cooperative multithreading programs available in the *Extended Intermediate Verification Language* (XIVL) format. The XIVL extends the SystemC IVL [11,15], which has been designed to capture the simulation semantics of SystemC programs [2,10,13], with a small core of OOP features to facilitate the translation of C++ code [16]. For verification purpose the XIVL supports computations with symbolic expressions and the *assume* and *assert* functions with their usual semantic. Our tool and set of XIVL examples is available at [1].

Verification of (cooperative) multithreading programs is difficult due to the large state space caused by all possible inputs and thread interleavings. Symbolic Simulation, a combination of symbolic execution [4,14] and *Partial Order Reduction* (POR) [8,9] has been shown to be particularly effective to tackle state explosion [5,6,15]. Recently *Compiled Symbolic Simulation* (CSS) has been proposed as further improvement [12]. CSS works by integrating the symbolic execution engine and POR based scheduler together with the multithreading program, e.g. available in the XIVL format, into a C++ program. Then, a standard C++ compiler is used to generate a native binary, whose execution performs exhaustive verification of the multithreading program. In contrast to traditional verification methods based on interpretation, CSS can provide significant simulation speed-ups especially by native execution of concrete operations.

This work was supported in part by the German Federal Ministry of Education and Research (BMBF) within the project EffektiV under contract no. 01IS13022E and by the German Research Foundation (DFG) within the Reinhart Koselleck project DR 287/23-1 and by the University of Bremen's graduate school SyDe, funded by the German Excellence Initiative.

© Springer International Publishing Switzerland 2016
S. Chaudhuri and A. Farzan (Eds.): CAV 2016, Part II, LNCS 9780, pp. 177–183, 2016.
DOI: 10.1007/978-3-319-41540-6_10

The implementation of our tool ParCoSS is based on CSS and additionally supports parallelization to further improve simulation performance. Compared to the original CSS approach our tool uses a *fork/join* based state space exploration instead of manually cloning the execution states to handle non-deterministic choices due to symbolic branches and scheduling decisions. A *fork/join* based architecture most notably has the following advantages: (1) It allows to generate more efficient code. (2) It drastically simplifies the implementation.

In particular, we avoid the layer of indirection necessary for variable access when manually tracking execution states and use native execution for all function calls by employing coroutines. Besides very efficient context switch implementation, coroutines allow natural implementation of algorithms without unwinding the native stack and without using state machines to resume execution on context switches. Additionally, manual state cloning of complex internal data structures is error prone and difficult to implement efficiently, whereas the *fork* system call is already very mature and highly optimized. Finally, our architecture allows for straightforward and efficient parallelization by leveraging the process scheduling and memory sharing capabilities of the underlying operating system.

2 Extended Intermediate Verification Language (XIVL)

An example cooperative multithreading program illustrating the core features of the XIVL is shown in Fig. 1. The program is using two threads to compute the sum of odd numbers up to the bound specified by the variable x, which is initialized using a symbolic expression of type *int* in Line 2 and constrained in Line 28. The threads synchronize using the *wait* and *notify* functions on the global event e. The XIVL syntax resembles C++, supports integer and boolean data types with all arithmetic and logic operators, arrays and pointers, is using high-level control flow structures and has a small set of OOP features including classes, inheritance and virtual methods with overrides and dynamic dispatch.

```
 1  event e;                        17  }
 2  int x = ?(int);                 18
 3  int sum = 0;                    19  thread B {
 4                                  20     while (x > 0) {
 5  bool is_odd(int i) {            21        x -= 1;
 6     return (i % 2) != 0;         22        notify(e, 0);
 7  }                               23        wait_time(1);
 8                                  24     }
 9  thread A {                      25  }
10     int i = 0;                   26
11     while (true) {               27  main {
12        wait_event(e);            28     assume(x >= 8 && x <= 10);
13        i += 1;                   29     start;
14        if (is_odd(i))            30     assert(sum <= 25);
15           sum = sum + i;         31  }
16     }
```

Fig. 1. XIVL example program

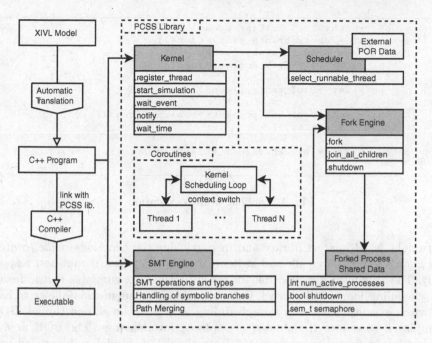

Fig. 2. Tool overview

3   Implementation Details

To simplify development, facilitate code re-use and the translation process from XIVL to C++ we have implemented the PCSS (Parallel CSS) library, which provides common building blocks for parallel symbolic simulation. The PCSS library is linked with the C++ program during compilation. An overview of our tool is shown in Fig. 2. In the following we will describe our PCSS library, provide more details on the *fork/join* based exploration and briefly sketch the translation process from XIVL to C++.

3.1   PCSS Library

The right hand side of Fig. 2 shows the main components, and their interaction, of the PCSS library. Essentially it consists of the following components: kernel, scheduler, SMT engine, fork engine and some process shared data.

The kernel provides a small set of functions which directly correspond to the XIVL kernel related primitives (e.g. *wait* and *notify*) and allows to simulate the SystemC event-driven simulation semantics. Furthermore, all thread functions of the XIVL model are registered in the kernel. The kernel will allocate a coroutine with every thread function as entry point. Coroutines naturally implement context switches as they allow to jump execution between arbitrarily nested functions while preserving the local data. Our implementation is using the

```
1  bool on_branch(const SmtExpr &cond) {
2    auto stat = check_branch_status(cond);
3    if (stat == BranchStatus::BothFeasible) {
4      bool is_child = fork_engine->fork();
5      if (is_child)
6        pc = smt->bool_and(pc, cond);
7      else
8        pc = smt->bool_and(pc, smt->bool_not(cond));
9      return is_child;
10   }
11   return stat == BranchStatus::FalseOnly ? false : true;
12 }
```

Fig. 3. Symbolic branch execution

lightweight *boost context* library and in particular the functions *make_fcontext* and *jump_fcontext* to create and switch execution between coroutines, respectively. The scheduler is responsible for selecting the next runnable thread inside the scheduling loop of the kernel. Our coroutine implementation allows to easily switch execution between the scheduling loop and the chosen thread. POR is employed to reduce the number of explored interleavings. The POR dependency relation is statically generated from the XIVL model and encoded into the C++ program during translation. At runtime it is passed to the scheduler during initialization.

The SMT engine provides common functionality required for symbolic execution. It keeps track of the current path condition, handles the *assume* and *assert* functions, and checks the feasibility of symbolic branch conditions. Furthermore, the SMT engine provides SMT types and operations. Essentially this is a lightweight layer around the underlying SMT solver and allows to transparently swap the employed SMT solver.

The fork engine is responsible to split the execution process into two independent processes in case of a non-deterministic choice. This happens when both branch directions are feasible in the SMT engine or multiple thread choices are still available in the scheduler after applying POR. One of the forked processes will continue exploration while the other is suspended until the first terminates. This approach simulates a depth first search (DFS) of the state space. As an optimization, the fork engine allows to run up to N processes in parallel, where N is a command line parameter to the compiled C++ program. Parallelization is very efficient as the processes explore disjoint state spaces independently.

3.2 Fork/Join Based State Space Exploration

Executing Symbolic Branches. The *on_branch* function in the SMT engine, shown in Fig. 3, accepts a symbolic branch condition and returns a concrete decision, which is then used to control native C++ control flow structures. The *check_branch_status* checks the feasibility of both branch directions by checking the satisfiability of the branch condition and its negation. In case both branch

```
 1  bool ForkEngine::fork() {
 2    int pid = ::fork();
 3    if (pid != 0) {
 4      num_children++;
 5      while (!try_fork(shared_data, N)) {
 6        if (num_children > 0) {
 7          join_any_child();
 8        } else {
 9          usleep(1); // wait for someone else to join child
10        }
11      }
12    } else {
13      num_children = 0;
14    }
15    return pid == 0;
16  }
```

Fig. 4. Implementation of parallelized forking

directions are feasible, the execution will fork (Line 4) into two independent processes and update the path condition (pc) with the normal (Line 6) or negated condition (Line 8), respectively. Please note that the execution is not forked and the path condition is not extended when only a single branch direction is feasible.

Parallelization. The forked processes communicate using anonymous shared memory, which is created during initialization in the first process using the *mmap* system call and thus accessible from all forked child processes. The shared memory essentially contains three information: (1) counter variable to ensure that no more than N processes will run in parallel, (2) shutdown flag to gracefully stop the simulation, e.g. when an assertion violation is detected, (3) unnamed semaphore to synchronize access. The semaphore is initialized and modified using the *sem_init*, *sem_post* and *sem_wait* functions. Furthermore, each process locally keeps track of the number of forked child processes (*num_children*). Figure 4 shows an implementation of the *fork* function. First the *fork* system call is executed. The child process (*pid* is zero) will never block, since executing only one process will not increase the number of active processes. The parent process however will first try to atomically check and increment the shared counter in Line 5. When this fails, i.e. the maximum number N of processes is already working, the parent process will wait until a working processes finishes, by either awaiting one of its own children (Line 7) or until some other process joins its children (Line 9).

3.3 XIVL to C++ Translation

We use the XIVL example from Fig. 1 to illustrate the XIVL to C++ translation process, which basically performs five steps: (1) Replace native data types (integer and boolean) and operations with SMT types and operations where necessary

Table 1. Experiment results, T.O. denotes timeout (limit 750 s)

Benchmark	Kratos	ISS	ParCoSS		
			P-1	P-4	P-8
buffer-ws-p5	1.400	65.951	9.086	2.882	1.987
mem-slave-tlm-bug-50	T.O	3.731	<0.1	<0.1	<0.1
mem-slave-tlm-sym-50	T.O	3.940	<0.1	<0.1	<0.1
pressure-15	1.281	219.300	17.182	5.312	3.855
pressure-bug-50	444.781	0.897	<0.1	<0.1	<0.1
irqmp-8	–	108.670	32.719	10.815	8.237
irqmp-12	–	T.O	530.705	178.108	128.257

(here variable x). Variables which are never assigned a symbolic value (here variables i and sum) can keep their native type and perform native operations. (2) Instrument control flow code to query the SMT engine for a concrete decision. The branch condition $x > 0$ will be transformed into an SMT expression, e.g. as $smt \rightarrow bv\_gt(x, smt \rightarrow bv\_val(0))$, and wrapped by the on_branch function of the smt_engine. (3) Generate static POR information for the scheduler. Essentially, a static analysis is employed to detect *read/write* and *notify/wait* dependencies. A flow- and context-insensitive pointer analysis is used to increase the precision. (4) Redirect builtin XIVL functions to the SMT engine (*assume* and *assert*) and kernel instance (e.g. *wait_event* and *notify*). (5) Add a new main function that will initialize the PCSS library and call the main function of the XIVL model. It will initialize the global data of the XIVL model and then enter the scheduling loop of the kernel by calling the *start_simulation* function.

4   Evaluation and Conclusion

We have evaluated our tool on a set of SystemC benchmarks from the literature [3,7,15] and the TLM model of the *Interrupt Controller for Multiple Processors* (IRQMP) of the LEON3-based virtual prototype SoCRocket [17]. All experiments have been performed on a Linux system using a 3.5 GHz Intel E3 Quadcore with Hyper-Threading. We used Clang 3.5 for compilation of the C++ programs and Z3 v4.4.1 in the SMT Layer. The time (memory) limit have been set to 750 s (6 GB), respectively. T.O. denotes that time limit has been exceeded. The results are shown in Table 1. It shows the simulation time in seconds for Kratos [7], *Interpreted Symbolic Simulation* (ISS) [6,15], and our tool ParCoSS with a single process (P-1) and parallelized with four (P-4) and eight processes (P-8). Comparing P-4 with P-8 allows to observe the effect of Hyper-Threading. The results demonstrate the potential of our tool and show that our parallelization approach can further improve results. As expected, CSS can be considerably faster than ISS. On some benchmarks Kratos is faster due to its abstraction technique, but the difference is not significant. Furthermore, Kratos is not applicable to the *irqmp* benchmark due to missing C++ language features. For future work we plan to integrate dynamic information, for POR and selection of code blocks for native execution, into our CSS framework.

References

1. www.systemc-verification.org/ParCoSS
2. Accellera Systems Initiative. SystemC (2012). http://www.systemc.org
3. Blanc, N., Kroening, D.: Race analysis for SystemC using model checking. ACM Trans. Des. Autom. Electron. Syst. **15**(3), 21:1–21:32 (2010)
4. Cadar, C., Dunbar, D., Engler, D.: Klee: unassisted and automatic generation of high-coverage tests for complex systems programs. In: OSDI, pp. 209–224 (2008)
5. Chou, C.-N., Chu, C.-K., Huang. C.-Y.R.: Conquering the scheduling alternative explosion problem of SystemC symbolic simulation. In: ICCAD, pp. 685–690 (2013)
6. Chou, C.-N., Ho, Y.-S., Hsieh, C., Huang. C.-Y: Symbolic model checking on SystemC designs. In: DAC, pp. 327–333 (2012)
7. Cimatti, A., Narasamdya, I., Roveri, M.: Software model checking SystemC. IEEE Trans. CAD Integr. Circuits Syst. **32**(5), 774–787 (2013)
8. Flanagan, C. Godefroid, P.: Dynamic partial-order reduction for model checking software. In: POPL, pp. 110–121 (2005)
9. Godefroid, P. (ed.): Partial-Order Methods for the Verification of Concurrent Systems. LNCS, vol. 1032. Springer, Heidelberg (1996)
10. Große, D., Drechsler, R.: Quality-Driven SystemC Design. Springer, The Netherlands (2010)
11. Herdt, V., Le, H.M., Drechsler, R.: Verifying SystemC using stateful symbolic simulation. In: DAC, pp. 49:1–49:6 (2015)
12. Herdt, V., Le, H.M., Große, D., Drechsler. R.. Compiled symbolic simulation for SystemC In: ICCAD (2016)
13. IEEE. IEEE Standard SystemC Language Reference Manual. IEEE Std. 1666 (2011)
14. King, J.C.: Symbolic execution and program testing. Commun. ACM **19**(7), 385–394 (1976)
15. Le, H.M., Große, D., Herdt, V., Drechsler, R.: Verifying SystemC using an intermediate verification language and symbolic simulation. In: DAC, pp. 116:1–116:6 (2013)
16. Le, H.M., Herdt, V., Große, D., Drechsler. R.: Towards formal verification of real-world SystemC TLM peripheral models - a case study. In: DATE (2016)
17. Schuster, T., Meyer, R., Buchty, R., Fossati, L., Berekovic. M.: SoCRocket - a virtual platform for the European Space Agency's SoC development. In: ReCoSoC, pp. 1–7 (2014). http://github.com/socrocket

Constraint Solving II

XSat: A Fast Floating-Point Satisfiability Solver

Zhoulai Fu[✉] and Zhendong Su

University of California, Davis, USA
zhoulai.fu@gmail.com, su@cs.ucdavis.edu

Abstract. The Satisfiability Modulo Theory (SMT) problem over floating-point arithmetic is a major hurdle in applying SMT techniques to real-world floating-point code. Solving floating-point constraints is challenging in part because floating-point semantics is difficult to specify or abstract. State-of-the-art SMT solvers still often run into difficulties when solving complex, non-linear floating-point constraints.

This paper proposes a new approach to SMT solving that does not need to directly reason about the floating-point semantics. Our insight is to establish the equivalence between floating-point satisfiability and a class of mathematical optimization (MO) problems known as unconstrained MO. Our approach (1) systematically reduces floating-point satisfiability to MO, and (2) solves the latter via the Monte Carlo Markov Chain (MCMC) method.

We have compared our implementation, XSat, with MathSat, Z3 and Coral, state-of-the-art solvers that support floating-point arithmetic. Evaluated on 34 representative benchmarks from the SMT-Competition 2015, XSat significantly outperforms these solvers. In particular, it provides both 100 % consistent satisfiability results as MathSat and Z3, and an average speedup of more than 700X over MathSat and Z3, while Coral provides inconsistent results on 10 of the benchmarks.

1 Introduction

Floating-point constraint solving has received much recent attention to support the testing and verification of programs that involve floating-point computation. Existing decision procedures, or Satisfiability Modulo Theory (SMT) solvers, are usually based on the DPLL(T) framework [19,33], which combines a Boolean satisfiability solver (SAT) for the propositional structure of constraints and a specialized theory solver. These decision procedures can cope with logical constraints over many theories, but since they are bit-level satisfiability solvers (SAT), their theory-specific SMT components can run into difficulties when dealing with complex, non-linear floating-point constraints.

This work proposes a new approach for solving floating-point satisfiability. Our approach does not need to directly reason about floating-point semantics. Instead, it transforms a floating-point constraint to a floating-point function that represents the models of the constraint as its minimum points. This "representing function" is similar to *fitness functions* used in search-based testing in the sense both reduce a search problem to a function minimization problem [30].

S. Chaudhuri and A. Farzan (Eds.): CAV 2016, Part II, LNCS 9780, pp. 187–209, 2016.
DOI: 10.1007/978-3-319-41540-6_11

However, unlike search-based testing, which uses fitness functions as heuristics, our approach uses the representing function as an essential element in developing precise, systematic methods for solving floating-point satisfiability.

Representing Function. Let π be a floating-point constraint, and $\mathsf{dom}(\pi)$ be the value domain of its variables. Our insight is to derive from π a floating-point program R that represents how far a value $x \in \mathsf{dom}(\pi)$ is from being a model of π. As illustrated in Fig. 1, we can imagine R as a distance from $x \in \mathsf{dom}(\pi)$ to the models of π: It is non-negative everywhere, becomes smaller when x goes closer to the set of π's models, and vanishes when x goes inside (*i.e.*, when x becomes a model of π). Thus, such a function R allows us to view the SMT constraint π as function minimization problem of function R. We call R a *representing function*.[1]

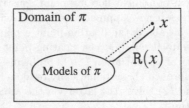

Fig. 1. Illustration of the representing function R for a floating-point constraint π.

It is a common need to minimize/maximize scalar functions in science and engineering. The research field dedicated to the subject is known as *mathematical optimization* (MO) [17]. MO works by iteratively evaluating its *objective function*, *i.e.*, the function that MO attempts to minimize. In other words, the representing function allows the transformation of an SMT problem to an MO problem, which enables floating-point constraint solving by *only* executing its representing function, without the need to directly reason about floating-point semantics—a key benefit of such an SMT-MO problem reduction.

Note, however, that an MO formulation of the SMT problem does not, by itself, provide a panacea to SMT solving, since many MO problems are themselves intractable. However, efficient algorithms have been successfully applied to difficult MO problems. A classic example is the traveling salesman problem. The problem is NP-hard, but has been nicely handled by simulated annealing [26], a stochastic MO technique. Another example is the Monte Carlo Markov Chain method (MCMC) [9], which has been successfully applied in testing and verification [12,18,38].

The insight of this work is that, if we carefully design the representing functions so that certain rules are respected, we can reduce floating-point constraint

---

[1] The term "representing function" in English should first appear in Kleene's book [27], where the author used it to define recursive functions. "Representing function" is also called "characteristic function" or "indicator function" in the literature.

solving to a category of MO problems known as unconstrained MO that can be efficiently solved. Thus, our high-level approach is: (1) systematically transform a floating-point constraint in conjunctive normal format (CNF) to its representing function, and (2) adapt MCMC to minimize the representing function to output a model of the constraint or report unsat.

We have compared our implementation, XSat, with Z3 [16], MathSat [14], and Coral [39], three solvers that can handle floating-point arithmetic. Our evaluation results on 34 representative benchmarks from the SMT-Competition 2015 show that XSat significantly outperforms these solvers in both correctness and efficiency. In particular, XSat provides 100 % consistent satisfiability results as MathSat and Z3, and an average speedup of more than 700X over MathSat and Z3, while Coral provides inconsistent results on 16 of the 34 benchmarks.

Contributions. We introduce a new SMT solver for the floating-point satisfiability problem. Our main contributions follow:

- We show, via the use of representing functions, how to systematically reduce floating-point constraint solving to a class of MO problems known as unconstrained MO;
- We establish a theoretical guarantee for the equivalence between the original floating-point satisfiability problem and the class of MO problems.
- We realize our approach in the XSat solver and show empirically that XSat significantly outperforms the state-of-the-art solvers.

The rest of the paper is organized as follows. Section 2 gives an overview of our approach, and Sect. 3 presents its theoretical underpinning. Section 4 presents the algorithm design of the XSat solver, while Sect. 5 describes its overall implementation and our evaluation of XSat. Finally, Sect. 6 surveys related work, and Sect. 7 concludes.

2   Approach Overview

This section presents a high-level overview of our approach. Its main goal is to illustrate, via examples, that (1) it is possible to reduce a floating-point satisfiability problem to a class of mathematical optimization (MO) problems, and (2) efficient solutions exist for solving those MO problems.

2.1   Preliminaries on Mathematical Optimization

A general Mathematical Optimization (MO) problem can be written as follows:

$$\begin{aligned} \text{minimize} \quad & f(x) \\ \text{subject to} \quad & x \in S \end{aligned} \tag{1}$$

where f is called the objective function, and S the search space [17].

MO techniques can be divided into two categories. One focuses on how functions are shaped at local regions and where a local minimum can be found near the given inputs. This *local optimization* is classic, involving techniques dated back to the 17th century (*e.g.*, Newton's approach or gradient-based search). Local optimization not only provides the minimum value of a function within a neighborhood of the given input points, but also aids *global optimization*, another, more active body of research, which determines the minimum value of a function over an entire search space.

Let f be a function over a metric space with d as its distance. We call x^* a *local minimum point* if there exists a *neighborhood* of x^*, namely $\{x \mid d(x, x^*) < \delta\}$ for some $\delta > 0$, so that all x in the neighborhood satisfy $f(x) \geq f(x^*)$. The value of $f(x^*)$ is called the *local minimum* of the function f. If $f(x^*) \leq f(x)$ for all $x \in S$, we call $f(x^*)$ the *global minimum* of the function f, and x^* a *global minimum point*.

In this presentation, if we say minimum (resp. minimum point), we mean global minimum (resp. global minimum point). It should be clear that a function may have more than one minimum point but only one minimum.

2.2   From SMT to Unconstrained Mathematical Optimization

Suppose we want to solve the simple floating-point constraint

$$x \leq 1.5 \tag{2}$$

Here, we aim to illustrate the feasibility of reducing an SMT problem to an MO problem. In fact, each model of $x \leq 1.5$ is a global minimum point of the formula

$$f_1(x) = \begin{cases} 0 & \text{if } x \leq 1.5 \\ (x - 1.5)^2 & \text{otherwise} \end{cases} \tag{3}$$

and conversely, each global minimum point of f_1 is also a model of $x \leq 1.5$, since $f_1(x) \geq 0$ and $f_1(x) = 0$ iff $x \leq 1.5$ (see Sect. 3 for a formalization). In the MO literature, the kind of problem of minimizing f_1 is called *unconstrained* MO, meaning that its search space is the whole domain of the objective function. Unconstrained MO problems are generally regarded easier to solve than constrained MO[2] since they can be efficiently solved if the objective function f_1 is smooth to some degree [34]. Figure 2 shows the curve of f_1 and a common local optimization method, which uses tangents of the curve to quickly converge to the minimum point. The smoothness makes it possible to deduce information about the function's behavior at points of the neighborhood of a particular point x by using objective and constraint information at x.

---

[2] For example, it is common practice to transform a constrained MO problem by replacing its constraints with penalized terms in the objective function and to solve the problem as an unconstrained MO [34].

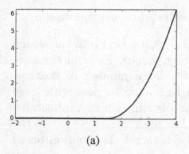
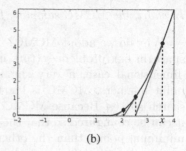

(a)   (b)

Fig. 2. (a) The curve of f_1 (Eq. 3) and (b) illustration of a classic local optimization method for finding a minimum point of f_1. The method uses tangents of the curve to quickly converge to a minimum point. (Color figure online)

2.3 Efficiently Solve MO Problems via MCMC

Suppose we slightly complicate constraint (2) by adding a non-linear conjunct:

$$x \leq 1.5 \wedge (x-1)^2 = 4. \tag{4}$$

This SMT problem can still be reduced to an unconstrained MO problem, with objective function

$$f_2(x) = f_1(x) + ((x-1)^2 - 4)^2 \tag{5}$$

where f_1 is as in Eq. (3). The equivalence of the two problems follows from the fact that $f_2(x) = 0$ if and only if $f_1(x) = 0$ and $((x-1)^2 - 4)^2 = 0$. The curve of f_2 is shown in Fig. 3(a), which has local minimum points at both $x = -1$ and $x = 3$, and only $x = -1$ is the global minimum point. It is more difficult to locate the global minimum point of this function, because local optimization methods such as the one illustrated in the previous example can be trapped in local minimum points, e.g., terminating and returning $x = 3$ in Fig. 3.

In this paper, we use a *Monte Carlo Markov Chain* (MCMC) method [9] as a general approach for unconstrained MO problems. MCMC is a random sampling technique used to simulate a target distribution. Consider, for example, the target distribution of coin tossing, with 0.5 probability for having the head or tail. An MCMC sampling is a sequence of random variables $x_1, \ldots, x_n$, such that the probability of x_n being "head", denoted by P_n, converges to 0.5, i.e., $\lim_{n \to \infty} P_n = 0.5$. The fundamental fact regarding MCMC sampling can be summarized as the lemma below [9]. For simplicity, we only show the result with discrete-valued probabilities here.

Lemma 1. *Let x be a random variable, A be an enumerable set of the possible values of x. Let f be a target distribution function for each $a \in A$. Then, for an MCMC sampling sequence $x_1, \ldots, x_n \ldots$ and a probability density function $P(x_i = a)$ for each x_i, we have:*

$$P(x_n = a) \to f(a). \tag{6}$$

In short, the MCMC sampling follows the target distribution asymptotically.

Why do we adopt MCMC? There are multiple advantages. First, the search space in our problem setting involves floating-point values. Even in the one-dimensional case, a very small interval contains a large number of floating-point numbers. MCMC is known as an effective technique to deal with large search spaces. Because MCMC samples follow the distribution asymptotically, it can be configured so that the sampling process has more chance to attain the minimum points than the others (by sampling for a target distribution based on $\lambda x : \exp^{-f(x)}$ for example, where f is the function to minimize). Second, MCMC has many mature techniques and implementations that integrate well with classic local search techniques. These implementations have proven efficient for real-world problems with a large number of local minimum points, and can even handle functions beyond classic MO, *e.g.*, discontinuous objective functions. Other MO techniques, *e.g.*, genetic programming, may also be used for our problem setting, which we leave for future investigation.

Figure 3(b) illustrates the iteration of MCMC sampling combined with a local optimization. As in the previous example, the local optimization can quickly converge (shown as steps $p_0 \to p_1$ and $p_2 \to p_3$ in the figure). The MCMC step, shown as the $p_1 \to p_2$ step, allows the search to escape from being trapped in local minimum points. This MCMC step is random, but follows a probability model which we will explain in Sect. 4.

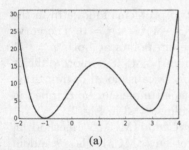
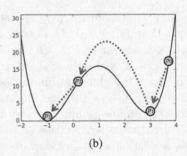

(a)   (b)

Fig. 3. (a) The curve of f_2 (Eq. 5); (b) Illustration of how MCMC can be combined with local optimization for locating the global minimum point $x = -1$. MCMC starts from p_0, converges to local minimum p_1, then performs a random move to p_2 (called a Monte-Carlo step, see Sect. 4) and converges to p_3, which is the global minimum point.

3   Technical Formulation

This section presents the theoretical underpinning of our approach. We write $\mathbb{F}$ for the set of floating-point numbers. Given a function f, we call x a zero of f if $f(x) = 0$.

Language. The language of interest is modeled as the set of quantifier-free floating-point constraints. Each constraint π is a conjunction or disjunction of arithmetic comparisons.

Constraints of FP $\qquad \pi := \pi_1 \wedge \pi_2 \mid \pi_1 \vee \pi_2 \mid e_1 \bowtie e_2$

Arithmetic expressions $\qquad e := c \mid X \mid \mathtt{foo}(e_1, \cdots e_n) \mid e_1 \oplus e_2$

where $\bowtie \in \{\leq, <, \geq, >, ==, \neq\}$, $\oplus \in \{+, -, *, /\}$, c is a floating-point numeral, X is a floating-point variable, and $\mathtt{foo}$ is an *interpreted* floating-point function, which can be a library function, *e.g.*, trigonometric, logarithmic or user-defined ones. We denote the language by FP.

Let $\pi \in$ FP be a constraint with variables $X_1, \cdots, X_N$. We write $\mathsf{dom}(\pi)$ for the value domain of its variables. Usually, $\mathsf{dom}(\pi) = \mathbb{F}^N$. We say a vector of floating-point numbers $(x_1, \cdots, x_N)$ is a model of π, denoted by $(x_1, \cdots, x_N) \models \pi$, if π becomes a tautology by substituting X_i with the corresponding x_i for all $i \in [1, N]$. In the following, we shall use a meta-variable x for a vector of floating-point numbers $(x_1, \cdots, x_N)$.

As mentioned in Sect. 1, our idea is to derive from π a floating-point program that represents how far a floating-point input, *i.e.*, $(x_1, \cdots, x_N)$, is from being a model of π. We specify this program as below:

Definition 1. *Given a floating-point constraint π, a floating-point program R of type $\mathsf{dom}(\pi) \to \mathbb{F}$ is called a* representing function *of π if the following properties hold:*

R1. $\mathrm{R}(x) > 0$ *for all $x \in \mathsf{dom}(\pi)$,*
R2. *Every zero of R is a model of π: $\forall x \in \mathsf{dom}(\pi), \mathrm{R}(x) = 0 \implies x \models \pi$, and*
R3. *The zeros of R include all models of π: $\forall x \in \mathsf{dom}(\pi), x \models \pi \implies \mathrm{R}(x) = 0$.*

The concept of representing functions allows us to establish an equivalence between the floating-point satisfiability problem and an MO problem. This is shown in the theorem below:

Theorem 1. *Let π be a floating-point constraint, and R be its representing function. Let x^* be a global minimum point of R. Then we have*

$$\pi \text{ is satisfiable } \Leftrightarrow \mathrm{R}(x^*) = 0. \tag{7}$$

Proof. Let x^* be an arbitrary global minimum point of R. If π is satisfiable with x being one of its models, then we have $\mathrm{R}(x) = 0$ by R3. By R1, x is also a global minimum point of R. Thus $\mathrm{R}(x^*) = \mathrm{R}(x) = 0$ since at most one global minimum exists. The proof for the "$\Leftarrow$" part follows directly from R2.

A simple procedure for solving floating-point constraints follows from Theorem 1.

Procedure P: Let π be a floating-point constraint $\pi \in$ FP.

P1. Construct a floating-point program R such that R1-3 hold with regard to π.
P2. Minimize R. Let x^* be the calculated global minimum point.
P3. Check whether $R(x^*) = 0$. If yes, return x^* as a model, or unsat otherwise.

Analysis of Procedure P. One challenge faced with procedure P lies in step P2. In general, global optimization may not return a true global minimum point. To make this point clear, we use the notation $\hat{x^*}$ for the global minimum point produced by the MO tool, and x^* for a true global minimum point. Then we have

$$R(\hat{x^*}) \geq R(x^*). \tag{8}$$

We consider two cases in analyzing procedure P. In the first case, if procedure P reports sat, we have $R(\hat{x^*}) = 0$. Thus, $R(x^*) = 0$ as well because of Eq. (8) and condition R1. Following Theorem 1, we conclude that π is necessarily satisfiable in this case. As for the second case, if procedure P reports unsat, we have $R(\hat{x^*}) > 0$. In this case, it is still possible that π is satisfiable, meaning that step P2 produces a conservative global minimum point, *i.e.*, $R(\hat{x^*}) > 0$ but $R(x^*) = 0$. To summarize, the following lemma holds:

Lemma 2. *Let π be a floating-point constraint of* FP. *Procedure P has the following two properties: (1) Soundness: If procedure P reports* sat, *π is necessarily satisfiable, and (2) Incompleteness: Procedure P may incorrectly report* unsat *when π is actually satisfiable. This case happens if the MO tool at step P2 calculates a wrong global minimum point.*

In the next section, we present XSat, a solver that realizes procedure P. As we will show in Sect. 5, by carefully designing the representing function, the incompleteness in theory can be largely mitigated in practice.

4   The XSat Solver

This section presents the algorithmic design of XSat, an SMT solver to handle quantifier-free floating-point constraints. XSat is an instance of Procedure P (Sect. 3).

Notation. Given a set A, we write $|A|$ to denote its cardinality. We adopt C's ternary operator "$p ? a : b$" to denote a code fragment that evaluates to a if p holds, or b otherwise. As in the previous section, we use $\mathbb{F}$ for the set of floating-point numbers, and FP for the language of quantifier-free floating-point constraints that we have defined.

Let π be a floating-point constraint of FP in the form of a conjunction. If we have a representing function for each of the conjuncts, we can construct the representing function of π as

$$R_{\pi_1 \wedge \pi_2} = R_{\pi_1} + R_{\pi_2}. \tag{9}$$

Similarly, if π is in the form of a disjunction, we can use

$$R_{\pi_1 \vee \pi_2} = R_{\pi_1} * R_{\pi_2}. \tag{10}$$

Above, both "+" and "*" denote the operations as given by IEEE floating-point arithmetic. Clearly, both $R_{\pi_1 \wedge \pi_2}$ and $R_{\pi_1 \vee \pi_2}$ satisfy conditions R1–3 since both R_{π_1} and R_{π_2} do, and since $\forall a, b \geq 0$, we have $a + b = 0 \Leftrightarrow a = 0 \wedge b = 0$ and $a * b = 0 \Leftrightarrow a = 0 \vee b = 0$.

To construct R for arithmetic comparisons, we need to introduce a helper function θ. Its idea is similar to the *representation distance* implemented in Boost [2], which counts the number of floating-point numbers between two bit-pattern representations. Because the IEEE-754 standard ensures that the next higher representable floating point value from a floating-point number a is a simple integer increment up from the previous one [21], we can view $\theta(a, b)$ for $a, b \in \mathbb{F} \setminus \{NaN, Inf, -Inf\}$ as

$$\theta(a, b) = |\{x \in \mathbb{F} \mid \min(a, b) < x < \max(a, b)\}|. \tag{11}$$

In general, for arbitrary $a, b \in \mathbb{F}$, $\theta(a, b)$ always returns a non-negative integer; it vanishes if and only if a and b hold the same floating-point value. Then, we use

$$R_{e_1 \leq e_2} \stackrel{\text{def}}{=} e_1 \leq e_2 \, ? \, 0 \, : \, \theta(e_1, e_2) \tag{12}$$

The representing function for the other arithmetic comparisons can be derived using the lemma below. The lemma directly follows from Definition 1.

Lemma 3. *Given* $\pi, \pi' \in$ FP *such that* $\pi \Leftrightarrow \pi'$ *(logical equivalence), any representing function of* π *is also a representing function of* π'.

Now, we can define $R_{x \geq y}$ as $R_{y \leq x}$, $R_{x == y}$ as $R_{x \geq y \wedge x \leq y}$. For the strict inequalities, we use the notation x^- for the largest floating point that is strictly smaller than x, and reduce $R_{x < y}$ to $R_{x \leq y^-}$, $R_{x > y}$ to $R_{y < x}$, and $R_{x \neq y}$ to $R_{x < y \vee x > y}$. We summarize the representing function used in XSat in the theorem below:

Theorem 2. *Let* F *be a conjunctive normal form of* FP:

$$F \stackrel{\text{def}}{=} \bigwedge_{j \in J} \bigvee_{i \in I} e_{i,j} \bowtie_{i,j} e'_{i,j} \tag{13}$$

where $e_{i,j}$ *and* $e'_{i,j}$ *are quantities to be interpreted over floating-point numbers or expressions, and* $\bowtie_{i,j} \in \{\leq, \geq, ==, <, >, \neq\}$. *Then, the function below is a representing function of* F:

$$\sum_{j \in J} \prod_{i \in I} d(\bowtie, e_{i,j}, e'_{i,j}) \tag{14}$$

where

$$d(==, x, y) \stackrel{def}{=} \theta(x, y) \tag{15}$$

$$d(\leq, x, y) \stackrel{def}{=} x \leq y \ ? \ 0 \ : \ \theta(x, y) \tag{16}$$

$$d(\geq, x, y) \stackrel{def}{=} x \geq y \ ? \ 0 \ : \ \theta(x, y) \tag{17}$$

$$d(<, x, y) \stackrel{def}{=} x < y \ ? \ 0 \ : \ \theta(x, y) + 1 \tag{18}$$

$$d(>, x, y) \stackrel{def}{=} x > y \ ? \ 0 \ : \ \theta(x, y) + 1 \tag{19}$$

$$d(\neq, x, y) \stackrel{def}{=} x \neq y \ ? \ 0 \ : \ 1 \tag{20}$$

Algorithm 1 shows the main steps of the XSat algorithm. (**Line 1–5**): The algorithm follows the three steps in procedure P, except that in practice, more than one starting points are used to launch MCMC. (Such a technique is commonly used in the MO literature, since most MO algorithms are sensible to its starting points [34].) If none of these starting points leads to a minimum point x^* such that $R(x^*) = 0$, unsat is reported. (**Line 7–15**): The function GEN is a simple code generator that generates the representing function. It works by recursively walking through the logical and arithmetic expressions of the language FP. (**Lines 16–27**): Each iteration of the loop can be regarded as an MCMC sampling over the space of the local minimum points [29]. In Algorithm 1, Line 17 enforces that the initial x is already a local minimum point. Each iteration (Lines 18–25) is composed of the two phases that are classic in the *Metropolis-Hasting* algorithm family of MCMC [13]. In Phase 1 (Lines 19-20), the algorithm *proposes* a new sample x^* from the current sample x. Then, the algorithm relies on a local minimization procedure to only propose local minimum points. Phase 2 (Lines 21–25) decides whether x^* should be *accepted*. As an algorithm of Metropolis-Hasting family, we use $f(x^*)/f(x)$ as the acceptance ratio. If $f(x^*) < f(x)$, the proposed x^* will be accepted. Otherwise, x^* may still be accepted, but only with the probability $\exp(f(x) - f(x^*))$.[3]

Example. Consider the floating-point formula

$$A(x) \stackrel{def}{=} (x == \text{SIN}(x) \land x \geq 1\text{E-}10) \tag{21}$$

where SIN is an implementation of the sine function, say, from glibc 2.21 [4]. Deciding $A(x)$ is challenging for traditional SAT/SMT solvers. In fact, the part $x == \text{SIN}(x)$ is unsatisfiable in the theory of reals (because $x = \text{SIN}(x) \Leftrightarrow x = 0$ in reals) but it can be satisfied in the floating-point semantics ($\text{SIN}(x) = x$ if $|x| < 2^{-26}$ in glibc's implementation).

---

[3] In a general Metropolis-Hasting algorithm, in the case of $f(x^*) > f(x)$, x^* is to be accepted with the probability of $\exp(-\frac{f(x^*)-f(x)}{T})$, where T is the "annealing temperature" [26]. Our algorithm sets $T = 1$ for simplicity.

Algorithm 1. The XSat solver.

Input:
- π Quantifier-free floating-point constraint of FP
- LM   Local minimization procedure
- **iter** MCMC iteration number

Output: sat with a model of π, if such a model can be found, or unsat otherwise

1 Let R be the floating-point program:

```
double R(double X){return g ;}
```

where g refers to the expression generated by GEN (π), and X is the variable in π.

/* Iteration of procedure P with n_start starting points.   */

2 **for** $j = 1$ to n_start **do**
3   Let sp be a randomly generated starting point
4   Let $x^* = $ Metropolis-Hasting(R, sp)
5   **if** $R(x^*) == 0$ **then return** x^*

6 **return** unsat

7 **Function** GEN (π)
8   **if** π is in the form of $\pi_1 \wedge \pi_2$ **then**
9   **return** '(' GEN(π_1) '+' GEN(π_1) ')'
10   **if** π is in the form of $\pi_1 \vee \pi_2$ **then**
11   **return** '(' GEN(π_1) '*' GEN(π_1) ')'
12   **if** π is in the form of $e_0 \bowtie e_1$, where $\bowtie$ is an arithmetic comparison **then**
13   **return** '$d($' $\bowtie$ ',' GEN(π_1) ',' GEN(π_2) ')'
14   **if** π is a floating-point constant **then**
15   **return** the constant as a string

16 **Function** Metropolis-Hasting (f, x)
17     $x = $ LM(f, x)
18   **for** $k = 1$ **to** iter **do**
19   Let d be a random perturbation generation from a predefined distribution
20   Let $x^* = $ LM$(f, x + d)$
21   **if** $f(x^*) < f(x)$ **then** $accept = true$
22   **else**
23   Let m randomly generated from the uniform distribution on $[0, 1]$
24   Let $accept$ be the Boolean $m < \exp(f(x) - f(x^*))$
25   **if** $accept$ **then** $x = x^*$
26   **return** x

Following Theorem 2, we use a representing function

$$\theta(x, \text{SIN}(x)) + (x \geq 1\text{E-}10 \ ? \ \ 0 \ : \ \theta(x, 1\text{E-}50)). \tag{22}$$

Two models of $A(x)$ that XSat finds are 1.1E-8 and 9.5E-9.

Discussion. The example above illustrates that XSat is execution-based—XSat executes the function (22) (so to minimize it) rather than analyzing the semantics of the logic formula (21). While this feature allows XSat to handle floating-point formulas that are difficult for traditional solvers, it also implies that XSat may be affected by floating-point inaccuracy: Let R be the representing function and x^* be its minimal point. Imagine that $\text{R}(x^*) > 0$ but the calculating $\text{R}(x^*)$ incorrectly gives 0 due to a truncation error. Then, XSat reports sat for an unsatisfiable formula. To overcome this issue, we test the original constraint to confirm the satisfiability (Sect. 5.1). Also, we have designed XSat's representing function using θ to sense small perturbations when calculating R. In the literature of search-based algorithms [28, 30], fitness functions have been proposed based on an absolute-value norm or Euclidean distance. They are valid representing functions in the sense of R1–3, but may trigger floating-point inaccuracies.

5   Experiments

5.1   Implementation

As a proof-of-concept demonstration, we have implemented XSat as a research prototype. Our implementation is written in Python and C. It is composed of two building blocks.

(B1). The front-end uses Z3's parser_smt_file API [8] to parse an SMT2-Lib file to its syntax tree representation, which is then transformed to a representing function following Lines 7–15 and Line 1 of Algorithm 1. The transformed program is compiled by Clang with optimization level -O2 and invoked via Python's C extension.

(B2). The back-end uses an implementation of a variant of MCMC, known as Basinhopping, taken from the scipy.optimize library of Python [6]. This MCMC tool has multiple options, including notably (1) the number of Monte-Carlo iterations and (2) the local optimization algorithm. These options are used in Algorithm 1 as the input parameters iter and LM respectively. In the experiment, we set iter = 100 and LM = "Powell" (which refers to Powell's algorithm [36]). To ensure that XSat does not returns sat yet the formula is unsatisfiable, we have used Z3's front-end to check XSat's calculated model.

The XSat solver does not yet support all floating-point operations that are specified in the SMT-LIB 2 standard [37]. The floating-point operators currently supported by XSat mainly include the common arithmetic operations: fp.leq, fp.lt, fp.geq, fp.gt, fp.eq, fp.neg, fp.add, fp.mult, fp.sub and fp.div. To extend XSat with other operators such as fp.min, fp.max, fp.abs and fp.sqrt, *etc.* should be straightforward since they can be directly translated into arithmetic expressions. XSat currently only accepts the rounding mode RNE (round to nearest). Other rounding modes can be easily supported in the front-end by setting appropriate floating-point flags in the C program. For example, the rounding mode RTZ (round toward zero) can be realized by introducing fesetround(FE_TOWARDZERO) in the representing function. The unsupported features listed above do not occur in the tested floating-point benchmarks (see below).

It is worth noting that, as mentioned in Sect. 4, XSat has the potential to handle floating-point constraints beyond the current SMT2-LIB's specification, because interpreted functions, such as trigonometric functions or any user-defined functions, can be readily implemented by translating them to their corresponding C implementations. An illustrative example of dealing with the sine function is given in Sect. 4.

5.2   Experimental Setup

Tested Floating-Point Benchmarks. We have evaluated XSat over a set of more than 200 benchmark SMT2 formulas. These benchmarks are proposed by Griggio (a main contributor of MathSat.[4]) for SMT-COMP 2015. They are accessible online [1]. To present our experimental results, we first divide Griggio's benchmarks into three parts:

(1) <=10K in file size: 131 SMT2 files
(2) 11K – 20K in size: 34 SMT2 files
(3) >20K in size: 49 SMT2 files

We have run XSat on *all* these benchmarks. This section presents our experiments on (2). We include our experimental results on (1) and (3) in Appendices A and B.

Compared Floating-Point Solvers. We have compared XSat with MathSat, Z3 and Coral, state-of-the-art solvers that are freely available online. MathSat and Z3 competed in the QF_FP (quantifier-free floating-point) track of the 2015 SMT Competition (SMT-COMP) [7]. The Coral solver was initially used in symbolic execution. It uses a search based approach to solve path constraints [25]. Unlike MathSat or Z3, Coral does not directly support the SMT2 language. Thus, we have transformed the benchmarks in the SMT2 language to the input language of Coral [3].

---

[4] Griggio initially used these benchmarks for comparing MathSat and Z3 [23].

For each solver, we use its default setting for running the benchmarks. All experiments were performed on a laptop with a 2.6 GHz Intel Core i7 and 16 GB RAM running MacOS 10.10.

Evaluation Objectives. There are two specific evaluation objectives:

- *Correctness testing*: For each benchmark, we run all solvers and check the consistency of their satisfiability results. MathSat's result is used as the reference because the selected benchmarks are initially used and provided by the MathSat developers.
- *Efficiency testing*: For each benchmark, we run all solvers with 48 h as the timeout limit. The time is wall time measured by the standard Unix command "time".

5.3 Quantitative Results

This subsection presents the empirical evaluation results with respect to the correctness and the efficiency of the solvers (Table 1).

Correctness. We sort the 34 benchmark programs by size in Table 1 (Col. 1-2), show each benchmark's number of variables (Col. 3) and report its satisfiability result (Col. 4–7). As mentioned above, MathSat's satisfiability results (Col. 4) are used as the reference. It shows that Z3 provides consistent results except for the benchmark sin.2.c.10, for which it times out after 48 h. Coral cannot solve 15 of the benchmarks with the wrong results marked by a framed box. For the benchmark sin2.c.10, Coral crashes due to an internal error (java.lang.NullPointerException).[5] Col. 7 shows the results of XSat, which is 100 % consistent compared with MathSat. We have summarized the correctness ratio for each solver on the last row of the table: 100 % for Z3,[6] 54.6 % for Coral,[7] and 100 % for XSat.

Efficiency. Table 1 also reports the time used by the solvers (the last four columns). Both Z3 and Mathsat show large performance variances over different benchmarks. Some of the benchmarks take very long time, such as sin.2.c.10 for MathSat, which takes 43438.34 s (¿ 12 h) or test_v7_r7_vr5_c1_s19694 for Z3, which takes 20862.74 s. On average, both MathSat and Z3 need more than 2,000 s (shown in the last row of the table).[8] By contrast, Coral and XSat (the last two

---

[5] More precisely, our JVM reports errors at coral. util. visitors. adaptors. Typed-VisitorAdaptor. visitSymBoolOperations (TypedVisitorAdaptor.java: 94). We are unsure whether this is due to bugs in Coral or our misusing it.

[6] The benchmark that Z3 times out on, sin2.c.10, is not included in calculating Z3's correctness.

[7] The one that Coral crashes on, sin2.c.10, is not included when calculating Coral's correctness.

[8] The one that Z3 times out on, sin2.c.10, is omitted in calculating Z3's performance.

Table 1. Comparison of MathSat, Z3, Coral and XSat on the SMT-Competition 2015 benchmarks proposed by Griggio, of file sizes 11K-20K.

Benchmark			Satisfiability				Time (seconds)			
SMT2-LIB program	size (byte)	#var	MathSat	Z3	Coral	XSat	MathSat	Z3	Coral	XSat
div2.c.30	11430	32	sat	sat	unsat	sat	131.73	14633.28	2.43	7.41
mult1.c.30	11478	33	sat	sat	unsat	sat	293.28	14.55	1.37	0.80
div3.c.30	11497	33	sat	sat	unsat	sat	139.30	212.68	1.37	0.76
div.c.30	11527	33	sat	sat	unsat	sat	90.75	140.09	1.37	0.75
mult2.c.30	11567	34	sat	sat	unsat	sat	358.77	12.87	1.39	0.77
test_v7_r7_vr10_c1_s24535	14928	7	sat	sat	sat	sat	35.27	85.56	0.78	0.77
test_v5_r10_vr5_c1_s13195	15013	5	sat	sat	sat	sat	160.30	260.32	0.54	0.76
div2.c.40	15060	42	sat	sat	unsat	sat	419.57	6011.65	3.38	11.90
mult1.c.40	15088	43	sat	sat	unsat	sat	726.95	31.88	1.57	0.83
test_v7_r7_vr1_c1_s24449	15090	7	unsat	unsat	unsat	unsat	359.42	669.88	1.34	3.93
div3.c.40	15117	43	sat	sat	sat	sat	301.53	226.78	0.92	0.80
div.c.40	15157	43	sat	sat	unsat	sat	290.41	375.42	1.57	0.79
mult2.c.40	15177	44	sat	sat	unsat	sat	1680.93	30.03	1.59	0.77
test_v7_r7_vr5_c1_s3582	15184	7	sat	sat	sat	sat	101.78	78.10	0.55	0.83
test_v7_r7_vr1_c1_s22845	15273	7	sat	sat	sat	sat	138.76	2619.23	0.72	0.78
test_v7_r7_vr5_c1_s19694	15275	7	sat	sat	sat	sat	705.91	20862.74	0.64	0.86
test_v7_r7_vr5_c1_s14675	15277	7	sat	sat	sat	sat	66.90	227.70	0.53	0.76
test_v7_r7_vr10_c1_s32506	15277	7	sat	sat	sat	sat	291.32	1401.88	0.74	0.96
test_v7_r7_vr10_c1_s10625	15277	7	sat	sat	sat	sat	2971.82	1335.51	0.53	0.76
test_v7_r7_vr1_c1_s4574	15279	7	sat	sat	sat	sat	90.80	2381.56	0.80	0.77
test_v5_r10_vr5_c1_s8690	15393	5	unsat	unsat	unsat	unsat	264.36	563.48	1.37	1.58
test_v5_r10_vr1_c1_s32538	15393	5	unsat	unsat	unsat	unsat	38.88	153.65	1.35	2.22
test_v5_r10_vr5_c1_s13679	15395	5	sat	sat	unsat	sat	256.88	1748.58	1.36	0.76
test_v5_r10_vr10_c1_s15708	15395	5	unsat	unsat	unsat	unsat	3586.89	9000.07	1.35	1.80
test_v5_r10_vr10_c1_s7608	15400	5	unsat	unsat	unsat	unsat	2098.50	4941.08	1.36	1.89
test_v5_r10_vr1_c1_s19145	15486	5	sat	sat	sat	sat	125.61	190.75	0.88	0.76
test_v5_r10_vr1_c1_s13516	15488	5	sat	sat	sat	sat	107.16	89.15	0.89	0.76
test_v5_r10_vr10_c1_s21502	15488	5	unsat	unsat	unsat	unsat	1810.06	4174.55	1.35	2.00
sin2.c.10	17520	37	sat	>48h	crash	sat	43438.34	timeout	crash	26.64
div2.c.50	18755	52	sat	sat	unsat	sat	972.07	1803.04	4.57	15.81
mult1.c.50	18757	53	sat	sat	unsat	sat	2742.47	61.49	1.71	1.32
div3.c.50	18798	53	sat	sat	unsat	sat	350.13	473.64	1.72	0.99
mult2.c.50	18848	54	sat	sat	unsat	sat	2890.08	106.22	1.71	0.96
div.c.50	18849	53	sat	sat	unsat	sat	464.64	554.38	1.70	0.97
SUMMARY			-	100.0 %	54.6 %	100.0 %	2014.75	2290.05	1.38	2.80

columns) perform significantly better than MathSat or Z3. Both can finish most benchmarks within seconds. On average, Coral requires 1.38 s, which is less than XSat (2.80 s). Note that Coral only obtains accurate satisfiability results on 54.6 % of the benchmarks.

Appendices A and B list our experimental results of XSat versus Z3 and Mathsat on the rest of Griggio's benchmarks. Similar to Table 1, the results in Tables 2 and 3 show an important performance improvement of XSat over

MathSat and Z3. Note that on five of the listed benchmarks, XSat reports unsat while MathSat and Z3 report sat. We have recognized such incompleteness in Lemma 2. Thus, although XSat has achieved significantly better results than the other evaluated solvers, it is generally unable to *prove* unsat, while Z3 and MathSat can. Therefore, XSat does not compete, but rather complements these solvers.

6   Related Work

The study on floating-point theory is relatively sparse compared to other theories. Eager approaches encode floating-point constraints as propositional formulas [15, 35], relying on a SAT solver as the backend; the lazy approaches, on the other hand, use a propositional CDCL solver [24] to reason about the Boolean structure and an ad-hoc floating-point procedures for theory reasoning. The issues of these decision procedures are well-known: The eager approaches may produce large propositional encoding, which can be a considerable time burden for the worst-case exponential SAT solvers, while the lazy approaches may have difficulties to deal with nontrivial numerical (*e.g.*, non-linear) operations that are frequent in real-world floating-point code. Although, we have seen active development and enhancement for these solutions, such as the mixed abstractions [11], theory-based heuristics [22], or the natural domain SMT [23], state-of-the-art floating-point decision procedures still face performance challenges.

The idea of using numerical methods in program reasoning has been explored. As an example, the SMT-solver dReal [20] combines numerical search with logical techniques for solving problems that can be encoded as first-order logic formulas over the real numbers. There is also a body of work on symbolic and numerical methods [28, 31, 32] for test generation in scientific programs.

Perhaps the closely related work to XSat is the Coral solver [10, 39]. It involves mostly heuristic-based fitness functions integrated in symbolic execution [25], which has been successfully integrated in Java Pathfinder [5]. However, to the best of our knowledge, it has not seen much adoption. Compared to XSat, Coral does not provide a precise and systematic solution for using mathematical optimization in solving floating-point constraints.

7   Conclusion

We have introduced XSat, a floating-point satisfiability solver that is grounded on the concept of representing functions. Given constraint π and program R such that R1-3 hold, the theoretical guarantee of Theorem 1 stipulates that the problem of deciding π can be equivalently solved via minimizing R and checking whether $R(x^*) = 0$ where x^* is a global minimum point of R.

The key challenge of such an approach lies in minimizing the representing function R, which involves an unconstrained mathematical optimization problem. While many MO problems are intractable, our sight is that carefully designed representing functions can lead to MO problems efficiently solvable in practice. We have implemented the XSat solver to empirically validate our theory. XSat systematically transforms quantifier-free floating-point formulas into representing functions, and minimizes them via MCMC methods. We have compared XSat with the state-of-the-art floating-point solvers, MathSat, Z3 and Coral. Evaluated on benchmarks taken from the SMT-Competition 2015, XSat is shown to significantly outperform these solvers.

Acknowledgments. We thank the anonymous reviewers for their useful comments on earlier versions of this paper. Our special thanks go to Viktor Kuncak for his thoughtful feedback. This work was supported in part by NSF Grant No. 1349528. The information presented here does not necessarily reflect the position or the policy of the Government and no official endorsement should be inferred.

A   Experimental Results for Griggio's Benchmarks (<=10K)

Table 2 shows that XSat produces the same satisfiability as MathSat and Z3 on nearly all benchmarks of file sizes <=10K. XSat does not support mul_03_03_1 (shown as unsupported in the table) because it currently does not handle NaN involved in its formula. XSat reports unsat for sqrt.c.5 whereas MathSat and Z3 report sat; this phenomenon also appears in Table 2 (which we have explained at the end of Sect. 5). Regarding the performance, XSat significantly outperforms both MathSat and Z3 in average: 2473.95 and 992.03 s for MathSat and Z3 respectively, and 2.63 s for XSat.[9]

B   Experimental Results for Griggio's Benchmarks (>20K)

Table 3 shows that XSat produces the same results as MathSat and Z3 for most benchmarks of sizes > 20K where MathSat or Z3 does not timeout; Observe that XSat reports unsat on four benchmarks (sqrt.c.10, sqrt.c.15, sqrt.c.20 and sqrt.c.25) which are satisfiable according to Z3.

---

[9] The benchmarks that Z3 or MathSat timeouts are not included when measuring their mean times (the last row of Table 2).

Table 2. Comparison of MathSat, Z3 and XSat. The table lists all 131 SMT2 files of size <=10K in Griggio's benchmarks. The timeout bound is 48 h.

Benchmark SMT2-LIB program	size (byte)	Satisfiability			Time (seconds)		
		MathSat	Z3	XSat	MathSat	Z3	XSat
test_v5_r15_vr10_c1_s11127	492	sat	sat	sat	0.01	0.18	2.03
square	1182	unsat	unsat	unsat	0.49	0.17	2.52
e1_2.c	1361	sat	sat	sat	0.12	0.50	1.03
e1_1.c	1361	sat	sat	sat	0.11	0.52	0.55
e1.c	1587	sat	sat	sat	0.13	0.56	1.02
pow5	1622	unsat	unsat	unsat	107.76	564.23	2.06
e2a_3.c	1788	sat	sat	sat	0.11	0.34	1.01
div2.c.3	1821	sat	sat	sat	1.01	3.31	1.03
e2a_1.c	1884	sat	sat	sat	0.12	0.05	0.55
div3.c.3	1911	sat	sat	sat	1.48	2.78	1.01
div.c.3	1914	sat	sat	sat	0.77	2.50	1.01
mult1.c.3	1917	sat	sat	sat	0.16	0.56	1.03
e2a_2.c	1979	sat	sat	sat	0.12	0.32	1.02
mult2.c.3	2004	sat	sat	sat	0.24	0.63	1.02
sine.1.0.i	2502	sat	sat	sat	7.16	3.87	1.02
e3_2.c	2529	sat	sat	sat	2.57	2.72	1.02
e2_3.c	2540	sat	sat	sat	0.15	0.36	1.03
e2_1.c	2588	sat	sat	sat	0.74	2.23	1.03
f23	2607	sat	sat	sat	7.33	11.64	0.54
sine.8.0.i	2617	unsat	unsat	unsat	9.87	45.71	1.15
sine.7.0.i	2617	unsat	unsat	unsat	12.81	45.31	1.13
sine.6.0.i	2617	unsat	unsat	unsat	5.22	40.68	1.13
sine.5.0.i	2617	unsat	unsat	unsat	35.32	38.48	1.16
sine.4.0.i	2617	unsat	unsat	unsat	409.29	32.98	0.65
sine.3.0.i	2617	unsat	unsat	unsat	18.34	45.26	1.13
sine.2.0.i	2617	unsat	unsat	unsat	12.63	30.68	1.13
e2_2.c	2636	sat	sat	sat	0.11	0.36	0.65
e3_1.c	2692	sat	sat	sat	0.85	4.00	1.02
square.8.0.i	2817	unsat	unsat	unsat	8.12	17.86	1.13
square.7.0.i	2817	unsat	unsat	unsat	3.43	13.29	0.67
square.6.0.i	2817	unsat	unsat	unsat	3.50	23.61	1.13
square.5.0.i	2817	unsat	unsat	unsat	12.83	20.05	1.12
square.4.0.i	2817	unsat	unsat	unsat	3.41	19.09	0.65
square.3.0.i	2817	unsat	unsat	unsat	5.69	13.34	1.13
square.2.0.i	2817	unsat	unsat	unsat	3.88	30.35	1.13
square.1.0.i	2817	unsat	unsat	unsat	3.42	12.92	1.13
e2.c	3279	sat	sat	sat	0.83	2.28	0.65
newton.8.1.i	3461	sat	sat	sat	3.76	5.36	1.04
newton.5.1.i	3461	sat	sat	sat	24.12	14.87	1.03
newton.7.1.i	3552	sat	sat	sat	12.80	6.65	0.54
newton.6.1.i	3552	sat	sat	sat	12.79	8.32	1.03
newton.4.1.i	3552	sat	sat	sat	5.10	9.41	1.03
newton.3.1.i	3552	unsat	unsat	unsat	3460.87	458.06	1.25
newton.2.1.i	3552	unsat	unsat	unsat	12419.87	341.96	1.25
newton.1.1.i	3552	unsat	unsat	unsat	912.12	241.52	0.74
e3.c	4011	unsat	unsat	unsat	0.67	3.49	16.06
test_v3_r3_vr5_c1_s26769	4103	sat	sat	sat	1.23	2.89	1.02

(Continued)

Table 2. *(Continued)*

Benchmark		Satisfiability			Time (seconds)		
SMT2-LIB program	size (byte)	MathSat	Z3	XSat	MathSat	Z3	XSat
test_v3_r3_vr5_c1_s16867	4103	sat	sat	sat	0.66	2.17	0.54
test_v3_r3_vr5_c1_s16641	4103	sat	sat	sat	0.77	2.23	1.05
test_v3_r3_vr1_c1_s6731	4103	unsat	unsat	unsat	4.46	10.94	2.69
test_v3_r3_vr1_c1_s5578	4103	unsat	unsat	unsat	1.22	4.40	2.06
test_v3_r3_vr1_c1_s10392	4103	sat	sat	sat	1.76	5.13	1.04
test_v3_r3_vr10_c1_s29304	4103	sat	sat	sat	0.84	2.20	1.04
test_v3_r3_vr10_c1_s24300	4103	sat	sat	sat	2.75	3.03	1.02
test_v3_r3_vr10_c1_s14052	4103	sat	sat	sat	2.55	4.89	1.02
add_01_1_4	4118	unsat	unsat	unsat	54.09	39.66	2.26
add_01_1_3	4118	unsat	unsat	unsat	48.12	30.98	2.27
add_01_1_2	4118	unsat	unsat	unsat	34.99	22.37	2.29
add_01_1_1	4118	unsat	unsat	unsat	8.52	20.30	2.29
add_01_10_4	4118	unsat	unsat	unsat	48.78	24.67	2.25
add_01_10_3	4118	unsat	unsat	unsat	22.62	23.94	2.36
add_01_10_2	4118	unsat	unsat	unsat	9.14	14.52	2.30
add_01_10_1	4118	unsat	unsat	unsat	3.32	8.48	2.26
add_01_100_4	4118	unsat	unsat	unsat	35.53	25.66	2.17
add_01_100_3	4118	unsat	unsat	unsat	15.13	19.12	2.27
add_01_100_2	4118	unsat	unsat	unsat	3.65	8.31	2.26
add_01_100_1	4118	unsat	unsat	unsat	1.47	4.55	2.27
add_01_1000_4	4118	unsat	unsat	unsat	11.03	16.22	2.16
add_01_1000_3	4118	unsat	unsat	unsat	3.88	9.61	2.18
add_01_1000_2	4118	unsat	unsat	unsat	1.08	4.66	2.28
add_01_1000_1	4118	unsat	unsat	unsat	1.25	3.57	2.47
mul_03_3_1	4211	sat	sat	unsupported	20.01	7.52	unsupported
mul_03_30_4	4211	unsat	unsat	unsat	235.55	503.51	2.53
mul_03_30_1	4211	unsat	unsat	unsat	11.65	43.26	2.65
mul_03_3000_1	4211	timeout	timeout	unsat	>48 h	>48 h	2.48
mul_000003_30000_1	4211	timeout	unsat	unsat	>48 h	16906.61	2.46
div2.c.10	4264	sat	sat	sat	65.87	21.25	1.13
mult1.c.10	4346	sat	sat	sat	12.70	3.40	1.02
div3.c.10	4347	sat	sat	sat	50.33	9.95	1.01
div.c.10	4357	sat	sat	sat	7.23	12.98	1.03
mult2.c.10	4433	sat	sat	sat	13.52	4.25	1.02
mul_03_30_7	4459	unsat	unsat	unsat	16.70	50.67	2.47
mul_03_30_6	4459	unsat	unsat	unsat	10.46	52.32	2.35
mul_03_30_5	4459	unsat	unsat	unsat	9.28	48.58	2.57
mul_03_30_3	4459	unsat	unsat	unsat	10.43	41.03	2.47
mul_03_30_2	4459	unsat	unsat	unsat	9.19	40.61	2.38
newton.8.2.i	5061	sat	sat	sat	7.18	10.42	1.05
newton.5.2.i	5061	unsat	unsat	unsat	72647.46	5486.77	0.54
sqrt.c.2	5070	sat	sat	sat	225.06	71.90	7.10
newton.7.2.i	5152	sat	sat	sat	81.02	20.90	1.06
newton.6.2.i	5152	sat	sat	sat	8.95	11.36	1.05
newton.4.2.i	5152	unsat	unsat	unsat	5488.06	4900.28	0.54
newton.3.2.i	5152	unsat	unsat	unsat	25240.14	3360.73	1.28
newton.2.2.i	5152	unsat	unsat	unsat	8889.74	3806.77	1.26
newton.1.2.i	5152	unsat	unsat	unsat	5681.05	4262.89	1.27

(Continued)

Table 2. *(Continued)*

Benchmark		Satisfiability			Time (seconds)		
SMT2-LIB program	size (byte)	MathSat	Z3	XSat	MathSat	Z3	XSat
sin2.c.2	5242	sat	sat	sat	18.90	7.80	9.18
square_and_power_inverse	6494	sat	sat	sat	0.01	0.01	0.84
newton.8.3.i	6669	sat	sat	sat	41.29	15.84	1.11
newton.5.3.i	6669	timeout	unsat	unsat	>48 h	15519.38	1.41
newton.7.3.i	6762	sat	sat	sat	586.00	13.54	1.12
newton.6.3.i	6762	sat	sat	sat	135.75	307.57	0.55
newton.4.3.i	6762	unsat	unsat	unsat	63877.95	12611.50	1.32
newton.3.3.i	6762	unsat	unsat	unsat	51598.07	11232.12	1.32
newton.2.3.i	6762	timeout	unsat	unsat	>48 h	17982.84	1.32
newton.1.3.i	6762	unsat	unsat	unsat	59252.23	13776.82	1.32
div2.c.20	7818	sat	sat	sat	127.18	50.76	7.29
mult1.c.20	7886	sat	sat	sat	98.25	4.32	1.04
div3.c.20	7895	sat	sat	sat	135.78	77.00	1.05
div.c.20	7915	sat	sat	sat	40.17	68.29	1.04
mult2.c.20	7975	sat	sat	sat	71.30	13.59	1.03
qurt.c.2	8332	unsat	unsat	unsat	48.25	16.43	15.64
test_v3_r8_vr5_c1_s8257	8359	unsat	unsat	unsat	20.65	20.14	1.58
test_v3_r8_vr5_c1_s10746	8361	unsat	unsat	unsat	31.51	38.80	2.38
test_v3_r8_vr1_c1_s733	8448	unsat	unsat	unsat	22.77	21.76	2.19
test_v3_r8_vr10_c1_s18214	8448	unsat	unsat	unsat	45.47	31.62	1.67
test_v3_r8_vr1_c1_s23752	8450	unsat	unsat	unsat	11.97	5.64	2.20
test_v3_r8_vr1_c1_s20372	8450	unsat	unsat	unsat	10.64	6.47	1.76
test_v3_r8_vr10_c1_s5590	8450	sat	sat	sat	33.42	68.78	1.04
test_v3_r8_vr5_c1_s1507	8452	unsat	unsat	unsat	18.78	19.66	1.66
test_v3_r8_vr10_c1_s4660	8454	unsat	unsat	unsat	41.24	34.78	2.08
test_v5_r5_vr1_c1_s14623	8628	sat	sat	sat	58.75	86.74	1.15
test_v5_r5_vr1_c1_s16138	8715	sat	sat	sat	22.96	58.91	1.14
test_v5_r5_vr10_c1_s7194	8715	sat	sat	sat	78.97	120.72	1.04
test_v5_r5_vr10_c1_s5379	8717	sat	sat	sat	53.81	36.80	1.05
test_v5_r5_vr5_c1_s9855	8721	sat	sat	sat	36.09	136.86	1.06
test_v5_r5_vr5_c1_s2800	8721	sat	sat	sat	121.14	660.37	1.25
test_v5_r5_vr1_c1_s15604	8721	sat	sat	sat	19.30	39.96	1.04
test_v5_r5_vr10_c1_s5996	8721	sat	sat	sat	9.56	18.63	0.54
test_v5_r5_vr5_c1_s24018	8723	sat	sat	sat	53.83	70.01	1.16
sin2.c.5	9817	sat	sat	sat	513.95	11640.31	81.31
sqrt.c.5	11235	sat	sat	unsat	362.19	2033.94	33.78
MEAN					2473.95	992.03	2.63

Table 3. Comparison of MathSat, Z3 and XSat. The table lists all 49 SMT2 files of size >20K in Griggio's benchmarks. The timeout bound is 600 s.

Benchmark		Time (seconds)			Satisfiability		
SMT2-LIB program	size (byte)	MathSat	Z3	XSat	MathSat	Z3	XSat
sqrt.c.10	21694	510.21	>600s	25.39	sat	timeout	unsat
test_v5_r15_vr5_c1_s8246	21786	>600s	>600s	5.43	timeout	timeout	unsat
test_v5_r15_vr1_c1_s26845	21806	205.72	>600s	4.25	unsat	timeout	unsat
test_v5_r15_vr10_c1_s25268	21811	>600s	>600s	4.16	timeout	timeout	unsat
test_v5_r15_vr5_c1_s26657	22065	1516.29	>600s	4.40	unsat	timeout	unsat
test_v5_r15_vr5_c1_s23844	22067	>600s	>600s	4.97	timeout	timeout	unsat
test_v5_r15_vr1_c1_s8236	22067	88.61	>600s	4.12	unsat	timeout	unsat
test_v5_r15_vr1_c1_s32559	22067	177.08	154.21	4.68	unsat	unsat	unsat
test_v5_r15_vr10_c1_s14516	22245	>600s	>600s	3.95	timeout	timeout	unsat
qurt.c.5	23164	30.09	180.65	16.87	unsat	unsat	unsat
test_v7_r12_vr5_c1_s29826	23733	6742.22	>600s	1.65	sat	timeout	sat
test_v7_r12_vr10_c1_s15994	23825	>600s	>600s	1.44	timeout	timeout	sat
test_v7_r12_vr10_c1_s30410	24063	>600s	>600s	7.26	timeout	timeout	sat
test_v7_r12_vr5_c1_s14336	24247	301.37	>600s	2.21	sat	timeout	sat
test_v7_r12_vr5_c1_s8938	24248	57.62	536.56	1.93	sat	sat	sat
test_v7_r12_vr1_c1_s10576	24267	>600s	>600s	9.48	timeout	timeout	unsat
test_v7_r12_vr1_c1_s22787	24338	>600s	>600s	6.81	timeout	timeout	unsat
test_v7_r12_vr10_c1_s18160	24430	>600s	>600s	7.42	timeout	timeout	unsat
test_v7_r12_vr1_c1_s703	24434	>600s	>600s	8.99	timeout	timeout	unsat
sin2.c.15	25228	>600s	>600s	214.19	timeout	timeout	sat
gaussian.c.25	29880	>600s	489.56	89.84	timeout	sat	sat
sqrt.c.15	32189	484.49	>600s	35.82	sat	timeout	unsat
test_v7_r17_vr5_c1_s2807	32704	>600s	>600s	7.81	timeout	timeout	unsat
test_v7_r17_vr1_c1_s30331	32869	>600s	>600s	9.13	timeout	timeout	unsat
test_v7_r17_vr5_c1_s25451	32957	>600s	>600s	7.95	timeout	timeout	unsat
sin2.c.20	33009	>600s	>600s	226.16	timeout	timeout	sat
test_v7_r17_vr10_c1_s8773	33144	>600s	>600s	7.55	timeout	timeout	sat
test_v7_r17_vr5_c1_s4772	33215	>600s	>600s	7.91	timeout	timeout	unsat
test_v7_r17_vr1_c1_s24331	33219	>600s	>600s	9.50	timeout	timeout	unsat
test_v7_r17_vr1_c1_s23882	33219	>600s	>600s	2.58	timeout	timeout	sat
test_v7_r17_vr10_c1_s3680	33328	>600s	>600s	6.90	timeout	timeout	unsat
test_v7_r17_vr10_c1_s18654	33403	>600s	>600s	2.39	timeout	timeout	sat
sin.c.25	40529	>600s	>600s	372.76	timeout	timeout	sat
sin2.c.25	40740	>600s	>600s	>600s	timeout	timeout	timeout
sqrt.c.25	46801	147.34	>600s	131.43	sat	timeout	unsat
sqrt.c.20	46801	151.93	>600s	153.13	sat	timeout	unsat
qurt.c.10	47941	33.34	490.03	55.50	unsat	unsat	unsat
qurt.c.15	73120	35.16	1.50	134.12	unsat	unsat	unsat
gaussian.c.75	89683	>600s	>600s	>600s	timeout	timeout	timeout
qurt.c.25	93119	51.39	>600s	194.27	unsat	timeout	unsat
qurt.c.20	93119	58.78	>600s	190.35	unsat	timeout	unsat
sin2.c.75	119783	>600s	>600s	>600s	timeout	timeout	timeout
sin.c.75	119787	>600s	>600s	>600s	timeout	timeout	timeout
gaussian.c.125	150785	>600s	>600s	>600s	timeout	timeout	timeout
sin2.c.125	200496	>600s	>600s	>600s	timeout	timeout	timeout
sin.c.125	200496	>600s	>600s	>600s	timeout	timeout	timeout
gaussian.c.175	210704	>600s	>600s	>600s	timeout	timeout	timeout
sin2.c.175	280955	>600s	>600s	>600s	timeout	timeout	timeout
sin.c.175	280977	>600s	>600s	>600s	timeout	timeout	timeout

References

1. Benchmarks of the QF_FP track in SMT-COMP (2015). http://www.cs.nyu.edu/~barrett/smtlib/QF_FP_Hierarchy.zip. Accessed 29 Jan 2016
2. Boost c++ libraries. www.boost.org/. Accessed 27 Jan 2016
3. Coral input language. http://pan.cin.ufpe.br/coral/InputLanguage.html. Accessed 24 Jan 2016
4. The GNU C library (glibc). https://www.gnu.org/software/libc/. Accessed 28 Jan 2016
5. The main page for Java Pathfinder. http://babelfish.arc.nasa.gov/trac/jpf. Accessed 29 Jan 2016
6. Scipy optimization package. http://docs.scipy.org/doc/scipy-dev/reference/optimize.html#module-scipy.optimize. Accessed 29 Jan 2016
7. SMT-COMP (2015). http://smtcomp.sourceforge.net/2015/. Accessed 24 Jan 2016
8. Z3py API. http://z3prover.github.io/api/html/namespacez3py.html. Accessed 29 Jan 2016
9. Andrieu, C., de Freitas, N., Doucet, A., Jordan, M.I.: An introduction to MCMC for machine learning. Mach. Learn. **50**, 5–43 (2003)
10. Borges, M., d'Amorim, M., Anand, S., Bushnell, D., Pasareanu, C.S.: Symbolic execution with interval solving and meta-heuristic search. In: Proceedings of the 2012 IEEE Fifth International Conference on Software Testing, Verification and Validation, ICST 2012, Washington, DC, USA, pp. 111–120. IEEE Computer Society (2012)
11. Brillout, A., Kroening, D., Wahl, T.: Mixed abstractions for floating-point arithmetic. In: FMCAD, pp. 69–76 (2009)
12. Chen, Y., Zhendong, S.: Guided differential testing of certificate validation in SSL/TLS implementations. In: Proceedings of the 2015 10th Joint Meeting on Foundations of Software Engineering, ESEC/FSE 2015, Bergamo, Italy, 30 August–4 September 2015, pp. 793–804 (2015)
13. Chib, S., Greenberg, E.: Understanding the metropolis-hastings algorithm. Am. Stat. **49**(4), 327–335 (1995)
14. Cimatti, A., Griggio, A., Schaafsma, B.J., Sebastiani, R.: The mathSAT5 SMT solver. In: Piterman, N., Smolka, S.A. (eds.) TACAS 2013 (ETAPS 2013). LNCS, vol. 7795, pp. 93–107. Springer, Heidelberg (2013)
15. Clarke, E., Kroning, D., Lerda, F.: A tool for checking ANSI-C programs. In: Jensen, K., Podelski, A. (eds.) TACAS 2004. LNCS, vol. 2988, pp. 168–176. Springer, Heidelberg (2004)
16. de Moura, L., Bjørner, N.S.: Z3: an efficient SMT solver. In: Ramakrishnan, C.R., Rehof, J. (eds.) TACAS 2008. LNCS, vol. 4963, pp. 337–340. Springer, Heidelberg (2008)
17. Espírito-Santo, I.A., Costa, L.A., Rocha, A.M.A.C., Azad, M.A.K., Fernandes, E.M.G.P.: On Challenging Techniques for Constrained Global Optimization. Springer, Heidelberg (2013)
18. Zhoulai, F., Bai, Z., Zhendong, S.: Automated backward error analysis for numerical code. In: OOPSLA, pp. 639–654 (2015)
19. Ganzinger, H., Hagen, G., Nieuwenhuis, R., Oliveras, A., Tinelli, C.: DPLL(T): fast decision procedures. In: Alur, R., Peled, D.A. (eds.) CAV 2004. LNCS, vol. 3114, pp. 175–188. Springer, Heidelberg (2004)
20. Gao, S., Kong, S., Clarke, E.M.: dReal: an SMT solver for nonlinear theories over the reals. In: Bonacina, M.P. (ed.) CADE 2013. LNCS, vol. 7898, pp. 208–214. Springer, Heidelberg (2013)

21. Goldberg, D.: What every computer scientist should know about floating point arithmetic. ACM Comput. Surv. **23**(1), 5–48 (1991)
22. Goldwasser, D., Strichman, O., Fine, S.: A theory-based decision heuristic for DPLL(T). In: FMCAD, pp. 1–8 (2008)
23. Haller, L., Griggio, A., Brain, M., Kroening, D.: Deciding floating-point logic with systematic abstraction. In: FMCAD, pp. 131–140 (2012)
24. Bayardo Jr., R.J., Schrag, R.: Using CSP look-back techniques to solve real-world SAT instances. In: Proceedings of the Fourteenth National Conference on Artificial Intelligence and Ninth Innovative Applications of Artificial Intelligence Conference, AAAI 1997, IAAI 1997, 27–31 July 1997, pp. 203–208. Providence, Rhode Island (1997)
25. King, J.C.: Symbolic execution and program testing. Commun. ACM **19**(7), 385–394 (1976)
26. Kirkpatrick, S., Gelatt, C.D., Vecchi, M.P.: Optimization by simulated annealing. Science **220**(4598), 671–680 (1983)
27. Kleene, S.C.: Introduction to Metamathematics. North-Holland, Amsterdam (1962)
28. Lakhotia, K., Tillmann, N., Harman, M., de Halleux, J.: Flopsy-search-based floating point constraint solving for symbolic execution. In: Petrenko, A., Simão, A., Maldonado, J.C. (eds.) ICTSS 2010. LNCS, vol. 6435, pp. 142–157. Springer, Heidelberg (2010)
29. Li, Z., Scheraga, H.A.: Monte Carlo-minimization approach to the multiple-minima problem in protein folding. In: Proceedings of the National Academy of Sciences of the United States of America, vol. 84, No. 19, pp. 6611–6615 (1987)
30. McMinn, P.: Search-based software test data generation: a survey: research articles. Softw. Test. Verif. Reliab. **14**(2), 105–156 (2004)
31. Meinke, K., Niu, F.: A learning-based approach to unit testing of numerical software. In: Petrenko, A., Simão, A., Maldonado, J.C. (eds.) ICTSS 2010. LNCS, vol. 6435, pp. 221–235. Springer, Heidelberg (2010)
32. Miller, W., Spooner, D.L.: Automatic generation of floating-point test data. IEEE Trans. Softw. Eng. **2**(3), 223–226 (1976)
33. Nieuwenhuis, R., Oliveras, A., Tinelli, C.: Solving SAT and SAT modulo theories: from an abstract Davis-Putnam-Logemann-Loveland procedure to DPLL(T). J. ACM **53**(6), 937–977 (2006)
34. Nocedal, J., Wright, S.J.: Numerical Optimization. Springer, Berlin (2006)
35. Peleska, J., Vorobev, E., Lapschies, F.: Automated test case generation with SMT-solving and abstract interpretation. In: Bobaru, M., Havelund, K., Holzmann, G.J., Joshi, R. (eds.) NFM 2011. LNCS, vol. 6617, pp. 298–312. Springer, Heidelberg (2011)
36. Press, W.H., Teukolsky, S.A., Vetterling, W.T., Flannery, B.P.: Numerical Recipes: The Art of Scientific Computing, 3rd edn. Cambridge University Press, New York (2007)
37. Rümmer, P., Wahl, T.: An SMT-LIB theory of binary floating-point arithmetic. In: Informal proceedings of 8th International Workshop on Satisfiability Modulo Theories (SMT) at FLoC, Edinburgh, Scotland (2010)
38. Schkufza, E., Sharma, R., Aiken, A.: Stochastic optimization of floating-point programs with tunable precision. In: PLDI, pp. 53–64 (2014)
39. Souza, M., Borges, M., d'Amorim, M., Păsăreanu, C.S.: CORAL: solving complex constraints for symbolic pathfinder. In: Bobaru, M., Havelund, K., Holzmann, G.J., Joshi, R. (eds.) NFM 2011. LNCS, vol. 6617, pp. 359–374. Springer, Heidelberg (2011)

Effectively Propositional Interpolants

Samuel Drews and Aws Albarghouthi[✉]

University of Wisconsin–Madison, Madison, USA
aws@cs.wisc.edu

Abstract. We present a novel interpolation algorithm for *effectively propositional logic* (EPR), a decidable fragment of first-order logic that enjoys a small-model property. EPR is a powerful fragment of quantified formulas that has been used to model and verify a range of programs, including heap-manipulating programs and distributed protocols. Our interpolation technique *samples finite models* from two sides of the interpolation problem and *generalizes* them to learn a quantified interpolant. Our results demonstrate our technique's ability to compute universally-quantified, existentially-quantified, as well as alternation-free interpolants and inductive invariants, thus improving the state of the art.

1 Introduction

Craig interpolation techniques have played an important role in the advancement of automated analysis and verification: from hardware verification [18], to software verification [12,19], to error diagnosis [10], and even to modeling of cyber-physical systems [4]. By representing program executions as first-order formulas, interpolants can be used to concisely conjecture *why* the program is correct. Expanding the scope of interpolation-based verification requires investigating and developing interpolation techniques for different logical theories that enable modeling of various program features.

In this paper, we investigate the problem of computing Craig interpolants for *effectively propositional logic* (EPR), also known as the Bernays-Schönfinkel-Ramsey fragment of first-order logic. EPR is the class of formulas of the form $\exists^* \forall^* \varphi$, where the quantifier-free formula φ has no function symbols. Two interesting aspects motivate our study of this fragment: (*i*) decidability of its satisfiability and (*ii*) its surprising applicability to modeling a range of complex program features. For instance, EPR has been used to model programs manipulating linked-list data structures and arrays [13–15,17,26], software-defined networking programs [5], eventually consistent data stores [29], parameterized distributed protocols [22], amongst others [23–25]. Indeed, the power of EPR lies primarily in its ability to model unbounded structures. Thus, progress in interpolation can open the door to verification in a large spectrum of domains.

We propose a *sampling*-based technique for computing an interpolant I for two inconsistent EPR formulas, A and B. A key insight in our approach is that we can use an EPR satisfiability procedure as an oracle to systematically sample finite models of A and B and *generalize* them to monotonically *grow* an

© Springer International Publishing Switzerland 2016
S. Chaudhuri and A. Farzan (Eds.): CAV 2016, Part II, LNCS 9780, pp. 210–229, 2016.
DOI: 10.1007/978-3-319-41540-6_12

interpolant. A finite model of an EPR formula can be viewed as a relational structure—a hypergraph—over a finite set of nodes. Our algorithm thus samples hypergraphs from A and B and generalizes them into infinite *sets* of structurally similar hypergraphs.

Our presented technique ensures that computed interpolants do not contain quantifier alternation—that is, they are of the form $\exists^* \varphi$, $\forall^* \varphi$, or Boolean combinations of those. This pragmatic constraint is motivated by the fact that computed interpolants are typically used in verification engines, and thus form inductive invariant conjectures. To check if an interpolant $I(\boldsymbol{x})$ is an inductive invariant with respect to a transition relation $T(\boldsymbol{x}, \boldsymbol{x}')$, one needs to check satisfiability of $I(\boldsymbol{x}) \wedge T(\boldsymbol{x}, \boldsymbol{x}') \wedge \neg I(\boldsymbol{x}')$. If I has quantifier alternation, we leave the decidable confines of the EPR fragment—due to the negation of I, which makes it of the form $\forall^* \exists^* \varphi$. Thus, by finding alternation-free interpolants, we maintain decidability of inductiveness checking.

Contributions. To our knowledge, this paper is the first comprehensive investigation of EPR interpolation. We summarize our key contributions as follows:

- We first present an interpolation algorithm that can construct an *existentially-quantified interpolant*, of the form $\exists^* \varphi$, or detect its non-existence. The algorithm monotonically grows an interpolant by sampling finite models and generalizing them using the model-theoretic notion of *diagrams* [9].
- We present an interesting proof of soundness and completeness of our algorithm and identify EPR fragments and conditions for which it is complete.
- We show that, by solving the *dual* interpolation problem, our algorithm can also be used to construct *universally-quantified interpolants*, of the form $\forall^* \varphi$.
- We then show how, by systematically decomposing the interpolation problem, we can leverage this procedure to construct *alternation-free interpolants* with Boolean combinations of universal and existential quantifiers.
- We validate our interpolation algorithm by implementing it alongside a simple interpolation-based verifier. We show that the verifier (i) is competitive with recent PDR-based algorithms [15,17] for computing universal invariants, and (ii) is able to compute alternation-free invariants, a fragment that is out of scope for existing techniques.

2   Illustrative Example

In this section, we illustrate our technique with simple examples.

Existential Interpolants. Consider the following formulas in EPR:

$$A \triangleq \exists a. \forall b. (p(a) \vee q(a)) \wedge r(b) \qquad B \triangleq \exists c. \forall d. \neg p(d) \wedge \neg q(d) \wedge s(c)$$

where p, q, r, s are unary relations. $A \wedge B$ is unsatisfiable, and we would like to find an interpolant I such that (i) $A \Rightarrow I$, (ii) $I \Rightarrow \neg B$, and (iii) I is over the shared vocabulary of A and B: the relations p and q, only.

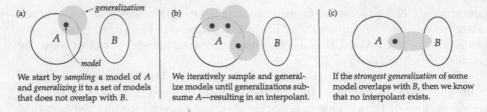

(a) We start by *sampling* a model of A and *generalizing* it to a set of models that does not overlap with B.

(b) We iteratively sample and generalize models until generalizations subsume A—resulting in an interpolant.

(c) If the *strongest generalization* of some model overlaps with B, then we know that no interpolant exists.

Fig. 1. High-level illustration of unidirectional interpolation.

We will search for an interpolant in EPR that is restricted to existential quantifiers, i.e., contains no universal quantifiers. To do so, we will use an algorithm we call *unidirectional interpolation* (UITP), illustrated at a high-level in Fig. 1. UITP grows an interpolant by sampling models of A only (hence, unidirectional) and generalizing them. EPR satisfiability is decidable and EPR formulas have finite models, which we can find using a reduction to SAT (or using, e.g., the Z3 SMT solver [20]). The problem is that models in this fragment correspond to a universe of anonymous elements that satisfy the formula. The question is: how can we generalize such a model to a set of models and represent it as a formula?

Let us begin by sampling the following model (structure) m from A: the singleton universe of elements $\{u_1\}$, where $p(u_1)$ and $r(u_1)$ hold, but $q(u_1)$ does not. Observe that this model satisfies A, denoted $m \models A$. Now, we can generalize this model to a set of models using the model-theoretic notion of *diagrams* [9,17], restricted to the shared vocabulary of A and B.

A diagram is analogous to a *cube* in the propositional setting, in that it is a conjunction of the facts the model satisfies. However, since our model is a collection of anonymous elements, we need to abstract them using quantified variables as follows:

$$diag(m) \triangleq \exists x_{u_1} . p(x_{u_1}) \wedge \neg q(x_{u_1})$$

There are *three* important aspects to observe:

(i) $m \models diag(m)$, and the diagram generalized m to a set of infinitely many models that have *at least* one element satisfying p but not q;
(ii) the relation r does not appear in the diagram, since it is not in the shared vocabulary of A and B; and
(iii) $diag(m) \wedge B$ is unsatisfiable.

At a high-level, a model defines a relational structure between a set of elements—perhaps a graph, linked list, or tree. Generically, models represent hypergraphs. A diagram then abstracts a model into a formula defining an infinite set of *structurally similar* hypergraphs, as illustrated in Fig. 2.

Our goal is to sample enough models such that the disjunction of their diagrams *covers* (subsumes) A and is unsatisfiable with B. In this example, A is not subsumed by $diag(m)$, and therefore we sample a model of A that is not a

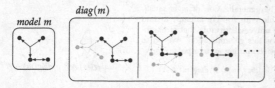

A model m can be viewed as a *hypergraph*, with nodes representing the universe of m and edges representing relations. The formula $diag(m)$ is an infinite set of hypergraphs that are structurally similar to m.

Fig. 2. Illustration of diagrams as sets of models

model of $diag(m)$. Suppose we get the model m' with the universe $\{u_2\}$, where $q(u_2)$ and $r(u_2)$ hold, but $p(u_2)$ does not. From m', we construct the following:

$$diag(m') \triangleq \exists x_{u_2}.\,\neg p(x_{u_2}) \wedge q(x_{u_2})$$

The formula $diag(m')$ is unsatisfiable with B, but together with $diag(m)$ does not yet subsume A. We sample a third model of A that is neither a model of $diag(m)$ nor $diag(m')$. Suppose we get the model m'' with the universe $\{u_3\}$, where $p(u_3)$, $q(u_3)$, and $r(u_3)$ hold. From m'', we construct the following: $diag(m'') \triangleq \exists x_{u_3}.\,p(x_{u_3}) \wedge q(x_{u_3})$. The formula $diag(m'')$ is unsatisfiable with B and, together with $diag(m)$ and $diag(m')$, subsumes A. Therefore,

$$diag(m) \vee diag(m') \vee diag(m'')$$

is an interpolant of (A, B). In practice, we weaken the interpolant further, and hasten convergence, by dropping unnecessary conjuncts appearing in the diagrams; we do so using UNSAT cores, as described in Sect. 4.1.

Detecting that no Interpolant Exists. Not all EPR formulas have existentially-quantified interpolants. Consider the following example [7]:

$$A \triangleq \forall x.\,p(y, x) \qquad\qquad B \triangleq \forall x.\,\neg p(x, z)$$

An interpolant for A and B has to have a quantifier alternation, for instance, $\exists y.\,\forall x.\,p(y, x)$. If we run UITP on the pair (A, B), we can detect that no existentially-quantified interpolant exists. Suppose that we sample the model m with universe $\{u\}$ where $p(u, u)$ holds. Then, $diag(m)$ is $\exists x_u.\,p(x_u, x_u)$. This diagram is satisfiable with B (see Fig. 1(c)). A diagram of m is the strongest possible existentially-quantified formula in the shared vocabulary of (A, B) for which m is a model; therefore, we can conclude that there is no existentially-quantified interpolant for (A, B).

Universal Interpolants. Suppose that a pair of formulas (A, B) only has a universally-quantified interpolant. By definition of an interpolant, this means that the dual interpolation problem over (B, A) has an existentially-quantified interpolant. Therefore, to compute a universally-quantified interpolant for (A, B), we can simply use UITP to compute an interpolant for (B, A) and negate it, as negation *flips* the existential quantifier into a universal one (see Sect. 4.1).

Alternation-Free Interpolants. Let us now consider an example that requires a Boolean combination of $\exists^*\varphi$ and $\forall^*\varphi$ formulas—i.e., an alternation-free EPR

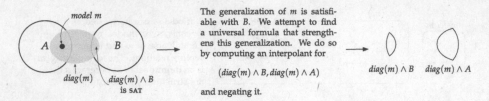

Fig. 3. High-level illustration of one recursive step of bidirectional interpolation.

formula. The UITP algorithm described above is insufficient in this case, as it cannot compute interpolants with Boolean combinations of existential and universal quantifiers. To construct such an interpolant, we will use UITP as a subprocedure, but we will *decompose* the interpolation problem and invoke UITP on a dual problem when requiring universal quantifiers. We call this approach *bidirectional interpolation*, BITP, as it alternates sampling between the A and B sides of the interpolation problem.

Consider the following interpolation problem:

$$A \triangleq \exists x, z. \forall y. \neg r(x, z) \land p(y, y) \qquad B \triangleq \exists y \forall x, z. \neg r(x, z) \land \neg p(y, y)$$

We begin by invoking UITP on the above, and it will immediately discover a model m of A whose diagram overlaps with B. Suppose UITP discovers the following diagram for some model m:

$$diag(m) \triangleq \exists x. \neg r(x, x) \land p(x, x)$$

It happens that $diag(m)$ overlaps with B. Intuitively, the *region* of overlap, $diag(m) \land B$, cannot be isolated by the interpolant using only existential quantifiers. Therefore, we need to strengthen the diagram using a universal formula. To do so, we attempt to find a universal interpolant between $diag(m) \land A$ and $diag(m) \land B$. Specifically, we invoke UITP on the interpolation problem

$$(diag(m) \land B, diag(m) \land A)$$

and negate the result—this produces a universally-quantified formula with which we can strengthen $diag(m)$. Notice that B now appears on the left side of the interpolation problem; thus, sampling now proceeds from the region in B that overlaps with $diag(m)$ (see Fig. 3 for an illustration).

Once we get a universal interpolant, we use it to strengthen $diag(m)$. In this example, after more sampling, we finally arrive at the following interpolant:

$$(\exists x, z. \neg r(x, z)) \land (\forall y. p(y, y))$$

We have demonstrated how BITP uses UITP as a base procedure to compute alternation-free interpolants. In a nutshell, the algorithm proceeds as if an existential interpolant exists, and when it finds out that is not the case, it switches direction to find the universal subformulas required to strengthen the interpolant. We describe this process in detail in Sect. 4.3.

3   Preliminaries

In this section, we formalize definitions needed for the rest of the paper.

Effectively Propositional Logic. We shall use $\mathcal{L}$ to denote the class of all EPR formulas. An EPR formula ψ is a first-order formula that, when written in prenex normal form, is of the form

$$\exists x_1, \ldots, x_n . \forall y_1, \ldots, y_m . \varphi,$$

where x_i and y_i are quantified variables, and φ is a quantifier-free formula over quantified variables, free variables, and relations. Note that φ has *no* function symbols. (We elide constants for clarity of presentation.) Throughout the paper, we shall refer to EPR formulas as if they are written in prenex normal form. We shall use $vocab(\psi)$ to denote the set of free variables and relation symbols appearing in ψ. We shall also refer to the following EPR subfragments:

- $\mathcal{L}_\forall$: the class of formulas that only contain universal quantifiers,
- $\mathcal{L}_\exists$: the class of formulas that only contain existential quantifiers, and
- $\mathcal{L}_{AF}$: the class of formulas that do not contain quantifier alternation.

Observe that $(\mathcal{L}_\exists \cup \mathcal{L}_\forall) \subset \mathcal{L}_{AF} \subset \mathcal{L}$.

Finite Models. Given a $\mathcal{L}$ formula ψ with a set V of free variables and a set R of relation symbols, a *finite model* m of ψ, denoted $m \models \psi$, is a tuple (U, A, T), where

- U is a finite set of elements, called the *universe* of m;
- A is an assignment function mapping free variables V and existentially-quantified variables of ψ to elements of U; and
- T is an interpretation function that maps each relation $r \in R$ to a set of tuples over U such that, for r with arity n, $(u_1, ..., u_n) \in U^n$ is in the relation r if and only if $(u_1, ..., u_n) \in T(r)$.

As is standard, given a model m of ψ, if ψ is instantiated with A and T, it evaluates to *true* under the universe U. The *cardinality* of m is the size of its universe. Despite the fact that $\mathcal{L}$ formulas may have infinite models, we will always use model to refer to finite models.

It is important to note that formulas in $\mathcal{L}$ have a *small-model property*, meaning that a formula is satisfiable *iff* it has a model whose universe is smaller than or equal to the sum of the number of free and existentially-quantified variables (see Theorem 3 below).

Diagrams. We now define the model-theoretic notion of a *diagram*, which allows us to *abstract* a model m into a set of models.

Given a model $m = (U, A, T)$, a set of variables V, and a set of relations R, we construct the diagram of m with respect to V and R, denoted $diag(m, V, R)$ (or $diag(m)$, when V and R are clear from context) as follows:

- For each element $u_i \in U$, introduce a fresh variable x_{u_i}.
- Let φ_{elem} be the conjunction of the following terms:
    For each distinct $u_i, u_j \in U$, the term $x_{u_i} \neq x_{u_j}$.
    For each $x \in V$, the term $x = x_u$, where $A(x) = u$.
- Let φ_{rel} be the conjunction of terms described as follows:
    For each $r \in R$ and $(u_1, \ldots, u_n) \in T(r)$, the term $r(x_{u_1}, \ldots, x_{u_n})$.
    For each $r \in R$ and $(u_1, \ldots, u_n) \notin T(r)$, the term $\neg r(x_{u_1}, \ldots, x_{u_n})$.
- Finally, $diag(m, V, R) = \exists x_{u_1}, \ldots, x_{u_{|U|}} . \varphi_{elem} \wedge \varphi_{rel}$

Observe that $m \models diag(m, V, R)$. The diagram abstracts the anonymous elements of the universe of a model as existential variables. As a result the diagram of m is the set of all models that have a *substructure* isomorphic to m (see definition of substructure below, and recall Fig. 2 for a visualization).

Example 1. Let $\psi \triangleq P(x) \wedge \forall y. (\neg P(y) \vee \neg Q(y))$. A possible model $m \models \psi$ is:

- $U = \{u_1, u_2\}$
- $A = \{x \mapsto u_2\}$
- $T = \{P \mapsto \{(u_2)\}, Q \mapsto \emptyset\}$

The diagram of the model m with respect to $V = \{x\}$ and $R = \{P\}$ is:

$$\exists x_{u_1}, x_{u_2} . x_{u_2} \neq x_{u_1} \wedge x = x_{u_2} \wedge P(x_{u_2}) \wedge \neg P(x_{u_1})$$

If we had considered instead a model m' with a single element in its universe, we would have obtained that $diag(m', V, R)$ is $\exists x_u . x = x_u \wedge P(x_u)$. ∎

Substructure. We briefly define the model-theoretic substructure relation. Given a model $m = (U, A, T)$, a *substructure* of m is a model $m' = (U', A', T')$ such that $U' \subset U$ and A' and T' are restrictions of A and T to U'. We will use $m' \preceq m$ to denote that m' is isomorphic to a substructure of m. The notion of a substructure admits many desirable properties:

Theorem 1. *If $m_1 \preceq m_2$ and $\varphi \in \mathcal{L}_\exists$, then $m_1 \models \varphi \Rightarrow m_2 \models \varphi$.*

Corollary 1. *$m_1 \preceq m_2$ if and only if $m_2 \models diag(m_1)$.*

Proof. The forward direction is a consequence of Theorem 1. For the reverse, if $m_2 \models diag(m_1)$, then, by construction of $diag$, there is a subset of m_2 that is isomorphic to m_1, so $m_1 \preceq m_2$. ∎

Theorem 2. *If $m_1 \preceq m_2$ and $\varphi \in \mathcal{L}_\forall$, then $m_2 \models \varphi \Rightarrow m_1 \models \varphi$.*

Corollary 2. *Given $\varphi \in \mathcal{L}_{AF}$, written as a Boolean combination of $\mathcal{L}_\forall$ and $\mathcal{L}_\exists$ subformulas, if $m_1 \preceq m_2$ and each $\mathcal{L}_\exists$ subformula ψ of φ has the property that $m_2 \models \psi \Rightarrow m_1 \models \psi$, then $m_2 \models \varphi \Rightarrow m_1 \models \varphi$.*

Proof. From the given and from Theorem 2, we know that m_1 satisfies at least as many subformulas of φ as m_2 does, and thus $m_1 \models \varphi$. ∎

Small Models. Additionally, given an arbitrary model $m \models \varphi$ for $\varphi \in \mathcal{L}$, there exists a *small* model $m' \preceq m$ such that $m' \models \varphi$.

Theorem 3. *If φ is a satisfiable* EPR *formula written in prenex normal form*

$$A \triangleq \exists x_1, \ldots, x_n \forall y_1, \ldots, y_k. \, \varphi(x_1, \ldots, x_n, y_1, \ldots, y_k, c_1, \ldots, c_\ell)$$

where $c_1, \ldots, c_\ell$ are free variables, then there exists a model of φ with size $|U| \leqslant n + \ell$.

Proof. Let m be a model of φ. Consider $m' = (U', A, T')$ where

- U' is the restriction of U to φ, i.e. the elements to which existentially-quantified variables $x_1, \ldots, x_n$ and free variables $c_1, \ldots, c_\ell$ are mapped.
- T' is the restriction of T to U'.

Then, it follows immediately that m' is also a model of φ with $U' \leqslant n + \ell$.   ∎

Interpolants. Given a pair of $\mathcal{L}$ formulas, (A, B), where $A \wedge B$ is unsatisfiable, an interpolant I for the *interpolation problem* (A, B) is a formula such that

- $A \Rightarrow I$ is valid,
- $I \Rightarrow \neg B$ is valid, and
- $vocab(I) \subseteq vocab(A) \cap vocab(B)$.

Given an interpolation problem (A, B), we call (B, A) the *dual interpolation problem*. For the purposes of this paper, we will restrict interpolants to formulas in the alternation-free subfragment of EPR, namely, $\mathcal{L}_{\mathrm{AF}}$.

4   Effectively Propositional Interpolation

In this section, we describe our algorithms for computing interpolants for EPR formulas. We first present a *unidirectional interpolation* algorithm, which can compute interpolants in $\mathcal{L}_\exists$ and $\mathcal{L}_\forall$ by sampling from *one side* (i.e., formula) of the interpolation problem. We then discuss *bidirectional interpolation*, which alternates its sampling between the two sides to construct an interpolant in $\mathcal{L}_{\mathrm{AF}}$.

4.1   Unidirectional Interpolation

Algorithm Description. The unidirectional interpolation algorithm, UITP, is used to find an interpolant in $\mathcal{L}_\exists$ for a pair of formulas (A, B) or to detect that no such interpolant exists. The high-level idea is to *grow* an interpolant—starting from *false*—by sampling models of A. Of course, A likely has infinitely many models; the algorithm thus *generalizes* sampled models using diagrams until they subsume all of A or until a model's diagram overlaps with B, in which case we know there does not exist an existentially-quantified interpolant.

UITP is presented in Algorithm 1 as a set of guarded rules that update a set of samples S, which contains diagrams of models of A. Initially, the set S is empty;

the rule SAMPLE finds a model of A that is not a model of one of the diagrams in S and adds its diagram to S. The diagrams are taken with respect to the set of variables V and relations R in the shared vocabulary, $vocab(A) \cap vocab(B)$.

Observe that S is a set of existentially-quantified formulas of the form

$$\exists X.\, a_1 \wedge \ldots \wedge a_n,$$

where a_i is an atomic predicate. At any point the *candidate* interpolant is $\bigvee S$, i.e., the disjunction of all diagrams in S. Thus, the candidate interpolant begins as being *false*, and every time the rule SAMPLE is applied, the candidate interpolant is weakened. Note that all formulas in $\mathcal{L}_\exists$ can be written as disjunctions of existentially-quantified conjunctions of atoms.

The algorithm succeeds in finding an interpolant when the rule ITP applies— that is, when $A \Rightarrow \bigvee S$ and $\bigvee S \Rightarrow \neg B$ are valid. Observe that all of these satisfiability checks lie within EPR, and are therefore decidable.

If the algorithm detects a diagram in S that is satisfiable with B, using rule FAIL, it concludes that no interpolant in $\mathcal{L}_\exists$ exists for (A, B). The intuition here is as follows: Given a model $m \models A$, $diag(m)$ is the strongest formula in $\mathcal{L}_\exists$ for which m is a model. Therefore, if $diag(m)$ overlaps with B, we cannot find an interpolant in $\mathcal{L}_\exists$ that *includes* the model m. (See Theorem 5.)

Finally, the rule ABSTRACT attempts to *weaken* a diagram *up to B*—that is, it takes a diagram in S and removes some of its conjuncts such that the result is still unsatisfiable with B. In practice, this is performed using UNSAT cores, when checking whether the diagram is satisfiable with B. Whereas this rule is not needed for soundness or completeness, it is of crucial importance in practice, as otherwise diagrams are overly specific (this is further discussed below).

Computing $\mathcal{L}_\forall$ Interpolants. UITP can also be used to compute universally-quantified interpolants in $\mathcal{L}_\forall$. This can be easily done as follows: Suppose that (A, B) has an interpolant $I_\forall$ in $\mathcal{L}_\forall$. By definition of an interpolant, we know that

(i) $B \Rightarrow \neg I_\forall$ is valid and
(ii) $\neg I_\forall \Rightarrow \neg A$ is valid.

In other words, $\neg I_\forall$ is an interpolant for the dual interpolation problem, (B, A). Observe that $\neg I_\forall$ is in $\mathcal{L}_\exists$, since the negation turns the universal quantifier into an existential one. Therefore, to find a universal interpolant for (A, B), we can simply use UITP to find an existential interpolant for (B, A) and take its negation. Viewed differently, by solving the dual interpolation problem, we are essentially *modifying* UITP to sample from the B side of the interpolation problem instead of the A side, and this allows us to compute universally-quantified interpolants.

Interpolant Strength. For any two formulas, there is typically a spectrum of interpolants. Depending on the order in which the UITP rules are applied, we may arrive at different interpolants.

On one extreme, if we avoid using the ABSTRACT rule, we ensure that whatever interpolant we find is the strongest possible one. This is because, for every sampled model m of A, UITP will add the strongest possible formula in $\mathcal{L}_\exists$ that

$$\frac{}{S \leftarrow \emptyset} \text{ INIT} \qquad \frac{m \models A \wedge \bigwedge_{s \in S} \neg s}{S \leftarrow S \cup \{diag(m, V, R)\}} \text{ SAMPLE}$$

$$\frac{s \in S \quad s \triangleq \exists X. \bigwedge D \quad s' \triangleq \exists X. \bigwedge D' \quad D' \subset D \quad s' \wedge B \text{ is UNSAT}}{S \leftarrow (S \setminus \{s\}) \cup \{s'\}} \text{ ABSTRACT}$$

$$\frac{s \in S \quad s \wedge B \text{ is SAT}}{\text{no } \mathcal{L}_\exists \text{ interpolant exists for } (A, B)} \text{ FAIL}$$

$$\frac{A \wedge \bigwedge_{s \in S} \neg s \text{ is UNSAT} \qquad B \wedge \bigvee S \text{ is UNSAT}}{\bigvee S \text{ is an } \mathcal{L}_\exists \text{ interpolant for } (A, B)} \text{ ITP}$$

Algorithm 1. Unidirectional interpolation

contains m (its diagram) to the set of samples S. Any interpolant that is stronger will thus have to exclude one of the models of A.

On the other extreme, if at every step ABSTRACT is applied exhaustively—i.e., until it is no longer applicable to any $s \in S$—then we arrive at a maximal interpolant. (This is equivalent to taking a *minimal* UNSAT core of each diagram with respect to B, which can result in sampling exponentially fewer models.) A maximal interpolant I is one that cannot be weakened while remaining an interpolant—i.e., there does not exist an interpolant I' such that $I \Rightarrow I'$ and $I \not\equiv I'$. Note that there maybe a number of incomparable maximal interpolants.

The following theorem states that different applications of the rules can result in all interpolants, from the weakest to the strongest.

Theorem 4. *For every interpolant $I \in \mathcal{L}_\exists$ of (A, B), there exists a run of UITP that will compute it.*

4.2   Theoretical Properties of UITP

We now investigate soundness and completeness of UITP.

Soundness. The following theorem states that UITP is sound.

Theorem 5 (Soundness). *If UITP, invoked on (A, B), returns a formula $I \in \mathcal{L}_\exists$, then I is an interpolant of (A, B). If the FAIL rule applies, then there is no interpolant in $\mathcal{L}_\exists$ for (A, B).*

Proof. The first statement follows from the fact that (i) the candidate interpolant $\bigvee S$ is in $\mathcal{L}_\exists$; (ii) following the rule SAMPLE, the candidate interpolant is over the shared vocabulary of A and B; and (iii) the rule ITP ensures that the returned formula I is such that $A \Rightarrow I$ and $I \Rightarrow \neg B$.

We prove the latter statement by contradiction. Suppose $I \in \mathcal{L}_\exists$ is an interpolant for (A, B), but the FAIL rule applies. Then, there is a model $m \models A$ such that $diag(m) \wedge B$ is satisfiable. I can be written as $\bigvee_i \psi_i$, where ψ_i is an $\mathcal{L}_\exists$ formula of the form $\exists^* \varphi_i$, where φ_i is a conjunction of atoms. If $m \models A$, then, since I subsumes A, $m \models I$. In particular, for some i, $m \models \exists^* \varphi_i$. By construction, $diag(m)$ is at least as strong as $\exists^* \varphi_i$, so since $diag(m) \wedge B$ is satisfiable, so is $I \wedge B$—but this contradicts the definition of an interpolant. ∎

Completeness. We now consider completeness of UITP: meaning that it is always able to find an interpolant if one exists or detect its non-existence in a finite number of steps. The key insight in our proof is the observation that every EPR formula A has a *finite set* of *small models* that characterize an $\mathcal{L}_\exists$ formula that subsumes A. The following lemma formalizes this observation, which we prove using EPR's small-model property.

Lemma 1 ($\mathcal{L}_\exists$ basis). *Given $A \in \mathcal{L}$, let $M = \{m \mid m$ is a small model of $A\}$. Then M is a finite set, called an $\mathcal{L}_\exists$ basis, such that*

$$A \Rightarrow \left(\bigvee_{m \in M} diag(m) \right) \text{ is valid.} \tag{1}$$

Proof. For any model $m \models A$, there is a small model $m' \models A$ such that $m' \preceq m$, and therefore $diag(m) \Rightarrow diag(m')$. It follows that every model of A is a model of $\bigvee_{m \in M} diag(m)$, and since the small models have an upper bound on their cardinality, there are finitely many of them. Therefore, Formula 1 is well-formed and holds. ∎

Using Lemma 1, we are now ready to state completeness of UITP. The following theorem assumes a fair application of UITP rules.

Theorem 6 (Completeness of UITP). *Let c be the maximum of the small-model cardinality bounds of A and B. If UITP is invoked under the additional constraint that each sampled model has cardinality at most c, then eventually one of the rules ITP or FAIL applies.*

Proof. First, consider the case that an interpolant exists. By Lemma 1, A has an $\mathcal{L}_\exists$ basis M' where each model has size at most c. So, if an interpolant exists in $\mathcal{L}_\exists$, we eventually find it by enumerating the finitely many models (up to isomorphism) of size at most c.

Second, consider the case where no interpolant exists. The algorithm will eventually find a model $m \models A$ such that $diag(m) \wedge B$ is satisfiable. This follows from Lemma 1, as if no such model is found, the existence of an $\mathcal{L}_\exists$ basis would induce an interpolant. ∎

Complete Theories. The above completeness theorem assumes that sampling produces models of bounded cardinality. This can be enforced by adding the constraint $card(c)$ to the formula:

$$card(c) \triangleq \exists x_1, \dots, x_c. \forall y. \bigvee_{1 \leqslant i \leqslant c} y = x_i \tag{2}$$

Require: $A \wedge B$ is UNSAT
1: **function** BITP(A, B)
2:      *apply* INIT
3:      **while** ITP *does not apply* **do**
4:          **if** $\exists s \in S. s \wedge B$ is SAT **then**
5:              $I \leftarrow$ BITP$(s \wedge B, s \wedge A)$
6:              $s \leftarrow s \wedge \neg I$
7:          **end if**
8:          *apply* SAMPLE
9:      **end while**
10:     **return** $\bigvee S$ is an interpolant
11: **end function**

Algorithm 2. Bidirectional interpolation

$card(c)$ restricts sampling to models of size at most c. In practice, however, we are typically operating on formulas from a specific domain, which might have desirable properties that allow us to elide the potentially costly cardinality restriction for completeness.

Consider, for example, EPR formulas representing *linear orders* [14,21], which can be used to model linked and doubly-linked lists. Linear orders restrict relations to be at most of binary arity and to be reflexive, transitive, and antisymmetric. We shall call this subset of formulas $\mathcal{L}_{\text{LO}}$. As very recently discovered by Padon et al. [21], this EPR theory forces a *well-quasi-order* on models. This ensures that there is no infinite sequence of models that are incomparable according to the substructure relation. Using this result, we can show that UITP is complete for $\mathcal{L}_{\text{LO}}$, without the model cardinality restrictions from Theorem 6.

Theorem 7 (Completeness under linear ordering). *Given $A, B \in \mathcal{L}_{\text{LO}}$, if UITP is invoked on (A, B), it eventually terminates.*

Proof. We prove this by contradiction. Suppose that UITP does not terminate on some (A, B). Then, there are infinitely many calls to SAMPLE, and therefore an infinite sequence of computed models $m_1, m_2, \ldots$ of A. By Padon et al. [21, Theorem 6.2], we know that this sequence of models forms a well-quasi-order that is equivalent to the substructure relation: there exist models m_i and m_j, with $i < j$, such that $m_i \preceq m_j$. This means that $m_j \models diag(m_i)$, which cannot happen by definition of SAMPLE: once we have considered m_i, we only obtain model m_j if $m_j \not\models diag(m_i)$. ∎

The proof of the above theorem only exploits the fact that models of $\mathcal{L}_{\text{LO}}$ form a well-quasi-order under the $\sqsubseteq_{\forall*}$ ordering of Padon et al. [21, Theorem 6.2]. Thus, as a direct corollary, we can show completeness of UITP for any theory with such property—and not only linear orders.

4.3 Bidirectional Interpolation

Algorithm Description. We now switch attention to computing alternation-free interpolants in $\mathcal{L}_{AF}$, i.e., with Boolean combinations of formulas in $\mathcal{L}_\exists$ and $\mathcal{L}_\forall$. Recall that, by solving the dual interpolation problem, we can compute universal interpolants using UITP. Bidirectional interpolation exploits this property to compute interpolants in $\mathcal{L}_{AF}$. Specifically, BITP proceeds as if an $\mathcal{L}_\exists$ interpolant exists, and when it discovers that it is not the case, it recursively switches to solving a dual interpolation problem in order to find the required subformulas needed to strengthen the interpolant.

BITP is described in Algorithm 2. BITP uses the rules of UITP to construct an interpolant, and, like UITP, maintains the set of diagrams S and a candidate interpolant $\bigvee S$. The algorithm begins by applying INIT and iteratively samples models, using SAMPLE, until an interpolant is found. When an $\mathcal{L}_\exists$ interpolant exists, BITP behaves as a determinization of UITP's rules. The difference from UITP, however, is when a diagram $s \in S$ overlaps with B.

Recall that sampling adds $\mathcal{L}_\exists$ formulas to S. If one $s \in S$ overlaps with B, we attempt to strengthen it with a universally-quantified formula by recursively calling BITP on $(s \wedge B, s \wedge A)$ and negating the result (see lines 5 and 6). In other words, we focus on the region in B that overlaps with s, and we attempt to strengthen s in order to excise that region from the candidate interpolant.

4.4 Theoretical Properties of BITP

We now discuss soundness and completeness of BITP. Observe that calling BITP in line 5 may require further recursive calls if no $\mathcal{L}_\exists$ interpolant exists for $(s \wedge B, s \wedge A)$—i.e., the interpolant for $(s \wedge B, s \wedge A)$ is still in $\mathcal{L}_{AF}$. If these recursive calls never terminate by finding an $\mathcal{L}_\exists$ interpolant at some depth, then the algorithm produces an infinite sequence of models (at least one per recursive call). We can show that the existence of such an infinite sequence is the exact criterion to determine that no $\mathcal{L}_{AF}$ interpolant exists for (A, B). Accordingly, we prove the relative completeness of BITP—that when an $\mathcal{L}_{AF}$ interpolant exists, the algorithm terminates with such an interpolant.

The following lemma states the conditions required to show that the no $\mathcal{L}_{AF}$ interpolant exists for a pair of formulas (A, B).

Lemma 2 (Non-existence of $\mathcal{L}_{AF}$ interpolants). *Let $A, B \in \mathcal{L}$, and suppose there is an infinite alternating chain of models of A and B: $m_1^A, m_2^B, m_3^A, m_4^B, \ldots$ with the three properties*

- $m_i^A \models A$ *and* $m_j^B \models B$, *for all odd i and even j*
- $\mathrm{diag}(m_1^A) \Leftarrow \mathrm{diag}(m_2^B) \Leftarrow \mathrm{diag}(m_3^A) \Leftarrow \ldots$
- $|m_1^A| < |m_2^B| < |m_3^A| < \ldots$

Then, there is no $\mathcal{L}_{AF}$ interpolant for (A, B).

Proof. We will prove this lemma by showing that for every formula $\varphi \in \mathcal{L}_{AF}$ s.t. $A \Rightarrow \varphi$, we have that $\varphi \wedge B$ is SAT, thus implying that no $\mathcal{L}_{AF}$ interpolant exists for (A, B). The proof relies on Theorem 1 and Corollary 2.

First, define $num(\varphi) = n + m + c$, where $\varphi \in \mathcal{L}$ is a prenex normal form formula $\exists x_1, \ldots, x_n. \forall y_1, \ldots y_m. \phi$ and c is the number of free variables in φ. We shall use $|m|$ to denote the number of elements in the universe of a model m.

Let $\Phi = \{\varphi \in \mathcal{L}_{AF} \mid \forall i. m_i^A \models \varphi\}$. That is, the set Φ is that of all $\mathcal{L}_{AF}$ formulas whose models contain $\{m_i^A\}$; thus the set of possible $\mathcal{L}_{AF}$ interpolants for (A, B) is contained in Φ. Assume each φ_i is written as a Boolean combination of universal and existential subformulas. Now, pick some $\varphi \in \Phi$ and some model m_i^A such that $|m_i^A| > num(\varphi)$.

By definition of Φ, we know that $m_i^A \models \varphi$ and $m_{i+2}^A \models \varphi$. We now show that this entails that $m_{i+1}^B \models \varphi$:

- Since the number of existentially quantified variables in φ is less than $|m_i^A|$, we know that m_i^A and m_{i+2}^A satisfy the same existential subformulas of φ.
- Since $m_i^A \preceq m_{i+1}^B$, by Theorem 1, m_{i+1}^B also satisfies all existential subformulas of φ.
- Since $m_{i+1}^B \preceq m_{i+2}^A$, by Corollary 2, we know that $m_{i+1}^B \models \varphi$.

Therefore there is no $\mathcal{L}_{AF}$ interpolant for (A, B), since any $\mathcal{L}_{AF}$ formula $I \in \Phi$, where $A \Rightarrow I$, is such that $I \wedge B$ is SAT.   ∎

We are now ready to state BITP's soundness and relative completeness.

Theorem 8 (Soundness and relative completeness of BITP). *Given two formulas* $A, B \in \mathcal{L}$, *where* $A \wedge B$ *is* UNSAT,

1. *if* BITP(A, B) *returns a formula, then it is an interpolant of* (A, B);
2. *if* A *and* B *have an* $\mathcal{L}_{AF}$ *interpolant, then* BITP(A, B) *returns a formula and terminates.*

Proof. If BITP returns an interpolant, then it is correct by construction.

We will prove relative completeness (point 2 in theorem statement) by the contrapositive: If BITP(A, B) does not terminate, then there is no $\mathcal{L}_{AF}$ interpolant for (A, B). For the purposes of the proof, let us assume that the algorithm always samples a model of the smallest cardinality possible. Now, suppose that the algorithm does not terminate. This could happen in two places:

1. the loop (line 3) in some recursion depth d executes indefinitely, or
2. there is an infinite chain of recursive calls to BITP.

Case 1: We first show that case 1 is impossible. Suppose that at recursive depth d the algorithm is called on (A', B'). Suppose the loop does not terminate. Since models are sampled in increasing cardinality, at some point the variable I is of the form

$$I \equiv \bigvee_{m \models A' \text{ and } |m| \leqslant num(A')} diag(m) \wedge \neg \text{BITP}(diag(m) \wedge B', diag(m) \wedge A')$$

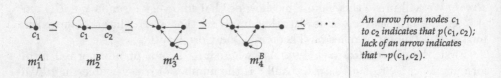

An arrow from nodes c_1 to c_2 indicates that $p(c_1, c_2)$; lack of an arrow indicates that $\neg p(c_1, c_2)$.

Fig. 4. Illustration of an infinite, alternating sequence of models satisfying conditions of Lemma 2, where $A \triangleq \forall x.\, p(y, x)$ and $B \triangleq \forall x.\, \neg P(x, z)$

In other words, at some point during the assumed infinite execution of the loop, the variable I will contain all diagrams of models of size $\leqslant num(A')$ (and any required strengthening). Since the loop keeps executing beyond this point, this means there is a model m s.t. $m \models A'$ and $m \not\models I$. But since $|m| > num(A')$, this means that there is a substructure $m' \preceq m$, where $m' \models A$, $|m'| \leqslant num(A)$, and $diag(m) \Rightarrow diag(m')$. But since $m' \models I$, it is also true that $m \models I$. By contradiction, the loop terminates.

Case 2: Now, consider case 2. Suppose there is an infinite chain of recursive calls. By definition of BITP, there is an infinite sequence of models (samples) m_1^A, m_2^B, m_3^A, m_4^B, ... such that

$$diag(m_1^A) \Leftarrow diag(m_2^B) \Leftarrow diag(m_3^A) \Leftarrow \ldots \tag{3}$$

$$|m_1^A| < |m_2^B| < |m_3^A| < \ldots \tag{4}$$

$$\text{for all } m_i^X, \ diag(m_i^X) \wedge A \text{ is SAT and } diag(m_i^X) \wedge B \text{ is SAT} \tag{5}$$

This happens by construction due to the alternation of BITP: in the first recursive call, it conjoins $diag(m_1^A)$ to A and B; then, in the second recursive call, $diag(m_2^B)$ is conjoined to A and B, where $m_2^B \models diag(m_1^A)$, etc. As a result, we get constraint 3. Constraint 4 is implied by the fact that $A \wedge B$ is UNSAT. (If there is i such that $|m_i^A| = |m_{i+1}^B|$ or $|m_i^B| = |m_{i+1}^A|$ this means that A and B have the same model.) Constraint 5 is implied by the fact that the sequence is infinite.

Following Lemma 2, non-termination means there is no $\mathcal{L}_{AF}$ interpolant. ∎

4.5 BITP Examples

The following example illustrates a successful run of BITP.

Example 2. Consider the following formulas, and suppose we call BITP on (A, B).

$$A \triangleq \exists x.\, \forall y.\, x = y \wedge p(x) \qquad\qquad B \triangleq \exists x, y.\, p(x) \wedge p(y) \wedge y \neq x$$

Initially, $S = \emptyset$ and the candidate interpolant $\bigvee S \equiv false$. So, we start by sampling (line 8) the model m with the following diagram, $s_m \triangleq \exists x_u.\, p(x_u)$. In the next iteration around the loop, we will notice that $s_m \wedge B$ is SAT (line 4);

therefore, we call UITP on $(s_m \wedge B, s_m \wedge A)$. The result we get is the following: $I \equiv \exists x, y. \, p(x) \wedge p(y) \wedge x \neq y$. As shown in line 6, we now strengthen s_m by setting it to $s_m \wedge \neg I$. At this point, s_m is an interpolant, and therefore the algorithm terminates.   ∎

We now demonstrate BITP on an example with no $\mathcal{L}_{AF}$ interpolant.

Example 3. We use the same example as in Sect. 2:

$$A \triangleq \forall x. \, p(y, x) \qquad\qquad B \triangleq \forall x. \, \neg p(x, z)$$

BITP might begin by sampling the model m_1^A of A with $diag(m_1^A) \triangleq \exists c_1. \, p(c_1, c_1)$. Model m_1^A is shown pictorially on the left side of Fig. 4. BITP now recursively looks for an interpolant of $(B \wedge diag(m_1^A), A \wedge diag(m_1^A))$.

At this point, BITP samples from $B \wedge diag(m_1^A)$ the model m_2^B of cardinality 2 with the diagram:

$$diag(m_2^B) \triangleq \exists c_1, c_2. \, c_1 \neq c_2 \wedge p(c_1, c_1) \wedge \neg p(c_1, c_2) \wedge \neg p(c_2, c_2) \wedge p(c_2, c_1)$$

Note that $diag(m_2^B) \wedge (A \wedge diag(m_1^A))$ is still satisfiable, so BITP will make yet another recursive call to $(A \wedge diag(m_1^A) \wedge diag(m_2^B), B \wedge diag(m_1^A) \wedge diag(m_2^B))$. We will notice that the cardinality of sampled models keeps increasing as BITP continues to run, and in fact, BITP will never terminate, since there is no $\mathcal{L}_{AF}$ interpolant for (A, B).

Specifically, BITP will end up constructing an infinite alternating sequence of models $m_1^A, m_2^B, m_3^A, m_4^B, \dots$. A possible infinite alternating sequence of models of A and B is illustrated in Fig. 4. Observe that this sequence satisfies the conditions of Lemma 2 for non-existence of an $\mathcal{L}_{AF}$ interpolant.   ∎

5   Implementation and Evaluation

Implementation. We have implemented prototypes of UITP and BITP using the Z3 SMT solver [20] as a black box. To evaluate the performance and utility of our algorithms, we built a simple interpolation-based verifier, ITPV, for transition systems in EPR. ITPV expects a transition system $TS = (init, trans, bad)$. ITPV unrolls the transition relation and uses our interpolation algorithms to compute interpolants and discover a safe inductive invariant for TS.

Evaluation. We applied ITPV on singly- and doubly-linked-list benchmarks [15, 17]. We compared the performance of ITPV against two tools: (i) PDR$_\alpha$ [15], a predicate-abstraction-based verifier based on property-directed reachability (PDR), and (ii) PDR$_\forall$ [17], a PDR-based verifier that uses diagrams for generalizing counterexamples. To our knowledge, these are the only two other techniques for automated verification of programs encoded in EPR. Note, however, that both PDR$_\alpha$ and PDR$_\forall$ can only compute universally-quantified invariants (in $\mathcal{L}_\forall$). We considered a set of benchmarks that require $\mathcal{L}_\forall$ invariants, and another a set that require $\mathcal{L}_{AF}$ invariants, as detailed below.

Table 1. Experimental results: (a) $\mathcal{L}_\forall$ benchmarks and (b) $\mathcal{L}_{AF}$ benchmarks

Benchmarks	ITPV Time D		PDR$_\alpha$ Time D		PDR$_\forall$ Time D	
singly-linked						
concat	0.22	3	$\boldsymbol{X}_\alpha$		0.61	3
create	0.07	0	2.37	3	0.68	3
delete-at	0.11	2	14.14	4	0.96	3
deleteAll	0.11	2	2.82	5	0.39	3
insert-at	0.51	3	8.25	4	1.3	4
insert	0.19	3	2.66	3	1.1	3
merge	4.68	4	$\boldsymbol{X}_\alpha$		5.2	6
split	39.96	6	25.49	6	4.86	6
reverse	0.24	3	3.35	5	1.74	6
sorted-insert	0.22	3	36.65	4	1.24	3
bubble-sort	0.19	0	2.11	4	1.35	5
nested-split	2.14	4	8.37	2	4.2	4
shared-delete	15.78	5	$\boldsymbol{X}_t$		33.38	5
ladder	18.89	5	12.3	4	7.37	6
filter	74.64	7	6.6	4	0.73	3
doubly-linked						
create	0.32	3	71.5	3	2.39	4
delete	0.38	3	344.5	6	1.07	3
insert-at	0.8	3	242.4	3	1.99	3

(a)

Benchmark	ITPV Time D		PDR$_\alpha$ Time	PDR$_\forall$ Time
shared-tail	3.56	5	$\boldsymbol{X}_\alpha$	$\boldsymbol{X}_\alpha$
shared-tailc	3.46	5	$\boldsymbol{X}_\alpha$	$\boldsymbol{X}_\alpha$
concat	0.37	3	$\boldsymbol{X}_\alpha$	$\boldsymbol{X}_\alpha$
create	0.86	3	$\boldsymbol{X}_\alpha$	$\boldsymbol{X}_\alpha$
deleteAll	0.25	2	$\boldsymbol{X}_\alpha$	$\boldsymbol{X}_\alpha$
insert	0.47	3	$\boldsymbol{X}_\alpha$	$\boldsymbol{X}_\alpha$
ladder	66.16	4	$\boldsymbol{X}_\alpha$	$\boldsymbol{X}_\alpha$

(b)

Universal Proofs. Table 1(a) shows the results of applying ITPV, PDR$_\alpha$, and PDR$_\forall$ to proving memory safety of a set of list-manipulating benchmarks drawn from [15,17].[1] All of these benchmarks require inductive invariants in $\mathcal{L}_\forall$. The symbol $\boldsymbol{X}_t$ indicates that the tool did not return a solution within a 10 min time limit, and $\boldsymbol{X}_\alpha$ indicates that the predicate abstract domain of PDR$_\alpha$ is not precise enough to compute a safe inductive invariant. Column D indicates the depth of the unrolling (PDR frames or transition relation unrollings) an algorithm required to compute a safe inductive invariant.

Our results primarily indicate that our interpolation technique (i) is a viable means for verifying non-trivial EPR transition relations and (ii) results in a verification tool that is comparable to the state-of-the-art in EPR verification. Digging deeper into the results, we see that ITPV is almost consistently superior to PDR$_\alpha$. Compared to PDR$_\forall$, we witness comparable performance. On benchmarks 8 and 15, however, we observe that ITPV is slower than PDR$_\forall$. We discovered that this occurs when one needs to interpolate over a *deep* unrolling of the transition relation in order to find an inductive invariant (on these examples, D is 6 and 7). This is an artifact of two factors: (i) the satisfiability algorithm in Z3 and (ii) the algorithmic differences between interpolation-based verification and property-directed reachability. PDR techniques do not explicitly unroll the transition relation, and therefore tend to make more but smaller SAT queries.

---

[1] Time measurements for all tools do not contain Z3 expression manipulation time, due to the avoidable substantial overhead incurred by the Python API.

Interpolation techniques unroll the transition relation, resulting in large SAT queries. The performance of the EPR satisfiability procedure in Z3 suffers when we give it large formulas, leading to slower verification when deep unrollings are needed. We thus hope that the benchmarks generated through this work would influence the design of more efficient EPR satisfiability procedures; for instance, linear orders [14,17,21] can benefit from specialized quantifier instantiation that exploits their transitivity and antisymmetry [6].

Alternating Proofs. Table 1(b) shows a set of benchmarks requiring inductive invariants in $\mathcal{L}_{AF}$. The first two benchmarks are from [17], where it is shown that PDR$_\forall$ declares that no universally-quantified invariant exists. The rest of the benchmarks are modifications of the ones appearing in Table 1(a), where we manually modified the program to require existential as well as universal quantifiers in the proof. To our knowledge, ITPV is the first tool to be able to automatically compute inductive invariants over the rich class of $\mathcal{L}_{AF}$ formulas.

6 Related Work

Interpolation and EPR. Our algorithm is inspired by the recent model-based interpolation techniques that rely on sampling models of A and B to construct a simple interpolant [2,28]. Thus far these techniques have been limited to linear arithmetic. Whereas our work here also constructs an interpolant by generalizing from models, the underlying methodology is very different.

The line of work by Itzhaky et al. [13–15] and Karbyshev et al. [17] showed us how to encode linear data structures in EPR. The model generalization technique our algorithm uses is similar to the notion of *diagrams* used in the recent property-directed reachability [8] algorithm for EPR [17]. Our interpolation technique enables construction of both universal, existential, and mixed quantifier interpolants—and therefore invariants. This is in contrast to existing verification techniques that only compute universal invariants. Additionally, the notion of interpolants is general and of independent interest outside of safety checking.

Another close work to ours is that of Bjørner et al. [7]: in a short paper, the authors sketch out a model-based EPR interpolation algorithm. However, unlike our work, it does not guarantee that the interpolants are alternation-free. There are also a number of works on interpolation techniques for arrays and heap-manipulating programs [1,3,16,31]. Our work differs in that it targets the EPR fragment of first-order logic, which none of those works apply to.

Symbolic Abstraction. Our work has connections with *symbolic abstraction* [27], in which a formula in a rich logic is abstracted into one that subsumes it in a weaker logic. The approach of Reps et al. [27] performs this abstraction by sampling models and growing the abstraction starting from *bottom*. Thakur defined the notion of *abstract interpolants* [30], which are interpolants in a restricted logic, and showed how to use symbolic abstraction to compute them. Our techniques can be viewed through this lens, as we restrict interpolants to a sub-fragment of EPR and iteratively grow interpolants. Another work in the same vein is that on learning quantified data automata [11] for verifying linear data structures. The similarity between our works is that both use a black box *teacher* to learn quantified invariants. Our technique, however, can compute invariants with combinations of quantifiers, and operates in the setting of EPR.

Acknowledgements. We would like to thank Shachar Itzhaky for giving us access to his PDR implementation. We would like to thank Thomas Reps and the programming languages group at UW–Madison for their insightful comments. We would like thank Paris Koutris for pointing out the connection between our proof of relative completeness and Pebble-like games. Finally, we would like to thank our shepherd, Mooly Sagiv, who gave us in-depth comments that helped fix earlier inconsistencies in our arguments.

References

1. Albargouthi, A., Berdine, J., Cook, B., Kincaid, Z.: Spatial interpolants. In: Vitek, J. (ed.) ESOP 2015. LNCS, vol. 9032, pp. 634–660. Springer, Heidelberg (2015)
2. Albarghouthi, A., McMillan, K.L.: Beautiful interpolants. In: Sharygina, N., Veith, H. (eds.) CAV 2013. LNCS, vol. 8044, pp. 313–329. Springer, Heidelberg (2013)
3. Alberti, F., Bruttomesso, R., Ghilardi, S., Ranise, S., Sharygina, N.: SAFARI: SMT-based abstraction for arrays with interpolants. In: Madhusudan, P., Seshia, S.A. (eds.) CAV 2012. LNCS, vol. 7358, pp. 679–685. Springer, Heidelberg (2012)
4. Alur, R., Singhania, N.: Precise piecewise affine models from input-output data. In: Mitra, T., Reineke, J. (eds.) EMSOFT, pp. 3:1–3:10. ACM (2014)
5. Ball, T., Bjørner, N., Gember, A., Itzhaky, S., Karbyshev, A., Sagiv, M., Schapira, M., Valadarsky, A.: Vericon: towards verifying controller programs in software-defined networks. In: O'Boyle, M.F.P., Pingali, K. (eds.) PLDI, p. 31. ACM (2014)
6. Bjørner, N.: Personal communication
7. Bjørner, N., Gurfinkel, A., Korovin, K., Lahav, O.: Instantiations, zippers and EPR interpolation. In: McMillan, K.L., Middeldorp, A., Sutcliffe, G., Voronkov, A. (eds.) LPAR (short papers). EPiC Series, vol. 26, pp. 35–41. EasyChair (2013)
8. Bradley, A.R.: SAT-based model checking without unrolling. In: Jhala, R., Schmidt, D. (eds.) VMCAI 2011. LNCS, vol. 6538, pp. 70–87. Springer, Heidelberg (2011)
9. Chang, C.C., Keisler, J.: Model Theory. Studies in Logic and the Foundations of Mathematics, vol. 73. North-Holland, Amsterdam (1973). 3rd edn., 1990
10. Ermis, E., Schäf, M., Wies, T.: Error invariants. In: Giannakopoulou, D., Méry, D. (eds.) FM 2012. LNCS, vol. 7436, pp. 187–201. Springer, Heidelberg (2012)
11. Garg, P., Löding, C., Madhusudan, P., Neider, D.: Learning universally quantified invariants of linear data structures. In: Sharygina, N., Veith, H. (eds.) CAV 2013. LNCS, vol. 8044, pp. 813–829. Springer, Heidelberg (2013)
12. Henzinger, T.A., Jhala, R., Majumdar, R., McMillan, K.L.: Abstractions from proofs. In: Jones, N.D., Leroy, X. (eds.) POPL, pp. 232–244. ACM (2004)
13. Itzhaky, S., Banerjee, A., Immerman, N., Lahav, O., Nanevski, A., Sagiv, M.: Modular reasoning about heap paths via effectively propositional formulas. In: Jagannathan, S., Sewell, P. (eds.) POPL, pp. 385–396. ACM (2014)
14. Itzhaky, S., Banerjee, A., Immerman, N., Nanevski, A., Sagiv, M.: Effectively-propositional reasoning about reachability in linked data structures. In: Sharygina, N., Veith, H. (eds.) CAV 2013. LNCS, vol. 8044, pp. 756–772. Springer, Heidelberg (2013)

15. Itzhaky, S., Bjørner, N., Reps, T., Sagiv, M., Thakur, A.: Property-directed shape analysis. In: Biere, A., Bloem, R. (eds.) CAV 2014. LNCS, vol. 8559, pp. 35–51. Springer, Heidelberg (2014)

16. Jhala, R., McMillan, K.L.: Array abstractions from proofs. In: Damm, W., Hermanns, H. (eds.) CAV 2007. LNCS, vol. 4590, pp. 193–206. Springer, Heidelberg (2007)

17. Karbyshev, A., Bjørner, N., Itzhaky, S., Rinetzky, N., Shoham, S.: Property-directed inference of universal invariants or proving their absence. In: Kroening, D., Pǎsǎreanu, C.S. (eds.) CAV 2015. LNCS, vol. 9206, pp. 583–602. Springer, Heidelberg (2015)

18. McMillan, K.L.: Interpolation and SAT-based model checking. In: Hunt Jr., W.A., Somenzi, F. (eds.) CAV 2003. LNCS, vol. 2725, pp. 1–13. Springer, Heidelberg (2003)

19. McMillan, K.L.: Lazy abstraction with interpolants. In: Ball, T., Jones, R.B. (eds.) CAV 2006. LNCS, vol. 4144, pp. 123–136. Springer, Heidelberg (2006)

20. de Moura, L., Bjørner, N.S.: Z3: an efficient SMT solver. In: Ramakrishnan, C.R., Rehof, J. (eds.) TACAS 2008. LNCS, vol. 4963, pp. 337–340. Springer, Heidelberg (2008)

21. Padon, O., Immerman, N., Shoham, S., Karbyshev, A., Sagiv, M.: Decidability of inferring inductive invariants. In: Bodik, R., Majumdar, R. (eds.) POPL, pp. 217–231. ACM (2016)

22. Padon, O., McMillan, K.L., Panda, A., Sagiv, M., Shoham, S.: Ivy: interactive verification of parameterized systems via effectively propositional reasoning. In: PLDI. ACM (2016)

23. Navarro-Pérez, J.A., Voronkov, A.: Encodings of bounded LTL model checking in effectively propositional logic. In: Pfenning, F. (ed.) CADE 2007. LNCS (LNAI), vol. 4603, pp. 346–361. Springer, Heidelberg (2007)

24. Navarro-Pérez, J.A., Voronkov, A.: Encodings of problems in effectively propositional logic. In: Marques-Silva, J., Sakallah, K.A. (eds.) SAT 2007. LNCS, vol. 4501, pp. 3–3. Springer, Heidelberg (2007)

25. Navarro-Pérez, J.A., Voronkov, A.: Planning with effectively propositional logic. In: Voronkov, A., Weidenbach, C. (eds.) Programming Logics. LNCS, vol. 7797, pp. 302–316. Springer, Heidelberg (2013)

26. Piskac, R., de Moura, L.M., Bjørner, N.: Deciding effectively propositional logic using DPLL and substitution sets. JAR 44(4), 401–424 (2010)

27. Reps, T., Sagiv, M., Yorsh, G.: Symbolic Implementation of the Best Transformer. In: Steffen, B., Levi, G. (eds.) VMCAI 2004. LNCS, vol. 2937, pp. 252–266. Springer, Heidelberg (2004)

28. Sharma, R., Nori, A.V., Aiken, A.: Interpolants as classifiers. In: Madhusudan, P., Seshia, S.A. (eds.) CAV 2012. LNCS, vol. 7358, pp. 71–87. Springer, Heidelberg (2012)

29. Sivaramakrishnan, K.C., Kaki, G., Jagannathan, S.: Declarative programming over eventually consistent data stores. In: Grove, D., Blackburn, S. (eds.) PLDI, pp. 413–424. ACM (2015)

30. Thakur, A.: Symbolic Abstraction: Algorithms and Applications. Ph.D. thesis, University of Wisconsin-Madison (2014)

31. Totla, N., Wies, T.: Complete instantiation-based interpolation. In: Giacobazzi, R., Cousot, R. (eds.) POPL, pp. 537–548. ACM (2013)

Array Folds Logic

Przemysław Daca[✉], Thomas A. Henzinger, and Andrey Kupriyanov[✉]

IST Austria, Klosterneuburg, Austria
{przemek,andrey.kupriyanov}@ist.ac.at

Abstract. We present an extension to the quantifier-free theory of integer arrays which allows us to express counting. The properties expressible in Array Folds Logic (AFL) include statements such as "the first array cell contains the array length," and "the array contains equally many minimal and maximal elements." These properties cannot be expressed in quantified fragments of the theory of arrays, nor in the theory of concatenation. Using reduction to counter machines, we show that the satisfiability problem of AFL is PSPACE-complete, and with a natural restriction the complexity decreases to NP. We also show that adding either universal quantifiers or concatenation leads to undecidability.

AFL contains terms that fold a function over an array. We demonstrate that folding, a well-known concept from functional languages, allows us to concisely summarize loops that count over arrays, which occurs frequently in real-life programs. We provide a tool that can discharge proof obligations in AFL, and we demonstrate on practical examples that our decision procedure can solve a broad range of problems in symbolic testing and program verification.

1 Introduction

Arrays and lists (or, more generally, sequences) are fundamental data structures both for imperative and functional programs: hardly any real-life program can work without processing sequentially-ordered data. Testing and verification of array- and list-manipulating programs is thus a task of crucial importance. Almost any non-trivial property about these data structures requires some sort of universal quantification; unfortunately, the full first-order theories of arrays and lists are undecidable. This has motivated researches to investigate fragments with restricted quantifier prefixes, and has given rise to numerous logics that can describe interesting properties of sequences, such as partitioning or sortedness. These logics have efficient decision procedures and have been successfully applied to verify some important aspects of programs working with arrays and lists: for example, the correctness of sorting algorithms.

This research was supported in part by the European Research Council (ERC) under grant 267989 (QUAREM) and by the Austrian Science Fund (FWF) under grants S11402-N23 (RiSE and SHiNE) and Z211-N23 (Wittgenstein Award).

S. Chaudhuri and A. Farzan (Eds.): CAV 2016, Part II, LNCS 9780, pp. 230–248, 2016.
DOI: 10.1007/978-3-319-41540-6_13

```
min = max = a[0];
j = k = 0;
for(i=0;i<size(a);i++) {
  if(a[i]<min) { min=a[i]; j=1; }
  if(a[i]==min) j++;
}
for(i=0;i<size(a);i++) {
  if(a[i]>max) { max=a[i]; k=1; }
  if(a[i]==max) k++;
}
assert(j==k);
```

$\exists\, min, max, i_1, i_2, j, k\ .$

$0 \leq i_1 < |a| \land 0 \leq i_2 < |a| \land$

$a[i_1] = min \land a[i_2] = max \land$

$\forall i.(a[i] \geq min) \land$

$\forall i.(a[i] \leq max) \land$

$j = |\{i \mid a[i] = min\}| \land$

$k = |\{i \mid a[i] = max\}| \land$

$j = k$

(a) C language　　　　　　　　　(b) Quantified arrays + cardinality

$$0 \leq i_1 < |a| \land 0 \leq i_2 < |a| \land a[i_1] = min \land a[i_2] = max \land$$
$$fold_a \binom{0}{0} \binom{e = min \Rightarrow c_1\text{++}}{e > min \Rightarrow skip} = \binom{|a|}{j} \land fold_a \binom{0}{0} \binom{e = max \Rightarrow c_1\text{++}}{e < max \Rightarrow skip} = \binom{|a|}{k} \land j = k$$

(c) Array Folds Logic

Fig. 1. A toy array problem

However, an important class of properties, namely, *counting* over arrays, has eluded researchers' attention so far. In addition to the examples from the abstract, this includes statements such as "the histogram of the input data satisfies the given distribution," or "the packet adheres to the requirements of the given type length value (TLV) encoding (e.g., of the IPv6 options)." Such properties, though crucial for many applications, cannot be expressed in decidable fragments of the first-order theory of arrays, nor in the decidable extensions of the theory of concatenation.

In this paper we present *Array Folds Logic* (*AFL*), which is an extension of the quantifier-free theory of integer arrays. But instead of introducing quantifiers, we introduce counting in the form of *fold* terms. Folding is a well-known concept in functional languages: as the name suggests, it folds some function over an array, i.e., applies it to every element of the array in sequence, while preserving the intermediate result.

To illustrate the kind of problems we are dealing with, consider the following toy example: given an array, accept it if the number of minimum elements in the array is the same as the number of maximum elements in the array. E.g., the array $[1, 2, 7, 4, 1, 3, 7, 5]$ is accepted (because there are two 1's and two 7's), while the array $[1, 2, 7, 4, 1, 3, 6, 5]$ is rejected (because there is only one 7).

Written in a programming language like C, the problem can be solved by the piece of code shown in Fig. 1a, but such *explicit* solution cannot express verification conditions for *symbolic* verification and testing. We can use the quantified theory of arrays mixed with assertions about cardinality of sets, as in Fig. 1b.

Unfortunately, such a combination is undecidable (by a reduction from Hilbert's Tenth Problem: replace *fold*s with cardinalities in the proof of Theorem 2).

The solution we propose is shown in Fig. 1c: in the example formula, the first *fold* applies a function to array a. The vector in the first parentheses gives initial values for the array index and counter c_1; the function is folded over the array starting from the initial index. Index variable i is implicit, and it is incremented at each iteration. The function itself is given in the second parentheses, and has two branches. The first branch *counts* the number of positions with elements equal to *min* in counter c_1. The second branch *skips* when the current array element e is greater than the (guessed, existentially quantified) variable *min*. When $e < min$, the implicit *break* statement is executed, and the *fold* terminates prematurely. The result of the *fold* is compared to the vector which asserts that the final value of the array index equals to the array size $|a|$ (which means no *break* was executed), and the final value of c_1 equals to j. The positions where elements are equal to *max*, are counted in the second *fold*, and the equality between these two counts is asserted. The ability to count over arrays with unbounded elements is a unique feature of Array Folds Logic.

This paper makes the following contributions:

1. We define a new logic, called AFL, that can express interesting and non-trivial properties of counting over arrays, which are orthogonal to the properties expressible by other logics. Additionally, AFL can concisely summarize loops with internal branching that traverse arrays and perform counting, enabling verification and symbolic testing of programs with such loops.

2. We show that the satisfiability problem for AFL is **PSPACE**-complete, and with a natural restriction the complexity decreases to **NP**. We provide a decision procedure for AFL, which works by a reduction to the emptiness of (symbolic) reversal-bounded counter machines, which in turn reduces to the satisfiability of existential Presburger formulas. We show that adding either universal quantifiers or concatenation leads to undecidability.

3. We implemented tool AFOLDER [13] that can discharge proof obligations in AFL, and we demonstrate on real-life examples that our decision procedure can solve a broad range of problems in symbolic testing and program verification.

Related Work. Our logic is related to the quantified fragments of the theory of arrays such as [4, 10, 21, 22]. These logics allow restricted quantifier prefixes, and their decision procedures work by rewriting to the (parametric) theories of array indices and elements (Presburger arithmetic being the most common case) [4, 10], or by reduction to flat counter automata with difference bound constraints [21, 22]. An interesting alternative is provided in [35], where the quantification is arbitrary, but array elements must be bounded by a constant given a priori; the decision procedure works by a reduction to WS1S. A separate line of work is presented by the theory combination frameworks of [16, 18], where the quantifier-free theory of arrays is extended by *injective* predicate and *domain* function [18], or with *map* and *constant-value* combinators [16]. The theory of concatenation and its extensions [11, 17, 29] are also related; their decision procedures work by reduction to Makanin's algorithm for solving word equations [30].

AFL can express some properties that are also expressible in these logics, such as *boundedness*, *partitioning*, or *periodicity*; other properties, such as *sortedness*, are not expressible in AFL. The counting properties that constitute the core of AFL are not expressible in any of the above logics. We compare the expressive power of AFL and other logics in Sect. 2.3.

There are numerous works on loop acceleration and summarization [8,12,27], also in the context of verification and symbolic testing [9,19,24,33] and array-manipulating programs [3,5,7]. Our logic allows one to summarize loops with internal branching and counting, which are outside of the scope of these works.

The decision procedure for AFL is based on decidability results for emptiness of reversal-bounded counter machines [20,25,26], on the encoding of this problem into Presburger arithmetic [23], and on the computation of Parikh images for NFAs [34]. In Sect. 5 we extend the encoding procedure to symbolic counter machines, and present some substantial improvements that make it efficient for solving practical AFL problems.

2 Array Folds Logic

We assume familiarity with the standard syntax and terminology of many-sorted first-order logics. We use vector notation: $v = (v_1, \ldots, v_n)$ denotes an ordered sequence of terms. For two vectors u and v, we write their concatenation as uv.

Within this paper we consider the domains of arrays, array indices, and array elements to be $A = \mathbb{Z}^*$, $\mathbb{N} = \{0, 1, \ldots\}$, and $\mathbb{Z} = \{\ldots, -1, 0, 1, \ldots\}$ respectively.

Presburger arithmetic has the signature $\Sigma_{\mathbb{Z}} = \{0, 1, +, <\}$; we use it for array indices and elements, as well as other arithmetic assertions, possibly with embedded array terms. We write *true* and *false* to denote a valid and an unsatisfiable Presburger formula, respectively.

The theory of integer-indexed arrays extends Presburger arithmetic with functions *read*, and *write*, and has the signature $\Sigma_A = \Sigma_{\mathbb{Z}} \cup \{\cdot[\cdot], \cdot\{\cdot \leftarrow \cdot\}\}$. The *read* function $a[i]$ returns the i-th element of array a, and the *write* function $a\{i \leftarrow x\}$ returns array a where the i-th element is replaced by x. These functions should satisfy the *read*-over-*write* axioms as described by McCarthy [32].

2.1 Syntax

Array Folds Logic (AFL) extends the quantifier-free theory of integer arrays with the ability to perform counting. The extension works by incorporating *fold* terms into arithmetic expressions; such a term folds some function over the array by applying it to each array element consecutively.

AFL contains the following sorts: array sort ASort, integer sort ISort, Boolean sort BSort, and two enumerable sets of sorts for integer vectors VSort^m and functional constants FSort^m = VSort^m × ISort → VSort^m, for each $m \in \mathbb{N}$, $m > 0$. The syntax of the AFL terms is shown in Table 1; a and b denote array variables, x denotes an integer variable, n and m denote integer constants.

Table 1. Syntax of AFL.

$$
\begin{aligned}
A &::= a \mid a\{T \leftarrow T\} \\
T &::= n \mid x \mid T + T \mid a[T] \mid |a| \\
B &::= a = b \mid T = T \mid T < T \mid \neg B \mid B \wedge B \mid V^m = V^m \\
V^m &::= \begin{pmatrix} T \\ \cdots \\ T \end{pmatrix} \mid fold_a\, V^m\, F^m \\
F^m &::= \begin{pmatrix} grd \Rightarrow upd \\ \cdots \\ grd \Rightarrow upd \end{pmatrix} \\
grd &::= \mathbf{e} \approx T \mid \mathbf{i} \approx T \mid \mathbf{c}_m \approx T \mid \mathbf{s} \approx n \mid grd \wedge grd & (\approx\; \in\; \{>, <, =, \neq\}) \\
upd &::= \mathbf{c}_m \mathrel{+}= n \mid \mathbf{s} \leftarrow n \mid skip \mid break \mid upd\,;\,upd
\end{aligned}
$$

Array terms A of sort ASort are represented either by an array variable a, or by the *write* term $a\{T \leftarrow T\}$.

Integer terms T of sort ISort can be integer constants $n \in \mathbb{Z}$, integer variables x, integer addition, *read* term $a[T]$ for the index represented as an integer term, or the term $|a|$, which represents the length of array a.

Boolean terms B of sort BSort are formed by array equality, usual Presburger and Boolean operators, and equality between vectors of sort VSort^m.

Vector terms V^m of sort VSort^m are either a list of m integer terms, or a *fold* term. The former is written as a vertical list in parentheses; they can be omitted when $m = 1$. The latter, written as $fold_a\, v\, f$, represents the result of the transformation of an input vector v of sort VSort^m by folding a functional constant f of sort FSort^m over an array a. The first element of v specifies an initial value of the array index; the remaining elements give initial values for the counters that can be used inside f. The resulting vector after the transformation gives the final values for the array index and the counters.

Functional constants (when no confusion can arise, we call them *functions*) F^m of sort FSort^m can only be a parenthesized list of branches (guarded commands); the length of the list is unrelated to m. A function f of sort FSort^m can refer to the following implicitly declared variables: $\mathbf{e}$ for the currently inspected array element; $\mathbf{i}$ for the current array index; $\mathbf{c}_1, \ldots, \mathbf{c}_{m-1}$ for the counters; $\mathbf{s}$ for the state (control flow) variable. All other variables that occur inside f are considered as free variables of sort ISort.

Guards are conjunctions of *atomic guards*, which can compare array elements, indices, and counters to integer terms; the state variable can only be compared to integer constants. *Updates* are lists of *atomic updates*; they can increment or decrease counters by a constant, assign a constant to the state variable, *skip*, i.e. perform no updates, or execute a *break* statement, which terminates the *fold* at the current position. Counter or state updates define a function $\mathbb{Z} \to \mathbb{Z}$. Guards and updates translate into logical formulas that either constraint the current variable values, or relate the current and the next-state (primed) variable values in the obvious way; we denote this translation by Φ. E.g., the update $upd \equiv (\mathbf{c}_1 \mathrel{+}= n)$ defines the formula $\Phi(upd) \equiv (\mathbf{c}_1' = \mathbf{c}_1 + n)$.

We require that guards of all branches are mutually exclusive. There is an implicit "catch-all" branch with the *break* statement, whose guard evaluates to *true* exactly when guards of all other branches evaluate to *false*. We also require that each branch contains at most one update for each implicit variable.

We restrict the control flow in functions, which is defined by state variable **s**. Notice that **s** is syntactically finite state. Thus, given a set of function branches Br, we define an edge-labeled control flow graph $G = \langle S, E, \gamma \rangle$, where:

- states $S = \{0\} \cup \{ n \mid \mathbf{s} \leftarrow n \in Br \}$;
- edges $E = \bigcup_{grd \Rightarrow upd \,\in\, Br} \{ (s_1, s_2) \mid s_1 \models grd \wedge s_2 = ite(\mathbf{s} \leftarrow n \in upd, n, s_1) \}$;
- γ is the labeling of edges with the set of formulas $\Phi(grd)$ and $\Phi(upd)$ for each guard or update which occurs in the same branch.

We require that edges in the strongly-connected components of G are labeled with counter updates that are, for each counter, all non-decreasing, or all non-increasing. Thus, G is a DAG of SCCs, where counters within each SCC behave in a monotonic way. We use this restriction to derive from f a reversal-bounded counter machine (see Definition 2).

The presented syntax is minimal and can be extended with convenience functions and predicates such as $\{-, n\cdot, \leq, \geq, \vee, \text{++}, \text{--}, \text{-}=n\}$ in the usual way. We allow to use $*$ to denote the absence of constraints: this is useful for vector notation. We replace each $*$ in the formula with a unique unconstrained variable.

2.2 Semantics

For a given AFL formula ϕ, we denote the sets of free variables of ϕ of sort ASort and ISort by Var_A and Var_I, respectively. All free variables are implicitly existentially quantified. For functions of sort FSort^m, we denote by FV^m the set of their implicit variables $\{\mathbf{i}, \mathbf{c}_1, \ldots, \mathbf{c}_{m-1}, \mathbf{s}\}$.

Array equalities partition the set of array variables into equivalence classes; all other constraints are then translated into constraints over a representative of the corresponding equivalence class.

An *interpretation* for AFL is a tuple $\sigma = \langle \lambda, \mu \rangle$, where $\lambda : Var_I \to \mathbb{Z}$ assigns each integer variable an integer, and $\mu : Var_A \to \mathbb{Z}^*$ assigns each array variable a finite sequence of integers.

The semantics of an AFL term t under the given interpretation σ is defined by the *evaluation* $[t]^\sigma$. Terms that constitute functions are evaluated in the additional *context* κ. For a function f of sort FSort^m, $\kappa : FV^m \to \mathbb{Z}^{m+1}$ maps internal variables of f to integers. The evaluation of Presburger, Boolean, and array terms is standard; the remaining ones are shown in Table 2. We give some explanations here (the remaining semantic rules are self-explanatory):

1. Vector equality resolves to a conjunction of equalities between components.
2. A *fold* term evaluates in the initial context that is defined by the given initial vector of counters v, and assigns 0 to state variable **s**.

Table 2. Semantics of AFL

1. $\left[\left(\begin{smallmatrix} t_1^1 \\ \cdots \\ t_m^1 \end{smallmatrix}\right) = \left(\begin{smallmatrix} t_1^2 \\ \cdots \\ t_m^2 \end{smallmatrix}\right)\right]^\sigma$ $\equiv$ $\left([t_1^1]^\sigma = [t_1^2]^\sigma\right) \wedge \ldots \wedge \left([t_m^1]^\sigma = [t_m^2]^\sigma\right)$

2. $[fold_a\ v\ f]^\sigma$ $\equiv$ $[fold_a\ v\ f]^{\sigma,\kappa}$, where $\kappa(FV^m) = \left(\begin{smallmatrix} v \\ 0 \end{smallmatrix}\right)$

3. $[fold_a\ v\ f]^{\sigma,\kappa}$ $\equiv$ if $([\mathbf{i}]^\kappa < 0)$ or $([\mathbf{i}]^\kappa \geq |a|)$ or $(false \in [f]^{\sigma,\kappa})$ then v

   $\qquad$ else $[fold_a\ v'\ f]^{\sigma,\kappa'}$, where $\kappa'(FV^m) = \left(\begin{smallmatrix} v' \\ \mathbf{s}' \end{smallmatrix}\right) = [f]^{\sigma,\kappa}\left(\kappa(FV^m)\right)$

4. $[f]^{\sigma,\kappa}\left(\begin{smallmatrix} v_1 \\ \cdots \\ v_m \end{smallmatrix}\right)$ $\equiv$ $\left(\begin{smallmatrix} v_1' \\ \cdots \\ v_m' \end{smallmatrix}\right)$, where $v_j' \equiv$ if $upd(v_j) \in [f]^{\sigma,\kappa}$ then $upd(v_j)$, else v_j

5. $\left[\left(\begin{smallmatrix} grd_1 \Rightarrow upd_1 \\ \cdots \\ grd_m \Rightarrow upd_m \end{smallmatrix}\right)\right]^{\sigma,\kappa}$ $\equiv$ $\{\mathbf{i}' = \mathbf{i} + 1\} \cup [grd_1 \Rightarrow upd_1]^{\sigma,\kappa} \cup \ldots \cup [grd_m \Rightarrow upd_m]^{\sigma,\kappa}$

6. $[grd \Rightarrow upd]^{\sigma,\kappa}$ $\equiv$ if $[grd]^{\sigma,\kappa} = true$ then $[upd]^{\sigma,\kappa}$ else $\emptyset$

7. $[\mathbf{e} \approx t]^{\sigma,\kappa}$ $\equiv$ $[\mathbf{e}]^\kappa \approx [t]^\sigma$ $\qquad$ (similarly for $\mathbf{i} \approx T$, $\mathbf{c}_m \approx T$, $\mathbf{s} \approx n$)

8. $[grd_1 \wedge grd_2]^{\sigma,\kappa}$ $\equiv$ $[grd_1]^{\sigma,\kappa} \wedge [grd_2]^{\sigma,\kappa}$

9. $[upd_1; upd_2]^{\sigma,\kappa}$ $\equiv$ $[upd_1]^{\sigma,\kappa} \cup [upd_2]^{\sigma,\kappa}$

10. $[\mathbf{c}_m \mathrel{+}= n]^{\sigma,\kappa}$ $\equiv$ $\{\mathbf{c}_m' = \mathbf{c}_m + n\}$

11. $[\mathbf{s} \leftarrow n]^{\sigma,\kappa}$ $\equiv$ $\{\mathbf{s}' = n\}$

12. $[skip]^{\sigma,\kappa}$ $\equiv$ $\emptyset$

13. $[break]^{\sigma,\kappa}$ $\equiv$ $\{false\}$

3. A contextual *fold* term checks whether the array index is out of bounds, or a *break* statement is executed in the current context (this is the only way for $[f]^{\sigma,\kappa}$ to contain *false*). If yes, *fold* terminates, and returns the current vector v. Otherwise *fold* continues with the updated vector and context.

4. If an update $upd(v_j)$ for some variable v_j is present in the function evaluation, then it is applied. Otherwise, the old variable value is preserved.

5. An evaluation of a function, represented by a list of branches, is a union of updates from its branch evaluations. Index $\mathbf{i}$ is always incremented by 1.

6. A guarded command evaluates to its update if its guard evaluates to *true*.

7. A comparison over an internal variable evaluates it in the context κ, and the comparison term is evaluated in the interpretation σ.

2.3 Expressive Power

Here we give some example properties that are expressible in AFL, and compare its expressive power to other decidable array logics.

1. **Boundedness.** All elements of array a belong to the interval $[l, u]$.

$$fold_a(0)\left(l \leq \mathbf{e} \leq u \Rightarrow skip\right) = |a|$$

2. **Partitioning.** Array a is partitioned if there is a position p such that all elements before p are smaller or equal than all elements at or after p.

$$fold_a(0)\left(\begin{smallmatrix} \mathbf{i} < p \,\wedge\, \mathbf{e} \leq a[p] \Rightarrow skip \\ \mathbf{i} \geq p \,\wedge\, \mathbf{e} \geq a[p] \Rightarrow skip \end{smallmatrix}\right) = |a|$$

3. **Periodicity.** Array a is of the form $(01)^*$:

$$fold_a(0)\left(\begin{smallmatrix} s=0 \,\wedge\, e=0 \,\Rightarrow\, s\leftarrow1 \\ s=1 \,\wedge\, e=1 \,\Rightarrow\, s\leftarrow0 \end{smallmatrix}\right) = |a|$$

4. **Pumping.** Array a is of the form 0^n1^n (a canonical non-regular language; $0^n1^n2^n$, a non-context-free language, is equally expressible):

$$fold_a\left(\begin{smallmatrix} 0 \\ 0 \\ 0 \end{smallmatrix}\right)\left(\begin{smallmatrix} s=0 \,\wedge\, e=0 \,\Rightarrow\, c_1\text{++} \\ s=0 \,\wedge\, e=1 \,\Rightarrow\, c_2\text{++} \,\wedge\, s\leftarrow1 \\ s=1 \,\wedge\, e=1 \,\Rightarrow\, c_2\text{++} \end{smallmatrix}\right) = \left(\begin{smallmatrix} |a| \\ n \\ n \end{smallmatrix}\right)$$

5. **Equal Count.** Arrays a and b have equal number of elements greater than l:

$$\left(\begin{smallmatrix} |a| \\ n \end{smallmatrix}\right) = fold_a\left(\begin{smallmatrix} 0 \\ 0 \end{smallmatrix}\right)\left(\begin{smallmatrix} e>l \,\Rightarrow\, c_1\text{++} \\ e\leq l \,\Rightarrow\, skip \end{smallmatrix}\right) \,\wedge\, \left(\begin{smallmatrix} |b| \\ n \end{smallmatrix}\right) = fold_b\left(\begin{smallmatrix} 0 \\ 0 \end{smallmatrix}\right)\left(\begin{smallmatrix} e>l \,\Rightarrow\, c_1\text{++} \\ e\leq l \,\Rightarrow\, skip \end{smallmatrix}\right)$$

6. **Histogram.** The histogram of the input data in array a satisfies the distribution $H(\{i \mid a[i] < 10\}) \geq 2H(\{i \mid a[i] \geq 10\})$:

$$fold_a\left(\begin{smallmatrix} 0 \\ 0 \end{smallmatrix}\right)\left(\begin{smallmatrix} e<10 \,\Rightarrow\, c_1\text{++} \\ e\geq10 \,\Rightarrow\, skip \end{smallmatrix}\right) = \left(\begin{smallmatrix} |a| \\ h_1 \end{smallmatrix}\right) \,\wedge\, fold_a\left(\begin{smallmatrix} 0 \\ 0 \end{smallmatrix}\right)\left(\begin{smallmatrix} e\geq10 \,\Rightarrow\, c_1\text{++} \\ e<10 \,\Rightarrow\, skip \end{smallmatrix}\right) = \left(\begin{smallmatrix} |a| \\ h_2 \end{smallmatrix}\right) \,\wedge\, h_1 \geq 2h_2$$

7. **Length of Format Fields.** The array contains two variable-length fields. The first two elements of the array define the length of each field; they are followed by the fields themselves, separated by 0:

$$len_1 = a[0] \,\wedge\, len_2 = a[1] \,\wedge\, fold_a\left(\begin{smallmatrix} 2 \\ 0 \\ 0 \end{smallmatrix}\right)\left(\begin{smallmatrix} s=0 \,\wedge\, e\neq0 \,\Rightarrow\, c_1\text{++} \\ s=0 \,\wedge\, e=0 \,\Rightarrow\, s\leftarrow1 \\ s=1 \,\wedge\, e\neq0 \,\Rightarrow\, c_2\text{++} \end{smallmatrix}\right) = \left(\begin{smallmatrix} |a| \\ len_1 \\ len_2 \end{smallmatrix}\right)$$

Comparison with Other Logics. Most decidable array logics can specify universal properties over a *single* index variable like (1) above; AFL uses *folds* to express such universal quantification. Properties that require universal quantification over *several* index variables, like sortedness, are inexpressible in AFL (it can simulate some of such properties, like partitioning (2), using a combination of *folds* with existential guessing). Periodic facts like (3) are inexpressible in [10], but AFL as well as [17,21] can express it. Counting properties such as (4)–(7), which constitute the core of AFL, are not expressible in other decidable logics over arrays and sequences.

3   Motivating Example

As a motivating example to illustrate applications of our logic, we consider a parser for the Markdown language as implemented in the Redcarpet project, hosted on GitHub [2]. Redcarpet is a popular implementation of the language, used by many other projects, in particular by the GitHub itself. Figure 2 shows the excerpt from the function `parse_table_header`, which can be found in the file `markdown.c`.

The function considered in the example parses the header of a table in the Markdown format. The first line of the header specifies column titles; they are separated by pipe symbols ('|'); the first pipe is optional. Thus, the number of

```
1: static size_t parse_table_header(uint8_t *a, size_t size, ...)
2:   size_t i=0, pipes=0;
```

$$\left\{ i_0 = 0 \wedge p_0 = 0 \right\}$$

```
3:   while (i < size && a[i] != '\n')
4:     if (a[i++] == '|') pipes++;
```

$$\left\{ \binom{i_1}{p_1} = fold_a \binom{i_0}{p_0} \left(\begin{matrix} e=P \Rightarrow c_1\text{++} \\ e \neq P \wedge e \neq N \Rightarrow skip \end{matrix} \right) \right\}$$

```
5:   if (a[0] == '|') pipes--;
```

$$\left\{ \binom{*}{p_2} = fold_a \binom{0}{p_1} \left(i = 0 \wedge e = P \Rightarrow c_1\text{--} \right) \right\}$$

```
6:   i++;
7:   if (i < size && a[i] == '|') i++;
```

$$\left\{ i_2 = i_1 + 1 \wedge i_3 = fold_a(i_2)\left(i = i_2 \wedge e = P \Rightarrow skip \right) \right\}$$

```
8:   end = i;
9:   while (end < size && a[end] != '\n') end++;
```

$$\left\{ e_0 = i_3 \wedge e1 = fold_a(e_0)\left(e \neq N \Rightarrow skip \right) \right\}$$

```
10:   for (col = 0; col<pipes && i<end; ++col) {
11:     size_t dashes = 0;
```

$$\left\{ c_0 = 0 \wedge c_0 < p_2 \wedge i_3 < e_1 \wedge d_0 = 0 \right\}$$

```
12:     if (a[i] == ':') { i++; dashes++; column_data[col] |= ALIGN_L; }
```

$$\left\{ \binom{i_4}{d_1} = fold_a \binom{i_3}{d_0}\left(i = i_3 \wedge e = C \Rightarrow c_1\text{++} \right) \right\}$$

```
13:     while (i < end && a[i] == '-') { i++; dashes++; }
```

$$\left\{ \binom{i_5}{d_2} = fold_a \binom{i_4}{d_1}\left(i < e_1 \wedge e = D \Rightarrow c_1\text{++} \right) \right\}$$

```
14:     if (a[i] == ':') { i++; dashes++; column_data[col] |= ALIGN_R; }
```

$$\left\{ \binom{i_6}{d_3} = fold_a \binom{i_5}{d_2}\left(i = i_5 \wedge e = C \Rightarrow c_1\text{++} \right) \right\}$$

```
15:     if (i < end && a[i] != '|' && a[i] != '+') break;
16:     if (dashes < 3) break;
17:     i++;
```

$$\left\{ \left(i_6 \geq end_1 \vee a[i_6] = P \vee a[i_6] = A \right) \wedge d_3 \geq 3 \wedge i_7 = i_6 + 1 \wedge c_1 = c_0 + 1 \right\}$$

```
18:   }
19:   if (col < pipes) return 0;
```

$$\left\{ c_1 \geq p_2 \right\}$$

Fig. 2. An excerpt from the Redcarpet Markdown parser with AFL annotations

pipes defines the number of columns in the table. The second line describes the alignment for each column, and should contain the same number of columns; in between each pair of pipes there should be at least three dash ('-') or colon (':') symbols. A colon on the left or on the right side of the dashes defines left or right alignment; colons on both sides mean centered text. Thus, the two lines "|One|Two|Three|" and "|:--|:--:|--:|" specify three columns which are left-, center-, and right-aligned. Replacing the second line with either "|:-|:--:|--:|" or "|:--|:--:|" would result in the ill-formed input: the former doesn't contain enough dashes in the first column, while the latter doesn't specify the format for the last column.

Suppose, we are interested in the symbolic testing of the parser implementation; in particular, we want to cover all branches in the code for a reasonably long input. For that we postulate that the first input line contains at least n columns (we add the condition assert(col>=n) after line 19).

Now, consider the last conditional statement at line 19. The if branch is satisfied by an empty second input line; and indeed, such concolic testers as CREST can easily cover it. The else branch, however, poses serious problems. In order to cover it, a well-formed input that respects all constraints should be generated; in particular the smallest length of such input, e.g., for n equal to 3, is 17. The huge number of combinations to test exceeds the capabilities of the otherwise very efficient concolic tester: for $n = 2$ CREST needs 800 s to generate a test, and for $n = 3$ it is not able to finish within 3 h.

Let us now examine the encoding of the implementation semantics in Array Folds Logic. The AFL assertions are shown in Fig. 2 intertwined with the source code: they encode the semantics of the preceding code lines in the SSA form. To shorten the presentation we use the following conventions: variables i, a, pipes, end, col, and dashes are represented by (SSA-indexed) logical variables i, a, p, e, c, and d respectively; characters '\n', '|', ':', '-', and '+' by logical constants N, P, C, D, and A respectively; finally, the subscript denotes the SSA index of a variable.

The Presburger constraints such as those after line 2 are standard and we do not elaborate on them here. The first AFL-specific annotation goes after line 4: it directly reflects the loop semantics. The *fold* term encodes the computation of the number of pipes: they are computed in the counter c_1, which gets its initial value equal to p_0, and its final value is equal to p_1. Similarly, array index i is initialized with i_0; and its final value is asserted to be equal to i_1. Both for counter c_1 and for index i (which is a special type of a counter) their initial and final values can be both constant and symbolic: in fact, arbitrary Presburger terms are allowed.

Notice that the loop at lines 3-4 is outside of the class of loops that can be accelerated by previous approaches. In particular, the difficulty here is the combination of the iteration over arrays with the branching structure inside the loop. On the contrary, AFL can summarize the loop in a concise logical formula.

The next conditional statement at line 5, takes care of the optional pipe at the beginning of the input. The annotation shown demonstrates that conditional statements are also easily represented by *fold* terms. In particular, here the function is folded over a starting from 0; the final index is unconstrained. The branch checks that the index is 0 (to prevent going further over the array), and that the symbol at this position is '|'. Counter c_1 is decremented only if these two conditions are met; otherwise, the *fold* terminates. An equivalent encoding using only array reads is possible: $(a[0] = P \wedge p_2 = p_1 - 1) \vee (a[0] \neq P \wedge p_2 = p_1)$, but this encoding involves a disjunction.

The other program statements of the motivating example are encoded in a similar fashion. The encoding shown is for one unfolding of the for loop at line 10; several unfoldings are encoded similarly. We have checked the resulting proof obligations with our solver for AFL formulas, called AFOLDER; it can discharge them and generate the required test input in less than 2 minutes for $n = 3$.

4   Complexity

A counter machine is a finite automaton extended by a vector $\boldsymbol{\eta} = (\eta_1, \dots, \eta_k)$ of k counters. Every counter in $\boldsymbol{\eta}$ stores a non-negative integer, and a counter machine can compare it to constant, and increment/decrease its value by a constant. For the formal definition of counter machines consult, e.g., [26].

We extend counter machines to symbolic counter machines (SCMs), which accept sequences (arrays) of integers. We denote the symbolic value of an array cell by a special integer variable x_e. Let X be a set of integer variables, where $x_e \notin X$. An *atomic input constraint* is of the form $x_e \approx c$ or $x_e \approx x$, where $c \in \mathbb{N}$, $x \in X$, and $\approx \in \{<, \leq, >, \geq, =, \neq\}$. Similarly, an *atomic counter constraint* is a formula of the form $\eta_i \approx c$ or $\eta_i \approx x$. An *input constraint* (resp. a *counter constraint*) is either a conjunction of $n \geq 1$ atomic input constraints (resp. atomic counter constraints), or the formula *true*. We denote by $\mathsf{IC}(X)$ (resp. $\mathsf{CC}_k(X)$) the set of all input constraints (resp. counter constraints with counters not greater than k) over variables in X.

Definition 1. *A symbolic k-counter machine is a tuple* $\mathcal{M} = (\boldsymbol{\eta}, X, Q, \delta, q^{\mathrm{init}})$, *where:*

- $\boldsymbol{\eta} = (\eta_1, \dots, \eta_k)$ *is a vector of k counter variables,*
- X *is a finite set of integer variables,*
- Q *is a finite set of states,*
- $\delta \subseteq Q \times \mathsf{CC}_k(X) \times \mathsf{IC}(X) \times Q \times \mathbb{Z}^k$ *is a transition relation,*
- $q^{\mathrm{init}} \in Q$ *is the initial state.*

A transition $(q_1, \alpha, \beta, q_2, \boldsymbol{\kappa}) \in \delta$ moves the SCM from state q_1 to q_2 if the counters satisfy the constraint α and the inspected array cell satisfies β; the counters are incremented by $\boldsymbol{\kappa}$, and the machine moves to the next cell. A machine is called *deterministic* if δ is functional. A counter machine makes a *reversal* if it makes an alternation between non-increasing and non-decreasing some counter. A machine is *reversal-bounded* if there exists a constant $c \geq 0$ such that on all accepting runs every counter makes at most c reversal.

Definition 2. *We define the translation of a functional constant f of sort $FSort^m$, occurring in a formula ϕ, as an SCM $\mathcal{M}(f) = (\eta, X, Q, \delta, q^{init})$. Let $G = \langle S, E, \gamma \rangle$ be the edge-labeled graph for f as defined in Sect. 2.1. Then $\eta = \{i, c_1, \ldots, c_{m-1}\}$, X are fresh free variables for each integer term T in f, $Q = S$, $q^{init} = 0$, and for each edge $(s_1, s_2) \in E$, δ contains a transition from s_1 to s_2 labeled with a conjunction of all constraints labeling the edge. For each integer term T in f and the corresponding variable $x \in X$, we replace T by x in f, and add the assertion $(x = T)$ as a conjunction at the outermost level of ϕ. Due to the constraint on G, we have that $\mathcal{M}(f)$ is reversal-bounded.*

Thus, we can translate a *fold* term into an SCM. A *parallel composition* of SCMs captures the scenario when several *folds* operate over the same array.

Definition 3. *The parallel composition (product) of two SCMs $\mathcal{M}_1$ and $\mathcal{M}_2$, where $\mathcal{M}_i = (\eta_i, X_i, Q_i, \delta_i, q_i^{init})$, is an SCM $\mathcal{M} = (\eta, X, Q, \delta, q^{init})$ such that:*

- $\eta = \eta_1 \eta_2$,
- $X = X_1 \cup X_2$,
- $Q = Q_1 \times Q_2$,
- *for each pair of transitions $(q_i, \alpha_i, \beta_i, p_i, \boldsymbol{w}_i) \in \delta_i$, where $i = 1..2$, there is the transition $((q_1, q_2), \alpha_1 \wedge \alpha_2, \beta_1 \wedge \beta_2, (p_1, p_2), \boldsymbol{w}_1\boldsymbol{w}_2) \in \delta$, which are the only transitions in δ,*
- $q^{init} = (q_1^{init}, q_2^{init})$.

One of the fundamental questions that can be asked about a logic concerns the size of its models. The following lemma shows that models of bounded size are enough to check satisfiability of an AFL formula.

Lemma 1 (Small model property). *There exists a constant $c \in \mathbb{N}$, such that an AFL formula ϕ is satisfiable iff there exists a model σ such that a) for each integer variable x in ϕ, σ maps x to an integer $\leq 2^{|\phi|^c}$, and b) for each array variable in ϕ, σ maps the variable to a sequence of $\leq 2^{|\phi|^c}$ integers, where each integer is $\leq 2^{|\phi|^c}$.*

Proof (sketch; see [14] for the full proof). One direction of the proof is trivial. For the other direction, assume that ϕ has a model σ. We construct a formula ψ that is a conjunction of all atomic formulas of ϕ: in positive polarity if σ satisfies the atomic formula, and in negative otherwise. Let $s = |\psi|$, and note that $s \leq 3|\phi|$. We observe that (1) σ is a model of ψ, (2) every model of ψ is a model of ϕ. In the remaining part of the proof we show that ψ has a small model, and as a consequence so does ϕ.

Let a be some array in ψ. We translate each *fold* term over a to an SCM $\mathcal{M}_j$ as in Definition 2; let SCM $\mathcal{M}$ be the product of all $\mathcal{M}_j$. We extend the technique of [20] to show that there exist a sufficiently short run of $\mathcal{M}$. Under the interpretation σ, all variables in counter constraints become constants. Let $\boldsymbol{c} = (c_1, \ldots c_n)$ be a non-decreasing vector of constants that appear in the counter constraints of $\mathcal{M}$ after fixing σ. Vector $\boldsymbol{c}$ gives rise to the set of regions

$$\mathcal{R} = \{[0, c_1], [c_1, c_1], [c_1 + 1, c_2 - 1], [c_2, c_2], \ldots, [c_l, \infty]\}.$$

The size of $\mathcal{R}$ is at most $2\dim(c) + 1 \leq 3s$. A mode of $\mathcal{M}$ is a tuple in $\mathcal{R}^k$ that describes the region of each counter. Let us observe that each counter can traverse at most $|\mathcal{R}|$ modes before it makes an additional reversal. Thus, $\mathcal{M}$ in any run can traverse at most $max = r \cdot k \cdot |\mathcal{R}| \leq \mathcal{O}(s^3)$ different modes.

We take some accepting run Tr of $\mathcal{M}$ that traverses at most max modes, and partition sequences of transition in Tr into equivalence classes. We create an integer linear program LP that encodes an accepting run of $\mathcal{M}$ that traverses at most max modes, as well as all non-fold constraints of ψ. The variables of LP correspond to (1) the integer variables of ψ, (2) the counter values of $\mathcal{M}$, (3) the number of times sequences from each equivalence class are taken, and (4) the solutions to each input constraint of $\mathcal{M}$.

We show that LP has a solution p, where each variable is at most $\leq 2^{|\phi|^c}$, for a fixed c. We use p to construct a small model for ψ. From p we immediately get interpretation for integer variables of ψ. Solution p implies that there is an accepting run of $\mathcal{M}$ of length at most $\leq 2^{|\phi|^c}$, which also gives a bound on the length of the input array. Finally, for every array cell we may use a solution to the specific input constraint. □

As a consequence of Lemma 1 we obtain a result on the complexity of AFL satisfiability checking.

Theorem 1. *The satisfiability problem of AFL is* **PSPACE**-*complete.*

Proof. Membership. By Lemma 1, if an AFL formula ϕ is satisfiable, then it has a model where integer variables have value $\leq 2^{|\phi|^c}$, and arrays have length $\leq 2^{|\phi|^c}$, and where each array cell stores a number $\leq 2^{|\phi|^c}$. A non-deterministic Turing machine can use a polynomial number of bits to: (1) guess the value of integer variables and store them using $|\phi|^c$ bits, (2) guess one-by-one the value of at most $2^{|\phi|^c}$ array cells, and simulate the *fold*s. The Turing machine needs $|\phi|^c$ bits for counting the number of simulated cells. The maximum constant used in a counter increment can be at most $2^{|\phi|}$. Then, the maximal value a *fold* counter can store after traversing the array is at most $2^{|\phi|^{c+1}}$, therefore polynomial space is also sufficient to simulate *fold* counters.

Hardness. We reduce from the emptiness problem for intersection of deterministic finite automata, which is **PSPACE**-complete [28]. We are given a sequence $A_1, \ldots, A_n$ of deterministic finite automata, where each automaton A_i accepts the language $\mathcal{L}(A_i)$. The problem is to decide whether $\bigcap_{i=1}^{n} \mathcal{L}(A_i) \neq \emptyset$. We simulate automata A_i with a *fold* expression $fold_a^i$ over a single counter, where input constraints correspond to the alphabet symbols of the automata. The expression $fold_a^i$ returns an even number on array a if and only if the interpretation of a represents a word in $\mathcal{L}(A_i)$. To check emptiness of the automata intersection, it is enough to check whether there exists an array such that all folds $fold_a^1, \ldots, fold_a^n$ return an even number. The reduction can be done in polynomial time. □

4.1   Undecidable Extensions

We show that two natural extensions to our logic lead to undecidability.

Theorem 2. *Array Folds Logic with an $\exists^*\forall^*$ quantifier prefix is undecidable.*

Proof. We prove by a reduction from Hilbert's Tenth Problem [31]; since addition is already in the logic, we only show how to encode multiplication. The following $\exists^*\forall^*$ AFL formula has a model iff array a is a repetition of z segments, and each segment is of length y and has the shape $00...01$; thus, it asserts that $x = y \cdot z$:

$$|a| = x \;\wedge\; fold_a\binom{0}{0}\binom{\mathsf{e}=0 \,\Rightarrow\, skip}{\mathsf{e}=1 \,\Rightarrow\, \mathsf{c}_1\mathsf{++}} = \binom{|a|}{z} \;\wedge$$
$$\forall j.0 \le j < |a| \;\Longrightarrow\; fold_a\binom{j}{0}\binom{\mathsf{i} \le j+y \,\wedge\, \mathsf{e}=0 \,\Rightarrow\, skip}{\mathsf{i} \le j+y \,\wedge\, \mathsf{e}=1 \,\Rightarrow\, \mathsf{c}_1\mathsf{++}} = \binom{*}{1} \qquad \square$$

In [11], the following is proved about the theory of concatenation:

Theorem 3 ([11], Corollary 4; see also [17], Proposition 1).
Solvability of equations in the theory $\langle \{1,2\}^*, e, \circ, Lg_1, Lg_2 \rangle$, where $Lg_p(x) \equiv \{y \in p^* \mid y \text{ has the same number of } p\text{'s as } x\}$, is undecidable.

Corollary 1. *Extension of AFL with concatenation operator $\circ$ is undecidable.*

Proof. For an array x, we can define another array $Lg_1(x)$ in AFL as follows:

$$\binom{|x|}{|Lg_1(x)|} = fold_x\binom{0}{0}\binom{\mathsf{e}=1 \,\Rightarrow\, \mathsf{c}_1\mathsf{++}}{\mathsf{e}\ne 1 \,\Rightarrow\, skip} \;\wedge\; \big(|Lg_1(x)|\big) = fold_{Lg_1(x)}\binom{0}{}\big(\mathsf{e}=1 \,\Rightarrow\, skip\big) \qquad \square$$

5 Decision Procedure

In Sect. 4 we described how a non-deterministic Turing machine can decide AFL satisfiability in **PSPACE**. Now we present a deterministic procedure that translates AFL formulas to equisatisfiable quantifier-free Presburger formulas. As a consequence of the procedure, we show that under certain restrictions satisfiability of AFL is **NP**-complete.

Deterministic Procedure. We are given an AFL formula ϕ such that there are at most m *fold*s over each array; clearly m can be at most $|\phi|$. We translate ϕ to the quantifier-free Presburger formula $\psi = \psi_n \wedge \psi_e \wedge \psi_l$. For the procedure we assume that there exists a fixed order $x_1 \le \cdots \le x_n$ on variables that appear in the counter constraints.

Formula ψ_n. The formula ψ_n is the part of ϕ that does not contain *fold*s.

Formula ψ_e. For an array a_j in ϕ, let $F_j = \{fold_a^1, \ldots, fold_a^m\}$ be the set of *fold*s in ϕ over a_i. We translate each $fold_a^i \in F_j$ to a symbolic counter machine $\mathcal{M}_j^i$. Each $\mathcal{M}_j^i$ has at most $|\phi|$ transitions, and the sum of the counters and the number of reversals among all $\mathcal{M}_j^i$ is at most $|\phi|$. Next, we construct the symbolic counter machine $\mathcal{M}_j$ as the product of all machines $\mathcal{M}_j^i$. The machine $\mathcal{M}_j$ has at most $k = |\phi|$ counters, $t = |\phi|^m$ transitions and makes at most $r = |\phi|$ reversals.

We translate the reachability problem of $\mathcal{M}_j$ to the quantifier-free Presburger formula ψ_e^j by applying an extension of the method described in [23]. In formula

ψ_e^j, two configurations of $\mathcal{M}_j$ are described symbolically: initial ζ, and final ζ'. The formula ψ_e^j is satisfiable iff there is an array a_j such that $\mathcal{M}_j$ reaches ζ' from ζ on reading a_j. The formula ψ_e is the conjunction ψ_e^j for all arrays a_j.

The formula ψ_e^j consists of two parts $\psi_e^j = \psi_p^j \wedge \psi_c^j$. For simplicity we assume that the counter constrains of $\mathcal{M}_j$ are defined only over variables $\{x_1, \cdots, x_n\}$. By assumption, there is a fixed order $x_1 \leq \ldots \leq x_n$, which gives rise a to the set of $\leq 2|\phi| + 1$ regions $\mathcal{R} = \{[0, x_1], [x_1, x_1], [x_1 + 1, x_2 - 1], \cdots, [c_l, \infty]\}$. As an optimization, we construct regions separately for each counter, which allows us to obtain a tighter bound on the number of regions that need to be encoded.

Each counter may traverse at most $|\mathcal{R}|$ regions before it makes a reversal, so an accepting computation of $\mathcal{M}_j$ traverses at most $max = r \cdot k \cdot |\mathcal{R}| = \mathcal{O}(|\phi|^3)$ modes. We construct an NFA $\mathcal{A}_j$ by making max copies of the control-flow structure of $\mathcal{M}_j$. Every run of $\mathcal{A}_j$ gives a correct sequence of states in $\mathcal{M}_j$, but may violate counter constraints. By using the procedure of [34] we can encode the Parikh image of $\mathcal{A}_j$ as the formula ψ_p^j that is polynomial in the size of $\mathcal{A}$. Similar to [23], the formula ψ_c^j puts additional constraints on the Parikh image to ensure that by executing the transitions of $\mathcal{A}_j$ we obtain counter values that satisfy the counter constraints of $\mathcal{M}_j$.

The size ψ_e^j is of the order $\mathcal{O}(|\phi|^3 t) = \mathcal{O}(|\phi|^{m+3})$. The formula ψ_e is the conjunction of formulas ψ_e^j for each array a_j. There can be at most $|\phi|$ arrays, so the size of ψ_e is $\mathcal{O}(|\phi|^{m+4})$.

Formula ψ_l. Finally, formula ψ_l links the initial and final configurations in ψ_e to the variables in ψ_p.

Formula size. The size of the formula ψ is $\mathcal{O}(|\phi|^{m+4})$. By keeping m constant, the encoding size is polynomial in the size of the AFL formula ϕ.

Restricted Fragment of AFL. We write m-AFL for formulas that have at most m *fold* expressions per array. As a consequence of the deterministic decision procedure, restriction on m reduces the complexity of deciding satisfiability.

Lemma 2. *The m-AFL satisfiability problem, for a fixed m, is **NP**-complete.*

Proof. Membership follows from the decision procedure above. For hardness observe that any quantifier-free Presburger formula is an 0-AFL formula.   □

Model Generation. Given a Presburger encoding ψ of an AFL formula ϕ, we may use the solution to ψ to generate a model of ϕ. The solution to ψ immediately gives us interpretation for the integer variables in ϕ. To obtain an interpretation for the array variables in ϕ, we observe that folds are implicitly encoded in ψ as counter machines, and that the solution to ψ describes the Parikh vector for each machine. We use the method of [34] to get a concrete sequence of transitions in each counter machine that produces the specific Parikh vector. We construct a multigraph by repeating each transition in $\mathcal{A}_j$ according to its Parikh image, and then find an Eulerian path in the multigraph. From the sequence of transitions in counter machines, and the interpretation of input constraints in ψ we obtain an interpretation for the arrays in ϕ.

6   Experiments

We implemented the decision procedure described in Sect. 5 in a prototype tool AFOLDER; the tool is available at [13]. The tool is written in C++ and uses Z3 [15] as the solver for Presburger formulas. We evaluated our decision procedure on a number of testing and verification tasks described below.

The experimental results are shown in Table 3; all experiments were performed on a Ubuntu-14.04 64-bit machine running on an Intel Core i5-2540M CPU of 2.60 GHz. For every example we report the size $|\phi|$ of the AFL formula measured as "the number of logical operators" + "the number of branches in folds." The table also shows the number of *fold* expressions in a formula, and the maximum number of folds per array (MFPA). Next, we report the time for translating the problem to a Presburger formula, the time for solving the formula, and whether the formula is satisfiable. If this is the case, we report the length of a satisfying array generated by our tool; in case of several arrays, we show the longest.

Markdown. This program is described in Sect. 3. The experiments are parametrized by the required number n of columns in the input.

perf_bench_numa. This example is part of a benchmark program for non-uniform memory access (NUMA) [1]. The program maintains a list of threads,

Table 3. Experimental results for AFOLDER.

Example	$|\phi|$	Folds	MFPA	Transl. time	Solving time	Result	Array length
Markdown(1)	62	6	3	$< 1\,s$	$< 1\,s$	sat	8
Markdown(2)	69	7	4	$1\,s$	$< 1\,s$	sat	14
Markdown(3)	76	8	5	$1.3\,s$	$79\,s$	sat	17
perf_bench_numa(10)	93	10	1	$< 1s$	$< 1s$	sat	100
perf_bench_numa(20)	183	20	1	$< 1s$	$< 1s$	sat	100
perf_bench_numa(40)	363	40	1	$< 1s$	$< 1s$	sat	100
standard_minInArray	10	3	3	$< 1s$	$< 1s$	unsat	-
linear_sea.ch_true	13	3	3	$< 1s$	$< 1s$	unsat	-
array_call3	11	2	3	$< 1s$	$< 1s$	unsat	-
standard_sentinel	14	3	3	$< 1s$	$< 1s$	unsat	-
standard_find	11	3	3	$< 1s$	$< 1s$	unsat	-
standard_vararg	11	3	3	$< 1s$	$< 1s$	unsat	-
histogram(8)	58	8	8	$< 1s$	$1.3\,s$	sat	9
histogram(9)	65	9	9	$< 1s$	$6.9\,s$	sat	10
histogram(10)	72	10	10	$2\,s$	$55\,s$	sat	11
histogram(11)	79	11	11	$8\,s$	$368\,s$	sat	12
histogram_unsat(11)	80	11	11	$9\,s$	$19\,s$	unsat	-

and for each thread a separate array of size 100 that describes processors assigned to the thread. The data is processed in a nested loop: the outer loop iterates over threads, and the inner loop counts the number of assigned processors. The outer loop also maintains the minimum, and maximum number of processors assigned to any thread. We model a testing scenario like in Sect. 3, where a symbolic execution tool unrolls the outer loop n times, and the inner loop is summarized by a fold expression. The testing goal is to provide a valid processor mapping such that each thread is assigned to exactly one processor. In Table 3 we show results for this benchmark parametrized by the number n of threads. The example scales well, since there a single fold per each processor array (see Lemma 2).

SV-COMP. Examples "standard_minInArray" to "standard_vararg" are taken from the SV-COMP benchmarks suite [6]. They model simple verification problems for loops, such as finding the position of an element in array, finding the minimum, or counting the number of positive elements. We model these programs as formulas that are unsatisfiable if the program is safe. Although the programs are simple, most verification tools competing in SV-COMP fail to prove their safety.

Histogram. We performed experiments on the histogram example in Sect. 2.3, parametrized by the number of range values. We observe that solving time grows rapidly with the number of folds. Example "histogram_unsat" is an unsatisfiable variation that requires two different counts in the same range.

7   Conclusion and Future Work

We presented Array Folds Logic (AFL), which extends the quantifier-free theory of arrays with *folding*, a well-known concept from functional languages. The extension allows us to express counting properties, occurring frequently in real-life programs. Additionally, AFL is able to concisely summarize loops with internal branching and counting over arrays. We have analyzed the complexity of satisfiability checking for AFL formulas, and presented an efficient decision procedure via an encoding to the quantifier-free Presburger arithmetic. Finally, we have implemented a tool called AFOLDER, which efficiently discharges AFL proof obligations, and demonstrated its practical applicability on numerous examples.

For the future work, we plan to investigate possible combinations with other decidable fragments of the theory of arrays (to allow some restricted form of quantifier alternation). We also plan to automate the generation of proof obligations and the summarization of loops, and want to improve the efficiency of our decision procedure by implementing suitable optimizations and heuristics.

References

1. Benchmark for non-uniform memory access (NUMA). http://lxr.free-electrons. com/source/tools/perf/bench/numa.c?v=3.9. Accessed 29 Jan 2016
2. Markdown parser of the Redcarpet project. https://github.com/vmg/redcarpet/ blob/master/ext/redcarpet/markdown.c. Accessed 20 Jan 2016
3. Alberti, F., Ghilardi, S., Sharygina, N.: Booster: an acceleration-based verification framework for array programs. In: Cassez, F., Raskin, J.-F. (eds.) ATVA 2014. LNCS, vol. 8837, pp. 18–23. Springer, Heidelberg (2014)
4. Alberti, F., Ghilardi, S., Sharygina, N.: Decision procedures for flat array properties. J. Autom. Reason. **54**(4), 327–352 (2015)
5. Alberti, F., Ghilardi, S., Sharygina, N.: A new acceleration-based combination framework for array properties. In: Lutz, C., Ranise, S. (eds.) FroCoS 2015. LNCS, vol. 9322, pp. 169–185. Springer, Heidelberg (2015). doi:10.1007/ 978-3-319-24246-0_11
6. Beyer, D.: Software verification and verifiable witnesses. In: Baier, C., Tinelli, C. (eds.) TACAS 2015. LNCS, vol. 9035, pp. 401–416. Springer, Heidelberg (2015)
7. Bozga, M., Habermehl, P., Iosif, R., Konečný, F., Vojnar, T.: Automatic verification of integer array programs. In: Bouajjani, A., Maler, O. (eds.) CAV 2009. LNCS, vol. 5643, pp. 157–172. Springer, Heidelberg (2009)
8. Bozga, M., Iosif, R., Konečný, F.: Fast acceleration of ultimately periodic relations. In: Touili, T., Cook, B., Jackson, P. (eds.) CAV 2010. LNCS, vol. 6174, pp. 227–242. Springer, Heidelberg (2010)
9. Bozga, M., Iosif, R., Konecný, F., Vojnar, T.: Tool demonstration of the FLATA counter automata toolset. In: Voronkov, A., Kovács, L., Bjørner, N. (eds.) Second International Workshop on Invariant Generation, WING 2009, York, UK, 29 March 2009 and Third International Workshop on Invariant Generation, WING 2010, Edinburgh, UK, 21 July 2010, EPiC Series, vol. 1, p. 75. EasyChair (2010)
10. Bradley, A.R., Manna, Z., Sipma, H.B.: What's decidable about arrays? In: Emerson, E.A., Namjoshi, K.S. (eds.) VMCAI 2006. LNCS, vol. 3855, pp. 427–442. Springer, Heidelberg (2006)
11. Büchi, J.R., Senger, S.: Definability in the existential theory of concatenation and undecidable extensions of this theory. Math. Log. Q. **34**(4), 337–342 (1988)
12. Comon, H., Jurski, Y.: Multiple counters automata, safety analysis and presburger arithmetic. In: Hu, A.J., Vardi, M.Y. (eds.) CAV 1998. LNCS, vol. 1427, pp. 268–279. Springer, Heidelberg (1998)
13. Daca, P.: AFolder. https://github.com/pdaca/AFolder
14. Daca, P., Henzinger, T.A., Kupriyanov, A.: Array folds logic. CoRR, abs/1603.06850 (2016)
15. de Moura, L.M., Bjørner, N.S.: Z3: an efficient SMT solver. In: Ramakrishnan, C.R., Rehof, J. (eds.) TACAS 2008. LNCS, vol. 4963, pp. 337–340. Springer, Heidelberg (2008)
16. de Moura, L.M., Bjørner, N.: Generalized, efficient array decision procedures. In: Proceedings of 9th International Conference on Formal Methods in Computer-Aided Design, FMCAD 2009, 15–18 November 2009, Austin, Texas, USA, pp. 45–52. IEEE (2009)
17. Furia, C.A.: What's decidable about sequences? In: Bouajjani, A., Chin, W.-N. (eds.) ATVA 2010. LNCS, vol. 6252, pp. 128–142. Springer, Heidelberg (2010)
18. Ghilardi, S., Nicolini, E., Ranise, S., Zucchelli, D.: Decision procedures for extensions of the theory of arrays. Ann. Math. Artif. Intell. **50**(3–4), 231–254 (2007)

19. Godefroid, P., Luchaup, D.: Automatic partial loop summarization in dynamic test generation. In: Proceedings of the 20th International Symposium on Software Testing and Analysis, ISSTA 2011, Toronto, ON, Canada, 17–21 July 2011, pp. 23–33 (2011)
20. Gurari, E.M., Ibarra, O.H.: The complexity of decision problems for finite-turn multicounter machines. In: Even, S., Kariv, O. (eds.) Automata, Languages and Programming. LNCS, vol. 115, pp. 495–505. Springer, Berlin (1981)
21. Habermehl, P., Iosif, R., Vojnar, T.: A logic of singly indexed arrays. In: Cervesato, I., Veith, H., Voronkov, A. (eds.) LPAR 2008. LNCS (LNAI), vol. 5330, pp. 558–573. Springer, Heidelberg (2008)
22. Habermehl, P., Iosif, R., Vojnar, T.: What else is decidable about integer arrays? In: Amadio, R.M. (ed.) FOSSACS 2008. LNCS, vol. 4962, pp. 474–489. Springer, Heidelberg (2008)
23. Hague, M., Lin, A.W.: Model checking recursive programs with numeric data types. In: Gopalakrishnan, G., Qadeer, S. (eds.) CAV 2011. LNCS, vol. 6806, pp. 743–759. Springer, Heidelberg (2011)
24. Hojjat, H., Iosif, R., Konečný, F., Kuncak, V., Rümmer, P.: Accelerating interpolants. In: Chakraborty, S., Mukund, M. (eds.) ATVA 2012. LNCS, vol. 7561, pp. 187–202. Springer, Heidelberg (2012)
25. Ibarra, O.H.: Reversal-bounded multicounter machines and their decision problems. J. ACM 25(1), 116–133 (1978)
26. Ibarra, O.H., Su, J., Dang, Z., Bultan, T., Kemmerer, R.A.: Counter machines and verification problems. Theoret. Comput. Sci. 289(1), 165–189 (2002)
27. Knoop, J., Kovács, L., Zwirchmayr, J.: Symbolic loop bound computation for WCET analysis. In: Clarke, E., Virbitskaite, I., Voronkov, A. (eds.) PSI 2011. LNCS, vol. 7162, pp. 227–242. Springer, Heidelberg (2012)
28. Kozen, D.: Lower bounds for natural proof systems. In: FOCS, pp. 254–266 (1977)
29. Lin, A.W., Barceló, P.: String solving with word equations and transducers: towards a logic for analysing mutation XSS. In: Proceedings of the 43rd Annual ACM SIGPLAN-SIGACT Symposium on Principles of Programming Languages, POPL 2016, St. Petersburg, FL, USA, 20–22 January 2016, pp. 123–136 (2016)
30. Makanin, G.S.: The problem of solvability of equations in a free semigroup. Sb. Math. 32(2), 129–198 (1977)
31. Matijasevič, J.V.: The Diophantineness of enumerable sets. Dokl. Akad. Nauk SSSR 191, 279–282 (1970)
32. McCarthy, J.: Towards a mathematical science of computation. In: IFIP Congress, pp. 21–28 (1962)
33. Saxena, P., Poosankam, P., McCamant, S., Song, D.: Loop-extended symbolic execution on binary programs. In: Proceedings of the Eighteenth International Symposium on Software Testing and Analysis, ISSTA 2009, Chicago, IL, USA, 19–23 July 2009, pp. 225–236 (2009)
34. Seidl, H., Schwentick, T., Muscholl, A., Habermehl, P.: Counting in trees for free. In: Díaz, J., Karhumäki, J., Lepistö, A., Sannella, D. (eds.) ICALP 2004. LNCS, vol. 3142, pp. 1136–1149. Springer, Heidelberg (2004)
35. Zhou, M., He, F., Wang, B.-Y., Gu, M., Sun, J.: Array theory of bounded elements and its applications. J. Autom. Reason. 52(4), 379–405 (2014)

Automata and Games

Compositional Synthesis of Reactive Controllers for Multi-agent Systems

Rajeev Alur[1], Salar Moarref[1(✉)], and Ufuk Topcu[2]

[1] CIS Department, University of Pennsylvania, Levine 609, 3330 Walnut Street,
Philadelphia, PA 19104, USA
{alur,moarref}@seas.upenn.edu
[2] Department of Aerospace Engineering and Engineering Mechanics,
University of Texas at Austin, W. R. Woolrich Laboratories, C0600,
210 East 24th Street, Austin, TX 78712-1221, USA
utopcu@utexas.edu

Abstract. In this paper we consider the controller synthesis problem
for multi-agent systems that consist of a set of controlled and uncontrolled agents. Controlled agents may need to cooperate with each other
and react to the actions of uncontrolled agents in order to fulfill their
objectives. Besides, the controlled agents may be imperfect, i.e., only
partially observe their environment, for example due to the limitations
in their sensors. We propose a framework for controller synthesis based
on compositional reactive synthesis. We implement the algorithms symbolically and apply them to a robot motion planning case study where
multiple robots are placed on a grid-world with static obstacles and other
dynamic, uncontrolled and potentially adversarial robots. We consider
different objectives such as collision avoidance, keeping a formation and
bounded reachability. We show that by taking advantage of the structure of the system, compositional synthesis algorithm can significantly
outperform centralized synthesis approach, both from time and memory perspective, and can solve problems where the centralized algorithm
is infeasible. Our findings show the potential of symbolic and compositional reactive synthesis methods as planning algorithms in the presence
of dynamically changing and possibly adversarial environment.

1 Introduction

Complex systems often consist of multiple agents (or components) interacting
with each other and their environment to achieve certain objectives. For example, teams of robots are employed to perform tasks such as monitoring, surveil-
lance, and disaster response in different domains including search and rescue [1],
object transportation [2], and formation control [3]. With growing complexity
of autonomous systems and their safety-critical nature, the need for *automated*

This research was partially supported by awards NSF Expeditions in Computing
CCF 1138996, AFRL $FA8650-15-C-2546$, ONR $N000141310778$, ARO $W911NF$-
15-1-0592, NSF 1550212 and DARPA $W911NF$-16-1-0001.

S. Chaudhuri and A. Farzan (Eds.): CAV 2016, Part II, LNCS 9780, pp. 251–269, 2016.
DOI: 10.1007/978-3-319-41540-6_14

and *reliable* design and analysis methods and tools is increasing. To this end, an ambitious goal in system design and control is to automatically synthesize controllers for controllable parts of the system that guarantee the satisfaction of the specified objectives. Given a model of the system describing the interaction of a controllable plant with its environment and an objective in a formal language such as linear temporal logic (LTL), controller synthesis problem seeks to construct a finite-state controller that ensures that the system satisfies the objective, regardless of how its environment behaves. In this paper we consider the controller synthesis problem for multi-agent systems.

One of the main challenges in automated synthesis of systems is the scalability problem. This issue becomes more evident for multi-agent systems, as adding each agent can often increase the size of the state space exponentially. The pioneering work by Pnueli et al. [4] showed that reactive synthesis from LTL specifications is intractable which prohibited the practitioners from utilizing synthesis algorithms in practice. Distributed reactive synthesis [5] and multi-player games of incomplete information [6] are undecidable in general. Despite these discouraging results, recent advances in this growing research area have enabled automatic synthesis of interesting real-world systems [7], indicating the potential of the synthesis algorithms for solving realistic problems. The key insight is to consider more restricted yet practically useful subclasses of the general problem, and in this paper we take a step toward this direction.

The main motivation for our work is the growing interest in robotic motion planning from rich high-level specifications, e.g., LTL [8–10]. In most of these works, all agents are controlled and operate in static and fully-observable environments, and the applications of synthesis algorithms are restricted to very small examples due to the well-known state explosion problem. Since the reactive synthesis from LTL specifications is intractable, no algorithm will be efficient for all problems. Nevertheless, one can observe that in many application domains such as robot motion planning, the systems are structured, a fact that can be exploited to achieve better scalability.

In this paper, we consider a special class of multi-agent systems that are referred to as *decoupled* and are inspired by robot motion planning, decentralized control [11,12], and swarm robotics [13,14] literature. Intuitively, in a decoupled multi-agent system the transition relations (or dynamics) of the agents are decoupled, i.e., at any time-step, agents can make decisions on what action to take based on their own local state. For example, an autonomous vehicle can decide to slow down or speed up based on its position, velocity, etc. However, decoupled agents are coupled through objectives, i.e., an agent may need to cooperate with other agents or react to their actions to fulfill a given objective (e.g., it would not be a wise decision for an autonomous vehicle to speed up when the front vehicle pushes the break if collision avoidance is an objective.) In our framework, multi-agent systems consist of a set of controlled and uncontrolled agents. Controlled agents may need to cooperate with each other and react to the actions of uncontrolled agents in order to fulfill their objectives. Besides, controlled agents may be imperfect in the sense that they can only partially observe their environment, for example due to the limitations in their sensors. The goal is to synthesize controllers for each controlled agent such that the objectives are enforced in the resulting system.

To solve the controller synthesis problem for multi-agent systems one can directly construct the model of the system by composing those of the agents, and solve the problem centrally for the given objectives. However, the centralized method lack flexibility, since any change in one of the components requires the repetition of the synthesis process for the whole system. Besides the resulting system might be exponentially larger than the individual parts, making this approach infeasible in practice. Compositional reactive synthesis aims to exploit the structure of the system by breaking the problem into smaller and more manageable pieces and solving them separately. Then solutions to sub-problems are merged and analyzed to find a solution for the whole problem. The existing structure in multi-agent systems makes them a potential application area for compositional synthesis techniques.

To this end, we propose a compositional framework for decoupled multi-agent systems based on automatic decomposition of objectives and compositional reactive synthesis using maximally permissive strategies [15]. We assume that the objective of the system is given in conjunctive form. We make an observation that in many cases, each conjunct of the global objective only refers to a small subset of agents in the system. We take advantage of this structure to decompose the synthesis problem: for each conjunct of the global objective, we only consider the agents that are involved, and compute the maximally permissive strategies for those agents with respect to the considered conjunct. We then intersect the strategies to remove potential conflicts between them, and project back the constraints to subproblems, solving them again with updated constraints, and repeating this process until the strategies become fixed.

We implement the algorithms symbolically using binary decision diagrams (BDDs) and apply them to a robot motion planning case study where multiple robots are placed on a grid-world with static obstacles and other dynamic, uncontrolled and potentially adversarial robots. We consider different objectives such as collision avoidance, keeping a formation and bounded reachability. We show that by taking advantage of the structure of the system, the proposed compositional synthesis algorithm can significantly outperform the centralized synthesis approach, both from time and memory perspective, and can solve problems where the centralized algorithm is infeasible. Furthermore, using compositional algorithms we managed to solve synthesis problems for systems with multiple agents, more complex objectives and for grid-worlds of sizes that are much larger than the cases considered in similar works. Our findings show the potential of symbolic and compositional reactive synthesis methods as planning algorithms in presence of dynamically changing and possibly adversarial environment.

Contributions. The main contributions of the paper are as follow. We propose a framework for modular specification and compositional controller synthesis for multi-agent systems with imperfect controlled agents. We implement the methods symbolically using BDDs and apply them to a robot motion planning case study. We report on our experimental results and show that the compositional algorithm can significantly outperform the centralized approach.

Related Work. Compositional reactive synthesis has been considered in some recent works. Kupferman et al. [16] propose a compositional algorithm for LTL realizability and synthesis based on a Safraless approach that transforms the synthesis problem into a Büchi game. Baier et al. [17] give a compositional framework for treating multiple linear-time objectives inductively. Sohail et al. [18] propose an algorithm to compositionally construct a parity game from conjunctive LTL specifications. Alur et al. [19] show how local specifications of components can be refined compositionally to ensure satisfaction of a global specification. Lustig et al. [20] study the problem of LTL synthesis from libraries of reusable components. Alur et al. [21] propose a framework for compositional synthesis from a library of parametric and reactive controllers. Filiot et al. [15] reduce the LTL realizability problem to solving safety games. They show that, for LTL specifications written as conjunction of smaller LTL formulas, the problem can be solved compositionally by first computing winning strategies for each conjunct. Moreover, they show that compositional algorithms can handle fairly large LTL specifications. To the best of our knowledge, algorithms in [15] seems to be the most successful application of compositional synthesis in practice.

Two-player games of imperfect information are studied in [22–25], and it is shown that they are often more complicated than games of perfect information. The algorithmic difference is exponential, due to a subset construction that turns a game of imperfect information into an equivalent game of perfect information. In this paper, we build on the results of [15,25] and extend and adapt their methods to treat multi-agent systems with imperfect agents. To the best of our knowledge, compositional reactive synthesis is not studied in the context of multi-agent systems and robot motion planning.

The controller synthesis problem for systems with multiple controllable agents from a high-level temporal logic specification is also considered in many recent works (e.g., [8,26,27]). A common theme is based on first computing a discrete controller satisfying the LTL specification over a discrete abstraction of the system, which is then used to synthesize continues controllers guaranteed to fulfill the high-level specification. In many of these works (e.g., [28,29]) the agents' models are composed (either from the beginning or incrementally) to obtain a central model. The product of the central model with the specification automaton is then constructed and analyzed to compute a strategy. In [9], authors present a compositional motion planning framework for multi-robot systems based on a reduction to satisfiability modulo theories. However, their model cannot handle uncertain or dynamic environment. In [8,30] it is proposed that systems with multiple components can be treated in a decentralized manner by considering one component as a part of the environment of another component. However, these approaches cannot address the need for joint decision making and cooperative objectives. In this paper we consider compositional and symbolic algorithms for solving games in presence of a dynamic and possibly adversarial environment.

2   Preliminaries

Linear temporal logic (LTL). We use LTL to specify system objectives. LTL is a formal specification language with two types of operators: logical connectives (e.g., $\neg$ (negation) and $\wedge$ (conjunction)) and temporal operators (e.g., $\bigcirc$ (next), $\mathcal{U}$ (until), $\Diamond$ (eventually), and $\square$ (always)). Let $\mathcal{V}$ be a finite set of Boolean variables. A formula with no temporal operator is a Boolean formula or a *predicate*. Given a predicate ϕ over variables $\mathcal{V}$, we say $s \in 2^{\mathcal{V}}$ satisfies ϕ, denoted by $s \models \phi$, if the formula obtained from ϕ by replacing all variables in s by `true` and all other variables by `false` is valid. We call the set of all possible assignments to variables $\mathcal{V}$ *states* and denote them by $\Sigma_{\mathcal{V}}$, i.e., $\Sigma_{\mathcal{V}} = 2^{\mathcal{V}}$. An LTL formula over variables $\mathcal{V}$ is interpreted over infinite words $w \in (\Sigma_{\mathcal{V}})^{\omega}$. The language of an LTL formula Φ, denoted by $\mathcal{L}(\Phi)$, is the set of infinite words that satisfy Φ, i.e., $\mathcal{L}(\Phi) = \{w \in (\Sigma_{\mathcal{V}})^{\omega} \mid w \models \Phi\}$. We assume some familiarity of the reader with LTL. We often use predicates over $\mathcal{V} \cup \mathcal{V}'$ where $\mathcal{V}'$ is the set of primed versions of the variables in $\mathcal{V}$. Given a subset of variables $\mathcal{X} \subseteq \mathcal{V}$ and a state $s \in \Sigma_{\mathcal{V}}$, we denote by $s_{|\mathcal{X}}$ the projection of s to $\mathcal{X}$. For a set $\mathcal{Z} \subseteq \mathcal{V}$, let $Same(\mathcal{Z}, \mathcal{Z}')$ be a predicate specifying that the value of the variables in $\mathcal{Z}$ stay unchanged during a transition. Ordered binary decision diagrams (OBDDs) can be used for obtaining concise representations of sets and relations over finite domains [31]. If R is an n-ary relation over $\{0, 1\}$, then R can be represented by the BDD for its *characteristic function*: $f_R(x_1, \cdots, x_n) = 1$ if and only if $R(x_1, \cdots, x_n) = 1$. With a little bit abuse of notation and when it is clear from the context, we treat sets and functions as their corresponding predicates.

Game Structures. A game structure $\mathcal{G}$ of imperfect information is a tuple $\mathcal{G} = (\mathcal{V}, \Lambda, \tau, \mathcal{OBS}, \gamma)$ where $\mathcal{V}$ is a finite set of variables, Λ is a finite set of actions, τ is a predicate over $\mathcal{V} \cup \Lambda \cup \mathcal{V}'$ defining $\mathcal{G}$'s transition relation, $\mathcal{OBS}$ is a finite set of observable variables, and $\gamma : \Sigma_{\mathcal{OBS}} \to 2^{\Sigma_{\mathcal{V}}} \setminus \emptyset$ maps each observation to its corresponding set of states. We assume that the set $\{\gamma(o) \mid o \in \Sigma_{\mathcal{OBS}}\}$ partitions the state space $\Sigma_{\mathcal{V}}$ (this assumption can be weakened to a covering of the state space where observations can overlap [24,25].) A game structure $\mathcal{G}$ is called *perfect information* if $\mathcal{OBS} = \mathcal{V}$ and $\gamma(s) = \{s\}$ for all $s \in \Sigma_{\mathcal{V}}$. We omit $(\mathcal{OBS}, \gamma)$ in the description of games of perfect information.

In this paper, we consider two-player turn-based game structures where player-1 and player-2 alternate in taking turns. Let $t \in \mathcal{V}$ be a special variable with domain $\{1, 2\}$ determining which player's turn it is during the game. Without loss of generality, we assume that player-1 always start the game. Let $\Sigma_{\mathcal{V}}^i = \{s \in \Sigma_{\mathcal{V}} \mid s_{|t} = i\}$ for $i = 1, 2$ denote player-i's states in the game structure. At any state $s \in \Sigma_{\mathcal{V}}^i$, the player-$i$ chooses an action $\ell \in \Lambda$ such that there exists a successor state $s' \in \Sigma_{\mathcal{V}'}$ where $(s, \ell, s') \models \tau$. Intuitively, at a player-i state, she chooses an available action according to the transition relation τ and the next state of the system is chosen from the possible successor states. For every state $s \in \Sigma_{\mathcal{V}}$, we define $\Gamma(s) = \{\ell \in \Lambda \mid \exists s' \in \Sigma_{\mathcal{V}'}.\ (s, \ell, s') \models \tau\}$ to be the set of available actions at that state. A *run* in $\mathcal{G}$ from an initial state $s_{init} \in \Sigma_{\mathcal{V}}$ is a sequence of states $\pi = s_0 s_1 s_2 \cdots$ such that $s_0 = s_{init}$ and for all $i > 0$, there is an action $\ell_i \in \Lambda$ with $(s_{i-1}, \ell_i, s_i') \models \tau$, where s_i' is obtained by replacing the variables in s_i by their primed copies. A run π is maximal if either it is infinite or it ends in a state $s \in \Sigma_\mathcal{V}$ where $\Gamma(s) = \emptyset$. The *observation sequence* of π is the unique sequence $Obs(\pi) = o_0 o_1 o_2 \cdots$ such that for all $i \geq 0$, we have $s_i \in \gamma(o_i)$.

Strategies. A *strategy* S in $\mathcal{G}$ for player-i, $i \in \{1, 2\}$, is a function $\mathsf{S} : (\Sigma_\mathcal{V})^* . \Sigma_\mathcal{V}^i \to \Lambda$. A strategy S in $\mathcal{G}$ for player-2 is *observation-based* if for all prefixes $\rho_1, \rho_2 \in (\Sigma_\mathcal{V})^* . \Sigma_\mathcal{V}^2$, if $Obs(\rho_1) = Obs(\rho_2)$, then $\mathsf{S}(\rho_1) = \mathsf{S}(\rho_2)$. In this paper, we are interested in the existence of observation-based strategies for player-2. Given two strategies S_1 and S_2 for player-1 and player-2, the *possible outcomes* $\Omega_{\mathsf{S}_1, \mathsf{S}_2}(s)$ from a state $s \in \Sigma_\mathcal{V}$ are runs: a run $s_0 s_1 s_2 \cdots$ belongs to $\Omega_{\mathsf{S}_1, \mathsf{S}_2}(s)$ if and only if $s_0 = s$ and for all $j \geq 0$ either s_j has no successor, or $s_j \in \Sigma_\mathcal{V}^i$ and $(s_j, \mathsf{S}_i(s_0 \cdots s_j), s_{j+1}') \models \tau$ where $s_j \in \Sigma_\mathcal{V}^i$.

Winning Condition. A game $(\mathcal{G}, \phi_{init}, \Phi)$ consists of a game structure $\mathcal{G}$, a predicate ϕ_{init} specifying an initial state $s_{init} \in \Sigma_\mathcal{V}$, and an LTL objective Φ for player-2. A run $\pi = s_0 s_1 \cdots$ is winning for player-2 if it is infinite and $\pi \in \mathcal{L}(\Phi)$. Let Π be the set of runs that are winning for player-2. A strategy S_2 is winning for player-2 if for all strategies S_1 of player-1, we have $\Omega_{\mathsf{S}_1, \mathsf{S}_2}(s_{init}) \subseteq \Pi$, that is, all possible outcomes are winning for player-2. Note that We assume the nondeterminism is always on player-1's side. We say the game $(\mathcal{G}, \phi_{init}, \Phi)$ is realizable if and only if the system has a winning strategy in the game $(\mathcal{G}, \phi_{init}, \Phi)$.

Constructing the Knowledge Game Structure. For a game structure $\mathcal{G} = (\mathcal{V}, \Lambda, \tau, \mathcal{OBS}, \gamma)$ of imperfect information, a game structure $\mathcal{G}^K$ of perfect information can be obtained using a subset construction procedure such that for any objective Φ, there exists a deterministic observation-based strategy for player-2 in $\mathcal{G}$ with respect to Φ if and only if there exists a deterministic winning strategy for player-2 in $\mathcal{G}^K$ for Φ [22, 25]. Intuitively, each state in $\mathcal{G}^K$ is a set of states of $\mathcal{G}$ that represents player-2's knowledge about the possible states in which the game can be after a sequence of observations. In the worst case, the size of $\mathcal{G}^K$ is exponentially larger than the size of $\mathcal{G}$. We refer to $\mathcal{G}^K$ as the *knowledge* game structure corresponding to $\mathcal{G}$. In the rest of this section, we only consider game structures of perfect information.

Solving Games. In this paper, we use the bounded synthesis approach [15, 32] to solve the synthesis problems from LTL specifications. In [15], it is shown how LTL formulas can be reduced to *safety games*. Formally, a safety game is a game $(\mathcal{G}, \phi_{init}, \Phi)$ with a special safety objective $\Phi = \Box(\mathbf{True})$. That is, any infinite run in the game structure $\mathcal{G}$ starting from an initial state $s \models \phi_{init}$ is winning for player-2. We drop Φ from description of safety games as it is implicitly defined. Intuitively, in a safety game, the goal of player-2 is to avoid the dead-end states, i.e., states that there is no available action. We refer the readers to [15, 33] for details of reducing LTL formulas to safety games and solving them. Composition of two game structures $\mathcal{G}_1 = (\mathcal{V}^1, \Lambda^1, \tau^1), \mathcal{G}_2 = (\mathcal{V}^2, \Lambda^2, \tau^2)$ of perfect information, denoted by $\mathcal{G}^\otimes = \mathcal{G}_1 \otimes \mathcal{G}_2$, is a game structure $\mathcal{G}^\otimes = (\mathcal{V}^\otimes, \Lambda^\otimes, \tau^\otimes)$ of perfect information where $\mathcal{V}^\otimes = \mathcal{V}^1 \cup \mathcal{V}^2$, $\Lambda^\otimes = \Lambda^1 \cup \Lambda^2$, and

$\tau^{\otimes} = \tau^1 \wedge \tau^2$. To solve a game $(\mathcal{G}, \phi_{init}, \Phi)$, we first obtain the game structure $\mathcal{G}^{\Phi}$ corresponding to Φ using the methods proposed in [15], and then solve the safety game $(\mathcal{G} \otimes \mathcal{G}^{\Phi}, \phi_{init})$ to determine the winner of the game and compute a winning strategy for player-2, if one exists.

Maximally Permissive Strategies. Safety games are *memory-less deter-mined*, i.e., player-2 wins the game if and only if there exists a strategy $\mathsf{S} : \Sigma_{\mathcal{V}}^2 \to \Lambda$. Intuitively, a memory-less strategy only depends on the current state and is independent from the history of the game. Let $(\mathcal{G}, \phi_{init})$ be a safety game, where $\mathcal{G} = (\mathcal{V}, \Lambda, \tau)$ is a perfect information game. Assume $W \subseteq \Sigma_{\mathcal{V}}$ be the set of winning states for player-2, i.e., from any state $s \in W$ there exists a strategy S_2 such that for any strategy S_1 chosen by player-1, all possible outcomes $\pi \in \Omega_{\mathsf{S}_1,\mathsf{S}_2}(s)$ are winning. The *maximally permissive strategy* $\mathcal{S} : \Sigma_{\mathcal{V}}^2 \to 2^{\Lambda}$ for player-2 is defined as follows: for all $s \in \Sigma_{\mathcal{V}}^2$, $\mathcal{S}(s) = \{\ell \in \Lambda \mid \forall r \in \Sigma_{\mathcal{V}'}. \ (s, \ell, r) \models \tau_s \to r \in W\}$, i.e., the set of actions ℓ where all ℓ-successors belong to the set of winning states. It is well-known that $\mathcal{S}$ subsumes all winning strategies of player-2 in the safety game $(\mathcal{G}, \Phi_{init})$. Composition of two maximally permissive strategies $\mathcal{S}_1, \mathcal{S}_2 : \Sigma_{\mathcal{V}}^2 \to 2^{\Lambda}$, denoted by $\mathcal{S} = \mathcal{S}_1 \otimes \mathcal{S}_2$, is defined as $\mathcal{S}(s) = \mathcal{S}_1(s) \cap \mathcal{S}_2(s)$ for any $s \in \Sigma_{\mathcal{V}}$, i.e., the set of allowed actions by $\mathcal{S}$ at any state $s \in \Sigma_{\mathcal{V}}$ is the intersection of the allowed actions by $\mathcal{S}_1$ and $\mathcal{S}_2$. The restriction of the game structure $\mathcal{G}$ with respect to its maximally permissive strategy $\mathcal{S}$ is the game structure $\mathcal{G}[\mathcal{S}] = (\mathcal{V}, \Lambda, \tau \wedge \phi_{\mathcal{S}})$ where $\phi_{\mathcal{S}}$ is the predicate encoding $\mathcal{S}$, i.e., for all $(s, \ell) \in \Sigma_{\mathcal{V}}^2 \times \Lambda$, $(s, \ell) \models \phi_{\mathcal{S}}$ if and only if $\ell \in \mathcal{S}(s)$. Intuitively, $\mathcal{G}[\mathcal{S}]$ is the same as $\mathcal{G}$ but player-2's actions are restricted according to $\mathcal{S}$.

3 Multi-agent Systems

In this section we describe how we model multi-agent systems and formally state the problem that is considered in the rest of the paper. Typically game structures arise from description of open systems in a particular language [34]. In our framework, we use *agents* to specify a system in a modular manner. An agent $\mathsf{a} = (\texttt{type}, \mathcal{I}, \mathcal{O}, \Lambda, \tau, \mathcal{OBS}, \gamma)$ is a tuple where $\texttt{type} \in \{\texttt{controlled}, \texttt{uncontrolled}\}$ indicates whether the agent can be controlled or not, $\mathcal{O}$ ($\mathcal{I}$) is a set of output (input) variables that the agent can (cannot, respectively) control by assigning values to them, Λ is a set of actions for the agent, and τ is a predicate over $\mathcal{I} \cup \mathcal{O} \cup \Lambda \cup \mathcal{O}'$ that specifies the possible transitions of the agent where $\mathcal{O}'$ is the primed copies of the variables $\mathcal{O}$, $\mathcal{OBS}$ is a set of observable variables, and $\gamma : \Sigma_{\mathcal{OBS}} \to 2^{\Sigma_{\mathcal{I} \cup \mathcal{O}}}$ is the observation function that maps agent's observations to its corresponding set of states. Intuitively, τ defines what actions an agent can choose at any state $s \in \Sigma_{\mathcal{I}} \times \Sigma_{\mathcal{O}}$ and what are the possible next valuations over agent's output variables for the chosen action. That is, $(i, o, \ell, o') \models \tau$ for $i \in \Sigma_{\mathcal{I}}$, $o \in \Sigma_{\mathcal{O}}, \ell \in \Lambda$, and $o' \in \Sigma_{\mathcal{O}'}$ means that at any state s of the system with $s_{|\mathcal{I}} = i$ and $s_{|\mathcal{O}} = o$, the agent can take action ℓ, and a state with component o' is a possible successor. A *perfect agent* is an agent with $\mathcal{OBS} = \mathcal{I} \cup \mathcal{O}$ and $\gamma(s) = \{s\}$ for all $s \in \Sigma_{\mathcal{I}} \times \Sigma_{\mathcal{O}}$. We omit $(\mathcal{OBS}, \gamma)$ in the description of perfect agents.

An agent a is called *local* if and only if its transition relation τ is a predicate over $\mathcal{O} \cup \Lambda \cup \mathcal{O}'$, i.e., it does not depend on any uncontrolled variable $v \in \mathcal{I}$.

A multi-agent system $\mathcal{M} = \{a_1, a_2, \cdots, a_n\}$ is defined as a set of agents $a_i = (\mathtt{type}_i, \mathcal{I}_i, \mathcal{O}_i, \Lambda_i, \tau_i, \mathcal{OBS}_i, \gamma_i)$ for $1 \leq i \leq n$. Let $\mathcal{V} = \bigcup_{i=1}^{n} \mathcal{O}_i$ be the set of agents' output variables. We assume that the set of output variables of agents are pairwise disjoint, i.e., $\forall 1 \leq i \leq n$. $\mathcal{O}_i \cap \mathcal{O}_j = \emptyset$, and the set of input variables $\mathcal{I}_i$ for each agent $a_i \in \mathcal{M}$ is a subset of variables controlled by other agents, i.e., $\mathcal{I}_i \subseteq \mathcal{V} \backslash \mathcal{O}_i$. We further make some simplifying assumptions. First, we assume that all uncontrolled agents are perfect, i.e., uncontrolled agent has perfect information about the state of the system at any time-step. Second, we assume that all controlled agents are *cooperative* while uncontrolled ones can play adversarially, i.e., the controlled agents cooperate with each other and make joint decisions to enforce the global objective. Finally, we assume that the observation variables for controlled agents are pairwise disjoint, i.e., $\forall 1 \leq i \leq n$. $\mathcal{OBS}_i \cap \mathcal{OBS}_j = \emptyset$, and that each controlled agent has perfect knowledge about other controlled agents' observations. That is, controlled agents share their observations with each other. Intuitively, it is as if the communication between controlled agents is instantaneous and error-free, i.e., they have perfect communication and tell each other what they observe. This assumption helps us preserve the two-player game setting and to stay in a decidable subclass of the more general problem of multi-player games with partial information. Note that multiplayer games of incomplete information are undecidable in general [6].

In this paper we focus on a special setting where all agents are local. A multi-agent system $\mathcal{M} = \{a_1, a_2, \cdots, a_n\}$ is *dynamically decoupled* (or decoupled in short) iff all agents $a \in \mathcal{M}$ are local. Intuitively, agents in a decoupled multi-agent system can choose their action based on their own local state and regardless of the local states of other agents in the system. That is, the availability of actions for each agent in any state of the system is only a function of the agent's local state. Such setting arises in many applications, e.g., robot motion planning, where possible transitions of agents are independent from each other. For example, how a robot moves around a room is usually based on its own characteristics and motion primitives [9]. Note that this does not mean that the controlled agents are completely decoupled, as the objectives might concern different agents in the system, e.g., collision avoidance objective for a system consisting of multiple controlled robots, which requires cooperation between agents.

In our framework, the user describes the agents and specifies the objective as a conjunctive LTL formula. From description of the agents, a game structure is obtained that encodes how the state of the system evolves. Formally, given a decoupled multi-agent system $\mathcal{M} = \mathcal{M}^u \uplus \mathcal{M}^c$ partitioned into a set $\mathcal{M}^u = \{u_1, \cdots, u_m\}$ of uncontrolled agents and a set $\mathcal{M}^c = \{c_1, \cdots, c_n\}$ of controlled agents, the turn-based game structure $\check{\mathcal{G}}^{\mathcal{M}}$ induced by $\mathcal{M}$ is defined as $\mathcal{G}^{\mathcal{M}} = (\mathcal{V}, \Lambda, \tau, \mathcal{OBS}, \gamma)$ where $\mathcal{V} = \{t\} \cup \bigcup_{a \in \mathcal{M}} \mathcal{O}_a$ is the set of all variables in $\mathcal{M}$ with t as a turn variable, $\Lambda = \bigcup_{a \in \mathcal{M}} \Lambda_a$ is the set of actions, $\mathcal{OBS} = \bigcup_{c \in \mathcal{M}^c} \mathcal{OBS}_c$ is the set of all observation variables of controlled agents (note that we assume all uncontrolled agents are perfect,) and τ and γ are defined as follows:

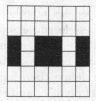

Fig. 1. Grid-world with static obstacles

$$\tau = \tau_e \vee \tau_s$$

$$\tau_e = t = 1 \wedge t' = 2 \wedge \bigwedge_{u \in \mathcal{M}^u} \tau_u \wedge \bigwedge_{c \in \mathcal{M}^c} Same(\mathcal{O}_c, \mathcal{O}'_c)$$

$$\tau_s = t = 2 \wedge t' = 1 \wedge \bigwedge_{c \in \mathcal{M}^c} \cdot \tau_c \wedge \bigwedge_{u \in \mathcal{M}^u} Same(\mathcal{O}_u, \mathcal{O}'_u)$$

$$\gamma = \bigwedge_{c \in \mathcal{M}^c} \gamma_c$$

Intuitively, at each step, uncontrolled agents take actions consistent with their transition relations, and their variables get updated while the controlled agents' variables stay unchanged. Then the controlled agents react concurrently and simultaneously by taking actions according to their transition relations, and their corresponding variables get updated while the uncontrolled agents' variables stay unchanged.

Example 1. Let R_1 and R_2 be two robots in an $n \times n$ grid-world similar to the one shown in Fig. 1. Assume R_1 is an uncontrolled robot, whereas R_2 can be controlled. In the sequel, let i range over $\{1, 2\}$. At each time any robot R_i can move to one of its neighboring cells by taking an action from the set $\Lambda_i = \{up_i, down_i, right_i, left_i\}$. Furthermore, assume that R_2 has imperfect sensors and can only observe R_1 when R_1 is in one of its adjacent cells. Let (x_i, y_i) represent the position of robot R_i in the grid-world at any time[1]. We define $\mathcal{O}_i = \{x_i, y_i\}$ and $\mathcal{I}_i = \mathcal{O}_{3-i}$ as the output and input variables, respectively. Note that the controlled variables by one agent are the input variables of the other agent. Transition relation $\tau_i = \bigwedge_{\ell \in \Lambda_i} \tau_\ell$ is defined as conjunction of four parts corresponding to robot's action where

$$\tau_{up_i} = (y_i > 1) \wedge up_i \wedge (y'_i \leftrightarrow y_i - 1) \wedge Same(x_i, x'_i)$$
$$\tau_{down_i} = (y_i < n) \wedge down_i \wedge (y'_i \leftrightarrow y_i + 1) \wedge Same(x_i, x'_i)$$
$$\tau_{left_i} = (x_i > 1) \wedge left_i \wedge (x'_i \leftrightarrow x_i - 1) \wedge Same(y_i, y'_i)$$
$$\tau_{right_i} = (x_i < n) \wedge right_i \wedge (x'_i \leftrightarrow x_i - 1) \wedge Same(y_i, y'_i)$$

---

[1] Note that variables x_i and y_i are defined over a bounded domain and can be encoded by a set of Boolean variables. To keep the example simple, we use their bounded integer representation here.

Intuitively, each τ_ℓ for $\ell \in \Lambda_i$ specifies whether the action is available in the current state and what is its possible successors. For example, τ_{up_i} indicates that if R_i is not at the top row ($y_i > 1$), then the action up_i is available and if applied, in the next state the value of y_i is decremented by one and the value of x_i does not change. Next we define the observation function γ_2 for R_2. It is easier and more intuitive to define γ_2^{-1}, and since observations partition the state space $\gamma_2 = (\gamma_2^{-1})^{-1}$ is defined. Formally,

$$\gamma_2^{-1}(a, b, c, d) = \begin{cases} (a, b, c, d) & \text{if } a - 1 \leq c \leq a + 1 \wedge b - 1 \leq d \leq b + 1 \\ (\bot, \bot, c, d) & \text{otherwise} \end{cases}$$

Let $\mathcal{OBS}_2 = \{x_1^o, y_1^o, x_2^o, y_2^o\}$ where $x_1^o, y_1^o \in \{\bot, 1, 2, \cdots, n\}$ and $x_2^o, y_2^o \in \{1, \cdots, n\}$. Intuitively, R_2 observes its own local state perfectly. Furthermore, if R_1 is in one of its adjacent cells, its position is observed perfectly, otherwise, R_1 is away and its location cannot be observed. γ_2 can be symbolically encoded as $\bigvee_{o \in \Sigma_{OBS}} (o \wedge \phi_{\gamma(o)})$ where $\phi_{\gamma(o)}$ is the predicate specifying the set $\gamma(o)$. Finally, we let $R_1 = (\text{uncontrolled}, \mathcal{I}_1, \mathcal{O}_1, \Lambda_1, \tau_1)$ and $R_2 = (\text{controlled}, \mathcal{I}_2, \mathcal{O}_2, \Lambda_2, \mathcal{OBS}_2, \gamma_2)$. Note that R_1 (R_2) is modeled as a perfect (imperfect, respectively) local agent.

The game structure $\mathcal{G}^{\mathcal{M}}$ of imperfect information corresponding to multi-agent system $\mathcal{M} = \{R_1, R_2\}$ is a tuple $\mathcal{G}^{\mathcal{M}} = (\mathcal{V}, \Lambda, \tau, \mathcal{OBS}, \gamma)$ where $\mathcal{V} = \{t\} \cup \mathcal{O}_1 \cup \mathcal{O}_2$, $\Lambda = \Lambda_1 \cup \Lambda_2$, $\tau = \tau_e \vee \tau_s$, $\tau_e = t = 1 \wedge t' = 2 \wedge \tau_1 \wedge Same(\mathcal{O}_2, \mathcal{O}_2')$, $\tau_s = t = 2 \wedge t' = 1 \wedge \tau_2 \wedge Same(\mathcal{O}_1, \mathcal{O}_1')$, $\mathcal{OBS} = \mathcal{OBS}_2$, and $\gamma = \gamma_2$.   □

We now formally define the problem we consider in this paper.

Problem 1. Given a decoupled multi-agent system $\mathcal{M} = \mathcal{M}^u \uplus \mathcal{M}^c$ partitioned into uncontrolled $\mathcal{M}^u = \{u_1, \cdots, u_m\}$ and controlled agents $\mathcal{M}^c = \{c_1, \cdots, c_n\}$, a predicate ϕ_{init} specifying an initial state, and an objective $\Phi = \Phi_1 \wedge \cdots \wedge \Phi_k$ as conjunction of $k \geq 1$ LTL formulas Φ_i, compute strategies $S_1, \cdots, S_n$ for controlled agents such that the strategy $S = S_1 \otimes \cdots \otimes S_n$ defined as composition of the strategies is winning for the game $(\mathcal{G}^{\mathcal{M}}, \phi_{init}, \Phi)$, where $\mathcal{G}^{\mathcal{M}}$ is the game structure induced by $\mathcal{M}$.

4   Compositional Controller Synthesis

We now explain our solution approach for Problem 1 stated in Sect. 3. Algorithm 1 summarizes the steps for compositional synthesis of strategies for controlled agents in a multi-agent system. It has three main parts. First the synthesis problem is automatically decomposed into subproblems by taking advantage of the structure in the multi-agent system and given objective. Then the subproblems are solved separately and their solutions are composed. The composition may restrict the possible actions that are available for agents at some states. The composition is then projected back to each subproblem and the subproblems are solved again with new restrictions. This process is repeated until either a subgame becomes unrealizable, or computed solutions for subproblems

---

Algorithm 1. Compositional Controller Synthesis

Input: A decoupled multi-agent system $\mathcal{M} = \{u_1, \cdots, u_m, c_1, \cdots, c_n\}$, ϕ_{init}
specifying initial state, and an objective $\Phi = \Phi_1 \wedge \cdots \wedge \Phi_k$

Output: A set of strategies $(\mathcal{S}_1, \cdots, \mathcal{S}_n)$ one for each controlled agent, if one
exists

1 /* Decompose the problem based on agents' involvement in conjuncts*/
2 **for** all $\Phi_i, 1 \leq i \leq k$ **do**
3 $\quad$ $\mathcal{INV}_i := \textbf{Involved}(\Phi_i)$;
4 $\quad$ $\mathcal{G}_i := \textbf{CreateGameStructure}(\mathcal{INV}_i)$;
5 $\quad$ $\mathcal{X}_i := \bigcup_{a \in \mathcal{INV}_i} \mathcal{O}_a$; /* the set of variables controlled by involved agents */
6 $\quad$ $\phi^i_{init} := \textbf{Project}(\phi_{init}, \mathcal{X}_i)$;
7 $\quad$ $\mathcal{G}^K_i := \textbf{CreateKnowledgeGameStructure}(\mathcal{G}_i)$;
8 $\quad$ $(\mathcal{G}^d_i, \phi^i_{init}) := \textbf{ToSafetyGame}(\mathcal{G}^K_i, \phi^i_{init}, \Phi_i)$;
9 /*Compositional synthesis*/
10 **while true do**
11 $\quad$ **for** $i = 1 \cdots k$ **do**
12 $\quad\quad$ $\mathcal{S}^d_i := \textbf{SolveSafetyGame}(\mathcal{G}^d_i, \phi^i_{init})$;
13 $\quad$ $\mathcal{S} := \bigotimes^m_{i=1} \mathcal{S}^d_i$; /* compose the strategies */
14 $\quad$ **for** $i = 1 \cdots k$ **do**
15 $\quad\quad$ Let $\mathcal{Y}_i = \mathcal{V}^d_i \cup \Lambda^d_i$ be the set of variables and actions in $\mathcal{G}^d_i$;
16 $\quad\quad$ $\mathcal{C}_i := \textbf{Project}(\mathcal{S}, \mathcal{Y}_i)$; /* project the strategies */
17 $\quad$ **if** $\forall 1 \leq i \leq k, \mathcal{S}^d_i = \mathcal{C}_i$ **then**
18 $\quad\quad$ break; /* a fixed point is reached over strategies */
19 $\quad$ **for** $i = 1 \cdots k$ **do**
20 $\quad\quad$ $\mathcal{G}^d_i := \mathcal{G}^d_i[\mathcal{C}_i]$; /* Restrict the subgames for the next iteration */
21 $(\mathsf{S}_1, \cdots, \mathsf{S}_n) := \textbf{Extract}(\mathcal{S})$;
22 return $(\mathsf{S}_1, \cdots, \mathsf{S}_n)$,

---

reach a fixed point. Finally, a set of strategies, one for each controlled agent, is
extracted by decomposing the strategy obtained in the previous step. Next, we
explain Algorithm 1 in more detail.

4.1 Decomposition of the Synthesis Problem

The synthesis problem is decomposed into subproblems in lines $2 - 9$ of
Algorithm 1. The main idea behind decomposition is that in many cases, each
conjunct Φ_i of the objective Φ only refers to a small subset of agents. This observation is utilized to obtain a game structure from description of those agents that
are *involved* in Φ_i, i.e., only agents are considered to form and solve a game with
respect to Φ_i that are relevant. In other words, each subproblem corresponds to
a conjunct Φ_i of the global objective Φ and the game structure obtained from
agents involved in Φ_i.

For each conjunct Φ_i, $1 \leq i \leq k$, Algorithm 1 first obtains the set $\mathcal{INV}_i$
of involved agents using the procedure **Involved**. Formally, let $\mathcal{V}_{\Phi_i} \subseteq \mathcal{V}$ be
the set of variables appearing in Φ_i's formula. The set of involved agents are

those agents whose controlled variables appear in the conjunt's formula, i.e., $\textbf{Involved}(\Phi_i) = \{a \in \mathcal{M} \mid \mathcal{O}_a \cap \mathcal{V}_{\Phi_i} \neq \emptyset\}$.

A game structure $\mathcal{G}_i$ is then obtained from the description of the agents $\mathcal{INV}_i$ using the procedure **CreateGameStructure** as explained in Sect. 3. The projection ϕ^i_{init} of the predicate ϕ_{init} with respect to the involved agents is computed next. The procedure **Project** takes a predicate ϕ over variables $\mathcal{V}_\phi$ and a subset $\mathcal{X} \subseteq \mathcal{V}_\phi$ of variables as input, and projects the predicate with respect to the given subset. Formally, $\textbf{Project}(\phi, \mathcal{X}) = \{s_{|\mathcal{X}} \mid s \in \Sigma_{\mathcal{V}_\phi}\}$.

The knowledge game structure $\mathcal{G}^K_i$ corresponding to $\mathcal{G}_i$ is obtained at line 7. Note that this step is not required if the system only includes perfect agents that can observe the state of the game perfectly at any time-step. Finally, the objective Φ_i is transformed into a game structure using the algorithms in [15, 33] and composed with $\mathcal{G}^K_i$ to obtain a safety game $(\mathcal{G}^d_i, \phi^i_{init})$. The result of decomposition phase is k safety games $\{(\mathcal{G}^d_1, \phi^1_{init}), \cdots, (\mathcal{G}^d_k, \phi^k_{init})\}$ that form the subproblems for the compositional synthesis phase.

Example 2. Let R_i for $i = 1, \cdots, 4$ be four robots in an $n \times n$ grid-world, where R_4 is uncontrolled and other robots are controlled. For simplicity, assume that all agents are perfect. At each time-step any robot R_i can move to one of its neighboring cells by taking an action from the set $\{up_i, down_i, right_i, left_i\}$ with their obvious meanings. Consider the following objective $\Phi = \Phi_1 \wedge \Phi_2 \wedge \Phi_3 \wedge \Phi_{12} \wedge \Phi_{23}$ where Φ_i for $i = 1, 2, 3$ specifies that R_i must not collide with R_4, and Φ_{12} (Φ_{23}) specifies that R_1 and R_2 (R_2 and R_3, respectively) must avoid collision with each other. Sub-formulas Φ_i, $i = 1, 2, 3$, only involve agents R_i and R_4, i.e., $\mathcal{INV}(\Phi_i) = \{R_i, R_4\}$. Therefore, the game structures $\mathcal{G}_i$ induced by agents R_i and R_4 are composed with the game structure computed for Φ_i to form a subproblem as a safety game. Similarly, we obtain safety games for objectives Φ_{12} and Φ_{23} with $\mathcal{INV}(\Phi_{12}) = \{R_1, R_2\}$ and $\mathcal{INV}(\Phi_{23}) = \{R_2, R_3\}$, respectively. $\square$

Remark 1. The decomposition method used here is not the only way to decompose the problem, neither it is necessarily optimal. More efficient decomposition technique can be used to obtain quicker convergence in Algorithm 1 for example by different grouping of conjuncts. Nevertheless, the decomposition technique explained above is simple and it was effective in our experiments.

4.2 Compositional Synthesis

The safety games obtained in decomposition phase are compositionally solved in lines $9 - 21$ of Algorithm 1. At each iteration of the main loop, the subproblems $(\mathcal{G}^d_i, \phi^i_{init})$ are solved, and a maximally permissive strategy $\mathcal{S}^d_i$ is computed for them, if one exists. Computed strategies are then composed in line 11 of Algorithm 1 to obtain a strategy $\mathcal{S}$ for the whole system. The strategy $\mathcal{S}$ is then projected back to sub-games, and it is compared if all the projected strategies are equivalent to the strategies computed for the subproblems. If that is the case, the main loop terminates, while $\mathcal{S}$ is winning for the game $(\mathcal{G}^d, \phi_{init})$ where $(\mathcal{G}^d, \phi_{init})$ is the safety game associated with the multi-agent system $\mathcal{M}$ and objective Φ. Otherwise, at least one of the subproblems needs to be restricted. Each sub-game is restricted by the computed projection, and the process is repeated. The loop terminates either if at some iteration a subproblem becomes unrealizable, or if permissive strategies $S_1, \cdots, S_k$ reach a fixed point. In the latter case, a set of strategies, one for each controlled agent is extracted from S as explained below.

4.3   Computing Strategies for the Agents

Let $\mathcal{V}^\otimes = \bigcup_{i=1}^k \mathcal{V}_{\mathcal{G}_i^d}$ be the set of all variables used to encode the game structures $\mathcal{G}_i^d$, and $\Lambda^c = \Lambda_{c_1} \times \cdots \times \Lambda_{c_n}$ be the set of controlled agents' actions. Once a permissive strategy $\mathcal{S} : \Sigma_{\mathcal{V}^\otimes} \to 2^{\Lambda^c}$ is computed, a winning strategy $S_d : \Sigma_{\mathcal{V}^\otimes} \to \Lambda^c$ is obtained from $\mathcal{S}$ by restricting the non-deterministic action choices of the controlled agents to a single action. The strategy S_d is then decomposed into strategies $S_1 : \Sigma_{\mathcal{V}^\otimes} \to \Lambda_{c_1}, \cdots, S_n : \Sigma_{\mathcal{V}^\otimes} \to \Lambda_{c_n}$ for the agents simply by projecting the actions over system transitions to their corresponding agents. Formally, for any $s \in \Sigma_{\mathcal{V}^\otimes}$ such that $\mathcal{S}(s)$ is defined, let $S_d(s) = \sigma \in \mathcal{S}(s)$ where $\sigma = (\sigma_1, \cdots, \sigma_n) \in \Lambda^c$ is an arbitrary action chosen from possible actions permitted by $\mathcal{S}$ in the state s. Agents' strategies are defined as $S_i(s) = \sigma_i$ for $i = 1, \cdots, n$. Note that we assume each controlled agent has perfect knowledge about other controlled agents' observations. The following theorem establishes the correctness of Algorithm 1.

Theorem 1. *Algorithm 1 is sound*[2].

Proof. Note that Algorithm 1 always terminates, that is because either eventually a fixed point over strategies is reached, or a sub-game becomes unrealizable which indicates that the objective cannot be enforced. Consider the permissive strategies $\mathcal{S}_i^d$ and their projections $\mathcal{C}_i$. We have $\mathcal{C}_i(s) \subseteq \mathcal{S}_i^d(s)$ for any $s \in \Sigma_{\mathcal{V}}$, and as a result of composing and projecting intermediate strategies, we will obtain more restricted sub-games. As the state space and available actions in any state is finite, at some point, either a sub-game becomes unrealizable because the system player becomes too restricted and cannot win the game, or all strategies reach a fixed point. Therefore, the algorithm always terminates.

We now show that Algorithm 1 is sound, i.e., if it computes strategies $(S_1, \cdots, S_n)$, then the strategy $S = \bigotimes_{i=1}^n S_i$ is a winning strategy in the game $(\mathcal{G}^\mathcal{M}, \phi_{init}, \Phi)$, where $\mathcal{G}^\mathcal{M}$ is the game structure induced by $\mathcal{M}$. Let $\mathcal{S}^* = \bigotimes_{i=1}^k \mathcal{S}_i^d$ be the fixed point reached over the strategies. First note that any run in $\mathcal{G}_i^d[\mathcal{S}_i^d]$ starting from a state $s \models \phi_{init}^i$ for $1 \leq i \leq k$ satisfies the conjunct Φ_i since $\mathcal{S}_i^d$ is winning in the corresponding safety game. That is, the restriction of the game structure $\mathcal{G}_i^d$ to the strategy $\mathcal{S}_i^d$ satisfies Φ_i. Consider any run $\pi = s_0 s_1 s_2 \cdots$ in the restricted game structure $\mathcal{G}^d[\mathcal{S}^*]$ starting from the

---

[2] In [15] it is shown that bounded synthesis is complete by proving the existence of a sufficiently large bound. Following their result, it can be shown that Algorithm 1 is also complete. However, in practice, the required bound is rather high and instead an incremental approach is used for synthesis.

initial state $s_0 \models \phi_{init}$ where $\mathcal{G}^d = \bigotimes_{i=1}^k \mathcal{G}_i^d$. Let $\pi^i = s_0^i s_1^i s_2^i \cdots$ for $1 \leq i \leq k$ be the projection of π with respect to variables $\mathcal{V}_i^d$ of the game structure $\mathcal{G}_i^d$, i.e., $s_j^i = s_{j_{|\mathcal{V}_i^d}}$ for $j \geq 0$. Since $s_0^i \models \phi_{init}^i$ and $\mathcal{S}_i^d$ is equivalent to the projection of $\mathcal{S}^*$ with respect to variables and actions in the game structure $\mathcal{G}_i^d$, it follows that π^i is a winning run in the safety game $(\mathcal{G}_i^d[\mathcal{S}_i^d], \Phi_i)$, i.e., $\pi^i \models \Phi_i$. As $\pi^i \models \Phi_i$ for $1 \leq i \leq k$, we have $\pi \models \Phi = \bigwedge_{i=1}^k \Phi_i$. It follows that $\mathcal{S}^*$ is winning in the safety game $(\mathcal{G}^d, \phi_{init})$. Moreover, $\mathcal{S}^*$ is also winning with respect to the original game as $(\mathcal{G}^d, \phi_{init})$ is the safety game associated with $(\mathcal{G}^{\mathcal{M}}, \phi_{init}, \Phi)$ [15]. It is easy to see that the set $(\mathsf{S}_1, \cdots, \mathsf{S}_n)$ of strategies extracted from $\mathcal{S}^*$ by Algorithm 1 is winning for the game $(\mathcal{G}^{\mathcal{M}}, \phi_{init}, \Phi)$. □

Remark 2. Algorithm 1 is different from compositional algorithm proposed in [15] in two ways. First, it composes maximally permissive strategies in contrast to composing game structures as proposed in [15]. The advantage is that strategies usually have more compact symbolic representations compared to game structures[3]. Second, in the compositional algorithm in [15], sub-games are composed and a symbolic step, i.e., a post or pre-image computation, is performed over the composite game. In our experiments, performing a symbolic step over composite game resulted in a poor performance, often worse than the centralized algorithm. Algorithm 1 removes this bottleneck as it is not required in our setting. This leads to a significant improvement in algorithm's performance since image and pre-image computations are typically the most expensive operations performed by symbolic algorithms [35].

5   Case Study

We now demonstrate the techniques on a robot motion planning case study similar to those that can be found in the related literature (e.g., [8–10].) Consider a square grid-world with some static obstacles similar to the one depicted in Fig. 1. We consider a multi-agent system $\mathcal{M} = \{\mathsf{u}_1, \cdots, \mathsf{u}_m, \mathsf{c}_1, \cdots, \mathsf{c}_n\}$ with uncontrolled robots $\mathcal{M}^u = \{\mathsf{u}_1, \cdots, \mathsf{u}_m\}$ and controlled ones $\mathcal{M}^c = \{\mathsf{c}_1, \cdots, \mathsf{c}_n\}$. At any time-step, any controlled robot c_i for $1 \leq i \leq n$ can move to one of its neighboring cells by taking actions $up_i, down_i, left_i,$ and $right_i$, or it can stay put by taking the action *stop*. Any uncontrolled robot u_j for $1 \leq j \leq m$ stays on the same row where they are initially positioned, and at any time-step can move to their left or right neighboring cells by taking actions $left_j$ and $right_j$, respectively. We consider the following objectives for the systems, (Φ_1) collision avoidance, i.e., controlled robots must avoid collision with static obstacles and other robots, (Φ_2) formation maintenance, i.e., each controlled robot c_i must keep a linear formation (same horizontal or vertical coordinate) at all times with the subsequent controlled robot c_{i+1} for $1 \leq i < n$, (Φ_3) bounded reachability,

---

[3] Strategies are mappings from states to actions while game structures include more variables and typically have more complex BDD representation as they refer to states, actions, and next states.

i.e., controlled robots must reach the bottom row in a pre-specified number of steps. We consider two settings. First we assume all agents are perfect, i.e., all agents have full-knowledge of the state of the system at any time-step. Then we assume controlled agents are imperfect and can observe uncontrolled robots only if they are nearby and occupying an adjacent cell, similar to Example 1.

We apply two different methods to synthesize strategies for the agents. In the *Centralized* method, a game structure for the whole system is obtained first, and then a winning strategy is computed with respect to the considered objective. In the *Compositional* approach, the strategy is computed compositionally using Algorithm 1. We implemented the algorithms in Java using the BDD package JDD [36]. The experiments are performed on an Intel core i7 3.40 GHz machine with 16 GB memory. In our experiments, we vary the number of uncontrolled and controlled agents, size of the grid-world, and the objective of the system as shown in Tables 1 and 2. The columns show the number of uncontrolled and controlled robots, considered objective, size of the grid-world, number of variables in the system, and the time and memory usage for different approaches, respectively. Furthermore, we define $\Phi_{12} = \Phi_1 \wedge \Phi_2$, $\Phi_{13} = \Phi_1 \wedge \Phi_3$, and $\Phi = \Phi_1 \wedge \Phi_2 \wedge \Phi_3$.

Table 1. Experimental results for systems with perfect agents.

					Centralized		Compositional	
$|\mathcal{M}^u|$	$|\mathcal{M}^c|$	Objective	Size	$|\mathcal{V}|$	Time	Mem (MB)	Time	Mem (MB)
1	1	Φ_1	64×64	52	**72 ms**	6.6	105 ms	6.6
1	1	Φ_1	128×128	60	**93 ms**	6.6	101 ms	6.6
1	2	Φ_{13}	10×10	79	14.0 min	365.5	**1.2 s**	**19.3**
1	2	Φ_{13}	32×32	95	mem out	mem out	**34.4 s**	**50.8**
1	2	Φ	16×16	79	400.3 s	239.7	**5.1 s**	**19.4**
1	2	Φ	32×32	95	155.8 min	1209	**33.1 s**	**38.3**
1	3	Φ_{13}	4×4	66	22 s	50.8	**0.8 s**	**6.8**
1	3	Φ_{13}	8×8	88	mem out	mem out	**98.4 s**	**101.2**
2	1	Φ	8×8	51	106.4 s	322	**33 ms**	**6.6**
2	1	Φ	128×128	107	mem out	mem out	**3.5 s**	**6.7**
2	2	Φ	4×4	56	3.2 s	19.4	**201 ms**	**6.6**
2	2	Φ	8×8	76	10.6 min	460	**14.4 s**	**19.4**
2	3	Φ_{13}	4×4	75	19.1 min	497.8	**8.4 s**	**25.9**
2	3	Φ_{13}	8×8	101	mem out	mem out	**30.2 min**	**800.2**
2	3	Φ	8×8	101	mem out	mem out	**12.7 min**	**302.6**

Multi-agent Systems with Perfect Agents. Table 1 shows some of our experimental results for the setting where all agents are perfect (more experimental data is provided in the technical report.) Note that the compositional algorithm does not always perform better than the centralized alternative. Indeed, if the conjuncts of objectives involve a large subset of agents, compositional

Table 2. Experimental results for systems with imperfect agents

$|\mathcal{M}^u|$	$|\mathcal{M}^c|$	Objective	Size	$|\mathcal{V}|$	Centralized		Compositional	
					Time	Mem (MB)	Time	Mem (MB)
1	2	Φ_{12}	4×4	127	1.7 s	6.7	**0.6 s**	6.7
1	2	Φ_{12}	6×6	235	28.6 s	31.9	**10.2 s**	**19.3**
1	2	Φ_{12}	8×8	235	229.7 s	126.6	**95 s**	**57.1**
1	2	Φ_{12}	9×9	375	time out	time out	**306 s**	**94.9**
1	2	Φ_{12}	10×10	375	time out	time out	**9.7 min**	**176.7**
1	2	Φ_{13}	4×4	143	1.4 s	6.7	**303 ms**	6.7
1	2	Φ_{13}	6×6	255	38.2 s	57.1	**5 s**	**13**
1	2	Φ_{13}	8×8	255	8.9 min	252.2	**38.3 s**	**51**
1	2	Φ_{13}	9×9	395	time out	time out	**114.9 s**	**88.6**
1	2	Φ_{13}	10×10	395	time out	time out	**279.9 s**	**157.8**
1	2	Φ	4×4	143	2.3 s	6.7	**0.7 s**	**6.7**
1	2	Φ	6×6	255	46.2 s	50.8	**10 s**	**19.3**
1	2	Φ	8×8	255	344.5 s	202.1	**129.9 s**	**57.1**
1	2	Φ	9×9	395	time out	time out	**309.9 s**	**101.2**
1	2	Φ	10×10	395	time out	time out	**9.6 min**	**176.7**
1	3	Φ_1	4×4	186	144.3 s	69.7	**0.9 s**	**6.7**
1	3	Φ_1	6×6	346	time out	time out	**17.7 s**	**38.2**
1	3	Φ_1	8×8	346	time out	time out	**190.9 s**	**176.7**
1	3	Φ_1	10×10	554	time out	time out	**24.6 min**	**730.6**
1	3	Φ_{13}	4×4	210	265.8 s	214.5	**0.9 s**	**6.7**
1	3	Φ_{13}	6×6	376	time out	time out	**49.2 s**	**57.1**
1	3	Φ_{13}	8×8	376	time out	time out	**483.9 s**	**214.5**
1	3	Φ_{13}	9×9	584	time out	time out	**31.7 min**	**441.1**
1	3	Φ	6×6	376	time out	time out	**36 s**	**50.8**
1	3	Φ	8×8	376	time out	time out	**343.4 s**	**201.9**
1	3	Φ	10×10	584	time out	time out	**39.6 min**	**774.7**

algorithm comes closer to the centralized algorithm. Intuitively, if the agents are "strongly" coupled, the overhead introduced by compositional algorithm is not helpful, and the central algorithm performs better. For example, when the system consists of a controlled robot and an uncontrolled one along with a single safety objective, compositional algorithm coincides with the centralized one, and centralized algorithm performs slightly better. However, if the sub-problems are "loosely" coupled, which is the case in many practical problems, the compositional algorithm significantly outperforms the centralized one, both from time and memory perspective, as we increase the number of agents and make the objectives more complex, and it can solve problems where the centralized algorithm is infeasible.

Multi-agent Systems with Imperfect Controlled Agents. Not surprisingly, scalability is a bigger issue when it comes to games with imperfect information due to the subset construction procedure, which leads to yet another reason for compositional algorithm to perform better than the centralized alternative. Table 2 shows some of our experimental results for the setting where controlled agents are imperfect. While the centralized approach fails to compute the knowledge game structure due to the state explosion problem, the compositional algorithm performs significantly better by decomposing the problem and performing subset construction on smaller and more manageable game structures of imperfect information.

6   Conclusions and Future Work

We proposed a framework for controller synthesis for multi-agent systems. We showed that by taking advantage of the structure in the system to compositionally synthesize the controllers, and by representing and exploring the state space symbolically, we can achieve better scalability and solve more realistic problems. Our preliminary results shows the potential of reactive synthesis as planning algorithms in the presence of dynamically changing and adversarial environment.

In our implementation, we performed the subset construction procedure symbolically and we only constructed the part of it that is reachable from the initial state. One of our observations was that by considering more structured observation functions for game structures of imperfect information, such as the ones considered in our case study where the robots show a "local" observation behavior, the worst case exponential blow-up in the constructed knowledge game structure does not occur in practice. In future, we plan to investigate how considering more restricted yet practical observation functions can enable us to handle systems with imperfect agents of larger size.

References

1. Jennings, J.S., Whelan, G., Evans, W.F.: Cooperative search and rescue with a team of mobile robots. In: 8th International Conference on Advanced Robotics. IEEE (1997)
2. Rus, D., Donald, B., Jennings, J.: Moving furniture with teams of autonomous robots. In: Proceedings of IEEE/RSJ International Conference on Intelligent Robots and Systems. IEEE (1995)
3. Balch, T., Arkin, R.C.: Behavior-based formation control for multirobot teams. IEEE Trans. Robot. Autom. **14**(6), 926–939 (1998)
4. Pnueli, A., Rosner, R.: On the synthesis of a reactive module. In: Proceedings of the 16th ACM SIGPLAN-SIGACT Symposium on Principles of Programming Languages. ACM (1989)

5. Pnueli, A., Rosner, R.: Distributed reactive systems are hard to synthesize. In: 31st Annual Symposium on Foundations of Computer Science. IEEE (1990)
6. Peterson, G., Reif, J., Azhar, S.: Lower bounds for multiplayer noncooperative games of incomplete information. Comput. Math. Appl. **41**(7), 957–992 (2001)
7. Bloem, R., Jobstmann, B., Piterman, N., Pnueli, A., Sa'ar, Y.: Synthesis of reactive (1) designs. J. Comput. Syst. Sci. **78**(3), 911–938 (2012)
8. Kress-Gazit, H., Fainekos, G.E., Pappas, G.J.: Temporal-logic-based reactive mission and motion planning. IEEE Trans. Robot. **25**(6), 1370–1381 (2009)
9. Saha, I., Ramaithitima, R., Kumar, V., Pappas, G.J., Seshia, S.A.: Automated composition of motion primitives for multi-robot systems from safe ltl specifications. In: IEEE/RSJ International Conference on Intelligent Robots and Systems. IEEE (2014)
10. Ayanian, N., Kallem, V., Kumar, V.: Synthesis of feedback controllers for multiple aerial robots with geometric constraints. In: IEEE/RSJ International Conference on Intelligent Robots and Systems. IEEE (2011)
11. Keviczky, T., Borrelli, F., Balas, G.J.: Decentralized receding horizon control for large scale dynamically decoupled systems. Automatica **42**(12), 2105–2115 (2006)
12. Dunbar, W.B., Murray, R.M.: Distributed receding horizon control for multi-vehicle formation stabilization. Automatica **42**(4), 549–558 (2006)
13. Sahin, E., Girgin, S., Bayindir, L., Turgut, A.E.: Swarm robotics. In: Blum, C., Merkle, D. (eds.) Swarm Intelligence. Springer, Berlin (2008)
14. Shi, Z., Tu, J., Zhang, Q., Liu, L., Wei, J.: A survey of swarm robotics system. In: Tan, Y., Shi, Y., Ji, Z. (eds.) ICSI 2012, Part I. LNCS, vol. 7331, pp. 564–572. Springer, Heidelberg (2012)
15. Filiot, E., Jin, N., Raskin, J.F.: Antichains and compositional algorithms for LTL synthesis. Formal Methods Syst. Des. **39**(3), 261–296 (2011)
16. Kupferman, O., Piterman, N., Vardi, M.Y.: Safraless compositional synthesis. In: Ball, T., Jones, R.B. (eds.) CAV 2006. LNCS, vol. 4144, pp. 31–44. Springer, Heidelberg (2006)
17. Baier, C., Klein, J., Klüppelholz, S.: A compositional framework for controller synthesis. In: Katoen, J.-P., König, B. (eds.) CONCUR 2011. LNCS, vol. 6901, pp. 512–527. Springer, Heidelberg (2011)
18. Sohail, S., Somenzi, F.: Safety first: a two-stage algorithm for LTL games. In: Formal Methods in Computer-Aided Design. IEEE (2009)
19. Alur, R., Moarref, S., Topcu, U.: Pattern-based refinement of assume-guarantee specifications in reactive synthesis. In: Baier, C., Tinelli, C. (eds.) TACAS 2015. LNCS, vol. 9035, pp. 501–516. Springer, Heidelberg (2015)
20. Lustig, Y., Vardi, M.Y.: Synthesis from component libraries. Int. J. Softw. Tools Technol. Transf. **15**(5–6), 603–618 (2013)
21. Alur, R., Moarref, S., Topcu, U.: Compositional synthesis with parametric reactive controllers. In: Proceedings of the 19th International Conference on Hybrid Systems: Computation and Control. ACM (2016)
22. Reif, J.H.: The complexity of two-player games of incomplete information. J. Comput. Syst. Sci. **29**(2), 274–301 (1984)
23. Chatterjee, K., Henzinger, T.A.: Semiperfect-information games. In: Sarukkai, S., Sen, S. (eds.) FSTTCS 2005. LNCS, vol. 3821, pp. 1–18. Springer, Heidelberg (2005)
24. De Wulf, M., Doyen, L., Raskin, J.-F.: A lattice theory for solving games of imperfect information. In: Hespanha, J.P., Tiwari, A. (eds.) HSCC 2006. LNCS, vol. 3927, pp. 153–168. Springer, Heidelberg (2006)

25. Chatterjee, K., Doyen, L., Henzinger, T.A., Raskin, J.-F.: Algorithms for omega-regular games with imperfect information'. In: Ésik, Z. (ed.) CSL 2006. LNCS, vol. 4207, pp. 287–302. Springer, Heidelberg (2006)

26. Wongpiromsarn, T., Topcu, U., Murray, R.M.: Receding horizon temporal logic planning. IEEE Trans. Autom. Control **57**(11), 2817–2830 (2012)

27. Kress-gazit, H., Wongpiromsarn, T., Topcu, U.: Correct, reactive robot control from abstraction and temporal logic specifications

28. Wongpiromsarn, T., Ulusoy, A., Belta, C., Frazzoli, E., Rus, D.: Incremental synthesis of control policies for heterogeneous multi-agent systems with linear temporal logic specifications. In: IEEE International Conference on Robotics and Automation. IEEE (2013)

29. Kloetzer, M., Belta, C.: Automatic deployment of distributed teams of robots from temporal logic motion specifications. IEEE Trans. Robot. **26**(1), 48–61 (2010)

30. Ozay, N., Topcu, U., Murray, R.M.: Distributed power allocation for vehicle management systems. In: 50th IEEE Conference on Decision and Control and European Control Conference. IEEE (2011)

31. Clarke, E.M., Grumberg, O., Peled, D.: Model Checking. MIT Press, Cambridge (1999)

32. Schewe, S., Finkbeiner, B.: Bounded synthesis. In: Namjoshi, K.S., Yoneda, T., Higashino, T., Okamura, Y. (eds.) ATVA 2007. LNCS, vol. 4762, pp. 474–488. Springer, Heidelberg (2007)

33. Ehlers, R.: Symbolic bounded synthesis. Formal Methods Syst. Des. **40**(2), 232–262 (2012)

34. Alur, R., Henzinger, T.A., Kupferman, O.: Alternating-time temporal logic. J. ACM **49**(5), 672–713 (2002)

35. Bloem, R., Gabow, H.N., Somenzi, F.: An algorithm for strongly connected component analysis in n log n symbolic steps. In: Johnson, S.D., Hunt Jr., W.A. (eds.) FMCAD 2000. LNCS, vol. 1954, pp. 37–54. Springer, Heidelberg (2000)

36. Vahidi, A.: Jdd. http://javaddlib.sourceforge.net/jdd/index.html

Solving Parity Games via Priority Promotion

Massimo Benerecetti[1], Daniele Dell'Erba[1], and Fabio Mogavero[2(✉)]

[1] Università Degli Studi di Napoli Federico II, Naples, Italy
[2] Oxford University, Oxford, UK
fabio.mogavero@cs.ox.ac.uk

Abstract. We consider *parity games*, a special form of two-player infinite-duration games on numerically labelled graphs, whose winning condition requires that the maximal value of a label occurring infinitely often during a play be of some specific parity. The problem has a rather intriguing status from a complexity theoretic viewpoint, since it belongs to the class UPTIME ∩ COUPTIME, and still open is the question whether it can be solved in polynomial time. Parity games also have great practical interest, as they arise in many fields of theoretical computer science, most notably logic, automata theory, and formal verification. In this paper, we propose a new algorithm for the solution of the problem, based on the idea of promoting vertices to higher priorities during the search for winning regions. The proposed approach has nice computational properties, exhibiting the best space complexity among the currently known solutions. Experimental results on both random games and benchmark families show that the technique is also very effective in practice.

1 Introduction

Parity games [45] are perfect-information two-player turn-based games of infinite duration, usually played on finite directed graphs. Their vertices, labelled by natural numbers called *priorities*, are assigned to one of two players, named *Even* and *Odd* or, simply, 0 and 1, respectively. The game starts at an arbitrary vertex and, during its evolution, each player can take a move only at its own positions, which consists in choosing one of the edges outgoing from the current vertex. The moves selected by the players induce an infinite sequence of vertices, called play. If the maximal priority of the vertices occurring infinitely often in the play is *even*, then the play is winning for player 0, otherwise, player 1 takes it all.

Parity games have been extensively studied in the attempt to find efficient solutions to the problem of determining the winner. From a complexity theoretic perspective, this decision problem lies in NPTIME ∩ CONPTIME [18,19], since it is *memoryless determined* [17,37,38,45]. It has been even proved to belong to UPTime ∩ CoUPTime [31], a status shared with the *factorisation problem*

F. Mogavero—Sponsored by the Engineering and Physical Sciences Research Council of the United Kingdom, grant EP/M005852/1.

© Springer International Publishing Switzerland 2016
S. Chaudhuri and A. Farzan (Eds.): CAV 2016, Part II, LNCS 9780, pp. 270–290, 2016.
DOI: 10.1007/978-3-319-41540-6_15

[1,24,25]. They are the simplest class of games in a wider family with similar complexities and containing, *e.g.*, *mean payoff games* [16,30], *discounted payoff games* [55], and *simple stochastic games* [15]. In fact, polynomial time reductions exist from parity games to the latter ones. However, despite being the most likely class among those games to admit a polynomial-time solution, the answer to the question whether such a solution exists still eludes the research community.

The effort devoted to provide efficient solutions stems primarily form the fact that many problems in formal verification and synthesis can be reformulated in terms of solving parity games. Emerson, Jutla, and Sistla [18,19] have shown that computing winning strategies for these games is linear-time equivalent to solving the modal μCALCULUS model checking problem [20]. Parity games also play a crucial role in automata theory [17,36,44], where, for instance, they can be applied to solve the complementation problem for alternating automata [29] and the emptiness of the corresponding nondeterministic tree automata [36]. These automata, in turn, can be used to solve the satisfiability and model checking problems for expressive logics, such as the modal [53] and alternating [2,51] μCALCULUS, ATL* [2,50], Strategy Logic [14,40,41,43], Substructure Temporal Logic [4,5], and fixed-point extensions of guarded first-order logics [7,8].

Previous solutions mainly divide into two families: those based on decomposing the game into subsets of winning regions, called dominions, and those trying to directly build winning strategies for the two players on the entire game. To the first family belongs the *divide et impera* solution originally proposed by McNaughton [39] for Muller games and adapted to parity games by Zielonka [54]. More recent improvements to that recursive algorithm have been proposed by Jurdziński, Paterson, and Zwick [33,34] and by Schewe [48]. Both approaches rely on finding suitably closed dominions, which can then be removed from a game to reduce the size of the subgames to be recursively solved. To the second family belongs the procedure proposed by Jurdziński [32], which exploits the connection between the notions of progress measures [35] and winning strategies. An alternative approach was proposed by Jurdziński and Vöge [52], based on the idea of iteratively improving an initial non-winning strategy. This technique was later optimised by Schewe [49]. From a purely theoretical viewpoint, the best asymptotic behaviour obtained to date is the one exhibited by the solution proposed in [48], which runs in time $O\left(e \cdot n^{\frac{1}{3}k}\right)$, where n and e are the number of vertices and edges of the underlying graph and k is the number of priorities. As far as space consumption is concerned, we have two incomparable best behaviours: $O(k \cdot n \cdot \log n)$, for the small progress measure procedure of [32], and $O(n^2)$, for the optimised strategy improvement method of [49]. Due to their inherent recursive nature, the algorithms of the first family require $O(e \cdot n)$ memory, which could be reduced to $O(n^2)$, by representing subgames implicitly through their sets of vertices. All these bounds do not seem to be amenable to further improvements, as they appear to be intrinsic to the corresponding solution techniques. Polynomial time solutions are only known for restricted versions of the problem, where one among the tree-width [22,23,46], the dag-width [6], the clique-width [47] and the entanglement [9] of the underlying graph is bounded.

The main contribution of the paper is a new algorithm for solving parity games, based on the notions of *quasi dominion* and *priority promotion*. A quasi dominion Q for player $\alpha \in \{0, 1\}$, called a *quasi α-dominion*, is a set of vertices from each of which player α can enforce a winning play that never leaves the region, unless one of the following two conditions holds: *(i)* the opponent $\overline{\alpha}$ can escape from Q or *(ii)* the only choice for player α itself is to exit from Q (*i.e.*, no edge from a vertex of α remains in Q). Quasi dominions can be ordered by assigning to each of them a priority corresponding to an under-approximation of the best value the opponent can be forced to visit along any play exiting from it. A crucial property is that, under suitable and easy to check assumptions, a higher priority quasi α-dominion Q_1 and a lower priority one Q_2, can be merged into a single quasi α-dominion of the higher priority, thus improving the approximation for Q_2. For this reason we call this merging operation a priority promotion of Q_2 to Q_1. The underlying idea of our approach is to iteratively enlarge quasi α-dominions, by performing sequences of promotions, until an α-dominion is obtained.

We prove soundness and completeness of the algorithm. Moreover, a bound $O\left(e \cdot (3\frac{n-2}{k-2})^{k-1}\right)$ on the time complexity and a $O(n \cdot \log k)$ bound on the memory requirements are provided. Experimental results, comparing our algorithm with the state of the art solvers, also show that the proposed approach perform very well in practice, most often significantly better than existing ones, on both random games and benchmark families proposed in the literature.

2   Parity Games

Let us first briefly recall the notation and basic definitions concerning parity games that expert readers can simply skip. We refer to [3,54] for a comprehensive presentation of the subject.

Given a partial function $f : A \rightharpoonup B$, by $\mathsf{dom}(f) \subseteq A$ and $\mathsf{rng}(f) \subseteq B$ we denote the domain and range of f, respectively.

A two-player turn-based *arena* is a tuple $\mathcal{A} = \langle \mathrm{Ps}^0, \mathrm{Ps}^1, Mv \rangle$, with $\mathrm{Ps}^0 \cap \mathrm{Ps}^1 = \emptyset$ and $\mathrm{Ps} \triangleq \mathrm{Ps}^0 \cup \mathrm{Ps}^1$, such that $\langle \mathrm{Ps}, Mv \rangle$ is a finite directed graph. Ps^0 (*resp.* Ps^1) is the set of positions of player 0 (*resp.*, 1) and $Mv \subseteq \mathrm{Ps} \times \mathrm{Ps}$ is a left-total relation describing all possible moves. A *path* in $\mathrm{V} \subseteq \mathrm{Ps}$ is a finite or infinite sequence $\pi \in \mathrm{Pth}(\mathrm{V})$ of positions in V compatible with the move relation, *i.e.*, $(\pi_i, \pi_{i+1}) \in Mv$, for all $i \in [0, |\pi| - 1[$. For a finite path π, with $\mathsf{lst}(\pi)$ we denote the last position of π. A positional *strategy* for player $\alpha \in \{0, 1\}$ on $\mathrm{V} \subseteq \mathrm{Ps}$ is a partial function $\sigma_\alpha \in \mathrm{Str}^\alpha(\mathrm{V}) \subseteq (\mathrm{V} \cap \mathrm{Ps}^\alpha) \rightharpoonup \mathrm{V}$, mapping each α-position $v \in \mathsf{dom}(\sigma_\alpha)$ to position $\sigma_\alpha(v)$ compatible with the move relation, *i.e.*, $(v, \sigma_\alpha(v)) \in Mv$. With $\mathrm{Str}^\alpha(\mathrm{V})$ we denote the set of all α-strategies on V. A *play* in $\mathrm{V} \subseteq \mathrm{Ps}$ from a position $v \in \mathrm{V}$ *w.r.t.* a pair of strategies $(\sigma_0, \sigma_1) \in \mathrm{Str}^0(\mathrm{V}) \times \mathrm{Str}^1(\mathrm{V})$, called $((\sigma_0, \sigma_1), v)$-*play*, is a path $\pi \in \mathrm{Pth}(\mathrm{V})$ such that $\pi_0 = v$ and, for all $i \in [0, |\pi| - 1[$, if $\pi_i \in \mathrm{Ps}^0$ then $\pi_{i+1} = \sigma^0(\pi_i)$ else $\pi_{i+1} = \sigma^1(\pi_i)$. The *play function* play : $(\mathrm{Str}^0(\mathrm{V}) \times \mathrm{Str}^1(\mathrm{V})) \times \mathrm{V} \to \mathrm{Pth}(\mathrm{V})$ returns, for each position $v \in \mathrm{V}$ and pair of strategies $(\sigma_0, \sigma_1) \in \mathrm{Str}^0(\mathrm{V}) \times \mathrm{Str}^1(\mathrm{V})$, the maximal $((\sigma_0, \sigma_1), v)$-play $\mathsf{play}((\sigma^0, \sigma^1), v)$.

A *parity game* is a tuple $\partial = \langle \mathcal{A}, \text{Pr}, \text{pr} \rangle$, where $\mathcal{A}$ is an arena, $\text{Pr} \subset \mathbb{N}$ is a finite set of priorities, and $\text{pr} : \text{Ps} \rightarrow \text{Pr}$ is a *priority function* assigning a priority to each position. The priority function can be naturally extended to games and paths as follows: $\text{pr}(\partial) \triangleq \max_{v \in \text{Ps}} \text{pr}(v)$; for a path $\pi \in \text{Pth}$, we set $\text{pr}(\pi) \triangleq \max_{i \in [0,|\pi|[} \text{pr}(\pi_i)$, if π is finite, and $\text{pr}(\pi) \triangleq \limsup_{i \in \mathbb{N}} \text{pr}(\pi_i)$, otherwise. A set of positions $V \subseteq \text{Ps}$ is an α-*dominion*, with $\alpha \in \{0,1\}$, if there exists an α-strategy $\sigma_\alpha \in \text{Str}^\alpha(V)$ such that, for all $\overline{\alpha}$-strategies $\sigma_{\overline{\alpha}} \in \text{Str}^{\overline{\alpha}}(V)$ and positions $v \in V$, the induced play $\pi = \text{play}((\sigma_o, \sigma_1), v)$ is infinite and $\text{pr}(\pi) \equiv_2 \alpha$. In other words, σ_α only induces on V infinite plays whose maximal priority visited infinitely often has parity α. By $\partial \setminus V$ we denote the maximal subgame of ∂ with set of positions Ps' contained in $\text{Ps} \setminus V$ and move relation Mv' equal to the restriction of Mv to Ps'.

The α-predecessor of V, in symbols $\text{pre}^\alpha(V) \triangleq \{v \in \text{Ps}^\alpha : Mv(v) \cap V \neq \emptyset\} \cup \{v \in \text{Ps}^{\overline{\alpha}} : Mv(v) \subseteq V\}$, collects the positions from which player α can force the game to reach some position in V with a single move. The α-attractor $\text{atr}^\alpha(V)$ generalizes the notion of α-predecessor $\text{pre}^\alpha(V)$ to an arbitrary number of moves. Thus, it corresponds to the least fix-point of that operator. When $V = \text{atr}^\alpha(V)$, we say that V is α-maximal. Intuitively, V is α-maximal if player α cannot force any position outside V to enter this set. For such a V, the set of positions of the subgame $\partial \setminus V$ is precisely $\text{Ps} \setminus V$. Finally, the α-*escape* of V, formally $\text{esc}^\alpha(V) \triangleq \text{pre}^\alpha(\text{Ps} \setminus V) \cap V$, contains the positions in V from which α can leave V in one move, while the dual notion of α-*interior*, defined as $\text{int}^\alpha(V) \triangleq (V \cap \text{Ps}^\alpha) \setminus \text{esc}^\alpha(V)$, contains the α-positions from which α cannot escape with a single move.

3   A New Idea

A solution for a parity game $\partial = \langle \mathcal{A}, \text{Pr}, \text{pr} \rangle \in \text{PG}$ over an arena $\mathcal{A} = \langle \text{Ps}^o, \text{Ps}^1, Mv \rangle$ can trivially be obtained by iteratively computing dominions of some player, namely sets of positions from which that player has a strategy to win the game. Once an α-dominion D for player $\alpha \in \{0,1\}$ is found, its α-attractor $\text{atr}_\partial^\alpha(D)$ gives an α-maximal dominion containing D, *i.e.*, α cannot force any position outside D to enter this set. The subgame $\partial \setminus \text{atr}_\partial^\alpha(D)$ can then be solved by iterating the process. Therefore, the crucial problem to address consists in computing a dominion for some player in the game. The difficulty here is that, in general, no unique priority exists which satisfies the winning condition for a player along all the plays inside the dominion. In fact, that value depends on the strategy chosen by the opponent. Our solution to this problem is to proceed in a bottom-up fashion, starting from a weaker notion of α-dominion, called *quasi α-dominion*. Then, we compose quasi α-dominions until we obtain an α-dominion. Intuitively, a quasi α-dominion is a set of positions on which player α has a strategy whose induced plays either remain in the set forever and are winning for α or can exit from it. This notion is formalised by the following definition.

Definition 1 (Quasi Dominion). *Let $\partial \in \text{PG}$ be a game and $\alpha \in \{0,1\}$ a player. A non-empty set of positions $Q \subseteq \text{Ps}_\partial$ is a* quasi α-dominion *in ∂*

if there exists an α-strategy $\sigma_\alpha \in \mathrm{Str}_\partial^\alpha(Q)$ such that, for all $\overline{\alpha}$-strategies $\sigma_{\overline{\alpha}} \in \mathrm{Str}_\partial^{\overline{\alpha}}(Q)$, with $\mathrm{int}_\partial^{\overline{\alpha}}(Q) \subseteq \mathrm{dom}(\sigma_{\overline{\alpha}})$, and positions $v \in Q$, the induced play $\pi = \mathrm{play}_\partial((\sigma_0, \sigma_1), v)$ satisfies $\mathrm{pr}_\partial(\pi) \equiv_2 \alpha$, if π is infinite, and $\mathrm{lst}(\pi) \in \mathrm{esc}_\partial^{\overline{\alpha}}(Q)$, otherwise.

The additional requirement that the opponent strategies be defined on all interior positions discards those strategies in which the opponent deliberately chooses to forfeit the play by declining to take any move at some of its positions. We say that a quasi α-dominion Q is α-*open* (*resp.*, α-*closed*) if $\mathrm{esc}_\partial^{\overline{\alpha}}(Q) \neq \emptyset$ (*resp.*, $\mathrm{esc}_\partial^{\overline{\alpha}}(Q) = \emptyset$). In other words, in a closed quasi α-dominion, player α has a strategy whose induced plays are all infinite and winning. Hence, when closed, a quasi α-dominion is a dominion for α in ∂. The set of pairs $(Q, \alpha) \in 2^{\mathrm{Ps}_\partial} \times \{0, 1\}$, where Q is a quasi α-dominion, is denoted by QD_∂, and is partitioned into the sets QD_∂^- and QD_∂^+ of open and closed quasi α-dominion pairs, respectively.

Note that quasi α-dominions are loosely related with the concept of snares, introduced in [21] and used for completely different purposes, namely to speed up the convergence of strategy improvement algorithms.

During the search for a dominion, we explore a suitable partial order, whose elements, called *states*, record information about the open quasi dominions computed so far. The search starts from the top element, where the quasi dominions are initialised to the sets of nodes with the same priority. At each step, a query is performed on the current state to extract a new quasi dominion, which is then used to compute a successor state, if it is open. If, on the other hand, it is closed, the search is over. Different query and successor operations can in principle be defined, even on the same partial order. However, such operations cannot be completely independent. To account for this intrinsic dependence, we introduce a compatibility relation between states and quasi dominions that can be extracted by the query operation. Such a relation also forms the domain of the successor function. The partial order together with the query and successor operations and the compatibility relation forms what we call a *dominion space*.

Definition 2 (Dominion Space). *A dominion space for a game $\partial \in \mathrm{PG}$ is a tuple $\mathcal{D} \triangleq \langle \partial, \mathcal{S}, \succ, \Re, \downarrow \rangle$, where (1) $\mathcal{S} \triangleq \langle \mathrm{S}, \top, \prec \rangle$ is a well-founded partial order w.r.t. $\prec \subseteq \mathrm{S} \times \mathrm{S}$ with distinguished element $\top \in \mathrm{S}$, (2) $\succ \subseteq \mathcal{S} \times \mathrm{QD}_\partial^-$ is the compatibility relation, (3) $\Re : \mathrm{S} \to \mathrm{QD}_\partial$ is the query function mapping each element $s \in \mathrm{S}$ to a quasi dominion pair $(Q, \alpha) \triangleq \Re(s) \in \mathrm{QD}_\partial$ such that, if $(Q, \alpha) \in \mathrm{QD}_\partial^-$ then $s \succ (Q, \alpha)$, and (4) $\downarrow : \succ \to \mathrm{S}$ is the successor function mapping each pair $(s, (Q, \alpha)) \in \succ$ to the element $s^\star \triangleq s \downarrow (Q, \alpha) \in \mathrm{S}$ with $s^\star \prec s$.*

The *depth* of a dominion space $\mathcal{D}$ is the length of the longest chain in the underlying partial order $\mathcal{S}$ starting from $\top$. Instead, by *execution depth* of $\mathcal{D}$ we mean the length of the longest chain induced by the successor function $\downarrow$. Obviously, the execution depth is always bound by the depth.

Different dominion spaces can be associated to the same game. Therefore, in the rest of this section, we shall simply assume a function Γ mapping every game ∂ to a dominion space $\Gamma(\partial)$. Given the top element of $\mathcal{D} = \Gamma(\partial)$, Algorithm 1 searches for a dominion of either one of the two players by querying the current state s for a region pair (Q, α). If this is closed in $\eth$, it is returned as an α-dominion. Otherwise, a successor state $s \downarrow_{\mathcal{D}} (Q, \alpha)$ is computed and the search proceeds recursively from it. Clearly, since the partial order is well-founded, termination of the $\mathsf{src}_{\mathcal{D}}$ procedure is guaranteed. The total number of recursive calls is, therefore, the execution depth $\mathsf{d}_{\mathcal{D}}(n, e, k)$ of the dominion space $\mathcal{D}$, where n, e, and k are the number of positions, moves, and priorities, respectively. Hence, $\mathsf{src}_{\mathcal{D}}$ runs in time $O(\mathsf{d}_{\mathcal{D}}(n, e, k) \cdot (\mathsf{T}_{\Re}(n, e) + \mathsf{T}_{\downarrow}(n, e)))$, where $\mathsf{T}_{\Re}(n, e)$ and $\mathsf{T}_{\downarrow}(n, e)$ denote the time needed by the query and successor functions, respectively. Thus, the total time to solve a game is $O(e + n \cdot \mathsf{d}_{\mathcal{D}}(n, e, k) \cdot (\mathsf{T}_{\Re}(n, e) + \mathsf{T}_{\downarrow}(n, e)))$. Since the query and successor functions of the dominion space considered in the rest of the paper can be computed in linear time $w.r.t.$ both n and e, the whole procedure terminates in time $O(n \cdot (n + e) \cdot \mathsf{d}_{\mathcal{D}}(n, e, k))$. As to the space requirements, observe that $\mathsf{src}_{\mathcal{D}}$ is a tail recursive algorithm. Hence, the upper bound on memory only depends on the space needed to encode the states of a dominion space, namely $O(\log \|\mathcal{D}\|)$, where $\|\mathcal{D}\|$ is the size of the partial order $\mathcal{S}$ associated with $\mathcal{D}$.

Soundness of the approach follows from the observation that quasi α-dominions closed in the entire game are winning for player α and so are their α-attractors. *Completeness*, instead, is ensured by the nature of dominion spaces. Indeed, algorithm $\mathsf{src}_{\mathcal{D}}$ always terminates by well-foundedness of the underlying partial order and, when it eventually does, a dominion for some player is returned. Therefore, the correctness of the algorithm reduces to proving the existence of a suitable dominion space, which is the subject of the next section.

Algorithm 1. The Searcher.

signature $\mathsf{src}_{\Gamma} : \mathrm{PG} \to_{\eth} \mathrm{QD}_{\eth}^+$
function $\mathsf{src}_{\Gamma}(\eth)$

1 | **return** $\mathsf{src}_{\Gamma(\eth)}(\top_{\Gamma(\eth)})$

signature $\mathsf{src}_{\mathcal{D}} : \mathrm{S}_{\mathcal{D}} \to \mathrm{QD}_{\eth_{\mathcal{D}}}^+$
function $\mathsf{src}_{\mathcal{D}}(s)$

1 | $(Q, \alpha) \leftarrow \Re_{\mathcal{D}}(s)$
2 | **if** $(Q, \alpha) \in \mathrm{QD}_{\eth_{\mathcal{D}}}^+$ **then**
3 | | **return** (Q, α)
   | **else**
4 | | **return** $\mathsf{src}_{\mathcal{D}}(s \downarrow_{\mathcal{D}}(Q, \alpha))$

---

4   Priority Promotion

In order to compute dominions, we shall consider a restricted form of quasi dominions that constrains the escape set to have the maximal priority in the game. Such quasi dominions are called *regions*.

Definition 3 (Region). *A quasi α-dominion R is an α-region if $\mathsf{pr}(\eth) \equiv_2 \alpha$ and all the positions in $\mathsf{esc}_{\eth}^{\overline{\alpha}}(R)$ have priority $\mathsf{pr}(\eth)$, i.e. $\mathsf{esc}_{\eth}^{\overline{\alpha}}(R) \subseteq \mathsf{pr}^{-1}(\mathsf{pr}(\eth))$.*

As a consequence of the above definition, if the opponent $\overline{\alpha}$ can escape from an α-region, it must visit a position with the highest priority in the region, which is of parity α. Similarly to the case of quasi dominions, we shall denote with $\mathrm{Rg}_{\eth}$ the set of region pairs in $\eth$ and with $\mathrm{Rg}_{\eth}^-$ and $\mathrm{Rg}_{\eth}^+$ the sets of open and closed region pairs, respectively. A closed α-region is clearly an α-dominion.

At this point, we have all the tools to explain the crucial steps underlying the search procedure. Open regions are not winning, as the opponent can force plays exiting from them. Therefore, in order to build a dominion starting from open regions, we look for a suitable sequence of regions that can be merged together until a closed one is found. Obviously, the merging operation needs to be applied only to regions belonging to the same player, in such a way that the resulting set of position is still a region of that player. To this end, a mechanism is proposed, where an α-region R in some game $\eth$ and an α-dominion D in a subgame of $\eth$ not containing R itself are merged together, if the only moves exiting from $\overline{\alpha}$-positions of D in the entire game lead to higher priority α-regions and R has the lowest priority among them. As we shall see, this ensures that the new region $R^\star \triangleq R \cup D$ has the same associated priority as R. This merging operation, based on the following proposition, is called *promotion* of the lower region to the higher one.

Proposition 1 (Region Merging). *Let $\eth \in \mathrm{PG}$ be a game, $R \subseteq \mathrm{Ps}_\eth$ an α-region, and $D \subseteq \mathrm{Ps}_{\eth \setminus R}$ an α-dominion in the subgame $\eth \setminus R$. Then, $R^\star \triangleq R \cup D$ is an α-region in $\eth$. Moreover, if both R and D are α-maximal in $\eth$ and $\eth \setminus R$, respectively, then $R^\star$ is α-maximal in $\eth$ as well.*

Proof. Since R is an α-region, there is an α-strategy σ_R such that, for all $\overline{\alpha}$-strategies $\sigma_{\overline{\alpha}} \in \mathrm{Str}_\eth^{\overline{\alpha}}(R)$, with $\mathrm{int}_\eth^{\overline{\alpha}}(R) \subseteq \mathrm{dom}(\sigma_{\overline{\alpha}})$, and positions $v \in R$, the play induced by the two strategies is either winning for α or exits from R passing through a position of the escape set $\mathrm{esc}_\eth^{\overline{\alpha}}(R)$, which must be one of the position of maximal priority in $\eth$ and of parity α. Set D is, instead, an α-dominion in the game $\eth \setminus R$, therefore an α-strategy $\sigma_D \in \mathrm{Str}_{\eth \setminus R}$ exists that is winning for α from every position in D, regardless of the strategy $\sigma_{\overline{\alpha}}' \in \mathrm{Str}_{\eth \setminus R}^{\overline{\alpha}}(D)$, with $\mathrm{int}_{\eth \setminus R}^{\overline{\alpha}}(D) \subseteq \mathrm{dom}(\sigma_{\overline{\alpha}}')$, chosen by the opponent $\overline{\alpha}$. To show that $R^\star$ is an α-region, it suffices to show that the following three conditions hold: *(i)* it is a quasi α-dominion; *(ii)* the maximal priority of $\eth$ is of parity α; *(iii)* the escape set $\mathrm{esc}_\eth^{\overline{\alpha}}(R^\star)$ is contained in $\mathrm{pr}_\eth^{-1}(\mathrm{pr}(\eth))$.

Condition *(ii)* immediately follows from the assumption that R is an α-region in $\eth$. To show that also Condition *(iii)* holds, we observe that, since D is an α-dominion in $\eth \setminus R$, the only possible moves exiting from $\overline{\alpha}$-positions of D in game $\eth$ must lead to R, *i.e.*, $\mathrm{esc}_\eth^{\overline{\alpha}}(D) \subseteq R$. Hence, the only escaping positions of $R^\star$, if any, must belong to R, *i.e.* $\mathrm{esc}_\eth^{\overline{\alpha}}(R^\star) \subseteq \mathrm{esc}_\eth^{\overline{\alpha}}(R)$. Since R is an α-region in $\eth$, it hods that $\mathrm{esc}_\eth^{\overline{\alpha}}(R) \subseteq \mathrm{pr}_\eth^{-1}(\mathrm{pr}(\eth))$. By transitivity, we conclude that $\mathrm{esc}_\eth^{\overline{\alpha}}(R^\star) \subseteq \mathrm{pr}_\eth^{-1}(\mathrm{pr}(\eth))$.

Let us now consider Condition *(i)* and let the α-strategy $\sigma_{R^\star} \triangleq \sigma_R \cup \sigma_D$ be defined as the union of the two strategies above. Note that, being D and R disjoint sets of positions, $\sigma_{R^\star}$ is a well-defined strategy. We have to show that every path π compatible with $\sigma_{R^\star}$ and starting from a position in $R^\star$ is either winning for α or ends in a position of the escape set $\mathrm{esc}_\eth^{\overline{\alpha}}(R^\star)$.

First, observe that $\mathrm{esc}_\eth^{\overline{\alpha}}(R^\star)$ contains only those positions in the escaping set of R from which α cannot force to move into D, *i.e.* $\mathrm{esc}_\eth^{\overline{\alpha}}(R^\star) = \mathrm{esc}_\eth^{\overline{\alpha}}(R) \setminus \mathrm{pre}_\eth^{\alpha}(D)$.

Let now π be a play compatible with σ_{R^*}. If π is an infinite play, then it remains forever in R^* and we have three possible cases. If π eventually remains forever in D, then it is clearly winning for α, since σ_{R^*} coincides with σ_D on all the positions in D. Similarly, if π eventually remains forever in R, then it is also winning for α, as σ_{R^*} coincides with σ_R on all the positions in R. If, on the other hand, π passes infinitely often through both R and D, it necessarily visits infinitely often an escaping position in $\mathsf{esc}_\partial^{\overline{\alpha}}(R) \subseteq \mathsf{pr}_\partial^{-1}(\mathsf{pr}(\partial))$, which has the maximal priority in ∂ and is of parity α. Hence, the parity of the maximal priority visited infinitely often along π is α and π is winning for player α. Finally, if π is a finite play, then it must end at some escaping position of R from where α cannot force to move to a position still in R^*, i.e., it must end in a position of the set $\mathsf{esc}_\partial^{\overline{\alpha}}(R) \setminus \mathsf{pre}_\partial^\alpha(D) = \mathsf{esc}_\partial^{\overline{\alpha}}(R^*)$. Therefore, $\mathsf{lst}(\pi) \in \mathsf{esc}_\partial^{\overline{\alpha}}(R^*)$. We can then conclude that R^* also satisfies Condition (i).

Let us now assume, by contradiction, that R^* is not α-maximal. Then, there must be at least one position v belonging to $\mathsf{atr}_\partial^\alpha(R^*) \setminus R^*$, from which α can force entering R^* in one move. Assume first that v is an α-position. Then there is a move from v leading either to R or to D. But this means that v belongs to either $\mathsf{atr}_\partial^\alpha(R) \setminus R$ or $\mathsf{atr}_{\partial \setminus R}^\alpha(D) \setminus D$, contradicting α-maximality of those sets. If v is a $\overline{\alpha}$-position, instead, all its outgoing moves must lead to $R \cup D$. If all those moves lead to R, then $v \in \mathsf{atr}_\partial^\alpha(R) \setminus R$, contradicting α-maximality of R in ∂. If not, then in the subgame $\partial \setminus R$, the remaining moves from v must all lead to D. But then, $v \in \mathsf{atr}_{\partial \setminus R}^\alpha(D) \setminus D$, contradicting α-maximality of D in $\partial \setminus R$.

During the search, we keep track of the computed regions by means of an auxiliary priority function $\mathsf{r} \in \Delta_\partial \triangleq \mathsf{Ps}_\partial \to \mathsf{Pr}_\partial$, called *region function*, which formalises the intuitive notion of priority of a region described above. Initially, the region function coincides with the priority function pr_∂ of the entire game ∂. Priorities are considered starting from the highest one. A region of the same parity $\alpha \in \{0, 1\}$ of the priority p under consideration is extracted from the region function, by collecting the set of positions $\mathsf{r}^{-1}(p)$. Then, its attractor $R \triangleq \mathsf{atr}_{\partial^*}^\alpha(\mathsf{r}^{-1}(p))$ is computed w.r.t. the subgame ∂^*, which is derived from ∂ by removing the regions with priority higher than p. The resulting set forms an α-maximal set of positions from which the corresponding player can force a visit to positions with priority p. This first phase is called *region extension*. If the α-region R is open in ∂^*, we proceed and process the next priority. In this case, we set the priority of the newly computed region to p. Otherwise, one of two situations may arise. Either R is closed in the whole game ∂ or the only $\overline{\alpha}$-moves exiting from R lead to higher regions of the same parity. In the former case, R is a α-dominion in the entire game and the search stops. In the latter case, R is only an α-dominion in the subgame ∂^*, and a promotion of R to a higher region $R^\natural$ can be performed, according to Proposition 1. The search, then, restarts from the priority of $R^\natural$, after resetting to the original priorities in pr_∂ all the positions of the lower priority regions. The region R^* resulting from the union of $R^\natural$ and R will then be reprocessed and, possibly, extended in order to make it α-maximal. If R can be promoted to more than one region, the one with the lowest priority is chosen, so as to ensure the correctness of the merging operation. Due to the property of maximality, no $\overline{\alpha}$-moves from R to higher priority $\overline{\alpha}$-regions exist. Therefore, only regions of the same parity are considered in the promotion step. The correctness of region extension operation above, the remaining fundamental step in the proposed approach, is formalised by the following proposition.

Proposition 2 (Region Extension). *Let* $\partial \in \mathrm{PG}$ *be a game and* $\mathrm{R}^\star \subseteq \mathrm{Ps}_\partial$ *an* α*-region in* ∂*. Then,* $\mathrm{R} \triangleq \mathrm{atr}_\partial^\alpha(\mathrm{R}^\star)$ *is an* α*-maximal* α*-region in* ∂*.*

Proof. Since $\mathrm{R}^\star$ is an α-region in ∂, then the maximal priority in ∂ is of parity α and $\mathrm{esc}_\partial^{\overline{\alpha}}(\mathrm{R}^\star) \subseteq \mathrm{pr}_\partial^{-1}(\mathrm{pr}(\partial))$. Hence, any position v in ∂ must have priority $\mathrm{pr}_\partial(v) \leq \mathrm{pr}(\partial)$. Player α can force entering $\mathrm{R}^\star$ from every position in $\mathrm{atr}_\partial^\alpha(\mathrm{R}^\star) \setminus \mathrm{R}^\star$, with a finite number of moves. Moreover, $\mathrm{R}^\star$ is a quasi α-dominion and the priorities of the positions in $\mathrm{Ps}_\partial \setminus \mathrm{R}^\star$ are lower than or equal to $\mathrm{pr}(\partial) \equiv_2 \alpha$. Hence, every play that remains in R forever either eventually remains forever in $\mathrm{R}^\star$ and is winning for α, or passes infinitely often through $\mathrm{R}^\star$ and $\mathrm{atr}_\partial^\alpha(\mathrm{R}^\star) \setminus \mathrm{R}^\star$. In the latter case, that path must visit infinitely often a position in $\mathrm{esc}_\partial^{\overline{\alpha}}(\mathrm{R}^\star)$ that has the maximal priority in ∂ and has parity α. Hence, the play is winning for α. If, on the other hand, $\overline{\alpha}$ can force a play to exit from R, it can do so only by visiting some position in $\mathrm{esc}_\partial^{\overline{\alpha}}(\mathrm{R}^\star)$. In other words, $\mathrm{esc}_\partial^{\overline{\alpha}}(\mathrm{R}) \subseteq \mathrm{esc}_\partial^{\overline{\alpha}}(\mathrm{R}^\star) \subseteq \mathrm{pr}_\partial^{-1}(\mathrm{pr}(\partial))$. In either case, we conclude that R is an α-region in ∂. Finally, being R the result of an α-attractor, it is clearly α-maximal. $\square$

Table 1. PP simulation.

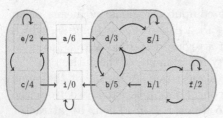

	1	2	3	4	5	6	7
6	a↓	⋯	⋯	⋯	⋯	a,b,d,g,i↓	⋯
5	b,f,h↓	⋯	⋯	b,d,f,g,h↓	⋯		
4	c↓	c,e↓	⋯	c↓	c,e↓	c↓	c,e,f,h↑6
3	d↓	d↓	d,g↑5				
2	e↑4			e↑4		e, f, h↑4	
1		g↑3					
0					i↑6		

Fig. 1. Running example.

Figure 1 and Table 1 illustrate the search procedure on an example game, where diamond shaped positions belong to player 0 and square shaped ones to the opponent 1. Player 0 wins from every position, hence the 0-region containing all the positions is a 0-dominion in this case. Each cell of the table contains a computed region. A downward arrow denotes a region that is open in the subgame where it is computed, while an upward arrow means that the region gets to be promoted to the priority in the subscript. The index of each row corresponds to the priority of the region. Following the idea sketched above, the first region obtained is the single-position 0-region {a}, which is open because of the two moves leading to d and e. At priority 5, the open 1-region {b, f, h} is formed by attracting both f and h to b, which is open in the subgame where {a} is removed. Similarly, the 0-region {c} at priority 4 and the 1-region {d} at priority 3 are open, once removed $\{a, b, f, h\}$ and $\{a, b, c, f, h\}$, respectively, from the game. At priority 2, the 0-region $\{e\}$ is closed in the corresponding subgame. However, it is not closed in the whole game, since it has a move leading to c, *i.e.*, to region 4. A promotion of $\{e\}$ to 4 is then performed, resulting in the new 0-region $\{c, e\}$. The search resumes at the corresponding priority and, after computing the extension of such a region via the attractor, we obtain that it is still open in the corresponding subgame. Consequently, the 1-region of priority 3 is recomputed and, then, priority 1 is processed to build the 1-region $\{g\}$. The latter is closed in the associated subgame, but not in the original game, because of a move leading to position d. Hence, another promotion is performed, leading to closed region in Row 3 and Column 3, which in turn triggers a promotion to 5. Observe that every time a promotion to a higher region is performed, all positions of the regions at lower priorities are reset to their original priorities. The iteration of the region forming and promotion steps proceeds until the configuration in Column 7 is reached. Here only two 0-regions are present: the open region 6 containing $\{a, b, d, g, i\}$ and the closed region 4 containing $\{c, e, f, h\}$. The second one has a move leading to the first one, hence, it is promoted to its priority. This last operation forms a 0-region containing all the positions of the game. It is obviously closed in the whole game and is, therefore, a 0-dominion.

Note that, the positions in 0-region $\{c, e\}$ are reset to their initial priorities, when 1-region $\{d, g\}$ in Column 3 is promoted to 5. Similarly, when 0-region $\{i\}$ in Column 5 is promoted to 6, the priorities of the positions in both regions $\{b, d, f, g, h\}$ and $\{c, e\}$, highlighted by the grey areas, are reset. This is actually necessary for correctness, at least in general. In fact, if region $\{b, d, f, g, h\}$ were not reset, the promotion of $\{i\}$ to 6, which also attracts b, d, and g, would leave $\{f, h\}$ as a 1-region of priority 5. However, according to Definition 3, this is not a 1-region. Even worse, it would also be considered a closed 1 region in the entire game, without being a 1-dominion, since it is actually an open 0-region. This shows that, in principle, promotions to an higher priority require the reset of previously built regions of lower priorities.

In the rest of this section, we shall formalise the intuitive idea described above. The necessary conditions under which promotion operations can be applied are also stated. Finally, query and successor algorithms are provided, which ensure that the necessary conditions are easy to check and always met when promotions are performed.

The PP *Dominion Space*. In order to define the dominion space induced by the *priority-promotion mechanism* (PP, for short), we need to introduce some additional notation. Given a priority function $r \in \Delta_{\partial}$ and a priority $p \in \text{Pr}$, we denote by $r^{(\geq p)}$ (*resp.*, $r^{(>p)}$ and $r^{(<p)}$) the function obtained by restricting the domain of r to the positions with priority greater than or equal to p (*resp.*, greater than and lower than p). Formally, $r^{(\geq p)} \triangleq r{\restriction}\{v \in \text{dom}(r) : r(v) \geq p\}$, $r^{(>p)} \triangleq r{\restriction}\{v \in \text{dom}(r) : r(v) > p\}$, and $r^{(<p)} \triangleq r{\restriction}\{v \in \text{dom}(r) : r(v) < p\}$. By $\partial_r^{\leq p}$ we denote the largest subgame contained in the structure $\partial \setminus \text{dom}(r^{(>p)})$, which is obtained by removing from ∂ all the positions in the domain of $r^{(>p)}$.

A priority function $r \in \mathbb{R}_{\Game} \subseteq \Delta_{\Game}$ in $\Game$ is a *region function* iff, for all priorities $q \in \text{rng}(r)$ with $\alpha \triangleq q \bmod 2$, it holds that $r^{-1}(q) \cap \text{Ps}_{\Game_r^{\leq q}}$ is an α-region in the subgame $\Game_r^{\leq q}$, if non-empty. In addition, we say that r is *maximal* above $p \in \text{Pr}$ iff, for all $q \in \text{rng}(r)$ with $q > p$, we have that $r^{-1}(q)$ is α-maximal in $\Game_r^{\leq q}$ with $\alpha \triangleq q \bmod 2$.

To account for the current status of the search of a dominion, the states s of the corresponding dominion space need to contain the current region function r and the current priority p reached by the search in $\Game$. To each of such states $s \triangleq (r, p)$, we then associate the *subgame at s* defined as $\Game_s \triangleq \Game_r^{\leq p}$, representing the portion of the original game that still has to be processed.

We can now formally define the *Priority Promotion* dominion space, by characterising the corresponding state space and compatibility relàtion. Moreover, algorithms for the query and successor functions of that space are provided.

Definition 4 (State Space). *A state space is a tuple $\mathcal{S}_{\Game} \triangleq \langle S_{\Game}, \top_{\Game}, \prec_{\Game} \rangle$, where its components are defined as prescribed in the following:*

1. *$S_{\Game} \subseteq \mathbb{R}_{\Game} \times \text{Pr}_{\Game}$ is the set of all pairs $s \triangleq (r, p)$, called* states, *composed of a region function $r \in \mathbb{R}_{\Game}$ and a priority $p \in \text{Pr}_{\Game}$ such that (a) r is maximal above p and (b) $p \in \text{rng}(r)$, and (c) $r^{(<p)} \subseteq \text{pr}_{\Game}^{(<p)}$;*
2. *$\top_{\Game} \triangleq (\text{pr}_{\Game}, \text{pr}(\Game))$;*
3. *for any two states $s_1 \triangleq (r_1, p_1), s_2 \triangleq (r_2, p_2) \in S_{\Game}$, it holds that $s_1 \prec_{\Game} s_2$ iff either (a) there exists a priority $q \in \text{rng}(r_1)$ with $q \geq p_1$ such that (a.i) $r_1^{(>q)} = r_2^{(>q)}$ and (a.ii) $r_2^{-1}(q) \subset r_1^{-1}(q)$, or (b) both (b.i) $r_1 = r_2$ and (b.ii) $p_1 < p_2$ hold.*

The state space specifies the configurations in which the priority promotion procedure can reside and the relative order that the successor function must satisfy. In particular, for a given state $s \triangleq (r, p)$, every region $r^{-1}(q)$, with priority $q > p$, recorded in the region function r has to be α-maximal, where $\alpha = q \bmod 2$. This implies that $r^{-1}(q) \subseteq \text{Ps}_{\Game_r^{\leq q}}$. Moreover, the current priority p of the state must be the priority of an actual region in r. As far as the order is concerned, a state s_1 is strictly smaller than another state s_2 if either there is a region recorded in s_1 at some higher priority that strictly contains the corresponding one in s_2 and all regions above are equal in the two states, or state s_1 is currently processing a lower priority than the one of s_2.

At this point, we can determine the regions that are compatible with a given state. They are the only ones that the query function is allowed to return and that can then be used by the successor function to make the search progress in the dominion space. Intuitively, a region pair (R, α) is compatible with a state $s \triangleq (r, p)$ if it is an α-region in the current subgame $\Game_s$. Moreover, if such region is α-open in that game, it has to be α-maximal,

---

Algorithm 2. Query Function.

signature $\mathfrak{R}_{\Game} : S_{\Game} \to (2^{\text{Ps}_{\Game}} \times \{0, 1\})$
function $\mathfrak{R}_{\Game}(s)$

    let $(r, p) = s$ **in**

1      $\alpha \leftarrow p \bmod 2$

2      $R \leftarrow \text{atr}_{\Game_s}^{\alpha}(r^{-1}(p))$

3   **return** (R, α)

and it has to necessarily contain the current region $r^{-1}(p)$ of priority p in r. These three accessory properties ensure that the successor function is always able to cast R inside the current region function r and obtain a new state.

Definition 5 (Compatibility Relation). *An open quasi dominion pair* $(R, \alpha) \in QD_{\partial}^{-}$ *is compatible with a state* $s \triangleq (r, p) \in S_{\partial}$, *in symbols* $s \succ_{\partial} (R, \alpha)$, *iff* (1) $(R, \alpha) \in Rg_{\partial_s}$ *and* (2) *if R is* α-*open in* ∂_s *then* (2.a) *R is* α-*maximal in* ∂_s *and* (2.b) $r^{-1}(p) \subseteq R$.

Algorithm 2 provides a possible implementation for the query function compatible with the priority-promotion mechanism. Let $s \triangleq (r, p)$ be the current state. Line 1 simply computes the parity α of the priority to process in that state. Line 2, instead, computes in game ∂_s the attractor *w.r.t.* player α of the region contained in r at the current priority p. The resulting set R is, according to Proposition 2, an α-maximal α-region in ∂_s containing $r^{-1}(p)$.

Before continuing with the description of the implementation of the successor function, we need to introduce the notion of *best escape priority* for player $\overline{\alpha}$ *w.r.t.* an α-region R of the subgame ∂_s and a region function r in the whole game ∂. Informally, such a value represents the best priority associated with an α-region contained in r and reachable by $\overline{\alpha}$ when escaping from r. To formalise this concept, let $I \triangleq Mv_{\partial} \cap ((R \cap Ps_{\partial}^{\overline{\alpha}}) \times (\text{dom}(r) \setminus R))$ be the *interface relation* between R and r, *i.e.*, the set of $\overline{\alpha}$-moves exiting from R and reaching some position within a region recorded in r. Then, $\text{bep}_{\partial}^{\overline{\alpha}}(R, r)$ is set to the minimal priority among those regions containing positions reachable by a move in I. Formally, $\text{bep}_{\partial}^{\overline{\alpha}}(R, r) \triangleq \min(\text{rng}(r \restriction \text{rng}(I)))$. Note that, if R is a closed α-region in ∂_s, then $\text{bep}_{\partial}^{\overline{\alpha}}(R, r)$ is necessarily of parity α and greater than the priority p of R. This property immediately follows from the maximality of r above p in any state of the dominion space. Indeed, no move of an $\overline{\alpha}$-position can lead to a $\overline{\alpha}$-maximal $\overline{\alpha}$-region. For instance, in the example of Fig. 1, for 0-region $R = \{e, f, h\}$ with priority equal to 2 in column 6, we have that $I = \{(e, c), (h, b)\}$ and $r \restriction \text{rng}(I) = \{(c, 4), (b, 6)\}$. Hence, $\text{bep}_{\partial}^{1}(R, r) = 4$.

In the following, to reset the priority of some the positions in the game, after a promotion of a given region is performed, we define the *completing operator* $\uplus$ that, taken a partial function $f : A \rightharpoonup B$ and a total function $g : A \to B$, returns the total function $g \uplus f \triangleq (g \setminus \text{dom}(f)) \cup f : A \to B$. The result is equal to f on its domain and assumes the same values of g on the remaining part of the set A.

Algorithm 3 implements the successor function informally described

---

Algorithm 3. Successor Function.

signature $\downarrow_{\partial} : \succ_{\partial} \to \Delta_{\partial} \times Pr_{\partial}$
function $s \downarrow_{\partial} (R, \alpha)$
    let $(r, p) = s$ **in**
1   **if** $(R, \alpha) \in Rg_{\partial_s}^{-}$ **then**
2        $r^{\star} \leftarrow r[R \mapsto p]$
3        $p^{\star} \leftarrow \max(\text{rng}(r^{\star(<p)}))$
      else
4        $p^{\star} \leftarrow \text{bep}_{\partial}^{\overline{\alpha}}(R, r)$
5        $r^{\star} \leftarrow pr_{\partial} \uplus r^{(\geq p^{\star})}[R \mapsto p^{\star}]$
6   **return** $(r^{\star}, p^{\star})$

---

at the beginning of the section. Given the current state s and a compatible region pair (R, α) open in the whole game as inputs, it produces a successor state $s^\star \triangleq (r^\star, p^\star)$ in the dominion space. It first checks whether R is open also in the subgame ∂_s (Line 1). If this is the case, it assigns priority p to region R and stores it in the new region function $r^\star$ (Line 2). The new current priority $p^\star$ is, then, computed as the highest priority lower than p in $r^\star$ (Line 3). If, on the other hand, R is closed in ∂_s, a promotion merging R with some other α-region contained in r is required. The next priority $p^\star$ is set to the bep of R for player $\overline{\alpha}$ in the entire game ∂ $w.r.t.$ r (Line 4). Region R is, then, promoted to priority $p^\star$ and all the priorities below $p^\star$ in the current region function r are reset (Line 5). The correctness of this last operation follows from Proposition 1.

As already observed in Sect. 3, a dominion space, together with Algorithm 1, provides a sound and complete solution procedure. The following theorem states that the priority-promotion mechanism presented above is indeed a dominion space. The proof will be provided in the extended version of the paper.

Theorem 1 (Dominion Space). *For a game ∂, the structure $\mathcal{D}_\partial \triangleq \langle \partial, \mathcal{S}_\partial, \succ_\partial, \Re_\partial, \downarrow_\partial \rangle$, where $\mathcal{S}_\partial$ is given in Definition 4, $\succ_\partial$ is the relation of Definition 5, and $\Re_\partial$ and $\downarrow_\partial$ are the functions computed by Algorithms 2 and 3 is a dominion space.*

Complexity of* PP *Dominion Space. To conclude, we estimate the size and depth of dominion space $\mathcal{R}_\partial$. This provides upper bounds on both the time and space needed by the search procedure $\mathsf{src}_{\mathcal{R}_\partial}$ computing dominions. By looking at the definition of state space $\mathcal{S}_\partial$, it is immediate to see that, for a game ∂ with n positions and k priorities, the number of states is bounded by k^n. Indeed, there are at most k^n functions $r : \mathrm{Ps}_\partial \to \mathrm{Pr}_\partial$ from positions to priorities that can be used as region function of a state. Note that the associated current priority is uniquely determined by the content of the region function. Measuring the depth is a little trickier. A coarse bound can be obtained by observing that there is an homomorphism from $\mathcal{S}_\partial$ to the well-founded partial order, in which the region function r of a state is replaced by a partial function $f : \mathrm{Pr}_\partial \rightharpoonup [1, n]$ with the following properties: it assigns to each priority $p \in \mathrm{rng}(r)$ the size $f(p)$ of the associated region $r^{-1}(p)$. The order $(f_1, p_1) \prec (f_2, p_2)$ between two pairs is derived from the one on the states, by replacing $r_2^{-1}(q) \subset r_1^{-1}(q)$ with $f_2(q) < f_1(q)$. This homomorphism ensures that every chain in $\mathcal{S}_\partial$ corresponds to a chain in the new partial order. Moreover, there are exactly $\binom{n+k}{k}$ partial functions f such that $\sum_{p \in \mathrm{dom}(f)} f(p) \leq n$. Consequently, every chain cannot be longer than $\binom{n+k}{k} \leq \left(e(\frac{n}{k} + 1) \right)^k$, where e is the Euler constant. By further exploiting the structure of the space, one can obtain a recurrence relation expressing a slightly better upper bound, whose explicit solution is $3 \cdot \sum_{i=0}^{k-2} \binom{n-2}{i}$. Then, by applying a standard approximation via geometric series based on the inequality $\left(\frac{h-i}{n-h+i} \right)^i \leq \binom{m}{h-i} / \binom{m}{h} \leq \left(\frac{h}{n-h+1} \right)^i$, we derive the asymptotic bound stated by the following theorem. A formal account of the recurrence relation will be provided in the extended version of this article.

Theorem 2 (Size & Depth Upper Bounds). *The size of a PP dominion space $\mathcal{R}$ with $n \in \mathbb{N}_+$ positions and $k \in [1, n]$ priorities is bounded by k^n. Moreover, if $2 \leq k$, its depth is bounded by $3 \cdot \sum_{i=0}^{k-2} \binom{n-2}{i}$, which is less than $3\frac{n-k+1}{n-2k+3}\left(e\frac{n-2}{k-2}\right)^{k-2}$, if $k < n/2$, and less than $3(2^{n-2} - c(\frac{n-2}{k-2})^{k-2})$, for a constant $c > 0$, otherwise.*

Unfortunately, due to the reset operations performed after each promotion, an exponential worst-case can actually be built. Indeed, consider the game $\partial_{m,h}$ having all positions ruled by player 0 and containing h chains of length $2m + 1$ that converge into a single position of priority 0 with a self loop. The i-th chain has a head of priority $4k - i$ and a body composed of m blocks of two positions having priority $2i - 1$ and $2i$, respectively. The first position in each block also has a self loop. An instance of this game with $m = 2$ and $h = 4$ is depicted in Fig. 2. The labels of the positions correspond to the associated priorities and the highlighted area at the bottom of the figure groups together the last blocks of the chains. Intuitively, the execution depth of the PP dominion space for this game is exponential, since the consecutive promotion operations performed on each chain can simulate the increments of a counter up to m. Also, the priorities are chosen in such a way that, when the i-th counter is incremented, all the j-th counters with $j \in]i, h]$ are reset. Therefore, the whole game simulates a counter with h digits taking values from 0 to m. Hence, the overall number of performed promotions is $(m + 1)^h$. The search procedure on $\partial_{2,4}$ starts by building the four open 1-regions $\{15\}$, $\{13\}$, $\{11\}$, and $\{9\}$ and the open 0-region $\{8', 7'', 8''\}$, where we use apices to distinguish different positions with the same priority. This state represents the configuration of the counter, where all four digits are set to 0. The closed 1-region $\{7'\}$ is then found and promoted to 9. Consequently, the previously computed 0-region with priority 8 is reset and the new region is maximised to obtain the open 1-region $\{9, 7', 8'\}$. Now, the counter is set to 0001.

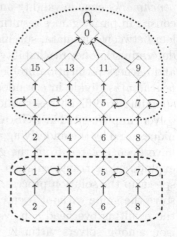

After that, the open 0-region $\{8''\}$ and the closed 1-region $\{7''\}$ are computed. The latter one is promoted to 9 and maximised to attract position 8''. This completes the 1-region containing the entire chain ending in 9. The value of the counter is now 0002. At this point, immediately after the construction of the open 0-region $\{6', 5'', 6''\}$, the closed 1-region $\{5'\}$ is found, promoted to 11, and maximised to absorb position 6'. Due to the promotion, the positions in the 1-region with priority 9 are reset to their original priority and all the work done to build it gets lost. This last operation represents the reset of the least significant digit of the counter, caused by the increment of the second one, *i.e.*, the counter displays 0010. Following similar steps, the process carries on until each chain is

Fig. 2. The $\partial_{2,4}^{PP}$ game.

grouped in a single region. The corresponding state represents the configuration of the counter in which all digits are set to m. Thus, after an exponential number promotions, the closed 0-region $\{0\}$ is eventually obtained as solution.

Theorem 3 (Execution-Depth Lower Bounds). *For all numbers $h \in \mathbb{N}$, there exists a PP dominion space $\mathcal{R}_h$ with $k = 2h + 1$ positions and priorities, whose execution depth is $3 \cdot 2^h - 2 = \Theta 2^{k/2}$. Moreover, for all numbers $m \in \mathbb{N}_+$, there exists a PP dominion space $\mathcal{R}_{m,h}$ with $n = (2m + 1) \cdot h + 1$ positions and $k = 3h + 1$ priorities, whose execution depth is $((3m+1) \cdot (m+1)^h - 1)/m - 2 = O\left((3n/(2(k-1)))^{k/3}\right).$*

Observe that, in the above theorem, we provide two different exponential lower bounds. The general one, with $k/3$ as exponent and a parametric base, is the result of the game $\partial_{m,h}$ described in the previous paragraph, where $k = 3h + 1$. The other bound, instead, has a base fixed to 2, but the worse exponent $k/2$. We conjecture that the given upper bound could be improved to match the exponent $k/2$ of this lower bound. In this way, we would obtain an algorithm with an asymptotic behaviour comparable with the one exhibited by the small-progress measure procedure [32]. This study will be further pursued in the extended version of the article.

5   Experimental Evaluation

In order to assess the effectiveness of the proposed approach, the new technique described above has been implemented in the tool PGSOLVER [28], which collects implementations of several parity game solvers proposed in the literature. This software framework, implemented in OCaml, also provides a benchmarking tool, which can generate different forms of parity games. The available benchmarks divide into concrete problems and synthetic ones. The *concrete benchmarks* encode validity and verification problems for temporal logics. They consist in parity games resulting from encodings of the language inclusion problem between automata, specifically a non-deterministic Büchi automaton and a deterministic one, reachability problems, namely the Tower of Hanoi problem, and fairness verification problems, the Elevator problem (see [28]). The *synthetic benchmarks* divide into randomly generated games and various families corresponding to difficult cases (clique and ladder-like games) and worst cases of the solvers implemented in PGSOLVER. To fairly compare the different solution techniques used by the underlying algorithms, the solvers involved in the experiments have been isolated from the generic solver implemented in PGSOLVER, which exploits game transformation and decomposition techniques in the attempt to speed up the solution process. However, those optimisations can, in some cases, solve the game without even calling the selected algorithm, and, in other cases, the resulting overhead can even outweigh the solver time, making the comparison among solvers virtually worthless [28]. Experiments were also conducted with different optimisations enabled and the results exhibit the same pattern emerging in the following experimental evaluation.

The algorithms considered in the experimentation are the Zielonka algorithm *Rec* [54], its two dominion decomposition variants, *Dom* [33,34] and *Big* [48], the strategy improvement algorithm *Str* [52], and the one proposed in this article, PP. Small progress measure [32] is not included, since it could not solve any of the tested benchmarks within the available computational resources[1].

Special Families. Table 2 displays the results of all the solvers involved on the benchmark families available in PGSOLVER. We only report on the biggest instances we could deal with, given the available computational resources[2]. The parameter Size refers to the number of positions in the games and the best performance are emphasised in bold. The first three rows consider

Table 2. Execution times in seconds on several benchmark families. Time out (†) is set to 600 s and memory out (‡) to 7.5 Gb.

Benchmark	Size	Dom	Big	Str	Rec	PP
Hanoi	6.3M	21.4	21.4	‡	17.4	**14.2**
Elevator	7.7M	†	‡	‡	‡	**43.3**
Lang. Incl	5M	†	‡	‡	145.5	**21.1**
Ladder	4M	†	‡	‡	35.0	**17.1**
Str. Imp	4.5M	81.0	82.8	†	71.0	**50.0**
Clique	8K	†	‡	†	†	**21.7**
MC. Lad	7.5M	†	‡	‡	**4.3**	6.5
Rec. Lad	50K	†	‡	**0.6**	‡	311.2
Jurdziński	40K	†	†	**188.2**	†	314.4

the concrete verification problems mentioned above. On the Tower of Hanoi problem all the solvers perform reasonably well, except for *Str* due its high memory requirements. The Elevator problem proved to be very demanding in terms of memory for all the solvers, except for our new algorithm and *Dom*, which, however, could not solve it within the time limit of 10 min. Our solver performs extremely well on both this benchmark and on Language Inclusion, which could be solved only by *Rec* among the other solvers. On the worst case benchmarks, it performs quite well also on Ladder, Strategy Improvement, and Clique, which proved to be considerably difficult for all the other solvers. It was outperformed only on the last three ones: the Modelchecker, the Recursive Ladder, and Jurdziński games. Despite this fact, the new solver exhibit the most consistent behaviour overall on these benchmarks. Indeed, in all those benchmarks, the priority promotion algorithm requires no promotions regardless of the input parameters, except for the elevator problem, where it performs only two promotions.

Random Games. Figure 3 compares the running times (left-hand side) and memory requirements (right-end side) of the new algorithm PP against *Rec* and *Str* on 2000 random games of size ranging from 5000 to 20000 positions and

---

[1] Experiments were carried out on a 64-bit 3.1 GHz INTEL® quad-core machine, with i5-2400 processor and 8 GB of RAM, running UBUNTU 12.04 with LINUX kernel version 3.2.0. PGSOLVER was compiled with OCaml version 2.12.1.

[2] The instances were generated with the following PGSOLVER commands: towersofhanoi 13, elevatorgame 8, langincl 500 100, laddergame 4000000, stratimprgen -pg friedmannsubexp 1000, modelcheckerladder 2500000, clique game 8000, recursiveladder 10000, and jurdzinskigame 100 100.

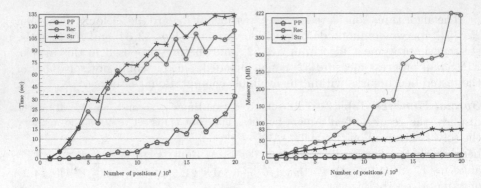

Fig. 3. Time and auxiliary memory on random games with 2 moves per position.

2 outgoing moves per position. Interestingly, these random games proved to be quite challenging for all the considered solvers. We set a time-out to 180 s (3 min). Both *Dom* and *Big* perform quite poorly on those games, hitting the time-out already for very small instances, and we decided to leave them out of the picture. The behaviour of the solvers is typically highly variable even on games of the same size and priorities. To summarise the results, the average running time on clusters of games seemed the most appropriate choice in this case. Therefore, each point in the graph shows the average time over a cluster of 100 different games of the same size: for each size value n, we chose a number $k = n \cdot i/10$ of priorities, with $i \in [1, 10]$, and 10 random games were generated for each pair of n and k. The new algorithm perform significantly better than the others on those games. The right-hand side graph also shows that the theoretical improvement on the auxiliary memory requirements of the new algorithm has a considerable practical impact on memory consumption compared to the other solvers. We also experimented on random games with a higher number of moves per position. The resulting games turn out to be much easier to solve for all the solvers. This behaviour might depend on the specific random generator provided by PGSOLVER. However, those experiments still show better performance by the new algorithm *w.r.t.* the competitor ones. Due to the space constraints, the corresponding results will be reported in the extended version of the paper.

6   Discussion

We considered the problem of solving *Parity Games*, a special form of infinite-duration games over graphs having relevant applications in various branches of Theoretical Computer Science. We proposed a novel solution technique, based on a *priority-promotion mechanism*. Based on this approach, a new solution algorithm have been presented and studied. We gave proofs of its correctness and provided an accurate analysis of its time and space complexities.

As far as time complexity is concerned, an exponential upper bound in the number of priorities has been given. A lower bound for the worst-case was also presented in the form of a family of parity games on which the new technique exhibits an exponential behaviour. On the bright side, the new solution exhibits the best space complexity among the currently known algorithms for parity games. In fact, we showed that the maximal additional space needed to solve a parity game is linear in the number of positions, logarithmic in the number of priorities, and independent from the number of moves in the game. This is an important result, in particular considering that in practical applications we often need to deal with games having a very high number of positions, moves, and, in some cases, priorities. Therefore, low space requirements are essential for practical scalability.

To assess the effectiveness of the new approach, experiments were carried out against concrete and synthetic problems. We compared the new algorithm with the state-of-the-art solvers implemented in PGSolver. The results are very promising, showing that the proposed approach is extremely effective in practice, often substantially better than existing ones. This suggests that the new approach is worth pursuing further. Therefore, we are currently investigating new and clever priority-promotion policies that try to minimise the number of region resets after a priority promotion.

It would be interesting to investigate the applicability of the priority promotion approach to related problems, such as *prompt-parity games* [42] and similar conditions [12,26,27], and even in wider contexts like *mean-payoff games* [13,16] and *energy games* [10,11].

References

1. Agrawal, M., Kayal, N., Saxena, N.: PRIMES is in P. Ann. Math. **160**(2), 781–793 (2004)
2. Alur, R., Henzinger, T., Kupferman, O.: Alternating-time temporal logic. JACM **49**(5), 672–713 (2002)
3. Apt, K., Grädel, E.: Lectures in Game Theory for Computer Scientists. Cambridge University Press, Cambridge (2011)
4. Benerecetti, M., Mogavero, F., Murano, A.: Substructure temporal logic. In: LICS 2013, pp. 368–377. IEEE Computer Society (2013)
5. Benerecetti, M., Mogavero, F., Murano, A.: Reasoning about substructures and games. TOCL **16**(3), 25:1–25:46 (2015)
6. Berwanger, D., Dawar, A., Hunter, P., Kreutzer, S.: DAG-width and parity games. In: Durand, B., Thomas, W. (eds.) STACS 2006. LNCS, vol. 3884, pp. 524–536. Springer, Heidelberg (2006)
7. Berwanger, D., Grädel, E.: Games and model checking for guarded logics. In: Nieuwenhuis, R., Voronkov, A. (eds.) LPAR 2001. LNCS (LNAI), vol. 2250, pp. 70–84. Springer, Heidelberg (2001)
8. Berwanger, D., Grädel, E.: Fixed-point logics and solitaire games. TCS **37**(6), 675–694 (2004)
9. Berwanger, D., Grädel, E., Kaiser, L., Rabinovich, R.: Entanglement and the complexity of directed graphs. TCS **463**, 2–25 (2012)
10. Chatterjee, K., Doyen, L.: Energy parity games. TCS **458**, 49–60 (2012)

11. Chatterjee, K., Doyen, L., Henzinger, T., Raskin, J.-F.: Generalized mean-payoff and energy games. In: FSTTCS 2010. LIPIcs, vol. 8, pp. 505–516. Leibniz-Zentrum fuer Informatik (2010)

12. Chatterjee, K., Henzinger, T., Horn, F.: Finitary winning in omega-regular games. TOCL **11**(1), 1:1–1:26 (2010)

13. Chatterjee, K., Henzinger, T., Jurdziński, M.: Mean-payoff parity games. In: LICS 2005, pp. 178–187. IEEE Computer Society (2005)

14. Chatterjee, K., Henzinger, T., Piterman, N.: Strategy Logic. IC **208**(6), 677–693 (2010)

15. Condon, A.: The complexity of stochastic games. IC **96**(2), 203–224 (1992)

16. Ehrenfeucht, A., Mycielski, J.: Positional strategies for mean payoff games. IJGT **8**(2), 109–113 (1979)

17. Emerson, E., Jutla, C.: Tree automata, mucalculus, and determinacy. In: FOCS 1991, pp. 368–377. IEEE Computer Society (1991)

18. Emerson, E.A., Jutla, C.S., Sistla, A.P.: On model-checking for fragments of μ-calculus. In: Courcoubetis, C. (ed.) CAV 1993. LNCS, vol. 697, pp. 385–396. Springer, Heidelberg (1993)

19. Emerson, E., Jutla, C., Sistla, A.: On model checking for the mucalculus and its fragments. TCS **258**(1–2), 491–522 (2001)

20. Emerson, E., Lei, C.-L.: Temporal reasoning under generalized fairness constraints. In: Monien, B., Vidal-Naquet, G. (eds.) STACS 1986. LNCS, vol. 210, pp. 267–278. Springer, Heidelberg (1986)

21. Fearnley, J.: Non-oblivious strategy improvement. In: Clarke, E.M., Voronkov, A. (eds.) LPAR-16 2010. LNCS, vol. 6355, pp. 212–230. Springer, Heidelberg (2010)

22. Fearnley, J., Lachish, O.: Parity games on graphs with medium tree-width. In: Murlak, F., Sankowski, P. (eds.) MFCS 2011. LNCS, vol. 6907, pp. 303–314. Springer, Heidelberg (2011)

23. Fearnley, J., Schewe, S.: Time and parallelizability results for parity games with bounded treewidth. In: Czumaj, A., Mehlhorn, K., Pitts, A., Wattenhofer, R. (eds.) ICALP 2012, Part II. LNCS, vol. 7392, pp. 189–200. Springer, Heidelberg (2012)

24. Fellows, M., Koblitz, N.: Self-witnessing polynomial-time complexity and prime factorization. In: CSCT 1992, pp. 107–110. IEEE Computer Society (1992)

25. Fellows, M., Koblitz, N.: Self-witnessing polynomial-time complexity and prime factorization. DCC **2**(3), 231–235 (1992)

26. Fijalkow, N., Zimmermann, M.: Cost-parity and cost-streett games. In: FSTTCS 2012. LIPIcs, vol. 18, pp. 124–135. Leibniz-Zentrum fuer Informatik (2012)

27. Fijalkow, N., Zimmermann, M.: Cost-parity and cost-streett games. LMCS **10**(2), 1–29 (2014)

28. Friedmann, O., Lange, M.: Solving parity games in practice. In: Liu, Z., Ravn, A.P. (eds.) ATVA 2009. LNCS, vol. 5799, pp. 182–196. Springer, Heidelberg (2009)

29. Grädel, E., Thomas, W., Wilke, T. (eds.): Automata, Logics, and Infinite Games: A Guide to Current Research. LNCS, vol. 2500. Springer, Heidelberg (2002)

30. Gurvich, V., Karzanov, A., Khachivan, L.: Cyclic games and an algorithm to find minimax cycle means in directed graphs. USSRCMMP **28**(5), 85–91 (1990)

31. Jurdziński, M.: Deciding the winner in parity games is in UP ∩ co-Up. IPL **68**(3), 119–124 (1998)

32. Jurdziński, M.: Small progress measures for solving parity games. In: Reichel, H., Tison, S. (eds.) STACS 2000. LNCS, vol. 1770, pp. 290–301. Springer, Heidelberg (2000)

33. Jurdziński, M., Paterson, M., Zwick, U.: A deterministic subexponential algorithm for solving parity games. In: SODA 2006, pp. 117–123. Society for Industrial and Applied Mathematics (2006)

34. Jurdziński, M., Paterson, M., Zwick, U.: A deterministic subexponential algorithm for solving parity games. SJM **38**(4), 1519–1532 (2008)

35. Klarlund, N., Kozen, D.: Rabin measures and their applications to fairness and automata theory. In: LICS 1991, pp. 256–265. IEEE Computer Society (1991)

36. Kupferman, O., Vardi, M.: Weak alternating automata and tree automata emptiness. In: STOC 1998, pp. 224–233. Association for Computing Machinery (1998)

37. Martin, A.: Borel determinacy. Ann. Math. **102**(2), 363–371 (1975)

38. Martin, A.: A purely inductive proof of borel determinacy. In: SPM 1982. Recursion Theory, pp. 303–308. American Mathematical Society and Association for Symbolic Logic (1985)

39. McNaughton, R.: Infinite games played on finite graphs. APAL **65**, 149–184 (1993)

40. Mogavero, F., Murano, A., Perelli, G., Vardi, M.Y.: What makes ATL* decidable? a decidable fragment of strategy logic. In: Koutny, M., Ulidowski, I. (eds.) CONCUR 2012. LNCS, vol. 7454, pp. 193–208. Springer, Heidelberg (2012)

41. Mogavero, F., Murano, A., Perelli, G., Vardi, M.: Reasoning about strategies: on the model-checking problem. TOCL **15**(4), 34:1–34:42 (2014)

42. Mogavero, F., Murano, A., Sorrentino, L.: On promptness in parity games. In: McMillan, K., Middeldorp, A., Voronkov, A. (eds.) LPAR-19 2013. LNCS, vol. 8312, pp. 601–618. Springer, Heidelberg (2013)

43. Mogavero, F., Murano, A., Vardi, M.: Reasoning About Strategies. In: FSTTCS 2010. LIPIcs, vol. 8, pp. 133–144. Leibniz-Zentrum fuer Informatik (2010)

44. Mostowski, A.: Regular expressions for infinite trees and a standard form of automata. In: Skowron, A. (ed.) SCT 1984. LNCS, vol. 208, pp. 157–168. Springer, Heidelberg (1984)

45. Mostowski, A.: Games with Forbidden Positions. University of Gdańsk, Gdańsk, Poland, Technical report (1991)

46. Obdržálek, J.: Fast mu-calculus model checking when tree-width is bounded. In: Hunt Jr., W.A., Somenzi, F. (eds.) CAV 2003. LNCS, vol. 2725, pp. 80–92. Springer, Heidelberg (2003)

47. Obdržálek, J.: Clique-width and parity games. In: Duparc, J., Henzinger, T.A. (eds.) CSL 2007. LNCS, vol. 4646, pp. 54–68. Springer, Heidelberg (2007)

48. Schewe, S.: Solving parity games in big steps. In: Arvind, V., Prasad, S. (eds.) FSTTCS 2007. LNCS, vol. 4855, pp. 449–460. Springer, Heidelberg (2007)

49. Schewe, S.: An optimal strategy improvement algorithm for solving parity and payoff games. In: Kaminski, M., Martini, S. (eds.) CSL 2008. LNCS, vol. 5213, pp. 369–384. Springer, Heidelberg (2008)

50. Schewe, S.: ATL* satisfiability is 2EXPTIME-complete. In: Aceto, L., Damgård, I., Goldberg, L.A., Halldórsson, M.M., Ingólfsdóttir, A., Walukiewicz, I. (eds.) ICALP 2008, Part II. LNCS, vol. 5126, pp. 373–385. Springer, Heidelberg (2008)

51. Schewe, S., Finkbeiner, B.: Satisfiability and finite model property for the alternating-Time μ-calculus. In: Ésik, Z. (ed.) CSL 2006. LNCS, vol. 4207, pp. 591–605. Springer, Heidelberg (2006)

52. Vöge, J., Jurdziński, M.: A discrete strategy improvement algorithm for solving parity games. In: Emerson, E.A., Sistla, A.P. (eds.) CAV 2000. LNCS, vol. 1855, pp. 202–215. Springer, Heidelberg (2000)

53. Wilke, T.: Alternating tree automata, parity games, and modal mu calculus. BBMS **8**(2), 359–391 (2001)
54. Zielonka, W.: Infinite games on finitely coloured graphs with applications to automata on infinite trees. TCS **200**(1–2), 135–183 (1998)
55. Zwick, U., Paterson, M.: The complexity of mean payoff games on graphs. TCS **158**(1–2), 343–359 (1996)

A Simple Algorithm for Solving Qualitative Probabilistic Parity Games

Ernst Moritz Hahn[1], Sven Schewe[2], Andrea Turrini[1], and Lijun Zhang[1(✉)]

[1] State Key Laboratory of Computer Science, Institute of Software,
CAS, Beijing, China
{hahn,zhanglj}@ios.ac.cn
[2] University of Liverpool, Liverpool, UK

Abstract. In this paper, we develop an approach to find strategies that guarantee a property in systems that contain controllable, uncontrollable, and random vertices, resulting in probabilistic games. Such games are a reasonable abstraction of systems that comprise partial control over the system (reflected by controllable transitions), hostile nondeterminism (abstraction of the unknown, such as the behaviour of an attacker or a potentially hostile environment), and probabilistic transitions for the abstraction of unknown behaviour neutral to our goals. We exploit a simple and only mildly adjusted algorithm from the analysis of non-probabilistic systems, and use it to show that the qualitative analysis of probabilistic games inherits the much celebrated sub-exponential complexity from 2-player games. The simple structure of the exploited algorithm allows us to offer tool support for finding the desired strategy, if it exists, for the given systems and properties. Our experimental evaluation shows that our technique is powerful enough to construct simple strategies that guarantee the specified probabilistic temporal properties.

1 Introduction

The automated synthesis of reactive protocols (strategies, policies) from temporal specifications has recently attracted considerable attention in numerous applications. Such a scenario can present both nondeterministic and probabilistic behaviours, so the resulting model can be seen as a Markov Decision Process (MDP) [31]. MDPs can also be viewed as $1\frac{1}{2}-player\ games$, where the full player decides which action to perform when resolving nondeterministic choices, and the $\frac{1}{2}$-player (or: random player) resolves the probabilistic choices.

This game can be enriched with a second player, e.g. an environment player, who controls some of the nondeterministic choices. Usually, the second player acts in a hostile manner: he tries to prevent the first (full) player from reaching her goal. The resulting game is known as a $2\frac{1}{2} - player\ game$. Examples of $2\frac{1}{2}$-player games are security and communication protocols [24,28,29,34,35] and robots playing in pursuit-evasion games [20].

A particular application in software engineering is the development of probabilistic reactive protocols and interfaces for probabilistic components. Such an

© Springer International Publishing Switzerland 2016
S. Chaudhuri and A. Farzan (Eds.): CAV 2016, Part II, LNCS 9780, pp. 291–311, 2016.
DOI: 10.1007/978-3-319-41540-6_16

interface would restrict the interactions a component offers to its environment. This technically corresponds to choosing a strategy for the component in a game with its environment, where the goal of the component is to satisfy its specification, while the goal of the environment is to violate it.

The contribution of this paper is to provide an efficient algorithm to synthesise strategies for the controllable player in $2\frac{1}{2}$-player games that are equipped with a *parity* winning condition. Parity conditions are very general winning conditions that can be used to represent all ω-regular properties. In particular, parity objectives contain temporal logics such as LTL (linear temporal logic [30]), which are useful in specifying system and program properties. Because of this, we can handle LTL with a probabilistic semantics, i.e. the qualitative fragment of PLTL [1], in our synthesis framework.

We focus on computing the regions of the game, in which one of the players is almost sure winning [9]. The algorithm from [9] is based on translating the stochastic parity game into a simple parity game [8] (a parity game without random vertices / a 2-player game) using a so called "gadget" construction, albeit to the cost of a blow-up by a factor linear in the number of priorities. For a small number of priorities, or colours, the complexity of this algorithm is better than the algorithm we suggest here, because solving the blown-up simple parity game with [21] or [32] provides better bounds. This advantage is, however, purely theoretical: even for non-stochastic parity games on which these algorithms can be applied directly without requiring a costly transformation, they do not perform well in practice [14], such that a nested fixed-point algorithm [13, 27] would be the natural choice for analysing the blown-up game.

Our algorithm is an adaptation of the classical nested fixed-point algorithm of McNaughton [13, 27] for the analysis of non-probabilistic systems. In particular, it does not involve a translation of the game. Thus, we avoid the practical problems existing algorithms with good complexity have [14]. The simple structure of the exploited algorithm also allows us to offer tool support by implementing a protocol synthesiser.

Present algorithms with the best theoretical complexity bounds for solving 2-player parity games with a low or fixed number of priorities are described in [21, 32]. However, the ranking based approach from [21] does not perform very well in practice [14], and the hybrid approach from [32] will inherit these practical draw-backs.

The direct algorithm we describe has exponential worst-case complexity. In the paper, we exploit the simple structure of our algorithm to lift the sub-exponential algorithm for 2-players games of Jurdiński, Paterson, and Zwick [22] to the qualitative analysis of $2\frac{1}{2}$-player games.

Related Work. There is a rich body of literature of algorithms for parity games in a two player setting [13, 21, 22, 27, 32, 36], and a few for multi player games with concurrent moves [3–5], in which players make simultaneous choices in every move. All of these algorithms share an $n^{\mathcal{O}(n)}$ running time.

Some experiments have suggested that the algorithm proposed in [13, 27, 36] performs best among them, in particular because it can be implemented

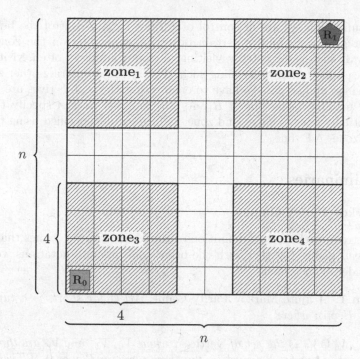

Fig. 1. Robot arena.

symbolically. In this paper, we are considering non-concurrent games. We have adjusted McNaughton's algorithm [13,27,36] for solving these $2\frac{1}{2}$-player games. Such games have also been considered in the literature, for instance in [2,6,9, 15,16]. Like 2-player games, they have pure memoryless optimal strategies.

Algorithms for solving probabilistic games have been implemented among others in PRISM-games [11]. This tool can, however, only handle a restricted class of properties, namely PCTL [19], which does not support nested temporal operators. As mentioned above, our approach can handle properties specified in the logics PLTL [1], as it translates such properties to parity objectives.

2   A Motivating Example

In a two-dimensional battlefield (cf. Fig. 1), there are two robots, R_0 and R_1, and four marked zones, $zone_1, \ldots, zone_4$. The battlefield is surrounded by a solid wall and has a square tiled floor of n fields in breadth and width. Each tile can be occupied by at most one robot. The robots act in strict alternation. When it is the turn of a robot, this robot can move as follows: decide a direction and move one field forward; decide a direction and attempt to move two fields forward. In the latter case, the robot moves two fields forward with a probability of 50 %, but only one field forward with a probability of 50 %. If the robot would run into a wall or into the other robot, it stops at the field before the obstacle.

We assume that we are in control of R_0 but cannot control the behaviour of R_1. Our goal is to fulfil a certain objective depending on the zones with probability 1, such as repeatedly visiting all zones infinitely often, visiting the zones in a specific order, performing such visits without entering other zones in the meanwhile, and so on. We have to ensure that these objectives are fulfilled under any possible behaviour of R_1. As an example, we can specify that the robot eventually reaches $zone_1$ and $zone_2$, which can be specified using the LTL formula $\mathbf{F}\, zone_1 \wedge \mathbf{F}\, zone_2$.

3   Preliminaries

3.1   Markov Parity Games

We now introduce the formal definition of the Markov parity games that model the $2\frac{1}{2}$-player games together with the other concepts and notations we use in the remainder of the paper.

Definition 1. *A finite Markov Parity Game, MPG for short, is a tuple* $\mathcal{P} = (V_0, V_1, V_r, E, \mathsf{pri})$, *where*

- $V = V_0 \cup V_1 \cup V_r$ *is the set of* vertices, *where* V_0, V_1, *and* V_r *are three finite disjoint sets of vertices owned by the three players: Player 0, Player 1, and Player random, respectively;*
- $E \subseteq V \times V$ *is a set of* edges *such that* (V, E) *is a* sinkless *directed graph, i.e. for each* $v \in V$ *there exists* $v' \in V$ *such that* $(v, v') \in E$; *and*
- $\mathsf{pri} \colon V \to \mathbb{N}$ *is the priority function mapping each vertex to a natural number. We call the image of* pri *the set of* priorities *(or:* colours*), denoted by* $\mathcal{C}$.

Note that, since the set of vertices V is finite, $\mathcal{C}$ is finite as well. For an MPG $\mathcal{P} = (V_0, V_1, V_r, E, \mathsf{pri})$, we call the tuple $\mathfrak{A} = (V_0, V_1, V_r, E)$ the *arena* of $\mathcal{P}$. For ease of notation, we sometimes use games when we refer to their arenas only. We also use the common intersection and subtraction operations on directed graphs for arenas and games: given an MPG $\mathcal{P}$ with arena $\mathfrak{A} = (V_0, V_1, V_r, E)$,

- $\mathcal{P} \cap V'$ denotes the Markov parity game $\mathcal{P}'$ we obtain when we restrict the arena $\mathfrak{A}$ to $\mathfrak{A} \cap V' = (V_0 \cap V', V_1 \cap V', V_r \cap V', E \cap (V' \times V'))$.
- $\mathcal{P} \setminus V'$ denotes the Markov parity game $\mathcal{P}'$ with arena $\mathfrak{A} \setminus V' = \mathfrak{A} \cap (V \setminus V')$, where $V = V_0 \cup V_1 \cup V_r$.

Note that the result of such an intersection may or may not be sinkless. While we use these operations freely in intermediate constructions, we make sure that, wherever they are treated as games, they have no sinks (cf. Lemma 4).

Plays. One can view the dynamics of a parity game as a board game, played by moving a pebble over the game arena. When the pebble is on a vertex v, the next vertex v' is chosen by the player owning the vertex v, that is, by Player 0 if $v \in V_0$, by Player 1 if $v \in V_1$, and by Player random if $v \in V_r$. The respective player chooses a proper successor v' of v, i.e. a vertex v' with $(v, v') \in E$, and pushes the pebble forward to v'. This way, they together construct an infinite play. If $V_0 = \emptyset$ or $V_1 = \emptyset$, we arrive at the model of *Markov decision processes* (MDPs).

A *play* is an infinite sequence $\pi = v_0 v_1 v_2 v_3 \ldots$ such that $(v_i, v_{i+1}) \in E$ for all $i \in \mathbb{N}$. Each play is evaluated by the lowest priority that occurs infinitely often. Player 0 wins a play $\pi = v_0 v_1 v_2 v_3 \ldots$ if the lowest priority that occurs infinitely often in the sequence $\mathsf{pri}(v_0)\mathsf{pri}(v_1)\mathsf{pri}(v_2)\mathsf{pri}(v_3)\ldots$, $\mathsf{pri}(\pi) = \liminf_{i \to \infty} \mathsf{pri}(v_i)$ is even, while Player 1 wins if $\mathsf{pri}(\pi)$ is odd. Below, we formalise *winning strategies* and *winning regions* for a given MPG:

Definition 2. *For a given MPG $\mathcal{P}$, we say*

- *For $\sigma \in \{0, 1\}$, a strategy f_σ of Player σ is a mapping $f_\sigma \colon V_\sigma \to V$ from the vertices of Player σ to their successor states, i.e. for each $v \in V_\sigma$, $(v, f_\sigma(v)) \in E$. A play $\pi = v_0 v_1 v_2 v_3 \ldots$ is called f_σ-conform if, for all $i \in \mathbb{N}$, if $v_i \in V_\sigma$, then $v_{i+1} = f_\sigma(v_i)$. A strategy f_σ for the player σ defines an MDP, namely the MDP where each vertex $v \in V_\sigma$ has exactly one successor, $f_\sigma(v)$.*
- *Given a vertex $v \in V$, a strategy f_0 for Player 0 is called v-winning if, starting from v, Player 0 wins almost surely in the MDP defined by f_0; a strategy f_1 for Player 1 is called v-winning if, starting from v, Player 1 wins with non-zero probability in the MDP defined by f_1, that is, Player 1 does not lose almost surely in the MDP defined by f_1.*
- *For $\sigma \in \{0, 1\}$, a vertex v in V is v-winning for Player σ if Player σ has a v-winning strategy f_σ. We call the set of v-winning vertices for Player σ the winning region of Player σ, denoted W_σ.*

As we concentrate on finding almost surely winning/losing regions, it suffices to assume that there is an $\varepsilon > 0$, such that all choices of Player random are made with probability of at least ε. We therefore omit the probabilities in our model.

4 McNaughton's Algorithm and Memoryless Determinacy

In this section, we adjust the classic algorithm for solving 2-player parity games to Markov parity games. The classic algorithm dates back to McNaughton [27] and was first published in this form by Emerson and Lei [13] and Zielonka [36].

The algorithm is the algorithmic version of a simple proof of the memoryless determinacy for parity games. The proof uses an inductive argument over the number of vertices. As an induction basis, games with only one game vertex are clearly memoryless determined: there is only one strategy, and it is memoryless. The game is won by Player 0 if the priority of this vertex is even and by Player 1 if the priority of this vertex is odd. We provide an algorithm for determining where Player 0 wins almost surely, i.e. its winning region W_0. Similarly, we compute the winning region W_1, in which Player 1 wins with non-zero probability. Adjusting it to finding sure winning sets for Player 1 is straight forward.

Procedure $prob-McNaughton(\mathcal{P})$: $(\mathcal{P} = (V_0, V_1, V_r, E, \mathsf{pri}))$

1. <u>if</u> $V = \emptyset$ <u>then</u> <u>return</u> $(\emptyset, \emptyset)$ (note that $V = V_0 \cup V_1 \cup V_r$)
2. set c to the minimal priority occurring in $\mathcal{P}$
3. <u>if</u> the image of pri is even <u>then</u> <u>return</u> $(V, \emptyset)$
4. <u>if</u> the image of pri is odd <u>then</u> <u>return</u> $(\emptyset, V)$
5. <u>if</u> c is even <u>then</u>
   (a) set W_1 to $\emptyset$
   (b) <u>repeat</u>
       i. set $\mathcal{P}'$ to $\mathcal{P} \setminus \mathsf{satr}_0(\mathsf{pri}^{-1}(c), \mathcal{P})$
       ii. set (W_0', W_1') to $prob-McNaughton(\mathcal{P}')$
       iii. <u>if</u> $W_1' = \emptyset$ <u>then</u>
            A. set W_0 to $V \setminus W_1$
            B. <u>return</u> (W_0, W_1)
       iv. set W_1 to $W_1 \cup \mathsf{satr}_1(W_1', \mathcal{P})$
       v. set $\mathcal{P}$ to $\mathcal{P} \setminus \mathsf{satr}_1(W_1', \mathcal{P})$
6. set W_0 to $\emptyset$
7. <u>repeat</u>
   (a) set $\mathcal{P}'$ to $\mathcal{P} \setminus \mathsf{satr}_1(\mathsf{pri}^{-1}(c), \mathcal{P})$
   (b) set (W_0', W_1') to $prob-McNaughton(\mathcal{P}')$
   (c) <u>if</u> $W_0' = \emptyset$ <u>then</u>
       i. set W_1 to $V \setminus W_0$
       ii. <u>return</u> (W_0, W_1)
   (d) set W_0 to $W_0 \cup \mathsf{watr}_0(W_0', \mathcal{P})$
   (e) set $\mathcal{P}$ to $\mathcal{P} \setminus \mathsf{watr}_0(W_0', \mathcal{P})$
       adding a sink vertex reachable from the random vertices adjacent to W_0 (cf. Lemma 7); this sink is a technicality and does not count when we check $W_0' = \emptyset$ in line 7.c

Fig. 2. The algorithm $prob-McNaughton(\mathcal{P})$ returns the ordered pair (W_0, W_1) of winning regions of Player 0 and Player 1, respectively. V and pri denote the states and the priority function of the parity game $\mathcal{P}$.

Lemma 1. *If, for a game* $(V_0, V_1, V_r, E, \mathsf{pri})$, *the image of* pri *consists only of even priorities, then Player 0 wins (surely) from all vertices, and* $W_0 = V$.

If, for a game $(V_0, V_1, V_r, E, \mathsf{pri})$, *the image of* pri *consists only of odd priorities, then Player 1 wins (surely) from all vertices, and* $W_1 = V$.

For general parity games $\mathcal{P}$ with lowest priority c, our adjustment of the McNaughton's algorithm, the procedure '$prob-McNaughton$' shown in Fig. 2, first determines the set $\mathsf{pri}^{-1}(c)$ of vertices with priority c, i.e. the vertices with minimal priority. If c is even, then Player 0 wins on all plays, where c occurs infinitely often. The algorithm then constructs the region, from which Player 1 cannot almost surely avoid to reach a vertex with priority c. This is obtained using attractors.

4.1   Attractors

Attractors are usually defined for classical 2-player games. For an arena $\mathfrak{A} = (V_0, V_1, E)$, a set $T \subseteq V$ of target vertices, and a player $\sigma \in \{0, 1\}$, the $\sigma-$ *attractor of* T is the set of game vertices from which Player σ can force the pebble into the set T of target vertices. The σ-attractor A of a set T can be defined as the least fixed point of sets that contain T and that contain a vertex v of Player σ if it contains some successor of v and a vertex v of Player $1 - \sigma$ if it contains all the successors of v. Equivalently, the σ-attractor $\sigma-Attractor(T, \mathfrak{A})$ of T in the arena $\mathfrak{A}$ can be defined as $A = \bigcup_{j \in \mathbb{N}} A_j$ where

$$A_0 = T,$$
$$A_{j+1} = A_j \cup \{ v \in V_\sigma \mid \exists v' \in A_j . (v, v') \in E \}$$
$$\cup \{ v \in V_{1-\sigma} \mid \forall (v, v') \in E . v' \in A_j \}.$$

This definition also provides a memoryless strategy for Player σ to move the pebble to T from all vertices in A: for a vertex $v \in A$, there is a minimal $i \in \mathbb{N}$ such that $v \in A_i$. For $i > 0$ (i.e. for $v \notin T$) and $v \in V_\sigma$, v has a successor in A_{i-1}, and Player σ can simply choose such a successor. (For $v \in V_{1-\sigma}$, all successors are in A_{i-1}.) Likewise, A itself provides a memoryless strategy to keep the pebble out of A (and hence out of T) for Player $1 - \sigma$ when starting from a vertex $v \notin A$, namely to never enter A.

For $2\frac{1}{2}$-player games, we distinguish two different types of attractors: strong attractors, where the random player co-operates with the player σ who wants to push the pebble into the target set (denoted $\mathsf{satr}_\sigma(T, \mathcal{P})$ when Player σ tries to move the pebble to T in the arena of $\mathcal{P}$); and weak attractors, where the target needs to be reached almost surely. (The 'strong' and 'weak' in their names are inspired by $\mathsf{satr}_\sigma(T, \mathcal{P}) \supseteq \mathsf{watr}_\sigma(T, \mathcal{P})$, which makes the first attractor stronger.) Note that the principle of the attractor construction is not affected by the co-operation for the strong attractor: we simply treat the random vertices as vertices of player σ and apply the normal attractor construction from 2-player games.

Lemma 2. *For an arena $\mathfrak{A}$ and a set T of target states, the strong σ-attractor of T can be constructed in time linear in the edges of $\mathfrak{A}$.*

The construction of weak attractors is more complex since it requires solving a singly nested fixed-point. Consider an MPG $\mathcal{P}$, a set $T \subseteq V$, and the player σ; the weak σ-attractor $\mathsf{watr}_\sigma(T, \mathcal{P})$ of the set T is defined as follows:

$$S_0 = \mathsf{satr}_\sigma(T, \mathcal{P}),$$
$$C_j = \mathsf{satr}_{1-\sigma}(V \setminus S_j, \mathcal{P} \setminus T),$$
$$S_{j+1} = \mathsf{satr}_\sigma(T, \mathcal{P} \setminus C_j),$$
$$\mathsf{watr}_\sigma(T, \mathcal{P}) = \bigcap_{j \in \mathbb{N}} S_j.$$

As a singly nested fixed point, constructing weak attractors can be reduced to solving Büchi games, which can be done in $O(n^2)$ time [7]. (We have implemented the classic $O(m \cdot n)$ iterated fixed point algorithm.)

Lemma 3. *For an arena $\mathfrak{A}$ and a set T of target states, the weak σ-attractor of T can be constructed in time quadratic in the states of $\mathfrak{A}$.*

Note that the co-games of attractors are proper games: they have no sinks.

Lemma 4. *For an arena $\mathfrak{A}$ and a set T of target states, $\mathfrak{A}' = \mathfrak{A} \setminus \mathsf{satr}_\sigma(T, \mathfrak{A})$ and $\mathfrak{A}'' = \mathfrak{A} \setminus \mathsf{watr}_\sigma(T, \mathfrak{A})$ are arenas for $\sigma \in \{0, 1\}$.*

For strong attractors, this is because every vertex in $(V_\sigma \cup V_r) \setminus \mathsf{satr}_\sigma(T, \mathfrak{A})$ has the same successors in $\mathfrak{A}'$ and $\mathfrak{A}$, while every vertex in $V_{1-\sigma} \setminus \mathsf{satr}_\sigma(T, \mathfrak{A})$ has some successor in $\mathfrak{A}'$. For weak attractors, every vertex in $V_\sigma \setminus \mathsf{watr}_\sigma(T, \mathfrak{A})$ has the same successors in $\mathfrak{A}''$ and $\mathfrak{A}$, while every vertex in $(V_{1-\sigma} \cup V_r) \setminus \mathsf{watr}_\sigma(T, \mathfrak{A})$ has some successor in $\mathfrak{A}'$.

4.2 Traps and Paradises

After constructing $A = \mathsf{satr}_{c_{\min} \bmod 2}(\mathsf{pri}^{-1}(c_{\min}), \mathcal{P})$, the co-game $\mathcal{P}' = \mathcal{P} \setminus A$ of $\mathcal{P}$ is solved.

A $\sigma - trap$ $T_\sigma \subseteq V$ is a set of vertices Player σ cannot force to leave, not even with some probability greater than 0 (she is trapped there). A set T_σ is a σ-trap if it is the co-set of a strong σ-attractor, i.e. if it satisfies $V \setminus T_\sigma = \mathsf{satr}_\sigma(V \setminus T_\sigma, \mathcal{P})$.

The co-game $\mathcal{P}'$ is smaller than $\mathcal{P}$: compared to $\mathcal{P}$, it has less vertices. By induction hypothesis, it is therefore memoryless determined. By induction over the size of the game, $\mathcal{P}'$ can therefore be solved by a recursive call of the algorithm.

The following picture shows how the first part of the algorithm works. We first determine the minimal priority in the game (line 2 of $prob{-}McNaughton$). Let $c := c_{\min}$ denote the minimal priority, and select the target to be $T = \mathsf{pri}^{-1}(c)$, shown as the solid green area in the top right corner. We then construct the respective strong attractor $A = \mathsf{satr}_\sigma(T, \mathcal{P})$ with $\sigma = c \bmod 2$, shown as T plus the NE hatched part around T, and consider the co-game $\mathcal{P}'$ (lines 5.b.i and 7.a of $prob{-}McNaughton$).

We then solve $\mathcal{P}'$, resulting in the winning regions $W'_{1-\sigma}$, shown in solid red, and W'_σ, the green SW hatched part below (lines 5.b.ii and 7.b of the procedure $prob{-}McNaughton$) (Fig. 3).

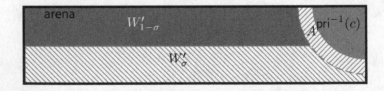

Fig. 3. First part of the algorithm; c is the minimal priority and $\sigma = c \bmod 2$

We fix the target set T. We call a subset $P_0 \subseteq W_0$ of the winning region of Player 0 a 0-*paradise* if it is a 1-trap and Player 0 has a memoryless strategy f, which is v-winning for all $v \in P_0$ in the game $\mathcal{P} \cap P_0$, such that P_0 cannot be left in any f-conform play.

We call a subset $P_1 \subseteq W_1$ of the winning region of Player 1 a 1-*paradise* if Player 1 has a memoryless strategy f, which is v-winning for all vertices $v \in P_1$, such that the probability measure of the plays π with odd $\mathrm{pri}(\pi)$ that never leave P_1 is non-zero for all vertices in P_1. (Note that it suffices for this property to define f on P_1.) In particular, all vertices in $v \in P_1$ are v-winning for Player 1.

Returning to the picture, $W'_{1-\sigma}$—the solid red area—is a $(1-\sigma)$-paradise for the game $\mathcal{P}$.

Lemma 5. *For a parity game $\mathcal{P}$ with a σ-trap T_σ and a $(1-\sigma)$-paradise $W_{1-\sigma}$ of $\mathcal{P}' = \mathcal{P} \cap T_\sigma$, $W_{1-\sigma}$ is a $(1-\sigma)$-paradise for $\mathcal{P}$.*

The lemma is obvious: Player $1-\sigma$ can simply use the same winning strategy f for $\mathcal{P}$ as for $\mathcal{P}'$ on T_σ: as T_σ is a σ-trap, neither Player σ nor Player random have additional moves in $\mathcal{P}$, and every f-conform play that starts in $W_{1-\sigma}$ in $\mathcal{P}$ is also an f-conform play in $\mathcal{P}'$. The winning region $W'_{1-\sigma}$ of $\mathcal{P}'$ is therefore a $(1-\sigma)$-paradise in $\mathcal{P}$.

This property can be easily extended to paradises using attractor operations (strong attractor for player odd and weak attractor for player even):

Lemma 6. *The strong 1-attractor $A = \mathrm{satr}_1(P_1, \mathcal{P})$ of a 1-paradise P_1 for a parity game $\mathcal{P}$ is a 1-paradise for $\mathcal{P}$, and the weak 0-attractor $A = \mathrm{watr}_0(P_0, \mathcal{P})$ of a 0-paradise P_0 for a parity game $\mathcal{P}$ is a 0-paradise for $\mathcal{P}$. A winning strategy for the respective player σ on A can be composed of the winning strategy for Player σ on P_σ and an attractor strategy on $A \setminus P_\sigma$.*

As a result, for a given 0-paradise P_0 for Player 0 in a parity game $\mathcal{P}$, we can reduce solving $\mathcal{P}$ to computing the weak 0-attractor $A = \mathrm{watr}_0(P_0, \mathcal{P})$ of P_0, and solving $\mathcal{P} \setminus A$.

Lemma 7. *Let $\mathcal{P}$ be a parity game, P_0 be a 0-paradise with weak 0-attractor $A = \mathrm{watr}_0(P_0, \mathcal{P})$, and W'_0 and W'_1 be the winning regions of Player 0 and Player 1, respectively, on $\mathcal{P}'$, which is obtained from the game $\mathcal{P}'' = \mathcal{P} \setminus A$ by adding a random vertex s, a sink with a self-loop and even priority, which is reachable from the random vertices that have (in the parity game $\mathcal{P}$) a successor in A. Then*

- $W_1 = W'_1$ *is the winning region of Player 1 on $\mathcal{P}$, and he can win by following his winning strategy from $\mathcal{P}'$ on his winning region, and*
- $W_0 = W'_0 \cup A \setminus \{s\}$ *is the winning region of Player 0 and she can win by following her winning strategy for A on A and her winning strategy from $\mathcal{P}'$ on W'_0.*

Proof. Player 0 wins with her strategy from every vertex in A by a composition of the attractor strategy on $A \setminus P_0$ and her winning strategy on P_0 by Lemma 6.

Let g_0 be a winning strategy for Player 0 on W'_0 in $\mathcal{P}'$. Consider a probability distribution on $\mathcal{P}'$ that summarises the probabilities to transfer to A in each situation to the same probability to transfer to s, and a fixed counter strategy f

of her opponent. As the likelihood of winning is 1 after transferring to A (with the strategy from above by Lemma 6) in $\mathcal{P}$ and in $\mathcal{P}'$ (as all plays that reach s are winning), the chance of winning is equal in both cases. Vertices in $W_0' \setminus \{s\}$ are therefore winning for the composed strategy.

Similarly, let g_1 be a winning strategy for Player 1 on W_1' in $\mathcal{P}'$. We consider a probability distribution on $\mathcal{P}'$ that summarises the probabilities to transfer to A in each situation to the same probability to transfer to s, and a fixed counter strategy f of his opponent. Estimating the chance of winning to 0 after reaching A results in the same likelihood of winning in $\mathcal{P}$ and $\mathcal{P}'$. As this is larger than 0, Player 1 wins with an extension of the same strategy on his winning region.   □

For our implementation, we have, instead of adding a sink with even priority, reduced the priority of all random vertices having s as successor to 0 (it could be set to any other even priority not greater than any priority of the vertices in $\mathcal{P} \setminus A$). This change is safe to implement: both players have the same memoryless strategies as in the game with the additional edges. Assume the players play according to fixed memoryless strategies f (Player 0) and g (Player 1), such that only stochastic decisions are left open. Player 0 will win almost surely from a vertex v if, and only if, for all leaf SCCs reachable from v the minimal priority among all priorities of the states in this leaf SCC is even. The leaf SCCs reachable from a vertex v other than the singleton leaf SCC $\{s\}$ from Lemma 7 are exactly those leaf SCCs reachable after re-prioritising, that do not contain a vertex whose priority is changed to 0. Thus, the same leaf SCCs with minimal odd priority are reachable. Consequently, the same vertices in A are winning for Player 0 (and for Player 1) in both constructions.

Corollary 1. *Let $\mathcal{P}$ be a parity game, P_0 be a 0-paradise with weak 0-attractor $A = \mathsf{watr}_0(P_0, \mathcal{P})$, and W_0' and W_1' be the winning regions of Player 0 and Player 1, respectively, on $\mathcal{P}'$, which is obtained from the game $\mathcal{P}'' = \mathcal{P} \setminus A$ by changing the priority of the random vertices that have (in the parity game $\mathcal{P}$) a successor in A to 0. Then*

- $W_1 = W_1'$ *is the winning region of Player 1 on $\mathcal{P}$, and he can win by following his winning strategy from $\mathcal{P}'$ on his winning region, and*
- $W_0 = W_0' \cup A \setminus \{s\}$ *is the winning region of Player 0 and she can win by following her winning strategy for A on A and her winning strategy from $\mathcal{P}'$ on W_0'.*

Note that this change of priority is, like adding the sink s, introduced recursively on a level in the call tree. While it is inherited in calls from there, the changes introduced in a level of the call tree (in line 7.e) are revoked when returning the values (in line 7.c.ii).

For a given 1-paradise P_1 for Player 1 in a parity game $\mathcal{P}$, we can reduce the qualitative analysis of a parity game $\mathcal{P}$ to computing the *strong* 1-attractor $A = \mathsf{satr}_1(P_1, \mathcal{P})$ of P_1, and solving $\mathcal{P} \setminus A$.

Lemma 8. *Let $\mathcal{P}$ be a parity game, P_1 be a 1-paradise with winning strategy f_1 and strong 1-attractor $A = \mathsf{satr}_1(P_1, \mathcal{P})$, and W_0' and W_1' be the winning regions of Player 0 and Player 1, respectively, on $\mathcal{P}' = \mathcal{P} \setminus A$. Then*

– $W_1 = W_1' \cup A$ is the winning region of Player 1 on $\mathcal{P}$, and he can win by following his winning strategy for A on A and his winning strategy g_1 from $\mathcal{P}'$ on W_1', and
– $W_0 = W_0'$ is the winning region of Player 0, and she can win by following her winning strategy g_0 from $\mathcal{P}'$ on W_0.

Proof. Player 0 wins with her winning strategy, g_0, on her complete winning region W_0 of $\mathcal{P} \setminus A$, since Player 1 has no additional choices in W_0 in $\mathcal{P}$. Consequently, the set of g_0-conform plays in $\mathcal{P}$ that start in W_0 coincides with the set of g_0-conform plays (with the same probability distribution on them) in $\mathcal{P} \setminus A$ that start in W_0.

Similarly, Player 1 wins with his strategy from every vertex in A, by a composition of his attractor strategy on $A \setminus P_1$ and his winning strategy f_1 on P_1 by Lemma 6.

Let g_1 be a winning strategy for Player 1 in $\mathcal{P}'$. Then every g_1-conform play in $\mathcal{P}$ that starts in a vertex in W_1' either eventually reaches A, and is then almost surely followed by a tail (remainder of the play) in $\mathcal{P}$ that starts in A, which is winning for Player 1 with a likelihood strictly greater than 0 by Lemma 6; or it stays for ever in the sub-game $\mathcal{P}'$. But these plays are also won by Player 1 with a non-zero likelihood. $\square$

We now distinguish two cases: firstly, if $W_{1-\sigma}'$ is non-empty, we can reduce solving $\mathcal{P}$ to constructing the weak or strong, respectively, $(1-\sigma)$-attractor $U_{1-\sigma}$ of $W_{1-\sigma}'$, and solving the co-game $\mathcal{P}'' = \mathcal{P} \setminus U_{1-\sigma}$ by Lemma 7 or 8, respectively. The co-game $\mathcal{P}''$ is simpler than $\mathcal{P}$: compared to $\mathcal{P}$, it contains less vertices (though not necessarily less priorities). By induction over the size of the game, $\mathcal{P}''$ can therefore be solved by a recursive call of the algorithm.

The figure below aligns this to our algorithm. We have seen that $W_{1-\sigma}'$ from the previous picture, shown again in solid red, is a $(1-\sigma)$-paradise, and so is its (weak or strong) $(1-\sigma)$-attractor $U_{1-\sigma}$ (the complete red area, full and hatched). It is constructed in lines 5.b.iv and 7.d, respectively, of *prob−McNaughton* (Fig. 4).

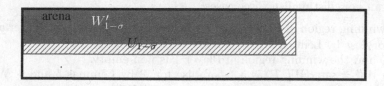

Fig. 4. Attractor of the player $1 - \sigma$ where c is the minimal priority and $1 - \sigma = c$ mod 2

Secondly, if $W_{1-\sigma}'$ is empty, we can compose the winning strategy for Player σ on $\mathcal{P}'$ with his attractor strategy for $\mathrm{pri}^{-1}(c)$ to a winning strategy on $\mathcal{P}$.

Lemma 9. *Let $\mathcal{P}$ be a parity game with minimal priority c, $\sigma = c \bmod 2$ be the player who wins if c occurs infinitely often, A be the strong σ-attractor of $\mathrm{pri}^{-1}(c)$, and f be an attractor strategy for Player σ on her vertices on $A \setminus \mathrm{pri}^{-1}(c)$. If Player σ has a winning strategy f' for every vertex in $\mathcal{P}' = \mathcal{P} \setminus A$, then f and f' can be composed to a winning strategy for Player σ for every vertex in $\mathcal{P}$.*

Proof. Let g be a strategy for Player σ that agrees with f and f' on their respective domain. We distinguish two types of g-conform plays: those that eventually stay in $\mathcal{P}'$, and those that visit A infinitely often. The latter plays almost surely contain infinitely many vertices with priority c and are therefore almost surely winning for Player σ. Games that eventually stay in $\mathcal{P}'$ consist of a finite prefix, followed by an f'-conform play in $\mathcal{P}'$. The lowest priority occurring infinitely often is therefore almost surely even for $\sigma = 0$ and odd with a likelihood strictly greater than 0 for $\sigma = 1$, respectively.   □

Theorem 1. *For each parity game $\mathcal{P} = (V_0, V_1, V_r, E, \mathrm{pri})$, the game vertices are partitioned into a winning region W_0 of Player 0 and a winning region W_1 of Player 1. Moreover, Player 0 and Player 1 have memoryless strategies that are v-winning for every vertex v in their respective winning region.*

In the following proof, we do not count the sink that is added by Lemma 7.

Proof. Games with a single vertex are trivially won by the player winning on the priority of this vertex (induction basis).

For the induction step, assume that the memoryless determinacy holds for games with up to n vertices. For a parity game with $n + 1$ vertices, we can then select the lowest priority $c_{\min}$, set σ to $c_{\min} \bmod 2$ to identify the Player σ who wins if $c_{\min}$ occurs infinitely often (note that $c_{\min}$ is the dominating priority in this case), and set $A = \mathrm{satr}_\sigma(\mathrm{pri}^{-1}(c_{\min}), \mathcal{P})$.

Then $\mathcal{P}' = \mathcal{P} \setminus A$ is a—possibly empty—parity game with strictly less states and priorities. (Note that, by the attractor construction, every vertex in $\mathcal{P}'$ has a successor, and the co-set of A is a σ-trap.)

By induction hypothesis, $\mathcal{P}'$ vertices are partitioned into winning regions of the two players, and both players have memoryless winning strategies on their winning regions.

We can now distinguish three cases:

1. The winning region of Player $1 - \sigma$ on $\mathcal{P}'$ is empty. In this case, Player σ wins memoryless by Lemma 9.
2. $\sigma = 0$ and the winning region of Player 1 is non-empty.
   Then $W_1'' = \mathrm{satr}_1(W_1', \mathcal{P})$ is a 1-paradise for $\mathcal{P}$ by Lemmas 5 and 6. We can therefore solve the remainder of the game, $\mathcal{P} \setminus W_1''$, individually and use the respective winning regions and (by induction) memoryless winning strategies of the players by Lemma 8.
3. $\sigma = 1$ and the winning region of Player 0 is non-empty.
   Then $W_0'' = \mathrm{watr}_0(W_1', \mathcal{P})$ is a 0-paradise for $\mathcal{P}$ by Lemmas 5 and 6. We can therefore solve the remainder of the game, $\mathcal{P} \setminus W_0''$, individually and use the respective winning regions and (by induction) memoryless winning strategies of the players by Lemma 7.

In case (1) we are done, in (2), (3) we reduced the problem to solving games with less states. By induction, memoryless determinacy extends to the complete game.   □

The worst case running time of this extension to McNaughton's algorithm [13, 27, 36] (cf. Procedure $prob-McNaughton$ of Fig. 2) occurs if $U_{1-\sigma}$ is always small and exactly one vertex with minimal priority c belongs to $U_{1-\sigma}$. For parity games with c priorities, n vertices, and m edges, the adjusted algorithm based on McNaughton's requires $\mathcal{O}\left(m \cdot \left(\frac{n}{c} + 1\right)^{c-1}\right)$ steps when the highest priority of the game is even, like McNaughton's algorithm itself [13, 36]: the cost of the attractor constructions is always dominated by the cost of the recursive calls, and the complexity analysis is the same.

When the highest priority is odd, the higher complexity for the weak attractor construction leads to a $\mathcal{O}\left(\left(\frac{n}{c} + 1\right)^{c+1}\right)$ complexity, and to an $\mathcal{O}\left(m \cdot \left(\frac{n}{c} + 1\right)^{c}\right)$ complexity of our implementation, due to the cost of constructing weak attractors of $\mathcal{O}(n^2)$ and $\mathcal{O}(m \cdot n)$ in our implementation, respectively. (The only point where this complexity is not dominated by other steps is when only the highest and the second highest priority are left. When the second highest priority is even, only strong attractors are used.)

The presented algorithm has a theoretical drawback: its running time is exponential in the number of priorities, which in turn can be as high as the number of states. For parity games without random vertices, the development of a deterministic subexponential algorithm [22] was considered a breakthrough, which also led to better bounds for games with a small number of priorities [32].

Theorem 2. *Parity games with n vertices can be solved in time $n^{\mathcal{O}(\sqrt{n})}$.*

The proof is completely analogously to the one from [22]. It uses the fact that the proofs do not rely on the way intermediate paradises are constructed. It is therefore possible to try out all small sets of vertices (i.e. all sets of vertices up to size $\sqrt{n}$) and check if they are paradises for the player who loses on the minimal priority. This can be done using brute force and takes $n^{\mathcal{O}(\sqrt{n})}$ time. Afterwards, one builds their union, computes the attractor for the set obtained this way, and performs a recursive call to decide the remaining game.

The progress obtained in one step, consisting of trying out all small sets of vertices, followed by a recursive call, is therefore at least $\sqrt{n}$ – unless the call returns an empty set, in which case we are finished. This provides a call tree of size $n^{\mathcal{O}(\sqrt{n})}$, with cost $n^{\mathcal{O}(\sqrt{n})}$ on each node of the call tree, such that the total cost is $n^{\mathcal{O}(\sqrt{n})} \cdot n^{\mathcal{O}(\sqrt{n})} = n^{\mathcal{O}(\sqrt{n})}$.

5   Implementation and Experimental Results

5.1   Overview of the Algorithm

We have written a prototypical implementation for the approach of this paper. In Fig. 5, we sketch how we analyse properties of formal models. Our tool reads

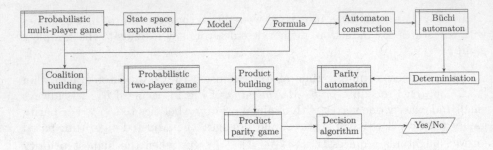

Fig. 5. Overview of the algorithm

a model specification in the input language of the probabilistic model checker PRISM-games [11]. This input language is an extension of probabilistic guarded-commands language of the probabilistic model checker PRISM [25]. We extend the recent probabilistic model checker IscasMC [17,18] that also supports this language. Each state of the model semantics is assigned to a specific player. When being in a state, a player can choose from several guarded commands. In each state, the player controlling this state can choose to execute one of the commands the guard of which is valid in the state. Afterwards, one of the possible effects of the command is chosen according to the probability of this effect. The next state is decided according to this effect. The models specified in this way may contain more than two players, and they do not contain any winning condition.

The property specification we use in our tool is also inspired by PRISM-games [11]. Its general form is $\langle\langle coalition\rangle\rangle\mathcal{P}_{\geq 1}[\phi]$. Here, coalition is a subset of the players from the model specification, and $\mathcal{P}_{\geq 1}[\phi]$ is a qualitative probabilistic LTL formula. This formula requires that the coalition of the players of coalition (by subsuming all of them into a single player) can enforce that ϕ holds with probability 1 under all possible behaviours of the players not in coalition. Variants like $\langle\langle coalition\rangle\rangle\mathcal{P}_{>0}[\phi]$ requiring only positive probability can be computed by minor adaptation of our algorithm.

To obtain the actual parity game to apply our algorithm on we proceed as follows. We first construct the explicit-state semantics of the model originally given in the high-level input language of PRISM-games. This semantics is thus a probabilistic multi-player game without a winning condition. Then, in this semantics we subsume the players of coalition to the single even player and the remaining players to the odd player, so as to obtain a probabilistic two-player game, still without a winning condition. We then transform ϕ into a generalised Büchi automaton using the tool SPOT [12]. Afterwards, we transform the Büchi into a deterministic parity automaton, using the algorithm from [33]. Simultaneously, we build a product of the model with this parity automaton, so as to fix the winning condition according to the property we want to decide. This on-the-fly approach allows us to only construct the states of the parity automaton which will actually be needed to construct the product. A state of this product is thus a tuple of a state from the two-player model and a state of the parity automaton.

The algorithm from [33] produces automata whose priorities are on the transitions (rather than on states). The product we produce is however a state-labelled parity game as in Definition 1: when building the product of the model with the automaton, the current state fixes the successor transition of the deterministic parity automaton. Therefore, we can label the product state with the priority of this successor transition. The first component of the successor states consists of a successor state of the model state. The second one consists of the single successor state of the parity automaton.

Finally, we can apply the algorithm discussed on the resulting MPG and decide whether all initial states of the product are winning, which means deciding whether the specification holds for all initial states of the model. If it does, we also obtain a winning strategy.

As stated before, the mutually optimal strategies are memoryless. However, this only holds for the game we are computing strategies for. If we map back these strategies to the original PRISM-games model, indeed memory might be required. This is because we have to remember the current state of the parity automaton with which the model had been composed to obtain the product on which we finally apply our algorithm.

5.2   Robots

Reconsider our robot example introduced in Sect. 2. We have applied our tool to construct the state-space of several instantiations of this model which we have modelled in the input language of PRISM-games. The machine we used is a 3.6 GHz Intel Core i7-4790 with 16 GB 1600 MHz DDR3 RAM of which 12 GB assigned to the tool; the timeout has been set to 30 min. In Table 1 we provide for each size "n" of the battlefield we consider, the number of vertices of the corresponding multiplayer game ("vertices") and the time in seconds required to construct it ("t_{constr}").

We remark that the constructed game encodes the behaviour of the robots on the battlefield without winning conditions, i.e. without considering the formula to be checked; as seen, the state-space contains millions of vertices for larger battlefield sizes n (it grows with $\mathcal{O}(n^4)$). Note that we cannot compare to PRISM-games because it does not support general PLTL formulas, and we are not aware of other tools to compare with.

We have applied our tool on a number of properties that require the robot R_0 to visit the different zones in a certain order. In Table 2 we report the

Table 1. Arena construction

n	Vertices	t_{constr}
12	370 656	1
16	1 175 040	3
20	2 872 800	6
24	5 961 600	13
28	11 049 696	25
32	18 855 936	47
36	30 209 760	69
40	46 051 200	112

performance measurements for these properties. In the column "property" we state the PLTL formula we consider, column "n" states the width of the battlefield instance, and "sat" shows whether the formula is satisfied. For the "game

Table 2. Robots analysis: different reachability properties

Property	n	sat	Game construction			Gadget construction		Solving time		
			vertices	colours	t_{prod}	vertices	t_{gadg}	t_{gMcN}	t_{gJur}	t_{pMcN}
Reachability	12	true	1 324 704	2	2	5 351 584	3	0	4	0
	16	true	4 418 592	2	9	17 996 832	13	3	24	1
$\langle\langle R_0 \rangle\rangle \mathcal{P}_{\geq 1}$	20	true	11 050 656	2	22	45 166 752	28	8	84	3
[**F** zone$_1$	24	true	23 211 552	2	51	95 045 152	58	18	219	7
$\wedge$**F** zone$_2$]	28	true	43 334 304	2	102	177 634 464	115	35	–MO–	14
	32	true	74 294 304	2	197	-	–MO–	-	-	24
	36	-	-	-	–MO–	-	-	-	-	-
	40	-	-	-	–MO–	-	-	-	-	-
Repeated	12	true	1 324 704	2	2	6 010 528	3	1	5	0
Reachability	16	true	4 418 592	2	9	20 085 792	15	3	25	1
	20	true	11 050 656	2	20	50 273 952	29	9	85	3
$\langle\langle R_0 \rangle\rangle \mathcal{P}_{\geq 1}$	24	true	23 211 552	2	44	105 643 552	59	21	227	8
[**GF** zone$_1$	28	true	43 334 304	2	88	197 278 368	121	38	–MO–	15
$\wedge$**GF** zone$_2$	32	true	74 294 304	2	180	-	–MO–	-	-	27
$\wedge$**GF** zone$_3$	36	-	-	-	–MO–	-	-	-	-	-
$\wedge$**GF** zone$_4$]	40	-	-	-	–MO–	-	-	-	-	-
Repeated	12	true	693 048	5	0	4 009 976	2	0	3	0
Ordered	16	true	2 264 184	5	3	13 206 072	9	2	16	0
Reachability	20	true	5 611 320	5	6	32 844 792	17	6	50	1
	24	true	11 729 784	5	14	68 787 512	62	13	129	4
$\langle\langle R_0 \rangle\rangle \mathcal{P}_{\geq 1}$	28	true	21 836 088	5	27	128 198 136	69	24	282	7
[**GF**(zone$_1 \wedge$	32	true	37 367 928	5	54	219 543 096	135	–MO–	–MO–	13
F zone$_2$)]	36	true	59 984 184	5	65	-	–MO–	-	-	21
	40	true	91 564 920	5	121	-	–MO–	-	-	36
Reach-avoid	12	true	1 616 400	4	2	7 656 720	4	1	–TO–	0
	16	true	5 452 848	4	14	25 820 208	15	6	–TO–	1
$\langle\langle R_0 \rangle\rangle \mathcal{P}_{\geq 1}$	20	true	13 703 184	4	35	64 877 328	33	19	–TO–	5
[$\neg$zone$_1$ **U** zone$_2$	24	true	28 855 728	4	79	136 606 128	116	40	–TO–	11
$\wedge\neg$zone$_4$ **U** zone$_2$	28	true	53 951 760	4	171	255 402 000	135	–MO–	–MO–	21
$\wedge\neg$zone$_4$ **U** zone$_1$	32	true	92 585 520	4	323	-	–MO–	-	-	38
$\wedge$**F**zone$_4$]	36	-	-	-	–MO–	-	-	-	-	-
	40	-	-	-	–MO–	-	-	-	-	-

construction" part, we present the number of "vertices" of the resulting MPG, the number of "colours", and the time "t_{prod}" required to generate the MPG. The construction of [8] to turn a stochastic parity game into a non-stochastic parity game replaces each stochastic node by a so-called "gadget", which consists of a combination of player odd and even nodes. Applying this construction thus leads to a game which can be solved using existing methods, although at the cost of increasing the number of vertices and the time to perform the transformation. The "gadget construction" part of the table shows the total number of "vertices" after applying this construction and the time "t_{gadg}" spent to do so.

Finally, the "solving time" part shows the time spent by the specific solvers: t_{gMcN} and t_{gJur} correspond to the gadget construction solved by using the classical non-stochastic McNaughton and Jurdziński approach, respectively, while t_{pMcN} refers to our *prob−McNaughton* algorithm proposed in Fig. 2. Note that these times represent only the actual time spent by the solver on the final MPG.

Entries marked by "–TO–" and "–MO–" mean that the corresponding phase has failed by time-out or has gone out of memory; entries marked by "-" mean that the phase has not been executed due to a failure in a previous phase.

The results show that our approach can be used to solve games with several million vertices, even though it is currently only implemented as an explicit-state solver. In particular, the part of the process that consumes the largest share of time is not the solution algorithm itself, but the preprocessing steps: most of the time was spent on constructing the product of the battlefield and the parity automaton. The largest amount of time spent in the solver was 38 s for a parity game with more than 90 million vertices. Despite the exponential complexity of the algorithm, our prototype performs quite well on the large state-spaces of this model. One reason is that the maximal number of different priorities seen was just 5, and the implementation was often able to use the lines 3 and 4 of the algorithm $prob-McNaughton$ in Fig. 2 to terminate the construction quickly. Indeed, we did not see more than 5 recursive calls of the algorithm. It is worthwhile to remark that, even if all properties are satisfied, not all vertices are winning for the robot R_0: for instance, for the reach-avoid property, around $1/3$ of the vertices are winning for the robot R_1; R_0 is anyway able to avoid such vertices and win with probability 1.

In comparison, the solution methods based on the gadget construction have an additional phase that takes quite some time and memory to be completed, so this affects their performances as they have to work on much larger games. While the classical non-stochastic McNaughton algorithm has a reasonable performance on these games, it still consumes much more resources than our approach $prob-McNaughton$. Jurdziński's approach turns out to be really slow in practice, confirming the previous results of [14]. As the results in the table show, our approach really outperforms the methods based on gadget construction: for instance for the reach-avoid property for $n = 24$, our approach takes only 11 seconds instead of 40 (plus 79 for the gadget construction) taken by the classical McNaughton and the time-out of 30 min by the Jurdziński algorithm.

5.3   Two Investors

As a further small case study, which provides similar results regarding the performance of the Jurdziński theoretical better algorithm, we consider an example originally from [26] in the version of [10]. In this version of the model, there are two investors, who are able to make investments in *futures*. Buying a future means to reserve an amount of company shares at a certain point of time and will be delivered at a later point of time to the market price the share has then. In this version of the model, there are three players: investor 1, investor 2, and the market. We considered a number of properties for which we provide results in Table 3; the meaning of the formulas is as follows:

1. Investor 1 is able to ensure (against the market and the other investor) that the share has eventually a value of at least 5 without ever stopping to invest.
2. She can ensure that the share repeatedly has a value of 5.

3. She can guarantee a permanent value of at least 5.
4. She can ensure that the probability of this event is non-zero.
5. If all players collaborate, this event is certain.

The parity game constructed to decide these properties contains less than 1.5 million vertices. Therefore, the time to decide the properties is also almost negligible: all experiments have taken a total of one or two seconds to complete, except for the Jurdziński approach that went time-out on all except one property.

Table 3. Two investors analysis.

	Property	sat	Game construction			Gadget construction		Solving time		
			vertices	colours	t_{prod}	vertices	t_{gadg}	t_{gMcN}	t_{gJur}	t_{pMcN}
1	$\langle\langle investor_1 \rangle\rangle \mathcal{P}_{\geq 1}$ $[\mathbf{G}\neg done_1 \wedge \mathbf{F}$ $v \geq 5]$	true	410 531	4	0	1 001 645	1	0	–TO–	0
2	$\langle\langle investor_1 \rangle\rangle \mathcal{P}_{\geq 1}$ $[\mathbf{G}\neg done_1 \wedge$ $\mathbf{GF}v \geq 5]$	false	410 531	4	0	1 265 755	1	0	–TO–	0
3	$\langle\langle investor_1 \rangle\rangle \mathcal{P}_{\geq 1}$ $[\mathbf{G}\neg done_1 \wedge$ $\mathbf{FG}v \geq 5]$	false	413 171	5	0	1 486 783	1	0	–TO–	0
4	$\langle\langle investor_1 \rangle\rangle \mathcal{P}_{>0}$ $[\mathbf{G}\neg done_1 \wedge$ $\mathbf{FG}v \geq 5]$	true	413 171	5	0	1 486 783	1	0	0	0
5	$\langle\langle investor_1,$ $investor_2,$ $market \rangle\rangle \mathcal{P}_{\geq 1}$ $[\mathbf{G}\neg done_1 \wedge$ $\mathbf{FG}v \geq 5]$	false	413 171	5	0	1 486 783	1	0	–TO–	0

6   Conclusions and Future Work

We have introduced a simple and effective algorithm for solving Markov games with a parity winning condition and implemented the algorithm as an explicit-state prototype as an extension of the model checker IscasMC [17,18]. The algorithm has proven to be capable of handling rather large examples, obtaining strategies that almost surely obtain their goal or demonstrating that such strategies do not exist. This is a very encouraging result for the automated construction of simple probabilistic reactive protocols, as they are already used in leader election problems.

The construction of such protocols is already difficult for deterministic systems, and new protocols (as well as the old ones) had been discovered when they had been recently synthesised [23]. Some complicated programming problems like mutual exclusion, leader election, and variations thereof, have complete specifications. Yet, they are very difficult to implement, e.g. due to problems arising through context switches. While such problems have proven to be difficult to implement for human developers due to parallelism and nondeterminism in traditional systems, allowing for randomness does—while potentially simplifying the algorithm—add another layer of difficulty for the human developer. We believe that this establishes the need for synthesis techniques, and in this light it is a very good news that the solution we have developed in this paper shows potential. In future work, we will extend this efficient technique to the quantitative analysis of systems.

Acknowledgement. This work is supported by the National Natural Science Foundation of China (Grants No. 61472473, 61532019, 61550110249, 61550110506), by the National 973 Program (No. 2014CB340701), by the CDZ project CAP (GZ 1023), by the Chinese Academy of Sciences Fellowship for International Young Scientists, by by the CAS/SAFEA International Partnership Program for Creative Research Teams, and by the Engineering and Physical Sciences Research Council (EPSRC) through grant EP/M027287/1 (Energy Efficient Control).

References

1. Bianco, A., de Alfaro, L.: Model checking of probabilistic and nondeterministic systems. In: Thiagarajan, P.S. (ed.) FSTTCS 1995. LNCS, vol. 1026, pp. 499–513. Springer, Heidelberg (1995)
2. Chatterjee, K.: Stochastic ω-regular games. Ph.D. thesis, University of California at Berkeley (2007)
3. Chatterjee, K.: Qualitative concurrent parity games: bounded rationality. In: Baldan, P., Gorla, D. (eds.) CONCUR 2014. LNCS, vol. 8704, pp. 544–559. Springer, Heidelberg (2014)
4. Chatterjee, K., de Alfaro, L., Henzinger, T.A.: Strategy improvement for concurrent reachability games. In: QEST, pp. 291–300. IEEE Computer Society (2006)
5. Chatterjee, K., de Alfaro, L., Henzinger, T.A.: Qualitative concurrent parity games. ACM Trans. Comput. Log. **12**(4), 28 (2011)
6. Chatterjee, K., Doyen, L., Gimbert, H., Oualhadj, Y.: Perfect-information stochastic mean-payoff parity games. In: Muscholl, A. (ed.) FOSSACS 2014 (ETAPS). LNCS, vol. 8412, pp. 210–225. Springer, Heidelberg (2014)
7. Chatterjee, K., Henzinger, M.: An $O(n^2)$ time algorithm for alternating Büchi games. In: SODA, pp. 1386–1399. SIAM (2012)
8. Chatterjee, K., Jurdziński, M., Henzinger, T.A.: Simple stochastic parity games. In: Baaz, M., Makowsky, J.A. (eds.) CSL 2003. LNCS, vol. 2803, pp. 100–113. Springer, Heidelberg (2003)
9. Chatterjee, K., Jurdziński, M., Henzinger, T.A.: Quantitative stochastic parity games. In: SODA 2004, pp. 121–130 (2004)
10. Chen, T., Forejt, V., Kwiatkowska, M.Z., Parker, D., Simaitis, A.: Automatic verification of competitive stochastic systems. Formal Methods Syst. Des. **43**(1), 61–92 (2013)
11. Chen, T., Forejt, V., Kwiatkowska, M., Parker, D., Simaitis, A.: PRISM-games: a model checker for stochastic multi-player games. In: Piterman, N., Smolka, S.A. (eds.) TACAS 2013 (ETAPS 2013). LNCS, vol. 7795, pp. 185–191. Springer, Heidelberg (2013)
12. Duret-Lutz, A.: LTL translation improvements in Spot. In: VECoS, pp. 72–83 (2011)

13. Emerson, E.A., Lei, C.: Efficient model checking in fragments of the propositional μ-calculus. In: Proceedings of LICS, pp. 267–278. IEEE Computer Society Press (1986)
14. Friedmann, O., Lange, M.: Solving parity games in practice. In: Liu, Z., Ravn, A.P. (eds.) ATVA 2009. LNCS, vol. 5799, pp. 182–196. Springer, Heidelberg (2009)
15. Gawlitza, T.M., Seidl, H.: Games through nested fixpoints. In: Bouajjani, A., Maler, O. (eds.) CAV 2009. LNCS, vol. 5643, pp. 291–305. Springer, Heidelberg (2009)
16. Gimbert, H., Zielonka, W.: Perfect information stochastic priority games. In: Arge, L., Cachin, C., Jurdziński, T., Tarlecki, A. (eds.) ICALP 2007. LNCS, vol. 4596, pp. 850–861. Springer, Heidelberg (2007)
17. Hahn, E.M., Li, G., Schewe, S., Turrini, A., Zhang, L.: Lazy probabilistic model checking without determinisation. In: CONCUR. LIPIcs, vol. 42, pp. 354–367 (2015)
18. Hahn, E.M., Li, Y., Schewe, S., Turrini, A., Zhang, L.: ISCASMc: a web-based probabilistic model checker. In: Jones, C., Pihlajasaari, P., Sun, J. (eds.) FM 2014. LNCS, vol. 8442, pp. 312–317. Springer, Heidelberg (2014)
19. Hansson, H., Jonsson, B.: A logic for reasoning about time and reliability. FAC 6(5), 512–535 (1994)
20. Hespanha, J.P., Kim, H.J., Sastry, S.: Multiple-agent probabilistic pursuit-evasion games. In: CDC, pp. 2432–2437 (1999)
21. Jurdziński, M.: Small progress measures for solving parity games. In: Reichel, H., Tison, S. (eds.) STACS 2000. LNCS, vol. 1770, pp. 290–301. Springer, Heidelberg (2000)
22. Jurdziński, M., Paterson, M., Zwick, U.: A deterministic subexponential algorithm for solving parity games. SIAM J. Comput. 38(4), 1519–1532 (2008)
23. Katz, G., Peled, D.A.: Genetic programming and model checking: synthesizing new mutual exclusion algorithms. In: Cha, S.S., Choi, J.-Y., Kim, M., Lee, I., Viswanathan, M. (eds.) ATVA 2008. LNCS, vol. 5311, pp. 33–47. Springer, Heidelberg (2008)
24. Kremer, S., Raskin, J.: A game-based verification of non-repudiation and fair exchange protocols. J. Comput. Secur. 11(3), 399–430 (2003)
25. Kwiatkowska, M., Norman, G., Parker, D.: PRISM 4.0: verification of probabilistic real-time systems. In: Gopalakrishnan, G., Qadeer, S. (eds.) CAV 2011. LNCS, vol. 6806, pp. 585–591. Springer, Heidelberg (2011)
26. McIver, A., Morgan, C.: Results on the quantitative mu-calculus qMu. ACM Trans. Comput. Logic 8(1) (2007). Article No.3
27. McNaughton, R.: Infinite games played on finite graphs. Ann. Pure Appl. Logic 65(2), 149–184 (1993)
28. Park, T., Shin, K.G.: Lisp: a lightweight security protocol for wireless sensor networks. ACM Trans. Embed. Comput. Syst. 3, 634–660 (2004)
29. Perrig, A., Szewczyk, R., Wen, V., Culler, D., Tygar, J.D.: SPINS: Security protocols for sensor networks. Wirel. Netw. 189–199 (2001)
30. Pnueli, A.: The temporal logic of programs. In: Proceedings of FOCS, pp. 46–57. IEEE Computer Society Press (1977)
31. Puterman, M.L.: Markov Decision Processes: Discrete Stochastic Dynamic Programming. Wiley, New York (1994)
32. Schewe, S.: Solving parity games in big steps. In: Arvind, V., Prasad, S. (eds.) FSTTCS 2007. LNCS, vol. 4855, pp. 449–460. Springer, Heidelberg (2007)

33. Schewe, S., Varghese, T.: Tight bounds for the determinisation and complementation of generalised Büchi automata. In: Chakraborty, S., Mukund, M. (eds.) ATVA 2012. LNCS, vol. 7561, pp. 42–56. Springer, Heidelberg (2012)
34. van der Hoek, W., Wooldridge, M.: Model checking cooperation, knowledge, and time - a case study. Res. Econ. **57**(3), 235–265 (2003)
35. Wu, L., Su, K., Chen, Q.: Model checking temporal logics of knowledge and its application in security verification. In: Hao, Y., Liu, J., Wang, Y.-P., Cheung, Y., Yin, H., Jiao, L., Ma, J., Jiao, Y.-C. (eds.) CIS 2005. LNCS (LNAI), vol. 3801, pp. 349–354. Springer, Heidelberg (2005)
36. Zielonka, W.: Infinite games on finitely coloured graphs with applications to automata on infinite trees. TCS **200**(1–2), 135–183 (1998)

Limit-Deterministic Büchi Automata for Linear Temporal Logic

Salomon Sickert[(✉)], Javier Esparza, Stefan Jaax, and Jan Křetínský

Technische Universität München, Munich, Germany
sickert@in.tum.de

Abstract. Limit-deterministic Büchi automata can replace deterministic Rabin automata in probabilistic model checking algorithms, and can be significantly smaller. We present a direct construction from an LTL formula φ to a limit-deterministic Büchi automaton. The automaton is the combination of a non-deterministic component, guessing the set of eventually true **G**-subformulas of φ, and a deterministic component verifying this guess and using this information to decide on acceptance. Contrary to the indirect approach of constructing a non-deterministic automaton for φ and then applying a semi-determinisation algorithm, our translation is compositional and has a clear logical structure. Moreover, due to its special structure, the resulting automaton can be used not only for qualitative, but also for quantitative verification of MDPs, using *the same* model checking algorithm as for deterministic automata. This allows one to reuse existing efficient implementations of this algorithm without any modification. Our construction yields much smaller automata for formulas with deep nesting of modal operators and performs at least as well as the existing approaches on general formulas.

1   Introduction

Translating Linear Temporal Logic (LTL) formulas into ω-automata is a fundamental problem of formal verification, which has been studied in depth. In the automata-theoretic approach to model checking, after computing the automaton for a formula one constructs its product with the state space of the system under consideration and analyses it. Since the product has up to $N \cdot m$ states, where N and m are the number of states of the system and the automaton, respectively, and typically $N \gg m$, it is important to construct automata as small as possible: even a small reduction of m can lead to a much larger reduction of $N \cdot m$.

Since non-deterministic ω-automata are typically much smaller than deterministic ones, for standard LTL model checking one translates formulas into non-deterministic Büchi automata. However, this is no longer possible for probabilistic model checking, and the standard approach is to use deterministic Rabin

Electronic supplementary material The online version of this chapter (doi:10. 1007/978-3-319-41540-6_17) contains supplementary material, which is available to authorized users.

S. Chaudhuri and A. Farzan (Eds.): CAV 2016, Part II, LNCS 9780, pp. 312–332, 2016.
DOI: 10.1007/978-3-319-41540-6_17

automata (DRA) instead—this is for instance the approach of the PRISM tool [3,22]. Translations of LTL into DRA have been thoroughly studied. Classical translations take a detour through Büchi automata as intermediate step [24–26], while more recent ones are direct translations [11,19].

It has been known for a long time that automata for probabilistic verification do not need to be fully deterministic: the automata-theoretic approach still works if *restricted* forms of non-determinism are allowed. For probabilistic verification of Markov chains one can use unambiguous Büchi automata (separated UBA [7], or even non-separated UBA [2]). The translation from LTL to separated UBA involves a single exponential blowup, while the translation to DRA is known to be double exponential. However, UBA cannot be used for the verification of Markov Decision Processes (MDPs). For qualitative verification of MDPs[1] one can use *limit-deterministic* Büchi automata (LDBA) [6,27] (also known as *semi-deterministic* or *deterministic-in-the-limit*). For quantitative verification of MDPs, limit-deterministic automata are not sufficient in general. However, recently [14], a more complex algorithm for probabilistic model checking was presented, considering products of the system and its parts with several different automata, including LDBA.

The translation LTL→LDBA is double exponential, and so in principle as expensive as the translation to DRA in the worst case. However, it is easy to find examples where the LDBA is much smaller than the DRA; in particular, in [16] it is shown that the LTL$_{\backslash \mathbf{GU}}$ fragment of LTL can be translated to LDBAs with a single-exponential blowup, while the translation to DRA is still double exponential. Further, efficient procedures for LDBA complementation exist [4].

In this paper, we give a compositional translation from *full* LTL to LDBAs, based on the one from LTL to DRAs recently presented in [11]. We then show that, due to the special form of the resulting LDBAs, the translation can also be used for *quantitative* model checking of MDPs, and in fact by means of *the same algorithm* as for DRAs. That is, in order to compute the maximal probability that an MDP M satisfies a formula φ we can just construct the product of M and the LDBA for φ obtained by our translation, and compute the maximal probability of reaching an accepting end component [3].

The translation of [11] becomes much simpler with LDBAs as target, instead of DRAs. In order to check if a word w satisfies a formula φ, our LDBAs use their restricted non-determinism to guess the set of **G**-subformulas of φ that are eventually satisfied by w (i.e., the subformulas $\mathbf{G}\varphi$ such that $w \models \mathbf{FG}\psi$), and the point at which all these subformulas have already become true. At this point the LDBA enters its deterministic component to check that the guess is correct, and that $w \models \varphi$ holds under the assumption that the guess is correct. We show that our translation produces LDBA of at most double exponential size, and exhibit a family of LTL formulas for which the smallest LDBA reaches this double exponential bound.

We conclude the paper with an experimental evaluation of an implementation of our construction on a large set of benchmarks. We compare the size of the generated LDBA with the size of the DRA provided by the Rabinizer tool, the DRA constructed by LTL2DSTAR, and the LDBA produced by the procedure of

---

[1] Recall that qualitative verification checks if the property holds with probability 1.

[6]: translate the formula into a Büchi automaton, apply the translation of Büchi automata to LDBA described in [6], and simplify the result. For the comparison we use the LTL3BA tool [1] and SPOT [8].

Outline. Sections 2 and 3 contain preliminaries. Section 4 presents an intuitive overview of the translation by means of an example. Section 5 formally defines the translation, Sect. 6 describes several optimisations, and Sect. 7 gives the complexity bounds. Quantitative verification is discussed in Sect. 8. Experimental results are presented in Sect. 9. Section 10 concludes and discusses future work.

2   Preliminaries

2.1   Linear Temporal Logic

We use a slightly unusual syntax for LTL. We consider formulas without negations and without the *Release* operator $\mathbf{R}$— the dual of the *Until* operator $\mathbf{U}$— but with both $\mathbf{F}$ and $\mathbf{G}$. Formulas in the usual syntax are transformed into equivalent formulas in our syntax by pushing negations inside, and—in the absence of $\mathbf{R}$—using the equivalence $\neg(\varphi\mathbf{U}\psi) = (\neg\psi\mathbf{U}(\neg\psi \wedge \neg\varphi)) \vee \mathbf{G}\neg\psi$. This may cause the formula to grow exponentially, when formulas are represented by their syntax trees. However, if they are represented by their syntax DAGs, then the transformation only causes a linear blowup.

Definition 1 (LTL). *A formula of LTL in* negation normal form *is given by the syntax:*

$$\varphi ::= \mathbf{tt} \mid \mathbf{ff} \mid a \mid \neg a \mid \varphi \wedge \varphi \mid \varphi \vee \varphi \mid \mathbf{X}\varphi \mid \mathbf{F}\varphi \mid \mathbf{G}\varphi \mid \varphi\mathbf{U}\varphi$$

where $a \in Ap$. An ω-word w is an infinite sequence of letters $w[0]w[1]w[2]\dots$. We denote the infinite suffix $w[i]w[i+1]\dots$ by w_i. The satisfaction relation $\models$ between ω-words and formulas is inductively defined as follows:

$$
\begin{aligned}
&w \models \mathbf{tt} & &w \not\models \mathbf{ff} & &w \models \mathbf{X}\varphi & &\textit{iff } w_1 \models \varphi \\
&w \models a & &\textit{iff } a \in w[0] & &w \models \mathbf{F}\varphi & &\textit{iff } \exists k.\, w_k \models \varphi \\
&w \models \neg a & &\textit{iff } a \notin w[0] & &w \models \mathbf{G}\varphi & &\textit{iff } \forall k.\, w_k \models \varphi \\
&w \models \varphi \wedge \psi & &\textit{iff } w \models \varphi \textit{ and } w \models \psi & &w \models \varphi\mathbf{U}\psi & &\textit{iff } \exists k.\, w_k \models \psi \textit{ and} \\
&w \models \varphi \vee \psi & &\textit{iff } w \models \varphi \textit{ or } w \models \psi & & & &\forall 0 \le j < k.\, w_j \models \varphi
\end{aligned}
$$

Given two formulas φ and ψ, we denote by $\varphi[\Phi/\psi]$ the result of substituting ψ for each maximal occurrence of a formula of Φ in φ (an occurrence is maximal if it is not a subformula of another occurrence). For example, $\mathbf{G}(a \vee \mathbf{G}b)[\{\mathbf{G}(a \vee \mathbf{G}b), \mathbf{G}b\}/\mathbf{tt}] = \mathbf{tt}$. Two formulas are *equivalent* if they are satisfied by the same words. We under-approximate this using propositional equivalence.

Definition 2 (Propositional Equivalence). *A subformula ψ of φ is called* proper, *if the root of its syntax tree is labelled by either a, $\neg a$, $\mathbf{F}$, $\mathbf{G}$, $\mathbf{U}$ or $\mathbf{X}$. Given a formula φ, we assign to it a propositional formula φ_P as follows: replace every maximal proper subformula ψ by a propositional variable x_ψ. Two* *formulas φ, ψ are propositionally equivalent, denoted $\varphi \equiv_P \psi$, iff φ_P and ψ_P are equivalent formulas of propositional logic. We denote by $[\varphi]_P$ the set of all formulas propositional equivalent to φ.*

For example, if $\varphi = \mathbf{X}b \vee (\mathbf{G}(a \vee \mathbf{X}b) \wedge \mathbf{X}b)$ with $\psi_1 = \mathbf{X}b$ and $\psi_2 = \mathbf{G}(a \vee \mathbf{X}b)$, then $\varphi_P = x_{\psi_1} \vee (x_{\psi_2} \wedge x_{\psi_1}) \equiv x_{\psi_1}$. Thus $\mathbf{X}b$ is propositionally equivalent to φ and $\mathbf{X}b \in [\varphi]_P$.

2.2 Formula Expansion

Our translation relies on the "After Function" $af(\varphi, w)$, read "φ after w" [11]. Intuitively, φ holds for ww' iff $af(\varphi, w)$ holds "after reading w", that is, if $w' \models af(\varphi, w)$.

Definition 3. *Let φ be a formula and $\nu \in 2^{Ap}$ a single letter. $af(\varphi, \nu)$ is then defined as follows:*

$$
\begin{aligned}
af(\mathbf{tt}, \nu) &= \mathbf{tt} & af(\varphi \wedge \psi, \nu) &= af(\varphi, \nu) \wedge af(\psi, \nu) \\
af(\mathbf{ff}, \nu) &= \mathbf{ff} & af(\varphi \vee \psi, \nu) &= af(\varphi, \nu) \vee af(\psi, \nu) \\
af(a, \nu) &= \begin{cases} \mathbf{tt} & \text{if } a \in \nu \\ \mathbf{ff} & \text{if } a \notin \nu \end{cases} & af(\mathbf{X}\varphi, \nu) &= \varphi \\
& & af(\mathbf{G}\varphi, \nu) &= af(\varphi, \nu) \wedge \mathbf{G}\varphi \\
af(\neg a, \nu) &= \begin{cases} \mathbf{ff} & \text{if } a \in \nu \\ \mathbf{tt} & \text{if } a \notin \nu \end{cases} & af(\mathbf{F}\varphi, \nu) &= af(\varphi, \nu) \vee \mathbf{F}\varphi \\
& & af(\varphi \mathbf{U} \psi, \nu) &= af(\psi, \nu) \vee (af(\varphi, \nu) \wedge \varphi \mathbf{U} \psi)
\end{aligned}
$$

Furthermore, we generalize the definition to finite words: $af(\varphi, \epsilon) = \varphi$; and $af(\varphi, \nu w) = af(af(\varphi, \nu), w)$ for every $\nu \in 2^{Ap}$ and every finite word w. Finally, we define the set of from ψ reachable formulas as $Reach(\varphi) = \{[\psi]_P \mid \exists w. \; \psi = af(\varphi, w)\}$.

Example 1. Let $Ap = \{a, b, c\}$ and $\varphi = a \vee (b \; \mathbf{U} \; c)$. We have $af(\varphi, \{a\}) = \mathbf{tt}$ $af(\varphi, \{b\}) = (b \; \mathbf{U} \; c)$, $af(\varphi, \{c\}) = \mathbf{tt}$, and $af(\varphi, \emptyset) = \mathbf{ff}$.

The following lemmas show that af has indeed the claimed property, and others.

Lemma 1 ([11] Lemma 7). *Let φ be a formula, and let $ww' \in (2^{Ap})^\omega$ be an arbitrary word. Then $ww' \models \varphi$ iff $w' \models af(\varphi, w)$.*

Lemma 2 ([11] Lemma 11). *Let φ be a $\mathbf{G}$-free formula and let w be a word. Then $w \models \varphi$ iff there exists $i > 0$ such that $af(\varphi, w_{0j}) \equiv_P \mathbf{tt}$ for every $j \geq i$.*

We now show that $Reach(\varphi)$ — a building block for the construction — is finite, and contains at most a double exponential number of elements.

Lemma 3. *For every formula φ and every finite word $w \in (2^{Ap})^*$:*

(1) $af(\varphi, w)$ is a boolean combination of proper subformulas of φ.
(2) If φ has n proper subformulas, then $Reach(\varphi)$ has at most size 2^{2^n}.

Proof. (1) By definition, every formula is a boolean combination of its proper subformulas. So it suffices to prove that every proper subformula of $af(\varphi, w)$ is also a proper subformula of φ. For $w = \nu$ this follows by an easy induction on φ, and for an arbitrary w by induction on $|w|$.

(2) By (1), every equivalence class $[\psi]_P \in Reach(\varphi)$ can be uniquely identified with a Boolean function over n variables, one for each proper subformula of φ. Since there are 2^{2^n} Boolean functions over n variables, we have at most so many equivalence classes. $\qquad\square$

Remark 1. It is easy to show by induction that $\varphi \equiv_P \psi$ implies $af(\varphi, w) \equiv_P af(\psi, w)$ for every finite word w. We extend af to equivalence classes by defining $af([\varphi]_P, w) := [af(\varphi, w)]_P$. Sometimes we abuse language and identify a formula and its equivalence class. For example, we write "the states of the automaton are pairs of formulas" instead of "pairs of equivalence classes of formulas".

3   Limit-Deterministic Büchi Automata

For convenience, we use Büchi automata with an accepting set of transitions, instead of an accepting set of places. We also consider generalized Büchi automata with several sets of accepting transitions. It is well known that all these classes accept the ω-regular languages and there are polynomial-time translations between them.

Definition 4 (Transition-Based Generalized Büchi Automata). *A generalized transition-based Büchi automaton (TGBA) is a tuple $\mathcal{B} = (\Sigma, Q, \Delta, q_0, \alpha)$ where Σ is an alphabet, Q is a finite set of states, $\Delta \colon Q \times \Sigma \to 2^Q$ is a transition function, q_0 is the initial state, and $\alpha = \{F_1, F_2, \ldots F_n\}$ with $F_i \subseteq Q \times \Sigma \times Q$ is an accepting condition.*

A run r of a TGBA $\mathcal{B}$ on the ω-word w is an infinite sequence of transitions $r = (q_0, w[0], q_1)(q_1, w[1], q_2) \ldots$ respecting the transition function, i.e. $r[i] \in \Delta$ for every $i \geq 0$. We denote by $\inf(r)$ the set of transitions occurring infinitely often in the run. A run is called accepting if for each set of transitions $F \in \alpha$ there is at least one transition in the run occurring infinitely often, i.e. if $\inf(r) \cap F \neq \emptyset$. An infinite word w is accepted by $\mathcal{B}$ and is in the language $L(\mathcal{B})$ if there exists an accepting run r for w.

Intuitively, a TGBA is limit-deterministic if it can be split into a non-deterministic component without accepting transitions, and a deterministic component. The automaton can only accept by "jumping" from the non-deterministic to the deterministic component, but after the jump must stay in the deterministic component forever.

Definition 5 (Limit-Determinism). *A TGBA $\mathcal{B} = (\Sigma, Q, \Delta, q_0, \alpha)$ is limit-deterministic if Q can be partitioned into two disjoint sets $Q = Q_\mathcal{N} \uplus Q_\mathcal{D}$, s.t.*

1. *$\Delta(q, \nu) \subseteq Q_\mathcal{D}$ and $|\Delta(q, \nu)| = 1$ for every $q \in Q_\mathcal{D}$, $\nu \in \Sigma$ and*
2. *$F \subseteq Q_\mathcal{D} \times \Sigma \times Q_\mathcal{D}$ for all $F \in \alpha$*

4 Overview of the Construction

We first explain the main ideas underlying our construction on the formula $\varphi = c \vee \mathbf{XG}(a \vee \mathbf{F}b)$, and then show how to generalise them to arbitrary formulas. We abbreviate $\psi := (a \vee \mathbf{F}b)$, and so we write $\varphi = c \vee \mathbf{XG}\psi$. The complete automaton for the formula is shown in Fig. 1.

Each state of the automaton for φ is labelled with a formula (the state is the equivalence class of this formula w.r.t. propositional equivalence). The words accepted from the state are exactly those satisfying the formula. We describe the initial and accepting components of the automaton, separated in Fig. 1 by the dashed line.

The Initial Component. The states of the initial component are the formulas of $Reach(\varphi)$, with φ as initial state. The non-ϵ transitions are given by the af-function: for every state φ' and letter ν there is a transition labelled by ν leading to $af(\varphi', \nu)$. With these transitions the component keeps track of the formula that must be satisfied by the rest of the word.

The only non-determinism is introduced by the "ϵ-jumps" into the accepting component. Imagine the automaton is currently at state φ'. The automaton

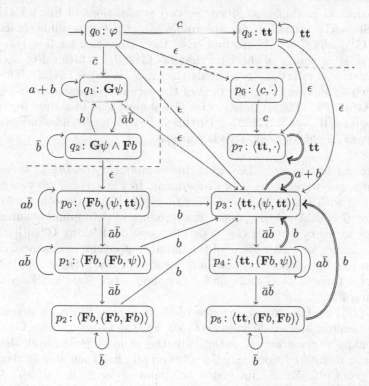

Fig. 1. Automaton $\mathcal{A}$ for $\varphi = c \vee \mathbf{XG}(a \vee \mathbf{F}b)$. Non-accepting sinks ($\langle \mathbf{ff}, \cdot \rangle$) and transitions to them have been removed. The initial component is above the dashed line, the accepting component below. States in the lower part are tuples of an auxiliary monitor and **G**-monitors.

has to check that φ' holds (more formally, that the rest of the run satisfies φ'). Intuitively, taking an ϵ-jump corresponds to picking a subset $\mathcal{G}$ of the **G**-subformulas of φ', guessing that they currently hold, and guessing further that φ' holds *even if no other* **G**-*subformula becomes true in the future*. In order to see how the automaton can check this guess, we introduce some notation.

Definition 6. *Given a formula φ and a set $\mathcal{G}$ of* **G**-*formulas, we denote $\varphi[\mathcal{G}]$ the result of substituting* **tt** *for every* **G**-*subformula of $\mathcal{G}$ and* **ff** *for every other* **G**-*subformula.*

We claim that after the jump the accepting component can check the guess by checking if (a) $\mathbf{G}(\psi[\mathcal{G}])$ holds for every $\mathbf{G}\psi \in \mathcal{G}$, and (b) $\varphi'[\mathcal{G}]$ holds.

Indeed, if $\mathbf{G}\psi \in \mathcal{G}$ holds now, then it always holds in the future, and so it can be replaced by **tt**. Similarly, if $\mathbf{G}\psi \notin \mathcal{G}$, then φ' should hold even if $\mathbf{G}\psi$ never holds in the future, which—since formulas are in negation normal form—is the case if φ' holds even after $\mathbf{G}\psi$ is replaced by **ff**.

The crucial point now is that the formulas of (a) are of the form $\mathbf{G}\psi'$, where ψ' is **G**-free, and the formula in (b) contains no occurrence of **G** at all. So for the accepting component (described below) it suffices to find deterministic automata for such formulas.

As a concrete example, consider the two ϵ-transitions of Fig. 1 leaving the state q_0. Since $\mathbf{G}\psi$ is the only **G**-subformula of φ, the two possible choices for $\mathcal{G}$ are $\mathcal{G} = \{\mathbf{G}\psi\}$ and $\mathcal{G} = \emptyset$. In the first case, the ϵ-transition for $\mathcal{G} = \{\mathbf{G}\psi\}$ must lead to a state in charge of checking that (a) $\mathbf{G}(\psi[\mathcal{G}]) = \mathbf{G}(a \vee \mathbf{F}b)$ holds, and (b) $\varphi[\mathbf{G}\psi/\mathbf{tt}] = c \vee \mathbf{X}\mathbf{tt} \equiv_P \textit{true}$ holds (in this case (b) is trivial). This is the state p_3, whose successors are the part of the accepting component in charge of checking $\mathbf{G}(a \vee \mathbf{F}b)$. The ϵ-transition for $\mathcal{G} = \emptyset$ must lead to a state in charge of checking $\varphi[\mathbf{G}\psi/\mathbf{ff}] = c \vee \mathbf{X}\mathbf{ff} \equiv_P c$ (if this holds, then φ' holds, independently of whether $\mathbf{G}\psi$ holds or not). This is state p_6.

The Accepting Component. The accepting component consists of several subcomponents, one for each set $\mathcal{G}$ of **G**-formulas. In Fig. 1 there are two subcomponents, one with states $\{p_0, \ldots, p_5\}$ for $\mathcal{G} = \{\mathbf{G}\psi\}$, and the other with states $\{p_6, p_7\}$ for $\mathcal{G} = \emptyset$. A subcomponent is a product of deterministic automata: a **G**-*monitor* for every formula $\mathbf{G}\psi \in \mathcal{G}$, in charge of checking $\mathbf{G}(\psi[\mathcal{G}])$, and an *auxiliary monitor* for each state φ' of the initial component, in charge of checking $\varphi'[\mathcal{G}]$. Consider for instance the subcomponent with states $\{p_0, \ldots, p_5\}$. It is the product of a three-state **G**-monitor for $\mathbf{G}\psi$, and a two-state auxiliary monitor for checking $\mathbf{F}b$.

Since $\varphi'[\mathcal{G}]$ contains no occurrence of **G**, it is easy to give a deterministic auxiliary monitor, and we do so in Sect. 5.2. For the **G**-*monitor* for $\mathbf{G}(\psi[\mathcal{G}])$ we use a breakpoint construction. Intuitively, the monitor must check that every suffix of the monitored word satisfies ψ', and so after each step it receives ψ' as new "proof obligation". Its states are pairs of formulas (ρ_1, ρ_2). At state (ρ_1, ρ_2) the monitor is currently taking care of the proof obligation ρ_1, and has put ρ_2 on hold. Initially $\rho_1 = \psi$ and $\rho_2 = \mathbf{tt}$. Transitions of the form $\delta((\rho_1, \rho_2), a) = (af(\rho_1, a), af(\rho_2, a) \wedge \psi')$. update the proof obligations according to the af-function, adding ψ' to the proof obligation on hold. If $\rho_1 = \mathbf{tt}$ then the current proof obligation can be discarded, and the monitor can take care of the one on hold; this is done by a transition $\delta((\mathbf{tt}, \rho_2), a) = (af(\rho_2, a) \wedge \psi', \mathbf{tt})$. These "discarding" transitions are accepting. If they are taken infinitely often, then all of the infinitely many proof obligations are eventually discarded.

5   Construction

For the formal presentation of the construction, let φ be a fixed formula and let Ap be the corresponding set of atomic propositions. Further, let $\mathbb{G}$ be the set of $\mathbf{G}$-subformulas of φ, i.e. the subformulas of φ of the form $\mathbf{G}\psi$. We first describe the initial component without ϵ-transitions, then the accepting component, and then the ϵ-transitions linking the two.

5.1   Initial Component

As already sketched, the component keeps track in its state of the formula that must be satisfied by the rest of the word.

Definition 7. *The initial component for a formula φ is the transition system:*

$$\mathcal{N} = (2^{Ap}, Reach(\varphi), af, \varphi)$$

5.2   Accepting Component

The accepting component for a subset $\mathcal{G} \subseteq \mathbb{G}$ of $\mathbf{G}$-subformulas is the product of one auxiliary monitor and one $\mathbf{G}$-monitor for each $\mathbf{G}\psi \in \mathcal{G}$. First, we show how to build a $\mathbf{G}$-monitor $\mathcal{U}$ for a single $\mathbf{G}$-free formula. Second, we construct a product $\mathcal{P}$ of these $\mathbf{G}$-monitors.

G-Monitor. Let ψ be a $\mathbf{G}$-free formula. We construct a deterministic Büchi automaton $\mathcal{U}$, called the $\mathbf{G}$-*monitor for* $\mathbf{G}\psi$, recognising $L(\mathbf{G}\psi)$. We first give the definition, and then explain the intuition behind it.

Definition 8 (G-Monitor). *Let ψ be a $\mathbf{G}$-free formula. The $\mathbf{G}$-monitor for ψ is the deterministic Büchi automaton*

$$\mathcal{U}(\mathbf{G}\psi) = (2^{Ap}, Reach(\psi) \times Reach(\psi), \delta, (\psi, \mathbf{tt}), F)$$

where

$$- \ \delta((\xi, \zeta), \nu) = \begin{cases} (af(\zeta, \nu) \wedge \psi, \mathbf{tt}) & \text{if } af(\xi, \nu) \equiv_P \mathbf{tt} \\ (af(\xi, \nu), af(\zeta, \nu) \wedge \psi) & \text{otherwise} \end{cases}$$

$$- \ F = \{((\xi, \zeta), \nu, p) \in Q \times 2^{Ap} \times Q \mid af(\xi, \nu) \equiv_P \mathbf{tt}\}$$

The states of the monitor are pairs (ϕ_1, ϕ_2) of formulas. Intuitively, from state (ϕ_1, ϕ_2) the automaton checks if the rest of the run satisfies $\phi_1 \wedge \phi_2$, but starting with ϕ_1 and putting ϕ_2 "on hold". The initial state is $(\psi, \mathbf{tt})$. After reading a letter, say ν_1, the automaton moves to $\delta(\psi, \mathbf{tt}) = (af(\psi, \nu_1), \psi)$. The meaning is: the automaton checks if the rest of the run satisfies $af(\psi, \nu_1) \wedge \psi$, but putting the check of ψ "on hold". If the next letter is, say, ν_2, then the automaton moves to $(af(\psi, \nu_1\nu_2), af(\psi, \nu_2) \wedge \psi)$, keeping the check of $af(\psi, \nu_2) \wedge \psi$ on hold. However, if $af(\psi, \nu_1\nu_2) = \mathbf{tt}$, then, the automaton knows already that the word $\nu_1\nu_2 \dots$ satisfies ψ, the first check is complete, and the automaton "transfers" the checks kept on hold to the first position, moving to the state $(af(\psi, \nu_2) \wedge \psi, \mathbf{tt})$. The accepting transitions are those at which the automaton completes a check. If the automaton completes infinitely many checks, then all suffixes of the run satisfy ψ, and so the run satisfies $\mathbf{G}\psi$.

Lemma 4. *Let ψ be a $\mathbf{G}$-free formula and let w be a word, then $w \models \mathbf{G}\psi$ iff $\mathcal{U}(\mathbf{G}\psi)$ accepts w.*

Proof. Assume $w \models \mathbf{G}\psi$. Hence $\forall i.\, w_i \models \psi$. Since ψ is a $\mathbf{G}$-free formula, af will eventually derive $\mathbf{tt}$ due to Lemma 2, that is, $\forall i.\, \exists j.\, af(\psi, w_{ij}) \equiv_P \mathbf{tt}$. Hence $\mathcal{U}(\mathbf{G}\psi)$ visits infinitely many states (ξ, ζ) such that $\xi \equiv_P \mathbf{tt}$, and so it accepts.

Assume $w \not\models \mathbf{G}\psi$. Let i be a point where w fails to satisfy ψ ($w_i \not\models \psi$). Thus $af(\psi, w_{ij}) \not\equiv_P \mathbf{tt}$ for any j. Once $af(\psi, w_{ij})$ is propagated from the second component to the first, $\mathcal{U}(\mathbf{G}\psi)$ never uses an accepting transition again and hence does not accept. $\qquad\square$

Example 2. The $\mathbf{G}$-monitor for $\mathbf{G}\psi = \mathbf{G}(a \vee \mathbf{F}b)$ is the automaton of Fig. 2.

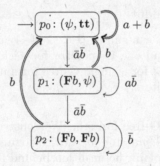

Fig. 2. $\mathbf{G}$-monitor for $\mathbf{G}\psi = \mathbf{G}(a \vee \mathbf{F}b)$.

Product of G-Monitors. Let φ be a formula, and let $\mathbb{G}$ be the set of all $\mathbf{G}$-subformulas of φ. Fix a set $\mathcal{G} = \{\mathbf{G}\psi_1, \dots, \mathbf{G}\psi_n\} \subseteq \mathbb{G}$. For every index $1 \leq i \leq n$, let $\mathcal{U}_i$ be the $\mathbf{G}$-monitor for the formula $\mathbf{G}(\psi_i[\mathcal{G}])$.

Definition 9 (Product of G-Monitors). *Let $\mathcal{U}_1, \dots, \mathcal{U}_n$ as above, and let $\mathcal{U}_i = (2^{Ap}, Q_i, \delta_i, q_{0i}, F_i)$. The product of $\mathbf{G}$-monitors of φ with respect to $\mathcal{G}$ is the generalized deterministic Büchi automaton*

$$\mathcal{P}(\mathcal{G}) = \left(\, 2^{Ap},\ \prod_{i=1}^{n} Q_i,\ \prod_{i=1}^{n} \delta_i,\ (q_{01}, \dots, q_{0n}),\ \{F_1', \dots, F_n'\}\, \right)$$

where $(\, (q_1, \dots, q_n), \nu, (q_1', \dots, q_n')\,) \in F_i'$ iff $(q_i, \nu, q_i') \in F_i$.

Lemma 5. *Let $\mathcal{G}$ be a set of $\mathbf{G}$-formulas and let w be a word. We have: $\mathcal{P}(\mathcal{G})$ accepts w iff $w \models \mathbf{G}(\psi[\mathcal{G}])$ for all $\mathbf{G}\psi \in \mathcal{G}$.*

Proof. Let $\mathcal{G} = \{\mathbf{G}\psi_1, \ldots, \mathbf{G}\psi_n\}$, and assume that the formulas are ordered so that if $\mathbf{G}\psi_i$ is a subformula of ψ_j then $j < i$ (so, in particular, $\mathbf{G}\psi_n$ is not a subformula of any of $\psi_1, \ldots, \psi_{n-1}$).

Assume $\mathcal{P}(\mathcal{G})$ accepts w. We prove $w \models \mathbf{G}(\psi_i[\mathcal{G}])$ for every $1 \leq i \leq n$ by induction on $n = |\mathcal{G}|$. If $n = 0$, then $\mathcal{P}(\emptyset)$ trivially accepts all words, and we are done. Let now $n > 0$. Since $\mathbf{G}\psi_n$ is not a subformula of any of $\psi_1, \ldots, \psi_{n-1}$, taking $\mathcal{G}' := \mathcal{G} \setminus \{\mathbf{G}\psi_n\}$ we have $\psi_i[\mathcal{G}] = \psi_i[\mathcal{G}']$ for every $\psi_i \in \mathcal{G}$. In particular, $\mathcal{P}(\mathcal{G})$ accepts w, then both $\mathcal{P}(\mathcal{G}')$ and $\mathcal{U}(\mathbf{G}(\psi_n[\mathcal{G}']))$ accept w too. By induction hypothesis we have $w \models \mathbf{G}(\psi_i[\mathcal{G}'])$ for every $1 \leq i \leq n - 1$. By Lemma 4 we obtain $w \models \mathbf{G}(\psi_n[\mathcal{G}'])$. Finally, since $\psi_i[\mathcal{G}] = \psi_i[\mathcal{G}']$ for every $\psi_i \in \mathcal{G}$, we get $w \models \mathbf{G}(\psi_i[\mathcal{G}])$ for every $1 \leq i \leq n$.

The other direction is analogous. $\qquad\square$

5.3   Connecting the Initial and Accepting Components

We now define the ϵ-transitions leading from states in the initial component to states in the accepting component. Intuitively, each ϵ-transition corresponds to a guess $\mathcal{G}$, and starts the corresponding product $\mathcal{P}(\mathcal{G})$. However, recall that if the source of the transition is the state φ', then the accepting component must also check that the formula $\varphi'[\mathcal{G}]$) holds. For example, for the state q_2 of Fig. 1 we have $\varphi' = \mathbf{G}\psi \wedge \mathbf{F}b$, and choosing $\mathcal{G} = \mathbf{G}\psi$ we get $\varphi'[\mathcal{G}] \equiv_P \mathbf{F}b$. So, intuitively, the state p_0 starts not only $\mathcal{P}(\mathcal{G})$, but also a deterministic automaton for $\mathbf{F}b$. More formally, p_0 is the initial state of the product of $\mathcal{P}(\mathcal{G})$ and this deterministic automaton.

The deterministic automaton for $\varphi'' := \varphi'[\mathcal{G}]$ is very simple. Since φ'' contains no occurrences of $\mathbf{G}$, by Lemma 2 we can just take the automaton $(2^{Ap}, Reach(\varphi''), af, \varphi'', \{\mathbf{tt}\})$. That is, the automaton keeps tracking the formula that the rest of the run must satisfy, and accepts iff eventually the formula is $\mathbf{tt}$. Comparing with the initial component $\mathcal{N}$, we observe that this automaton is nothing but $\mathcal{N}$ with $\mathbf{tt}$ as single accepting state, meaning all outgoing transitions are accepting. We can now define the complete limit-deterministic automaton for a formula φ.

Definition 10. *Let φ be a formula. Let $\mathcal{N} = (2^{Ap}, Q_{\mathcal{N}}, \delta_{\mathcal{N}}, q_{0\mathcal{N}})$ be the transition system of Definition 7. Furthermore, for every set $\mathcal{G}$ of $\mathbf{G}$-subformulas of φ, let $\mathcal{P}(\mathcal{G}) = (2^{Ap}, Q_{\mathcal{P}(\mathcal{G})}, \delta_{\mathcal{P}(\mathcal{G})}, q_{0\mathcal{P}(\mathcal{G})}, \{F_{(\mathcal{G}, \mathbf{G}\psi)} \mid \mathbf{G}\psi \in \mathcal{G}\})$ be the product of Definition 9. The limit-deterministic automaton $\mathcal{A}$ is defined as*

$$\mathcal{A} = (2^{Ap}, Q_{\mathcal{N}} \cup Q_{Acc}, \delta_{\mathcal{N}} \cup \Delta_{\epsilon} \cup \Delta_{Acc}, \varphi, \{F_{\xi} \mid \xi \in \mathbb{G}\})$$

where

$$Q_{Acc} = \bigcup_{\mathcal{G} \subseteq \mathbb{G}} (Q_{\mathcal{N}} \times Q_{\mathcal{P}(\mathcal{G})}) \quad and \quad \Delta_{Acc} = \bigcup_{\mathcal{G} \subseteq \mathbb{G}} (\delta_{\mathcal{N}} \times \delta_{\mathcal{P}(\mathcal{G})})$$

$$\Delta_{\epsilon} = \{(\chi, \epsilon, (\chi[\mathcal{G}], q_{0\mathcal{G}})) \mid \chi \in Q_{\mathcal{N}}, \mathcal{G} \subseteq \mathbb{G}\}$$

$$F_{\xi} = \bigcup_{\mathcal{G} \subseteq \mathbb{G}} \{((\mathbf{tt}, q), \nu, (\mathbf{tt}, q')) \mid (q, \nu, q') \in F_{(\mathcal{G}, \xi)}\}$$

Example 3. The complete automaton $\mathcal{A}$ for $\varphi = c \vee \mathbf{XG}(a \vee \mathbf{F}b)$, displayed in Fig. 1, consists of the initial component above the dashed line, and the products of the auxiliary monitor with the product automata $\mathcal{P}$ for $\mathcal{G}_1 = \{\}$ and $\mathcal{G}_2 = \{\mathbf{G}\psi\}$ (below the dashed line)

5.4   Correctness

We prove a stronger correctness statement: For every state $\psi \in Q_\mathcal{N}$ of the initial component, the words w accepted from ψ are exactly those that satisfy ψ. Before we proceed, we need the notion of a *stable set* of **G**-subformulas.

Definition 11. *A set $\mathcal{G} \subseteq \mathbb{G}$ of **G**-subformulas of φ is stable for a word w if the following holds:*

$$\forall \mathbf{G}\psi \in \mathcal{G}. \ \forall i \geq 0. \ w_i \models \mathbf{G}\psi$$
$$\forall \mathbf{G}\psi \in \mathbb{G} \setminus \mathcal{G}. \ \forall i \geq 0. \ w_i \not\models \mathbf{G}\psi$$

Observe that at most one set is stable for a given word, and some words have no stable set. Further, if a set is stable for a word, then it is stable for all its suffixes.

Lemma 6. *Let φ be a formula, and let w be a word with stable set $\mathcal{G}$. Then $w \models \varphi$ iff $w \models \varphi[\mathcal{G}]$.*

Proof. (Induction on φ) The only non-trivial case is $\varphi = \mathbf{G}\varphi'$. Consider two subcases. If $\mathbf{G}\varphi' \in \mathcal{G}$, then by the definition of stable set we have $w \models \varphi$ and by the definition of $\varphi[\mathcal{G}]$ we get $\varphi[\mathcal{G}] = \mathbf{tt}$, so $w \models \varphi[\mathcal{G}]$. If $\mathbf{G}\varphi' \notin \mathcal{G}$, then $w \not\models \mathbf{G}\varphi'$ and $\varphi[\mathcal{G}] = \mathbf{ff}$, so $w \not\models \varphi[\mathcal{G}]$.   □

Lemma 7. *Let φ be a formula, and let w be a word with stable set $\mathcal{G}$. If $w \models \varphi$ holds, then $\mathcal{A}$ has an accepting run r for w starting at φ. Moroever, r immediately switches from $\varphi \in Q_\mathcal{N}$ to the accepting component for $\mathcal{G}$.*

Proof. Assume $w \models \varphi$ and assume $\mathcal{G}$ is the stable set for w. Let r be the run starting at φ that immediately uses the ϵ-transition to jump to the accepting component for $\mathcal{G}$. We show that r is accepting. Since $\mathcal{G}$ is a stable set for w, the product automaton $\mathcal{P}(\mathcal{G})$ accepts w due to Lemma 5. It remains to prove that the auxiliary monitor eventually reaches $\mathbf{tt}$. By Lemma 6 we have $w \models \varphi[\mathcal{G}]$. Since $\varphi[\mathcal{G}]$ is **G**-free, we can apply Lemma 2 and obtain that the auxiliary monitor eventually reaches $\mathbf{tt}$.   □

Lemma 8. *Let w be a word and let $\varphi \in Q_\mathcal{N}$ be a state in the initial component of $\mathcal{A}$. We have: $w \models \varphi$ iff $\mathcal{A}$ has an accepting run r for w starting at φ.*

Proof. Assume $w \models \varphi$. Let $\mathcal{G} = \{\mathbf{G}\psi \in \mathbb{G} \mid w \models \mathbf{FG}\psi\}$ be the set of eventually true **G**-subformulas, and let i be an index such that $w_i \models \mathbf{G}\psi$ for every $\mathbf{G}\psi \in \mathcal{G}$. Then $\mathcal{G}$ is a stable set for w_i. Consider the run that first reads $w_{0(i-1)}$ in the initial component, reaching a state φ', and then jumps to the accepting component for the $\mathcal{G}$. By Lemma 1 we have $w_i \models \varphi'$, and by Lemma 7 the run is accepting.

Assume $\mathcal{A}$ accepts w. Let r be an accepting run. Let i be the point at which r switches to the accepting component for some set $\mathcal{G}$. By Lemma 5 we have $w_i \models \xi$ for each $\xi \in \mathcal{G}$. Since accepting transitions are only taken when the remaining obligations are fulfilled (that is, when the formula in the first position of the tuple is replaced by $\mathbf{tt}$), we also obtain from Lemma 1 $w_i \models af(\varphi, w_{0(i-1)})[\mathcal{G}]$. Because the formulas are in NNF and $\mathcal{G} \subseteq \{\xi \in \mathbb{G} \mid w_i \models \xi\}$, we have $w_i \models af(\varphi, w_{0(i-1)})$, and, by Lemma 1, we finally get $w \models \varphi$. $\square$

From this lemma we immediately obtain the correctness:

Theorem 1. *Let w be a word, then $w \models \varphi$ iff $\mathcal{A}$ accepts w.*

Further, staying for an arbitrary number of steps in the initial component is safe, because is it always possible to switch to a successful accepting component:

Lemma 9. *Let w be a finite word and let φ be a formula. We denote by $\mathsf{L}(q)$ the language accepted from state $q \in Q_{\mathcal{A}}$. Then the following inclusion holds:*

$$\bigcup_{q \in \delta(\varphi, w)} \mathsf{L}(q) \subseteq \mathsf{L}(\delta_{\mathcal{N}}(\varphi, w))$$

Proof. Let $q \in \delta(\varphi, w)$ be an arbitrary state in the accepting component reached after reading w. Let $w' \in \mathsf{L}(q)$ and let r' be an accepting run for w'. We extend r' to a run r for ww' starting in $\varphi \in Q_{\mathcal{N}}$ by taking the path from φ to q as a prefix for r'. Iteratively applying Lemmas 1 and 8 yields $w' \in \mathsf{L}(\delta_{\mathcal{N}}(\varphi, w))$:

$$ww' \in \mathsf{L}(\varphi) \text{ iff } ww' \models \varphi \text{ iff } w' \models af(\varphi, w) \text{ iff } w' \in \mathsf{L}(\delta_{\mathcal{N}}(\varphi, w))$$

Thus $\mathsf{L}(q) \subseteq \mathsf{L}(\delta_{\mathcal{N}}(\varphi, w))$ for all $q \in \delta(\varphi, w)$. $\square$

6   Optimisations

For the experimental evaluation we apply several optimisations to the presented construction:

First, *ϵ-transitions are removed* and replaced by the outgoing edges of the successor state. Second, *non-accepting sinks are removed*, as they can be easily recognised: from the state $\mathbf{ff}$ accepting edges are unreachable. Third, not all "ϵ-jumps" are necessary: A run starting in $\mathbf{G}\psi_1 \wedge \mathbf{G}\psi_2$ cannot be accepting in the component for $\emptyset$ or $\{\mathbf{G}\psi_1\}$, since the auxiliary monitor cannot reach $\mathbf{tt}$ from $\mathbf{ff}$ or $\mathbf{G}\psi_1 \wedge \chi$. Hence only jumps for (minimal) satisfying assignments of a state label (restricted to $\mathbf{G}$s) are constructed. Fourth, we call a state *transient* if every run can only visit the state at most once, e.g. it is labelled by $\mathbf{X}\varphi$. As shown in Lemma 9 a jump to the accepting component can safely be delayed. Thus jumps for transient states are not constructed.

While these four optimisations suppress the construction of states and edges, also the state labels can be optimised: Fifth, $\mathbf{G}$-monitors can safely replace (ξ, ζ)

by $(\xi, \mathbf{tt})$ if ξ implies ζ. In a similar way the auxiliary component removes terms already taken care of by $\mathbf{G}$-monitors. Sixth, all modal operators in state labels are unfolded, reducing the number of states: $\mathbf{FG}a$ is rewritten to $(\mathbf{FG}a) \vee (\mathbf{G}a)$ and merged with existing states.

7   Complexity

Upper Bound. Let n be the length of the formula φ. Since $Q_{\mathcal{U}(\mathbf{G}\psi)}$ and $Q_{\mathcal{N}}$ are defined using *Reach*, the size for $Q_{\mathcal{U}(\mathbf{G}\psi)}$ and $Q_{\mathcal{N}}$ is $\mathcal{O}(2^{2^n})$. For each $\mathcal{G} \subseteq \mathbb{G}$ the accepting component has at most $|\mathbb{G}|$ $\mathbf{G}$-monitors and one auxiliary monitor. Hence the size of the accepting component for a single $\mathcal{G}$ is at most $(|\mathbb{G}| + 1) \cdot \mathcal{O}(2^{2^n}) = \mathcal{O}(2^{2^{n+\log\log n}})$. Summing up to:

$$\mathcal{O}(2^{2^n}) + 2^{|\mathbb{G}|} \cdot \mathcal{O}(2^{2^{n+\log\log n}}) = \mathcal{O}(2^{2^{n+\log n+\log\log n}})$$

Lower Bound. This upper bound is matched by a double exponential (not tight) lower bound. The language used in the proof is an adaptation of [21].

Theorem 2. *There is a family of formulas ϕ_n of size $\mathcal{O}(n^2)$ such that the smallest limit-deterministic state-based Büchi automaton recognising $\mathsf{L}(\phi_n)$ has at least 2^{2^n} states.*

Proof. For every $n \in \mathbb{N}$, let r_n be the regular expression over the alphabet $\Sigma = \{0, 1, \#, \$, \%\}$, defined as

$$r_n := \sum_{w \in \{0,1\}^n} \% \,(0|1|\#)^* \, \# \, w \, \# \,(0|1|\#)^* \, \$ \, w$$

Since the language $\mathsf{L}(r_n^\omega)$ can be expressed by an LTL formula of size $\mathcal{O}(n^2)$ (Lemma 10) and the smallest limit-deterministic state-based Büchi automaton recognising $\mathsf{L}(r_n^\omega)$ has at least 2^{2^n} states (Lemma 11), the claim holds.   □

Lemma 10. *There exists an LTL formula of size $\mathcal{O}(n^2)$ defining $\mathsf{L}(r_n^\omega)$.*

Proof. The conjunction of the following LTL formulas of size $\mathcal{O}(n^2)$ defines $\mathsf{L}(r_n^\omega)$:

$$\% \wedge \mathbf{G}(\$ \to \mathbf{X}^{n+1}\%) \wedge \mathbf{G}(\bigvee_{\alpha \in \Sigma} (\alpha \wedge \bigwedge_{\beta \in \Sigma \setminus \{\alpha\}} \neg\beta)) \tag{1}$$

$$\mathbf{G}(\% \to \mathbf{X}((0 \vee 1 \vee \#) \,\mathbf{U}(\bigwedge_{1 \le i \le n}(\varphi(i,0) \vee \varphi(i,1)) \wedge \mathbf{X}^{n+1}\#))) \tag{2}$$

with $\varphi(i, \alpha) := \mathbf{X}^i \alpha \wedge ((0 \vee 1 \vee \#)\,\mathbf{U}(\$ \wedge \mathbf{X}^i \alpha))$. Formula 1 ensures the basic syntactic properties of r_n, and Formula 2 enforces that the literal $\%$ is always succeeded by a string of the form $(0|1|\#)^* \# w \# (0|1|\#)^* \$ w$ using $\varphi(i, \alpha)$ to guarantee the existence of matching substrings $\# w \#$ and $\$ w$.   □

Lemma 11. *The smallest limit-deterministic state-based Büchi automaton recognising* $\mathsf{L}(r_n^\omega)$ *has at least* 2^{2^n} *states.*

Proof. Let $\mathcal{A}_n$ be a limit-deterministic state-based Büchi automaton recognising $\mathsf{L}(r_n^\omega)$. A state q is called a *\$-successor* if there exists an accepting run r containing the transition $(p, \$, q)$ and q is in the deterministic component of $\mathcal{A}_n$. For every \$-successor q we denote by $\mathcal{W}(q) = \{u \in \{0,1\}^n \mid \exists w.\ uw \in \mathsf{L}(q)\}$ the set of prefixes of length n of $\mathsf{L}(q)$. We show that $\mathcal{A}_n$ has at least one distinct \$-successor q for each subset $\emptyset \neq \mathcal{S} \subseteq \{0,1\}^n$, such that $\mathcal{W}(q) = \mathcal{S}$. Thus $\mathcal{A}_n$ has at least 2^{2^n} states, since not all states can be \$-successors. We expose these states by the recursively defined sequence s. Let $\mathcal{S} = \{w_1, w_2, \ldots w_i\}$ be such a subset and let $k := |Q_n|$:

$$s(\mathcal{S}) := s_{|\mathcal{S}|}(\mathcal{S})$$
$$s_1(\mathcal{S}) := \%\#w_1\#\ldots\#w_i\#\$w_1$$
$$s_j(\mathcal{S}) := s_{j-1}(\mathcal{S})^k \cdot s_{j-2}(\mathcal{S})^k \cdot \ldots \cdot s_1(\mathcal{S})^k \%\#w_1\# \cdot \ldots \cdot \#w_i\#\$w_j \ \forall 1 < j \leq i$$

Since $s(\mathcal{S})^\omega \in L(r_n^\omega)$ holds for all non-empty $\mathcal{S}$, there exists for each $s(\mathcal{S})$ an accepting run r, such that the sequence is read in the deterministic component. Furthermore by construction we have for each \$-successor q encountered reading $s(\mathcal{S})$: $\mathcal{W}(q) \subseteq \mathcal{S}$. Showing that the converse also holds concludes the proof:

Proposition 1. *Let* $\mathcal{S} = \{w_1, \ldots w_i\}$, *and let* $1 \leq j \leq i$. *Furthermore, assume the sequence* $s_j(\mathcal{S})$ *is read in the deterministic part during an accepting run. Let* q_j *be the \$-successor transitioned to after the last \$ of* $s_j(\mathcal{S})$. *Then* q_j *satisfies* $\mathcal{W}(q_j) \supseteq \{w_1, \ldots, w_j\}$.

Proof (By induction on j) Case $j = 1$ is trivial. Case $j > 1$: By construction $s_j(\mathcal{S})$ is equal to $s_{j-1}(\mathcal{S})^{k+1}$ up to the last \$ and ends with w_j instead of w_{j-1}. Since $k = |Q_n|$ and the sequence is read in the deterministic component, q_j occurred previously in the run on $s_{j-1}(\mathcal{S})$ as a \$-successor. Hence we apply the induction hypothesis to q_j and obtain: $\mathcal{W}(q_j) \supseteq \{w_1, \ldots, w_{j-1}\}$. Since w_j occurs after the last \$-symbol in $s_j(\mathcal{S})$, we have $\mathcal{W}(q_j) \supseteq \{w_1, \ldots, w_j\}$. $\square$

8   Quantitative Probabilistic Model Checking

The problem of LTL probabilistic model checking [3] is to determine the probability that an LTL formula φ holds on a run generated by a given Markov chain $\mathcal{M}$, i.e., $\mathbb{P}_\mathcal{M}\{\text{run } \rho \mid \rho \models \varphi\}$, or more generally, for Markov decision process $\mathcal{M}$ the *maximal* probability that φ is satisfied, i.e., $\sup_\sigma \mathbb{P}_{\mathcal{M}^\sigma}\{\text{run } \rho \mid \rho \models \varphi\}$, where σ ranges over *schedulers* resolving the non-determinism of $\mathcal{M}$, and $\mathcal{M}^\sigma$ is the Markov chain resulting from application of σ to $\mathcal{M}$.

The automata-theoretic approach to model checking LTL over Markov decision processes amounts to (1) constructing the product $\mathcal{M} \times \mathcal{A}$ of the system $\mathcal{M}$ and an automaton $\mathcal{A}$ for the LTL formula, (2) computing *maximal end components (MECs)* in the product, (3) determining which MECs are accepting, and (4) determining the maximal probability to reach the accepting MECs.

However, as opposed to the non-probabilistic model checking case, in general the automaton $\mathcal{A}$ cannot be used if it is non-deterministic. Intuitively, resolving non-determinism of the automaton may depend on the yet unknown, probabilistically given future. For the same reason, limit-deterministic automata are in general applicable only to qualitative probabilistic model checking, i.e., determining whether the satisfaction probability is 0, 1, or neither. We show that our limit-deterministic automata can be used even in the quantitative-analysis algorithm outlined above without conversion to a fully deterministic automaton.

Notice that the only non-deterministic transitions present in our construction are ϵ-transitions. This allows us to represent the non-deterministic choice in our LDBA $\mathcal{A}$ by means of additional ϵ-actions in the product MDP where each ϵ-action only changes the automaton state. Formally, given a Markov decision process $\mathcal{M} = (S, \mathrm{Act}, \mathbf{P}, s_0, \mathrm{Ap}, L)$ with set of states S, set of actions Act, transition probability function $\mathbf{P} : S \times \mathrm{Act} \times S \to [0,1]$, initial state $s_0 \in S$ and labelling function L, and given an automaton $\mathcal{A} = (2^{\mathrm{Ap}}, Q, \delta, q_0, Acc)$ we define the product $(\mathcal{M} \times \mathcal{A}) = ((S \times Q), \mathrm{Act}', \mathbf{P}', (s_0, q_0), \mathrm{Ap}, L')$ of $\mathcal{M}$ and $\mathcal{A}$ as follows. Firstly, for every potential ϵ-transition in $\mathcal{A}$ to some state $q \in Q$ we add a corresponding action ϵ_q in the product:

$$\mathrm{Act}' := \mathrm{Act} \cup \{\epsilon_q \mid q \in Q\}$$

As usual, we define for all $(s, q), (s', q') \in S \times Q$ and $\alpha \in \mathrm{Act}$:

$$L'((s, q)) := L(s)$$

$$\mathbf{P}'((s, q), \alpha, (s', q')) := \begin{cases} \mathbf{P}(s, \alpha, s') & \text{if } q \xrightarrow{L(s')} q' \\ 0 & \text{otherwise} \end{cases}$$

Additionally, for all $(s, q), (s', q') \in S \times Q$, the transition probabilities of the ϵ-actions are given by

$$\mathbf{P}'((s, q), \epsilon_{\hat{q}}, (s', q')) := \begin{cases} 1 & \text{if } s = s' \text{ and } q \xrightarrow{\epsilon} q' = \hat{q} \\ 0 & \text{otherwise} \end{cases}$$

Now we are going to show that our product can indeed be used for quantitative model checking using the standard techniques.

Theorem 3. *For any formula φ, the automaton $\mathcal{A}$ can be used in the standard probabilistic model checking algorithm, i.e., for any Markov decision process $\mathcal{M}$,*

$$\sup_{\sigma} \mathbb{P}_{\mathcal{M}^\sigma}[\mathrm{L}(\mathcal{A})] = \sup_{\sigma} \mathbb{P}_{(\mathcal{M} \times \mathcal{A})^\sigma}[\Diamond X]$$

where $\Diamond X$ is the set of runs that reach an accepting MEC of $\mathcal{M} \times \mathcal{A}$.

Proof. The inequality "$\geq$" is trivial even for general non-deterministic automata. Indeed, every scheduler over $\mathcal{M} \times \mathcal{A}$ induces a scheduler over $\mathcal{M}$ (by elimination of ϵ-transitions and subsequent projection) such that for every run (ρ, π) reaching X, where acceptance is guaranteed, we have a run ρ of $\mathcal{M}$ that is accepted by $\mathcal{A}$ due to π. The scheduler thus resolved the non-determinism also of the automaton.

While the inequality "$\leq$" generally holds only for deterministic automata, we prove it also for our $\mathcal{A}$. We define a random variable $index$ mapping a run ρ of $\mathcal{M}$, corresponding to a word w, as follows: $index(\rho) := \min\{i \mid \forall \mathbf{G}\psi \in \mathbb{G}.\ w \models \mathbf{FG}\psi \implies w_i \models \mathbf{G}\psi\}$. Observe that every run has a finite index. From this point on, the run satisfies all $\mathbf{G}$-formulas that it will ever eventually satisfy; we call the set of these formulas $\mathcal{G}(\rho)$.

Given a scheduler σ, a state m of $\mathcal{M}^\sigma$ is called *decided* if almost all runs starting in m have index 0. In other words, almost all runs of $\mathcal{M}^\sigma$ starting in m satisfy each $\mathbf{G}$-formula already at the beginning or never. Intuitively, $\mathcal{G}$ is determined by m.

Lemma 12. *Let C be a bottom strongly connected component (BSCC) of a Markov chain. Then all states of C are decided and almost all runs ρ in C have the same $\mathcal{G}(\rho)$.*

Proof. Let $\mathbb{P}_s[\mathcal{L}]$ denote the probability that a run of the Markov chain starting in state s induces a word from language $\mathcal{L}$. Now let $\mathbf{G}\psi \in \mathbb{G}$. If for all $c \in C$, $\mathbb{P}_c[\mathsf{L}(\mathbf{G}\psi)] = 1$, then we are done. Let now $c \in C$ be such that $\mathbb{P}_c[\mathsf{L}(\mathbf{G}\psi)] < 1$. We show that for all $d \in C$, we have $\mathbb{P}_d[\mathsf{L}(\mathbf{G}\psi)] = 0$, thus also proving $\mathbb{P}_d[\mathsf{L}(\mathbf{FG}\psi)] = 0$. Since $\mathbb{P}_c[\mathsf{L}(\mathbf{G}\psi)] < 1$, we have $\mathbb{P}_c[\mathsf{L}(\mathbf{F}\neg\psi)] > 0$. Therefore, with every visit of c there is a positive probability p that ψ will be violated in the next n steps for some $n \in \mathbb{N}$. Since c is in a BSCC it will be visited infinitely often with probability 1 from any $d \in C$. Consequently, $\mathbb{P}_d[\mathsf{L}(\mathbf{G}\psi)] \leq \lim_{k\to\infty}(1-p)^k = 0$. $\square$

We are now ready to prove the inequality "$\leq$". Given a scheduler σ of $\mathcal{M}$, we define a scheduler σ' of $\mathcal{M} \times \mathcal{A}$ such that $\mathbb{P}_{\mathcal{M}^\sigma}[\mathsf{L}(\mathcal{A})] \leq \mathbb{P}_{(\mathcal{M}\times\mathcal{A})^{\sigma'}}[\Diamond X]$. The scheduler σ' follows the behaviour of σ up to the point where a BSCC is reached in $\mathcal{M}^\sigma$. A run on $\mathcal{M}^\sigma$ will almost surely reach some BSCC in $\mathcal{M}^\sigma$. Let m be the first visited state in a BSCC of $\mathcal{M}^\sigma$. By Lemma 12, m has unique decided $\mathcal{G}$, and σ' then chooses the unique ϵ-action ϵ_q such that $q \in Q_\mathcal{N} \times Q_{\mathcal{P}(\mathcal{G})}$. Having performed this ϵ-action, the scheduler σ' then continues to follow the behaviour of σ indefinitely. Note that apart from emulating σ, the constructed scheduler σ' only decides when to switch to the accepting component and with which $\mathcal{G}$.

Notice that by construction every run ρ_σ on $\mathcal{M}^\sigma$ corresponds to a run $\rho_{\sigma'}$ on $(\mathcal{M} \times \mathcal{A})^{\sigma'}$ with equal transition probabilities, except for the probability of the ϵ-action, which has neutral probability 1. It thus only remains to show that if a trace of ρ_σ is accepted by $\mathcal{A}$ then the corresponding run $\rho_{\sigma'}$, projected to the second component, is also an accepting run on $\mathcal{A}$. To this end, let All be the set of states where $\mathcal{A}$ can be after reading the run up to the point where m is reached. In particular, let $init, acc \in All$ be the source and the target of the ϵ-transition taken if σ' is followed, i.e. when the transition from $(m, init)$ to (m, acc) under action ϵ_{acc} is taken. Note that other elements of All correspond to runs of $\mathcal{A}$ that either switch at another time or to an accepting part $Q_\mathcal{N} \times Q_{\mathcal{P}(\mathcal{G}')}$ for a different $\mathcal{G}'$. In order to show that σ' always chooses an accepting run of $\mathcal{A}$ if there is one, we have to show that the following constraints are satisfied:

- Lingering in the initial part and delaying the switch to the acceptance part is safe. Formally:

$$\mathsf{L}(\mathit{init}) \supseteq \bigcup_{a \in \mathit{All}} \mathsf{L}(a) \tag{1}$$

This is shown in Lemma 9.
- Switching to the acceptance part is safe upon reaching the BSCC. Formally:

$$\mathbb{P}_m[\mathsf{L}(\mathit{init})] = \mathbb{P}_m[\mathsf{L}(\mathit{acc})] \tag{2}$$

From Lemma 12 we obtain a unique $\mathcal{G}$ for almost all runs starting in m. Let $\mathsf{L}(\mathcal{G})$ denote the set of runs satisfying $\mathbf{FG}\psi$ for all $\mathbf{G}\psi \in \mathcal{G}$ and not satisfying $\mathbf{FG}\psi$ for all $\mathbf{G}\psi \notin \mathcal{G}$. Further, the set of runs not in $\mathsf{L}(\mathcal{G})$ has zero probability, formally $\mathbb{P}_m[\overline{\mathsf{L}(\mathcal{G})}] = 0$. Hence it is sufficient to show $\mathsf{L}(\mathit{init}) \cap \mathsf{L}(\mathcal{G}) = \mathsf{L}(\mathit{acc}) \cap \mathsf{L}(\mathcal{G})$. Here $\supseteq$ is trivial and for $\subseteq$ let $w \in \mathsf{L}(\mathit{init}) \cap \mathsf{L}(\mathcal{G})$. Observe that $\mathcal{G}$ is a stable set for w. Let φ_{init} be the formula label of init. Because $w \in \mathsf{L}(\mathit{init})$, $w \models \varphi_{\mathit{init}}$. Thus we can apply Lemma 7 and obtain $w \in \mathsf{L}(\mathit{acc})$. $\square$

Remark 2. The limit-deterministic automata of [6] (making its first part deterministic, which is informally mentioned as an option in the paper) and the one of [14] (which is essentially the same) satisfy condition (1). Moreover, they satisfy condition (2), not necessarily upon reaching the BSCC of $\mathcal{M}^\sigma$, but at the latest upon reaching the BSCC of its product with the initial part of the automaton, see [14]. So they can also be used for quantitative probabilistic model checking using the standard algorithm, as implicitly suggested by the more complex on-the-fly variant of the algorithm of [14].

9   Experimental Evaluation

In our experimental evaluation we measure the state size and the number of acceptance sets. We compare our translation to state-of-the-art LTL-to-Büchi and LTL-to-deterministic-Rabin translators.

For the first group we use the semi-determinisation of [6] to obtain limit-deterministic systems where the first component only uses the non-determinism for jumping into the second component, starting a breakpoint construction. This approach enables quantitative model checking (see Remark 2). The algorithm is only applied when the automaton is non-deterministic and this translation is necessary. Apart from selecting state-based Büchi automata as output, the tools are left in their default configuration.

We compared the following tools[2] where each tool is given at most 4 GB of memory and 5 min computing time:

L3 (ltl3ba, 1.1.2) - An enhanced fork of ltl2ba with formula rewriting [1].
 S (ltl2tgba, 1.99.6) - The LTL translator from Spot. Features advanced formula simplification and several post-processing optimisations [9].

---

[2] ltl2ba was left out and the improved "successor" ltl3ba was used.

L2D (ltl2dstar, 0.5.3) - Translates LTL to deterministic Streett and Rabin
    automata. Configured to use Spot as a translator from LTL to NBA [17].
  R (Rabinizer, 3.1) - Constructs deterministic generalized Rabin automata
    avoiding Safra's construction. Configured to produce Rabin automata [19].
 LD (ltl2ldba) - Implementation of the proposed construction without any
    post-processing. Available at: www7.in.tum.de/~sickert/projects/ltl2ldba.

Table 1. Number of states and number of acceptance sets in parenthesis for the constructed automata. The smallest and second smallest state spaces are highlighted.
Each resource exhaustion is marked with an additional *. Abbreviated formulas:
$\varphi_1 = \mathbf{GF}(\mathbf{F}a \vee \mathbf{G}b \vee \mathbf{FG}(a \vee (\mathbf{X}b)))$, $\varphi_2 = \mathbf{FG}(\mathbf{G}a \vee \mathbf{F}\neg b \vee \mathbf{GF}(a \wedge \mathbf{X}b))$, $\varphi_3 = \mathbf{GF}(\mathbf{F}a \vee \mathbf{GX}b \vee \mathbf{FG}(a \vee \mathbf{XX}b))$

	Büchi Acceptance			Rabin Acceptance	
	L3	S	LD	L2D	R
$j = 1$	10 (1)	11 (1)	3 (1)	5 (4)	2 (4)
$j = 2$	21 (1)	21 (1)	4 (2)	17 (6)	3 (6)
$j = 3$	44 (1)	44 (1)	5 (3)	49 (8)	4 (8)
$j = 4$	95 (1)	95 (1)	6 (4)	129 (10)	5 (10)
$k = 2$	40 (1)	62 (1)	5 (2)	4385 (14)	13 (8)
$k = 3$	326 (1)	571 (1)	9 (3)	*	198 (16)
φ_1	37 (1)	12 (1)	9 (3)	6 (4)	7 (6)
φ_2	39 (1)	33 (1)	7 (3)	27 (4)	6 (6)
φ_3	35 (1)	14 (1)	19 (3)	7 (6)	13 (6)
$f(0,0)$	5 (1)	5 (1)	5 (1)	5 (2)	5 (4)
$f(0,2)$	16 (1)	16 (1)	10 (1)	10 (4)	7 (4)
$f(0,4)$	18 (1)	18 (1)	16 (1)	12 (4)	9 (4)
$f(1,0)$	51 (1)	64 (1)	6 (3)	196 (10)	17 (6)
$f(1,2)$	138 (1)	345 (1)	28 (3)	109839 (22)	33 (6)
$f(1,4)$	943 (1)	2450 (1)	58 (3)	*	70 (6)
$f(2,0)$	289 (1)	215 (1)	10 (4)	99793 (22)	41 (8)
$f(2,2)$	915 (1)	1061 (1)	46 (4)	*	94 (8)
$f(2,4)$	12314 (1)	14161 (1)	92 (4)	*	139 (8)
Σ [5]	55444 (353)***	29559 (356)	9518 (889)**	382350 (1670)*	10616 (2554)**

We consider the following five groups of formulas:

1. The first group of formulas in Table 1 are from the GR(1) fragment of LTL
   and parametrised by j: $\bigwedge_{i=1}^{j}(\mathbf{GF}a_i) \implies \bigwedge_{i=1}^{j}(\mathbf{GF}b_i)$. These have been
   previously used in [20].
2. The second group of formulas are fairness constraints, taken from [11], and
   are parametrised by k: $\bigwedge_{i=1}^{k}(\mathbf{GF}a_i \vee \mathbf{FG}b_i)$
3. The third section looks at formulas with light nesting of modal operators.

4. In the fourth section we explore the effect of deeply nesting modal operators using the parametrised formula f.

$$f(0,j) = (\mathbf{GF}a_0)\mathbf{U}(\mathbf{X}^j b) \qquad f(i+1,j) = (\mathbf{GF}a_{i+1})\mathbf{U}(\mathbf{G}f(i,j))$$

While the automata sizes are close to each other for $i, j = 0$, this immediately changes after increasing the parameters controlling the nesting depth.
5. The last entry is cumulative and sums up results for 359 formulas. These formulas are from the collection used in [5]. The authors collected these from existing sources, such as [10,12,13,23], and additionally included randomly generated formulas.

10   Conclusion

We present a direct translation from LTL formulas to limit-deterministic Büchi automata. The approach relies on decomposing the formula, constructing small automata for each $\mathbf{G}$ and building a product deciding acceptance. The complexity analysis shows that translating LTL to limit-deterministic automata is in the worst case double exponential, which is matched by existing constructions and the novel approach. The experimental section shows that for deeply nested formulas the presented approach outperforms existing tools and in the general case is as good as the other tools.

There are several open questions we want to investigate. First, we have not included the *Release*-operator in the syntax. While this does not have an impact on the expressiveness of the logic, direct support for it would be favourable. Second, it is open, if is possible to adapt the construction such that for the $\mathrm{LTL}_{\backslash\mathbf{GU}}$ fragment the size is also exponential as in [16]. Third, we would like to investigate the impact of specialised and standard post-processing steps on the size of the automaton. Fourth, we want to study the performance impact of using this construction for quantitative model checking.

Finally, in the area of reactive synthesis DRAs can be replaced by *good for games* Büchi automata [15,18]. Studying the connection to our translation, and a possibility of adapting our work for reactive synthesis is open.

Acknowledgments. The authors want to thank Orna Kupferman for suggesting the language for proving the lower complexity bound. This work is partially funded by the DFG Research Training Group "PUMA: Programm- und Modell-Analyse" (GRK 1480) and by the Czech Science Foundation Grant No. P202/12/G061.

References

1. Babiak, T., Křetínský, M., Řehák, V., Strejček, J.: LTL to Büchi automata translation: fast and more deterministic. In: Flanagan, C., König, B. (eds.) TACAS 2012. LNCS, vol. 7214, pp. 95–109. Springer, Heidelberg (2012)
2. Baier, C., Kiefer, S., Klein, J., Klüppelholz, S., Müller, D., Worrel, J.: Markov chains and unambiguous Büchi automata. In: CAV 2016 (2016) (to appear). http://arxiv.org/abs/1605.00950

3. Baier, C., Katoen, J.: Principles of Model Checking. MIT Press, Cambridge (2008)
4. Blahoudek, F., Heizmann, M., Schewe, S., Strejček, J., Tsai, M.-H.: Complementing semi-deterministic Büchi automata. In: Chechik, M., Raskin, J.-F. (eds.) TACAS 2016. LNCS, vol. 9636, pp. 770–787. Springer, Heidelberg (2016). doi:10.1007/978-3-662-49674-9_49
5. Blahoudek, F., Křetínský, M., Strejček, J.: Comparison of LTL to deterministic rabin automata translators. In: McMillan, K., Middeldorp, A., Voronkov, A. (eds.) LPAR-19 2013. LNCS, vol. 8312, pp. 164–172. Springer, Heidelberg (2013)
6. Courcoubetis, C., Yannakakis, M.: The complexity of probabilistic verification. J. ACM **42**(4), 857–907 (1995)
7. Couvreur, J., Saheb, N., Sutre, G.: An optimal automata approach to LTL model checking of probabilistic systems. In: Vardi, M.Y., Voronkov, A. (eds.) LPAR 2003. LNCS, vol. 2850, pp. 361–375. Springer, Heidelberg (2003)
8. Duret-Lutz, A.: Manipulating LTL formulas using spot 1.0. In: Van Hung, D., Ogawa, M. (eds.) ATVA 2013. LNCS, vol. 8172, pp. 442–445. Springer, Heidelberg (2013)
9. Duret-Lutz, A.: LTL translation improvements in spot 1.0. Int. J. Crit. Comput.-Based Syst. **5**(1/2), 31–54 (2014)
10. Dwyer, M.B., Avrunin, G.S., Corbett, J.C.: Patterns in property specifications for finite-state verification. In: ICSE, pp. 411–420 (1999)
11. Esparza, J., Křetínský, J.: From LTL to deterministic automata: a safraless compositional approach. In: Biere, A., Bloem, R. (eds.) CAV 2014. LNCS, vol. 8559, pp. 192–208. Springer, Heidelberg (2014)
12. Gastin, P., Oddoux, D.: Fast LTL to Büchi automata translation. In: Berry, G., Comon, H., Finkel, A. (eds.) CAV 2001. LNCS, vol. 2102, pp. 53–65. Springer, Heidelberg (2001)
13. Geldenhuys, J., Hansen, H.: Larger automata and less work for LTL model checking. In: Valmari, A. (ed.) SPIN 2006. LNCS, vol. 3925, pp. 53–70. Springer, Heidelberg (2006)
14. Hahn, E.M., Li, G., Schewe, S., Turrini, A., Zhang, L.: Lazy probabilistic model checking without determinisation. In: Aceto, L., de Frutos Escrig, D. (eds.) CONCUR 2015. LIPIcs, vol. 42, pp. 354–367. Schloss Dagstuhl–Leibniz-Zentrum fuer Informatik, Dagstuhl (2015)
15. Henzinger, T.A., Piterman, N.: Solving games without determinization. In: Ésik, Z. (ed.) CSL 2006. LNCS, vol. 4207, pp. 395–410. Springer, Heidelberg (2006)
16. Kini, D., Viswanathan, M.: Limit deterministic and probabilistic automata for LTL \ GU. In: Baier, C., Tinelli, C. (eds.) TACAS 2015. LNCS, vol. 9035, pp. 628–642. Springer, Heidelberg (2015)
17. Klein, J., Baier, C.: Experiments with deterministic ω-automata for formulas of linear temporal logic. Theoret. Comput. Sci. **363**(2), 182–195 (2006)
18. Klein, J., Müller, D., Baier, C., Klüppelholz, S.: Are good-for-games automata good for probabilistic model checking? In: Dediu, A.-H., Martín-Vide, C., Sierra-Rodríguez, J.-L., Truthe, B. (eds.) LATA 2014. LNCS, vol. 8370, pp. 453–465. Springer, Heidelberg (2014)
19. Komárková, Z., Křetínský, J.: Rabinizer 3: safraless translation of LTL to small deterministic automata. In: Cassez, F., Raskin, J.-F. (eds.) ATVA 2014. LNCS, vol. 8837, pp. 235–241. Springer, Heidelberg (2014)
20. Křetínský, J., Esparza, J.: Deterministic automata for the (F,G)-fragment of LTL. In: Madhusudan, P., Seshia, S.A. (eds.) CAV 2012. LNCS, vol. 7358, pp. 7–22. Springer, Heidelberg (2012)
21. Kupferman, O., Vardi, M.Y.: From linear time to branching time. ACM Trans. Comput. Log. **6**(2), 273–294 (2005)

22. Kwiatkowska, M., Norman, G., Parker, D.: PRISM 4.0: verification of probabilistic real-time systems. In: Gopalakrishnan, G., Qadeer, S. (eds.) CAV 2011. LNCS, vol. 6806, pp. 585–591. Springer, Heidelberg (2011)
23. Pelánek, R.: BEEM: benchmarks for explicit model checkers. In: Bošnački, D., Edelkamp, S. (eds.) SPIN 2007. LNCS, vol. 4595, pp. 263–267. Springer, Heidelberg (2007)
24. Piterman, N.: From nondeterministic Büchi and Streett automata to deterministic parity automata. Log. Methods Comput. Sci. 3(3), 1–21 (2007)
25. Safra, S.: On the complexity of omega-automata. In: FOCS, pp. 319–327 (1988)
26. Schewe, S.: Tighter bounds for the determinisation of Büchi automata. In: de Alfaro, L. (ed.) FOSSACS 2009. LNCS, vol. 5504, pp. 167–181. Springer, Heidelberg (2009)
27. Vardi, M.Y.: Automatic verification of probabilistic concurrent finite-state programs. In: FOCS, pp. 327–338 (1985)

Slugs: Extensible GR(1) Synthesis

Rüdiger Ehlers[1](✉) and Vasumathi Raman[2]

[1] University of Bremen and DFKI GmbH, Bremen, Germany
ruediger.ehlers@uni-bremen.de
[2] United Technologies Research Center, Berkeley, CA, USA

Abstract. Applying reactive synthesis in practice often requires modifications of the synthesis algorithm in order to obtain useful implementations. We present slugs, a generalized reactivity(1) synthesis tool that has a powerful plugin architecture for modifying any aspect of the synthesis process to fit the application. Slugs comes pre-equipped with a variety of plugins that improve the quality of the synthesized solutions along criteria such as quick response, cost-optimality, and error-resilience. We demonstrate the utility and scalability of the tool on an example from robotics.

1 Introduction

Reactive synthesis automates the task of developing correct-by-construction finite-state machines: rather than writing an implementation and a specification for verifying the system, the engineer need only devise the specification, and the implementation is computed automatically. Of the many synthesis approaches available to the practitioner, *generalized reactivity(1) synthesis* [1], which is commonly abbreviated as *GR(1) synthesis*, has found widespread use for applications in robotics and control. Reasons for this success include its comparatively low, singly-exponential time complexity, and its amenability to symbolic computation using binary decision diagrams (BDDs).

The basic idea behind reactive synthesis is to capture *all* of the requirements of the desired implementation in the specification, and to then accept *any* implementation that satisfies the requirements. On a theoretical level, this is a compelling premise: if the obtained implementation is not good enough, the engineer can simply add additional requirements until it is. However, on a practical level, this approach is problematic: in many cases, system properties such as "quick response" or "few states" cannot be captured precisely in the specification without resorting to synthesis with a cost or payoff function. Introducing costs leads to a higher computational complexity, loss of ability to efficiently use BDDs as a computational data structure, and unfavourable theoretical properties, such as suboptimality of finite memory solutions. Having several optimization criteria in the specification can also create undecidable synthesis problems. Finally, some optimization criteria cannot be expressed quantitatively. Examples include minimizing the time spent waiting for environment fairness conditions

© Springer International Publishing Switzerland 2016
S. Chaudhuri and A. Farzan (Eds.): CAV 2016, Part II, LNCS 9780, pp. 333–339, 2016.
DOI: 10.1007/978-3-319-41540-6_18

(i.e. environment actions that can be assumed to be performed infinitely often) to hold, and cooperation with the environment on preserving the environment assumptions.

All these arguments advocate for a different approach to practical reactive synthesis: rather than encoding every qualitative requirement for the synthesized controller into the specification, why not adapt the synthesis algorithm itself to compute implementations that have the properties needed for practical applications? The simplicity of generalized reactivity(1) synthesis makes it particularly suitable as a starting point for demonstrating this approach to synthesis. Modifications of the standard GR(1) algorithm for synthesizing eager and cost-optimal implementations [2] or cooperative implementations [3] that still support symbolic computation have already been proposed in the past, along with semantic modifications for robotics applications [4] and techniques for debugging support [5].

The presented tool slugs offers a framework for GR(1) synthesis and its modifications. It has a small simple core implementation of the GR(1) synthesis algorithm that can be extended by user-written plugins. The architecture of slugs allows one to use multiple plugins at the same time, where each plugin only modifies a part of the synthesis process. A focus of the tool lies on *conciseness* and *readability* of the code, to make it easier for algorithms to be adapted for specific application domains. For example the realizability check on a specification, which amounts to evaluating the main fixpoint formula from [1], takes only 23 lines of code, and yet is very readable. The slugs synthesis tool comes with a specification debugger, using which the cause for realizability and unrealizability of a specification can be determined in an interactive fashion. The tool is written in C++ and is available under the permissive MIT open source license.

This paper is structured as follows: in the next section, we describe the particular view of GR(1) synthesis that slugs takes. Section 3 then provides an overview of slugs's architecture and the available plugins. Finally, Sect. 4 demonstrates slugs's performance on an example specification.

2   GR(1) Synthesis

Synthesis of reactive systems has been identified to have a high computational complexity for many specification logics. For generalized reactivity(1) specifications, the synthesis problem has a complexity that is only exponential in the number of atomic propositions in the specification (or polynomial in the size of the the state space of the *game structure* built in the synthesis process). Given sets of input positions $\mathcal{I}$ and $\mathcal{O}$, specifications in this fragment of linear temporal logic (LTL) are of the form

$$(\varphi_i^a \wedge \varphi_s^a \wedge \varphi_l^a) \rightarrow (\varphi_i^g \wedge \varphi_s^g \wedge \varphi_l^g),$$

where φ_i^a, φ_s^a, and φ_l^a are called the *assumptions*, and φ_i^g, φ_s^g, and φ_l^g are called the *guarantees* of the specification. The assumptions are used to state what we know about the behavior of the environment in which the synthesized system is intended to operate, whereas the guarantees contain the properties that the synthesized system needs to satisfy if the environment behaves as expected. In GR(1) specifications, all assumptions and guarantees must have a certain shape. The *initialization assumptions* φ_i^a and φ_i^g must be free of temporal operators and state valid variable valuations for $\mathcal{I}$ and $\mathcal{O}$ when the synthesized controller starts to operate. The safety properties φ_s^a and φ_s^g state how the proposition valuations for $\mathcal{I}$ and $\mathcal{O}$ can evolve during a step of the synthesized controller's execution. The *liveness properties* φ_l^a and φ_l^g state which transitions of $(\mathcal{I} \cup \mathcal{O})$'s valuations are supposed to happen infinitely often.

Synthesis from generalized reactivity(1) specifications is often reduced to solving a *fixpoint* equation on a *game structure* that is built from the specification. The transitions in the game structure are given by the safety assumptions and guarantees, and the liveness properties are translated to environment and system *goals*, which the system and environment player try to satisfy infinitely often in a play of the game, respectively. In contrast to [1], we use a modified fixpoint equation with only a single occurrence of the *enforceable predecessor operator* EnfPre to compute from which positions the *system player* can win the game:

$$W = \nu Z. \bigwedge_{j=1}^{n} \mu Y. \bigvee_{i=1}^{m} \nu X. \mathsf{EnfPre}((\varphi_{l,j}^g \wedge Z') \vee Y' \vee (\neg \varphi_{l,i}^a \wedge X'))$$

Here, ν is the *greatest fixpoint operator* whereas μ is the *least fixpoint operator*, while the number of liveness assumptions and guarantees are m and n, respectively. The EnfPre operator takes as input a set of *transitions* (the corresponding operator in [1] takes a set of *states*), and computes the set of positions of the game from which the system player can ensure that, after the next valuations to $\mathcal{I}$ and $\mathcal{O}$ have been selected by the environment and system players, respectively, the resulting transition is in the set of given transitions. The specification formula only explicitly mentions the liveness assumptions and guarantees of the specification, as the safety constraints are encoded in the game structure, and the initialization constraints only need to be considered after computing the set of winning positions in the game, W. If for every first environment player move, the system player can ensure that the resulting position satisfies $\varphi_i^a \rightarrow \varphi_i^g$ and is in W, then there exists an implementation for the specification, and it can be extracted from the sequence of transitions given to EnfPre during the evaluation of the least fixpoint, after all the greatest fixpoint operators have been fully evaluated.

The modified fixpoint formula makes it easier to alter the synthesis algorithm, as it channels the possible actions of the implementation to be synthesized through a single invocation of the EnfPre operator. Restricting or extending this set of actions thus amounts to simply adding or removing transitions from the operand of EnfPre. Also, the modified fixpoint formula makes the aims of the system player more explicit: in every step of the system's execution, the system should either reach a *system goal* (which need to be reached infinitely often for the liveness guarantees to hold), get closer to the system goal, or wait for some environment goal to be reached: this last option is only available until the current environment goal has been reached. Except in very simple specifications, it is commonly not under the control of the system which of these cases holds. The system must, however, ensure that at least one of them holds at every point in time. The conjunctions and disjunctions over i and j make sure that all liveness assumptions and guarantees are considered in order.

The presented tool `slugs` does not build the game structure explicitly, but rather uses binary decision diagrams (BDDs) as symbolic data structure. As the synthesis games have all valuations of $\mathcal{I} \cup \mathcal{O}$ as positions, position sets and transitions relations can be represented efficiently as BDDs with $|\mathcal{I}|+|\mathcal{O}|$ many or twice as many variables (one for each 'end' of a transition). All BDD operations are performed by the `CUDD` library [6].

3   Modifying GR(1) Synthesis

Reactive synthesis has many applications, but most of them require the adaptation of the synthesis approach in order to yield useful implementations **and** to scale to problems of relevant size at the same time.

As one example, when performing automated high-level planning in robotics, liveness assumptions are often used to model that *doors* in some workspace must be open infinitely often. For a robot that needs to perform a certain task, this allows the robot to wait for a door to open, for example if it has to pass through the door in order to perform its task. Yet, high-level robot controllers are often observed to wait needlessly for doors to open when alternative paths exist; this is considered to decrease the quality of the controller, even if the specification is satisfied. While lifting the specification to a *weighted* one could solve the problem, solving (synthesis) games symbolically with costs is substantially harder and leads to unfavourable theoretical properties (e.g. optimal strategies require infinitely many states for mean-payoff games with liveness objectives). As an alternative, `slugs` contains a simple modification to the GR(1) fixpoint formula that penalizes such "waiting": the implementation in slugs takes just 7 lines of C++ code.

As another example, in high-level robotics applications [7], the position of a robot in a workspace is commonly under the control of the robot. Safety guarantees constrain the motion of the robot such that it can only move to adjacent regions of a workspace. However, the robot does not have control over where in the workspace it is deployed. A synthesized controller should thus be able to deal with *any* initial robot position. This makes the initial position an input to the controller that is used exactly once, namely when the controller starts. Integrating this additional input into the specification would lead to many more variables in the BDDs during synthesis, which decreases performance. As an alternative, we can confirm that all possible initial locations for the robot are winning by testing for membership in W. This change in the synthesis process needs a single line of code.

The slugs tool offers many plugins that implement other such modifications to the synthesis process. It was designed exactly with such modifications in mind and is optimized towards being easily extensible. In particular, all core parts of the synthesis process have been kept short and easily readable, to enable modifying them with the least effort possible. Slugs uses C++ features such as operator overloading to make all BDD operations concise and easily readable. Furthermore, the input language of slugs is very simple to parse. This facilitates modifications of the synthesis process that are based on *preprocessing* the specification. An additional script to translate from a richer input language to slugs' simpler language is also provided for convenience.

The slugs distribution can be obtained from https://github.com/VerifiableRobotics/slugs and comes equipped with a few plugins that implement techniques that can be found in the literature on GR(1) synthesis:

- The two plugins mentioned above (producing implementations that wait less for the environment and system initialization robotics semantics).
- A plugin to compute implementations that cooperate with the environment to satisfy the environment assumptions [3].
- A plugin to compute a counterstrategy from an unrealizable specification.
- Plugins to compute symbolic and explicit implementations, the former being represented as BDDs.
- A plugin to compute *estimators* for incomplete information synthesis [8].
- A plugin that lets slugs execute a controller in an interactive way, such that it can be used as a tool for simulating the controller called from other tools.
- Various plugins to compute *specification reports*, which help with debugging formal specifications as in [5].
- A plugin that allows output variables to be divided into two classes, "fast" and "slow", and ensures that each transition in the solution is safe even if the faster actions complete first [9].
- A plugin that computes implementations with *recovery transitions*, which allow the system to continue operating after safety assumption failures that can be compensated, similarly to the approach in [10].
- A plugin that computes the permissive implementations from [11].
- A plugin implementing the two-dimensional cost notion from [2].
- A plugin that computes a weakening of the assumptions in case of a realizable specification such that the specification stays realizable under the weakening.

In addition, the slugs distribution comes with several Python scripts that augment its functionality:

- A script to modify a specification such that it encodes the *error-resilient* synthesis problem for the original specification [12].
- A debugger to simulate implementations for realizable specifications and to simulate a falsifying environment for unrealizable specifications.
- A compiler that converts specifications with integer variables and constraints to purely boolean specifications.
- A specification report generator similar to the one described in [5].

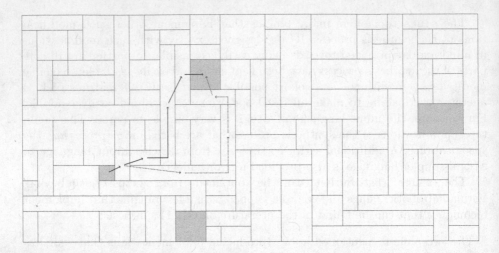

Fig. 1. A robot workspace and two paths to reach the respective next goal. The naive one is dotted, whereas the optimized one is not.

The `slugs` tool also allows to combine multiple plugins, provided that they have been marked as being compatible.

4   Slugs in Action

We now describe a concrete application made possible by a `slugs` plugin.

Consider the synthesis problem for a high level robot controller in which the robot operates on the workspace depicted in Fig. 1. The workspace is partitioned into regions, which all have different sizes. The position of the robot is under its control, but it can only move to adjacent cells in each step. There are four goals for the robot that each have to be visited infinitely often. For two of the goal regions, we have additional input bits. Those regions do not have to be reached if their respective input bit is **false**. The standard GR(1) synthesis algorithm does not use the relative sizes of the regions, and therefore the strategy that we synthesize in this setting is not optimal with respect to the physical grounding of the scenario. The figure shows one relatively complex path for getting from one gray region to another one that is part of the synthesized strategy.

To ensure that the physically more efficient strategy is obtained, the synthesis algorithm must be modified to incorporate worst-case costs on transitions between rooms. For this example, we use the difference between region centers as cost measure. `Slugs` comes with a plugin that implements GR(1) synthesis with a cost function, similar to the modifications described in [2]. The alternative path is shown in Fig. 1 as well. Note that the notion of optimality here is somewhat specific to the application domain, as we always optimize the cost for reaching the *next goal* of the robot, rather than using an optimization criterion such as mean-payoff.

To solve the realizability problem of the scenario, `slugs` needs 0.03 s on a
i5 1.6 GHz computer. Extracting an explicit-state implementation takes 0.1 s in
addition (1015 states), and synthesizing the optimal strategy takes another 14.9 s
(resulting in 3315 states).

Acknowledgements. This work was supported by NSF ExCAPE and the Institutional Strategy of the University of Bremen, funded by the German Excellence Initiative.

References

1. Bloem, R., Jobstmann, B., Piterman, N., Pnueli, A., Sa'ar, Y.: Synthesis of reactive(1) designs. J. Comput. Syst. Sci. **78**(3), 911–938 (2012)
2. Jing, G., Ehlers, R., Kress-Gazit, H.: Shortcut through an evil door: optimality of correct-by-construction controllers in adversarial environments. In: IEEE/RSJ International Conference on Intelligent Robots and Systems (IROS), pp. 4796–4802 (2013)
3. Ehlers, R., Könighofer, R., Bloem, R.: Synthesizing cooperative reactive mission plans. In: 2015 IEEE/RSJ International Conference on Intelligent Robots and Systems (IROS), pp. 3478–3485 (2015)
4. Raman, V., Piterman, N., Finucane, C., Kress-Gazit, H.: Timing semantics for abstraction and execution of synthesized high-level robot control. IEEE Trans. Robot. **31**(3), 591–604 (2015)
5. Ehlers, R., Raman, V.: Low-effort specification debugging and analysis. In: 3rd Workshop on Synthesis (SYNT), pp. 117–133 (2014)
6. Somenzi, F.: CUDD: CU Decision Diagram package release 3.0.0 (2015)
7. Kress-Gazit, H., Fainekos, G.E., Pappas, G.J.: Temporal-logic-based reactive mission and motion planning. IEEE Trans. Robot. **25**(6), 1370–1381 (2009)
8. Ehlers, R., Topcu, U.: Estimator-based reactive synthesis under incomplete information. In: 18th International Conference on Hybrid Systems: Computation and Control (HSCC), pp. 249–258 (2015)
9. Raman, V., Finucane, C., Kress-Gazit, H.: Temporal logic robot mission planning for slow and fast actions. In: IEEE/RSJ International Conference on Intelligent Robots and Systems (IROS), pp. 251–256 (2012)
10. Wong, K.W., Ehlers, R., Kress-Gazit, H.: Correct high-level robot behavior in environments with unexpected events. In: Robotics: Science and Systems (RSS) (2014)
11. Wen, M., Ehlers, R., Topcu, U.: Correct-by-synthesis reinforcement learning with temporal logic constraints. In: IEEE/RSJ International Conference on Intelligent Robots and Systems (IROS), pp. 4983–4990 (2015)
12. Ehlers, R., Topcu, U.: Resilience to intermittent assumption violations in reactive synthesis. In: 17th International Conference on Hybrid Systems: Computation and Control (HSCC), pp. 203–212 (2014)

Synthesis II

Synthesis of Fault-Attack Countermeasures for Cryptographic Circuits

Hassan Eldib, Meng Wu, and Chao Wang[⊠]

Department of ECE, Virginia Tech,
Blacksburg, VA 24061, USA
chaowang@vt.edu

Abstract. Fault sensitivity analysis (FSA) is a side-channel attack method that injects faults to cryptographic circuits through clock glitching and applies statistical analysis to deduce sensitive data such as the cryptographic key. It exploits the correlation between the circuit's signal path delays and sensitive data. A countermeasure, in this case, is an alternative implementation of the circuit where signal path delays are made independent of the sensitive data. However, manually developing such countermeasure is tedious and error prone. In this paper, we propose a method for synthesizing the countermeasure automatically to defend against FSA attacks. Our method uses a syntax-guided inductive synthesis procedure combined with a light-weight static analysis. Given a circuit and a set of sensitive signals as input, it returns a functionally-equivalent and FSA-resistant circuit as output, where all path delays are made independent of the sensitive signals. We have implemented our method and evaluated it on a set of cryptographic circuits. Our experiments show that the method is both scalable and effective in eliminating FSA vulnerabilities.

1 Introduction

The rising security risks in embedded computing devices in cyber physical systems (CPS) and the Internet of Things (IoT) have led to the pervasive use of cryptographic modules, often implemented in hardware, to guarantee secure authentication, privacy, and integrity [3]. In particular, various light-weight cryptographic primitives have been recommended for securing resource-constrained devices such as Smartcards and RFID tags [10,27]. Although these cryptographic algorithms are designed to be secure against brute-force attacks, their actual implementations may not be as secure. Indeed, there have been many reported cases of attacks on cryptographic modules in embedded systems, the majority of which were through side-channel attacks [5,33,36].

Fault sensitivity analysis (FSA) is a side-channel attack [20,32,37] that exploits the correlation between secret data and the time needed to propagate these data through a cryptographic circuit. In particular, there is a large number of reported cases of such attacks on lightweight block ciphers [4,21,23,24,29,30, 38,39,42]. With physical access to the circuit, an attacker can introduce clock

© Springer International Publishing Switzerland 2016
S. Chaudhuri and A. Farzan (Eds.): CAV 2016, Part II, LNCS 9780, pp. 343–363, 2016.
DOI: 10.1007/978-3-319-41540-6_19

glitches until logical errors occur in the output. The attacker measures the fault intensity *critical level* [24], which is the lowest fault intensity level where a faulty output first occurs. This critical level can be compared, via a statistical analysis [9], with a set of simulated critical levels computed *a priori*, to determine the most likely values of the secret signals [41].

A countermeasure is an alternative implementation of the circuit where all signal path delays are made independent of the sensitive data. However, manually developing such countermeasure is tedious and error prone. Therefore, we propose a new method for constructing the countermeasure automatically. Given a circuit C and a set S of sensitive signals as input, our method relies on inductive synthesis [2,25,40] to compute a functionally equivalent circuit that is guaranteed to be resistant to FSA attacks. More specifically, it first generates a candidate circuit C' that, at least for some input values, produces the same output as C, and is likely to have balanced delay along the sensitive paths. Then, it invokes a verification subroutine to check that C' and C are functionally equivalent for all input values and C' is FSA-resistant. If C' passes this verification step, then a countermeasure has been synthesized. Otherwise, we block this bad countermeasure and generate another candidate circuit. The iterative *guess-and-check* procedure continues until a valid solution is found, or it runs out of time or memory.

Although inductive synthesis has been successfully applied in main domains [2,13,25,26,31,40], this is the first time that it is used to mitigate fault attacks on cryptographic circuits. In practice, however, the bottleneck of applying inductive synthesis to practical applications is the limited scalability of the synthesis tool. Since the design space is enormous, directly applying inductive synthesis to large circuits often does not work. Fortunately, in this application, FSA-resistant circuits are amenable to compositional analysis. That is, the delay of a path in a circuit is the summation of the delays of its individual path segments. Based on this observation, we have developed a *divide-and-conquer* approach, which first divides the circuit into pieces, then synthesizes a countermeasure for each piece, and finally composes them to form the final solution. In this context, our verification subroutine is implemented as an equivalence checker for C' and C augmented with a static analysis procedure for computing the delays along their sensitive paths.

We have implemented our method and evaluated it on a set of realistic cryptographic circuits, including a set of nonlinear components of AES and MAC-Keccak. Our experimental results show that the new method is both scalable and effective in eliminating FSA vulnerabilities. Furthermore, the resulting circuits are consistently smaller than the countermeasures obtained by competing techniques. To summarize, this paper makes the following contributions:

- We propose the first fully automated method for synthesizing FSA-resistant cryptographic circuits.
- We develop a new partitioned synthesis procedure to improve the scalability of our method.

– We demonstrate the effectiveness of our new method on realistic cryptographic benchmarks.

The remainder of this paper is organized as follows. First, we illustrate our main ideas using examples in Sect. 2. Then, we establish the notation in Sect. 3 and present our baseline inductive synthesis algorithm in Sect. 4. We present our partitioned synthesis procedure in Sects. 5 and 6 and our experimental results in Sect. 7. We review related work in Sect. 8 and finally give our conclusions in Sect. 9.

2   Motivation

In this section, we illustrate the main ideas behind our countermeasure synthesis method using examples. Specifically, we use the PPRM1 AES S-box implementation proposed by Morioka and Satoh [34] as the original circuit, shown partially in Fig. 1. The standard Advanced Encryption Standard (AES) algorithm has four main functions that are repeated for a number of rounds depending on the required length of the secret key. Among the four functions, S-box is the only nonlinear function. In cryptographic engineering, nonlinear functions are often the hardest to implement and protect against side-channel attacks. In particular, the S-box implementation scheme in Fig. 1 is a widely used benchmark in the cryptography field. The entire circuit is constructed from two parts: a network of XOR gates and a network of AND gates. For simplicity, we only use the network of AND gates to illustrate our synthesis algorithm. Later in this paper, we will explain how our method can be applied to larger circuits, by first partitioning a circuit into smaller regions, then synthesizing a countermeasure for each region, and finally composing the partial solutions to form the countermeasure for the whole circuit.

The circuit in Fig. 1 is vulnerable to FSA attacks because the time taken for computing the output signals depends not only on the structure of the circuit but also on the values of the sensitive input signals (e.g., bits in the cryptographic key). Consider the output signal O_0 of the AND network and the two input signals In_2 and I_{chain}. Let $\tau(I_{chain})$ and $\tau(In_2)$ be the signal arrival times of I_{chain} and In_2, respectively. If we assume

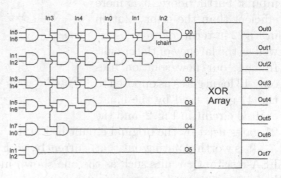

Fig. 1. PPRM1 AES S-box that is vulnerable to FSA.

that all input signals In_0-In_7 have the same arrival time, we have $\tau(I_{chain}) > \tau(In_2)$. Furthermore, the value of $\tau(I_{chain})$ depends on the value of the input signals $In_0, In_1, In_3, In_4, In_5, In_6$ as well as the number of gates along the path.

If we assume that In_2 is a sensitive signal, the aforementioned mismatch in the arrival time of the input signals of the last AND gate will make signal O_0 sensitive as well.

In the context of FSA attacks, we say that the output O_0 is statistically dependent on the sensitive variable In_2 for the following reasons. When the value of In_2 is logical 1, the delay $\tau(O_0)$ is determined by $\tau(I_{chain})$. In contrast, when the value of In_2 is logical 0, the delay $\tau(O_0)$ is determined by $\tau(In_2)$. Since $\tau(I_{chain}) > \tau(In_2)$, the dependency relation and the secret value of In_2 cause a leak of the sensitive information, which is recoverable by correlation-based statistical analysis techniques [32, 37].

Previously published countermeasures for FSA, typically hand-crafted by cryptographic system engineers [19, 22], rely on adding buffers (delay components) to certain input-output paths to eliminate such information leaks. For example, a recently-published countermeasure in Fig. 2 was implemented by manually analyzing the input-output signal paths for each output gate, and then adding buffers accordingly to make the delay along all sensitive paths equal. However, such countermeasures often result in an unnecessarily large number of logic gates inserted into the circuit, thus leading to higher area cost and energy cost.

Our method, in contrast, can generate more efficient countermeasures. Figure 3 illustrates the circuit synthesized by our method, which is functionally equivalent to the original circuit and at the same time guarantees to be FSA-resistant. That is, the path delays are independent of the sensitive inputs. Furthermore, it is more efficient than the prior solution in Fig. 2 in terms of area cost as well as the latency of the circuit. In fact, our new solution uses only 13 logic gates as opposed to the 41 gates used by the hand-crafted circuit in Fig. 2, and the 21 gates used by the original circuit in Fig. 1.

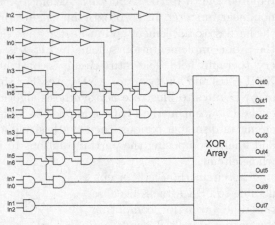

Fig. 2. S-box with buffered countermeasure [22].

It is worth pointing out that, currently, no EDA tool can be used to generate FSA-resistant circuits such as the one shown in Fig. 3. For example, traditional logic synthesis and optimization techniques, such as two- and multi-level minimizations [28], do not have the capability of identifying sensitive signal paths or ensuring that these paths exhibit the same delay. We will demonstrate this in the experiments section and explain why it is difficult to leverage state-of-the-art EDA algorithms, such as the ones implemented in the ABC tool [12], to generate FSA-resistant circuits.

Our new method leverages the idea of syntax-guided *inductive synthesis* to generate FSA countermeasures. Although inductive synthesis has been applied to many domains [2, 13, 25, 26, 31, 40], this is the first time it is used to eliminate FSA vulnerabilities in cryptographic circuits. When inductive synthesis techniques are applied to large circuits, however, scalability becomes a problem because

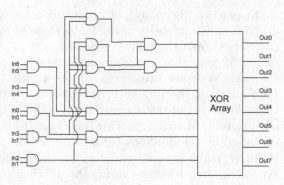

Fig. 3. S-box with our new countermeasure.

the synthesis procedure has to search an extremely large design space for an alternative and FSA-resistant implementation of the given circuit. As mentioned earlier, we propose to solve this scalability problem using a *partitioned* synthesis procedure. After establishing the notion and present our baseline synthesis algorithm in Sects. 3 and 4, we will explain how to leverage the *divide-and-conquer* principle to scale our synthesis method to large circuits.

3   Preliminaries

Fault attacks are typically conducted by changing the physical environment of the circuit to introduce logical errors. Although various fault injection techniques have been used in practice, in this work, we focus on faults injected by disturbing the external clock, and more specifically, by increasing the clock frequency beyond its normal range.

Fault Sensitivity Analysis (FSA). In digital circuits, the time taken by the output to change from logical 1 to logical 0 (or vice versa) in response to changes in the inputs may depend on the circuit structure as well as values of the input/internal signals. This is important to attackers, because it means the impact of an injected fault will be significantly different depending on the internal states of the circuit. Consider the AND gate in Fig. 4, where T_A and T_B are the arrival time of input signals A and B, respectively, and T_{AND} is the gate's propagation delay. When $T_A < T_B$, i.e., signal B arrives later than signal A, the time taken for signal C to stabilize (T_c) depends on the value of signal A. Specifically,

– when A is logical 0, we have $T_c = T_A + T_{AND}$; and
– when A is logical 1, we have $T_c = T_B + T_{AND}$.

In other words, by observing the difference in T_c we can deduce the (sensitive) value of A based on our knowledge of the circuit structure. Such dependency is not unique to AND gates; other logic gates have similar properties. For a large circuit, it is not uncommon for delays along input-to-output paths to depend on the values of sensitive signals. However, to launch a successful attack, merely injecting faults is not enough; these faults must become observable.

In practice, the chance of producing a faulty output depends on the intensity of the faults injected to the circuit, for example, through over-clocking [20,23], as shown in Fig. 5. Note that the information leak is specific to the *faults* as opposed to generic *timing* attacks. Without fault injection, the tiny delay variation in the combinational logic part of this sequential circuit $(C(i,o))$ would

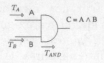

Fig. 4. Fault sensitivity of an AND gate.

not be visible to attackers. This is because the output signals (o) are always synchronized by the flip-flops before they are propagated to the next clock cycle. However, faults injected via clock glitching may destabilize the flip-flop based synchronization scheme, causing the information leak.

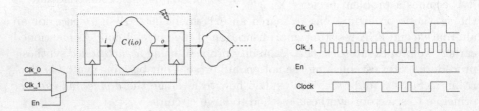

Fig. 5. Injecting faults via clock glitching [20,23]: (a) the circuit and (b) the timing diagram.

Following Ghalaty et al. [23], we define the *fault intensity* and *fault sensitivity* of a circuit as follows. The fault intensity is the strength of the faults by which a circuit is pushed outside of its normal operating condition. Since faults are introduced through clock-glitching, the fault intensity corresponds to the shortened clock cycle. The fault sensitivity is defined as the fault intensity where the circuit starts to generate faulty output. In our work, the fault intensity corresponds to the critical paths in the circuit. FSA, in particular, relies on exploiting the dependency between the values of sensitive input signals and the fault sensitivity critical level, or simply the *critical level*, under which injected faults become observable in the circuit's output.

Attacks and Countermeasures. We assume the attacker has knowledge of the circuit under attack. In this case, an FSA attack often consists of three steps:

1. The attacker injects faults through clock-glitching and measures the critical level of the circuit for a set of N randomly generated plaintexts (inputs);
2. The attacker computes, using computer simulation, the critical level for each of the N selected plaintexts and combinations of the sensitive data values;
3. The attacker performs a correlation analysis between the *measured* critical level and the *simulated* critical level for each combination of sensitive data values.

In the third step above, the sensitive data value combination that results in the highest correlation coefficient will be identified and used to deduce the sensitive data value.

Since the necessary condition for FSA attacks is having easily distinguishable fault sensitivity *critical levels* for various sensitive data value combinations, the goal of a countermeasure is to disable this condition. Generally speaking, among output signals whose arrival time depend on the sensitive data, the greater the difference in their arrival times, the more distinguishable the critical levels, and consequently, the higher the chance that attackers can successfully deduce the sensitive data. Therefore, the ideal countermeasure is an alternative and functionally-equivalent implementation of the original circuit that has the same delay for all its sensitive input-output signal paths.

Previously published FSA countermeasures [19,22] mainly rely on adding delay elements to certain parts of the circuit to make the arrival time of all output signals independent of the sensitive data. However, this approach may add an unnecessarily large number of delay elements (buffers), which results in higher area cost and power cost (Fig. 2). In contrast, our method can generate a potentially more efficient countermeasure (Fig. 3) using the new inductive synthesis technique.

4 Synthesis of FSA Countermeasures

Our method takes a circuit C and a set S of sensitive signals as input and returns an FSA-resistant circuit C' as output. It consists of a synthesis subroutine and a verification subroutine, where the synthesis subroutine guesses a candidate solution and the verification subroutine checks whether it is a valid solution. In this work, the verification subroutine has to check two properties: (1) the new circuit C' is functionally equivalent to C; and (2) the new circuit C' is FSA-resistant.

More formally, we say that two circuits $C(i, o)$ and $C'(i', o')$ are functionally equivalent if $(i = i') \rightarrow (o = o')$. Let $\pi_A(i'_A, o'_C)$ and $\pi_B(i'_B, o'_C)$ be two sensitive paths in C', where $i'_A, i'_B \in S$ are the sensitive inputs and $i'_A \neq i'_B$. Let $\tau_v(\pi)$ be the delay of the path π under the input valuation v – different input values can lead to different delays of the same path. We say that C' is FSA-resistant if $\tau_v(\pi_A(i'_A, o'_C)) = \tau_v(\pi_B(i'_B, o'_C))$ for *any two such* paths π_A and π_B and *any valuation* v of the input signals.

To reduce the computational cost, we choose to formulate the synthesis subproblem in a way that every solution C' is guaranteed to be FSA-resistant. Therefore, the verification subroutine only needs to check the functional equivalence of C and C'. The main idea behind our synthesis subroutine is to construct a *template circuit*, whose instantiations are guaranteed to be FSA-resistant. Without loss of generality, we assume all logic gates have *unit propagation delay*, and being FSA-resistant means that all paths from sensitive signals to the output have an equal number of logic gates. Consider the example in Fig. 1 again, whose template circuit is shown in Fig. 6. Gates and input/output signals in this diagram are distributed to five different levels, where Level 0 consists of only output signals, Level 4 consists of only input signals, and in between the two levels are the logic gates of various types. This is a template because neither the types of internal logic gates nor the connections between the gates have been fixed.

To make sure all instantiations of this template circuit are FSA-resistant, we require that (1) all sensitive input nodes are placed on the same level–although they do not have to be at the bottom level–and (2) the output and input of each node are constrained to be connected, respectively, to either a node of one level higher or a node of one level lower, to ensure that the level assigned to this node remains valid. Implicitly, the above constraints guarantee an equal number of gates between each output signal and the corresponding sensitive inputs. Note that the

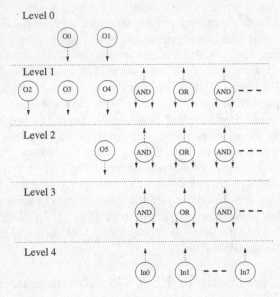

Fig. 6. FSA-resistant template circuit structure.

circuit only needs to have equal-delay paths for each output; it does not need to have the same delay for all outputs.

To reduce the computational overhead within the SyGuS tools, we also statically estimate the level where the output signals should be placed in the template circuit, based on the number of inputs they are connected to and the level required for each input. Since this is only an estimation, initially we assign the minimal depth needed to separate an output node from the sensitive input nodes to fit all nodes in between. If the depth turns out to be insufficient, the synthesis subroutine would fail to return a solution, in which case we shift the output nodes one level up to enlarge the design space, and invoke the synthesis subroutine again.

In principle, this synthesis subproblem can be specified using the SyGuS specification language and solved using the associated tools developed by Alur et al. [2] (or the Sketch tool by Solar-Lezama [40]). In practice, however, there are two significant challenges. The first challenge is due to a limitation in the implementation of SyGuS tools. Specifically, they are designed for synthesizing a function with a single output, whereas we need to synthesize a circuit with multiple output signals, and these output signals must share logic gates that fall in their cone-of-influence as much as possible. Although SyGus allows the use of multiple functions (each with a single output) to mimic a circuit with multiple output signals, in such case, the SyGuS tools would not return a solution where the internal nodes are shared among these functions. Therefore, we need to modify the SyGuS tools, so that internal nodes can be shared among multiple functions.

Figure 7 shows an example SyGuS specification. The original circuit is given by the function Spec, which defines the output signals O_o and O_1 of the circuit in Fig. 1. Note that **ite** is a special operator that we use as a *work-around* since SyGuS does not allow the output to be a concatenation of bits. Inside the SyGuS tool, we made some modification to permit the solver to return a circuit where different output signals share the same set of intermediate logic gates – this is crucial for us to generate a compact circuit. The template of the output circuit is given by the function Impl, which specifies the pool of components that can be used by the synthesizer, including the output node **Start**, and nodes on the remaining three levels: d0, d1 and d2. On each level, both AND and OR gates may be used. The primary inputs are i0 − i6. The constraint at the bottom of the file states that the two circuits are functionally equivalent. Given this specification as input, the SyGuS tool will generate the desired countermeasure.

```
1  (define-fun Spec ((i0 Bool)(i1 Bool)(i2 Bool)(i3 Bool)(i4 Bool)(i5 Bool)(i6
        Bool)) Int
2    (+ (ite (and i2 (and i1 (and i0 (and i4 (and i3 (and i5 i6)))))) 1 0 )
3       (ite (and i1 (and i0 (and i4 (and i3 (and i1 i2)))))  2 0 ) )
4  )
5  (synth-fun Impl ((i0 Bool)(i1 Bool)(i2 Bool)(i3 Bool)(i4 Bool)(i5 Bool)(i6
        Bool)) Int
6   ((Start Bool ( (+ (ite d0 1 0)
7                     (ite d0 2 0)) ) )
8     (d0 Bool ( (and d1 d1)
9                (or d1 d1) ) )
10    (d1 Bool ( (and d2 d2)
11               (or d2 d2) ) )
12    (d2 Bool ( (and d3 d3)
13               (or d3 d3) ) )
14    (d3 Bool ( i0 i1 i2 i3 i4 i5 i6 ) ) )
15 )
16 (constraint (= (Spec i0 i1 i2 i3 i4 i5 i6) (Impl i0 i1 i2 i3 i4 i5 i6) ) )
```

Fig. 7. Automatically generated synthesis subproblem for O_0 and O_1 (Fig. 1) in SyGuS language.

The second challenge is to scale up this new synthesis method to large circuits. Even with the optimizations mentioned above, state-of-the-art SyGuS tools can only handle small circuits, since as the circuit size increases, the design space that SyGuS has to search through increase dramatically. Although we believe the performance of SyGuS tools will continue to improve in the coming years, such improvement alone is unlikely to be sufficient for handling realistic circuits. Therefore, we propose a new method based on the idea of *divide-and-conquer*. It leverages a nice *compositionality* property of the FSA-resistant circuit: If each partition of a circuit is FSA-resistant, then the whole circuit is guaranteed to be FSA-resistant as well.

5   The Partitioned Synthesis Approach

To partition the given circuit, we first represent the combinational part as a directed acyclic graph (DAG), whose input nodes are either *primary inputs* or *pseudo primary inputs* (outputs of latches from the previous clock cycle). Then, we traverse the DAG in a topological order to identify the vulnerable (sensitive) output signals. Specifically, if there are discrepancies between the delays along different paths to the output from different sensitive inputs, we consider it to be vulnerable. For each vulnerable output signal, we build a circuit region by iteratively including logic gates in its fanin and fanout cones until the region size reaches a predefined limit. We invoke the SyGuS tool on each circuit region to synthesize the replacement circuit. By replacing the old circuit region with the new circuit, we can eliminate the vulnerability. This process of extracting, synthesizing, and replacing vulnerable circuit regions is repeated until no vulnerable circuit region exists any more.

5.1   The Overall Algorithm

The pseudocode of our partitioned synthesis procedure is shown in Algorithm 1, where P denotes the original circuit, *InputSort* denotes a map from each input of P to a type (sensitive or non-sensitive), *GatesPD* denotes a map from each gate in P to its propagation delay, and *GatesSyn* denotes a set of logic gates (components) to be used by SyGuS for synthesizing the new circuit. The parameter *lev* is a bound on the maximum number of levels of the new circuit region to be synthesized.

Algorithm 1. Partitioned FSA-countermeasure synthesis procedure.

```
 1:  GEN-COUNTERMEASURE (P, InputSort, GatesPD, GatesSyn, lev) {
 2:      while ( true ) {
 3:          for each ( gate g ∈ P ) {
 4:              MaxPD[g] ← GETMAXPD (g, GatesPD, P)
 5:              MinAr[g] ← GETMINAR (g, GatesPD, P)
 6:              MaxAr[g] ← GETMAXAR (g, GatesPD, P)
 7:          }
 8:          sGate ← GETSENSITIVE (MaxPD, MinAr, MaxAr, P)
 9:          if (sGate = ∅)
10:              return P;
11:          n ← 2^lev − 1
12:          newReg ← ∅
13:          while (newReg = ∅) {
14:              reg ← GETREG (sGate, MinAr, MaxAr, P, n)
15:              newReg ← SYNTHESIZE (reg, MinAr, GatesSyn, lev)
16:              n ← n − 1
17:          }
18:          P ← UPDATEREGION (P, reg, newReg)
19:      }
20: }
```

Our method first identifies a sensitive gate $sGate \in P$ (Lines 3–8), based on which it generates small circuit regions (Line 14). It starts by analyzing each gate $g \in P$ while creating three auxiliary tables:

- $MaxPD[g]$ denotes the maximum path delay from g to the output of P,
- $MinAr[g]$ denotes the minimum arrival time of any sensitive input to g, and
- $MaxAr[g]$ denotes the maximum arrival time of any sensitive input to g.

The subroutine GETSENSITIVE returns the next sensitive gate $sGate$, which is a gate $g \in P$ such that the maximum arrival time $MaxAr[g]$ differs from the minimum arrival time $MinAr[g]$. In the presence of multiple choices, this subroutine returns a gate with the smallest propagation delay from the sensitive inputs. In the case of a tie, the gate with the maximum propagation delay $MaxPD[g]$ to the primary output is selected. This heuristic helps our method find a small countermeasure circuit.

Next, it invokes the subroutine GETREG to extract a circuit region reg, consisting of logic gates in the fanin and fanout cones of $sGate$. From reg, we synthesize a new circuit $newReg$, which is functionally equivalent to reg and, at the same time, FSA-resistant. If the synthesis subroutine fails to find $newReg$ for reg, it will be invoked again for a circuit region reg with a smaller number of gates. There may not always exist an FSA-resistant $newReg$, for example, when the mismatch between the maximum and minimum arrival times of the inputs of reg exceeds the maximum depth of $newReg$ defined by lev. In such case, $newReg$ is synthesized with the goal of reducing the mismatch between the arrival times, and the residual mismatch will be eliminated in a later iteration. After finding the new region, we replace it with the old region in P. We keep updating P until no more sensitive gates remain in the circuit. At this point, the new circuit P is returned.

5.2   Region Selection

Inside the subroutine GETREG, the sensitive gate $sGate$ is added to reg first. Then, we expand reg by adding the sensitive fanout gates transitively. When no sensitive fanout gate exists, we add the sensitive fanin gates of $sGate$ transitively. When there are multiple sensitive fanin gates, we always add the gate with the minimum arrival time first, until reg reaches a predefined size limit n. This heuristic ensures that we follow a topological order and therefore avoids the need to re-synthesize countermeasures for the same gate. It also reduces the maximum mismatch in the arrival time by decreasing the circuit's maximum depth.

Given lev, which is controlled by the user, each new region would have a maximum size of $2^{lev} - 1$ gates. The maximum size occurs when all region inputs have equal arrival time from the inputs of P. If the region inputs have different arrival time, however, they will be assigned to different levels in the template circuit, which means the total number of gates would be less than $2^{lev} - 1$.

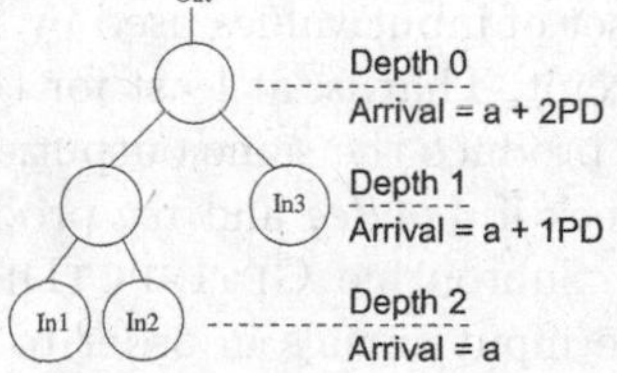

Fig. 8. The size of the new region.

For example, the region in Fig. 8 has $lev = 2$, but since the three inputs have arrival time of a, a and $a + 1$, respectively, the template circuit would have two nodes as opposed to the maximum $(2^2 - 1) = 3$ nodes.

In Algorithm 1, both *GatesSyn* and *lev* are parameters that may be controlled by the user. They are used to identify a sweet spot for the application with respect to several optimization factors. For example, by including more types of gates in *GatesSyn*, the number of solutions to be examined by the SyGuS tool will increase. It may lead to a more compact solution, but may also increase the search time. Similarly, having a larger *lev* will improve the quality of the synthesized circuit, since gate sharing is more likely in a larger circuit than in a smaller circuit. On the other hand, having a larger *lev* will significantly slow down the synthesis procedure.

6   The Synthesis Subroutine

Given a circuit region *reg*, the subroutine SYNTHESIZE searches for a functionally equivalent new circuit *newReg* that is also FSA-resistant. The pseudocode of this subroutine is shown in Algorithm 2, where the input consists of *reg*, the map *MinAr*, the set *GatesSyn* of logic gates (components) to used in creating *newReg*, and *lev*.

Algorithm 2. The synthesis subroutine based on SyGuS.

```
1:  SYNTHESIZE (reg, MinAr, GatesSyn, lev) {
2:     testEx ← ∅
3:     Depth ← GETINPUTDEPTH (reg, lev, MinAr)
4:     while (true) {
5:        newReg ← GENNEWREGION (reg, testEx, Depth, GatesSyn, lev)
6:        if (newReg exists) {
7:           test ← CHECKEQUIVALENCE (reg, newReg)
8:           if (test = ∅)
9:              return newReg;
10:          testEx ← testEx ∪ {test}
11:       }
12:       else
13:          return ∅;
14:    }
15: }
```

The subroutine starts by initializing the set *testEx* to an empty set. This is a set of input values used by SyGuS to generate a partially equivalent candidate circuit. That is, at least for these test input values, *newReg* and *reg* guaranteed to produce the same output. Later, we will invoke the verification subroutine to check if *newReg* and *reg* produce the same output for all possible input values.

Subroutine GETINPUTDEPTH computes the appropriate depth for each of the input signals in order to reduce the discrepancies among their arrival time at the outputs. At Line 4, the subroutine enters a while-loop that contains two main steps. In the first step, it calls SYNNEWREGION to search for *newReg*. In the second step, it calls CHECKEQUIVALENCE to prove the functional equivalence of *reg* and *newReg*. If they are not equivalent, a counterexample, denoted *test*, will be returned. This new input value will be added to *testEx* before the while-loop enters the next iteration. The larger the set *testEx*, the more likely that the next *newReg* is functionally equivalent to *reg*.

Computing the Input Depth. The subroutine GETINPUTDEPTH computes, for each input signal in *reg*, the allowed depth in *newReg* (the *level* as described in Fig. 6). Recall that each input signal in *reg* may have a different arrival time. Therefore, inside *newReg*, they need to be placed at different levels (or have different depths) in order to eliminate the mismatch in the time taken for them to arrive at the output. Consider, for example, the circuit in Fig. 9, which has different delay along different input-to-output paths in *reg* (boxed region). To eliminate the mismatch in *newReg*, node X should be placed one level closer to the output O than nodes A and B. The pseudocode for computing the depths of all input signals (for creating *newReg*) is shown in Algorithm 3.

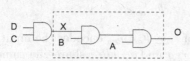

Fig. 9. Example of circuit *reg*.

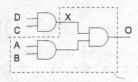

Fig. 10. Example of the *newReg*.

Algorithm 3. Computing the depths of the input nodes in *newReg*.

```
1: GETINPUTDEPTH (reg, lev, MinAr) {
2:    minMinAr ← minimum of MinAr[in] for all input in
3:    for each  (input signal in ∈ reg) {
4:       Δ_Ar ← MinAr[in] − minMinAr
5:       newRegDepth[in] ← MAX(2, (lev − Δ_Ar))
6:    }
7:    return newRegDepth;
8: }
```

Generating the Candidate Circuit. Subroutine SYNNEWREGION computes a candidate circuit that behaves the same as *reg* at least for the test cases in *testEx*. It follows our description in Sect. 4, where the template circuit is constructed using the SyGuS specification language. Then, it invokes the solvers in the SyGuS tool [2] to compute a solution. For example, a solution returned by SyGuS for the example in Fig. 9 is shown in the boxed region in Fig. 10. The resulting circuit, denoted *newReg*, is checked by the verification subroutine. If no candidate circuit exists and the subroutine SYNNEWREGION returns an empty set, Algorithm 1 will invoke it again on a smaller region.

More formally, using the SyGuS specification language, we construct a logical formula Φ for reg, whose satisfying assignment directly corresponds to a candidate solution for $newReg$. The logical formula Φ is defined as follows:

$$\Phi = \Phi_{reg} \wedge \Phi_{template} \wedge \Phi_{EqI} \wedge \Phi_{EqO} \wedge \Phi_{testEx},$$

where Φ_{reg} encodes the input-output relation of the original circuit reg, $\Phi_{template}$ encodes the input-output relation of the template circuit (as in Fig. 6), Φ_{EqI} asserts that reg and the template circuit share the same input values, Φ_{EqO} asserts that reg and the template circuit have the same output, and Φ_{testEx} restricts the input values to the examples in $testEx$.

Verifying the Equivalence. For each candidate circuit $newReg$, we also need to verify that it is equivalent to reg for all input values (not just the input values in $testEx$). This is a standard equivalence checking problem, for which we construct a logical formula Ψ such that Ψ is satisfiable if and only if $newReg$ and reg are not equivalent. The new formula Ψ is defined as follows:

$$\Psi = \Psi_{reg} \wedge \Psi_{newReg} \wedge \Psi_{EqI} \wedge \Psi_{UneqO},$$

where Ψ_{reg} encodes the input-output relation of reg, Ψ_{newReg} encodes the input-output relation of $newReg$, Ψ_{EqI} asserts that reg and $newReg$ share the same input values, and Ψ_{UneqO} asserts that reg and $newReg$ have different output values.

If Ψ is satisfiable, a test case (input value) will be generated to show why two regions are not equivalent. In such case, we add the new test to $testEx$ so that the bad solution will not be computed in the future. Then, we invoke SynNewRegion again.

7   Experiments

We have implemented our method using the SyGuS solvers [2] and conducted experiments on a set of circuits that implement various parts of the Advanced Encryption Standard (AES) and MAC-Keccak, which is the SHA-3 crypto-hashing algorithm recently standardized by NIST. Table 1 shows the statistics of these benchmarks, including the name, a brief description, the circuit size, as well as the number of input and output signals (bits). The source code of our synthesis tool as well as the input files and instructions to reproduce our experiments are available for artifact evaluation.

During the experiments, we used the AND, XOR, OR and NOT gates as components in *GatesSyn* for synthesizing new regions. We set the depth lev to 3. To compare with state-of-the-art techniques, we implemented the buffer insertion method as described in [19,22]. We also applied the logic optimization algorithms in the ABC tool [12], to check if standard algorithms in EDA tools can be used to generate FSA-resistant circuits (the answer is no). All our experiments were conducted on a computer with a 3.4 GHz Intel i7-2600 processor and 4 GB RAM.

Table 1. Statistics of the set of benchmark circuits used in our experiments.

Name	Circuit description	Nodes	Inputs	Outputs
C1	MAC-Keccak nonlinear masked Chi function 1 [8]	35	10	1
C2	MAC-Keccak nonlinear masked Chi function 2 [8]	35	10	1
C3	Generated MAC-Keccak nonlinear masked Chi function 1 [14]	44	10	1
C4	Generated MAC-Keccak nonlinear masked Chi function 2 [14]	44	10	1
C5	Unmasked MAC-Keccak nonlinear Chi function [8]	6	3	1
C6	AES S-Box design of nonlinear invg4 function [11]	83	4	4
C7	AES S-Box design of nonlinear mul4 function [11]	63	8	4
C8	AES S-Box single round nonlinear functions [11]	209	8	8
C9	Complete AES PPRM1 S-box design [34]	8,054	8	8
C10	Complete AES Boyar-Peralta S-box design [11]	156	8	8

Table 2 shows our experimental results. Columns 1-2 show the benchmark name and the number of nodes in the original circuit. Columns 3-4 show the number of nodes in the new circuit obtained by buffer insertion, and the node increase in percentage. Columns 5-6 show the number of nodes in the new circuit obtained by our method, and the node increase in percentage.

Table 2. Comparing our synthesis method with buffer insertion [19,22].

Name	Nodes	Buffer insertion		New method	
		Nodes	Increase	Nodes	Increase
C1	35	51	45 %	42	20 %
C2	35	48	37 %	40	14 %
C3	44	54	22 %	48	9 %
C4	44	59	34 %	45	2 %
C5	6	9	50 %	9	50 %
C6	83	134	61 %	98	18 %
C7	63	79	25 %	73	15 %
C8	209	292	39 %	244	16 %
C9	8,054	77,717	864 %	8,943	11 %
C10	156	9,585	6044 %	370	137 %

The results in Table 2 demonstrate the effectiveness of our method in synthesizing more compact countermeasures against FSA attacks. Compared to the buffer insertion method, the circuits produced by our method are consistently smaller. For example, our new circuit for C9 has only 11 % more nodes than the original circuit, whereas the circuit produced by the buffer insertion method has 864 % more nodes.

Table 3 shows the statistics of our iterative synthesis method, where Column 2 is the number of calls that we made to SyGuS to generate the new circuit regions. Among them, Column 3 shows the number of successful calls and Column 4 shows the number of failed calls. The results shows that calls to SyGuS almost always succeed – recall that when the SyGuS solver fails, the size of *reg* has to be reduced before we try again. Column 5 is the total time taken by our synthesis method to generate the final result.

Table 3. Statistics of our new synthesis method.

Name	Synthesis iterations	Successful iterations	Failed iterations	Total time [s]
C1	7	7	0	1.22
C2	5	5	0	0.10
C3	4	4	0	0.09
C4	2	2	0	0.06
C5	4	3	1	0.13
C6	23	23	0	0.48
C7	12	12	0	0.26
C8	47	47	0	1.11
C9	2,627	2,627	0	412.3
C10	219	217	2	13.7

For most benchmark circuits, the time taken by our method to synthesize the countermeasure is negligible. Furthermore, the synthesis time only increases moderately as the countermeasure circuit size increases. Finally, compared to prior techniques such as the buffer insertion method, our new method is more effective in reducing the area cost: as the circuit size increases, the saving also increases.

To confirm that standard EDA algorithms cannot generate FSA-resistant circuits, we also applied the ABC tool [12] to all the benchmark circuits. Specifically, ABC has a command called *balance*, which is designed to balance the delay along input-output paths in a circuit. To preform balancing, ABC starts by converting the circuit into an And-Inverter-Graph (AIG). This results in a circuit containing only AND gates and Inverters. Then ABC heuristically optimizes the new circuit by balancing the number of two-input AND gates between the circuit output and the primary inputs.

Unfortunately, ABC does not distinguish sensitive input signals from insensitive ones. As such, it cannot be used to target only the sensitive input-output paths. For the sake of comparison, we conducted the experiments using a variant of our method (a weakened version) that does not differentiate between the type of the primary inputs either. That is, as in ABC, we pretend that all input signals of the circuit are sensitive. Table 4 shows the results of our experiments. Here, the focus is on comparing the size of the new circuits and the depth of the circuits (longest path).

Table 4. Comparing our method with the *balance* command of ABC [12].

Name	Depth	ABC		Our new method	
		Node increase	Depth	Node increase	Depth
C1	8	300 %	27	20 %	5
C2	7	300 %	27	31 %	6
C3	7	273 %	25	20 %	6
C4	8	273 %	28	18 %	6
C5	3	233 %	7	50 %	3
C6	9	285 %	31	18 %	7
C7	7	322 %	21	16 %	7
C8	17	308 %	33	17 %	15
C9	156	80 %	586	11 %	17
C10	24	476 %	64	137 %	23

The results in Table 4 show a noticeable difference in the quality of the synthesized circuits. First, in all cases, our new circuits are significantly smaller than those obtained by ABC. Indeed, the node increase percentage by ABC ranges from 80 % to 476 % (the average is 285 %), whereas in our method, it only ranges from 2 % to 137 % (the average is 33 %). In addition, the longest path (Depth), measured by largest number of gate levels between any primary input and the circuit output, is also significantly smaller in the our new circuits.

8   Related Work

As we have mentioned earlier, our method is the first inductive synthesis based method for synthesizing FSA-resistant circuits. Although there is a large body of work on logic synthesis and optimization, traditional EDA algorithms cannot be used to solve this problem. Since our method relies on inductive synthesis, as opposed to matching some known patterns and then applying predefined transformations, it can search through a larger design space and therefore generate solutions that are better than hand-crafted countermeasures. In addition, our solutions are provably secure.

Ghalaty et al. [22] proposed a method for implementing FSA countermeasures based on the addition of delay elements at the inputs of certain gates in the circuit, to equalize the path delays from sensitive inputs. As we have demonstrated through experiments, their method can lead to countermeasures with significantly more logic gates. Furthermore, it does not guarantee to eliminate the mismatch in the arrival time of the input signals for all gate types; in particular, it ignores the XOR gates. Due to this reason, their countermeasure may still be vulnerable to FSA attacks.

Endo et al. [19] proposed another countermeasure to defend against FSA attacks based on adding a configurable buffer circuitry to delay the propagation of the output signals from the cryptographic module. However, their method is a post-silicon solution, which means it does not seek to modify the implementation of the original circuit as in our case. In general, a post-silicon solution is more expensive to implement, since the delay period needs to be configured after the chip is manufactured. To configure the delay, they first measure the delay needed for securing the manufactured cryptography module and then store the delays in an on-chip memory. As for the experimental evaluation, they implemented the countermeasure only for the benchmark C9, and reported a gate overhead of 10 % to 16 %, which is similar to our solution. However, their countermeasure was designed manually, whereas ours is generated automatically.

There is also a large body of work on verifying and synthesizing countermeasures against other types of side-channel attacks. They include, for example, the verification tools developed by Bayrak et al. [7], the *SC Sniffer* tool developed by Eldib et al. [15–18], the compiler assisted masking tool developed by Moss et al. [35], the code morphing method proposed by Agosta et al. [1], and the tool developed by Eldib et al. [14] for synthesizing masking countermeasures for cryptographic software. However, none of these existing tools can handle fault injection based attacks on cryptographic circuits. Although Barthe et al. [6] developed a method for systematic analysis of the security of cryptographic implementations against fault attacks, their focus was on finding fault attacks against cryptographic implementations, as opposed to synthesizing the countermeasures.

9 Conclusions

We have presented a new method for synthesizing cryptographic circuits to defend against fault sensitivity analysis based attacks. Our method relies on syntax-guided inductive synthesis to search for a new circuit that is functionally equivalent to the original circuit and at the same time FSA-resistant. It has the potential to discover more compact and efficient implementations than existing techniques. We have implemented the method and evaluated it on a set of cryptographic circuits. Our experiments show that the method is both scalable and effective in eliminating FSA vulnerabilities. For future work, we plan to evaluate the countermeasures synthesized by our new method on real hardware to assess its resistance against FSA attacks.

Acknowledgments. This work was primarily supported by the NSF under grant CNS-1128903. Partial support was provided by the ONR under grant N00014-13-1-0527. Any opinions, findings, and conclusions expressed in this material are those of the authors and do not necessarily reflect the views of the funding agencies.

References

1. Agosta, G., Barenghi, A., Pelosi, G.: A code morphing methodology to automate power analysis countermeasures. In: ACM/IEEE Design Automation Conference, pp. 77–82 (2012)
2. Alur, R., Bodík, R., Juniwal, G., Martin, M.M.K., Raghothaman, M., Seshia, S.A., Singh, R., Solar-Lezama, A., Torlak, E., Udupa, A.: Syntax-guided synthesis. In: International Conference on Formal Methods in Computer-Aided Design, pp. 1–8 (2013)
3. Atzori, L., Iera, A., Morabito, G.: The internet of things: a survey. Comput. Netw. **54**(15), 2787–2805 (2010)
4. Bagheri, N., Ebrahimpour, R., Ghaedi, N.: New differential fault analysis on PRESENT. EURASIP J. Adv. Sig. Proc. **2013**, 145 (2013)
5. Balasch, J., Gierlichs, B., Verdult, R., Batina, L., Verbauwhede, I.: Power analysis of Atmel CryptoMemory–recovering keys from secure EEPROMs. In: Dunkelman, O. (ed.) CT-RSA 2012. LNCS, vol. 7178, pp. 19–34. Springer, Heidelberg (2012)
6. Barthe, G., Dupressoir, F., Fouque, P., Grégoire, B., Zapalowic, J.: Synthesis of fault attacks on cryptographic implementations. In: ACM SIGSAC Conference on Computer and Communications Security, pp. 1016–1027 (2014)
7. Bayrak, A., Regazzoni, F., Brisk, P., Standaert, F.-X., Ienne, P.: A first step towards automatic application of power analysis countermeasures. In: ACM/IEEE Design Automation Conference, pp. 230–235 (2011)
8. Bertoni, G., Daemen, J., Peeters, M., Assche, G.V., Keer, R.V.: Keccak implementation overview. URL: http://keccak.neokeon.org/Keccak-implementation-3. 2.pdf
9. Biham, E.: Differential cryptanalysis. In: Encyclopedia of Cryptography and Security, 2nd edn., pp. 332–336 (2011)
10. Bogdanov, A.A., Knudsen, L.R., Leander, G., Paar, C., Poschmann, A., Robshaw, M., Seurin, Y., Vikkelsoe, C.: PRESENT: an ultra-lightweight block cipher. In: Paillier, P., Verbauwhede, I. (eds.) CHES 2007. LNCS, vol. 4727, pp. 450–466. Springer, Heidelberg (2007)
11. Boyar, J., Peralta, R.: A small depth-16 circuit for the AES S-Box. In: SEC, pp. 287–298 (2012)
12. Brayton, R., Mishchenko, A.: ABC: an academic industrial-strength verification tool. In: Touili, T., Cook, B., Jackson, P. (eds.) CAV 2010. LNCS, vol. 6174, pp. 24–40. Springer, Heidelberg (2010)
13. Eldib, H., Wang, C.: An SMT based method for optimizing arithmetic computations in embedded software code. IEEE Trans. CAD Integr. Circ. Syst. **33**(11), 1611–1622 (2014)
14. Eldib, H., Wang, C.: Synthesis of masking countermeasures against side channel attacks. In: Biere, A., Bloem, R. (eds.) CAV 2014. LNCS, vol. 8559, pp. 114–130. Springer, Heidelberg (2014)
15. Eldib, H., Wang, C., Schaumont, P.: Formal verification of software countermeasures against side-channel attacks. ACM Trans. Softw. Eng. Methodol. **24**(2), 11:1–11:24 (2014)
16. Eldib, H., Wang, C., Schaumont, P.: SMT based verification of software countermeasures against side-channel attacks. In: International Conference on Tools and Algorithms for Construction and Analysis of Systems (2014)
17. Eldib, H., Wang, C., Taha, M., Schaumont, P.: QMS: evaluating the side-channel resistance of masked software from source code, pp. 209:1–209:6 (2014)

18. Eldib, H., Wang, C., Taha, M., Schaumont, P.: Quantitative masking strength: quantifying the power side-channel resistance of software code. IEEE Trans. CAD Integr. Circ. Syst. **34**, 1558 (2015)

19. Endo, S., Li, Y., Homma, N., Sakiyama, K., Ohta, O., Fujimoto, D., Nagata, M., Katashita, T., Danger, J.-L., Aoki, T.: A silicon-level countermeasure against fault sensitivity analysis and its evaluation. IEEE Trans. Very Large Scale Integr. Syst. pp. 1–10 (2014)

20. Endo, S., Sugawara, T., Homma, N., Aoki, T., Satoh, A.: A configurable on-chip glitchy-clock generator for fault injection experiments. IEICE Trans. Fundam. Electron. Commun. Comput. Sci. **95–A**(1), 263–266 (2012)

21. Fuhr, T., Jaulmes, É., Lomné, V., Thillard, A.: Fault attacks on AES with faulty ciphertexts only. In: International Workshop on Fault Diagnosis and Tolerance in Cryptography, pp. 108–118 (2013)

22. Ghalaty, N.F., Aysu, A., Schaumont, P.: Analyzing and eliminating the causes of fault sensitivity analysis. In: Design, Automation and Test in Europe, pp. 1–6 (2014)

23. Ghalaty, N.F., Yuce, B., Schaumont, P.: Differential fault intensity analysis on PRESENT and LED block ciphers. In: Mangard, S., Poschmann, A.Y. (eds.) COSADE 2015. LNCS, vol. 9064, pp. 174–188. Springer, Heidelberg (2015)

24. Ghalaty, N.F., Yuce, B., Taha, M.M.I., Schaumont, P.: Differential fault intensity analysis. In:International Workshop on Fault Diagnosis and Tolerance in Cryptography, pp. 49–58 (2014)

25. Gulwani, S., Jha, S., Tiwari, A., Venkatesan, R.: Synthesis of loop-free programs. In: ACM SIGPLAN Conference on Programming Language Design and Implementation, pp. 62–73 (2011)

26. Gulwani, S., Srivastava, S., Venkatesan, R.: Program analysis as constraint solving. In : ACM SIGPLAN Conference on Programming Language Design and Implementation, pp. 281–292 (2008)

27. Guo, J., Peyrin, T., Poschmann, A., Robshaw, M.: The LED block cipher. In: Preneel, B., Takagi, T. (eds.) CHES 2011. LNCS, vol. 6917, pp. 326–341. Springer, Heidelberg (2011)

28. Hachtel, G.D., Somenzi, F.: Logic Synthesis and Verification Algorithms. Kluwer Academic Publishers, Boston (1996)

29. Järvinen, K., Blondeau, C., Page, D., Tunstall, M.: Harnessing biased faults in attacks on ECC-based signature schemes. In: International Workshop on Fault Diagnosis and Tolerance in Cryptography, pp. 72–82 (2012)

30. Jeong, K., Lee, C., Lim, J.: Improved differential fault analysis on lightweight block cipher lblock for wireless sensor networks. EURASIP J. Wireless Commun. Netw. **2013**, 151 (2013)

31. Kuncak, V., Mayer, M., Piskac, R., Suter, P.: Software synthesis procedures. Commun. ACM **55**(2), 103–111 (2012)

32. Li, Y., Sakiyama, K., Gomisawa, S., Fukunaga, T., Takahashi, J., Ohta, K.: Fault sensitivity analysis. In: Mangard, S., Standaert, F.-X. (eds.) CHES 2010. LNCS, vol. 6225, pp. 320–334. Springer, Heidelberg (2010)

33. Moradi, A., Barenghi, A., Kasper, T., Paar, C.: On the vulnerability of FPGA bitstream encryption against power analysis attacks-extracting keys from Xilinx Virtex-II FPGAs. In: IACR Cryptology (2011)

34. Morioka, S., Satoh, A.: An optimized S-Box circuit architecture for low power AES design. In: Kaliski, B.S., Koç, K., Paar, C. (eds.) Cryptographic Hardware and Embedded Systems-CHES 2002. LNCS, vol. 2523, pp. 172–186. Springer, Heidelberg (2003)

35. Moss, A., Oswald, E., Page, D., Tunstall, M.: Compiler assisted masking. In: Prouff, E., Schaumont, P. (eds.) CHES 2012. LNCS, vol. 7428, pp. 58–75. Springer, Heidelberg (2012)

36. Paar, C., Eisenbarth, T., Kasper, M., Kasper, T., Moradi, A.: Keeloq and side-channel analysis-evolution of an attack. In: Workshop on Fault Diagnosis and Tolerance in Cryptography, pp. 65–69 (2009)

37. Sakamoto, H., Li, Y., Ohta, K., Sakiyama, K.: Fault sensitivity analysis against elliptic curve cryptosystems. In: Workshop on Fault Diagnosis and Tolerance in Cryptography, pp. 11–20 (2011)

38. Sakiyama, K., Li, Y., Gomisawa, S., Hayashi, Y., Iwamoto, M., Homma, N., Aoki, T., Ohta, K.: Practical DFA strategy for AES under limited-access conditions. JIP **22**(2), 142–151 (2014)

39. Santis, F.D., Guillen, O.M., Sakic, E., Sigl, G.: Ciphertext-only fault attacks on PRESENT. In: International Workshop on Lightweight Cryptography for Security and Privacy, pp. 85–108 (2014)

40. Solar-Lezama, A.: Program sketching. Int. J. Softw. Tools Technol. Transfer **15**(5–6), 475–495 (2013)

41. Yuce, B., Ghalaty, N.F., Schaumont, P.: TVVF: estimating the vulnerability of hardware cryptosystems against timing violation attacks. In: IEEE International Symposium on Hardware Oriented Security and Trust, pp. 72–77 (2015)

42. Zhao, X., Guo, S., Zhang, F., Wang, T., Shi, Z., Ji, K.: Algebraic differential fault attacks on LED using a single fault injection. IACR Cryptology ePrint Archive 2012, p. 347 (2012)

A SAT-Based Counterexample Guided Method for Unbounded Synthesis

Alexander Legg[1]($\boxtimes$), Nina Narodytska[2], and Leonid Ryzhyk[2]

[1] Data61, CSIRO (formerly NICTA) and UNSW,
Sydney, Australia
`alexander.legg@nicta.com.au`
[2] Samsung Research America, Mountain View, USA

Abstract. Reactive synthesis techniques based on constructing the winning region of the system have been shown to work well in many cases but suffer from state explosion in others. A different approach, proposed recently, applies SAT solvers in a counterexample guided framework to solve the synthesis problem. However, this method is limited to synthesising systems that execute for a bounded number of steps and is incomplete for synthesis with unbounded safety and reachability objectives. We present an extension of this technique to unbounded synthesis. Our method applies Craig interpolation to abstract game trees produced by counterexample guided search in order to construct a monotonic sequence of may-losing regions. Experimental results based on SYNTCOMP 2015 competition benchmarks show this to be a promising alternative that solves some previously intractable instances.

1 Introduction

Reactive systems are ubiquitous in real-world problems such as circuit design, industrial automation, or device drivers. Automatic synthesis can provide a *correct by construction* controller for a reactive system from a specification. Reactive synthesis is formalised as a game between the *controller* and its *environment*. In this work we focus on safety games, in which the controller must prevent the environment from forcing the game into an error state.

The reactive synthesis problem is EXPTIME-complete (when starting from a symbolic representation of the game graph) so naïve algorithms are infeasible on anything but simple systems. There are several techniques that aim to mitigate this complexity by representing states and transitions of the system symbolically [4, 17, 19]. These techniques incrementally construct a symbolic representation of the set of discovered winning states of the game. The downside of this approach is that keeping track of all discovered winning states can lead to a space explosion even when using efficient symbolic representation such as BDDs or CNFs.

A. Legg—NICTA is funded by the Australian Government as represented by the Department of Broadband, Communications and the Digital Economy and the Australian Research Council through the ICT Centre of Excellence program.

N. Narodytska and L. Ryzhyk—Work completed at Carnegie Mellon University.

S. Chaudhuri and A. Farzan (Eds.): CAV 2016, Part II, LNCS 9780, pp. 364–382, 2016.
DOI: 10.1007/978-3-319-41540-6_20

An alternative approach, proposed by Narodytska et al. [18], is to eschew states and focus on *runs* of the game. The method works by exploring a subset of the concrete runs of the game and proving that these runs can be generalised into a winning strategy on behalf of one of the players. In contrast to other existing synthesis methods, it does not store, in either symbolic or explicit form, the set of winning states. Instead, it uses counterexample guided backtracking search to identify a small subset of runs that are sufficient to solve the game.

This method has been shown to outperform BDDs on certain classes of games; however it suffers from an important limitation: it is only able to solve games with a bounded number of rounds. In case of safety games, this means proving that the controller can keep the game within the safe region for a bounded number of steps. This is insufficient in most practical situations that require unbounded realisability.

In this paper, we extend the method by Narodytska et al. [18] to unbounded safety games. To this end we enhance the method with computational learning: every time the search algorithm discovers a new counterexample, the learning procedure analyzes the counterexample, extracting a subset of states winning for one of the players from it. The learning procedure ensures that reaching a fixed point in these sets is sufficient to establish unbounded realisability. Our method can be seen as a hybrid between the counterexample guided algorithm by Narodytska et al. and methods based on losing set computation: we use the former to guide the search, while we rely on the latter to ensure convergence.

We evaluate our method on the benchmarks of the 2015 synthesis competition (SYNTCOMP'15). While our solver solves fewer total instances than competitors, it solves the largest number of unique instances, i.e., instances that could not be solved by any other sequential solver. These results confirm that there exist classes of problems that are hard for traditional synthesis techniques, but can be efficiently solved by our method. While further performance improvements are clearly needed, in its current state the method may be a worthwhile addition to a portfolio solver.

Section 2 outlines the original bounded synthesis algorithm. In Sect. 3 we describe and prove the correctness of our extension of the algorithm to unbounded games. In the following sections we evaluate our methodology, and compare our approach to other synthesis techniques.

2   Background

A *safety game*, $G = \langle X, U, C, \delta, I, E \rangle$, is defined over boolean state variables X, uncontrollable action variables U, and controllable action variables C. We use $\mathcal{X}, \mathcal{U}$, and $\mathcal{C}$ to denote sets of valuations of variables X, U, and C respectively. I is the initial state of the game given as a valuation of state variables. $E(X)$ is the set of error states represented by its characteristic formula. The transition relation $\delta(X, U, C, X')$ of the game is a boolean formula that relates current state and action to the set of possible next states of the game. We assume deterministic games, where $\delta(x, u, c, x_1') \wedge \delta(x, u, c, x_2') \implies (x_1' = x_2')$.

At every round of the game, the *environment* picks an uncontrollable action, the *controller* responds by choosing a controllable action and the game transitions into a new state according to δ. A *run* of a game $(x_0, u_0, c_0), (x_1, u_1, c_1) \ldots (x_n, u_n, c_n)$ is a chain of state and action pairs s.t. $\delta(x_k, u_k, c_k, x_{k+1})$. A run is winning for the controller if $x_0 = I \wedge \forall i \in \{1..n\}(\neg E(x_i))$. In a *bounded game* with maximum bound κ all runs are restricted to length κ, whereas unbounded games consider runs of infinite length. Since we consider only deterministic games, a run is uniquely described by a list of assignments to U and C.

A *controller strategy* $\pi^c : \mathcal{X} \times \mathcal{U} \to \mathcal{C}$ is a mapping of states and uncontrollable inputs to controllable actions. A controller strategy is winning in a bounded game of maximum bound κ if all runs $(x_0, u_0, \pi^c(x_0, u_0)), (x_1, u_1, \pi^c(x_1, u_1)) \ldots (x_n, u_n, \pi^c(x_n, u_n))$ are winning. Bounded *realisability* is the problem of determining the existence of such a strategy for a bounded game.

An *environment strategy* $\pi^e : \mathcal{X} \to \mathcal{U}$ is a mapping of states to uncontrollable actions. A bounded run is winning for the environment if $x_0 = I \wedge \exists i \in \{1..n\}(E(x_i))$ and an environment strategy is winning for a bounded game if all runs $(x_0, \pi^e(x_0), c_0), (x_1, \pi^e(x_1), c_1) \ldots (x_n, \pi^e(x_n), c_n)$ are winning for the environment. Safety games are zero sum, therefore the existence of a winning controller strategy implies the nonexistence of a winning environment strategy and vice versa.

2.1 Counterexample Guided Bounded Synthesis

We review the bounded synthesis algorithm by Narodytska et al. [18], which is the main building block for our unbounded algorithm.

Example. *We introduce a running example to assist the explanation. We consider a simple arbiter system in which the environment makes a request for a number of resources (1 or 2), and the controller may grant access to up to two resources. The total number of requests grows each round by the number of environment requests and shrinks by the number of resources granted by the controller in the previous round. The controller must ensure that the number of unhandled requests does not accumulate to more than 2. Figure 1 shows the variables (Fig. 1a), the initial state of the system (Fig. 1b), and the formulas for computing next-state variable assignments (Fig. 1c) for this example. We use primed identifiers to denote next-state variables and curly braces to define the domain of a variable.*

This example is the $n = 2$ instance of the more general problem of an arbiter of n resources. For large values of n, the set of winning states has no compact representation, which makes the problem hard for BDD solvers. In Sect. 3 we will outline how the unbounded game can be solved without enumerating all winning states.

Our bounded synthesis algorithm constructs abstractions of the game that restrict actions available to one of the players. Specifically, we consider abstractions represented as trees of actions, referred to as *abstract game trees* (AGTs).

Controllable	Uncontrollable	State
request : {1, 2}	grant0 = {0, 1}	resource0 = {0, 1}
	grant1 : {0, 1}	resource1 = {0, 1}
		nrequests : {0, 1, 2, 3}

(a) Variables

resource0 = 0; resource1 = 0; nrequests = 0;

(b) Initial State

```
resource0' = grant0;
resource1' = grant1;
nrequests' = (nrequests + request >= resource0 + resource1)
        ? (nrequests + request - resource0 - resource1) : 0;
```

(c) Transition Relation

Fig. 1. Example

Figure 2b shows an example abstract game tree restricting the environment (abstract game trees restricting the controller are similar). In the abstract game, the controller can freely choose actions whilst the environment is required to pick actions from the tree. After reaching a leaf, the environment continues playing unrestricted. The tree in Fig. 2b restricts the first environment action to request=1. At the leaf of the tree the game continues unrestricted.

The root of the tree is annotated by the initial state s of the abstract game and the bound k on the number of rounds. We denote NODES(T) the set of all nodes of a tree T, LEAVES(T) the subset of leaf nodes. For edge e, ACTION(e) is the action that labels the edge, and for node n, HEIGHT(k, n) is the distance from n to the last round of a game bounded to k rounds. HEIGHT(k, T) is the height of the root node of the tree. For node n of the tree, SUCC(n) is the set of pairs $\langle e, n' \rangle$ where n' is a child node of n and e is the edge connecting n and n'.

Given an environment (controller) abstract game tree T a *partial strategy* $Strat$: NODES(T) → $\mathcal{C}$ ($Strat$: NODES(T) → $\mathcal{U}$) labels each node of the tree with the controller's (environment's) action to be played in that node. Given a partial strategy $Strat$, we can map each leaf l of the abstract game tree to $\langle s', i' \rangle =$ OUTCOME($\langle s, i \rangle, Strat, l$) obtained by playing all controllable and uncontrollable actions on the path from the root to the leaf. An environment (controller) partial strategy is *winning against T* if all its outcomes are states that are winning for the environment (controller) in the concrete game.

Example: Intuition behind the algorithm. *We present the intuition behind our bounded synthesis method by applying its simplified version to the running example. We begin by finding a trace of length k (here we consider k = 3) that is winning for the controller, i.e., that starts from the initial state and avoids the error set for three game rounds (see Fig. 2a). We use a SAT solver to find such*

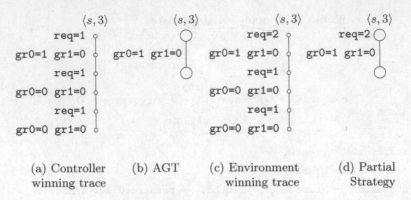

(a) Controller   (b) AGT   (c) Environment   (d) Partial
winning trace   winning trace   Strategy

Fig. 2. Abstract game trees.

a trace, precisely as one would do in bounded model checking. Given this trace we make an initial conjecture that any trace starting with action gr0=1 gr1=0 is winning for the controller. This conjecture is captured in the abstract game tree shown in Fig. 2b. We validate this conjecture by searching for a counterexample trace that reaches an error state with the first controller action fixed to gr0=1 gr1=0. Such a trace, that refutes the conjecture, is shown in Fig. 2c. In this trace, the environment wins by playing req=2 in the first round. This move represents the environment's partial strategy against the abstract game tree in Fig. 2b. This partial strategy is shown in Fig. 2d.

Next we strengthen the abstract game tree taking this partial strategy into account. To this end we again use a SAT solver to find a trace where the controller wins while the environment plays according to the partial strategy. In the resulting trace (Fig. 3a), the controller plays gr0=1 gr1=1 in the second round. We refine the abstract game tree using this move as shown in Fig. 3b. The environment's partial strategy was to make two requests in the first round, to which the controller responds by now granting an additional two resources in the second round.

When the controller cannot refine the tree by extending existing branches, it backtracks and creates new branches. Eventually, we obtain the abstract game tree shown in Fig. 3c for which there does not exist a winning partial strategy on behalf of the environment. We conclude that the bounded game is winning for the controller.

The full bounded synthesis algorithm is more complicated: upon finding a candidate partial strategy on behalf of player p against abstract game tree T, it first checks whether the strategy is winning against T. By only considering such strong candidates, we reduce the number of refinements needed to solve the game. To this end, the algorithm checks whether each outcome of the candidate strategy is a winning state for OPPONENT(p) by recursively invoking the synthesis algorithm on behalf of the opponent. Thus, our bounded synthesis algorithm

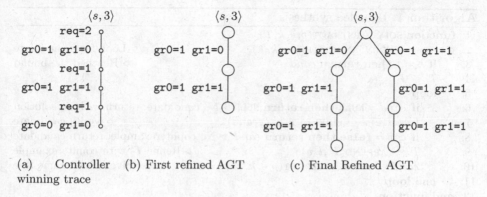

(a)   Controller   (b) First refined AGT   (c) Final Refined AGT
winning trace

Fig. 3. Refined abstract game trees.

can be seen as running two competing solvers, for the controller and for the environment.

The full procedure is illustrated in Algorithm 1. The algorithm takes a concrete game G with maximum bound κ as an implicit argument. In addition, it takes a player p (controller or environment), state s, bound k and an abstract game tree T and returns a winning partial strategy for p, if one exists. The initial invocation of the algorithm takes the initial state I, bound κ and an empty abstract game tree $\emptyset$. Initially the solver is playing on behalf of the environment since that player takes the first move in every game round. The empty game tree does not constrain opponent moves, hence solving such an abstraction is equivalent to solving the original concrete game.

The algorithm is organised as a counterexample-guided abstraction refinement (CEGAR) loop. The first step of the algorithm uses the FINDCANDIDATE function, described below, to come up with a candidate partial strategy that is winning when the opponent is restricted to T. If it fails to find a strategy, this means that no winning partial strategy exists against the opponent playing according to T. If, on the other hand, a candidate partial strategy is found, we need to verify if it is indeed winning for the abstract game T.

The VERIFY procedure searches for a *spoiling* counterexample strategy in each leaf of the candidate partial strategy by calling SOLVEABSTRACT for the opponent. The dual solver solves games on behalf of the opponent player.

If the dual solver can find no spoiling strategy at any of the leaves, then the candidate partial strategy is a winning one. Otherwise, VERIFY returns the move used by the opponent to defeat a leaf of the partial strategy, which is appended to the corresponding node in T in order to refine it in line (9).

We solve the refined game by recursively invoking SOLVEABSTRACT on it. If no partial winning strategy is found for the refined game then there is also no partial winning strategy for the original abstract game, and the algorithm returns a failure. Otherwise, the partial strategy for the refined game is *projected* on the original abstract game by removing the leaves introduced by refinements.

Algorithm 1. Bounded synthesis

```
 1: function SOLVEABSTRACT(p, s, k, T)
 2:     cand ← FINDCANDIDATE(p, s, k, T)                          ▷ Look for a candidate
 3:     if k = 1 then return cand                                ▷ Reached the bound
 4:     T' ← T
 5:     loop
 6:         if cand = NULL then return NULL ▷ No candidate: return with no solution
 7:         ⟨cex, l, u⟩ ← VERIFY(p, s, k, T, cand)                      ▷ Verify candidate
 8:         if cex = false then return cand ▷ No counterexample: return candidate
 9:         T' ← APPEND(T', l, u)                         ▷ Refine T' with counterexample
10:         cand ← SOLVEABSTRACT(p, s, k, T')                 ▷ Solve refined game tree
11:     end loop
12: end function
13: function FINDCANDIDATE(p, s, k, T)
14:     T̂ ← EXTEND(T)                              ▷ Extend the tree with unfixed actions
15:     f ← if p = cont then TREEFORMULA(k, T̂) else TREEFORMULA(k, T̂)
16:     sol ← SAT(s(X_T̂) ∧ f)
17:     if sol = unsat then
18:         if unbounded then                    ▷ Active only in the unbounded solver
19:             if p = cont then LEARN(s, T̂) else LEARN(s, T̂)
20:         end if
21:         return NULL                                          ▷ No candidate exists
22:     else
23:         return {⟨n, c⟩|n ∈ NODES(T), c = SOL(n)}        ▷ Fix candidate moves in T
24:     end if
25: end function
26: function VERIFY(p, s, k, T, cand)
27:     for l ∈ leaves(gt) do
28:         ⟨k', s'⟩ ← OUTCOME(s, k, cand, l)                ▷ Get bound and state at leaf
29:         u ← SOLVEABSTRACT(OPPONENT(p), s', k', ∅)          ▷ Solve for the opponent
30:         if u ≠ NULL then return ⟨true, l, u⟩            ▷ Return counterexample
31:     end for
32:     return ⟨false, ∅, ∅⟩
33: end function
```

The resulting partial strategy becomes a candidate strategy to be verified at the next iteration of the loop. In the worst case the loop terminates after all actions in the game are refined into the abstract game.

The CEGAR loop depends on the ability to guess candidate partial strategies in FINDCANDIDATE. For this purpose we use the heuristic that a partial strategy may be winning if each OUTCOME of the strategy can be extended to a run of the game that is winning for the current player. Clearly, if such a partial strategy does not exist then no winning partial strategy can exist for the abstract game tree. We can formulate this heuristic as a SAT query, which is constructed recursively by TREEFORMULA (for the controller) or TREEFORMULA (for the environment) in Algorithm 2.

The tree is first extended to the maximum bound with edges that are labeled with arbitrary opponent actions (Algorithm 1, line 14). For each node in the tree, new SAT variables are introduced corresponding to the state (X_T) and action (U_T or C_T) variables of that node. Additional variables for the opponent actions in the edges of T are introduced (U_e or C_e) and set to ACTION(e). The state and action variables of node n are connected to successor nodes SUCC(n) by an encoding of the transition relation and constrained to the winning condition of the player.

Algorithm 2. Tree formulas for Controller and Environment respectively

---

1: **function** TREEFORMULA(k, T)
2:     **if** HEIGHT(k, T) = 0 **then**
3:         **return** $\neg E(X_T)$
4:     **else**
5:         **return** $\neg E(X_T) \wedge$
6:
$$\bigwedge_{\langle e,n \rangle \in \text{SUCC}(T)} (\delta(X_T, U_e, C_T, X_n) \wedge U_e = \text{ACTION}(e) \wedge \text{TREEFORMULA}(k, n))$$

7:     **end if**
8: **end function**

9: **function** $\overline{\text{TREEFORMULA}}(k, T)$
10:     **if** HEIGHT(k, T) = 0 **then**
11:         **return** $E(X_T)$
12:     **else**
13:         **return** $E(X_T) \vee$
14:
$$\bigvee_{\langle e,n \rangle \in \text{SUCC}(T)} (\delta(X_T, U_T, C_e, X_n) \wedge C_e = \text{ACTION}(e) \wedge \overline{\text{TREEFORMULA}}(k, n))$$

15:     **end if**
16: **end function**

---

3   Unbounded Synthesis

Bounded synthesis can be used to prove the existence of a winning strategy for the environment on the unbounded game by providing a witness. For the controller, the strongest claim that can be made is that the strategy is winning as long as the game does not extend beyond the maximum bound.

It is possible to set a maximum bound such that all runs in the unbounded game will be considered. The naïve approach is to use size of the state space as the bound ($|\mathcal{X}|$) so that all states may be explored by the algorithm. A more nuanced approach is to use the diameter of the game [3], which is the smallest number d such that for any state x there is a path of length $\leq d$ to all other

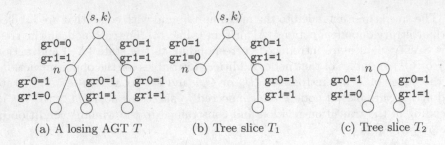

(a) A losing AGT T (b) Tree slice T_1 (c) Tree slice T_2

Fig. 4. Splitting of an abstract game tree by the learning procedure.

reachable states. However, the diameter is difficult to estimate and can still lead to infeasibly long games.

We instead present an approach that iteratively solves games of increasing bound while learning bad states from abstract games using interpolation. We show that reaching a fixed point in learned states is sufficient for completeness.

3.1   Learning States with Interpolants

We extend the bounded synthesis algorithm to learn states losing for one of the players from failed attempts to find candidate strategies. The learning procedure kicks in whenever FINDCANDIDATE cannot find a candidate strategy for an abstract game tree. We can learn additional losing states from the tree via interpolation. This is achieved in lines 18–20 in Algorithm 1, enabled in the unbounded version of the algorithm, which invoke LEARN or $\overline{\text{LEARN}}$ to learn controller or environment losing states respectively (Algorithm 3).

Example: Why we use interpolants. *Consider node n in Fig. 4a. At this node there are two controller actions that prevent the environment from forcing the game into an error state in one game round. We want to use this tree to learn the states from which the controller can win playing one of these actions.*

One option is using a BDD solver, working backwards from the error set, to find all losing states. One iteration of this operation on our example would give the set: $nrequests = 3 \vee (nrequests = 2 \wedge (resource0 = 0 \vee resource1 = 0)) \vee (nrequests = 1 \wedge (resource0 = 0 \wedge resource1 = 0))$. In the general case there is no compact representation of the losing set, so we try to avoid computing it by employing interpolation instead. The benefit of interpolation is that it allows approximating the losing states efficiently by obtaining an interpolant from a SAT solver.

Given two formulas F_1 and F_2 such that $F_1 \wedge F_2$ is unsatisfiable, it is possible to construct a Craig interpolant [9] $\mathcal{I}$ such that $F_1 \rightarrow \mathcal{I}$, $F_2 \wedge \mathcal{I}$ is unsatisfiable, and $\mathcal{I}$ refers only to the intersection of variables in F_1 and F_2. An interpolant can be constructed efficiently from a resolution proof of the unsatisfiability of $F_1 \wedge F_2$ [20].

Algorithm 3. Learning algorithms

Require: $s(X_T) \wedge$ TREEFORMULA$(k, T) \equiv \bot$
Require: *Must-invariant* holds
Ensure: *Must-invariant* holds
Ensure: $s(X_T) \wedge B^M \not\equiv \bot$ ▷ s will be added to B^M
1: **function** LEARN(s, T)
2:     **if** SUCC$(T) = \emptyset$ **then return**
3:     $n \leftarrow$ non-leaf node with min height
4:     $\langle T_1, T_2 \rangle \leftarrow$ GTSPLIT(T, n)
5:     $\mathcal{I} \leftarrow$ INTERPOLATE$(s(X_T) \wedge$ TREEFORMULA$(k, T_1),$ TREEFORMULA$(k, T_2))$
6:     $B^M \leftarrow B^M \vee \mathcal{I}$
7:     LEARN(s, T_1)
8: **end function**

Require: $s(X_T) \wedge \overline{\text{TREEFORMULA}}(k, T) \equiv \bot$
Require: *May-invariant* holds
Ensure: *May-invariant* holds
Ensure: $s(X_T) \wedge B^m[\text{HEIGHT}(k, T)] \equiv \bot$ ▷ s will be removed from B^m
9: **function** $\overline{\text{LEARN}}(s, T)$
10:    **if** SUCC$(T) = \emptyset$ **then return**
11:    $n \leftarrow$ non-leaf node with min height
12:    $\langle T_1, T_2 \rangle \leftarrow$ GTSPLIT(T, n)
13:    $\mathcal{I} \leftarrow$ INTERPOLATE$(s(X_T) \wedge \overline{\text{TREEFORMULA}}(k, T_1), \overline{\text{TREEFORMULA}}(k, T_2))$
14:    **for** $i = 1$ to HEIGHT(k, n) **do**
15:       $B^m[i] \leftarrow B^m[i] \setminus \mathcal{I}$
16:    **end for**
17:    $\overline{\text{LEARN}}(s, T_1)$
18: **end function**

We choose a non-leaf node n of T with maximal depth, i.e., a node whose children are leafs (Algorithm 3, line 3). We then split the tree at n such that both slices T_1 and T_2 contain a copy of n (line 4). Figure 4b shows T_1, which contains all of T except n's children, and T_2 (Fig. 4c), which contains only n and its children. There is no candidate strategy for T so $s \wedge \overline{\text{TREEFORMULA}}(k, T)$ is unsatisfiable. By construction, $\overline{\text{TREEFORMULA}}(k, T) \equiv \overline{\text{TREEFORMULA}}(k, T_1) \wedge \overline{\text{TREEFORMULA}}(k, T_2)$ and hence $s \wedge \overline{\text{TREEFORMULA}}(k, T_1) \wedge \overline{\text{TREEFORMULA}}(k, T_2)$ is also unsatisfiable.

We construct an interpolant with $F_1 = s(X_T) \wedge$ TREEFORMULA(k, T_1) and $F_2 =$ TREEFORMULA(k, T_2) (line 5). The only variables shared between F_1 and F_2 are the state variable copies belonging to node n. By the properties of the interpolant, $F_2 \wedge \mathcal{I}$ is unsatisfiable, therefore all states in $\mathcal{I}$ are losing against abstract game tree T_2 in Fig. 4c. We also know that $F_1 \rightarrow \mathcal{I}$, thus $\mathcal{I}$ contains all states reachable at n by following T_1 and avoiding error states.

Example. *At node n, the interpolant* $nrequests = 1 \wedge resource1 = 1$ *captures the information we need. Any action by the environment followed by one of the controller actions at n will be winning for the controller.*

Algorithm 4. Amended tree formulas for Controller and Environment

---

1: **function** TREEFORMULA(k, T)
2:     **if** HEIGHT$(k, T) = 0$ **then**
3:         **return** $\neg B^M(X_T)$
4:     **else**
5:         **return** $\neg B^M(X_T) \wedge$
6:

$$\bigwedge_{\langle e,n \rangle \in \text{SUCC}(T)} (\delta(X_T, U_e, C_n, X_n) \wedge U_e = \text{ACTION}(e) \wedge \text{TREEFORMULA}(k, n))$$

7:     **end if**
8: **end function**
9: **function** $\overline{\text{TREEFORMULA}}(k, T)$
10:     **if** HEIGHT$(k, T) = 0$ **then**
11:         **return** $\text{E}(X_T)$
12:     **else**
13:         **return** $B^m[\text{HEIGHT}(k, T)](X_T) \wedge$
14:

$$\left(\text{E}(X_T) \vee \bigvee_{\langle e,n \rangle \in \text{SUCC}(T)} (\delta(X_T, U_n, C_e, X_n) \wedge C_e = \text{ACTION}(e) \wedge \overline{\text{TREEFORMULA}}(k, n)) \right)$$

15:     **end if**
16: **end function**

We have discovered a set $\mathcal{I}$ of states losing for the environment. Environment-losing states are only losing for a particular bound: given that there does not exist an environment strategy that forces the game into an error state in k rounds or less; there may still exist a longer environment-winning strategy. We therefore record learned environment-losing states along with associated bounds. To this end, we maintain a conceptually infinite array of sets $B^m[k]$ that are may-losing for the controller, indexed by bound k. $B^m[k]$ are initialised to E for all k. Whenever an environment-losing set $\mathcal{I}$ is discovered for a node n with bound HEIGHT(k, n) in line 13 of Algorithm 3, this set is subtracted from $B^m[i]$, for all i less than or equal to the bound (lines 14–16).

The $\overline{\text{TREEFORMULA}}$ function is modified for the unbounded solver (Algorithm 4) to constrain the environment to the appropriate B^m. This enables further interpolants to be constructed by the learning procedure recursively splitting more nodes from T_1 (Algorithm 3, line 7) since the states that are losing to T_2 are no longer contained in B^m.

Learning of states losing from the controller is similar (LEARN in Algorithm 3). The main difference is that environment-losing states are losing for all bounds. Therefore we record these states in a single set B^M of must-losing states (Algorithm 3, line 6). This set is initialised to the error set E and grows as new losing states are discovered. The modified $\overline{\text{TREEFORMULA}}$ function (Algorithm 4) blocks must-losing states, which also allows for recursive learning over the entire tree.

3.2 Main Synthesis Loop

Figure 5 shows the main loop of the unbounded synthesis algorithm. The algorithm invokes the modified bounded synthesis procedure with increasing bound k until the initial state is in B^M (environment wins) or B^m reaches a fixed point (controller wins). We prove correctness in the next section.

Algorithm 5. Unbounded Synthesis

1: **function** SOLVEUNBOUNDED(T)
2:     $B^M \leftarrow E$
3:     $B^m[0] \leftarrow E$
4:     **for** $k = 1 \ldots$ **do**
5:         **if** SAT($I \wedge B^M$) **then return unrealisable**   ▷ Losing in the initial state
6:         **if** $\exists i < k.\ B^m[i] \equiv B^m[i+1]$ **then**   ▷ Reached fixed point
7:             **return realisable**
8:         $B^m[k] \leftarrow E$
9:         CHECKBOUND(k)
10:    **end for**
11: **end function**
Require: *May* and *must* invariants hold
Ensure: *May* and *must* invariants hold
Ensure: $I \notin B^m[k]$ if there exists a winning controller strategy with bound k
Ensure: $I \in B^M$ if there exists a winning environment strategy with bound k
12: **function** CHECKBOUND(k)
13:     **return** SOLVEABSTRACT(**env**, $I, k, \emptyset$)
14: **end function**

3.3 Correctness

We define two global invariants of the algorithm. The *may-invariant* states that sets $B^m[i]$ grow monotonically with i and that each $B^m[i+1]$ overapproximates the states from which the environment can force the game into $B^m[i]$. We call this operation $Upre$, the uncontrollable predecessor. So the *may-invariant* is:

$$\forall i < k.\ B^m[i] \subseteq B^m[i+1], Upre(B^m[i]) \subseteq B^m[i+1].$$

The *must-invariant* guarantees that the must-losing set B^M is an underapproximation of the actual losing set B:

$$B^M \subseteq B.$$

Correctness of SOLVEUNBOUNDED follows from these invariants. The must-invariant guarantees that the environment can force the game into an error state from B^M, therefore checking whether the initial state is in B^M (as in line 5) is sufficient to return **unrealisable**. The may-invariant tells us that if $B^m[i] \equiv$

$B^m[i+1]$ (line 6) then $Upre(B^m[i]) \subseteq B^m[i]$, i.e. $B^m[i]$ overapproximates the winning states for the environment. We know that $I \notin B^m[k]$ due to the postcondition of CHECKBOUND, and since the may-invariant tells us that B^m is monotonic then I must not be in $B^m[i]$. If $I \notin B^m[i]$ then I is not in the winning states for the environment and the controller can always win from I.

Both invariants trivially hold after B^m and B^M have been initialised in the beginning of the algorithm. The sets B^m and B^M are only modified by the functions LEARN and $\overline{\text{LEARN}}$. Below we prove that $\overline{\text{LEARN}}$ maintains the invariants. The proof of LEARN is similar.

3.4 Proof of $\overline{\text{learn}}$

We prove that postconditions of $\overline{\text{LEARN}}$ are satisfied assuming that its preconditions hold.

Lines (11 and 12) splits the tree T into T_1 and T_2, such that T_2 has depth 1. Consider formulas $F_1 = s(X_T) \wedge \overline{\text{TREEFORMULA}}(k, T_1)$ and $F_2 = \overline{\text{TREEFORMULA}}(k, T_2)$. These formulas only share variables X_n. Their conjunction $F_1 \wedge F_2$ is unsatisfiable, as by construction any solution of $F_1 \wedge F_2$ also satisfies $s(X_T) \wedge \overline{\text{TREEFORMULA}}(k, T)$, which is unsatisfiable (precondition (b)). Hence the interpolation operation is defined for F_1 and F_2.

Intuitively, the interpolant computed in line (13) overapproximates the set of states reachable from s by following the tree from the root node to n, and underapproximates the set of states from which the environment loses against tree T_2.

Formally, $\mathcal{I}$ has the property $\mathcal{I} \wedge F_2 \equiv \perp$. Since T_2 is of depth 1, this means that the environment cannot force the game into $B^m[\text{HEIGHT}(k, n) - 1]$ playing against the counterexample moves in T_2. Hence, $\mathcal{I} \cap Upre(B^m[\text{HEIGHT}(k, n) - 1]) = \emptyset$. Furthermore, since the may-invariant holds, $\mathcal{I} \cap Upre(B^m[i]) = \emptyset$, for all $i < \text{HEIGHT}(k, n)$. Hence, removing $\mathcal{I}$ from all $B^m[i], i \leq \text{HEIGHT}(k, n)$ in line (15) preserves the may-invariant, thus satisfying the first post-condition.

Furthermore, the interpolant satisfies $F_1 \rightarrow \mathcal{I}$, i.e., any assignment to X_n that satisfies $s(X_T) \wedge \overline{\text{TREEFORMULA}}(k, T_1)$ also satisfies $\mathcal{I}$. Hence, removing $\mathcal{I}$ from $B^m[\text{HEIGHT}(k, n)]$ makes $s(X_T) \wedge \overline{\text{TREEFORMULA}}(k, T_1)$ unsatisfiable, and hence all preconditions of the recursive invocation of $\overline{\text{LEARN}}$ in line (17) are satisfied.

At the second last recursive call to $\overline{\text{LEARN}}$, tree T_1 is empty, n is the root node, $\overline{\text{TREEFORMULA}}(k, T_1) \equiv B^m[\text{HEIGHT}(k, T_1)](X^T)$; hence $s(X_T) \wedge \overline{\text{TREEFORMULA}}(k, T_1) \equiv s(X_T) \wedge B^m[\text{HEIGHT}(k, T_1)](X^T) \equiv \perp$. Thus the second postcondition of $\overline{\text{LEARN}}$ holds.

The proof of LEARN is similar to the above proof of LEARN. An interpolant constructed from $F_1 = s(X_T) \wedge \text{TREEFORMULA}(k, T_1)$ and $F_2 = \text{TREEFORMULA}(k, T_2)$ has the property $\mathcal{I} \wedge F_2 \equiv \perp$ and the precondition ensures that the controller is unable to force the game into B^M playing against the counterexample moves in T_2. Thus adding $\mathcal{I}$ to B^M maintains the must-invariant satisfying the first postcondition.

Likewise, in the second last recursive call of LEARN with the empty tree T_1 and root node n: TREEFORMULA$(k, T_1) \equiv \neg B^M(X_T)$. Hence $s(X_T) \wedge$ TREEFORMULA$(k, T_1) \equiv s(X_T) \wedge \neg B^M(X_T) \equiv \bot$. Therefore $s(X_T) \wedge B^M(X_T) \not\equiv \bot$, the second postcondition, is true.

3.5 Proof of Termination

We must prove that CHECKBOUND terminates and that upon termination its postcondition holds, i.e., state I is removed from $B^m[\kappa]$ if there is a winning controller strategy on the bounded safety game of maximum bound κ or it is added to B^M otherwise. Termination follows from completeness of counterexample guided search, which terminates after enumerating all possible opponent moves in the worst case.

Assume that there is a winning strategy for the controller at bound κ. This means that at some point the algorithm discovers a counterexample tree of bound κ for which the environment cannot force into E. The algorithm then invokes the $\overline{\text{LEARN}}$ method, which removes I from $B^m[\kappa]$. Alternatively, if there is a winning strategy for the environment at bound κ then a counterexample losing for the controller will be found. Subsequently LEARN will be called and I added to B^M.

3.6 Optimisation: Generalising the Initial State

This optimisation allows us to learn may and must losing states faster. Starting with a larger set of initial states we increase the reachable set and hence increase the number of states learned by interpolation. This optimisation requires a modification to SOLVEABSTRACT to handle sets of states, which is not shown.

The optimisation is relatively simple and is inspired by a common greedy heuristic for minimising unsat cores. Initial state I assigns a value to each variable in X. If the environment loses $\langle I, k \rangle$ then we attempt to solve for a generalised version of I by removing one variable assignment at a time. If the environment loses from the larger set of states then we continue generalising. In this way we learn more states by increasing the reachable set. In our benchmarks we have observed that this optimisation is beneficial on the first few iterations of CHECKBOUND.

4 Evaluation

We evaluate our approach on the benchmarks of the 2015 synthesis competition (SYNTCOMP'15). Each benchmark comprises of controllable and uncontrollable inputs to a circuit that assigns values to latches. One latch is configured as the error bit that determines the winner of the safety game. The benchmark suite is a collection of both real-world and toy specifications including generalised buffers, AMBA bus controllers, device drivers, and converted LTL formulas. Descriptions of many of the benchmark families used can be found in the 2014 competition report [14].

Algorithm 6. Generalise I optimisation

---

function CHECKBOUND(k)
    $r \leftarrow$ SOLVEABSTRACT(**env**, $I, k, \emptyset$)
    if $r \neq \emptyset$ **then return** r
    $s' \leftarrow I$
    for $x \in X$ **do**
        $r \leftarrow$ SOLVEABSTRACT(**env**, $s' \setminus \{x\}, k, \emptyset$)
        if $r =$ NULL **then** $s' \leftarrow s' \setminus \{x\}$ ▷ Removes the assignment to x from s'
    end for
    return NULL
end function

The implementation of our algorithm uses GLUCOSE [2] for SAT solving and PERIPLO [21] for interpolant generation. We intend to open source the tool for SYNTCOMP'16. The benchmarks were run on a cluster of Intel Quad Core Xeon E5405 2 GHz CPUs with 16 GB of memory. The solvers were allowed exclusive access to a node for one hour to solve an instance.

The results of our benchmarking are shown, along with the synthesis competition results [1], in Table 1. The competition was run on Intel Quad Core 3.2 GHz CPUs with 32 GB of memory, also on isolated nodes for one hour per instance. The competition results differ significantly from our own benchmarks due to this more powerful hardware. For our benchmarks we report only the results for solvers we were able to run on our cluster. The unique column lists the number of instances that only that tool could solve in the competition (excluding our solver). In brackets is the number of instances that only that tool could solve, including our solver.

Table 1. Synthesis competition 2015 results

Solver	Solved (Competition)	Solved (Benchmarks)	Unique
Simple BDD Solver (2)	195	189	10 *(6)*
AbsSynthe (seq2)	187	139	2
Simple BDD Solver (1)	185	175	
AbsSynthe (seq3)	179	134	
Realizer (sequential)	179		
AbsSynthe (seq1)	173	139	1
Demiurge (D1real)	139	136	5 *(2)*
Aisy	98		
Unbounded Synthesis		*103*	*12*

Our implementation was able to solve 103 out of the 250 specification in the allotted time, including 12 instances that were not solved by any other solver in the sequential track of the competition. The unique instances we solved are listed in Table 2.

Table 2. Instances uniquely solved by our approach

1. 6s216rb0_c0to31	7. driver_c10n
2. cnt30y	8. stay18y
3. driver_a10n	9. stay20n
4. driver_a8n	10. stay20y
5. driver_b10y	11. stay22n
6. driver_b8y	12. stay22y

Five of the instances unique to our solver are device driver instances and another five are from the stay family. This supports the hypothesis that different game solving methodologies perform better on certain classes of specifications.

We also present a cactus plot of the number of instances solved over time (Fig. 5). We have plotted the best configuration of each solver we benchmarked. The solvers shown are DEMIURGE [4], the only SAT-based tool in the competition, the winner of the sequential realisability track SIMPLE BDD SOLVER 2 [22], and AbsSynthe (seq3) [6].

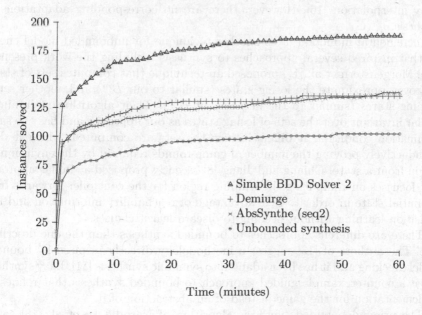

Fig. 5. Number of instances solved over time. (Color figure online)

Whilst our solver is unable to solve as many instances as other tools, it was able to solve more unique instances than any solver in the competition. This confirms that our methodology is able to fill gaps in a state of the art synthesis toolbox by more efficiently solving instances that are hard for other techniques. For this reason our solver would be a worthwhile addition to a portfolio solver. In the parallel track of the competition, DEMIURGE uses a suite of 3 separate but communicating solvers. The solvers relay unsafe states to one another, which is compatible with the set B^M in our solver. This technique can already solve each of the unique instances solved by our solver but there may still be value in the addition of this work to the portfolio. It remains future work to explore this possibility.

5   Related Work

Synthesis of safety games is a thoroughly explored area of research with most efforts directed toward solving games with BDDs [7] and abstract interpretation [6,22]. Satisfiability solving has been used previously for synthesis in a suite of methods proposed by Bloem et al. [4]. The authors propose employing competing SAT solvers to learn clauses representing bad states, which is similar to our approach but does not unroll the game. They also suggest QBF solver, template-based, and Effectively Propositional Logic (EPR) approaches.

SAT-based bounded model checking approaches that unroll the transition relation have been extended to unbounded by using conflicts in the solver [15], or by interpolation [16]. However, there are no corresponding adaptations to synthesis.

Incremental induction [5] is another technique for unbounded model checking that inspired several approaches to synthesis including the work presented here. Morgenstern et al. [17] proposed an technique that computes sets of states that overapproximate the losing states (similar to our B^m) and another set of winning states (similar to the negation of B^M). Their algorithm maintains a similar invariant over the sets of losing states as our approach and has the same termination condition. It differs in how the sets are computed, which it does by inductively proving the number of game rounds required by the environment to win from a state. Chiang and Jiang [8] recently proposed a similar approach that focusses on computing the winning region for the controller forwards from the initial state in order to take advantage of reachability information and bad transition learning without needing to discard learnt clauses.

There are different approaches to bounded synthesis than the one described here. The authors of [13] suggest a methodology directly inspired by bounded model checking and it has been adapted to symbolic synthesis [11]. Lazy synthesis [12] is a counterexample guided approach to bounded synthesis that refines an implementation for the game instead of an abstraction of it.

The original bounded synthesis algorithm of Narodytska et al. [18] solves realisability without constructing a strategy. In [10] the realisability algorithm is extended with strategy extraction. The technique relies on interpolation over abstract game trees to compute the winning strategy. In the present work we use interpolation in a different way in order to learn losing states of the game. In addition, this method could be easily adapted to the unbounded realisability algorithm presented here to generate unbounded strategies.

6   Conclusion

We presented an extension to an existing bounded synthesis technique that promotes it to unbounded safety games. The approach taken as whole differs from other synthesis techniques by combining counterexample guided game solving with winning set computation. Intuitively, the abstraction refinement framework of the bounded synthesis algorithm restricts the search to consider only moves that may lead to winning strategies. By constructing sets of bad states during this search we aim to consider only states that are relevant to a winning strategy while solving the unbounded game.

The results show that our approach is able to solve more unique instances than other solvers by performing well on certain classes of games that are hard for other methodologies.

Future work includes incorporating the solver into a parallel suite of communicating solvers [4]. There is evidence that different solvers perform well on different classes of games. Thus we hypothesise that the way forward for synthesis tools is to combine the efforts of many different techniques.

References

1. Syntcomp   2015   results.   http://syntcomp.cs.unisaarland.de/syntcomp2015/ experiments/. Accessed 29 Jan 2016
2. Audemard, G., Simon, L.: Lazy clause exchange policy for parallel SAT solvers. In: Sinz, C., Egly, U. (eds.) SAT 2014. LNCS, vol. 8561, pp. 197–205. Springer, Heidelberg (2014)
3. Biere, A., Cimatti, A., Clarke, E., Zhu, Y.: Symbolic model checking without BDDs. In: Cleaveland, W.R. (ed.) TACAS 1999. LNCS, vol. 1579, pp. 193–207. Springer, Heidelberg (1999)
4. Bloem, R., Könighofer, R., Seidl, M.: SAT-based synthesis methods for safety specs. In: McMillan, K.L., Rival, X. (eds.) VMCAI 2014. LNCS, vol. 8318, pp. 1–20. Springer, Heidelberg (2014)
5. Bradley, A.R.: SAT-based model checking without unrolling. In: Jhala, R., Schmidt, D. (eds.) VMCAI 2011. LNCS, vol. 6538, pp. 70–87. Springer, Heidelberg (2011)
6. Brenguier, R., Pérez, G.A., Raskin, J., Sankur, O.: AbsSynthe: abstract synthesis from succinct safety specifications. In: Workshop on Synthesis, SYNT, pp. 100–116 (2014)
7. Burch, J.R., Clarke, E.M., McMillan, K.L., Dill, D.L., Hwang, L.J.: Symbolic model checking: 10^{20} states and beyond. In: Symposium on Logic in Computer Science, pp. 428–439 (1990)

8. Chiang, T.W., Jiang, J.H.R.: Property-directed synthesis of reactive systems from safety specifications. In: Proceedings of the IEEE/ACM International Conference on Computer-Aided Design, ICCAD 2015, pp. 794–801 (2015)
9. Craig, W.: Linear reasoning. A new form of the Herbrand-Gentzen theorem. J. Symb. Log. **22**(3), 250–268 (1957)
10. Eèn, N., Legg, A., Narodytska, N., Ryzhyk, L.: SAT-based strategy extraction in reachability games. In: AAAI Conference on Artificial Intelligences, AAAI, pp. 3738–3745 (2015)
11. Ehlers, R.: Symbolic bounded synthesis. In: Touili, T., Cook, B., Jackson, P. (eds.) CAV 2010. LNCS, vol. 6174, pp. 365–379. Springer, Heidelberg (2010)
12. Finkbeiner, B., Jacobs, S.: Lazy synthesis. In: Kuncak, V., Rybalchenko, A. (eds.) VMCAI 2012. LNCS, vol. 7148, pp. 219–234. Springer, Heidelberg (2012)
13. Finkbeiner, B., Schewe, S.: Bounded synthesis. Softw. Tools Technol. Transf. STTF **15**(5–6), 519–539 (2013)
14. Jacobs, S., Bloem, R., Brenguier, R., Ehlers, R., Hell, T., Könighofer, R., Pérez, G.A., Raskin, J., Ryzhyk, L., Sankur, O., Seidl, M., Tentrup, L., Walker, A.: The first reactive synthesis competition (SYNTCOMP 2014). Computing Research Repository, CoRR abs/1506.08726 (2015). http://arxiv.org/abs/1506.08726
15. McMillan, K.L.: Applying SAT methods in unbounded symbolic model checking. In: Brinksma, E., Larsen, K.G. (eds.) CAV 2002. LNCS, vol. 2404, pp. 250–264. Springer, Heidelberg (2002)
16. Dransfield, M.R., Marek, V.W., Truszczyński, M.: Satisfiability and computing van der Waerden numbers. In: Giunchiglia, E., Tacchella, A. (eds.) SAT 2003. LNCS, vol. 2919, pp. 1–13. Springer, Heidelberg (2004)
17. Morgenstern, A., Gesell, M., Schneider, K.: Solving games using incremental induction. In: Johnsen, E.B., Petre, L. (eds.) IFM 2013. LNCS, vol. 7940, pp. 177–191. Springer, Heidelberg (2013)
18. Narodytska, N., Legg, A., Bacchus, F., Ryzhyk, L., Walker, A.: Solving games without controllable predecessor. In: Biere, A., Bloem, R. (eds.) CAV 2014. LNCS, vol. 8559, pp. 533–540. Springer, Heidelberg (2014)
19. Piterman, N., Pnueli, A., Sa'ar, Y.: Synthesis of reactive(1) designs. In: Emerson, E.A., Namjoshi, K.S. (eds.) VMCAI 2006. LNCS, vol. 3855, pp. 364–380. Springer, Heidelberg (2006)
20. Pudlák, P.: Lower bounds for resolution and cutting plane proofs and monotone computations. J. Symb. Log. **62**(3), 981–998 (1997)
21. Rollini, S.F., Alt, L., Fedyukovich, G., Hyvärinen, A.E.J., Sharygina, N.: PeRIPLO: a framework for producing effective interpolants in SAT-based software verification. In: McMillan, K., Middeldorp, A., Voronkov, A. (eds.) LPAR-19 2013. LNCS, vol. 8312, pp. 683–693. Springer, Heidelberg (2013)
22. Walker, A., Ryzhyk, L.: Predicate abstraction for reactive synthesis. In: Formal Methods in Computer-Aided Design FMCAD, pp. 219–226 (2014)

QLOSE: Program Repair
with Quantitative Objectives

Loris D'Antoni[1], Roopsha Samanta[2(✉)], and Rishabh Singh[3]

[1] University of Wisconsin-Madison, Madison, USA
loris@cs.wisc.edu
[2] IST Austria, Klosterneuburg, Austria
roopsha.samanta@ist.ac.at
[3] Microsoft Research, Redmond, USA
risin@microsoft.com

Abstract. The goal of automatic program repair is to identify a set of syntactic changes that can turn a program that is incorrect with respect to a given specification into a correct one. Existing program repair techniques typically aim to find *any* program that meets the given specification. Such "best-effort" strategies can end up generating a program that is quite different from the original one. Novel techniques have been proposed to compute syntactically minimal program fixes, but the smallest syntactic fix to a program can still significantly alter the original program's behaviour. We propose a new approach to program repair based on *program distances*, which can quantify changes not only to the program syntax but also to the program semantics. We call this the *quantitative program repair problem* where the "optimal" repair is derived using multiple distances. We implement a solution to the quantitative repair problem in a prototype tool called QLOSE (Quantitatively close), using the program synthesizer SKETCH. We evaluate the effectiveness of different distances in obtaining desirable repairs by evaluating QLOSE on programs taken from educational tools such as CodeHunt and edX.

1 Introduction

Recent years have seen the emergence of computer-aided personalized education as a new, important research field. Sophisticated techniques relying on formal methods, programming languages, and program synthesis have been designed to assist teachers in grading and providing feedback for introductory programming assignments [24], automata constructions [1], and geometric constructions [10,13]. In this paper, we propose a novel program repair framework that enhances the state of the art in automated feedback generation for students in introductory programming courses.

This research was supported in part by the European Research Council (ERC) under grant 267989 (QUAREM) and by the Austrian Science Fund (FWF) under grants S11402-N23 (RiSE) and Z211-N23 (Wittgenstein Award).

© Springer International Publishing Switzerland 2016
S. Chaudhuri and A. Farzan (Eds.): CAV 2016, Part II, LNCS 9780, pp. 383–401, 2016.
DOI: 10.1007/978-3-319-41540-6_21

The goal of automatic program repair is to identify a set of syntactic changes that can turn a program that is incorrect with respect to a given specification into a correct one. In the context of automated feedback generation, repairing a program corresponds to finding a "fix" to the student's incorrect solution. The specification can be as simple as a set of test cases.

Existing program repair techniques are typically "best-effort" and aim to find *any* repair that meets the given specification. Such techniques can end up generating a program that is quite different from the original one. Although this may be acceptable in some settings, in the context of education, the goal should be to slowly guide the students towards a correct solution. In particular, if a student solution is close to a correct one, a teacher wouldn't point the student to a completely different program, but would rather show how the student solution can be corrected with small changes. Advanced program repair techniques address this problem by computing syntactically minimal program repairs [19, 23, 24].

In this paper, we argue that even the smallest syntactic fix to a program can significantly alter its behaviour. We propose a new approach to program repair based on *program distances*, which quantify changes not only to the program syntax but also to the program semantics. While syntactic distances capture the number of edits to the program, semantic distances quantify the number of changes to the "behaviour" of a program with respect to a given set of tests. We formalize the *quantitative program repair problem* in which the "optimal" repair is defined as a correct program that minimizes an objective function over multiple program distances. Although our framework is general, we present two types of syntactic distances, three types of semantic distances, and propose a solution to the quantitative program repair problem with respect to these distances.

We have implemented our techniques in a prototype tool called QLOSE (Quantitatively close), which is built on top of the SKETCH synthesis system [26]. In QLOSE, we encode the functional correctness property of the student solution with respect to a set of tests as a *hard* constraint and the syntactic and semantic distances with respect to the original solution as *soft* constraints. The repair generated by SKETCH maximizes the number of soft constraints that can be satisfied, while satisfying the hard constraints. We evaluate QLOSE on 11 representative benchmark programs taken from student submissions to the Microsoft CodeHunt platform [29] and the Introduction to Programming course on the edX platform. Our preliminary results show that encoding quantitative program repair using syntactic and semantic distances is practically feasible for small student solutions and leads to more desirable repairs.

Contributions. This paper makes the following key contributions.

- We define new notions of syntactic and semantic distances between programs with respect to a given set of tests and use these notions to formalize the quantitative program repair problem (Sects. 3, 4).
- We encode the quantitative repair problem in a prototype tool called QLOSE, which is built on top of the SKETCH synthesis system (Sect. 5).
- We evaluate QLOSE and the strengths of the different distances on 11 representative student submissions taken from education platforms (Sect. 6).

2   Motivating Example

We use the example in Fig. 1 to show that semantic distances can sometimes yield more intuitive program repairs than syntactic distances.[1] Figure 1 contains a set of tests that is representative of the intended semantics of a desired program. Given this test set, the student has come up with the program FINDCBUGGY in Fig. 1(a) which fails the first test but passes the other ones. The desired program is one that given a string s, a character c, and an integer k outputs whether the character c appears in s at some position $j \leq k$. Besides a small imprecision, the student solution captures the intended algorithm in the sense that successful executions of the program are not far from those in the correct algorithm.

Test set

Input			Output	
s	c	k	expected	actual
ab?	?	2	true	false
aba?gc	?	5	true	true
?aba	?	3	true	true

```
1  FindCBuggy(str s, ch c, int k){
2    for(int j=0;j<k;j++)
3      if(s[j]==c)
4        return true;
5    return false;
6  }
```

(a)

```
1  FindCBadFix(str s, ch c, int k){
2    for(int j=0;j<k;j++)
3      if(c=='?') //new condition
4        return true;
5    return false;
6  }
```

(b)

```
1  FindCGoodFix(str s, ch c, int k){
2    for(int j=0;j<=k;j++) // new guard
3      if(s[j]==c)
4        return true;
5    return false;
6  }
```

(c)

Fig. 1. A buggy program (a) with two possible syntactic repairs (b) and (c).

Limitation of syntactic distances. To give feedback to the student, one can try fixing the student solution using existing program repair techniques that minimize the number of *syntactic changes* to an incorrect program. Techniques like the ones presented in [19,24] would return one of the two programs at the bottom of Fig. 1. Both of these programs differ from the one in Fig. 1(a) by exactly one expression. However, one of the repaired programs is, in some sense, more "disruptive" than the other. In particular, although the program in Fig. 1(b) simply changes the guard of the if-statement, its executions on previously correct tests are now very different: on all tests the loop is now executed only once! On the other hand, for the program in Fig. 1(c), the executions on correct tests are the same as for the original program. Syntactic program distances cannot distinguish between these two candidate repairs and are inadequate for this example.

Semantic distances. One can capture the intuition that the program in Fig. 1(c) is a better repair for the student solution than the program in Fig. 1(b) by examining the execution of these programs on successful tests. For example, if

---

[1] This example is a slight variation of the one appearing in Fig. 3 of [19].

we were to track the locations (lines of code) traversed by the three programs on the second input test with $s = $ aba?gc we would get the following sequences of locations: (a) $2, 3, 2, 3, 2, 3, 2, 3, 4$; (b) $2, 3, 4$; and (c) $2, 3, 2, 3, 2, 3, 2, 3, 4$. These sequences highlight that the program in Fig. 1(c) is *semantically closer* to the student solution.

A similar argument can be made for repairing using only a semantic distance as the repaired program may be syntactically very far from the original one. In summary, in order to repair programs in a meaningful way, it is often necessary to take into account multiple quantitative objectives such as the number of syntactic edits and the *distance* between program behaviours.

3   Program Repair

In this section, we formalize programs, correctness specifications, and permissible program edits. We then use these notions to define the program repair problem.

3.1   Programs

We fix a simple imperative programming language, in which a program P consists of a function definition $f(i_1, \ldots, i_q) : o$, a set of program variables V, and a sequence of labeled statements $\sigma = s_1 \ldots s_n$. A statement is one of the following: skip, return, assignment, conditional or loop statement.[2] Each statement in σ is labeled with a unique location identifier from the set $L = \{\ell_0, \ell_1, \ldots, \ell_p, exit\}$. The function f has a designated set of input variables $I = \{i_1, \ldots, i_q\}$ and a designated output variable o. The program statements are allowed to use an auxiliary set of variables $V = \{v_1, \ldots, v_r\}$. We assume a universe $\mathcal{U}$ of values. We also assume that all variables are associated with a given type and are only assigned values from $\mathcal{U}$ with the proper types.

We now define the semantics of our programs. The semantics of program statements is standard. Without loss of generality, we assume execution of a return statement assigns a value to the output variable and transfers control to a designated location $exit$.

A program configuration η is a pair (ℓ, ν) where $\ell \in L$ is a location and $\nu : I \cup \{o\} \cup V \mapsto \mathcal{U} \cup \{nd\}$ is a valuation function that assigns values to all variables. The element nd indicates that a variable has not been assigned a value yet or is out of scope. We write $(\ell, \nu) \to (\ell', \nu')$ if execution of the statement at location ℓ under variable valuation ν transfers control to location ℓ' with variable valuation ν'.

The execution $\pi(\nu)$ of program P on a valuation ν is a sequence of configurations $\eta_0, \eta_1, \ldots$, where $\eta_0 = (\ell_0, \nu)$ and for each h, $\eta_h \to \eta_{h+1}$. An execution terminates once the location $exit$ is reached.

Here we are only interested in executions for which the initial valuation ν is such that for every input variable $x \in I$, $\nu(x) \neq nd$, and for every non-input

---

[2] Our implementation supports a richer subset of the Python language including lists, strings, and function calls.

variable $y \in V \cup \{o\}$, $\nu(y) = nd$. Given a partial valuation $\nu_I : I \mapsto \mathcal{U}$ assigning values to the input variables, let ν_I^+ be the valuation such that for every input variable $x \in I$, $\nu_I^+(x) = \nu_I(x)$, and for every other variable $y \notin I$, $\nu_I^+(y) = nd$. We denote by $[\![P]\!] : (I \mapsto \mathcal{U}) \mapsto \mathcal{U}$ the partial function computed by a program P, and define it as $[\![P]\!](\nu_I) = res$ iff $\pi(\nu_I^+)$ terminates with output valuation ν' and $\nu'(o) = res$.

Example 1. Consider the program FINDCBUGGY in Fig. 1(a). The input variables I are $\{s, c, k\}$ and the designated output variable is o. The set of program variables is the singleton $\{j\}$. The execution of FINDCBUGGY on ν such that $\nu_I(s) = \text{ab?}, \nu_I(c) = ?, \nu_I(k) = 2$ is illustrated in the following table:

	η_0	η_1	η_2	η_3	η_4	η_5	η_6
loc	2	3	2	3	2	5	exit
s	ab?	ab?	ab?	ab?	ab?	ab?	ab?
c	?	?	?	?	?	?	?
k	2	2	2	2	2	2	2
j	nd	0	0	1	1	2	nd
o	nd	nd	nd	nd	nd	nd	false

We thus have $[\![\text{FINDCBUGGY}]\!](\text{ab?}, ?, 2) = \text{false}$.

3.2 Test Sets as Specifications

A test t is a pair (ν_I, res), where $\nu_I : I \mapsto \mathcal{U}$ is a valuation over the input variables, and $res \in \mathcal{U}$ is the expected output value. A program P satisfies a test t if $[\![P]\!](\nu_I) = res$. A program P satisfies a test set T if it satisfies all the tests $t \in T$.

We use $\dot{\pi}(t)$, read as "execution of a program on a test t", to refer to $\pi(\nu_I^+)$.

Example 2. Consider the test set and the program FINDCBUGGY in Fig. 1. Clearly, FINDCBUGGY does not satisfy the test set. In particular, on the first test from Example 1 we have $[\![\text{FINDCBUGGY}]\!](\text{ab?}, ?, 2) \neq \text{true}$.

3.3 The Program Repair Problem

In our repair model we permit program expressions to be changed, but not program statements. For example, we permit replacement of loop guards and right-hand sides of assignments and disallow replacement of an assignment with a **return** statement. Formally, a permissible program edit applied to a labeled statement ℓ : stmt in program P is any modification of stmt that replaces an expression in stmt with another expression over the same domain, and leaves the label ℓ unchanged.

Given program P and a subset of locations LOC $\subseteq L$ of P, let $\mathcal{R}_{\text{LOC}}(P)$ be the set of all programs that can be obtained by applying permissible program edits to labeled statements with labels in LOC. The following proposition holds trivially.

Proposition 1. *Given programs P, P', with locations L, L', the following statements are equivalent:*

   (i) *there exists unique* LOC $\subseteq L$ *such that* $P' \in \mathcal{R}_{\text{LOC}}(P)$
  (ii) *there exists unique* LOC$' \subseteq L'$ *such that* $P \in \mathcal{R}_{\text{LOC}'}(P')$
 (iii) $L = L'$ *and there exists unique* LOC $\subseteq L$ *such that* $P' \in \mathcal{R}_{\text{LOC}}(P)$ *and*
      $P \in \mathcal{R}_{\text{LOC}}(P')$.

Example 3. In Fig. 1, FINDCBADFIX $\in \mathcal{R}_{\{3\}}$(FINDCBUGGY) as FINDCBADFIX replaces the guard $s[j] == c$ in location 3 of FINDCBUGGY with the guard $c ==?$. Similarly, FINDCGOODFIX $\in \mathcal{R}_{\{2\}}$(FINDCBUGGY) as FINDCGOODFIX replaces the loop guard $j < k$ in location 2 of FINDCBUGGY with the guard $j \leq k^3$.

Given a program P and a test set T such that P does not satisfy T, the goal of program repair is to compute P' such that: (1) P' satisfies T, and (2) there exists LOC $\subseteq L$ such that $P' \in \mathcal{R}_{\text{LOC}}(P)$.

Example 4. Consider the programs in Fig. 1. The programs FINDCBADFIX and FINDCGOODFIX are possible repairs of the program FINDCBUGGY with respect to the test set shown in the figure. They are both correct on the test set and, from Example 3, FINDCBADFIX $\in \mathcal{R}_{\{3\}}$(FINDCBUGGY) and FINDCGOODFIX $\in \mathcal{R}_{\{2\}}$(FINDCBUGGY).

4   Quantitative Program Repair

In this section, we define program distances and the quantitative program repair problem. Given two programs P, P' and a test set T, a program distance[4] is a function over P, P' and T that quantifies how *close* are P and P' w.r.t. T. We classify program distances as *syntactic* and *semantic* distances. A syntactic program distance simply tracks the syntactic change between P and P', independent of the test set T. Hence, a syntactic program distance is a function over P and P'. A semantic program distance tracks the semantic differences between P and P' with respect to executions on the test set T. In particular, a semantic program distance tracks the differences in the executions of P and P' on all tests

---

[3] In our implementation, each location is associated with a single expression. To keep our presentation simple, we associate all 3 expressions in the **for** loop in FINDCBUGGY with location 2, instead of mapping each expression to a different location.

[4] Our program distances are not necessarily *distance metrics*. In particular, some of them are not symmetric in P and P'.

t such that both P and P' satisfy t. In what follows, we define several syntactic and semantic distances. One could easily define more sophisticated distances and we invite the reader to do so. The following distances sufficed for our "proof of concept" experiments with quantitative program repair.

4.1   Syntactic Distances

A syntactic distance between programs P and P' is defined modulo an *expression distance* ε. An expression distance tracks the syntactic difference between two expressions. In this work, we use two simple expression distances, defined below.

Boolean expression distance, $\varepsilon_{\text{BOOL}}$, is a Boolean-valued distance that simply tracks if two expressions are equal or not:

$$\varepsilon_{\text{BOOL}}(expr, expr') = \begin{cases} 0 & \text{if } expr = expr' \\ 1 & \text{otherwise.} \end{cases}$$

Expression-size distance, $\varepsilon_{\text{SIZE}}$, tracks the size of the repaired expression:

$$\varepsilon_{\text{SIZE}}(expr, expr') = \begin{cases} 0 & \text{if } expr = expr' \\ size(expr') & \text{otherwise,} \end{cases}$$

where $size(expr')$ can be defined in different ways. For example, $size(expr')$ could be the total number of symbols and operators in $expr'$. In Sect. 5, we present the definition of $size(expr')$ used in our implementation. Note that $\varepsilon_{\text{SIZE}}(expr, expr')$ is not a symmetric function.

A syntactic program distance between programs P and P' is finite only if P and P' can be obtained from each other by applying a set of permissible program edits. Given an expression distance ε, a syntactic program distance accumulates the expression distance across all expression changes between P and P'. Formally:

$$d_{syn}^{\varepsilon}(P, P') = \begin{cases} \infty & \text{if } \forall \text{LOC} : P' \notin \mathcal{R}_{\text{LOC}}(P) \\ \sum_{\ell \in \text{LOC}: P' \in \mathcal{R}_{\text{LOC}}(P)} \varepsilon(expr_\ell, expr'_\ell) & \text{otherwise.} \end{cases}$$

Note that Proposition 1 ensures the uniqueness of LOC in the second case. Here, $expr_\ell, expr'_\ell$ denote expressions in ℓ-labeled statements of P, P', respectively. Thus, if $\varepsilon = \varepsilon^{\text{BOOL}}$, $d_{syn}^{\varepsilon}(P, P')$ equals the number of permissible program edits required to transform P to P'. Similarly, if $\varepsilon = \varepsilon_{\text{SIZE}}$, $d_{syn}^{\varepsilon}(P, P')$ equals the total size of all new expressions in P'.

Example 5. Consider the programs in Fig. 1. For $\varepsilon = \varepsilon_{\text{BOOL}}$, one can see that $d_{syn}^{\varepsilon}(\text{FINDCBUGGY}, \text{FINDCBADFIX})$ and $d_{syn}^{\varepsilon}(\text{FINDCBUGGY}, \text{FINDCGOOD}\allowbreak\text{FIX})$ both equal 1, as there is exactly one permissible program edit in each case. For $\varepsilon = \varepsilon_{\text{SIZE}}$, if expression size is given by the total number of symbols and operators, $d_{syn}^{\varepsilon}(\text{FINDCBUGGY}, \text{FINDCBADFIX})$ and $d_{syn}^{\varepsilon}(\text{FINDCBUGGY}, \text{FINDCGOODFIX})$ both equal 3. Neither syntactic distance can distinguish between FINDCBADFIX and FINDCGOODFIX.

4.2 Semantic Distances

The semantic distance between programs P and P' with respect to a test set T is defined modulo an *execution distance* ζ. An execution distance tracks the differences between two executions. In this paper, we consider three types of execution distances, defined on terminating executions.

Let $T_{sat} \subseteq T$ consist of all tests t such that P and P' both satisfy t. Given a test t in T_{sat}, let $\dot{\pi}(t)$, $\dot{\pi}'(t)$ denote executions of P, P', respectively on t. In what follows, we fix $\dot{\pi}(t) = \eta_0, \eta_1, \ldots, \eta_M$ and $\dot{\pi}'(t) = \eta'_0, \eta'_1, \ldots, \eta'_K$. Recall that a configuration η_h is a tuple of the form (ℓ_h, ν_h).

Our execution distances essentially compute the Hamming distance between two executions, using different abstractions of configurations. For executions of equal lengths, this distance equals the minimum number of configuration substitutions required to transform one execution into another. For executions of differing lengths, this distance additionally includes the difference in the execution lengths. All three execution distances can be defined as follows:

$$\zeta(\dot{\pi}(t), \dot{\pi}'(t)) = \begin{cases} |M - K| + \sum_{h=0}^{min(M,K)} \texttt{diff}(\eta_h, \eta'_h) & \text{if } M, K < \infty \\ \infty & \text{otherwise,} \end{cases}$$

where the definition of $\texttt{diff}(\eta_h, \eta'_h)$ varies for each execution distance.

Concrete execution distance, ζ_{CONC}, compares both locations and variable values in two executions: $\texttt{diff}_{conc}(\eta_h, \eta'_h) = 0$ if $\eta_h = \eta'_h$ and 1 otherwise.

Value execution distance, ζ_{VAL}, only compares the variable values in two executions: $\texttt{diff}_{val}(\eta_h, \eta'_h) = 0$ if $\nu_h = \nu'_h$ and 1 otherwise.

Location execution distance, ζ_{LOCS}, only compares the locations in two executions: $\texttt{diff}_{loc}(\eta_h, \eta'_h) = 0$ if $\ell_h = \ell'_h$ and 1 otherwise.

A semantic program distance between programs P, P' w.r.t. test set T is finite only if P and P' can be obtained from each other by applying a set of permissible program edits and T_{sat} is not empty. Given an execution distance ζ and the set T_{sat}, a semantic program distance accumulates the execution distance between executions of P and P' on tests in T_{sat}. Formally:

$$d^{\zeta}_{sem}(P, P', T) = \begin{cases} \infty & \text{if } \forall \text{LOC} : P' \notin \mathcal{R}_{\text{LOC}}(P) \text{ or } T_{sat} \text{ is empty} \\ \sum_{t \in T_{sat}} \zeta(\dot{\pi}(t), \dot{\pi}'(t)) & \text{otherwise.} \end{cases}$$

Example 6. The executions of FINDCBUGGY and FINDCBADFIX from Fig. 1 on ν such that $\nu_I(s) = \texttt{aba?gc}, \nu_I(c) = ?, \nu_I(k) = 5$ are shown in Fig. 2. The last 3 rows of the table show $\texttt{diff}(\eta_h, \eta'_h)$ for $h = 0, 1, 2, 3$. Note that $\texttt{diff}_{val}$ doesn't distinguish between η_2 and η'_2 as these configurations share the same variable values. The difference in lengths of the given two executions is 6. Thus, for these executions, $\zeta_{\text{CONC}} = \zeta_{\text{LOCS}} = 6 + 2 = 8$, and $\zeta_{\text{VAL}} = 6 + 1 = 7$.

	step	0	1	2	3	4	5	6	7	8	9
	loc	2	3	2	3	2	3	2	3	4	exit
FINDCBUGGY	j	nd	0	0	1	1	2	2	3	3	exit
	o	nd	nd	nd	nd	nd	nd	nd	nd	nd	true
	loc	2	3	4	exit						
FINDCBADFIX	j	nd	0	0	exit						
	o	nd	nd	nd	true						
	$\mathtt{diff}_{conc}$	0	0	1	1						
diff	$\mathtt{diff}_{val}$	0	0	0	1						
	$\mathtt{diff}_{loc}$	0	0	1	1						

Fig. 2. Semantic distances between executions. We do not show the input variables s, c, and k as their values are never modified.

The execution of FINDCGOODFIX on the same ν with $\nu_I(s) = $ aba?gc, $\nu_I(c) = ?, \nu_I(k) = 5$ is exactly the same as the execution of FINDCBUGGY shown in Fig. 2. Hence, $\zeta_{\text{CONC}} = \zeta_{\text{LOCS}} = \zeta_{\text{VAL}} = 0$ for the executions of FINDCBUGGY and FINDCGOODFIX. Our semantic program distances can distinguish between FINDCBADFIX and FINDCGOODFIX.

4.3 The Quantitative Program Repair Problem

Given a program P and a test set T such that P does not satisfy T, syntactic distance functions $d^1_{syn}, \ldots, d^x_{syn}$, semantic distance functions $d^1_{sem}, \ldots, d^y_{sem}$, and *objective functions* $f_1, \ldots, f_z$ over $d^1_{syn}, \ldots, d^x_{syn}, d^1_{sem}, \ldots, d^y_{sem}$, the goal of quantitative program repair is to compute P' such that:

(1) P' satisfies T,
(2) there exists LOC $\subseteq L$ such that $P' \in \mathcal{R}_{\text{LOC}}(P)$, and
(3) $P' = \underset{\exists \widehat{\text{LOC}} \subseteq L : \widehat{P} \in \mathcal{R}_{\widehat{\text{LOC}}}(P)}{\arg\min} \underset{1 \leq i \leq z}{\text{AGGREGATE}} \{f_i(d^1_{syn}(P, \widehat{P}), \ldots, d^y_{sem}(P, \widehat{P}, T))\}$.

Here AGGREGATE allows multiple objective functions to be combined. For example, AGGREGATE could enforce Pareto optimality.

Example 7. Consider the programs in Fig. 1. In Example 4, we showed that both FINDCBADFIX and FINDCGOODFIX satisfy conditions (1) and (2) of the quantitative program repair problem for program FINDCBUGGY and the test set shown in Fig. 1.

In Example 5, we showed that both $d^\varepsilon_{syn}(\text{FINDCBUGGY}, \text{FINDCBADFIX})$ and $d^\varepsilon_{syn}(\text{FINDCBUGGY}, \text{FINDCGOODFIX})$ equal 1 for $\varepsilon = \varepsilon_{\text{BOOL}}$. For $\varepsilon = \varepsilon_{\text{SIZE}}$, $d^\varepsilon_{syn}(\text{FINDCBUGGY}, \text{FINDCBADFIX})$ and $d^\varepsilon_{syn}(\text{FINDCBUGGY}, \text{FINDCGOODFIX})$ both equal 3.

The set T_{sat} consists of the last two tests in the test set T in Fig. 1. Let the test with $s = $ aba?gc be denoted t_1 and the test with $s = $?aba be denoted t_2. Let $\dot{\pi}(t_1)$ and $\dot{\pi}(t_2)$ denote the executions of FINDCBUGGY on t_1 and t_2, respectively.

Let $\dot{\pi}'(t_1)$, $\dot{\pi}'(t_2)$ and $\dot{\pi}''(t_1)$, $\dot{\pi}''(t_2)$ denote the executions of FINDCBADFIX and FINDCGOODFIX on t_1, t_2, respectively.

We have seen in Example 6 that $\zeta_{\text{CONC}}(\dot{\pi}(t_1), \dot{\pi}'(t_1)) = 8$ and $\zeta_{\text{CONC}}(\dot{\pi}(t_1), \dot{\pi}''(t_1)) = 0$. It's not hard to see that $\zeta_{\text{CONC}}(\dot{\pi}(t_2), \dot{\pi}'(t_2)) = 0$ and $\zeta_{\text{CONC}}(\dot{\pi}(t_2), \dot{\pi}''(t_2)) = 0$. Thus, we can compute $d_{sem}^{\zeta_{\text{CONC}}}(\text{FINDCBUGGY}, \text{FINDCBADFIX}, T) = 8$ and $d_{sem}^{\zeta_{\text{CONC}}}(\text{FINDCBUGGY}, \text{FINDCGOODFIX}, T) = 0$.

If we choose $d_{syn}^{\varepsilon_{\text{BOOL}}}$, $d_{syn}^{\varepsilon_{\text{SIZE}}}$ as our syntactic distances, $d_{sem}^{\zeta_{\text{CONC}}}$ as our semantic distance and our objective function f to simply be the sum of $d_{syn}^{\varepsilon_{\text{BOOL}}}$, $d_{syn}^{\varepsilon_{\text{SIZE}}}$ and $d_{sem}^{\zeta_{\text{CONC}}}$, the value of f is 4 for FINDCGOODFIX and is 12 for FINDCBADFIX. Hence, this instance of the quantitative program repair problem will prefer the program FINDCGOODFIX as a repair candidate.

5 Quantitative Program Repair Using Sketch

In this section, we describe the formulation of the quantitative program repair problem as an instance of the MAX-SMT problem. We encode the program semantics using a symbolic Boolean encoding and specify the functional correctness of the program w.r.t the given test set T as a *hard* constraint. The syntactic and semantic distances are encoded using *soft* constraints. The repair generated by the MAX-SMT solver maximizes the number of soft constraints that can be satisfied while ensuring the satisfaction of the hard constraints. We perform a syntax-directed translation from the source imperative language to SKETCH [26], and use the minimization algorithm in SKETCH to solve the MAX-SMT constraints. Instead of using a general MAX-SMT solver, we use the SKETCH solver because of the ease in translation of the buggy programs into constraints. The SKETCH solver allows for optimization constraints similar to MAX-SMT, but uses several algorithmic optimizations before encoding the problem into low-level SMT constraints. We now describe the key ideas in the formulation and translation of the quantitative program repair problem using the SKETCH system.

5.1 Background on Sketch

SKETCH is a synthesis system for writing partial programs (with holes) together with some high-level specifications of the programs. The synthesis algorithm fills the holes automatically using a constraint-based, counterexample-guided inductive synthesis (CEGIS) algorithm such that the completed program satisfies the given specifications. For example, consider the SKETCH program shown in Fig. 3(a). One possible completion synthesized by the SKETCH system is shown in Fig. 3(b). The hole expressions ?? can take any constant integer value, and they can further be composed to construct more complex unknown expressions.

5.2 Space of Expression Edits

For our quantitative program repair encoding, we restrict the class of expressions that can potentially be modified by the solver to (i) the set of conditional

```
harness int triple(int x){          harness int triple(int x){
  int y = ?? * x;                     int y = 3 * x;
  if(x==10) assert y == 30;           if(x==10) assert y == 30;
  return y;                           return y;
}                                   }
```

(a)   (b)

Fig. 3. (a) A simple SKETCH program and (b) a possible completion.

expressions and (ii) the right hand side expressions of assignment statements. Furthermore, to restrict the space of possible repairs, we use an expression template corresponding to a linear combination of constants and all program variables in scope at the program location. In SKETCH, the modifiable expressions are replaced by functions that either allow for returning the original unmodified expression in the program or some instantiation of the expression template.

For example, the SKETCH translation for the buggy program in Fig. 1(a) is shown in Fig. 4(a). The conditional expressions and the right hand side expressions of the assignment statements are translated to *change functions* f_i. An example change function f_1 is shown in Fig. 4(b). Each change function f_i is associated with a Boolean variable b_{f_i} that indicates if the original expression is selected ($b_{f_i} = 0$) or some new expression is selected for the completion of the function f_i ($b_{f_i} = 1$). Each set of possible new expressions is represented as a linear combination of program variables of appropriate types where the coefficients of the variables are denoted using unknown values $??_{i,j}$. For expressions involving strings, the change function restricts the edit expression to consist of only 1 character from that string. The characters are then interpreted as integers in SKETCH.

```
bit FindCBuggySketch(str s, ch c, int k){      int f1(str s, ch c, int k){
  for(int j= f₁(s,c,k); f₂(j,s,c,k);             if (b_f₁ == 0)
      j=f₃(j,s,c,k))                                return 0;
    if(f₄(j,s,c,k))                              else
      return f₅(j,s,c,k);                          return ??₁,₁*s[??] +
  return f₆(j,s,c,k);                                     ??₁,₂ * c+??₁,₃*k + ??₁,₄;
}                                              }
```

(a)   (b)

Fig. 4. The SKETCH translation for the FINDCBUGGY program from Fig. 1(a).

5.3 Encoding Distances

We now describe how the syntactic and semantic distances are encoded as constraints in the SKETCH system.

Syntactic Distances. We encode our syntactic distances modulo our two expression distances in SKETCH as follows.

- *Boolean expression distance:* The syntactic distance d_{syn}^{ε} for $\varepsilon = \varepsilon_{\text{BOOL}}$ computes the number of expression changes that are performed by the solver and is computed as $\Sigma_i b_{f_i}$. The Boolean variable b_{f_i} is set to 0 if the expression corresponding to function f_i remains unchanged in the final solution and is set to 1 otherwise.
- *Expression-size distance:* The syntactic distance d_{syn}^{ε} for $\varepsilon = \varepsilon_{\text{SIZE}}$ computes the total size of modified expressions, where the size of a modified linear arithmetic expression corresponding to f_i is computed as the sum of all of its coefficients $|??_{i,j}|$. Thus, $d_{syn}^{\varepsilon_{\text{SIZE}}}$ is defined as $\Sigma_i \Sigma_j |??_{i,j}|$.

Semantic Distances. We encode our semantic distance modulo the *concrete execution distance*. The SKETCH translation is instrumented to capture program states at different program locations as shown in Fig. 5(a), where $S_\ell^t[j]$ denotes the program state for j^{th} loop iteration at program location ℓ for a test case t. The concrete execution distance ζ_{CONC} between the original program and the modified program on a test case t in T_{sat} is computed as $\Sigma_{\ell,j}\phi(S_\ell^t[j], S_\ell^{\text{orig},t}[j])$, where the function ϕ counts the number of variables that do not have equal values across two states $S_\ell^t[j]$ and $S_\ell^{\text{orig},t}[j]$, as shown in Fig. 5(b). Our encoding enforces a bound on the length of program executions by unrolling loops a fixed number of times.

```
m₂ = 0; m₃ = 0; m₄ = 0;
for(int j= f1(s,c,k); f2(j,s,c,k); j=f3(j,s,c,k)){
    S₂ᵗ[m₂++] = [j,s,c,k];
    if(f4(j,s,c,k)){
        S₃ᵗ[m₃++] = [j,s,c,k]; return f5(j,s,c,k);}
}
S₄ᵗ[m₄++] = [j,s,c,k];
return f6(j,s,c,k);
```

```
int semDistance(S,Sᵒʳⁱᵍ,Tₛₐₜ){
    dₗ = 0;
    foreach(test t ∈ Tₛₐₜ)
        foreach(loc ℓ ∈ |S|)
            dₗ+ = φ(Sₗᵗ,Sₗᵒʳⁱᵍ,ᵗ);
    return dₗ;
}
```

(a)   (b)

Fig. 5. Encoding semantic distance in SKETCH.

Quantitative Objective. The final quantitative objective in the SKETCH translation is encoded as the following constraint:

$$\texttt{assert } d_{syn}^{\varepsilon_{\text{BOOL}}} < N \wedge \texttt{minimize } (d_{syn}^{\varepsilon_{\text{SIZE}}} + d_{sem}^{\zeta_{\text{CONC}}})$$

We use a linear search to first find the minimum number of expression changes N that are needed to repair the buggy program using a linear iterative search. After computing the value n, we then add the minimization constraint to find a repair with minimum semantic distance $d_{sem}^{\zeta_{\text{CONC}}}$ and simpler expression modifications $d_{syn}^{\varepsilon_{SIZE}}$. The SKETCH solver uses an incremental search methodology to compute the repair that corresponds to the minimum objective function value [24]. The hard constraints specifying functional correctness w.r.t a test set T is encoded in a standard way using **assert** statements in SKETCH. If we refer back to the definition of quantitative program repair in Sect. 4.3, the resulting repaired program is

$$P' = \underset{\exists \widehat{LOC} \subseteq L: \widehat{P} \in \mathcal{R}_{\widehat{LOC}}(P)}{\arg\min} \langle d_{syn}^{\varepsilon_{BOOL}}(P, \widehat{P}), d_{syn}^{\varepsilon_{SIZE}}(P, \widehat{P}) + d_{sem}^{\zeta_{CONC}}(P, \widehat{P}) \rangle.$$

In this case, the aggregation operator is the one that first minimizes the left element of the pair and then the right one.

6 Evaluation

We implemented a prototype tool QLOSE that given a (simplified) C# program, a set of test cases, and the desired types of distances, constructs a SKETCH program with the corresponding constraints to encode the quantitative program repair problem. We evaluated QLOSE on 11 representative benchmark programs using the distances presented in Sect. 5. Our preliminary results suggest that QLOSE is practically feasible for small student solutions and generates more desirable repairs while using a combination of syntactic and semantic distances.[5]

6.1 Benchmarks

Our benchmark set consists of 11 representative buggy programs taken from student submissions to introductory programming courses and recent program repair literature. The LargestGap problem is taken from the Microsoft Code-Hunt platform [29] and asks students to write a program to compute the largest difference amongst any two values in a given input array of integers. The FindC program is the same as FINDCBUGGY in Fig. 1. The tcas-semfix benchmark is taken from the SEMFIX [20] system and corresponds to a code excerpt from the Tcas benchmark[6]. The max3 problem asks students to compute the maximum of 3 integers. The iterPower, epoly, and multIA problems are taken from the Introduction to Programming course taught on the edX platform. The iterPower problem asks students to write an iterative program that, given two integers m and n, computes the value m^n. The epoly problem evaluates a polynomial (defined using an array of integer coefficients) on an integer value, and the multIA problem requires students to write a program to compute multiplication of two integers using successive additions.

---

[5] The experiments were performed on a 40-core 2.4 GHz Intel Xeon CPU with 100 GB RAM, with a timeout of 20 min. Although this is powerful hardware, we point out that SKETCH only uses a single core and in our experiments the maximum memory usage was less than 500 MB RAM.

[6] http://www.irit.fr/wiki/doku.php?id=wtc:benchmarks:tcas.

The number of lines of code (LOC), the number of variables ($|\text{Vars}|$), and the number of test input-output pairs ($|T_{sat}|$) for each benchmark problem[7] is shown in Fig. 6. The number of lines in the benchmarks varied from 4 to 10 lines, whereas the number of variables and the number of test cases varied from 3 to 5. For the CodeHunt benchmarks, we reused the test input-output pairs automatically generated by the CodeHunt engine. For the `tcas-semfix` benchmark, we use the tests from the SEMFIX paper [20]. For the benchmarks obtained from the edX class, we manually selected the relevant test cases that exposed different corner case behaviors.

Problem	LOC	$|\text{Vars}|$	$|T_{sat}|$	Syntactic		Semantic		Syntactic + Semantic	
FindC	4	4	4	1.5s	✗	2.5s	✓	2.2s	✓
LargestGap-1	10	4	4	9.8s	✓	184.9s	✗	13.4s	✓
LargestGap-2	7	4	4	6.9s	✗	TO	-	18.2s	✓
LargestGap-3	8	4	4	7.3s	✓	15.7s	✓	14.4s	✓
tcas-semfix	10	4	5	12.6s	✓	27.8s	✓	18.4s	✓
max3	5	3	4	1.1s	✓	1.7s	✗	1.9s	✓
iterPower-1	7	3	4	2.3s	✗	10.3s	✓	3.4s	✓
iterPower-2	7	3	4	2.1s	✓	15.2s	✗	2.7s	✓
ePoly-1	8	4	3	1.8s	✗	3.6s	✓	2.5s	✓
ePoly-2	10	4	3	2.4s	✓	4.6s	✓	2.8s	✓
multIA	5	4	4	1.8s	✗	21.5s	✗	2.4s	✓

Fig. 6. Solving times and the desiredness of the generated repairs for different distances. TO denotes that the solver timed out ($> 20\,\text{min}$), The symbol ✓ (resp. ✗) denotes that the generated repair was (resp. wasn't) the desired one.

6.2   Desired Repairs

The experimental results obtained by running QLOSE on different benchmarks using different distances are shown in Fig. 6. We manually inspected the repairs generated using different distance metrics and classified them into desired (✓) or not (✗). For performing this classification, we did not inspect the reference code for the problem, but instead inspected the original buggy program and manually inferred the algorithm the student (or programmer) likely intended to implement. We then checked whether the repaired program matched the intended algorithm.

We can observe that using only syntactic or semantic distance sometimes leads to undesired repairs whereas combining the two distances always leads to the desired fixes in our benchmark set. For example, for the `LargestGap-2` program shown in Fig. 7(a), the syntactic distance encoding causes the solver to

---

[7] The benchmark problems and the translated SKETCH files are available at: bit.ly/cav16-qlose.

come up with a fix that sets the loop initialization variable i to 0 instead of 1. Although, this repair is correct on the test cases, it is less desirable than the repair that assigns $a[0]$ to the low variable l, which corresponds to the solution that student had in mind. QLOSE generates this repair when it uses both syntactic and semantic distances. A similar example of a desirable repair generated by QLOSE using both syntactic and semantic distances is illustrated in Fig. 7 for the ePoly-1 benchmark.

```
int LargestGap(int[] a){
  int h = a[0], l=0;
  int N = a.Length;
  for(int i=1; i<N;++i){
    h = max(h,a[i]);
    l = min(l,a[i]);
  }
  return h - l;
}
```

```
int LargestGap(int[] a){
  int h = a[0], l=0;
  int N = a.Length;
  for(int i=0; i<N;++i){
    h = max(h,a[i]);
    l = min(l,a[i]);
  }
  return h - l;
}
```

```
int LargestGap(int[] a){
  int h = a[0], l=a[0];
  int N = a.Length;
  for(int i=1; i<N;++i){
    h = max(h,a[i]);
    l = min(l,a[i]);
  }
  return h - l;
}
```

```
int ePoly-1(int[]p,int
    x){
  int n = p[0];
  int i = p.Length-1;
  while(i >= 0){
    n += p[i]*pow(x,i);
    i--;
  }
  return n;
}
```

```
int ePoly-1(int[]p,int
    x){
  int n = 0;
  int i = p.Length-1;
  while(i >= 0){
    n += p[i]*pow(x,i);
    i--;
  }
  return n;
}
```

```
int ePoly-1(int[]p,int
    x){
  int n = p[0];
  int i = p.Length-1;
  while(i > 0){
    n += p[i]*pow(x,i);
    i--;
  }
  return n;
}
```

(a) Original   (b) Syntactic   (c) Syntactic+Semantic

Fig. 7. (a) The original LargestGap-2 and ePoly-1 programs, (b) the repair generated by the syntactic distance, and (c) the repair generated by the combination of syntactic and semantic distances that corresponds to the desired repair.

6.3 Solving Time

The solving times for different combinations of syntactic and semantic distances are shown in Fig. 6. As expected, the syntactic distances take the smallest amount of time to resolve the sketches. For some problems, the semantic distances also resolve within a few seconds, but there are some cases where the solver takes much longer (including a case where the solver times out at 20 min). Our hypothesis for this phenomenon is that the semantic constraints by themselves under-constrain the space of repairs, which causes the solver to search a larger space for finding the optimal solution for the minimization objective. On the other hand, by combining syntactic and semantic distances, QLOSE can solve the sketches with minimization constraints within 20 s for each benchmark.

6.4 Repairs with Different Test Sets

In this experiment, we evaluate the effect of using different sets of tests on the repairs generated by QLOSE. We empirically observe that the combination of

Tests over variables s, c, and k	Syntactic Fix
(adb?,?,3),(bgc?cg,?,5),(?aba,?,3),(abcdd?,g,4)	`for(i=0;i<k;i++) if(c=='?')`
(adb?,?,3),(bgc?cg,?,5),(gaba,?,3),(abcdd?,g,4)	`for(i=0;s[i]!='e';i++) ...`
(ab?,?,2),(aba?cg,?,5), (?aba,?,3),(abcdd?,?,4)	`for(i=0;s[i]!='d';i++) ...`

Fig. 8. Repairs obtained for `FindC` with syntactic distance for different test sets.

syntactic and semantic distances is more robust with respect to changes in the test set as compared to individual distances. For example, if we look at Fig. 8, we can see that when we vary the test set for the `FindC` benchmark, using only syntactic distances yields different and undesired repairs. On the contrary, we obtain the same desired repair using the combined distance for these test sets.

7 Related Work

We review relevant work focussing on sequential, imperative software programs.

The authors in [30] were the first to emphasize the need to look for repaired programs that are semantically close to the original program. But they did not develop a quantitative formulation of the problem and relied on choosing sets of traces of the original program to be preserved exactly. There are several program repair approaches that aim to find repairs that are syntactically close to the original program [16,19,23,24]. As we have discussed in the paper, focussing just on syntactic changes can lead to non-intuitive repairs. The AUTOPROF system [24] uses the SKETCH solver to compute the minimum number of syntactic changes to incorrect student solutions based on a manual error model. QLOSE, on the other hand, uses additional syntactic and semantic distances, and generalizes the set of expression modifications using linear combinations of constants with program variables.

There is also a growing and interesting body of work on quantitative notions for verification and synthesis [4,5,11], which formalize distances between specifications and systems or between systems themselves. However, these distances mostly apply to reactive systems and temporal logic specifications. There have also been many proposals for scaling program repair and synthesis to large programs. These are based on techniques ranging from constraint-solving [20,27,28], winning strategies in games [14], abstractions [9,18,22], mutations [7], genetic algorithms [2,8], using contracts [31], and focusing on data structure manipulations [25,32]. As we develop QLOSE further, we hope to leverage some of these techniques and improve the scope of our approach.

Many fault localization algorithms are based on analyzing error traces [3,6, 15,33]. Some of these techniques can be used as a preprocessing step to improve the efficiency of our algorithm. A recent paper [17] finds the root cause of an equivalence failure in binaries using a notion of semantic similarity between programs. The problem setting is quite different from ours and the notions of similarity mostly refer to the program abstract semantics rather than to concrete executions. We wish to explore whether the distances proposed in [17] can be instantiated in our framework.

A more general question is whether the notions of program distances appearing in quantitative program analysis and program repair can be modeled in QLOSE. While simple limits on the number of syntactic edits clearly fall in our framework [19], some complex distances could take into account features that we currently do not model. For example [23] uses location-specific costs that cannot be captured using our current definitions. Extending QLOSE to more complex distances is an interesting research direction.

In this paper we use manual code inspection to decide which repair is most *natural*. Recently, many data-driven techniques have been proposed to reason about code *naturalness* [12,21]. These techniques learn language models of source code from a large code corpus and then use these models for several applications such as learning natural coding conventions, code suggestions and auto-completion, improving code style, suggesting variable and method names etc. Using such automatic techniques to classify repairs is an interesting direction.

8   Limitations and Conclusion

We introduce the *quantitative program repair* problem informally described as follows: *given a set D of syntactic and semantic distances, a program P, and a set of test cases T, find the closest program P' (with respect to some function over the distances in D) such that P' is correct on all the tests in T*. We differentiated ourselves from previous approaches by showing that, to find "natural" program repairs, both semantic and syntactic distances are necessary. Our techniques have been implemented in a prototype tool QLOSE, but some limitations need to be addressed. The most important ones are that the distances are tailored to specifications given as test sets and that QLOSE only handles programs with tens of lines of code. Addressing these limitations is part of our research agenda.

Acknowledgements. The authors would like to thank the anonymous reviewers for their insightful feedback. Roopsha Samanta would like to thank Krishnendu Chatterjee and Tom Henzinger for inspiring discussions on quantitative repair for reactive systems.

References

1. Alur, R., D'Antoni, L., Gulwani, S., Kini, D., Viswanathan, M.: Automated grading of dfa constructions. In: Proceedings of the Twenty-Third International Joint Conference on Artificial Intelligence, IJCAI 2013, pp. 1976–1982. AAAI Press (2013)
2. Arcuri, A.: On the automation of fixing software bugs. In: International Conference on Software Engineering (ICSE), pp. 1003–1006. ACM (2008)
3. Ball, T., Naik, M., Rajamani, S.K.: From symptom to cause: localizing errors in counterexample traces. In: Principles of Programming Languages (POPL), pp. 97–105. ACM (2003)

4. Cerný, P., Henzinger, T.A.: From Boolean to quantitative synthesis. In: Proceedings of the 11th International Conference on Embedded Software (EMSOFT), pp. 149–154 (2011)
5. Cerný, P., Henzinger, T.A., Radhakrishna, A.: Simulation distances. Theor. Comput. Sci. **413**(1), 21–35 (2012)
6. Chandra, S., Torlak, E., Barman, S., Bodik, R.: Angelic debugging. In: International Conference on Software Engineering (ICSE), pp. 121–130. ACM (2011)
7. Debroy, V., Wong, W.E.: Using mutation to automatically suggest fixes for faulty programs. In: Software Testing, Verification and Validation (ICST), pp. 65–74 (2010)
8. Goues, C.L., Dewey-Vogt, M., Forrest, S., Weimer, W.: A systematic study of automated program repair: fixing 55 out of 105 bugs for \$8 each. In: International Conference on Software Engineering (ICSE), pp. 3–13. IEEE Press (2012)
9. Griesmayer, A., Bloem, R., Cook, B.: Repair of Boolean programs with an application to C. In: Ball, T., Jones, R.B. (eds.) CAV 2006. LNCS, vol. 4144, pp. 358–371. Springer, Heidelberg (2006)
10. Gulwani, S., Korthikanti, V.A., Tiwari, A.: Synthesizing geometry constructions. SIGPLAN Not. **46**(6), 50–61 (2011)
11. Henzinger, T.A., Otop, J.: From model checking to model measuring. In: D'Argenio, P.R., Melgratti, H. (eds.) CONCUR 2013 – Concurrency Theory. LNCS, vol. 8052, pp. 273–287. Springer, Heidelberg (2013)
12. Hindle, A., Barr, E.T., Su, Z., Gabel, M., Devanbu, P.: On the naturalness of software. In: Proceedings of the 34th International Conference on Software Engineering, Piscataway, NJ, USA, ICSE 2012, pp. 837–847. IEEE Press (2012)
13. Itzhaky, S., Gulwani, S., Immerman, N., Sagiv, M.: Solving geometry problems using a combination of symbolic and numerical reasoning. In: McMillan, K., Middeldorp, A., Voronkov, A. (eds.) LPAR-19 2013. LNCS, vol. 8312, pp. 457–472. Springer, Heidelberg (2013)
14. Jobstmann, B., Griesmayer, A., Bloem, R.: Program repair as a game. In: Etessami, K., Rajamani, S.K. (eds.) CAV 2005. LNCS, vol. 3576, pp. 226–238. Springer, Heidelberg (2005)
15. Jose, M., Majumdar, R.: Cause clue clauses: error localization using maximum satisfiability. In: Programming Language Design and Implementation (PLDI), pp. 437–446. ACM (2011)
16. Könighofer, R., Bloem, R.: Automated error localization and correction for imperative programs. In: Formal Methods in Computer Aided Design (FMCAD), pp. 91–100 (2011)
17. Lahiri, S.K., Sinha, R., Hawblitzel, C.: Automatic rootcausing for program equivalence failures in binaries. In: Kroening, D., Păsăreanu, C.S. (eds.) CAV 2015. LNCS, vol. 9206, pp. 362–379. Springer, Heidelberg (2015)
18. Logozzo, F., Ball, T.: Modular and verified automatic program repair. In: Object Oriented Programming Systems Languages and Applications (OOPSLA), pp. 133–146. ACM (2012)
19. Mechtaev, S., Yi, J., Roychoudhury, A.: Directfix: looking for simple program repairs. In: Proceedings of the 37th International Conference on Software Engineering, Piscataway, NJ, USA, ICSE 2015, vol. 1, pp. 448–458. IEEE Press (2015)
20. Nguyen, H.D.T., Qi, D., Roychoudhury, A., Chandra, S.: Semfix: program repair via semantic analysis. In: Proceedings of the 2013 International Conference on Software Engineering, Piscataway, NJ, USA, ICSE 2013, pp. 772–781. IEEE Press (2013)

21. Partush, N., Yahav, E.: Abstract semantic differencing via speculative correlation. In: Proceedings of the 2014 ACM International Conference on Object Oriented Programming Systems Languages & Applications, OOPSLA 2014, part of SPLASH 2014, Portland, OR, USA, 20–24 October 2014, pp. 811–828 (2014)

22. Samanta, R., Deshmukh, J.V., Emerson, E.A.: Automatic generation of local repairs for Boolean programs. In: Formal Methods in Computer Aided Design (FMCAD), pp. 1–10 (2008)

23. Samanta, R., Olivo, O., Emerson, E.A.: Cost-aware automatic program repair. In: Müller-Olm, M., Seidl, H. (eds.) Static Analysis. LNCS, vol. 8723, pp. 268–284. Springer, Heidelberg (2014)

24. Singh, R., Gulwani, S., Solar-Lezama, A.: Automatic feedback generation for introductory programming assignments. In: Proceedings of Programming Language Design and Implementation (PLDI), pp. 15–26 (2013)

25. Singh, R., Solar-Lezma, A.: Synthesizing data-structure manipulations from storyboards. In: Foundations of Software Engineering (FSE), pp. 289–299 (2011)

26. Solar-Lezama, A.: Program sketching. STTT **15**(5–6), 475–495 (2013)

27. Solar-Lezama, A., Tancau, L., Bodik, R., Seshia, S., Saraswat, V.: Combinatorial sketching for finite programs. In: Architectural Support for Programming Languages and Operating Systems (ASPLOS), pp. 404–415. ACM (2006)

28. Srivastava, S., Gulwani, S., Foster, J.S.: From program verification to program synthesis. In: Principles of Programming Languages (POPL), pp. 313–326. ACM (2010)

29. Tillmann, N., de Halleux, J., Xie, T., Bishop, J.: Code hunt: gamifying teaching and learning of computer science at scale. In: Proceedings of the First ACM Conference on Learning @ Scale Conference, New York, NY, USA, L@S 2014, pp. 221–222. ACM (2014)

30. von Essen, C., Jobstmann, B.: Program repair without regret. In: Sharygina, N., Veith, H. (eds.) CAV 2013. LNCS, vol. 8044, pp. 896–911. Springer, Heidelberg (2013)

31. Wei, Y., Pei, Y., Furia, C.A., Silva, L.S., Buchholz, S., Meyer, B., Zeller, A.: Automated fixing of programs with contracts. In: International Symposium on Software Testing and Analysis (ISSTA), pp. 61–72. ACM (2010)

32. Nokhbeh Zaeem, R., Gopinath, D., Khurshid, S., McKinley, K.S.: History-aware data structure repair using SAT. In: Flanagan, C., König, B. (eds.) TACAS 2012. LNCS, vol. 7214, pp. 2–17. Springer, Heidelberg (2012)

33. Zeller, A., Hilebrandt, R.: Simplifying and isolating failure-inducing input. IEEE Trans. Softw. Eng. **28**(2), 183–200 (2002)

BDD-Based Boolean Functional Synthesis

Dror Fried, Lucas M. Tabajara$^{(\boxtimes)}$, and Moshe Y. Vardi

Department of Computer Science, Rice University, Houston, USA
lucasmt@rice.edu

Abstract. *Boolean functional synthesis* is the process of automatically obtaining a constructive formalization from a declarative relation that is given as a Boolean formula. Recently, a framework was proposed for Boolean functional synthesis that is based on Craig Interpolation and in which Boolean functions are represented as And-Inverter Graphs (AIGs). In this work we adapt this framework to the setting of Binary Decision Diagrams (BDDs), a standard data structure for representation of Boolean functions. Our motivation in studying BDDs is their common usage in *temporal synthesis*, a fundamental technique for constructing control software/hardware from temporal specifications, in which Boolean synthesis is a basic step. Rather than using Craig Interpolation, our method relies on a technique called *Self-Substitution*, which can be easily implemented by using existing BDD operations. We also show that this yields a novel way to perform quantifier elimination for BDDs. In addition, we look at certain BDD structures called *input-first*, and propose a technique called *TrimSubstitute*, tailored specifically for such structures. Experiments on scalable benchmarks show that both Self-Substitution and TrimSubstitute scale well for benchmarks with good variable orders and significantly outperform current Boolean-synthesis techniques.

1 Introduction

Boolean functions appear in all levels of computing, and can fairly be considered as one of the most fundamental building block of modern digital computers. Often, the most intuitive way of defining a Boolean function is not *constructively*, describing how the outputs can be computed from the inputs, but rather *declaratively*, as a *relation* between input and output values that must be satisfied [4]. Nevertheless, in order to implement a function in a practical format, such as in a circuit or program, a declarative definition is not enough, and a constructive description of how to compute the output from the input is necessary. The process of going from a declarative formalization to a constructive one is called *functional synthesis* [14]. This transformation is a challenging algorithmic problem, which we focus on in this paper.

In this work, we follow a framework proposed in [16,17] for algorithmically synthesizing a correct-by-construction constructive representation of a desired Boolean function from a relational specification. Such relation is given as a

S. Chaudhuri and A. Farzan (Eds.): CAV 2016, Part II, LNCS 9780, pp. 402–421, 2016.
DOI: 10.1007/978-3-319-41540-6_22

propositional formula that relates input and output variables. Our construction ensures that when the input is *realizable*, that is, there is a corresponding output for that specific input, the function that we synthesize produces this output. More formally, given a specification in the form of a characteristic function $f : \mathbb{B}^m \times \mathbb{B}^n \to \mathbb{B}$, where $f(x, y) = 1$ iff y is a correct output for the input x, we synthesize functions $r_f : \mathbb{B}^m \to \mathbb{B}$ and $g : \mathbb{B}^m \to \mathbb{B}^n$ with the guarantee that $r_f(x) = 1$ precisely when there exists some y for which $f(x, y) = 1$ and $f(x, g(x)) = 1$ for every input vector x for which $r_f(x) = 1$. As such, our framework consists of two phases. The first phase is the *realizability* phase, and requires the computation of the Boolean realizability function r_f. The second phase is the *function-construction* phase, in which we construct the function g.

The proposed framework in [17] is based on representing Boolean functions by means of And-Inverter Graphs (AIGs) [20]. In this paper we adapt this framework to the setting of Reduced Ordered Binary Decision Diagrams (BDDs) [6], a data structure designed for the efficient representation and manipulation of Boolean functions. BDDs provide easy-to-manipulate canonical (and minimal) representations of Boolean functions in which Boolean operations can be implemented efficiently. BDDs have found numerous applications in a variety of settings, including model checking [7], equivalence checking [24], and others. Our main motivation for using BDDs is that Boolean functional synthesis is also a basic step in *temporal synthesis*, a fundamental technique for constructing control software/hardware from temporal specifications [26], which is most often implemented by using BDDs, cf. [3]. Thus, our approach can be easily incorporated to temporal-synthesis tools. We discuss the differences between the AIG-based and BDD-based approaches below.

At the heart of our approach there is a technique we call *Self-Substitution*, a simplification of the Craig Interpolation-based approach that appears in [17]. A single-step Self-Substitution enables us to extract a function g *syntactically* from the function f for a case in which there is a single output variable. When there are multiple output variables, we iterate the single-step for each of the output variables. In this way we can use Self-Substitution both for quantifier elimination, in the realizability phase, and for constructing a function g, one output variable at a time. We use the software tool CUDD [28] for our implementation, and show that Self-Substitution can be efficiently implemented through basic BDD operations by using the CUDD API. Thus, Self-Substitution provides a novel way to perform quantifier elimination for BDDs, where the standard technique has been *Shannon Expansion* [6].

We begin the synthesis process by converting the relational specification f into a BDD. To obtain r_f we quantify out the output variables existentially one by one, which can be done by either Shannon Expansion or Self-Substitution. Eliminating the output variables one by one yields a *realizability sequence* $f_n, \ldots, f_0$ of BDDs, where f_n is the specification f, and f_0 is the desired realizability function r_f. In the function-construction phase again we use Self-Substitution, leveraging the realizability sequence $f_1, \ldots, f_n$ to construct a function, represented as a BDD, for each output variable. At the end, we obtain an n-rooted BDD for the implementation function g, where each root represents a single output variable. Motivated by [22], we study Self-Substitution on a specific BDD order called *input-first*. In input-first BDDs, all input variables precede output variables. We develop a novel method, *TrimSubstitute*, which tailors Self-Substitution for input-first BDDs.

Our experimental evaluation relies on *scalable* problem instances rather than a random collection of problem instances, so we can evaluate the scalability of our techniques. Our evaluations demonstrate that the proposed framework scales well when the problem admits a good variable order, which is a well-established property of BDDs [6]. Our comparisons also showed that our method outperforms the previous AIG-based approach and other state-of-the-art tools by orders of magnitude. We also compare Self-Substitution as a quantifier-elimination technique against the standard Shannon-Expansion technique, and show that in many cases Self-Substitution scales better than Shannon Expansion. In addition, we show that TrimSubstitute outperforms Self-Substitution on input-first BDDs. The tool we built to implement our framework, RSynth, is available on-line[1].

The contributions of this paper are as follows: We offer a BDD-based approach for Boolean Synthesis that is simple and requires only basic BDD procedures. We show that our method outperforms other synthesis tools on scalable benchmarks. Our method also suggests a novel way for BDD based quantifier elimination. In addition we also offer a technique for input-first BDD in which we tailor our method specifically to this BDD order and show that we outperform all others tools.

Related Work. Functional Boolean synthesis has been the goal of a number of different works over the years, focusing on different applications in both hardware and software design. In some literature, our definition of functional synthesis is also called *uniformization* [13]. Note however, that our definition is different than that of *logic synthesis*, which is used in tools such as ABC, in which a given circuit structure is transformed to meet certain criteria [5].

Several approaches have been proposed for functional Boolean synthesis, but one trend that can be observed among them is that BDDs seem to be a popular choice of data structure to use for the underlying representation of Boolean functions, despite a common concern regarding their scalability. Kuncak et al. developed a general framework for functional synthesis, focusing mainly on unbounded domains, such as integer arithmetic and sets with size constraints [22]. For Boolean logic, they suggest to start with a BDD following what we call an input-first order. Our work on input-first BDDs can be viewed as an elaboration of their work. Tronci considered synthesis of Boolean functions in a work that is focused on synthesizing optimal controllers [29]. He mentioned a basic form of Self-Substitution for function construction to extract an implementation function from a relational specification, but did not develop the idea and did not exploit Self-Substitution as a quantifier-elimination technique. Kukula and

---

[1] http://www.cs.rice.edu/~lm30/RSynth/.

Shiple [21] were the first to address explicitly the issue of converting relational to functional specifications. They present a direct mapping of a BDD for a relation to a circuit, where each node of the BDD is converted into a hardware module composed of several logic gates. Their approach is quite complex, and was not accompanied by an empirical evaluation. Bañeres, Cortadella, and Kishinevsky also addressed the problem for converting relational to functional specifications [1]. Their approach is based on a recursive search in which the cost function is a parameter. In this sense, their work is focused on optimizing the output size, rather than scalability, as in our work. Another search-based synthesis tool is Sketch [27], where the user specifies the behavior of a desired function, which the tool finds by searching through the space of possible implementations. A very recent work of [19] adapts [17] to synthesis for relations specified as large conjunctions of small formulas. Their work also makes use of Self-Substitution for function construction, but does not use BDDs. Certain QBF solvers [2,15] include the capability of producing witnesses from the proof of validity of a formula. For valid QBF formulas these witnesses can be computed fairly efficiently, but cannot be applied when the formula is not valid.

Boolean synthesis lies at the heart of temporal synthesis, as temporal synthesis for the temporal formula $\Box f$ ("globally f"), where f is a Boolean formula, essentially requires functional Boolean synthesis for the formula f. There are several tools for temporal synthesis [10,18,25], yet the focus of such tools is on dealing with temporal formulas, while dealing with the underlying Boolean formulas is ignored or delegated to Boolean-synthesis tools.

Our framework is based on that of Jiang [16,17], also concerned with extracting functions from Boolean relations. That work uses *and-inverters graphs* (AIGs) as the basic data structure, and uses Craig Interpolation for quantifier elimination and witness extraction. As seen below, our experiments have shown that this interpolation-based approach does not scale well and is very unpredictable. This has also been noted in [19].

Since our approach can also be used for quantifier elimination, we compare it with the standard quantifier elimination technique of Shannon Expansion. Other quantifier elimination techniques such as Goldberg and Mañolios [12], require the formulas to be in CNF form, rather than the BDD representation we use. In addition, these techniques eliminate variables in blocks, while to compute each witness variable separately, our synthesis requires the variables to be eliminated individually.

2   Preliminaries

Boolean Functions. We denote by $\mathbb{B} = \{0,1\}$ the set of Boolean values. For simplicity, we often conflate an m-ary Boolean function $f : \mathbb{B}^m \to \mathbb{B}$ with its representation by means of a Boolean formula f with m propositional variables. Then $f(\sigma) = 1$ if and only if $\sigma \in \mathbb{B}^m$ is a satisfying assignment for f. Two formulas $f(x)$ and $f'(x)$ are *logically equivalent*, denoted $f \equiv f'$, if $f(\sigma) = f'(\sigma)$ for every assignment σ for x. Given formulas

$f(x_1, \ldots, x_m)$ and $f'(y_1, \ldots, y_n)$, we use $f[x_i \mapsto f']$ to denote the formula $f(x_1, \ldots, x_{i-1}, f'(y_1, \ldots, y_n), x_{i+1}, \ldots, x_m)$, representing the functional composition of f in variable x_i with f'. A *Quantified Boolean Formula*, or QBF, is a Boolean formula in which some variables can be universally or existentially quantified. In this work we assume that all the QBF are in *prenex normal form* in which all the quantifiers are grouped together before the quantifier-free part of the formula. Every QBF can be converted into a logically equivalent quantifier-free formula through a process called *quantifier elimination*. This is usually performed using the technique of *Shannon Expansion* [6], where $\forall x f \equiv f[x \mapsto 0] \wedge f[x \mapsto 1]$, and $\exists x f \equiv f[x \mapsto 0] \vee f[x \mapsto 1]$. Given a QBF in prenex normal form, we can obtain its equivalent quantifier-free formula by eliminating the quantifiers from the inside out.

Binary Decision Diagrams. A *[Reduced Ordered] Binary Decision Diagram*, or BDD, is a data structure that represents a Boolean function as a directed acyclic graph [6]. BDDs can be seen as a reduced representation of a binary decision tree of a Boolean function. We require that variables are ordered the same way along every path of the BDD ("ordered") and that the BDD is minimized to eliminate duplication ("reduced"). For a given variable order, the reduced BDD is *canonical*. The variable order used can have a major impact on its size, and two BDDs representing the same function but with different orders can have an exponential difference in size. Consequently, finding a good variable order is essential for BDD-based Boolean reasoning. Since BDDs represent Boolean functions, they can be manipulated using standard Boolean operations. We overload the notation of the operators $\neg$, $\wedge$, $\vee$ and functional composition (e.g. $B[x_i \mapsto B']$) with equivalent semantics to their counterparts for Boolean formulas.

3 Theoretical Framework

3.1 Realizability and Synthesis

The problem of synthesis of Boolean functions is formally defined as follows.

Problem 1. Given a relation between two vectors of Boolean variables represented by the characteristic function $f : \mathbb{B}^m \times \mathbb{B}^n \to \mathbb{B}$, obtain a function $r_f : \mathbb{B}^m \to \mathbb{B}$ such that $r_f(\boldsymbol{x}) = 1$ exactly for the inputs $\boldsymbol{x} \in \mathbb{B}^m$ for which $\exists \boldsymbol{y} f(\boldsymbol{x}, \boldsymbol{y})$, and a function $g : \mathbb{B}^m \to \mathbb{B}^n$ such that $f(\boldsymbol{x}, g(\boldsymbol{x})) = 1$ if and only if $r_f(\boldsymbol{x}) = 1$.

In the context of this problem, f is called the *specification*, g is called the *implementation* or *witness function*, and r_f is called a *realizability function*. The specification is interpreted as describing a desired relationship between inputs and outputs of a function, and the implementation describes how to obtain an output from an input such that this relationship is maintained. The realizability function indicates for which inputs the specification can be satisfied.

in the expression $f(x, y)$, $x = (x_1, \ldots, x_m)$ are called the *input variables*, and $y = (y_1, \ldots, y_n)$ the *output variables*. The function that gives the i-th bit of $g(x)$ is called a *witness-bit function*, and is denoted by $g_i(x)$. A Boolean function $f(x, y)$ is said to be *realizable for an input* σ if $\exists y f(\sigma, y) \equiv 1$. We say that f is *realizable* if $\forall x \exists y f(x, y) \equiv 1$. For every assignment σ for x such that f is realizable for σ we will have that $r_f(\sigma) = 1$. In this case, $g(\sigma)$ is called a *witness* for σ. In case $r_f(\sigma) = 0$ we are not concerned about the output of g since f is unrealizable for σ.

Following [17], the structure of our solution takes two steps, (1) Realizability, where we obtain r_f by constructing a sequence of formulas with progressively fewer output variables, and (2) Function construction, in which we synthesize a witness-bit function from every formula in the sequence obtained in the realizability step.

To perform both steps, we suggest a novel method called *Self-Substitution*. In Sect. 2 we observed that Boolean quantifier elimination is usually performed via Shannon Expansion. More recently, it was proposed to use Craig Interpolation for quantifier elimination (see [16]). We now introduce Self-Substitution as an alternative quantifier-elimination technique.

Lemma 1 *(Self-Substitution for Quantifier Elimination). Let $\varphi = Qy f(x, y)$ be a QBF formula, where Q is either a universal or existential quantifier and f is quantifier-free. Let q be 0 if Q is universal and 1 if Q is existential. Then, $Qy f(x, y)$ is logically equivalent to $f(x, f(x, q))$, and is also logically equivalent to $f(x, \neg f(x, \neg q))$.*

Proof. If Q is an existential quantifier, we prove that for every assignment σ for x, $\exists y f(\sigma, y) = 0$ iff $f(\sigma, f(\sigma, 1)) = 0$. If $\exists y f(\sigma, y) = 0$, then $f(\sigma, y) = 0$ for all possible assignments of y. Since this includes $f(\sigma, 1)$, then $f(\sigma, f(\sigma, 1)) = 0$. On the other hand, if $f(\sigma, f(\sigma, 1)) = 0$, then it cannot be the case that $f(\sigma, 1) = 1$ (otherwise $f(\sigma, f(\sigma, 1)) = f(\sigma, 1) = 1$). Therefore, $f(\sigma, 1) = 0$, and so $f(\sigma, 0) = f(\sigma, f(\sigma, 1)) = 0$. Since both $f(\sigma, 1) = 0$ and $f(\sigma, 0) = 0$, then $\exists y f(\sigma, y) = 0$. The claim that for every assignment σ, $\exists y f(\sigma, y) = 0$ iff $f(\sigma, \neg f(\sigma, 0)) = 0$ is proved analogously. The proof when Q is a universal quantifier is derived by using the identity $\forall y f(x, y) \equiv \neg \exists y \neg f(x, y)$.   □

Following Lemma 1, quantifier elimination can be performed by replacing quantified formulas by their quantifier-free equivalents. Table 1 compares the formulas produced by quantifier elimination using Shannon Expansion and Self-Substitution.

The Self-Substitution method looks surprising at first glance. In the Shannon-Expansion method it is easy to see that the size of the quantifier-free formula becomes exponential compared to its quantified version, as it is a disjunction of all possible assignments. In Self-Substitution such a blow-up also takes place, but the encapsulation of all assignments is more subtle. The depth of the nested functions for a formula with n quantified variables is $n + 1$. Therefore all the possible assignments for the quantified variables can

Table 1. Equivalent formulas using each method of quantifier elimination

	$\forall y f(x,y)$	$\exists y f(x,y)$
Shannon Expansion	$f(x,0) \wedge f(x,1)$	$f(x,0) \vee f(x,1)$
Self-Substitution 1	$f(x, f(x,0))$	$f(x, f(x,1))$
Self-Substitution 2	$f(x, \neg f(x,1))$	$f(x, \neg f(x,0))$

be obtained recursively. For example let $q_i = 1$ if the quantifier Q_i is existential, and $q_i = 0$ if Q_i is universal. Then a possible expansion for two quantified variables is $Q_1 y_1 Q_2 y_2 f(x, y_1, y_2) = Q_1 y_1 f(x, y_1, f(x, y_1, q_2)) = f(x, f(x, q_1, f(x, q_1, q_2)), f(x, f(x, q_1, f(x, q_1, q_2)), q_2))$.

The following lemma which appeared in many forms in various places, e.g. [1, 17, 29], is derived from Lemma 1 and shows how Self-Substitution can be used for synthesis purposes.

Lemma 2 *(Synthesis by Self-Substitution). Let $f(x,y)$ be a Boolean formula with free variables x and y. Then $f(x,1)$ and $\neg f(x,0)$ are witness functions to $f(x,y)$.*

Proof. By Lemma 1, $\exists y f(x,y)$ is logically equivalent to $f(x, f(x,1))$ and to $f(x, \neg f(x,0))$. Since $r_f(x) = 1$ exactly for those x for which $\exists y f(x,y)$ holds, both $f(x, f(x,1))$ and $f(x, \neg f(x,0))$ return 1 if and only if $r_f(x) = 1$. Thus, $f(x,1)$ and $\neg f(x,0)$ are witness functions to $f(x,y)$. ☐

The witness $f(x,1)$ is called the *default*-1 witness, while the witness $\neg f(x,0)$ is called the *default*-0 witness. The observation in [17] is that when f is realizable for all x, the conjunction of the two formulas $\neg f(x,0)$ and $\neg f(x,1)$ is unsatisfiable. From a resolution proof of this unsatisfiability, one can extract a Craig interpolant, which may be smaller than either $f(x,1)$ or $\neg f(x,0)$. Our experimental evaluation for our benchmarks does not support this expectation, where we show the advantage of using the witness function $f(x,1)$ for synthesis and $f(x, f(x,1))$ for existential-quantifier elimination.

3.2 Realizability and Function-Construction Using BDDs

Similarly to [17], we separate the synthesis approach into two phases. We call the first the *realizability* phase, and the second the *function construction* phase. We assume that the input is in the form of a BDD B_f that describes the function $f(x,y)$. When f is obvious from the reference, we denote B_f by B.

Realizability. Our definition of r_f requires that r_f returns 1 exactly for those assignments of x for which $\exists y f(x,y)$. This means r_f can be obtained by applying quantifier elimination on the output variables. Recall that f has n output variables $y_1, \ldots, y_n$. Typically, the order of variables makes a major difference in constructing a BDD. However, in this section we assume no specific order.

The basic idea is as follows: from the input BDD B, we construct a sequence $\boldsymbol{B} = \{B_n, B_{n-1}, \ldots B_1, B_0\}$ of BDDs, where $B_n = B$, such that B_{i-1} is logically equivalent to $\exists y_i B_i$. Therefore, the BDD B_{i-1} is constructed from B_i by eliminating the existentially quantified variable y_i. The elimination process guarantees that B_0 represents the realizability function r_f.

The elimination of y_i from B_i can be done via either Shannon Expansion, or via Self-Substitution. For Shannon Expansion, we define $B_{i-1} = B_i[y_i \mapsto 0] \vee B_i[y_i \mapsto 1]$. To use the Self-Substitution method, we define either $B_{i-1} = B_i[y_i \mapsto B_i[y_i \mapsto 1]]$ to construct the default-1 witness for y_i or $B_{i-1} = B_i[y_i \mapsto \neg B_i[y_i \mapsto 0]]$ to construct the default-0 witness for y_i.

Function Construction. We next use the BDD sequence obtained in the realizability process to construct a sequence of BDDs $\boldsymbol{W} = \{W_n, W_{n-1}, \ldots, W_1\}$, each emitting an output bit.

By using Lemma 2, we perform the function-construction step as follows. Let $\boldsymbol{B} = \{B_n, B_{n-1}, \ldots, B_1, B_0\}$ be the BDD sequence obtained in the realizability step, and note that the output variables in the BDD B_i are $y_1, \ldots, y_i$. We first construct W_1 from B_1 by setting $W_1 = B_1[y_1 \mapsto 1]$ for a default-1 witness for y_1 or $W_1 = \neg B_1[y_1 \mapsto 0]$ for a default-0 witness for y_1. The structure of BDDs allows us to define both B_1 and $\neg B_1$ without extra effort. Next, we inductively define either $W_i = B_i[y_1 \mapsto W_1, \ldots, y_{i-1} \mapsto W_{i-1}, y_i \mapsto 1]$ for a default 1 witness for y_i, or $W_i = \neg B_i[y_1 \mapsto W_1, \ldots, y_{i-1} \mapsto W_{i-1}, y_i \mapsto 0]$ for a default 0 witness for y_i. Thus, every W_i has only the input variables $\boldsymbol{x}$, and represents the witness-bit function $g_i(\boldsymbol{x})$. Thus, the proof for the following theorem follows from Lemma 2.

Theorem 1. *For every assignment $\boldsymbol{\sigma}$ for $\boldsymbol{y}$, the sequence $(g_1(\boldsymbol{\sigma}), \ldots g_n(\boldsymbol{\sigma}))$ is a witness to $\boldsymbol{\sigma}$. Thus $\boldsymbol{W}$ describes a witness function for B.*

In practice, we chose, for simplicity, to use only the default-1 witnesses. In principle, one could always choose the best among the default-0 and default-1 witnesses. Since, however, we have n output variables, and the assignment of one of them affects the others, finding the optimal combination of bit-witness functions requires optimizing over an exponentially large space, which is an expensive undertaking. Finding such combinations of functions is a matter of future work.

3.3 Synthesis of Input-First BDD

An *input-first* BDD is a BDD in which all the input (universal) variables precede all the output (existential) variables. Synthesis using input-first BDDs was suggested in [22], but an explicit way to do it was not provided. This specific order of variables of input-first BDDs has led us to develop a method called *Trim-Substitute* for synthesis of input-first BDDs, in which we tailor Self-Substitution specifically for the input-first order. Given the input BDD, the running time of TrimSubstitute is at most quadratic in its size. In Sect. 4 we show that Trim-Substitute indeed outperforms Self-Substitution on input-first BDDs. In this section we give an outline of our method. Full proof with an example appears in the appendix. For simplicity TrimSubstitute produces default-1 witnesses. With minor modification the TrimSubstitute method can produce any desired combination of bit-witness functions.

An *output node* (resp. *input node*) in a BDD B is a node labeled with an output (resp. input) variable. Recall that every non-terminal node in B has exactly two children called *high-child* and *low-child*. Let B be an input-first BDD. We define $Fringe(B)$ to be the collection of all output nodes and terminal nodes in B that have an input node as an immediate parent. Note that $Fringe(B)$ can be found by performing standard graph-search operations (e.g. Depth-First-Search) on B. Also note that B is realizable exactly for those assignments for which the corresponding node in $Fringe(B)$ is not the terminal node 0.

Given an input-first BDD B, we assume without loss of generality that the order of the output variables in B is $y_1, \ldots y_n$. We construct a sequence of witness BDDs $\boldsymbol{W} = (W_1, \ldots, W_n)$, in which every W_i contains only input variables, and is the witness-bit function $g_i(\boldsymbol{x})$. To obtain $\boldsymbol{W}$, we construct a sequence of BDDs $\boldsymbol{B}' = (B_1', \ldots, B_n')$ in which every B_i' is an input-first BDD that contains all input variables, plus only output variables from $y_i, \ldots, y_n$. We obtain W_i from B_i' by an operation called "trim", and obtain B_{i+1}' from B_i' and W_i' by an operation called "substitute", hence our method's name TrimSubstitute. We next describe how $\boldsymbol{B}'$ and $\boldsymbol{W}$ are obtained.

We assume by induction on $i \leq n$ that B_i' is an input-first BDD that is realizable for exactly the same inputs as B, and that contains input variables plus only output variables from $y_i, \ldots, y_n$. Setting $B_1' = B$, we already satisfy these assumptions for the base case. We first construct W_i by "trimming" B_i', which means replacing each node v in $Fringe(B_i')$ with either the terminal node 0 or 1. Intuitively we construct W_i to produce an output bit for y_i in the "default-1" sense, i.e., W_i always produces 1 unless 1 is not a possible output bit for y_i. Formally, this is done as follows.

Note that if a $v \in Fringe(B_i')$ is the terminal node 0, then the assignment to y_i is irrelevant since the path to v corresponds to an unrealizable input, and so it can be left as 0. If v is a variable node, it cannot be that both children of v are the terminal node 0, as otherwise v itself would be reduced to 0. Therefore, if v is labeled by y_i, and the high-child of v is not the terminal node 0, replace v with the terminal node 1. Otherwise, if v is labeled by y_i and the high-child of v is 0 (then the low-child of v is not 0), replace v with the terminal node 0. For all other cases (v is labeled y_j, where $j > i$, or v is the terminal node 1), replace v with the terminal node 1. Note that W_i has only input variables.

Finally, we use B_i' and W_i to construct B_{i+1}'. To do that, we define $B_{i+1}' = B_i'[y_i \mapsto W_i]$. That is, B_{i+1}' is constructed from B_i' by "substituting" y_i with W_i. By construction we have that B_{i+1}' is an input-first BDD that is realizable for the same inputs as B and that contains input variables plus only output variables from $y_{i+1}, \ldots, y_n$. Therefore, the induction assumption is maintained. An example of the construction can be found in the appendix.

Theorem 2. *The BDD sequence* $\boldsymbol{W} = (W_1, \ldots, W_n)$ *describes a witness function for* B.

In the last induction step we obtain an additional BDD B'_{n+1} which is realizable for the same inputs as B, but contains only input variables. As such, B'_{n+1} encodes the realizability function r_f.

4 Experimental Evaluation

We compare our approach with two current state-of-the-art methods: the Craig Interpolation-based approach [17] and Sketch [27]. In addition, we compare between Shannon Expansion and Self-Substitution as quantifier-elimination methods to be used for the realizability phase. Finally, we see how the Trim-Substitute method, specialized to input-first BDDs, compares with the generic Self-Substitution method when using this type of BDD.

Rather than using a random collection of problem instances for our experiments, we selected a collection of *scalable* benchmarks, presented in Table 2, that operate over vectors of Boolean variables. Each entry in the table represents a class of benchmarks parameterized by the length n of the vectors. This allows us to produce benchmarks of different size to measure how our techniques scale. For our experiments we vary n in powers of 2 between 8 and 1024, totaling 42 benchmark instances. The first five benchmark classes represent linear-arithmetic functions in which the vectors encode the binary representation of integers in n bits, while the sixth represents the sorting of a bit array of size n. The first column in Table 2 describes the function we synthesize, where x and x' are vectors of input variables and y is a vector of output variables. The relational specification of these functions are shown in the second column. These specifications are translated to propositional-logic formulas (see appendix for details) and given as input to the algorithm, which then constructs a BDD for the relational specification and synthesizes the implementation function. All benchmarks are realizable for every input[2], therefore the realizability function is just the constant 1.

Table 2. Benchmark classes used for synthesis. See the appendix for translation into propositional-logic formulas.

	Function to synthesize	Specification
Subtraction	$y = x' - x$	$y + x = x'$
Maximum	$y = max(x, x')$	$(y \geq x) \wedge (y \geq x') \wedge ((y = x) \vee (y = x'))$
Minimum	$y = min(x, x')$	$(y \leq x) \wedge (y \leq x') \wedge ((y = x) \vee (y = x'))$
Floor of average	$y = \lfloor \dfrac{x + x'}{2} \rfloor$	$(2y = x + x') \vee (2y + 1 = x + x')$
Ceiling of average	$y = \lceil \dfrac{x + x'}{2} \rceil$	$(2y = x + x') \vee (2y = x + x' + 1)$
Sorting	$y = sort(x)$	$sorted(y) \wedge (\Sigma_{i=1}^{n} x_i = \Sigma_{j=1}^{n} y_j)$

---

[2] The *Subtraction* class of benchmarks is defined for subtraction modulo 2^n, or equivalently subtraction in two's complement, which is realizable for all inputs.

For purposes of evaluation we have constructed a tool, called RSynth, implemented in C++11 using the CUDD BDD library [28]. Self-Substitution was implemented using the built-in method Compose for BDD composition. That way, for a BDD B representing a function $f(x, y)$, the BDD for $f(x, f(x, 1))$ is computed as B.Compose(i, B.Compose(i, bddOne)), where bddOne is the BDD for the constant 1 and i is the index of variable y. All the experiments in this paper were carried out on a computer cluster consisting of 192 Westmere nodes of 12 processor cores each, running at 2.83 GHz with 4 GB of RAM per core, and 6 Sandy Bridge nodes of 16 processor cores each, running at 2.2 GHz with 8 GB of RAM per core. Since the algorithm has not been parallelized, the cluster was used solely to run different experiments simultaneously. The execution of each benchmark for a given n had a maximum time limit of 8 h.

Scalability Comparison with Previous Approaches. We compared the performance of RSynth with the Craig Interpolation approach from [17] that synthesizes functions in the format of AIGs, and the Sketch synthesis tool [27] that uses syntax-guided search-based synthesis. The original tool for Craig Interpolation from [17] was not available, therefore we used an implementation of the same method, which is called MonoSkolem, from [19].

Since BDD sizes can blow up if a poor variable order is chosen, causing initial BDD construction time to dominate the overall running time, we selected a variable order that can be expected to produce efficient BDDs for our benchmarks. For that, we chose an order called *fully interleaved*, in which the variables are ordered according to their index, alternating input and output variables.

We show the results of the comparison for the *Subtraction*, *Maximum* and *Ceiling of Average* benchmark classes in Fig. 1. Similar results were obtained for the other arithmetic benchmarks. Recall that n is the number of variables in each vector x, x' and y, therefore the total number of variables in each case is $3n$, with $2n$ input variables and n output variables.

Sketch is omitted from Fig. 1 because it was unable to synthesize the benchmarks for any n greater than 3, in all cases either timing out or running out of memory. For the two remaining approaches, it is noticeable that RSynth outperformed MonoSkolem by orders of magnitude, and scaled significantly better.

Although these results seem to lean considerably in favor of our approach, note that the benchmark classes used so far are deterministic (relations that have a unique implementation), while Craig Interpolation is reported to produce better results for non-deterministic relations by exploiting the flexibility in the

Table 3. Non-deterministic benchmark classes

	Input	Output	Specification
Decomposition	x	y, y'	$x = y + y'$
Equalization	x, x'	y, y'	$x + y = x' + y'$
Intermediate value	x, x'	y	$(x \leq y \wedge y \leq x') \vee (x' \leq y \wedge y \leq x)$

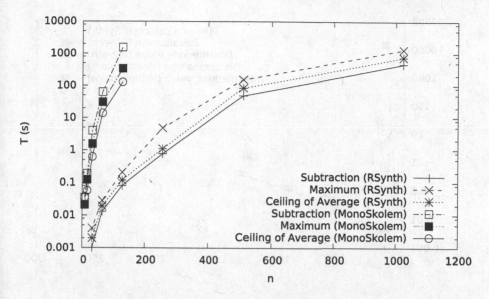

Fig. 1. Comparison of running time of RSynth against MonoSkolem

choice of witness. To address these factors, we added to the same setting an additional collection of linear arithmetic operations, represented in Table 3, this time of *non-deterministic* benchmarks.

Contrary to expectations, as Fig. 2 shows, our method gives better performance for the non-deterministic benchmark classes as well. From this we can conclude that despite the flexibility that Craig Interpolation provides, it does not necessarily exploit the don't-cares of the input specification efficiently. These results are supported by the ones obtained in [19], which reported that the quality of the results obtained when using Craig Interpolation depended strongly on the interpolation procedure of finding good interpolants, something which is not guaranteed to happen. Comparison of the size of the implementation between RSynth and MonoSkolem also showed that the functions constructed by Craig Interpolation are much larger.

These results allow us to conclude that with a good variable order to the function being synthesized, our method scales well and outperforms previous approaches. For linear arithmetic operations, we can identify fully-interleaved to be such an order.

Shannon Expansion vs. Self-Substitution. As mentioned in Sect. 3.2, the first step of the synthesis, realizability, requires quantifier elimination, which can be performed by either Shannon Expansion or Self-Substitution. We compared these two techniques by measuring the running time of the realizability phase using each of them. Our experiments show that the realizability step is responsible for only a small fraction of the running time of the synthesis. For the arithmetic benchmarks with fully-interleaved order, this step is performed in

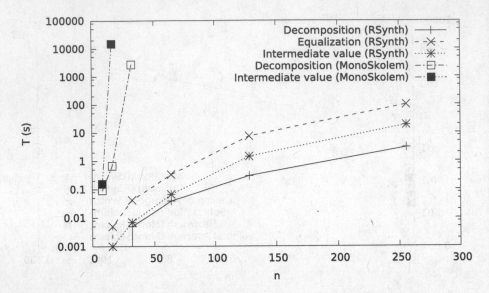

Fig. 2. Comparison of running time using non-deterministic benchmarks. The results for *Equalization* using MonoSkolem are not shown due to the synthesis timing out for $n > 8$.

under 1s in all cases, even for $n = 1024$. In order to better observe the difference between the two quantifier-elimination techniques, we measured them using the *Sorting* benchmark class, for which the BDD representation is not as efficient.

As can be seen in Fig. 3, as n grows Self-Substitution tends to perform better than Shannon Expansion, taking approximately 40 % less time to perform the realizability step for $n = 256$ (the same behavior was observed on the arithmetical benchmarks, using different variable orders). Thus, our experiments show an advantage in using Self-Substitution for quantifier elimination in the realizability step. Note that both Self-Substitution and Shannon Expansion are semantically equivalent, and thus produce identical BDDs. Therefore, the difference in performance between the two methods originates solely from the application of the CUDD operation itself over the constructed BDD. Shannon Expansion is currently the standard way of performing quantifier elimination on BDDs, but our experiments indicate that Self-Substitution interacts more efficiently with this type of data structure and should be considered as an alternative for practical applications.

Synthesis for Input-First BDDs. Following a suggestion in [22] for synthesis of propositional logic, we presented in Sect. 3.3 the TrimSubstitute method for BDDs that follow an input-first order. We compared the performance of Trim-Substitute with Self-Substitution (using Self-Substitution for both realizability and function construction) on input-first BDDs.

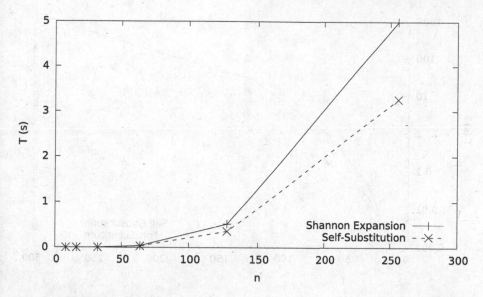

Fig. 3. Comparison of Shannon expansion and self-substitution for realizability, for the *Sorting* benchmark class

We first observed that construction time of the input-first BDD for the arithmetic benchmark classes scales poorly and was very large even for a relatively small n. The reason is that in the input-first order, the BDD is forced to keep track of all relevant information about the input before looking at the output variables. Thus, the constructed BDD must have a path for every possible output of the function being synthesized. Since in the arithmetic benchmarks, the number of such paths is 2^n, it does not pay off to use an input-first order for these benchmarks, regardless of the efficiency of the synthesis algorithm used.

On the other hand, for other classes of specifications the amount of information that must be memorized about the input can be polynomial or even linear in size. An example for that is the *Sorting* benchmark class, in which it is only necessary to keep track of the number of 1s in the input; thus, only n paths are required in the constructed BDD. In this case, although the construction time of the initial BDD still dominates the running time (experiments showed construction to take around 1200 s for $n = 256$), the size of the constructed BDD scales much better and makes synthesis feasible for a larger number of bits. The development of techniques to lessen the impact of construction time is a matter of future work.

Figure 4 shows a comparison of running time between the Self-Substitution and TrimSubstitute methods for *Sorting*. We can see that TrimSubstitute greatly improves over Self-Substitution, performing around 50 times faster for $n = 256$. These results imply that when the specification can be efficiently represented as an *input-first* BDD, TrimSubstitute can be used to obtain a significant improvement in synthesis time.

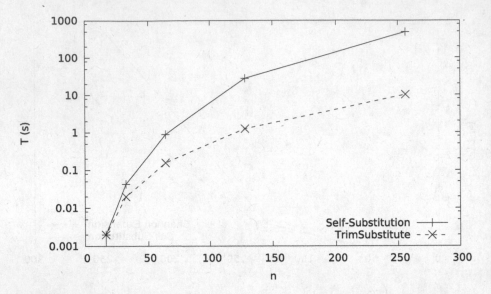

Fig. 4. Comparison of methods for synthesis using *input-first* BDDs for the *Sorting* benchmark class

5   Concluding Remarks

In this work we introduced BDD-based methods for synthesizing Boolean functions from relational specifications. We suggested a method called Self-Substitution for both quantifier elimination and function construction. We also suggested a method called TrimSubstitute, which outperforms Self-Substitution on input-first BDDs. We demonstrated that our methods scale well for benchmarks for which we have good BDD variable order, and outperform prior techniques.

A key challenge venue is to lessen the impact of the BDD size in the synthesis process. Factored representation of BDDs and early-quantification techniques, used in both symbolic model checking [8] and satisfiability testing [23], may be also helpful for synthesis. Another research direction is to find a good combination of bit-witness functions for specific benchmarks. There may also be BDD variants that can bring benefits in this area. For example, Free Binary Decision Diagrams (FBDDs) [11] relax the variable-order requirement in BDDs by allowing separate paths to use different orders. This might allow for more efficient representation of specifications in cases where an efficient global order is difficult to find. The Self-Substitution method as a technique for quantifier elimination calls for further research, both in applied settings, for example, in symbolic model checking [8], and in theoretical settings, for example, in the study of Post classes and algebraic clones [9]. Finally, we plan to explore the extension of our techniques to the setting of temporal synthesis.

Acknowledgement. This work is supported in part by NSF grants CCF-1319459 and IIS-1527668, by NSF Expeditions in Computing project "ExCAPE: Expeditions in Computer Augmented Program Engineering", by BSF grant 9800096, and by the Brazilian agencies CAPES and CNPq through the Ciência Sem Fronteiras program

A   APPENDIX

A.1   Proof of TrimSubstitute

We prove Theorem 2. Let B be an input-first BDD, and let $\boldsymbol{B'} = (B_1', \dots, B_n')$ and $\boldsymbol{W} = (W_1, \dots, W_n)$ as defined in Sect. 3.3. Figure 5 depicts our construction. Given a BDD D, and a node v in D, the subgraph D_v of D is obtained by restricting D to all the nodes that can be reached from v. Assume $z_1, \dots z_k$ are the variables of D. Then by following a partial assignment $\boldsymbol{\nu}$ to the variables of $z_1, \dots z_i$ for some i, we follow a unique path in D that ends up in a node v. Then the subgraph D_v is called the subgraph *reached* by following $\boldsymbol{\nu}$ in D.

Theorem 2. *The BDD sequence $\boldsymbol{W} = (W_1, \dots, W_n)$ describes a witness function for B.*

Proof. Let $g_i : \mathbb{B}^m \to \mathbb{B}$ be the function that describes W_i. The following facts are easily proved by induction on i.

1. Following the construction of W_i, for every realizable assignment σ to the input variables, the path followed by $(\sigma, g_i(\sigma))$ in B_i' does not end in the terminal node 0.
2. Following fact (1), and the construction of B_{i+1}', we have that for every realizable assignment σ to the input variables, the subgraph reached by following σ in B_{i+1}' is identical to the subgraph reached by following $(\sigma, g_i(\sigma))$ in B_i'. Therefore B_{i+1}' is realizable for σ as well.

As a result, we specifically have that for every realizable assignment σ to the input variables, the assignment $(\sigma, g_1(\sigma), \dots, g_n(\sigma))$ leads to the terminal node 1. This means that the BDD sequence $\boldsymbol{W} = (W_1, \dots, W_n)$ describes a witness function for B.   □

A.2   Encoding of Specifications in Propositional Logic

For completeness we show how to encode the specification given in Sect. 4, Table 2, into propositional logic formulas (later represented as a BDD). We assume that an integer is described by a vector of variables $z = (z_n, z_{n-1}, \dots, z_2, z_1)$, where z_n represents the most significant bit and z_1 the least significant bit. We now describe how specific operations used in the high-level specifications are encoded in propositional logic.

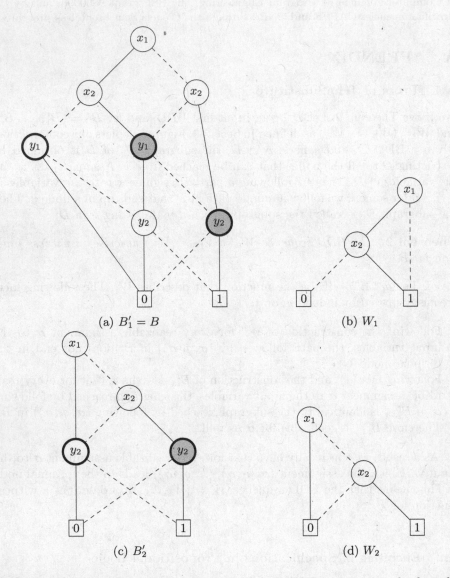

Fig. 5. Example of the TrimSubstitute method for a BDD representing the formula $(((x_1 \rightarrow \neg y_1) \land (x_1 \oplus x_2) \land (x_1 \oplus y_2)) \lor ((x_1 \leftrightarrow x_2) \land (y_1 \oplus y_2)))$. Nodes with bold outlines are in $Fringe(B'_i)$, and are either white if they should be replaced by the leaf node 0 or gray if they should be replaced by the leaf node 1.

Relational Operations. The formulas $(z = z')$, $(z \leq z')$ and $(z \geq z')$ are encoded respectively as $\varphi^=$, $\varphi^{\leq}$ and $\varphi^{\geq}$, as follows:

$$\varphi^= = \bigwedge_{i=1}^{n}(z_i \leftrightarrow z_i') \tag{1}$$

$$\varphi^{\leq} = \varphi_n, \text{ where } \varphi_i = (\neg z_i \wedge z_i') \vee ((z_i \leftrightarrow z_i') \wedge \varphi_{i-1}) \text{ and } \varphi_0 = 1 \tag{2}$$

$$\varphi^{\geq} = \varphi_n, \text{ where } \varphi_i = (z_i \wedge \neg z_i') \vee ((z_i \leftrightarrow z_i') \wedge \varphi_{i-1}) \text{ and } \varphi_0 = 1 \tag{3}$$

Addition. Since addition is an operation that returns an integer rather than a Boolean it cannot be implemented as a single Boolean formula. Rather, it produces n formulas $\varphi_n^+, \ldots, \varphi_1^+$ representing a new integer, which can be later combined into a single formula through one of the relational operators above. The encoding for the $+$ operator follows the usual representation of addition in binary: $\varphi_i^+ = z_i \oplus z_i' \oplus c_{i-1}$ where $c_i = (z_i \wedge z_i') \vee (z_i \wedge c_{i-1}) \vee (z_i' \wedge c_{i-1})$.

In this encoding, c_i represents the carry-out from the addition in the i-th position. The carry-in for the first position, c_0, is normally 0, but can be set to 1 to add an extra term of 1 to the sum, which is useful in the formulas for average.

Recall that in the *Subtraction* benchmark class, $+$ is interpreted as addition modulo n. On the other hand, in the high-level formulas for average we need the result of the addition with an extra bit added if necessary. This extra bit can be obtained by simply taking c_n. Therefore the comparisons in these formulas are actually performed over $(n + 1)$-bit integers.

Sorting. The specification for the *Sorting* benchmark class requires a more careful encoding. Recall that its high-level specification is given as $sorted(\boldsymbol{y}) \wedge (\Sigma_{i=1}^{n}x_i = \Sigma_{j=1}^{n}y_j)$ where $\boldsymbol{x}$ and $\boldsymbol{y}$ are interpreted as bit arrays. The first conjunct says that the output must be sorted, meaning that all 0 bits must precede all 1 bits. This is defined recursively for a range of consecutive positions $y_i, \ldots, y_j$ by saying that either all the variables are assigned to 1, or the first is 0 and the rest are sorted. The function $sorted(\boldsymbol{y})$ is defined as $sorted(y_i, \ldots, y_j) = 1$ if $i = j$ and $(\bigwedge_{k=i}^{j} y_k) \vee (\neg y_i \wedge sorted(y_{i+1}, \ldots, y_j))$ otherwise.

The second conjunct in the Sorting specification says that the output must have the same number of bits set to 1 as the input. In the high-level representation, this can be represented by $\Sigma_{i=1}^{n}x_i = \Sigma_{j=1}^{n}y_j$, but in practice it is not necessary to use summation in the encoding. Instead, the propositional logic formula for this property can be represented by a recurrence and constructed using dynamic programming:

$$\varphi_{0,0} = 1$$
$$\varphi_{i,0} = \neg x_i \wedge \varphi_{i-1,0}$$
$$\varphi_{0,j} = \neg y_j \wedge \varphi_{0,j-1}$$
$$\varphi_{i,j} = ((x_i \leftrightarrow y_j) \wedge \varphi_{i-1,j-1}) \vee (x_i \wedge \neg y_j \wedge \varphi_{i,j-1}) \vee (\neg x_i \wedge y_j \wedge \varphi_{i-1,j}) \tag{4}$$

In this encoding, $\varphi_{i,j}$ means that $x_1, \ldots, x_i$ has the same number of 1s as $y_1, \ldots, y_j$. This is obtained by matching each bit that is set to 1 in the input with a bit that is set to 1 in the output, and skipping bits that are set to 0.

Note that some of these encodings can be optimized, for example the specification for *Sorting* can be reduced by testing at the same time if the input is sorted and it has the same number of 1s as the output. This can shorten the construction time, but since it is logically equivalent to the original formula, by the canonicity property of BDDs, the resulting BDD for the specification will be the same.

References

1. Bañeres, D., Cortadella, J., Kishinevsky, M.: A recursive paradigm to solve Boolean relations. IEEE Trans. Comput. **58**(4), 512–527 (2009)
2. Benedetti, M.: sKizzo: a suite to evaluate and certify QBFs. In: Nieuwenhuis, R. (ed.) CADE 2005. LNCS (LNAI), vol. 3632, pp. 369–376. Springer, Heidelberg (2005)
3. Bloem, R., Galler, S., Jobstmann, B., Piterman, N., Pnueli, A., Weiglhofer, M.: Automatic hardware synthesis from specifications: a case study. In: Proceedings of Conference on Design, Automation and Test in Europe, pp. 1188–1193. ACM (2007)
4. Brayton, R.K., Somenzi, F.: Minimization of Boolean relations. In: IEEE International Symposium on Circuits and Systems, pp. 738–743. IEEE (1989)
5. Brayton, R., Mishchenko, A.: ABC: an academic industrial-strength verification tool. In: Touili, T., Cook, B., Jackson, P. (eds.) CAV 2010. LNCS, vol. 6174, pp. 24–40. Springer, Heidelberg (2010)
6. Bryant, R.E.: Graph-based algorithms for Boolean function manipulation. IEEE Trans. Comput. **35**(8), 677–691 (1986)
7. Burch, J.R., Clarke, E.M., McMillan, K.L., Dill, D.L., Hwang, L.J.: Symbolic model checking: 10^{20} states and beyond. Inf. Comput. **98**(2), 142–170 (1992)
8. Burch, J.R., Clarke, E.M., Long, D.E.: Representing circuits more efficiently in symbolic model checking. In: Proceedings of 28th ACM/IEEE Design Automation Conference, pp. 403–407. ACM (1991)
9. Couceiro, M., Foldes, S., Lehtonen, E.: Composition of Post classes and normal forms of Boolean functions. Discrete Math. **306**(24), 3223–3243 (2006)
10. Ehlers, R.: Symbolic bounded synthesis. In: Touili, T., Cook, B., Jackson, P. (eds.) CAV 2010. LNCS, vol. 6174, pp. 365–379. Springer, Heidelberg (2010)
11. Gergov, J., Meinel, C.: Boolean manipulation with free BDDs: an application in combinational logic verification. IFIP Congr. **1**, 309–314 (1994)
12. Goldberg, E., Manolios, P.: Quantifier elimination via clause redundancy. In: Formal Methods in Computer-Aided Design, FMCAD 2013, Portland, OR, USA, 20–23 October 2013, pp. 85–92 (2013)
13. Gurevich, Y., Shelah, S.: Rabin's uniformization problem. J. Symb. Log. **48**(4), 1105–1119 (1983)
14. Hachtel, G.D., Somenzi, F.: Logic Synthesis and Verification Algorithms. Kluwer Academic Publishers, Boston (1996)
15. Heule, M., Seidl, M., Biere, A.: Efficient extraction of Skolem functions from QRAT proofs. In: Formal Methods in Computer-Aided Design, FMCAD 2014, Lausanne, Switzerland, 21–24 October 2014, pp. 107–114 (2014)

16. Jiang, J.-H.R.: Quantifier elimination via functional composition. In: Bouajjani, A., Maler, O. (eds.) CAV 2009. LNCS, vol. 5643, pp. 383–397. Springer, Heidelberg (2009)

17. Jiang, J.R., Lin, H., Hung, W.: Interpolating functions from large Boolean relations. In: 2009 International Conference on Computer-Aided Design (ICCAD 2009), 2–5 November 2009, San Jose, CA, USA, pp. 779–784. IEEE (2009)

18. Jobstmann, B., Galler, S., Weiglhofer, M., Bloem, R.: Anzu: a tool for property synthesis. In: Damm, W., Hermanns, H. (eds.) CAV 2007. LNCS, vol. 4590, pp. 258–262. Springer, Heidelberg (2007)

19. John, A.K., Shah, S., Chakraborty, S., Trivedi, A., Akshay, S.: Skolem functions for factored formulas. In: Formal Methods in Computer-Aided Design, FMCAD 2015, Austin, Texas, USA, 27–30 September 2015, pp. 73–80 (2015)

20. Kuehlmann, A., Ganai, M., Paruthi, V.: Circuit-based Boolean reasoning. In: Proceedings of Design Automation Conference, pp. 232–237. IEEE (2001)

21. Kukula, J.H., Shiple, T.R.: Building circuits from relations. In: Emerson, E.A., Sistla, A.P. (eds.) CAV 2000. LNCS, vol. 1855, pp. 113–123. Springer, Heidelberg (2000)

22. Kuncak, V., Mayer, M., Piskac, R., Suter, P.: Complete functional synthesis. In: Zorn, B.G., Aiken, A. (eds.) Proceedings of the 2010 ACM SIGPLAN Conference on Programming Language Design and Implementation, PLDI 2010, Toronto, Ontario, Canada, 5–10 June 2010, pp. 316–329. ACM (2010)

23. Pan, G., Vardi, M.Y.: Symbolic techniques in satisfiability solving. J. Autom. Reason. **35**(1–3), 25–50 (2005)

24. Paruthi, V., Kuehlmann, A.: Equivalence checking combining a structural SAT-solver, BDDs, and simulation. In: Proceedings of the International Conference on Computer Design, pp. 459–464. IEEE (2000)

25. Piterman, N., Pnueli, A., Sa'ar, Y.: Synthesis of reactive(1) designs. In: Emerson, E.A., Namjoshi, K.S. (eds.) VMCAI 2006. LNCS, vol. 3855, pp. 364–380. Springer, Heidelberg (2006)

26. Pnueli, A., Rosner, R.: On the synthesis of a reactive module. In: Proceedings of 16th ACM Symposium on Principles of Programming Languages, pp. 179–190 (1989)

27. Solar-Lezama, A., Rabbah, R.M., Bodík, R., Ebcioglu, K.: Programming by sketching for bit-streaming programs. In: Proceedings of the ACM Conference on Programming Language Design and Implementation, pp. 281–294. ACM (2005)

28. Somenzi, F.: CUDD: CU Decision Diagram Package Release 2.5.0. (2012). http://vlsi.colorado.edu/fabio/CUDD/

29. Tronci, E.: Automatic synthesis of controllers from formal specifications. In: ICFEM, pp. 134–143 (1998)

SOUFFLÉ: On Synthesis of Program Analyzers

Herbert Jordan[1], Bernhard Scholz[2], and Pavle Subotić[3(✉)]

[1] University of Innsbruck, Innsbruck, Austria
[2] University of Sydney, Sydney, Australia
[3] University College London, London, UK
psubotic@gmail.com

Abstract. SOUFFLÉ is an open source programming framework that performs static program analysis expressed in Datalog on very large code bases, including points-to analysis on OpenJDK7 (1.4M program variables, 350K objects, 160K methods) in under a minute. SOUFFLÉ is being successfully used for Java security analyses at Oracle Labs due to (1) its high-performance, (2) support for rapid program analysis development, and (3) customizability. SOUFFLÉ incorporates the highly flexible Datalog-based program analysis paradigm while exhibiting performance results that are on-par with manually developed state-of-the-art tools. In this tool paper, we introduce the SOUFFLÉ architecture, usage and demonstrate its applicability for large-scale code analysis on the Open-JDK7 library as a use case.

1 Introduction

Among the reasons for the slow industrial adoption of static program analysis is the lack of sufficient customizability and scalability in tools. Recently, the use of Datalog-like languages, has had a resurgence in several computer science communities [9], particularly, in the area of program analysis [2–4,12,16,18] where tools such as μZ [10], LogicBlox [11] and bddbddb [18] have shown great promise. In these tools, Datalog acts as a domain specific language to express custom program analyses concisely, reducing the complexity of developing program analyzers. The drawback of this approach is that program analyses specified in Datalog typically experience reduced performance compared to manually implemented tools. A notable reason for this decrease in performance appears to be the "one size fits all" approach of evaluating Datalog programs, i.e., Datalog engines generally lack the ability to specialize their evaluation process for a given instance of a program analysis specification.

To close the performance gap, we have developed a tool called SOUFFLÉ that overcomes the performance limitations of standard Datalog evaluation by performing an efficient synthesis of Datalog specifications to executable C++ programs. As a result, SOUFFLÉ is able to perform analyses on-par with state-of-the-art manual tools while retaining the advantages of employing a domain specific

Parts of this research was conducted while visiting Oracle Labs, Australia as assistants and visiting professor.

S. Chaudhuri and A. Farzan (Eds.): CAV 2016, Part II, LNCS 9780, pp. 422–430, 2016.
DOI: 10.1007/978-3-319-41540-6_23

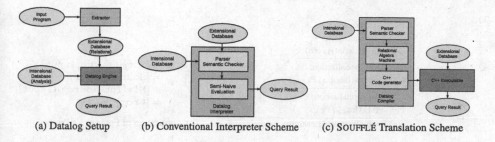

(a) Datalog Setup   (b) Conventional Interpreter Scheme   (c) SOUFFLÉ Translation Scheme

Fig. 1. Comparison: standard Datalog evaluation versus the architecture of SOUFFLÉ

language for expressing static program analyses. For example, [6] reports the ground-breaking capability of obtaining points-to analysis results for the Open-JDK library in under a minute. With the same dataset, SOUFFLÉ can obtain a similar performance (35s) using a general purpose analysis infrastructure on a multi-core commodity desktop system.

In this tool paper, we give an overview of the SOUFFLÉ framework; notably its architecture, optimizations and expected performance on very large code bases. We conclude with a summary of on-going developments of the SOUFFLÉ infrastructure.

2   How It Works

A Datalog program [1] consists of an extensional database, which is defined by facts, and an intensional database, which is defined by rules. In a setup for static program analysis, the extensional database represents an input program in relational form. The relational representation of an input program is obtained from an extractor [15] describing the relevant semantics of the input program for a given program analysis. The intensional database represents the program analysis specification phrased as Horn clause formulae over finite domains. Figure 1(a) illustrates the workflow for static program analysis in Datalog. The query result of the Datalog execution represents the actual result of the program analysis. While standard schemes for evaluating Datalog are generally optimized for reducing the amount of redundant computation, e.g., the conventional, interpreter-based semi-naïve evaluation scheme [1] as shown in Fig. 1(b), they lack the ability to specialize their evaluation for a given program analysis specification instance.

SOUFFLÉ takes a different approach: Instead of evaluating a Datalog program on-the-fly, we treat a Datalog program as a specification that is synthesized to a C++ program. The C++ program is compiled, and executed with the extensional database (i.e. facts) as an input. Essentially, the generated executable becomes an analyzer in its own right. Figure 1(c) depicts our translation scheme, where the Datalog specification is first parsed and semantically checked. The input specification is then translated internally to an imperative Relational Algebra Machine (RAM) program. The RAM program is further translated to a

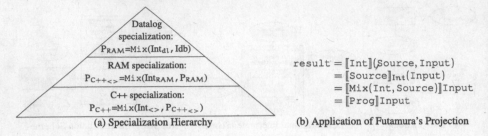

(a) Specialization Hierarchy

(b) Application of Futamura's Projection

Fig. 2. Specialization Hierarchy and First Futamura Projection of Semi-Naïve Evaluation

C++ program with OpenMP annotations for parallel execution and C++ template based meta-programming elements. In the last stage, an OpenMP/C++ compiler translates the generated code to a highly optimized, parallel program.

2.1 A Hierarchy of Specializations

To achieve a synthesis of Datalog specifications to C++, we follow a staged specialization hierarchy as depicted in Fig. 2(a). At each stage, a specialization step, as characterized by Futamura projections [8], is applied. The foundation is provided by an abstract transformation $\mathtt{Mix}$ that, given an interpreter $\mathtt{Int}$ and a source program $\mathtt{Source}$, yields a specialized program amalgamating the interpreter and the source program. The specialized program performs the same computation as the source program (executed by the interpreter) – yet more efficiently. In Fig. 2(b), the semantic equivalence is shown between evaluation under an interpreter $\mathtt{Int}$ and the program produced by the $\mathtt{Mix}$ transformation [8]. What is of particular interest, is that at each specialization phase, information is revealed that enables opportunities for code optimizations that were not possible at earlier stages. As a consequence, the binary code produced by our specialization hierarchy is on-par in terms of run-time and memory usage with state-of-the-art hand crafted code.

The first specialization $\mathtt{P_{RAM}}=\mathtt{Mix(Int_{dl},Idb)}$ sees the Semi-Naïve Evaluation [1] as the interpreter, $\mathtt{Int_{dl}}$. It is specialized with the intensional database, Idb, corresponding to the analysis specification. As a result, we receive a relational algebra machine program $\mathtt{P_{RAM}}$ that expresses the computation of the specified analysis as a series of fix-point computation steps over relational algebra operations. From a high-level viewpoint, the specialization of the Semi-Naïve evaluation is a translation of a declarative Datalog program to an imperative relational algebra program.

The next application of Futamura's projection is performed on the RAM program, i.e., $\mathtt{P_{C++_{<>}}} = \mathtt{Mix(Int_{RAM},P_{RAM})}$, that has been generated by the first stage and the RAM interpreter $\mathtt{Int_{RAM}}$. The conducted specializations target the efficient structuring of loop-based join operations and the identification of optimal index support, in order to reduce the worst-case runtime complexity

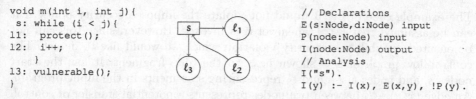

```
void m(int i, int j){                        // Declarations
  s: while (i < j){                          E(s:Node,d:Node) input
11:   protect();                             P(node:Node) input
12:   i++;                                   I(node:Node) output
  }                                          // Analysis
13: vulnerable();                           I("s").
}                                            I(y) :- I(x), E(x,y), !P(y).
```

Fig. 3. Java-like input program, a graphical representation of its control-flow, and security specification in SOUFFLÉ

of the RAM program. However, index management is expensive and a minimal number of indices is desirable. In SOUFFLÉ we employ a novel, optimal and polynomial-time algorithm that is inspired by Dilworth's theorem [7] to compute only necessary indices. The idea of the algorithm is to compute partitions of chains in a lattice of indices. From each chain, a maximum index is computed that subsumes all other indices in the chain. This optimization results in a large run-time improvement in the resulting analyzer. After specializing the relational algebra program, C++ code that makes extensive use of templates is generated.

The final specialization step, $P_{C++} = \texttt{Mix}(\texttt{Int}_{<>}, P_{C++_{<>}})$, is performed while compiling the generated C++ program. This Futamura projection is implemented using template-based meta-programming techniques [17]. With meta-programming techniques, data structures and algorithms are specialized by static information, thereby hoisting computations from run-time to compile-time. E.g., data structure interfaces are realized in form of C++ concepts rather than polymorphic C++ base classes to eliminate virtual-call dispatches and run-time type checks. The generated data structures are highly specialized towards the use of the corresponding relations in the input program. We employ efficient parallel variations of B-trees and Tries, with customized data element, node, and iterator types. Additionally, primary and secondary index support is provided for efficient operations on the represented relation in the program. For example, one of the most time-consuming operations with the use of indices is the comparison of two tuples. For this purpose we instantiate specialized versions of templatized lexicographical order functions in order to removing unnecessary control-flow and memory access overhead from the analysis run-time.

Our staged-translation approach using a specialization hierarchy coupled with standard Datalog optimizations and specialized relational data structures allows SOUFFLÉ to analyze very large code bases, previously considered to be impractical for Datalog-based engines. The generated C++ code is packaged in form of header files for a smooth integration with host applications.

2.2   An Example of the Specialization Process

Figure 3 illustrates a simple security analysis for an example assuming that there is a low and high security state in a program. The invocation of a security sensitive method `vulnerable` is permitted only in the high-security state. A call to the method `protect` transfers the security state from low to high if permitted.

The example code of Fig. 3 would not violate the imposed security policy if it can be assumed that $i < j$ whenever m is invoked. However, since this can not be ensured, m exhibits a security violation which we would like to detect. The control-flow graph of m is shown next to the code fragment. It has the start nodes s, and nodes ℓ_1, ℓ_2, and ℓ_3 representing statements in the input program. An edge $(x, y) \in E$ between two nodes represents a potential transfer of control. A statement $x \in P$ raises the security level.

A simple analysis verifying the imposed security policy computes all statements that can be reached without passing the protect function. If a call to vulnerable is included in this set, the security policy is violated. Such a security analysis is be specified by the SOUFFLÉ code listed next to the control-flow graph in Fig. 3. The first section of the program declares relations used in the SOUFFLÉ program. The relation E is defined as a binary relation between two Node elements and the sets P and I contain elements of type Node. The qualifier input denotes that the relations are an extensional database and are provided as an input when executing the analysis. The set I contains all nodes in the control-flow that are not secure and is denoted as a result of the analysis using the qualifier output. In particular, if node ℓ_3 which is a vulnerable call is in set I, the method m does not fulfill the security policy to be enforced and would thus be identified as insecure.

The analysis always assumes the entry node s to be insecure by adding it to set I via I("s"). The propagation rule

$$\text{I(y) :- I(x), E(x,y), !P(y).}$$

adds node y to the set of insecure nodes if (1) node x is insecure, (2) there is a control-flow from x to y, and (3) the target node y does not raise the security level.

SOUFFLÉ translates the given analysis specification in stages. The specialization hierarchy first fuses the semi-naïve evaluation with rules from the analysis as shown in Fig. 4: For the recursively defined set I code computing a fixed-point is generated. The set I is thereby supported by two auxiliary sets I' and Δ I. The set I' represents the newly gained knowledge within an iteration of the fix-point computation and set Δ I represents the newly gained knowledge of the previous iteration. The fix-point computation is performed in the while loop from line 2 to line 9 of the RAM program listed by Fig. 4(a). The first section of the loop body (lines 3 - 7) computes I' using Δ I as an input. The loop starting in line 4 iterates over all nodes in Δ I and the nested loop starting in line 5 iterates over all edges in the control flow graph. If any of those edges links some node x to a previously discovered insecure node y present in Δ I, where x is not a protect call itself and has not been marked as insecure before, it is add to the newly deduced set of insecure nodes I' (lines 6 and 7). In the last two statements of the loop body (i.e. lines 8 and 9) the newly gained knowledge of relation I' is added to relation I and I' becomes Δ I. The fixed-point calculation terminates if no new insecure nodes could be identified.

The pseudo-code of the Futamura projection is not optimal since it might have a worst-case complexity of $\mathcal{O}(n \cdot m)$ where n is the number of nodes in the

```
1   I = {s}; ΔI = I
2   while  ΔI ≠ ∅
3     I' = ∅
4     for  u ∈ ΔI do
5       for  (x,y) ∈ E do
6         if ( u = x ∧ y ∉ P ∧ y ∉ I )
7           I' = I' ∪ {y}
8     I = I ∪ I'
9     ΔI = I'
```

(a) Futamura Projection

```
1   I = {s}; ΔI = I
2   while  ΔI ≠ ∅
3     I' = ∅
4     for  u ∈ ΔI do
5       for  (_,y) ∈ E(u,_) do
6         if (y ∉ P ∧ y ∉ I )
7           I' = I' ∪ {y}
8     I = I ∪ I'
9     ΔI = I'
```

(b) Partial Evaluation of RAM Program

Fig. 4. Running example

control-flow graph and m is the number of edges in the control-flow graph. To improve the performance of the program, we specialize the loop traversal of the loop in line 5 by employing an index. The index filters out all pairs in the edge relation whose source is not node u, i.e., all the edges are selected which emanate of node u denoted by the set $E(u,\_)$. This specialization requires an index on relation E, yet significantly reduces the runtime complexity. Typical analyses result in potentially hundreds of indices, making index management expensive if performed naively. We therefore employ an optimal, minimal index selection technique based on Dilworth's theorem [7] to select only necessary indices since an index may subsume several indices. Suppose we had another access to relation E on both u and v attributes, i.e., $E(u,v)$. A naive implementation would be to have two indices defined by the lexicographical orders u and $u<v$, however, the minimal solution would be to have only one index, namely, $u<v$ as it subsumes the index with only u. Some information to our solution to this combinatorial problem can be found in [13].

To implement indices from the previous step, we employ templatized B-Trees that require a comparison function for two tuples in the relation. The comparison function is implemented as a lexicographical order in the form of a template as sketched below,

```
template<int...> struct Comperator;
template<int i, int ...  tail  > struct Comperator<i,tail...> {
  static  bool cmp(const tuple& a, const tuple& b){
    return a[i]  < b[i]  ||  (a[i]  == b[i] && Comperator<tail...>::cmp(a,b));
  }
};
template<> struct Comperator<> {
  static  bool cmp(const tuple&, const tuple&){ return true; }
};
```

The variadic template for the struct `Comperator` is parametrized by the columns in order. E.g., the call `Comperator<2,0>::cmp(a,b)` compares the tuples a and b by checking whether the third element of a is less than the third element of b. If the comparison results in a tie, the first elements of both tuples are compared to determine the order between the two tuples a and b. The operator is defined recursively: the base case is given by the struct `Comperator<>` considering every tuple equal, and the inductive case by struct Comperator<i,tail...>, comparing the i-th components and, if equal, delegating the comparison to Comperator<tail...>. The expansion of the template for a given instance such as Comperator<2,0> is performed at compile-time and delivers, in combination with function inlining, significant performance gains for index construction and retrieval. Without applying meta-programming techniques that rely on program specializations, i.e., pushing computations from runtime to compile-time, these performance gains would not be achievable.

3   Case Study: OpenJDK7

In this section we present our experience using SOUFFLÉ as a Java security analysis tool on the Java Development Kit (JDK). We point the reader to [5] for information on the Java vulnerabilities work at Oracle. For more detailed performance data on the techniques used in SOUFFLÉ, we refer the reader to [13].

In Table 1 we present three types of analyses performed on the OpenJDK7-b147. Due to the sheer size of OpenJDK7 (1.4M variables, 350K heap objects, 160K methods, 590K invocations and 17K types) such analyses are typically regarded as either impractical for most tools or at the very least, extremely challenging. The CI column refers to a *context-insensitive* points-to analysis and the CS refers to a *context-sensitive* points-to analysis. Points-to analysis is the main building block of most security analyses performed and are typically dominating the overall execution time. The last column, Security, refers to a large, composite security analysis similar to the *caller sensitive method* analysis in [5].

For our evaluation, we compare the performance of bddbddb [18], Z3's Datalog extension μZ [10], an SQLite based Datalog engine [14], and a 8-core parallel version of SOUFFLÉ. Each analysis has been ported to the respective Datalog variation of the evaluated tools. The resulting specifications typically comprise a few thousand lines of code. For the SOUFFLÉ based specifications, SOUFFLÉ's module system has been utilized to facilitate the reuse of code among the three analysis, reducing the necessary development effort.

Our experiments reveal the limited capability of pre-existing Datalog-based tools when analyzing very large code bases. The CI analysis represents a very simple points-to analysis that does not construct the call-graph on the fly. A

Table 1. Comparison of Datalog evaluation tools for analyses on the OpenJDK7 b147 library, executing on an 8 core Intel Xeon E5-2690 v2 @ 3.0 GHz server system. DNF = Did Not Finish within 18 h.

Tool	CI		CS		Security	
	Δt [hh:mm::ss]	Memory [GB]	Δt [hh:mm::ss]	Memory [GB]	Δt [hh:mm::ss]	Memory [GB]
bddbddb	0:30:00	5.7	DNF	DNF	DNF	DNF
SQLite	6:20:00	40.2	DNF	DNF	DNF	DNF
μZ	DNF	DNF	DNF	DNF	DNF	DNF
SOUFFLÉ	0:00:35	8.5	6:44:08	206.4	14:45:01	75.3

hand-crafted version of this analysis is reported to run under a minute [6]. For the CI analysis, bddbddb performs the analysis in a reasonable amount of time. However SOUFFLÉ outperforms bddbddb in terms of run-time by more than 50× consuming a comparable amount of memory. In the case of the CS and Security analyses, SOUFFLÉ is the only tool capable of performing the analyses within the 18 h time limit imposed by the computation resources available to us for our evaluations. The Z3 based versions did not manage to finish any of our evaluated analyses in time.

4   Conclusion and Current Developments

We have presented SOUFFLÉ, a Datalog-based analysis tool that instead of evaluating Datalog, performs several specialization and optimization steps to produce a compiled, binary analyzer that can handle very large code bases. SOUFFLÉ is publicly available[1] and is actively developed by both Oracle and several universities. SOUFFLÉ supports a range of Datalog language extensions to aid in the specification of program analyses and resulting analyzers may be directly included into host applications as a header-only library.

Acknowledgement. We would like to thank Cristina Cifuentes, Paddy Krishnan, and all our other colleagues from Oracle Labs, Brisbane. We would also like to thank Byron Cook, Yannis Smaragdakis, and our anonymous reviewers.

References

1. Abiteboul, S., Hull, R., Vianu, V.: Foundations of Databases. Addison-Wesley, Boston (1995)
2. Allen, N., Krishnan, P., Scholz, B.: Combining type-analysis with points-to analysis for analyzing java library source-code. In: Møller, A., Naik, M. (eds.) Proceedings of the 4th ACM SIGPLAN International Workshop on State of the Art in Program Analysis, SOAP@PLDI 2015, Portland, OR, USA, 15–17 June 2015, pp. 13–18. ACM (2015)
3. Allen, N., Scholz, B., Krishnan, P.: Staged points-to analysis for large code bases. In: Franke, B. (ed.) CC 2015. LNCS, vol. 9031, pp. 131–150. Springer, Heidelberg (2015)
4. Alpuente, M., Feliú, M.A., Joubert, C., Villanueva, A.: Datalog-based program analysis with BES and RWL. In: de Moor, O., Gottlob, G., Furche, T., Sellers, A. (eds.) Datalog 2010. LNCS, vol. 6702, pp. 1–20. Springer, Heidelberg (2011)
5. Cifuentes, C., Gross, A., Keynes, N.: Understanding caller-sensitive method vulnerabilities: a class of access control vulnerabilities in the java platform. In: Proceedings of the 4th ACM SIGPLAN International Workshop on State of the Art in Program Analysis. SOAP 2015, NY, USA, pp. 7–12. ACM, New York (2015)
6. Dietrich, J., Hollingum, N., Scholz, B.: Giga-scale exhaustive points-to analysis for java in under a minute. In: Proceedings of the 2015 ACM SIGPLAN International Conference on Object-Oriented Programming, Systems, Languages, and Applications. OOPSLA 2015, NY, USA. pp. 535–551. ACM, New York (2015)

---

[1] http://souffle-lang.github.io.

7. Dilworth, R.: A decomposition theorem for partially ordered sets. Ann. Math. **2**(51), 161–166 (1950)
8. Futamura, Y.: Partial evaluation of computation process - an approach to a compiler-compiler. High. Order Symbolic Comput. **12**(4), 381–391 (1999)
9. Green, T.J., Huang, S.S., Loo, B.T., Zhou, W.: Datalog and recursive query processing. Found. Trends Databases **5**(2), 105–195 (2013)
10. Hoder, K., Bjørner, N., de Moura, L.: μZ– an efficient engine for fixed points with constraints. In: Gopalakrishnan, G., Qadeer, S. (eds.) CAV 2011. LNCS, vol. 6806, pp. 457–462. Springer, Heidelberg (2011)
11. LogicBlox Inc.: Declartive cloud platform for applications that combine transactions & analytics. http://www.logicblox.com
12. Naik, M., Aiken, A., Whaley, J.: Effective static race detection for Java. SIGPLAN Not. **41**(6), 308–319 (2006)
13. Scholz, B., Jordan, H., Subotic, P., Westmann, T.: On fast large-scale program analysis in datalog. In: Zaks, A., Hermenegildo, M.V. (eds.) Proceedings of the 25th International Conference on Compiler Construction, CC 2016, Barcelona, Spain, 12–18 March 2016, pp. 196–206. ACM (2016)
14. Scholz, B., Vorobyov, K., Krishnan, P., Westmann, T.: A datalog source-to-source translator for static program analysis: an experience report. In: 24th Australasian Software Engineering Conference, ASWEC 2015, Adelaide, SA, Australia, 28 September – 1 October, 2015, pp. 28–37. IEEE Computer Society (2015)
15. Smaragdaiks, Y., Bravenboer, M., Kastrinis, G.: Doop: A framework for java pointer analysis. http://doop.program-analysis.org/
16. Smaragdakis, Y., Kastrinis, G., Balatsouras, G.: Introspective analysis: context-sensitivity, across the board. In: PLDI, NY, USA, pp. 485–495. ACM, New York (2014)
17. Veldhuizen, T.L.: C++ templates as partial evaluation. In: Danvy, O. (ed.) PEPM, pp. 13–18. University of Aarhus (1999). http://dblp.uni-trier.de/db/conf/pepm/pepm1999.html#Veldhuizen99
18. Whaley, J., Avots, D., Carbin, M., Lam, M.S.: Using datalog with binary decision diagrams for program analysis. In: Yi, K. (ed.) APLAS 2005. LNCS, vol. 3780, pp. 97–118. Springer, Heidelberg (2005)

Model Checking II

Property Directed Equivalence
via Abstract Simulation

Grigory Fedyukovich[1,2]([⊠]), Arie Gurfinkel[3], and Natasha Sharygina[1]

[1] USI, Lugano, Switzerland
{grigory.fedyukovich,natasha.sharygina}
@usi.ch
[2] UW, Seattle, USA
grigory@cs.washington.edu
[3] SEI/CMU, Pittsburgh, USA
arie@cmu.com

Abstract. We present a novel approach for automated incremental verification that employs both reusable and relational specifications of software to incrementally verify pairs of programs with possibly nested loops. It analyzes two programs, P - the one already verified, and Q - the one needed to be verified, and proceeds by detecting an abstraction αP of P and a simulation ρ, such that αP simulates Q via ρ. The key idea behind our simulation synthesis is to drive construction of both αP and ρ by the safe inductive invariants of P, thus guaranteeing the property preservations by the results. Finally, our approach allows effective lifting of the safe inductive invariants of P to Q using only αP and ρ. Based on our evaluation, in many cases when the absolute equivalence between programs cannot be proven, our approach is able to establish the *property directed equivalence*, confirming that the program Q is safe.

1 Introduction

Software development is a continuous process that repeatedly iterates between the stages of implementing a program and checking its safety. To satisfy quality standards, a software product should pass through a myriad of intermediate verification stages, each of which assures safety of a particular change against its baseline version. One of the most successful techniques to verify isolated software versions fully automatically and exhaustively is *Model Checking*.

Without detracting from the merits of the recent model checking solutions, there is a demand for new methods to make other steps in the typical "verify-bugfix-verify" workflow automated and exhaustive. In particular, there is a clear

This work is supported in part by the SNSF Fellowship P2T1P2_161971.

This material is based upon work funded and supported by the Department of Defense under Contract No. FA8721-05-C-0003 with Carnegie Mellon University for the operation of the Software Engineering Institute, a federally funded research and development center. Any opinions, findings and conclusions or recommendations expressed in this material are those of the author(s) and do not necessarily reflect the views of the United States Department of Defense. This material has been approved for public release and unlimited distribution. DM-0001771.

© Springer International Publishing Switzerland 2016
S. Chaudhuri and A. Farzan (Eds.): CAV 2016, Part II, LNCS 9780, pp. 433–453, 2016.
DOI: 10.1007/978-3-319-41540-6_24

need for new techniques that would make the software analysis more efficient by (1) finding a *reusable specification* of an already verified program version to be used while verifying another program version; and (2) finding a *relational specification* between program versions that describes how the versions relate to each other. When discovered, these specifications enable formal analysis of sequences of program versions called *Formal Incremental Verification* (FIV) and can be used for various tasks such as upgrade checking, compositional (modular) verification, change impact calculation, program repair, etc.

Model checkers for the programs with unbounded (and possibly nested) loops reduce the verification tasks to finding safe inductive invariants. Such invariants over-approximate all safe behaviors of the program and constitute so called *proof certificates*. Since the problem of inferring proofs is known to be undecidable in general [29], individual model-checking solutions are not guaranteed to deliver an appropriate invariant. On the other hand, in cases if model checking succeeded, the synthesized proof provides an important reusable specification that comes in handy whenever the program gets modified. In this paper, we address a challenge of migrating proofs across the different program versions.

Simulation is known to be the most general mapping to transfer proofs between program versions [17,26,27]. However, discovering a simulation relation is difficult and usually requires a manual guidance. One of the recent promising approaches for the simulation synthesis is SIMABS introduced in [16]. Despite providing a fully automated schema, it is unable to find simulations for pairs of program versions obtained after non-trivial program transformations. We experimented with SIMABS and observed that it discovered precise simulations only in 9 % of cases[1], while in the rest it either provided an *abstract simulation* (i.e., an abstraction of the already verified program version that simulates the precise modified program version) or diverged. In general, abstract simulations are not applicable for migrating proofs, since the delivered abstraction might not preserve all important safety properties of the verified program version.

In this paper, for the task of migrating proofs, we show that the precise simulation relation between program versions is not even needed. Instead, it is enough to deal with abstract simulations, but created in a particular way. It is crucial to ensure that the given invariant is safe for the delivered abstraction. For this reason, we propose to guide the abstraction generation by the proofs. If a simulation for such a *proof-based abstraction* is found then the proof can be lifted directly. We present an algorithm called ASSI (stands for *Abstract Simulation Synthesis with Invariants*) and an algorithm called PDE (stands for *Property Directed Equivalence*) that perform such reasoning completely automatically.

A distinguishing feature of ASSI and PDE is the ability to migrate the invariants through abstractions even if the abstractions do not preserve safety. PDE attempts to lift as much information from the invariant as possible and then strengthens it using a Horn-clause-based unbounded model checker.

We contribute the implementation of ASSI and PDE on the top of the LLVM-based model checker UFO [1] and provide extensive evaluation of

---

[1] See Sect. 6 for more details.

non-trivial LLVM-optimizations. In the same experimental setting as for SIMABS, ASSI discovered non-trivial abstract simulations in 82 % of cases, that further allowed PDE to migrate the proofs completely (34 %) or at least partially (48 %). Guided by the proofs, ASSI outperformed SIMABS by up to 2000**X**. In other words, it enabled scaling the entire simulation synthesis technology to solve more difficult problems and to do it more efficiently.

To sum up, PDE can be seen as the first technique to effectively exploit both, the *reusable specification* (by means of the proofs) and the *relational specification* (by means of the abstract simulations), to incrementally verify sequences of program versions with non-trivial loop structures and non-trivial transformations. The most important contributions can be classified as follows:

- A concept and a formalization of the PDE framework to incremental verification through abstract simulation and invariants.
- An algorithm ASSI for abstract simulation synthesis, designed to take the proofs into account and consider the proof-based abstractions.
- An LLVM-based evaluation on Software Verification Competition benchmarks that succeeds in establishing the property directed equivalence in many cases when the absolute equivalence between programs cannot be proven. In some other cases PDE was able to lift the proof partially and strengthen it further by means of the model checker UFO.

The rest of the paper is structured as follows. We start with a brief overview of the related methods (Sect. 2) followed by the background of unbounded verification (Sect. 3). Then, we formalize the underlying concepts behind simulation synthesis (Sect. 4) and use them to build the algorithms for ASSI and PDE (Sect. 5). Finally, we outline the evaluation of ASSI and PDE (Sect. 6) and conclude the paper (Sect. 7).

2 Related Work

We aim at checking the *property directed equivalence* (i.e., equivalence of programs with respect to some common property) automatically since it has a direct application in model checking. This is an alternative property to *absolute equivalence* (i.e., equivalence of programs with respect to any possible property) [3,12,19,21,28] that is rare in practice. The first automatic solutions to equivalence checking date back to hardware verification. Based on BDDs and SAT solving, the methods [5,9,30] aim at searching for a counter-example witnessing inequivalence of the two circuits. Most of them exploit structural similarities between the circuits that make them able to scale well with the circuit size. The further application of equivalence checking is to prove validity of compiler optimizations (e.g., [3,28,33]). The basis of most of work on Translation Validation is the idea of guessing a simulation relation between programs. Our algorithm also guesses relations, but before using them for PDE, it formally checks their validity with ASSI and drops those for which the check fails.

A step towards equivalence checking of software was made in [12] that proposed to check equivalence of a Verilog circuit and a C program through encoding and solving a quantifier-free SAT formula. A more recent solution [19] employs Bounded Model Checking [10] (BMC) to establish absolute equivalence between C programs. The method traverses the call graph bottom-up and separately checks whether identity of inputs implies identity of outputs for each pair of matched (e.g., by type annotation) functions, while all the nested calls are abstracted away using the same uninterpreted functions. A similar but language-agnostic approach is implemented in the SYMDIFF tool [21].

The problem of checking *non-absolute equivalence* between programs (also referred to as *incremental verification*) was addressed in a number of works, e.g. [2,4,7,13,15,18,24,31,34]. The main motivating idea behind this line of research is the ability of reusing efforts between verification runs, thus achieving performance speedup compared to verification of programs in isolation. EVOL-CHECK [31] extracts the over-approximating function summaries from one program satisfying the given property and then re-checks if summaries still over-approximate function behavior in another program. However, EVOLCHECK is based on BMC and relies on the user-provided bounds for loops and recursive function calls. Unbounded incremental verifier OPTVERIFY [15] is designed to lift inductive invariants across program transformations using a guessed variable mapping. Contrary to our approach, OPTVERIFY can be applied only to programs sharing the same loop-structure. A similar and generalized approach for CEGAR-based verification was proposed in [7]. It stores the level of abstraction needed to prove safety of one program (e.g., which predicates to use in predicate analysis). The predicates are then transferred and adapted to another program to obtain the initial level of abstraction from which the analysis starts (not from scratch). Note that none of the mentioned techniques relies on automatically derived relational specifications (like a mapping between variables or a type annotation) so they all require re-validating the artifacts migrated from the verified programs. In contrast, the technique presented in this paper benefits from using certified simulation relations between programs, thus confirming that the migrated invariants are always sound.

Alternatively, there are approaches [25,34] to reason not only about differences between behaviors, but also to analyze differences between properties in different programs. The technique called Verification Modulo Versions (VMV) [25] transforms assertions from one program into assumptions for another program. VMV then tries to find (or prove absence of) bugs that are present only in the latter program. The technique called Directed Incremental Symbolic Execution (DISE) [34] is driven by the *change impact* which in fact is the program slice obtained by symbolic execution of the syntactic delta between the programs. The change impact is, however, property-independent, so DISE still requires further analysis whether the requested properties hold or do not in both programs. PDE is also able to calculate the change impact as a side effect of incremental verification. In contrast, our change impact is always property-dependent that would make it potentially useful to identify program locations responsible for the particular property violations.

3   Programs, Abstractions and Proofs

In this paper, we consider "large-block" encoding (LBE) [6] of programs that allows representing complex control-flow graphs compactly. A *program* is a tuple $P = \langle Vars, CP, en, err, E, \tau \rangle$, where $Vars$ is a set of *real* and *boolean* variables, CP is a set of cutpoints (i.e., program locations which represent heads of loops); $en, err \in CP$ are respectively designated locations of the program entry and the error (i.e., the violation of some property of interest); $E \subseteq CP \times CP$ is the cutpoint-relation corresponding to the largest loop-free program fragments, and $\tau : E \to Expr(Vars)$ maps each element of E to a formula in first-order logic that encodes a transition relation of the corresponding program fragment. We refer to the graph $\langle CP, E \rangle$ as a *Cutpoint graph* (*CPG*) of the program P.

Throughout the paper, we consider only variables that appear as *source*- and *destination* arguments for the edges E of the program P. In the formulas encoding transition relations τ, the other (local) variables are implicitly existentially quantified. Let $V : E \to 2^{Vars}$ be the function that, given a cutpoint, returns a set of variables live at that cutpoint. We use primed notation for $Vars'$ to distinguish between the source and the destination arguments of each edge. To enable existential quantification over variables in a formula $e \in Expr$, we explicitly declare the variable sets over which e is expressed.

The goal of formal verification is to check whether the location err is unreachable by any program behavior starting at the location en. One of the most common ways of proving safety of a program is to construct an *inductive invariant* that over-approximates the sets of reachable states in the program, and to prove the unreachability of err for the invariant. In the context of LBE, (safe) inductive invariants are represented by a labeling of the cutpoints with logical formulas such that the condition(s) of the following definition hold.

Definition 1. *Given a program P, a mapping $\psi : CP \to Expr(Vars)$ is an inductive invariant if:*

$$\psi(en) = \top \tag{1}$$

$$\forall (u, v) \in E . \left(\psi(u)(\vec{x}) \wedge \tau(u, v)(\vec{x}, \vec{x}') \implies \psi(v)(\vec{x}') \right) \tag{2}$$

ψ *is a proof (or a safe inductive invariant) of P if additionally:*

$$\psi(err)(\vec{x}') \implies \bot \tag{3}$$

In (2), $\psi(u)$ is expressed over the source arguments of the CPG-edge (u, v), namely $\vec{x}$. In contrast, $\psi(v)$ is expressed over the destination arguments of the CPG-edge (u, v), namely $\vec{x}'$. Throughout the paper, we add the following mnemonic notation to emphasize whether (3) holds for an inductive invariant: $|\psi|$ (with vertical bars) to indicate that (1)–(2) hold, but (3) does not, and $\widehat{\psi}$ (with a hat) to indicate that all three conditions hold. If ψ is used without this mnemonic notation then in the current context it does not matter if (3) holds or not.

Since an inductive invariant over-approximates the sets of reachable states for each cutpoint of a program P, it allows more behaviors of P than specified

```
int x = 0;              int y = 0;              int z = 0;
while ( * ) {           while ( * ) {           while ( * && z < 12 ) {
    x++;                    if ( y == 12 ) {        z++;
}                               y = y + 2;      }
if ( x < 0 ) {              } else {            if ( z == 12 ) {
    error();                    y++;                z = z + 2;
}                           }                   }
                        }                       while ( * && z > 12 ) {
                        if ( y < 0 ||               z++;
                             y == 13 ) {        }
                            error();            if ( z < 0 || z == 13 ) {
                        }                           error();
                                                }
```

$\quad$ (a) P_0 $\qquad\qquad\qquad$ (b) Q_0 $\qquad\qquad\qquad\qquad$ (c) Q_1

Fig. 1. Programs P_0 and Q_0 and the loop-splitting optimization of Q_0.

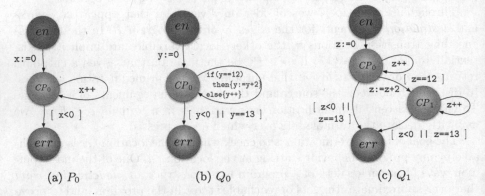

$\quad$ (a) P_0 $\qquad\qquad\qquad\qquad$ (b) Q_0 $\qquad\qquad\qquad\qquad$ (c) Q_1

Fig. 2. Cutpoint graphs of P_0, Q_0 and Q_1.

$$\tau_{P_0} = \begin{cases} (en, CP_0) \mapsto (x' = 0) \\ (CP_0, CP_0) \mapsto (x' = x + 1) \\ (CP_0, err) \mapsto (x' = x \wedge x' < 0) \end{cases} \qquad \widehat{\psi} = \begin{cases} (en) \mapsto \top \\ (CP_0) \mapsto x \geq 0 \\ (err) \mapsto \bot \end{cases}$$

$$\tau_{\alpha P_0} = \begin{cases} (en, CP_0) \mapsto (x' \geq 0) \\ (CP_0, CP_0) \mapsto (x' \geq x) \\ (CP_0, err) \mapsto (x < 0) \end{cases} \qquad \tau_{\beta P_0} = \begin{cases} (en, CP_0) \mapsto (x' \geq 0) \\ (CP_0, CP_0) \mapsto (x' \geq x) \\ (CP_0, err) \mapsto (x < 0) \vee (x = 13) \end{cases}$$

Fig. 3. Transition relations τ_{P_0}, $\tau_{\alpha P_0}$, $\tau_{\beta P_0}$ and proof $\widehat{\psi}$ of P_0.

by its transition relation τ. It can be used to represent programs that share the CPG-structure with P, but have less accurate transition relations. We say that such programs are the *abstractions* of P and describe them formally as follows.

Definition 2. *Given two programs* $P = \langle Vars, CP, en, err, E, \tau \rangle$ *and* $\alpha P = \langle Vars, CP, en, err, E, \tau_\alpha \rangle$, αP *is an* abstraction *of* P *if for some inductive invariant* ψ *of* P,

$$\forall (u, v) \in E \cdot \left(\psi(u)(\vec{x}) \wedge \tau(u, v)(\vec{x}, \vec{x}') \implies \tau_\alpha(u, v)(\vec{x}, \vec{x}') \right) \tag{4}$$

The use of an inductive invariant ψ in (4) makes the way of creating abstractions more flexible. Indeed, for each cutpoint $u \in CP$, the formula $\psi(u)$ might bring any additional information about the pre-states at the edge $(u, v) \in E$

learned inductively from the dependent CPG-edges. Note that $\tau(u,v)$ might be incomparable (and even inconsistent) with $\psi(u)$.

The simplest way to construct a program abstraction from the given inductive invariant ψ is to assign the transition relation of each CPG-edge by the invariant at the post-state of that edge. Thus, an abstraction of P can be constructed directly from ψ, and in rest of the paper we refer to it as to $\alpha^\psi P$. The following lemma assures that $\alpha^\psi P$ satisfies Definition 2.

Lemma 1. *Given $P = \langle Vars, CP, en, err, E, \tau \rangle$ and its invariant ψ, let $\alpha^\psi P = \langle Vars, CP, en, err, E, \tau_\alpha^\psi \rangle$ be defined as:*

$$\forall (u,v) \in E \,.\, \left(\tau_\alpha^\psi(u,v)(\vec{x}, \vec{x}') \triangleq \psi(v)(\vec{x}') \right) \tag{5}$$

Then $\alpha^\psi P$ is an abstraction of P.

If ψ is not trivial (i.e., $\exists u \in CP \,.\, \psi(u) \neq \top$) and some abstraction αP is as accurate as $\alpha^\psi P$ then αP provides a particular interest for incremental verification that is explained in Sect. 5. However, for the sake of completeness of presentation, we must admit that Definition 2 also allows other types of abstractions, abstract transition relation of which does not necessarily satisfy $\psi(v)$ for all post-states at (u,v).

Example 1. Consider a program P_0 shown in Fig. 1(a) that increments an integer counter[2] x, initially assigned to 0. The CPG_{P_0} is shown in Fig. 2(a) and consists of $CP = \{en, CP_0, err\}$ and $E = \{(en, CP_0), (CP_0, CP_0), (CP_0, err)\}$. Figure 3 shows: (1) transition relation τ_{P_0} labeling each edge in E, (2) the proof $\hat\psi$ labeling each cutpoint in CP, (3–4) transition relations of two abstractions αP_0 and βP_0 respectively. Compared to αP_0, βP_0 allows variable x to be equal to 13 in the cutpoint err.   □

4   Simulation Relations in LBE with Invariants

Given a pair of programs $P = \langle Vars_P, CP_P, en_P, err_P, E_P, \tau_P \rangle$ and $Q = \langle Vars_Q, CP_Q, en_Q, err_Q, E_Q, \tau_Q \rangle$. A simulation relation between P and Q specifies a matching of every program behavior of Q by some program behavior of P. In LBE, finding simulation relations is the two-steps procedure. First, it requires finding a simulation σ at the level of $CPGs$ (further referred to as *CPG-simulation*). Second, it requires finding a simulation ρ at the level of pairs of CPG-edges (further referred to as *edge-simulation*).

Definition 3. *Given two programs P and Q, we say that CPG_P simulates CPG_Q iff there exists a left-total relation $\sigma : CP_Q \to CP_P$ such that:*

$$\forall u_Q, v_Q \in CP_Q, u_P \in CP_P \,.\, (u_Q, v_Q) \in E_Q \wedge u_P = \sigma(u_Q) \implies$$
$$\exists v_P \in CP_P \,.\, (u_P, v_P) \in E_P \wedge v_P = \sigma(v_Q) \tag{6}$$

---

[2] Here and later in the paper we assume no arithmetic overflow.

When clear from the context, we omit the subscripts from u_Q, v_Q, etc.

Definition 4. *Program P simulates program Q iff (1) CPG_P simulates CPG_Q via some σ, and (2) for that σ and some inductive invariant ψ of P, there exists a left-total relation $\rho : CP_Q \times CP_P \to Expr(Vars_Q \cup Vars_P)$ such that:*

$$\forall(u,v) \in E_Q . \left(\psi(\sigma(u))(\vec{y}) \wedge \rho(u, \sigma(u))(\vec{x}, \vec{y}) \wedge \tau_Q(u,v)(\vec{x}, \vec{x}') \implies \right.$$
$$\left. \exists \vec{y}' . \rho(v, \sigma(v))(\vec{x}', \vec{y}') \wedge \tau_P(\sigma(u), \sigma(v))(\vec{y}, \vec{y}') \right) \tag{7}$$

For each edge (u, v) in (7), the existential quantifier in front of $\vec{y}'$ is served to encode existence of a valuation of the variables in $V_P'(\sigma(v))$. In contrast, valuations of the variables $\vec{x}$, $\vec{x}'$, $\vec{y}$ respectively of $V_Q(u)$, $V_Q(v)$ and $V_P(\sigma(u))$ are implicitly universally quantified. Thus, for each $\vec{x}$ and $\vec{y}$ matched by $\rho(u, \sigma(u))$ and $\vec{x}'$, there should exists $\vec{y}'$ such that $\vec{x}'$ and $\vec{y}'$ are matched by $\rho(v, \sigma(v))$. Additionally, the pairs $\vec{x}$ and $\vec{x}'$, and $\vec{y}$ and $\vec{y}'$ should belong to valid behaviors corresponding to their transition relations $\tau_Q(u, v)$ and $\tau_P(\sigma(u), \sigma(v))$ respectively. Note that those transition-relation formulas are conjoined with the different sides of the implication, so the validity of the $\forall\exists$-formula means that each behavior of $\tau_Q(u, v)$ is matched by a behavior of $\tau_P(\sigma(u), \sigma(v))$ (but it is still allowed to have unmatched behaviors of $\tau_P(\sigma(u), \sigma(v))$). For this, the simulation relation induced by formulas $\rho(u, \sigma(u))$ and $\rho(v, \sigma(v))$ is required to be left-total.

Whenever for a given pair of programs P and Q, there exists the pair of relations $\langle \sigma, \rho \rangle$ such that P simulates Q, we write $Q \preceq_{\langle \sigma, \rho \rangle} P$, or simply $Q \preceq P$ if $\langle \sigma, \rho \rangle$ are clear from the context.

It is important to note that our definition of simulation relation exploits an inductive invariant ψ of P that over-approximates the sets of reachable states for each cutpoint of P. In particular, for each CPG-edge (u, v) of Q, the condition of Definition 4 restricts the set of pre-states of $\tau_P(\sigma(u), \sigma(v))$ on $\psi(\sigma(u))$. Such restriction is sound, since it does not drop any behavioral information of P that can be potentially useful while constructing and checking a simulation of Q. Furthermore, for each behavior of Q requiring to be matched by some behavior of P, the invariant ψ reduces the search space of this matching.

Simulations are used to lift the proofs between programs. In fact, if the error location err_P is proven unreachable in P, and P simulates Q, then the error location err_Q is unreachable in Q. Interestingly, this fact can be further propagated to the level of inductive invariants [22,26] making the following lemma hold:

Lemma 2. *Given programs P and Q, let ψ be a (safe) inductive invariant of P and $Q \preceq_{\langle \sigma, \rho \rangle} P$. Consider a mapping $\varphi : CP_Q \to Expr(Vars_Q)$ defined for each $u \in CP_Q$ such that:*

$$\varphi(u)(\vec{x}) \triangleq \exists \vec{y} . \rho(u, \sigma(u))(\vec{x}, \vec{y}) \wedge \psi(\sigma(u))(\vec{y}) \tag{8}$$

Then φ is a (safe) inductive invariant of Q.

$$\tau_{Q_0} = \begin{cases} (en, CP_0) \mapsto (y' = 0) \\ (CP_0, CP_0) \mapsto ((y = 12 \wedge y' = y + 2) \vee (y \neq 12 \wedge y' = y + 1)) \\ (CP_0, err) \mapsto ((y' = y) \wedge (y' < 0 \vee y' = 13)) \end{cases}$$

$$\sigma = \begin{cases} en \mapsto en \\ CP_0 \mapsto CP_0 \\ err \mapsto err \end{cases} \qquad \rho = \begin{cases} (en, \sigma(en)) \mapsto \top \\ (CP_0, \sigma(CP_0)) \mapsto (x = y) \\ (err, \sigma(err)) \mapsto (x = y) \end{cases}$$

$$|\varphi| = \begin{cases} en \mapsto \top \\ CP_0 \mapsto \exists x . (x = y \wedge x \geq 0) \\ err \mapsto \exists x . (x = y \wedge x = 13) \end{cases} \qquad \widehat{\varphi} = \begin{cases} en \mapsto \top \\ CP_0 \mapsto (y \geq 0 \wedge y \neq 13) \\ err \mapsto \bot \end{cases}$$

Fig. 4. Simulation relation between Q_0 and βP_0, and lifted invariants.

$$\tau_{Q_1} = \begin{cases} (en, CP_0) \mapsto (z' = 0) \\ (CP_0, CP_0) \mapsto (z < 12 \wedge z' = z + 1) \\ (CP_0, CP_1) \mapsto (z = 12 \wedge z' = z + 2) \\ (CP_1, CP_1) \mapsto (z > 12 \wedge z' = z + 1) \\ (CP_0, err) \mapsto ((z' = z) \wedge (z' < 0 \vee z' = 13)) \end{cases} \qquad \sigma = \begin{cases} en \mapsto en \\ CP_0 \mapsto CP_0 \\ CP_1 \mapsto CP_0 \\ err \mapsto err \end{cases}$$

$$\rho = \begin{cases} (en, \sigma(en)) \mapsto \top \\ (CP_0, \sigma(CP_0)) \mapsto (y = z) \\ (CP_0, \sigma(CP_0)) \mapsto (y = z) \\ (err, \sigma(err)) \mapsto (y = z) \end{cases} \qquad \widehat{\pi} = \begin{cases} en \mapsto \top \\ CP_0 \mapsto (z \geq 0 \wedge z \neq 13) \\ CP_1 \mapsto (z \geq 0 \wedge z \neq 13) \\ err \mapsto \bot \end{cases}$$

Fig. 5. Simulation relation between Q_1 and Q_0, and lifted invariants.

Example 2. Suppose that P_0 (shown in Fig. 1(a)) evolved to a "lucky" program Q_0 (shown in Figs. 1(b), 2(b)) such that the counter jumps over the value "13": the new variable y appeared instead of x, and the program fragment corresponding to the looping edge (CF_0, CF_0) is replaced by if (y==12) then {y=y+2} else {y++}. More importantly, the property to hold in Q_0 is stronger than the one in P_1: in addition to be positive, y is restricted to be not equal to 13. CPG_{P_0} and CPG_{Q_0} are identical. Note that $Q_0 \not\preceq P_0$, $Q_0 \not\preceq \alpha P_0$, but $Q_0 \preceq \beta P_0$. Figure 4 shows: (1) transition relation τ_{Q_0}, (2) CPG-simulation between Q_0 and P_0 via the *identity* relation σ; (3) edge-simulation between Q_0 and βP_0 via ρ, (4) lifted inductive (but not safe) invariant $|\varphi|$ labeling each cutpoint in CP of Q_0, and (5) proof $\widehat{\varphi}$ of Q_0 obtained from $|\varphi|$ by some strengthening procedure.   □

In order to obtain the inductive invariant $|\varphi|$ for Example 2, we first need to weaken $\widehat{\psi}$ (as in Example 1) to be an inductive invariant of βP_0. Weakening can be done, e.g., by replacing the labeling $\widehat{\psi}(err)$ by a formula $x = 13$. Then $|\varphi|$ can be strengthened to $\widehat{\varphi}$ using an induction-based model checker to become safe.

Example 3. Consider a loop-splitting optimization Q_1 of Q_0 (shown in Figs. 1(c) and 2(c) respectively) produced by inserting an if-conditional out of the while-loop and a renaming of y to z. Thus, an extra loop (and an extra cutpoint CP_1) appeared in Q_1, but both loops were simplified to contain only an increment z++. Note that $Q_1 \preceq Q_0$. Figure 5 shows: (1) transition relation τ_{Q_1}, (2) CPG-simulation between Q_1 and Q_0 via σ, (3) edge-simulation between for Q_1 and Q_0 via ρ, and (4) lifted inductive (and safe) invariant $\widehat{\pi}$ of Q_1.   □

In the next section we elaborate on the way of computing simulation relations and lifting proofs, the results of which were demonstrated in Examples 2 and 3.

5   Property Directed Equivalence

Our key result is a new technique that exploits both, the *reusable specification* and the *relational specification*, to incrementally verify pairs of programs. We instantiate reusable specifications by the safe inductive invariants, and relational specification by the simulation relations. To the best of our knowledge, PDE is unique in a sense that all the competitors in the scope of FIV operate either by reusable or by relational specifications, but not by both.

Given an abstraction αP of P and a proof $\widehat{\psi}$ of P, we say that αP is $\widehat{\psi}$-*safe* iff $\widehat{\psi}$ is also a proof of αP. Not every abstraction of P is $\widehat{\psi}$-safe, but there might exist several $\widehat{\psi}$-safe abstractions of P of different precision, and the most precise one of those is P itself. Formally, it is reflected in the following definition.

Definition 5. *Given a program P and a proof $\widehat{\psi}$, an abstraction $\alpha P = \langle Vars, CP, en, err, E, \tau_\alpha \rangle$ of P is $\widehat{\psi}$-safe iff the following holds:*

$$\forall (u, v) \in E \, . \, \widehat{\psi}(u)(\vec{x}) \wedge \tau_\alpha(u, v)(\vec{x}, \vec{x}') \implies \widehat{\psi}(v)(\vec{x}') \tag{9}$$

Definition 6. *Programs P and Q are $\widehat{\psi}$-equivalent iff there exists another program R such that $P \preceq R, Q \preceq R$, and $\widehat{\psi}$ is a proof of R.*

Note that Definition 6 allows R to be either P or Q, in cases when $\widehat{\psi}$ is a proof of P or Q, respectively. Similarly, R is allowed to be an abstraction of P or Q.

Example 4. Programs P_0 and Q_0 (shown in Fig. 1(a) and (b) respectively) are not $\widehat{\psi}$-equivalent, since we cannot find a $\widehat{\psi}$-safe abstraction of P_0 (αP_0 is $\widehat{\psi}$-safe, but $Q_0 \npreceq \alpha P_0$, and βP_0 is not $\widehat{\psi}$-safe). Contrary to them, Q_0 and Q_1 (shown in Fig. 1(b) and (c) respectively) are $\widehat{\psi}$-equivalent, since we have shown in Example 3 that $Q_1 \preceq Q_0$.   □

The FIV-problem for P, Q and $\widehat{\psi}$ can be formulated as establishing a $\widehat{\psi}$-equivalence between P and Q. In this paper, we want to provide not only a generic, but also an efficient solution to the FIV-problem. One crucial obstacle on the way towards efficiency is that the simulation synthesis in general requires more efforts for solving than needed to verify Q from scratch. However, PDE does not require Q to be simulated by the precise program P via some total $\langle \sigma, \rho \rangle$. Instead, PDE aims at finding a $\widehat{\psi}$-safe abstraction αP that simulates Q via some abstract $\langle \sigma, \rho_\alpha \rangle$. Detecting ρ_α is expected to be easier than detecting ρ and to have more chances to converge.

Theorem 1. *Given programs P, αP and Q, let $\widehat{\psi}$ be a proof of P, and αP be a $\widehat{\psi}$-safe abstraction of P. If $Q \preceq \alpha P$ then P and Q are $\widehat{\psi}$-equivalent.*

The tie that binds the abstraction and the simulation in Theorem 1 is the proof $\widehat{\psi}$. In practice, synthesis of αP and $\langle \sigma, \rho_\alpha \rangle$ benefits from the guidance by $\widehat{\psi}$. Furthermore, when discovered, $\langle \sigma, \rho_\alpha \rangle$ is directly used to migrate $\widehat{\psi}$ from P to Q. In the rest of the section, we elaborate on these routines in more detail.

5.1   Simulation Synthesis

In our previous work [16], we presented SimAbs, the first algorithm to synthesize simulation relations completely automatically. Given programs P and Q, SimAbs attempts to deliver a total simulation relation[3] $\langle \sigma, \rho \rangle$ between P and Q such that $Q \preceq_{\langle \sigma, \rho \rangle} P$. If such *concrete* simulation cannot be found, SimAbs iteratively performs abstraction-refinement reasoning to detect an *abstract simulation*, i.e., an abstraction αP of P that simulates Q via some $\langle \sigma, \rho_\alpha \rangle$.

However, the results of SimAbs are not always useful for PDE, since it does not provide any guarantees of the strength and the property preservation of αP. In particular, SimAbs can unadvisedly abstract away some important details of P, so αP becomes not $\widehat{\psi}$-safe, and Theorem 1 becomes inapplicable. In this section, we present a novel algorithm ASSI that guides the simulation discovery by the invariants of P. Furthermore, ASSI supports a more general case when $CPG_Q \preceq_\sigma CPG_P$, and σ is not necessarily the identity relation. We outline ASSI and highlight its distinguishing features in Algorithm 1.

Synthesizing a CPG-simulation. The algorithm starts (lines 2–9) with synthesizing a CPG-simulation σ. It maintains a temporary graph G which is expected to be equivalent to CPG_P and by the end of the algorithm to become a supergraph of CPG_Q. Thus, G is initiated by CPG_P, and in the first iteration, ASSI checks whether G is a supergraph of CPG_Q. If the check succeeds, CPG_P simulates CPG_Q via identity, and ASSI directly proceeds to synthesizing ρ.

If G is not a supergraph of CPG_Q then ASSI attempts to *grow* G by introducing redundant nodes and edges, thus ensuring that G remains equivalent to CPG_P. The method CloneLoops has a relatively straightforward meaning: it finds a node in G with a looping edge (u, u), creates a new node u' and an edge (u', u'). Finally, it clones all the outgoing edges of u: (u, v) to (u', v) and all incoming edges of u: (v, u) to (v, u'). The information that u' obtains after copying u is book-kept and further used to recurrently create σ.

Checking whether one graph is a supergraph of another one is reduced to checking CPG-simulation via the identity relation and in turn to checking validity of the $\forall\exists$-formula (6). However, in the worst-case scenario, the procedure of cloning loops may keep iterating forever. Therefore, in practice, it makes sense to bound the iterations either by using some maximal number of cloned loops or by a timeout (method CanGrow).

The algorithm gets another challenge when Q has multiple loops that would require cloning different loops in a branch-and-bound manner. In general, it may lead to establishing multiple possible CPG-simulations, and each of those could be used to further establish its own edge-simulation ρ. To simplify presentation, we do not consider this case in the paper and assume that it is a rather engineering question of enhancing ASSI with backtracking to support multiple simulations.

---

[3] σ is limited to be the identity relation in the original algorithm.

Algorithm 1. ASSI (Q, P, ψ)

Input: programs Q and P, inductive invariant ψ of P
Output: abstraction αP, relation $\langle \sigma, \rho_\alpha \rangle$ such that $Q \preceq_{\langle \sigma, \rho_\alpha \rangle} \alpha P$
Data: universal abstraction $\mathbb{U}$, temporary graph G

```
1  G ← CPG_P;
2  while (⊤) do                                              ▷ Synthesize σ
3     if (ISSUPERGRAPH(G, CPG_Q)) then                ▷ Wait until G is big enough
4        σ ← GROWINGHISTORY(CPG_P, G);    ▷ Restore all changes in G since CPG_P
5        break;                                          ▷ And go to line 10
6     if (CANGROW(G)) then                          ▷ If G does not cover CPG_Q
7        G ← CLONELOOPS(G);                      ▷ Try growing G by cloning loops
8     else                                  ▷ Until no more loops can be cloned
9        return U, ∅;                             ▷ Or a timeout is exceeded
10 while (⊤) do                                  ▷ Use σ to synthesize ρ
11    ρ ← GUESS(P, Q, σ);         ▷ Guess some relation ρ over variables at each cutpoint
12    if (Q ⪯_{⟨σ,ρ⟩} P) then              ▷ Use ρ and σ in (7) and check ∀∃-validity
13       return P, ⟨ρ, σ⟩;         ▷ If ρ is an edge-simulation then the algorithm terminates
14    else                        ▷ If not, iteratively replace P by some of its abstractions:
15       P ← ABSTRACT(P, ψ);                  ▷ Try α^ψ first, then α^{ψ∃}
```

Algorithm 2. PDE $(P, Q, \widehat{\psi})$

Input: Programs P and Q, proof $\widehat{\psi}$ of P
Output: Verification result $res \in \{\text{SAFE}, \text{BUGGY}\}$, proof $\widehat{\varphi}$ of Q

```
1  αP, ⟨σ, ρ_α⟩ ← ASSI (Q, P, ψ̂);                  ▷ Find αP such that Q ⪯ αP
2  if (ISPSISAFE(αP, ψ̂)) then                          ▷ Check if (9) holds
3     return ⟨SAFE, ∃⟨σ, ρ_α⟩ψ̂⟩;    ▷ If αP is ψ̂-safe then lift the proof completely (Theorem 1)
4  else                              ▷ If not, attempt to lift the proof partially
5     |ψ| ← WEAKEN(ψ̂);         ▷ Weaken ψ̂ to |ψ| such that |ψ| is inductive for αP
6     |φ| ← ∃⟨σ, ρ_α⟩|ψ|;      ▷ Lift |ψ| to |φ| such that |φ| is inductive for Q (Lemma 2)
7     return VERIFY(Q, |φ|);    ▷ Strengthen |φ| to become safe for Q (if possible)
```

Synthesizing an edge-simulation. The further reasoning of ASSI (lines 10–15) proceeds by finding an edge-simulation ρ. Note that at this point σ is already synthesized, and each pair of CPG-edges is fixed due to valid $\forall\exists$-formula (6). Now, ASSI has to iteratively decide validity of another set of $\forall\exists$-formulas (7). Each such formula requires a guessed relation ρ over *live* variables at each pair of cutpoints matched by σ. ASSI makes a guess based on similarity (ideally, equality) of the variable names.

In cases when there is an invalid formula among (7), ASSI attempts to lower the precision of P by abstracting some (preferably, minimal amount of) details away. Intuitively, the goal is to weaken τ_P which is placed on the right-hand-side of the $\forall\exists$-formula such that the formula becomes valid. In general, ASSI is parametrized by the method ABSTRACT which performs such weakening automatically.

Due to an infinite number of possible abstractions, an arbitrary chosen implementation of ABSTRACT might not converge. The most distinguishing feature of ASSI compared to SIMABS, is that it guides the whole process of edge-simulation synthesis by invariants. That is, an invariant ψ is not only plugged into the formulas (7), but also used to create the abstraction $\alpha^\psi P$ (defined in Lemma 1). In practice, $\alpha^\psi P$ dramatically weakens τ_P, and ASSI earns much higher number of valid $\forall\exists$-formulas than SIMABS earns from the existential abstraction $\alpha^\exists P$ [11]. The latter simply treats some program variables nondeterministically and does not change the transition relation itself.

Since depending on the semantic delta between P and Q, the simulation check between Q and $\alpha^\psi P$ is still not guaranteed to succeed. In such cases, the other variants of ABSTRACT (e.g., the existential abstraction $\alpha^\exists$) might come in handy. In our implementation, we apply $\alpha^\exists$ to the result of a previous application of $\alpha^{\widehat\psi}$, thus delivering *not* $\widehat\psi$-safe abstractions of P (denoted $\alpha^{\widehat\psi\exists}P$).

Contrary to SIMABS, ASSI lacks a so called *Skolem-based refinement* that would attempt strengthening of abstract simulations, but still would not guarantee any success. But since ASSI is designed to deal with PDE, a necessary strengthening is performed on the level of proof generation. In the next Sect. 5.2, we show how weak abstractions could be still useful for lifting proofs partially.

5.2 Lifting Proofs Completely and Partially

The main practical importance of PDE is that it allows lifting a proof $\widehat\psi$ of program P directly to a proof $\widehat\varphi$ of program Q if there exists a $\widehat\psi$-safe abstraction of P that simulates Q (recall Theorem 1). In such a case, no additional analysis of Q is required unless one wants to eliminate existential quantifiers from the adapted proof. However, if the conditions of Theorem 1 are not met, we are still interested in accelerating the verification process for Q. In particular, if the detected abstraction αP of P is not $\widehat\psi$-safe, we still may be able to lift some (not safe, but) inductive invariant to be further strengthened by a Horn-clause-based model checker.

We address the problem of verifying Q using P and $\widehat\psi$. Our solution is outlined in Algorithm 2. PDE proceeds as follows. First (line 1) it invokes the two-steps procedure of ASSI: (1) obtaining a relation σ between cutpoints of P and Q via iterative growing of CPG_P and checking validity of the implication (6); (2) discovering an abstraction αP of P and a relation ρ_α such that $Q \preceq_{\langle\sigma,\rho_\alpha\rangle} \alpha P$.

The discovered abstraction αP is then checked for being $\widehat\psi$-safe (line 2). This is done by deciding validity of a set of implications (9) for each edge of CPG_P. If this check succeeds then the simulation relation ρ_α discovered by means of ASSI is combined with $\widehat\psi$ using existential quantification to obtain an inductive invariant $\exists\langle\sigma,\rho_\alpha\rangle\widehat\psi$ (a shortcut for the invariant defined in Lemma 2). By Theorem 1, $\exists\langle\sigma,\rho_\alpha\rangle\widehat\psi$ is also a *safe* inductive invariant, which entails that the program Q is safe.

If the abstraction αP delivered by ASSI is not $\widehat\psi$-safe then ρ_α cannot be directly used to lift invariants. But since $P \preceq \alpha P$ via the identity relation, $\widehat\psi$

can be weakened to become an inductive invariant $|\psi|$ of αP (line 5). Method WEAKEN can implement different methods including simple generation of the strongest postcondition (as in Example 5), or a counter-example-guided inductive weakening (method MKIND [15]) that constructs an inductive invariant out of a set of conjunctions of candidate formulas (also referred to as *lemmas*).

MKIND performs inductive weakening using an incremental SMT solver. MKIND assumes that each candidate invariant is represented by a conjunction of lemmas, and the weakening by itself is performed by dropping some lemmas from this conjunction. MKIND iterates over the set of CPG-edges in the Weak Topological Ordering [8] (in which inner loops are traversed before outer loops). For each edge, MKIND checks whether $\widehat{\psi}$ is inductive (i.e., formula (2) holds). If the check for some edge (u, v) fails, MKIND uses a counter-example provided by the SMT solver to identify all lemmas to be dropped from $\widehat{\psi}(v)$. Afterwards, the check is propagated to all the CPG-edges (v, w) outgoing from v. Effectiveness of MKIND requires the sets of candidate invariants to contain many small lemmas.

Example 5. Consider programs P_0 and Q_0 (shown in Fig. 1(a) and (b) respectively). Suppose, P_0 is verified and has a proof $\widehat{\psi}$ (shown in Fig. 3). Let us show how PDE operates in order to derive the proof $\widehat{\varphi}$ of Q_0 (envisioned in Fig. 4). First, PDE invokes ASSI to iteratively abstract P_0, e.g., to αP_0 and to βP_0 (both shown in Fig. 3) and check whether the abstraction simulates Q_0: the former does not, but the latter does. Second, PDE confirms that βP_0 is not $\widehat{\psi}$-safe and thus attempts to lift the proof partially.

The next step is to do WEAKEN and to obtain the inductive invariant $|\psi|$ of βP_0. For this, PDE exploits the efforts spent on checking that βP_0 is not $\widehat{\psi}$-safe. In particular, for all CPG-edges for which that check succeeded, the invariants at the pre- and post-states remain the same as specified by $\widehat{\psi}$ (i.e., $\widehat{\psi}(CP_0) = |\psi|(CP_0)$). But $\widehat{\psi}$ is broken for the edge (CP_0, err), i.e., the implication $(x \geq 0) \wedge ((x < 0) \vee (x = 13)) \implies \bot$ is invalid. This means that $\bot$ is too strong to label err in $|\psi|$, and a weaker formula should be discovered. Following MKIND, the labeling $|\psi|$ of cutpoint err would be aggressively assigned to $\top$, which would in turn require re-verification of Q_0 from scratch.

Alternatively, it can be assigned to $|\psi|(err) = (x = 13)$, which is the strongest postcondition for $\tau_{\beta P_0}(CP_0, err) = (x < 0) \vee (x = 13)$ and precondition $|\psi|(CP_0) = (x \geq 0)$. It is easy to see that $|\psi|$ constitutes an inductive invariant $|\psi|$ of βP_0. Finally, $|\psi|$ is lifted to become inductive invariant $|\varphi|$ (shown in Fig. 4) of Q_0 using the already established abstract simulation ρ_α.   □

The last bit in PDE is done by method VERIFY (line 7). At that stage, the partially lifted invariant $\exists \langle \sigma, \rho_\alpha \rangle |\psi|$ needs to be strengthened to finally become a proof of Q. Method VERIFY can exploit an off-the-shelf model checker as long as it is able to fight against the following two challenges. First, the model checker should deal with induction and avoid re-verifying Q from scratch. Second, the model checker should deal with existentially quantified variables of P and avoid expensive quantifier elimination.

5.3 Finding Inductive Invariants Without Quantifier Elimination

In this section, we focus on method VERIFY that strengthens an inductive invariant $\exists\langle\sigma,\rho_\alpha\rangle\psi$ for PDE. The key idea is based on the fact that adding invariants to the transition relation does not affect any behaviors of the program. In a nutshell, the invariants are extra constraints about pre- and post-states of each CPG-edge $(u,v) \in E$.

Given $(u,v) \in E$ and $\tau : E \to Expr(V(u) \cup V'(v))$, let $\widehat{\tau} : E \to Expr(V(u) \cup V'(v))$ denote the relation constrained by the invariants $\exists\langle\sigma,\rho_\alpha\rangle\psi$, i.e.:

$$\widehat{\tau}(u,v) = \exists\vec{y}.\rho_\alpha\big(u,\sigma(u)\big)(\vec{x},\vec{y}) \wedge \psi(u)(\vec{y}) \wedge \tau(u,v)(\vec{x},\vec{x}') \wedge \\ \exists\vec{y}'.\rho_\alpha\big(v,\sigma(v)\big)(\vec{x}',\vec{y}') \wedge \psi(v)(\vec{y}') \tag{10}$$

It is easy to see that a program $\widehat{Q} = \langle Vars, CP, en, err, E, \widehat{\tau}\rangle$ is equivalent to program $Q = \langle Vars, CP, en, err, E, \tau\rangle$, and the proof $\widehat{\psi}$ of Q is sufficient for $\widehat{Q}$. However, the opposite is not true, i.e., a proof $\widehat{\psi}$ of $\widehat{Q}$ might not be sufficient for Q.

Theorem 2. *Given Q and inductive invariant $\exists\langle\sigma,\rho_\alpha\rangle\psi$ of Q, let $\widehat{Q}$ be as in (10). If $\widehat{\varphi}$ is the proof of $\widehat{Q}$ then $\varphi = \widehat{\varphi} \wedge \exists\langle\sigma,\rho_\alpha\rangle\psi$ is the proof of Q.*

Method VERIFY reduces the task of obtaining $\widehat{\varphi}$ to solving a system of Constrained Horn Clauses [20]. This system consists of the rules that have a form (1), (2) or (3). The quantifier elimination is done lazily inside the solving engine. Note that such a model-checking approach is also applicable in cases when $\exists\langle\sigma,\rho_\alpha\rangle\psi$ is not only inductive, but also safe. If so, a constant mapping $\widehat{\varphi}(u,v) = \top$ for any (u,v) is a solution for the Horn system, and solving terminates immediately.

5.4 Calculating the Change Impact

In case when PDE (and in turn VERIFY) cannot prove safety (i.e., fails to strengthen the inductive invariant), it generates a so called *change impact* – an indication whether the change of the code in a particular edge of the CPG_P broke the proof. Change impact can be calculated cheaply as a by-product of checking whether an abstraction αP of P is $\widehat{\psi}$-safe for the proof $\widehat{\psi}$.

Definition 7. *Given P, Q, a proof $\widehat{\psi}$ of P and abstraction αP of P such that $Q \preceq_{\langle\sigma,\rho_\alpha\rangle} \alpha P$, the change impact δ of program Q is a mapping $\delta : E_Q \to \{\top,\bot\}$ such that for each $(u,v) \in E_Q$:*

$$\delta(u,v) \equiv \begin{cases} \top & \text{if } \widehat{\psi}(\sigma(u))(\vec{x}) \wedge \tau_\alpha\big(\sigma(u),\sigma(v)\big)(\vec{x},\vec{x}') \implies \widehat{\psi}(\sigma(v))(\vec{x}') \\ \bot & \text{else} \end{cases} \tag{11}$$

If calculated this way, the change impact is precise enough to indicate all CPG-edges that are responsible for a property violation. Together with a counter-example witnessing the property violation, the change impact is a step towards shrinking the search space of a possible bugfix.

Let us denote the set of edges $\Delta = \{(u,v) \in E_Q \mid \delta(u,v) = \bot\}$. In order to fix the given bug, the encoding τ of some of the CPG-edges from Δ must be rewritten, but the encoding τ of the edges in $E_Q \setminus \Delta$ can remain unchanged. In other words, program Q can be used to create a *partial program* Q_Δ that preserves the encoding of the edges $E_Q \setminus \Delta$ and contains *holes* to represent the absence of the encoding of Δ. Then, such a partial program Q_Δ is given as input to a program synthesizer, such as SKETCH [32] to automatically find instantiations of the holes. In our future work we plan to integrate an automatic program repairer with PDE.

6   Evaluating ASSI and PDE

We built PDE on the top of the model checker UFO [1] and the simulation synthesizer SIMABS. UFO relies on LLVM to create verification conditions for the input programs that involves inlining procedures, lowering memory to registers, extracting a CPG-representation. UFO synthesizes a proof by running the PDR engine [23] implemented in Z3 [14].

We evaluate ASSI and PDE for benchmarks from SVCOMP[4]. We focus our attention only on safe programs, i.e., those for which it is possible to generate a proof $\widehat{\psi}$. We further consider a program transformation from an original version P to a transformed version Q. Finally, we use $\widehat{\psi}$ to (1) find an abstraction αP of P that simulates Q via some ρ_α, (2) check whether αP is $\widehat{\psi}$-safe, and (3) use $\widehat{\psi}$ and ρ_α to incrementally verify Q.

One of the essential applications of discovering simulation relations is proving correctness of program optimizations. The users often perform optimizations and refactoring manually, and usually end up with the semantically different programs. Similarly, optimizations are performed *silently*, by compilers. PDE is insensitive to the source of program transformation and could be applicable to both types of optimizations. In our experiments, we focused on compiler optimizations, as a larger base of benchmarks.

For evaluation, we used two non-trivial LLVM-optimizations: `indvars` and `licm`. The `indvars` (stands for *Canonicalize Induction Variables*) transforms the loops to have a single canonical induction variable initially assigned to zero and being incremented by one. The `licm` (stands for *Loop Invariant Code Motion*) detects loop invariants and moves them outside of the loop body. Note that the combination of these optimizations is aggressive, and does not necessarily preserve the loop structure of the given program. We considered 115 programs, for which UFO is able to discover a proof $\widehat{\psi}$ within a given timeout of 700 s, and the correspondent LLVM-optimizations. The size of the programs ranges from 91 to 2904 lines of code, and the syntactic delta between versions ranges from 3 to 345 instructions.

---

[4] Software Verification Competition, http://sv-comp.sosy-lab.org/.

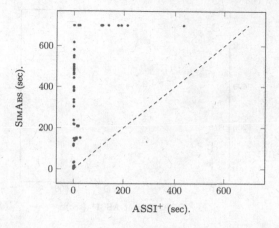

Fig. 6. Simulation synthesis by ASSI$^+$ compared to SIMABS.

Evaluating ASSI. We compared our novel algorithm ASSI$^+$ with SIMABS (Fig. 6). In our experiment[5], SIMABS delivers precise simulations only in 13 cases, and this result can be interpreted as the *absolute equivalence* between the original and the optimized programs. In 38 more cases, SIMABS ended up with an abstraction of P that simulates Q In the remaining 64 cases, SIMABS exceeds the timeout or diverged.

In contrast to SIMABS, ASSI$^+$ adds $\widehat{\psi}$ to the low-level $\forall\exists$-formulas and manipulates directly with the $\widehat{\psi}$-safe abstraction $\alpha^{\widehat{\psi}}P$ of P. These two improvements made the low-level $\forall\exists$-formulas smaller, as encoding of the original transition relation of P got replaced by more compact formulas representing $\widehat{\psi}$. All 115 experiments terminated. There were 39 $\widehat{\psi}$-safe abstractions (i.e., that are used to adapt the proof completely); 55 weaker abstractions (i.e., that are used to adapt the proof at least partially), and only 21 abstractions were trivial (i.e., too weak to adapt any invariant). Performance-wise, ASSI$^+$ was in order of magnitude faster than SIMABS, and in some cases outperformed its competitor by 2000**X**.

One can observe an interesting phenomenon that despite ASSI$^+$ never delivers concrete simulations, it is in general more precise than SIMABS. It can be explained by the fact that ASSI$^+$ is able to safely ignore some details of P that can break simulation synthesis in SIMABS. It is important to note that in cases when αP is trivial, ASSI$^+$ does not produce big overhead. In our experiments, the running time for such scenarios is less than 10 s.

Evaluating PDE. We compared the performance of PDE with the performance of the model checker UFO that verifies the optimized program from scratch (shown in the upper chart of Fig. 7). Provided with the proof and the abstract simulation, PDE outperformed UFO in 90 out of 115 cases. In the remaining cases, the performed optimizations dramatically simplified the program so it became easier to verify the optimized program from scratch.

---

[5] Full results are available at http://www.inf.usi.ch/phd/fedyukovich/niagara.

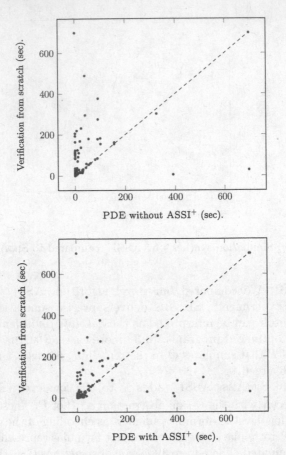

Fig. 7. Verification by PDE (with and without ASSI$^+$) compared to UFO.

Both simulation discovery and incremental verification (ASSI + PDE) were faster than UFO in 60 cases (shown in the lower chart of Fig. 7). This includes 1 case in which UFO exceeded timeout (i.e., PDE solved the problems that cannot be solved by UFO). In future, as a possible performance improvement, we may run ASSI + PDE and UFO in parallel, and terminate both processes whenever one of them returned a result. Thus, we can exploit benefits of incremental and non-incremental verification at the same time.

To summarize our case studies, we must mention that being an SMT-based framework, PDE currently supports only Linear Rational Arithmetic that makes it difficult to evaluate programs handling arrays, floating point arithmetic, bit-vectors and so on. PDE shown its potential to be the first working framework that is able to connect reusable and relational specifications of the versioned software, and we envision multiple improvements of its workflow in future.

7   Conclusion

In this paper, we formalized the concept of PDE that allows migrating safe inductive invariants across program transformations. We presented an algorithm ASSI for simulation relation synthesis with invariants and an algorithm PDE to address the FIV-problem using ASSI. We evaluated ASSI and PDE on the benchmarks from SVCOMP and LLVM-optimizations. It confirmed that in many cases when the absolute equivalence between programs cannot be proven, our approach is able to establish the property directed equivalence. In cases when the proof can be lifted only partially, our approach allows its further strengthening by means of a Horn-clause-based model checker.

References

1. Albarghouthi, A., Li, Y., Gurfinkel, A., Chechik, M.: UFO: a framework for abstraction- and interpolation-based software verification. In: Madhusudan, P., Seshia, S.A. (eds.) CAV 2012. LNCS, vol. 7358, pp. 672–678. Springer, Heidelberg (2012)
2. Backes, J., Person, S., Rungta, N., Tkachuk, O.: Regression verification using impact summaries. In: Bartocci, E., Ramakrishnan, C.R. (eds.) SPIN 2013. LNCS, vol. 7976, pp. 99–116. Springer, Heidelberg (2013)
3. Barrett, C.W., Fang, Y., Goldberg, B., Hu, Y., Pnueli, A., Zuck, L.D.: TVOC: a translation validator for optimizing compilers. In: Etessami, K., Rajamani, S.K. (eds.) CAV 2005. LNCS, vol. 3576, pp. 291–295. Springer, Heidelberg (2005)
4. Barthe, G., Crespo, J.M., Kunz, C.: Relational verification using product programs. In: Butler, M., Schulte, W, (eds.) FM 2011. LNCS, vol. 6664, pp. 200–214. Springer, Heidelberg (2011)
5. Berman, C.L., Trevillyan, L.H.: Functional comparison of logic designs for VLSI circuits. In: ICCAD, pp. 456–459. IEEE (1989)
6. Beyer, D., Cimatti, A., Griggio, A., Keremoglu, M.E., Sebastiani, R.: Software model checking via large-block encoding. In: FMCAD, pp. 25–32. IEEE (2009)
7. Beyer, D., Löwe, S., Novikov, E., Stahlbauer, A., Wendler, P.: Precision reuse for efficient regression verification. In: ESEC/FSE, pp. 389–399. ACM (2013)
8. Bourdoncle, F.A.: Efficient chaotic iteration strategies with widenings. In: Bjørner, D., Broy, M., Pottosin, I.V. (eds.) Formal Methods in Programming and Their Applications. LNCS, vol. 735, pp. 128–141. Springer, Heidelberg (1993)
9. Burch, J.R., Singhal, V.: Tight integration of combinational verification methods. In: ICCAD, pp. 570–576. IEEE (1998)
10. Clarke, E., Kroning, D., Lerda, F.: A tool for checking ANSI-C programs. In: Jensen, K., Podelski, A. (eds.) TACAS 2004. LNCS, vol. 2988, pp. 168–176. Springer, Heidelberg (2004)
11. Clarke, E.M., Grumberg, O., Long, D.E.: Model checking and abstraction. ACM Trans. Program. Lang. Syst. 16(5), 1512–1542 (1994)
12. Clarke, E.M., Kroening, D., Yorav, K.: Behavioral consistency of C and Verilog programs using bounded model checking. In: DAC, pp. 368–371. ACM (2003)

13. Conway, C.L., Namjoshi, K.S., Dams, D.R., Edwards, S.A.: Incremental algorithms for inter-procedural analysis of safety properties. In: Etessami, K., Rajamani, S.K. (eds.) CAV 2005. LNCS, vol. 3576, pp. 449–461. Springer, Heidelberg (2005)

14. de Moura, L., Bjørner, N.S.: Z3: an efficient SMT solver. In: Ramakrishnan, C.R., Rehof, J. (eds.) TACAS 2008. LNCS, vol. 4963, pp. 337–340. Springer, Heidelberg (2008)

15. Fedyukovich, G., Gurfinkel, A., Sharygina, N.: Incremental verification of compiler optimizations. In: Badger, J.M., Rozier, K.Y. (eds.) NFM 2014. LNCS, vol. 8430, pp. 300–306. Springer, Heidelberg (2014)

16. Fedyukovich, G., Gurfinkel, A., Sharygina, N.: Automated discovery of simulation between programs. In: Davis, M., Fehnker, A., McIver, A., Voronkov, A. (eds.) LPAR-20 2015. LNCS, vol. 9450, pp. 606–621. Springer, Heidelberg (2015). doi:10.1007/978-3-662-48899-7_42

17. Gjomemo, R., Namjoshi, K.S., Phung, P.H., Venkatakrishnan, V.N., Zuck, L.D.: From verification to optimizations. In: D'Souza, D., Lal, A., Larsen, K.G. (eds.) VMCAI 2015. LNCS, vol. 8931, pp. 300–317. Springer, Heidelberg (2015)

18. Godefroid, P., Lahiri, S.K., Rubio-González, C.: Statically validating must summaries for incremental compositional dynamic test generation. In: Yahav, E. (ed.) Static Analysis. LNCS, vol. 6887, pp. 112–128. Springer, Heidelberg (2011)

19. Godlin, B., Strichman, O.: Regression verification. In: DAC, pp. 466–471. ACM (2009)

20. Hoder, K., Bjørner, N.: Generalized property directed reachability. In: Cimatti, A., Sebastiani, R. (eds.) SAT 2012. LNCS, vol. 7317, pp. 157–171. Springer, Heidelberg (2012)

21. Kawaguchi, M., Lahiri, S.K., Rebelo, H.: Conditional equivalence. Technical report MSR-TR-2010-119, Microsoft Research (2010)

22. Kesten, Y., Pnueli, A.: Control and data abstraction: the cornerstones of practical formal verification. STTT 2(4), 328–342 (2000)

23. Komuravelli, A., Gurfinkel, A., Chaki, S.: SMT-based model checking for recursive programs. In: Biere, A., Bloem, R. (eds.) CAV 2014. LNCS, vol. 8559, pp. 17–34. Springer, Heidelberg (2014)

24. Leino, K.R.M., Wüstholz, V.: Fine-grained caching of verification results. In: Kroening, D., Păsăreanu, C.S. (eds.) CAV 2015. LNCS, vol. 9206, pp. 380–397. Springer, Heidelberg (2015)

25. Logozzo, F., Lahiri, S.K., Fähndrich, M., Blackshear, S.: Verification modulo versions: towards usable verification. In: PLDI, p. 32. ACM (2014)

26. Namjoshi, K.S.: Lifting temporal proofs through abstractions. In: Zuck, L.D., Attie, P.C., Cortesi, A., Mukhopadhyay, S. (eds.) VMCAI 2003. LNCS, vol. 2575, pp. 174–188. Springer, Heidelberg (2002)

27. Namjoshi, K.S., Zuck, L.D.: Witnessing program transformations. In: Logozzo, F., Fähndrich, M. (eds.) Static Analysis. LNCS, vol. 7935, pp. 304–323. Springer, Heidelberg (2013)

28. Necula, G.C.: Translation validation for an optimizing compiler. In: PLDI, pp. 83–94. ACM (2000)

29. Padon, O., Immerman, N., Shoham, S., Karbyshev, A., Sagiv, M.: Decidability of inferring inductive invariants. In: POPL, pp. 217–231. ACM (2016)

30. Paruthi, V., Kuehlmann, A.: Equivalence checking combining a structural SAT-solver, BDDs, and simulation. In: ICCD, pp. 459–464. IEEE (2000)

31. Sery, O., Fedyukovich, G., Sharygina, N.: Incremental upgrade checking by means of interpolation-based function summaries. In: FMCAD, pp. 114–121. IEEE (2012)
32. Solar-Lezama, A., Tancau, L., Bodík, R., Seshia, S.A., Saraswat, V.A.: Combinatorial sketching for finite programs. In: ASPLOS, pp. 404–415. ACM (2006)
33. Tristan, J., Govereau, P., Morrisett, G.: Evaluating value-graph translation validation for LLVM. In: PLDI, pp. 295–305. ACM (2011)
34. Yang, G., Khurshid, S., Person, S., Rungta, N.: Property differencing for incremental checking. In: ICSE, pp. 1059–1070. ACM (2014)

Combining Model Learning and Model Checking to Analyze TCP Implementations

Paul Fiterău-Broştean, Ramon Janssen, and Frits Vaandrager[(✉)]

Institute for Computing and Information Sciences,
Radboud University, P.O. Box 9010, 6500 GL Nijmegen, The Netherlands
F.Vaandrager@cs.ru.nl

Abstract. We combine model learning and model checking in a challenging case study involving Linux, Windows and FreeBSD implementations of TCP. We use model learning to infer models of different software components and then apply model checking to fully explore what may happen when these components (e.g. a Linux client and a Windows server) interact. Our analysis reveals several instances in which TCP implementations do not conform to their RFC specifications.

1 Introduction

Our society has become completely dependent on network and security protocols such as TCP/IP, SSH, TLS, BlueTooth, and EMV. Protocol specification or implementation errors may lead to security breaches or even complete network failures, and hence many studies have applied model checking to these protocols in order to find such errors. Since exhaustive model checking of protocol implementations is usually not feasible [24], two alternative approaches have been pursued in the literature. This article proposes a third approach.

A first approach, followed in many studies, is to use model checking for analysis of models that have been handcrafted starting from protocol standards. Through this approach many bugs have been detected, see e.g. [8,11,21,26,28, 45]. However, as observed in [10], the relationships between a handcrafted model of a protocol and the corresponding standard are typically obscure, undermining the reliability and relevance of the obtained verification results. In addition, implementations of protocols frequently do not conform to their specification. Bugs specific to an implementation can never be captured using this way of model checking. In [18], for instance, we showed that both the Windows 8 and Ubuntu 13.10 implementations of TCP violate the standard. In [40], new security flaws were found in three of the TLS implementations that were analyzed, all due

---

P. Fiterău-Broştean—Supported by NWO project 612.001.216, Active Learning of Security Protocols (ALSEP).

R. Janssen—Supported by STW project 13859, Supersizing Model-Based Testing (SUMBAT).

F. Vaandrager—Supported by STW project 11763, Integrating Testing And Learning of Interface Automata (ITALIA).

S. Chaudhuri and A. Farzan (Eds.): CAV 2016, Part II, LNCS 9780, pp. 454–471, 2016.
DOI: 10.1007/978-3-319-41540-6_25

to violations of the standard. In [13, 46] it was shown that implementations of a protocol for Internet banking and of SSH, respectively, violate their specification.

A second approach has been pioneered by Musuvathi and Engler [31]. Using the CMC model checker [32], they model checked the "hardest thing [they] could think of", the Linux kernel's implementation of TCP. Their idea was to run the *entire* Linux kernel as a CMC process. Transitions in the model checker correspond to events like calls from the upper layer, and sending and receiving packets. Each state of the resulting CMC model is around 250 kilobytes. Since CMC cannot exhaustively explore the state space, it focuses on exploring states that are the most different from previously explored states using various heuristics and by exploiting symmetries. Through their analysis, Musuvathi and Engler found four bugs in the Linux TCP implementation. One could argue that, according to textbook definitions of model checking [7, 17], what Musuvathi and Engler do is not model checking but rather a smart form of testing.

The approach we explore in this paper uses model learning. Model learning, or active automata learning [1, 6, 44], is emerging as a highly effective technique to obtain models of protocol implementations. In fact, all the standard violations reported in [13, 18, 40, 46] have been discovered (or reconfirmed) with the help of model learning. The goal of model learning is to obtain a state model of a black-box system by providing inputs to and observing outputs. This approach makes it possible to obtain models that fully correspond to the observed behavior of the implementation. Since the models are derived from a finite number of observations, we can (without additional assumptions) never be sure that they are correct: even when a model is consistent with all the observations up until today, we cannot exclude the possibility that there will be a discrepancy tomorrow. Nevertheless, through application of conformance testing algorithms [27], we may increase confidence in the correctness of the learned models. In many recent studies, state-of-the-art tools such as LearnLib [44] routinely succeeded to learn correct models efficiently. In the absence of a tractable white-box model of a protocol implementation, a learned model is often an excellent alternative that may be obtained at relatively low cost.

The main contribution of this paper is the combined application of model checking, model learning and abstraction techniques in a challenging case study involving Linux, Windows and FreeBSD implementations of TCP. Using model learning and abstraction we infer models of different software components and then apply model checking to explore what may happen when these components (e.g. a Linux client and a Windows server) interact.

The idea to combine model checking and model learning was pioneered in [36], under the name of *black box checking*. In [30], a similar methodology was introduced to use learning and model checking to obtain a strong model-based testing approach. Following [30, 36], model checkers are commonly used to analyze models obtained via automata learning. However, most of these applications only consider specifications of a single system component, and do not analyze networks of learned models. An exception is the work of Shahbaz and Groz [42] on integration testing, in which learned component models are composed and then analyzed using reachability analysis in order to find integration faults. Our results considerably extend our previous work on learning fragments of TCP [18] since we have (1) added inputs corresponding to calls from the upper layer, (2) added transmission of data, (3) inferred models of TCP clients in addition to servers, and (4) learned models for FreeBSD in addition to Windows and Linux. Abstraction is the key for scaling existing automata learning methods to realistic applications. In order to obtain tractable models we use the theory of abstractions from [2], which in turn is inspired by earlier work on predicate abstraction [16,29]. Our use of abstractions is similar to that of Cho et al. [14], who used abstractions to infer models of realistic botnet command and control protocols. Whereas in our previous studies on model learning the abstractions were implemented by ad-hoc Java programs, we now define them in a more systematic manner. We provide a language for defining abstractions, and from this definition we automatically generate mapper components for learning and model checking.

Our method may be viewed as a smart black-box testing approach that combines the strengths of model learning and model checking. The main advantage of our method compared to approaches in which models are handcrafted based on specifications is that we analyze the "real thing" and may find "bugs" in implementations. In fact, our analysis revealed several instances in which TCP implementations do not conform to the standard. Compared to the white-box approach of Musuvathi and Engler [31], our black-box method has several advantages. First of all, we obtain explicit component models that can be fully explored using model checking. Also, our method appears to be easier to apply and is more flexible. For instance, once we had learned a model of the Linux implementation it took just two days to learn a model of the Windows implementation. In the approach of [31], one first would need to get access to the proprietary code from Microsoft, and then start more or less from scratch from an entirely different code base. In contrast, using our approach it is possible to learn a model of any TCP implementation within a few days. Besides these practical benefits, there is also an important philosophical advantage. If one constructs a model of some real-world phenomenon or system and makes claims based on this model then, in line with Popper [37], we think this model ought to be falsifiable. Our model of the Windows8 TCP client is included in the paper in Fig. 2, and all Mealy machine and nuSMV models are available at http://www.sws.cs.ru.nl/publications/papers/fvaan/FJV16/. Our notion of state is clear and based on the Nerode congruence [33]: two traces lead to the same state unless there is a distinguishing suffix. Any researcher can study our models and point out mistakes. In contrast, the model of Musuvathi is specified implicitly through heuristics (when have we seen a state before?) that are programmed on top of the Linux implementation. As a result, falsification of their model is virtually impossible.

2 Background on Model Learning

Mealy Machines. During model learning, we represent protocol entities as Mealy machines. A *Mealy machine* is a tuple $\mathcal{M} = \langle I, O, Q, q^0, \rightarrow \rangle$, where I, O, and Q are finite sets of *input actions, output actions,* and *states,* respectively, $q^0 \in Q$ is the *initial state,* and $\to \subseteq Q \times I \times O \times Q$ is the *transition relation.* We write $q \xrightarrow{i/o} q'$ if $(q, i, o, q') \in \to$. We assume $\mathcal{M}$ to be *input enabled* (or *completely specified*) in the sense that, for each state q and input i, there is a transition $q \xrightarrow{i/o} q'$, for some o and q'. We call $\mathcal{M}$ *deterministic* if for each state q and input i there is exactly one output o and one state q' such that $q \xrightarrow{i/o} q'$. We call $\mathcal{M}$ *weakly deterministic* if for each state q, input i and output o there is exactly one state q' with $q \xrightarrow{i/o} q'$.

Let $\sigma = i_1 \cdots i_n \in I^*$ and $\rho = o_1 \cdots o_n \in O^*$. Then ρ is an *observation* triggered by σ in $\mathcal{M}$, notation $\rho \in A_{\mathcal{M}}(\sigma)$, if there are $q_0 \cdots q_n \in Q^*$ such that $q_0 = q^0$ and $q_{j-1} \xrightarrow{i_j/o_j} q_j$, for all j with $0 \leq j < n$. If $\mathcal{M}$ and $\mathcal{M}'$ are Mealy machines with the same inputs I and outputs O, then we write $\mathcal{M} \leq \mathcal{M}'$ if, for each $\sigma \in I^*$, $A_{\mathcal{M}}(\sigma) \subseteq A_{\mathcal{M}'}(\sigma)$. We say that $\mathcal{M}$ and $\mathcal{M}'$ are *(behaviorally) equivalent,* notation $\mathcal{M} \approx \mathcal{M}'$, if both $\mathcal{M} \leq \mathcal{M}'$ and $\mathcal{M}' \leq \mathcal{M}$.

If $\mathcal{M}$ is deterministic, then $A_{\mathcal{M}}(\sigma)$ is a singleton set for each input sequence σ. In this case, $\mathcal{M}$ can equivalently be represented as a structure $\langle I, O, Q, q^0, \delta, \lambda \rangle$, with $\delta : Q \times I \to Q$, $\lambda : Q \times I \to O$, and $q \xrightarrow{i/o} q' \Rightarrow \delta(q, i) = q' \wedge \lambda(q, i) = o$.

MAT Framework. The most efficient algorithms for model learning all follow the pattern of a *minimally adequate teacher (MAT)* as proposed by Angluin [6]. In the MAT framework, learning is viewed as a game in which a learner has to infer an unknown automaton by asking queries to a teacher. The teacher knows the automaton, which in our setting is a deterministic Mealy machine $\mathcal{M}$. Initially, the learner only knows the inputs I and outputs O of $\mathcal{M}$. The task of the learner is to learn $\mathcal{M}$ through two types of queries:

- With a *membership query,* the learner asks what the response is to an input sequence $\sigma \in I^*$. The teacher answers with the output sequence in $A_{\mathcal{M}}(\sigma)$.
- With an *equivalence query,* the learner asks whether a hypothesized Mealy machine $\mathcal{H}$ is correct, that is, whether $\mathcal{H} \approx \mathcal{M}$. The teacher answers *yes* if this is the case. Otherwise it answers *no* and supplies a *counterexample,* which is a sequence $\sigma \in I^*$ that triggers a different output sequence for both Mealy machines, that is, $A_{\mathcal{H}}(\sigma) \neq A_{\mathcal{M}}(\sigma)$.

Starting from Angluin's seminal L^* algorithm [6], many algorithms have been proposed for learning finite, deterministic Mealy machines via a finite number of queries. We refer to [23] for recent overview. In applications in which one wants to learn a model of a black-box reactive system, the teacher typically consists of a System Under Learning (SUL) that answers the membership queries, and a conformance testing tool [27] that approximates the equivalence queries using a set of *test queries.* A test query consists of asking to the SUL for the response to an input sequence $\sigma \in I^*$, similar to a membership query.

Abstraction. We recall relevant parts of the theory of abstractions from [2]. Existing model learning algorithms are only effective when applied to Mealy machines with small sets of inputs, e.g. fewer than 100 elements. Practical systems like TCP, however, typically have huge alphabets, since inputs and outputs carry parameters of type integer or string. In order to learn an over-approximation of a "large" Mealy machine $\mathcal{M}$, we place a transducer in between the teacher and the learner, which translates concrete inputs in I to abstract inputs in X, concrete outputs in O to abstract outputs in Y, and vice versa. This allows us to abstract a Mealy machine with concrete symbols in I and O to a Mealy machine with abstract symbols in X and Y, reducing the task of the learner to inferring a "small" abstract Mealy machine.

Formally, a *mapper* for inputs I and outputs O is a deterministic Mealy machine $\mathcal{A} = \langle I \cup O, X \cup Y, R, r_0, \delta, \lambda \rangle$, where I and O are disjoint sets of *concrete input and output symbols*, X and Y are disjoint sets of *abstract input and output symbols*, and $\lambda : R \times (I \cup O) \to (X \cup Y)$, the *abstraction function*, respects inputs and outputs, that is, for all $a \in I \cup O$ and $r \in R$, $a \in I \Leftrightarrow \lambda(r, a) \in X$.

Basically, the *abstraction* of Mealy machine $\mathcal{M}$ via mapper $\mathcal{A}$ is the Cartesian product of the underlying transition systems. Let $\mathcal{M} = \langle I, O, Q, q_0, \to_{\mathcal{M}} \rangle$ be a Mealy machine and let $\mathcal{A} = \langle I \cup O, X \cup Y, R, r_0, \delta_{\mathcal{A}}, \lambda_{\mathcal{A}} \rangle$ be a mapper. Then $\alpha_{\mathcal{A}}(\mathcal{M})$, the *abstraction of $\mathcal{M}$ via $\mathcal{A}$*, is the Mealy machine $\langle X, Y \cup \{\bot\}, Q \times R, (q_0, r_0), \to_\alpha \rangle$, where $\bot \notin Y$ is a fresh output and $\to_\alpha$ is given by the rules

$$\frac{q \xrightarrow{i/o}_{\mathcal{M}} q', \ r \xrightarrow{i/x}_{\mathcal{A}} r' \ \xrightarrow{o/y}_{\mathcal{A}} r''}{(q, r) \xrightarrow{x/y}_\alpha (q', r'')} \qquad \frac{\not\exists i \in I : r \xrightarrow{i/x}_{\mathcal{A}}}{(q, r) \xrightarrow{x/\bot}_\alpha (q, r)}$$

To understand how the mapper is utilized during learning, we follow the execution of a single input of a query. The learner produces an abstract input x, which it sends to the mapper. By inversely following abstraction function $\lambda_{\mathcal{A}}$, the mapper converts this to a concrete input i and updates its state via transition $r \xrightarrow{i/x}_{\mathcal{A}} r'$. The concrete input i is passed on to the teacher, which responds with a concrete output o according to $q \xrightarrow{i/o}_{\mathcal{M}} q'$. This triggers the transition $r' \xrightarrow{o/y}_{\mathcal{A}} r''$ in which the mapper generates the corresponding abstract output y and updates its state again. The abstract output is then returned to the learner.

We notice that the abstraction function is utilized invertedly when translating inputs. More precisely, the abstract input that the learner provides is an output for the mapper. The translation from abstract to concrete involves picking an arbitrary concrete value that corresponds with the given abstract value. It could be that multiple concrete values can be picked, in which case all values should lead to the same abstract behavior in order to learn a deterministic abstract model. It can also be that no values correspond to the input abstraction, in which case, by the second rule, $\bot$ is returned to the learner, without consulting the teacher. We define the *abstraction component* implementing $\alpha_{\mathcal{A}}$ as the transducer which follows from the mapper $\mathcal{A}$, but inverts the abstraction of inputs.

From the perspective of a learner, a teacher for $\mathcal{M}$ and abstraction component implementing $\alpha_{\mathcal{A}}$ together behave exactly like a teacher for $\alpha_{\mathcal{A}}(\mathcal{M})$. If $\alpha_{\mathcal{A}}(\mathcal{M})$ is deterministic, then the learner will eventually succeed in learning a deterministic machine $\mathcal{H}$ satisfying $\alpha_{\mathcal{A}}(\mathcal{M}) \approx \mathcal{H}$. In [2], also a *concretization* operator $\gamma_{\mathcal{A}}$ is defined. This operator is the adjoint of the abstraction operator: it turns any abstract machine $\mathcal{H}$ with symbols in X and Y into a concrete machine with symbols in I and O. If $\mathcal{H}$ is deterministic then $\gamma_{\mathcal{A}}(\mathcal{H})$ is weakly deterministic.

As shown in [2], $\alpha_{\mathcal{A}}(\mathcal{M}) \leq \mathcal{H}$ implies $\mathcal{M} \leq \gamma_{\mathcal{A}}(\mathcal{H})$. This tells us that when we apply mapper $\mathcal{A}$ during learning of some "large" Mealy machine $\mathcal{M}$, even though we may not be able to learn the behavior of $\mathcal{M}$ exactly, the concretization $\gamma_{\mathcal{A}}(\mathcal{H})$ of the learned abstract model $\mathcal{H}$ is an over-approximation of $\mathcal{M}$, that is, $\mathcal{M} \leq \gamma_{\mathcal{A}}(\mathcal{H})$. Similarly to the abstraction component, a *concretization component* for mapper $\mathcal{A}$ implements $\gamma_{\mathcal{A}}$. This component is again fully defined by a mapper, but handles abstraction of outputs invertedly. During model checking, the composition of the abstract model $\mathcal{H}$ and the concretization component for $\mathcal{A}$ provides us with an over-approximation of $\mathcal{M}$.

Framework for Mapper Definition. In order to apply our abstraction approach, we need an abstraction and a concretization component for a given mapper $\mathcal{A}$. We could implement these components separately in an arbitrary programming language, but then they would have to remain consistent with $\mathcal{A}$. Moreover, ensuring that translation in one component inverts the corresponding translation in the other is non-trivial, and difficult to maintain, as changes in one would have to be applied invertedly in the other.

We used an alternative approach, in which we first define a mapper and then derive the abstraction and concretization components automatically. To this end, we built a language for defining a mapper in terms of (finite) registers, and functions to encode transitions and outputs. Our language supports case distinctions with programming-style if-else-statements, and requires that every branch leads to exactly one output and updates registers exactly once, such that the translations are complete. Except for the restrictions of finiteness and determinism, our language has the expressiveness of a simple programming language and should thus be usable to abstract (and concretize reversely) a wide range of systems and protocols. Listing 1 shows the example of a mapper for a simple login system. The mapper stores the first password received, and compares subsequent passwords to it. The abstract passwords used by the learner are $\{true, false\}$, denoting a correct or incorrect password, respectively. At the first attempt, *true* invertedly maps to any concrete password, and *false* maps to $\perp$. Later on *true* invertedly maps to the value picked the first time, while *false* maps to any other value. For TCP, we define multiple abstraction functions for inputs and outputs, in terms of multiple parameters per input or output.

To derive the components, we need to implement the inverse of the abstraction function, for both inputs and outputs. This can be achieved using a constraint solver or by picking random concrete values and checking if they are translated to the sought after abstraction, by translating them with the mapper in the forward direction. The latter approach may be hard, as the concrete domain is usually very large. In addition to finding a corresponding concrete

Listing 1. A simple example mapper for a login system, in a simplified syntax

```
integer stored := −1;
map ENTER(integer password → boolean correct)
    if (stored = −1 ∧ password ≥ 0) ∨ stored = password then
        correct := true
    else
        correct := false
    end if
end map
update
    if stored = −1 ∧ password ≥ 0 then
        stored := password
    else
        stored := stored                    ▷ Every path explicitly assigns a value
    end if
end update
```

value, another purpose of executing abstractions invertedly is to test the abstraction: different possible values should lead to the same abstract behavior, as the learner cannot handle non-determinism. A constraint solver usually picks values in a very structured and deterministic way, which does not test the abstraction well. Picking concrete values randomly and checking the corresponding abstract value allows more control over obtaining a good test coverage, but is in general less scalable.

3   Learning Setup

3.1   TCP as a System Under Learning

In TCP there are two interacting entities, the *server* and the *client*, which communicate over a network through packets, comprising a header and application data. On both sides there is an application, initiating and using the connection through *socket calls*. Each entity is learned separately and is a SUL in the learning context. This SUL thus takes packets or socket calls as inputs. It can output packets or *timeout*, in case the system does not respond with any packet. RFC 793 [38] and its extensions, most notably [9,34], specify the protocol.

Packets are defined as tuples, comprising sequence and acknowledgement numbers, a payload and flags. By means of abstraction, we reduce the size of sequence and acknowledgement number spaces. Each socket call also defines an abstract and concrete input. Whereas packet configurations are the same for both client and server, socket calls differ. The server can *listen* for connections and *accept* them, whereas the client can actively *connect*. Both parties can *send* and *receive* data, or *close* an established connection (specifically, a half-duplex close [9, p. 88]). The server can additionally *close* its listening socket. Values returned by socket calls are not in the output alphabet to reduce setup complexity.

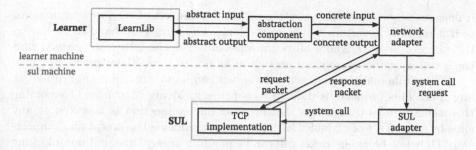

Fig. 1. Overview of the learning setup.

Figure 1 displays the learning setup used. The *learner* generates abstract inputs, representing packets or socket calls. The abstraction component concretizes each input by translating abstract parameters to concrete, and then updates its state. The concrete inputs are then passed on to the *network adapter*, which in turn transforms each input into a packet, sending it directly to the SUL, or into a socket call, which it issues to the SUL *adapter*. The SUL adapter runs on the same environment as the SUL and its sole role is to perform socket calls on the SUL. Each reponse packet generated by the SUL is received by the *network adapter*, which retrieves the concrete output from the packet or produces a *timeout* output, in case no packet was received within a predefined time interval. The output is then sent to the abstraction component, which computes the abstraction, updates its state again, and sends the abstract output to the learner.

The learner is based on LearnLib [39], a Java library implementing L^* based algorithms for learning Mealy machines. The abstraction component is also written in Java, and interprets and inverts a mapper. The network adapter is a Python program based on Scapy [41], Pcapy [35], and Impacket [22]. It uses Scapy to craft TCP packets, and Scapy together with a Pcapy and Impacket based sniffer to intercept responses. The network adapter is connected to the SUL adapter via a standard TCP connection. This connection is used for communicating socket calls to be made on the SUL. Finally, the SUL adapter is a program which performs socket calls on command, written in C to have low level access to socket options.

3.2   Viewing the SUL as a Mealy Machine

TCP implementations cannot be fully captured by Mealy Machines. To learn a model, we therefore need to apply some restrictions. As mentioned, the number of possible values for the sequence and acknowledgement numbers is reduced by means of abstractions. Furthermore, payload is limited to either 0 or 1 byte. Consequently, 1 byte of data is sent upon a *send*-call. Flags are limited to only the most interesting combinations, and we also abstract away from all other fields from the TCP layer or lower layers, allowing Scapy to pick default values.

TCP is also time-dependent. The SUL may, for instance, retransmit packets if they are not acknowledged within a specified time. The SUL may also reset if it does not receive the acknowledgement after a number of such retransmissions, or if it remains in certain states for too long. The former we handled by having the *network adapter* ignore all retransmissions. For the latter, we verified that the learning queries were short enough so as not to cause these resets.

TCP is inherently concurrent, as a server can handle multiple connections at any time. This property is difficult to capture in Mealy Machines. Overcoming this, the SUL adapter ensures that at most one connection is accepted at any time by using a set of variables for locking and unlocking the *accept* and *connect*-calls. Only one blocking socket call can be pending at any time, but non-blocking socket calls can always be called.

Furthermore, the backlog size parameter defines the number of connections to be queued up for an eventual *accept*-call by the server SUL. The model grows linearly with the this parameter, while only exposing repetitive behavior. For this reason we set the backlog to the value 1.

3.3   Technical Challenges

We overcame several technical challenges in order to learn models. Resetting the SUL and setting a proper timeout value are solved similarly to [18].

Our tooling for sniffing packets sometimes missed packets generated by the SUL, reporting erroneous *timeout* outputs. This induced non-deterministic behavior, as a packet may or may not be caught, depending on timing. Each observation is therefore repeated three times to ensure consistency. Consistent outputs are cached to speed up learning, and to check consistency with new observations. It also allows to restart learning with reuse of previous observations.

In order to remove time-dependent behavior we use several TCP settings. Most notably, we disable slow acknowledgements and enable quick acknowledgements where possible (on Linux and FreeBSD). The intuition is that we want the SUL to send acknowledgements whenever they can be issued, instead of delaying them. We also had to disable syn cookies in FreeBSD, as this option caused generation of the initial sequence number in a seemingly time dependent way, instead of using fresh values. For Linux, packets generated by a *send*-call were occasionaly merged with previous unacknowledged packets, so we could only learn a model by omitting *send*-call, although data packets could still be sent from the learner to the SUL.

3.4   Mapper Definition

The mapper is based on the work of Aarts et al. [5], and on the RFCs. Socket calls contain no parameters and do not need abstraction, so they are mapped simply with the identity relation. TCP packets are mapped by mapping their parameters individually. Flags are again retained by an identity relation. The sequence and acknowledgement numbers are mapped differently for inputs and outputs; input numbers are mapped to {*valid, invalid*}, and outputs are mapped to {*current, next, zero, fresh*}. After a connection is set up, the mapper keeps track of the sequence number which should be sent by the SUL and learner.

Valid inputs are picked according to this, whereas *current* and *next* represent repeated or incremented numbers, respectively. The abstract output *zero* simply denotes the concrete number zero, whereas *fresh* is used for all other numbers. If no connection is established, any sequence number is valid (as the RFCs then allow a fresh value), and the only valid acknowledgement number is zero.

Note that all concrete inputs with the same abstract value, should lead to an equivalent abstract behavior. Valid inputs are defined according to the RFC's. However, this is very hard for invalid inputs, as they may be accepted, ignored, they may lead to error recovery, or even undefined behavior. To learn the behavior for these inputs, abstractions should be defined precisely according to these behaviors, which is unfeasible to do by hand. As a result, we have excluded invalid inputs from the learning alphabet. To translate valid inputs, we first used a constraint solver which finds solutions for the transition relation. This is done by taking the disjunction of all path constraints, similar to symbolic execution techniques [25]. However, this did not test the abstraction well, as the constraint solver always picks zero if possible, for example. We therefore randomly picked concrete values to test with, and used values with the right corresponding abstract value, instead. Concrete values were picked with a higher probability if they were picked or observed previously during the same run, as well as the successors of those values. This approach sufficed to translate all values for our experiments.

4 Model Learning Results

Using the abstractions defined in Sect. 2, we learned models of the TCP client and server for Windows 8, Ubuntu 14.04 and FreeBSD 10.2. For testing we used the conformance testing algorithm described in [43] to generate efficient test suites which are parameterized by a middle section of length k. Generated exhaustively, these ensure learned model correctness, unless the respective implementation corresponds to a model with at least k more states. For each model, we first executed a random test suite with k of 4, up to 40000 tests for servers, and 20000 tests for clients. We then ran an exhaustive test suite with k of 2 for servers, respectively 3 for clients.

Table 1 describes the setting of each of these experiments together with statistics on learning and testing: (1) the number of states in the final model,

Table 1. Statistics for learning experiments

SUL		States	Hyp.	Memb. Queries	Tests to last Hyp.	Tests on last Hyp.
Client	Windows 8	13	2	1576	1322	50243
Server	Windows 8	38	10	11428	9549	65040
Client	Ubuntu 14.04	15	2	1974	15268	56174
Server	Ubuntu 14.04	57	14	17879	15681	66523
Client	FreeBSD 10.2	12	2	1456	1964	47387
Server	FreeBSD 10.2	55	18	22287	12084	75894

(2) the number of hypotheses found, (3) the total number of membership queries, (4) the total number of unique test queries run on the SUL before the last hypothesis, (5) the number of unique test queries run to validate the last hypothesis.

Figure 2 shows the model learned for the Windows 8 client. This model covers standard client behavior, namely connection setup, sending and receiving data and connection termination. Based on predefined access sequences, we identify each state with its analogous state in the RFC state diagram [38, p. 23], if such a state exists. Transitions taken during simulated communication between a Windows client and a server are colored green. These transitions were identified during model checking, on which we expand in Sect. 5.

Table 1 shows that the models for the Linux and FreeBSD servers have more states than for Windows, and all models have more states than described in the specification. We attribute this to several factors. We have already mentioned that model sizes grow linearly with the value of the backlog-parameter. While we set it to 1, the setting is overriden by operating system imposed minimum value of 2 for FreeBSD and Linux. Moreover, SUL behavior depends on blocking system calls and on whether the receive buffer is empty or not. Although specified, this is not modelled explicitly in the specification state diagram. As an example, the ESTABLISHED and CLOSE WAIT states from the standard each have multiple corresponding states in the model in Fig. 2.

Non-conformance of Implementations. Inspection of learned models revealed several cases of non-conformance to RFC's in the corresponding implementations.

A first non-conformance involves terminating an established connection with a CLOSE. The resulting output should contain a FIN if all data up to that point has been received. If there is data not yet received, the output should contain a RST, which would signal to the other side an aborted termination [9, p. 88]. Windows does not conform to this, as a CLOSE can generate a RST instead of a FIN even in cases where there is no data to be received, namely, in states where a RCV call is pending. Figure 2 marks this behavior in red. FreeBSD implementations are also non-compliant, as they always generate FIN packets on a CLOSE, regardless if all data has been received. This would arguably fall under the list of common bugs [34], namely "Failure to send a RST after Half Duplex Close". The learned Linux models fully comply to these specifications.

A second non-conformance has to do with the processing of SYN packets. On receiving a SYN packet in a synchronized state, if the sequence number is in "the window" (as it always is, in our case), the connection should be reset (via a corresponding RST packet) [38, p. 71]. Linux implementations conform for SYN packets but not for SYN+ACK packets, to which they respond by generating an acknowledgement with no change of state. Both Windows and FreeBSD respect this specification.

We note a final non-conformance in Windows implementations. In case the connection does not exist (CLOSED), a reset should be sent in response to any

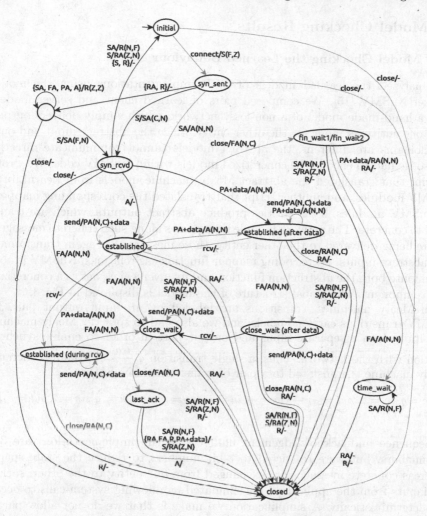

Fig. 2. Learned model for Windows 8 TCP Client. To reduce the size of the diagram, we eliminate all self loops with *timeout* outputs. We replace flags and abstractions by their capitalized initial letter, hence use *s* for *syn*, *a* for *ack*, *n* for *next*, etc. We omit input parameter abstractions, since they are the same for all packets, namely *valid* for both sequence and acknowledgement numbers. Finally, we group inputs that trigger a transition to the same state with the same output. Timeouts are denoted by '-'.

incoming packet except for another reset [38, p. 36], but Windows 8 sends nothing. FreeBSD can be configured to respond in a similar way to Windows, by changing the *blackhole setting*.[1] This behavior is claimed to provide "some degree of protention against stealth scans", and is thus intentional.

---

[1] https://www.freebsd.org/cgi/man.cgi?query=blackhole.

5   Model Checking Results

5.1   Model Checking the Learned Behaviour

We analyzed the learned models of TCP implementations using the model checker NuSMV [15]. We composed pairs of learned client and server models with a hand-made model of a non-lossy network, which simply delivers output from one entity as input for the other entity. Since the abstract input and output domains are different, the abstract models cannot communicate directly, and so we had to encode the concretized models within NuSMV code. We wrote a script that translated the abstract Mealy machine models from LearnLib to NuSMV modules, and another script that translated the corresponding mappers to NuSMV modules. TCP entities produce abstract outputs, which are translated to concrete. The network module then passes along such concrete messages. Before being delivered to the other entity, these messages are again transformed into abstract inputs. By encoding mapper functions as relations, NuSMV is able to compute both the abstraction function and its inverse, i.e., act as a concretization component. The global structure of the model is displayed in Fig. 3.

In Mealy machines, transitions are labeled by an input/output pair. In NuSMV transitions carry no labels, and we also had to split the Mealy machine transitions into a separate input and output part in order to enable synchronization with the network. Thus, a single transition $q \xrightarrow{i/o} q'$ from a (concrete) Mealy machine is translated to a pair of transitions in NuSMV:

$$(loc = q, in = .., out = ..) \rightarrow (loc = q, in = i, out = ..) \rightarrow (loc = q', in = i, out = o).$$

Sequence and acknowledgement numbers in the implementations are 32-bit numbers, but were restricted to 3-bit numbers to reduce the state space. Whereas concrete messages are exchanged from one entity to the other, socket call inputs from the application are simulated by allowing system-calls to occur non-deterministically. A simplification we make is that we do not allow parallel actions: an action and all resulting packets have to be fully processed until another action can be generated. Consequently, there can be at most one packet in the composite model at any time. For example, once a three way handshake

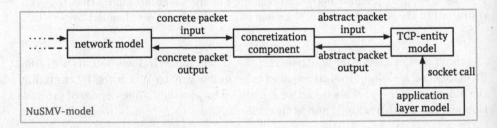

Fig. 3. Schematic overview of NuSMV-model. Only half of the setup is shown in detail, as the model is symmetric and another TCP-entity model is connected to the network.

is initiated between a client and a listening server via a *connect*-call, no more system-calls can be performed until the handshake is finalized.

5.2   Checking Specifications

After a model is composed, the interaction between TCP entities can be analyzed using the NuSMV model checker. However, it is important to realize that, since we used abstractions, the learned models of TCP servers and clients are over-approximations of the actual behaviors of these components. If Mealy machine $\mathcal{M}$ models the actual behavior of a component, $\mathcal{A}$ is the mapper used, and $\mathcal{H}$ is the abstract model that we learned then, as explained in Sect. 2, correctness of $\mathcal{H}$ implies $\mathcal{M} \leq \gamma_{\mathcal{A}}(\mathcal{H})$. Since $\gamma_{\mathcal{A}}(\mathcal{H})$ is weakly deterministic, in this case there exists a forward simulation relation from $\mathcal{M}$ to $\gamma_{\mathcal{A}}(\mathcal{H})$. This forward simulation is preserved by the translation from Mealy machines to NuSMV. Results from Grumberg and Long [20] then imply that, for any $\forall$CTL*-formula (which includes all LTL-formulas) we can transfer model checking results for $\gamma_{\mathcal{A}}(\mathcal{H})$ to the (unknown) model $\mathcal{M}$. Since simulations are preserved by composition, this result even holds when $\gamma_{\mathcal{A}}(\mathcal{H})$ is used as a component in a larger model.

Another essential point is that only a subset of the abstract inputs is used for learning. Hence invalid inputs (i.e. inputs with invalid parameters) are not included in our models. Traces with these inputs can therefore not be checked. Hence, the first property that we must check is a global invariant that asserts that invalid inputs will never occur. In case they do, NuSMV will provide a counterexample, which is used to find the cause of invalidity. During our initial experiments, NuSMV found several counterexamples showing that invalid inputs may occur. Based on analysis of these counterexamples we either refined/corrected the definition of one of the mappers, or we discovered a counterexample for the correctness of one of the abstract models. After a number of these iterations, we obtained a model in which invalid inputs can no longer occur. As mappers construction is done manually, these iterations are also not yet automated.

With only valid inputs, composite model may be checked for arbitrary $\forall$CTL* formulas. Within these formulas, we may refer to input and output packets and their constituents (sequence numbers, acknowledgements, flags,..). This yields a powerful language for stating properties, illustrated by a few examples below. These formulas are directy based on the RFC's.

Many properties that are stated informally in the RFC's refer to control states of the protocol. These control states, however, cannot be directly observed in our black-box setting. Nevertheless, we can identify states, e.g. based on inputs and outputs leading to and from it. For example, we base the proposition *established* on RFC 793, which states that: "The connection becomes 'established' when sequence numbers have been synchronized in both directions" [38, p. 11], and that only a CLOSE or ABORT socket call or incoming packets with a RST or FIN can make an entity leave the ESTABLISHED state [38, Sect. 3.9].

We first show a simple safety formula checking desynchonization: if one entity is in the ESTABLISHED state, the other cannot be in SYN_SENT and TIME_WAIT:

$$\mathsf{G}\neg(tcp1 - state = established \wedge (tcp2 - state = syn\_sent \vee tcp2 - state = time\_wait))$$

The next specification considers terminating an established connection with a CLOSE-input. The output should contain a FIN, except if there is unread data (in which case it should contain a RST). This corresponds to the first non-conformance case explained in Sect. 4. The specification is captured by the following formula, in which T is the triggered-operator as defined in NuSMV.

$$\mathsf{G}(state = established \rightarrow ((input = rcv\ \mathsf{T}\ input \neq packet\ with\ data) \wedge input = close)$$
$$\rightarrow (\mathsf{F}\ output = packet\ with\ \text{FIN})))$$

We have formalized and checked, in a similar way, specifications for all other non-conforming cases as well as many other specifications.

We have also checked which transitions in the abstract models are reachable in the composed system. For every transition, we take its input and starting state, and check whether they can occur together. In this way we can find the reachable parts of model. This proves useful when analysing models, as the reachable parts likely harbor bugs with the most impact. Similarly, comparing reachable parts helps reveal the most relevant differences between implementations. The first and third non-conformances in Sect. 4 occur in the reachable parts of the respective models. Figure 2 marks these parts in green.

6   Conclusions and Future Work

We combined model learning, model checking and abstraction techniques to obtain and analyze models of Windows, Linux and FreeBSD TCP server and client implementations. Composing these models together with the model of a network allowed us to perform model checking over the composite setup and verify that any valid number generated by one TCP entity is seen as valid number by the other TCP entity. We have also identified breaches of the RFC's in all operating systems, and confirmed them by formulating temporal specification and checking them. Our work suggests several directions for future work.

Based on our understanding of TCP, we manually defined abstractions (mappers) that made it possible to learn models of TCP implementations. Getting the mapper definitions right turned out to be tricky. In fact, we had to restrict our learning experiments to *valid* abstractions of the sequence and acknowledgement numbers. This proved limiting when searching for interesting rules to model check, like for example those that would expose known implementation bugs. Such rules often concern invalid parameters, which do not appear in the models we learned. Additionaly, we had to manually refine our mapper due to counterexamples found by the model checker. Learning algorithms that construct the abstractions automatically could potentially solve this problem. We hope that extensions of the learning algorithms for register automata as implemented in the Tomte [4] and RALib [12] tools will be able to construct abstractions for TCP fully automatically.

Our work was severely restricted by the lack of expressivity of Mealy machines. In order to squeeze the TCP implementation into a Mealy machine, we had to eliminate timing based behavior as well as re-transmissions. Other frameworks for modeling state machines might facilitate modelling these aspects. Obviously, we would also need learning algorithms capable of generating such state machines. There has been some preliminary work on extending learning algorithms to timed automata [19,47], and to I/O transition systems [3,48], with the additional benifit of approximate learning. Approximate learning learns an upper and lower boundary to the behaviour of the system, instead of an exact model. This may allow to abstract away the corner-cases in the model and the mapper, if they are not relevant for the specifications. Extensions of this work could eliminate some of the restrictions that we encountered.

References

1. Aarts, F.: Tomte: Bridging the Gap between Active Learning and Real-World Systems. Ph.D. thesis, Radboud University Nijmegen, October 2014
2. Aarts, F., Jonsson, B., Uijen, J., Vaandrager, F.W.: Generating models of infinite-state communication protocols using regular inference with abstraction. Formal Methods Syst. Des. **46**(1), 1–41 (2015)
3. Aarts, F., Vaandrager, F.: Learning I/O automata. In: Gastin, P., Laroussinie, F. (eds.) CONCUR 2010. LNCS, vol. 6269, pp. 71–85. Springer, Heidelberg (2010)
4. Aarts, F., Fiterau-Brostean, P., Kuppens, H., Vaandrager, F.: Learning register automata with fresh value generation. In: Leucker, M., Rueda, C., Valencia, F.D. (eds.) ICTAC 2015. LNCS, vol. 9399, pp. 165–183. Springer, Heidelberg (2015). doi:10.1007/978-3-319-25150-9_11
5. Aarts, F., Jonsson, B., Uijen, J., Vaandrager, F.W.: Generat-ing models of infinite-state communication protocols using regular inference withabstraction. Formal Methods Syst. Des. **46**(1), 1–41 (2015)
6. Angluin, D.: Learning regular sets from queries and counterexamples. Inf. Comput. **75**(2), 87–106 (1987)
7. Baier, C., Katoen, J.-P.: Principles of Model Checking. MIT Press, Cambridge (2008)
8. Berendsen, J., Gebremichael, B., Vaandrager, F.W., Zhang, M.: Formal specification and analysis of Zeroconf using Uppaal. ACM Trans. Embed. Comput. Syst. **10**(3), 1–32 (2011)
9. Braden, R.: RFC 1122 Requirements for Internet Hosts - Communication Layers. Internet Engineering Task Force, October 1989
10. Brinksma, E., Mader, A.: On verification modelling of embedded systems. Technical report TR-CTIT-04-03, Centre for Telematics and Information Technology, Univ. of Twente, The Netherlands, January 2004
11. Bruns, G., Staskauskas, M.G.: Applying formal methods to a protocol standard and its implementations. In: Proceedings International Symposium on Software Engineering for Parallel and Distributed Systems (PDSE 1998), 20–21 April 1998, Kyoto, Japan, pp. 198–205. IEEE Computer Society (1998)

12. Cassel, S.: Learning Component Behavior from Tests: Theory and Algorithms for Automata with Data. Ph.D. thesis, University of Uppsala (2015)
13. Chalupar, G., Peherstorfer, S., Poll, E., de Ruiter, J.: Automated reverse engineering using Lego. In: Proceedings 8th USENIX Workshop on Offensive Technologies (WOOT 2014), San Diego, California, Los Alamitos, CA, USA, IEEE Computer Society, August 2014
14. Cho, C.Y., Babic, D., Shin, E.C.R., Song, D.: Inference and analysis of formal models of botnet command and control protocols. In: Al-Shaer, E., Keromytis, A.D., Shmatikov, V. (eds.) ACM Conference on Computer and Communications Security, pp. 426–439. ACM (2010)
15. Cimatti, A., Clarke, E., Giunchiglia, E., Giunchiglia, F., Pistore, M., Roveri, M., Sebastiani, R., Tacchella, A.: NuSMV 2: an opensource tool for symbolic model checking. In: Brinksma, E., Larsen, K.G. (eds.) CAV 2002. LNCS, vol. 2404, pp. 359–364. Springer, Heidelberg (2002)
16. Clarke, E.M., Grumberg, O., Jha, S., Lu, Y., Veith, H.: Counterexample-guided abstraction refinement for symbolic model checking. J. ACM **50**(5), 752–794 (2003)
17. Clarke, E.M., Grumberg, O., Peled, D.: Model Checking. MIT Press, Cambridge (1999)
18. Fiterău-Broştean, P., Janssen, R., Vaandrager, F.: Learning fragments of the TCP network protocol. In: Lang, F., Flammini, F. (eds.) FMICS 2014. LNCS, vol. 8718, pp. 78–93. Springer, Heidelberg (2014)
19. Grinchtein, O., Jonsson, B., Leucker, M.: Learning of event-recording automata. Theor. Comput. Sci. **411**(47), 4029–4054 (2010)
20. Grumberg, O., Long, D.E.: Model checking and modular verification. ACM Trans. Program. Lang. Syst. **16**(3), 843–871 (1994)
21. Holzmann, G.J.: The SPIN Model Checker: Primer and Reference Manual. Addison Wesley, Reading (2004)
22. Impacket. http://www.coresecurity.com/corelabs-research/open-source-tools/impacket. Accessed 28 Jan 2016
23. Isberner, M: Foundations of Active Automata Learning: An Algorithmic Perspective. Ph.D. thesis, Technical University of Dortmund (2015)
24. Jhala, R., Majumdar, R.: Software model checking. ACM Comput. Surv. **41**(4), 21:1–21:54 (2009)
25. King, J.C.: Symbolic execution and program testing. Commun. ACM **19**(7), 385–394 (1976)
26. van Langevelde, I., Romijn, J.M.T., Goga, N.: Founding FireWire bridges through Promela prototyping. In: 8thInternational Workshop on Formal Methods for Parallel Programming: Theory and Applications (FMPPTA). IEEE Computer Society Press, April 2003
27. Lee, D., Yannakakis, M.: Principles and methods of testing finite state machines – a survey. Proc. IEEE **84**(8), 1090–1123 (1996)
28. Lockefeer, L., Williams, D.M., Fokkink, W.J.: Formal specification and verification of TCP extended with the window scale option. In: Lang, F., Flammini, F. (eds.) FMICS 2014. LNCS, vol. 8718, pp. 63–77. Springer, Heidelberg (2014)
29. Loiseaux, C., Graf, S., Sifakis, J., Boujjani, A., Bensalem, S.: Property preserving abstractions for the verification of concurrent systems. Formal Methods Syst. Des. **6**(1), 11–44 (1995)
30. Meinke, K., Sindhu, M.A.: Incremental learning-based testing for reactive systems. In: Gogolla, M., Wolff, B. (eds.) TAP 2011. LNCS, vol. 6706, pp. 134–151. Springer, Heidelberg (2011)

31. Musuvathi, M., Engler, D.R.: Model checking large network protocol implementations. In: Morris, R., Savage, S. (eds.) 1st Symposium on Networked Systems Design and Implementation (NSDI 2004), March 29–31, 2004, San Francisco, California, USA, Proceedings, pp. 155–168. USENIX (2004)

32. Musuvathi, M., Park, D.Y.W., Chou, A., Engler, D.R., Dill, D.L.: CMC: A pragmatic approach to model checking real code. In: Culler, D.E., Druschel, P. (eds.) 5th Symposium on Operating System Design and Implementation (OSDI 2002), Boston, Massachusetts, USA, December 9–11, 2002. USENIX Association (2002)

33. Nerode, A.: Linear automaton transformations. Proc. Am. Math. Soc. 9(4), 541–544 (1958)

34. Paxson, V., Allman, M., Dawson, S., Fenner, W., Griner, J., Heavens, I., Lahey, K., Semke, J., Volz, B.: Known TCP Implementation Problems. RFC 2525 (Informational), March 1999

35. Pcapy. http://www.coresecurity.com/corelabs-research/open-source-tools/pcapy. Accessed 28 Jan 2016

36. Peled, D., Vardi, M.Y., Yannakakis, M.: Black box checking. J. Autom. Lang. Comb. 7(2), 225–246 (2002)

37. Popper, K.R.: Logik der Forschung. Julius Springer Verlag, Vienna (1935)

38. Postel, J.: Transmission control protocol. RFC 793 (Standard), Updated by RFCs 1122, 3168, September 1981

39. Raffelt, H., Steffen, B., Berg, T., Margaria, T.: LearnLib: a framework for extrapolating behavioral models. STTT 11(5), 393–407 (2009)

40. de Ruiter, J., Poll, E.: Protocol state fuzzing of tls implementations. In: 24th USENIX Security Symposium (USENIX Security 15), pp. 193–206. SENIX Association, Washington, D.C., August 2015

41. Scapy. http://www.secdev.org/projects/scapy/. Accessed 28 Jan 2016

42. Shahbaz, M., Groz, R.: Analysis and testing of black-box component-based systems by inferring partial models. Softw. Test. Verif. Reliab. 24(4), 253–288 (2014)

43. Smeenk, W., Moerman, J., Vaandrager, F., Jansen, D.N.: Applying automata learning to embedded control software. In: Butler, M., Conchon, S., Zaïdi, F. (eds.) ICFEM 2015. LNCS, vol. 9407, pp. 67–83. Springer, Heidelberg (2015). doi:10.1007/978-3-319-25423-4_5

44. Steffen, B., Howar, F., Merten, M.: Introduction to active automata learning from a practical perspective. In: Bernardo, M., Issarny, V. (eds.) SFM 2011. LNCS, vol. 6659, pp. 256–296. Springer, Heidelberg (2011)

45. Stoelinga, M.: Fun with FireWire: A comparative study of formal verification methods applied to the IEEE 1394 root contention protocol. Formal Aspects Comput. J. 14(3), 328–337 (2003)

46. Verleg, P.: Inferring SSH state machines using protocol state fuzzing. Master thesis, Radboud University (2016)

47. Verwer, S.: Efficient Identification of Timed Automata – Theory and Practice. Ph.D. thesis, Delft University of Technology, March 2010

48. Volpato, M., Tretmans, J.: Active learning of nondeterministic systems from an ioco perspective. In: Margaria, T., Steffen, B. (eds.) ISoLA 2014, Part I. LNCS, vol. 8802, pp. 220–235. Springer, Heidelberg (2014)

BFS-Based Model Checking of Linear-Time Properties with an Application on GPUs

Anton Wijs[✉]

Eindhoven University of Technology, Eindhoven, The Netherlands
A.J.Wijs@tue.nl

Abstract. Efficient algorithms have been developed to model check liveness properties, such as the well-known Nested Depth-First Search, which uses a depth-first search (DFS) strategy. However, in some settings, DFS is not a suitable option. For instance, when considering distributed model checking on a cluster, or many-core model checking using a Graphics Processing Unit (GPU), Breadth-First Search (BFS) is a more natural choice, at least for basic reachability analysis. Liveness property checking, however, requires the detection of (accepting) cycles, and BFS is not very suitable to detect these on-the-fly. In this paper, we consider how a model checker that completely runs on a GPU can be extended to efficiently verify whether finite-state concurrent systems satisfy liveness properties. We exploit the fact that the state space is the product of the behaviour of several parallel automata. The result of this work is the very first GPU-based model checker that can check liveness properties.

1 Introduction

Model checking [2] is a formal verification technique to ensure that a model satisfies desired functional properties. Some of these properties may address infinite system behaviour. Such properties are called *liveness* properties; they express that some desired behaviour eventually happens [1].

In finite-state systems, infinite behaviour is only possible if some of the states are visited infinitely often. Therefore, in the state space of such a system, infinite behaviour is represented by a cycle and a path from the initial state leading to it. A counter-example to a liveness property is also some infinite behaviour through the product of the system behaviour and an automaton accepting any infinite behaviour that violates the property [2]. Linear-time properties, for instance expressed in the LTL temporal logic, can be represented by such automata, for instance Büchi and Rabin automata.

For explicit-state model checking, there are efficient algorithms to find counter-examples to liveness properties, e.g. [10, 14, 17, 29, 30]. All of these perform a search through the state space using a Depth-First Search (DFS) strategy. However, in some settings, Breadth-First Search (BFS) is a more natural choice

A. Wijs—We gratefully acknowledge the support of NVIDIA Corporation with the donation of the GeForce Titan X used for this research.

S. Chaudhuri and A. Farzan (Eds.): CAV 2016, Part II, LNCS 9780, pp. 472–493, 2016.
DOI: 10.1007/978-3-319-41540-6_26

for graph traversals than DFS. For instance, when model checking is done by several machines collaboratively in a network [5,7,11], and when General Purpose Graphics Processing Units (GPGPUs or GPUs) are employed for model checking. In the former case, information obtained through DFS traversals cannot efficiently by synchronised between workers. In the latter case, the availability of thousands of threads, and the requirement to occupy these to fully harness the computing power of the GPU, is at odds with a DFS-based search, in which a stack is used and the focus is always on the state at the top of the stack. One might consider running multiple randomised DFSs in parallel [12,23], but maintaining thousands of stacks would require too much overhead.

GPUs are being used to dramatically speed up computations. For explicit-state model checking, GPUs are used for on-the-fly state space exploration and safety property checking [6,35,36,39], offline property checking [3,8,9,34], counterexample generation [38], and state space decomposition and minimisation [33,37].

The next challenge in GPU model checking is the on-the-fly checking of general linear-time properties. In this paper, we consider doing this using a BFS-based approach. The best known way to find cycles using a BFS-like search is by *topological sorting* of the states [19], but it does not work on-the-fly, i.e. while discovering the state space. A more suitable algorithm is a heuristic search called *piggybacking* [13,16], in which a state that may be in a cycle of a counter-example, is carried (piggybacked) along the search. If at any point, a state is visited which is at that time also piggybacked, then a cycle is found. However, the algorithm is not complete; in many situations, it may fail to detect a cycle.

Contributions. Firstly, we define, to the best of our knowledge, for the first time a variant of piggybacking using *Rabin automata* to express properties. Secondly, we propose several new algorithms that can efficiently analyse the input model before the checking is started, to extract structural information that tends to make the piggybacking algorithm more effective. Thirdly, in earlier work [13], a post-processing phase was proposed to further analyse particular states that can be identified as 'promising' during piggybacking. This phase makes piggybacking complete for *bounded suffix model checking*, in which cycle detection is limited to cycles of a predetermined number of transitions. In [13], a depth-bounded DFS was initiated from each of those promising states to search for a cycle containing them. In this paper, we show that with the extracted structural information, the number of promising states can be reduced, thereby potentially speeding up the post-processing phase. Fourthly, we discuss how piggybacking can be implemented in a GPU model checking approach, focussing primarily on the data structures. Finally, we validate the effectiveness of our approach as a whole, and the application of the different algorithms in particular, on an implementation in the GPU model checker GPUEXPLORE [35,36].

It should be stressed that, even though we focus on using GPUs, our proposed enhancements of piggybacking may be of use in other contexts as well. For instance, in [25], several heuristics are used to incrementally verify liveness properties symbolically using saturation. Our proposed heuristics seem to be more refined than the ones they use; for instance, they consider every visiting of a state in a non-trivial strongly connected component to be an event that may close a cycle in the state space, whereas we can distinguish situations where this cannot be the case from cases where it can.

Piggybacking was first proposed in [16] and extended in [13], and a similar approach is used as an on-the-fly heuristic in the OTF-OWCTY algorithm [4]. Various different strategies to select and remove piggybacking states have been proposed, including piggybacking not one, but multiple states, to improve the algorithm. However, these variations tend to not fundamentally improve the original algorithm. We are the first to try to exploit the fact that the state space is the combination of behaviour of several interacting processes in the input model. One of the new algorithms, to identify so-called essential states, is inspired by [22]. They statically analyse cycles in processes to improve partial order reduction, and they consider state-based models. as opposed to our algorithm, which works for action-based models.

The structure of the paper is as follows. In Sect. 2, we discuss the basic notions. Section 3 presents the piggybacking algorithm and various algorithms to statically analyse input models. How these algorithms affect GPU model checking is explained in Sect. 4. Experimental results are given in Sect. 5, and finally, our conclusions are presented in Sect. 6.

2   Preliminaries

In this section, we discuss the basic notions involved to understand the problem, namely LTS, network of LTSs, and an action-based version of Rabin automata.

Labelled Transition Systems. We use Labelled Transition Systems (LTSs) to represent the semantics of finite-state systems. They are action-based descriptions, indicating how a system can change state by performing particular actions.

Definition 1 (Labelled Transition System). *An* LTS $\mathcal{G}$ *is a tuple* $\langle \mathcal{S}, \mathcal{A}, \mathcal{T}, \underline{s} \rangle$, *with*

- $\mathcal{S}$ *a finite set of states;*
- $\mathcal{A}$ *a set of action labels;*
- $\mathcal{T} \subseteq \mathcal{S} \times \mathcal{A} \times \mathcal{S}$ *a transition relation;*
- $\underline{s} \in \mathcal{S}$ *the initial state.*

Actions in $\mathcal{A}$ are denoted by a, b, c, etc. We use $s_1 \xrightarrow{a} s_2$ to denote $\langle s_1, a, s_2 \rangle \in \mathcal{T}$. If $s_1 \xrightarrow{a} s_2$, this means that an action a can be performed in state s_1, leading to state s_2; we call s_2 a *successor* of s_1. We refer with $\rightarrow^*$ and $\rightarrow^+$ to the reflexive, transitive closure, and the transitive closure of $\rightarrow$, respectively. We call $s_1 \rightarrow^* s_2$ and $s_1 \rightarrow^+ s_2$ *paths* through $\mathcal{G}$, and for a path π, we refer with $S(\pi)$ to the set of states that are part of π. A *cycle* is a path consisting of at least one transition, from a state s_1 to itself, i.e. $s_1 \rightarrow^+ s_1$. Finally, $inf(\pi)$ is the set of states in $S(\pi)$ that are part of a cycle in π. In particular, if π is a cycle, we have $S(\pi) = inf(\pi)$. In finite-state LTSs, a path involving a cycle is called an *infinite* path.

LTS *Networks.* We use LTS networks (Definition 2) to describe concurrent systems. They consist of a finite number of concurrent process LTSs and a set of synchronisation rules that define the possible interaction between the processes. We write $1..n$ for the set of integers ranging from 1 to n. A vector $\bar{v}$ of size n contains n elements indexed from 1 to n. For all $i \in 1..n$, $\bar{v}_i$ represents the ith element of vector $\bar{v}$.

Definition 2 (LTS network). *An* LTS *network* $\mathcal{N}$ *of size* n *is a pair* $\langle \Pi, \mathcal{V} \rangle$, *where*

- *Π is a vector of n concurrent process* LTSs. *For each $i \in 1..n$, we write $\Pi_i = \langle \mathcal{S}_i, \mathcal{A}_i, \mathcal{T}_i, \underline{s}_i \rangle$.*
- *$\mathcal{V}$ is a finite set of synchronisation rules. A synchronisation rule is a tuple $\langle a, T \rangle$, where a is an action label and $T \subseteq 1..n$.*

The synchronisation rules define how the processes can synchronise with each other. These rules allow m among n synchronisation between transitions of the same label. The fact that they must have the same label is a restriction of our definition of LTS networks, by which it differs from the one in [24]. Our rules can, for instance, express that a-transitions of different processes need to synchronise, and not that a- and b-transitions must synchronise with each other, and produce a transition with some other label, say c. The reason for having the restriction is due to our desire to compactly represent synchronisation rules in the GPU model checker [35, 36]. It does not restrict our ability to specify concurrent system behaviour, since any network with rules that do not adhere to this restriction can be rewritten to a network without such rules. It does remove the ability to rename transition labels, but on the other hand, this is not a limitation for the current application, in which renaming is never applied.

The explicit behaviour of an LTS network is defined by its *system* LTS (Definition 3).

Definition 3 (System LTS). *Given an* LTS *network* $\mathcal{N} = \langle \Pi, \mathcal{V} \rangle$, *its system* LTS *is defined by* $\mathcal{N}_\mathcal{G} = \langle \mathcal{S}_\mathcal{N}, \mathcal{A}_\mathcal{N}, \mathcal{T}_\mathcal{N}, \underline{s}_\mathcal{N} \rangle$, *with*

- $\mathcal{S}_\mathcal{N} = \mathcal{S}_1 \times \cdots \times \mathcal{S}_n$;
- $\mathcal{A}_\mathcal{N} = \bigcup_{i \in 1..n} \mathcal{A}_i$;
- $\underline{s}_\mathcal{N} = \langle \underline{s}_1, \ldots, \underline{s}_n \rangle$, *and*
- $\mathcal{T}_\mathcal{N}$ *is the smallest relation satisfying:*

$$\forall \bar{s} \in \mathcal{S}_\mathcal{N}, \langle a, T \rangle \in \mathcal{V}.(\forall i \in 1..n. \left(\begin{array}{c} (i \notin T \wedge \bar{s}_i = \bar{s}'_i) \\ \vee \, (i \in T \wedge \bar{s}_i \xrightarrow{a} \bar{s}'_i) \end{array} \right)) \implies \bar{s} \xrightarrow{a} \bar{s}'$$

The system LTS is obtained by combining the processes in Π according to the synchronisation rules in $\mathcal{V}$. In the following, we assume that the so-called *independent* transitions of a process, i.e. those that do not require synchronisation with other transitions, are always enabled. In other words, for each process Π_i ($i \in 1..n$) and independent action $a \in \mathcal{A}_i$, we assume that $\langle a, \{i\} \rangle \in \mathcal{V}$.

Rabin Automata. Model checking linear-time functional properties involves checking whether a system satisfies a property φ, written in some linear-time temporal logic. The property can be a liveness property addressing infinite system behaviour ("something good eventually happens"). Since we use the action-based LTS network formalism to express system behaviour, we also require an action-based way to express our properties (which can, for instance, be done using action-based LTL). For this, we extend the definition of LTS to obtain an action-based Rabin automaton [28].

Definition 4 (Rabin automaton). *A Rabin automaton (RA)* $\mathcal{R}$ *is a tuple* $\langle \mathcal{S}, \mathcal{A}, \mathcal{T}, \underline{s}, \mathcal{F} \rangle$, *with*

- $\langle \mathcal{S}, \mathcal{A}, \mathcal{T}, \underline{s} \rangle$ *an* LTS;
- $\mathcal{F}$ *a set of k pairs of state sets* $\{(L_i, K_i) \mid 0 \le i < k\}$, *with* $L_i, K_i \subseteq \mathcal{S}$.

An RA has an *acceptance condition*: an infinite path π is *accepted* iff there exists a pair $(L_i, K_i) \in \mathcal{F}$ such that $inf(\pi) \cap L_i = \emptyset$ and $inf(\pi) \cap K_i \ne \emptyset$ [2,21]. RAs are as expressive as ω-regular languages (and many linear-time properties are ω-regular). In fact, contrary to Büchi automata, deterministic versions of RAs already have the full power of ω-regular languages [15]. A deterministic automaton defines for each state and action label at most one successor state.

Verifying Linear-Time Properties. When checking functional properties, one must solve the emptiness problem for the product of $\mathcal{N}_\mathcal{G}$ and the property automaton $\mathcal{R}_{\neg\varphi}$, where $\mathcal{R}_{\neg\varphi}$ refers to the RA accepting all infinite paths described by the negation of φ [32]. In fact, this product is the system LTS $\mathcal{P}_\mathcal{G}$ of an LTS network $\mathcal{P} = \langle \Pi', \mathcal{V}' \rangle$ combining $\mathcal{N}$ and $\mathcal{R}_{\neg\varphi}$, in which for each $i \in 1..n$, $\Pi'_i = \Pi_i$, $\Pi'_{n+1} = \mathcal{R}_{\neg\varphi}$, and the synchronisation rules of $\mathcal{N}$ have been extended in $\mathcal{V}'$ to always involve synchronisation with $\mathcal{R}_{\neg\varphi}$, i.e. $\mathcal{V}' = \{\langle a, T \cup \{n+1\}\rangle \mid \langle a, T \rangle \in \mathcal{V}\}$.

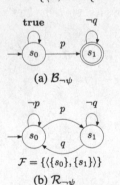

(a) $\mathcal{B}_{\neg\psi}$

(b) $\mathcal{R}_{\neg\psi}$

$\mathcal{F} = \{\langle \{s_0\}, \{s_1\}\rangle\}$

Fig. 1. Request-response automata

A counter-example for φ in $\mathcal{P}_\mathcal{G}$ exists iff there exists some path $\pi = \langle \underline{s_\mathcal{N}}, \underline{t}\rangle \to^* \langle \bar{s}, t\rangle$, with $\underline{t}$ the initial state of $\mathcal{R}_{\neg\varphi}$, and a path $\pi' = \langle \bar{s}, t\rangle \to^+ \langle \bar{s}, t\rangle$, that is accepted by $\mathcal{R}_{\neg\varphi}$. Let $C = \{t' \mid \langle \bar{s}', t'\rangle \in S(\pi')\}$, then the combination of π and π' is accepted iff there exists an $(L_i, K_i) \in \mathcal{F}$ such that $C \cap L_i = \emptyset$ and $C \cap K_i \ne \emptyset$. If this is the case, then π' is referred to as an *accepting cycle*. In other words, solving the emptiness problem boils down to checking for the reachability of accepting cycles.

Figure 1 shows a Büchi automaton $\mathcal{B}_{\neg\psi}$ (a), which accepts all paths that traverse through s_1 infinitely often, and a Rabin automaton $\mathcal{R}_{\neg\psi}$ (b). Both express the negation of a property $\psi =$ "after p, eventually q happens".[1] This property is of a very commonly used type, namely *request-response*. For our application, Rabin automata are often more suitable than Büchi automata. In GPU model checking (Sect. 4), the outgoing transitions of each state vector are constructed using multiple threads. In general, for this

---

[1] Note that this is an action-based property referring to the transition-labels, as opposed to a state-based property referring to state predicates.

construction, the more independent transitions are present in the processes, the more potential there is to explore them in parallel, which speeds up the successor construction. When using non-deterministic Büchi automata, we observe that the potential to avoid synchronisation is often smaller than when using (deterministic) Rabin automata. For instance, in $\mathcal{R}_{\neg\psi}$, we can ignore the self-loops, and combine $\mathcal{R}_{\neg\psi}$ with $\mathcal{N}_{\mathcal{G}}$ in such a way that p and q-transitions of $\mathcal{N}_{\mathcal{G}}$ need to synchronise with p and q-transitions of $\mathcal{R}_{\neg\psi}$, but other transitions do not, thereby avoiding many synchronisations. In $\mathcal{B}_{\neg\psi}$, however, we have a self-loop $\neg q$ at state s_1, which cannot be ignored in the same way, since we depend on q-transitions in $\mathcal{N}_{\mathcal{G}}$ being blocked whenever $\mathcal{R}_{\neg\psi}$ is in state s_1 in $\mathcal{P}_{\mathcal{G}}$. This could be solved by extending $\mathcal{B}_{\neg\psi}$, but an additional drawback is that unlike $\mathcal{R}_{\neg\psi}$, $\mathcal{B}_{\neg\psi}$ is non-deterministic for p at state s_0, thereby creating two branches in $\mathcal{P}_{\mathcal{G}}$ whenever a p-transition can be fired, which may increase the state space size. On the other hand, it should be noted that in general, Rabin automata tend to be larger than Büchi automata expressing the same property, but multiple techniques exist to keep the former reasonably small [20].

3 On-The-Fly BFS-Based Property Checking

3.1 A Piggyback Algorithm for Rabin Automata

It is well-known that BFS-based graph search algorithms are not as efficient in detecting cycles as DFS-based algorithms. This is because unlike in DFS, where a stack is employed that keeps track of the currently explored path, information on the individual paths in the state space is not maintained during a BFS. However, there is one exception to this, relating to the state s from which the BFS is initiated: if at any point in the BFS, s is reached again, we know that a cycle involving s exists.

Algorithm 1. Piggyback BFS

Require: network $\mathcal{P} = \langle \Pi', \mathcal{V}' \rangle$

    $\alpha \leftarrow \bullet$; $I \leftarrow \{i \mid (L_i, K_i) \in \mathcal{F} \wedge \underline{s}_{n+1} \in K_i\}$

2: **if** $I \neq \emptyset$ **then** $\alpha \leftarrow \underline{s}_{\mathcal{P}}$

    - $Open, Closed \leftarrow \{\langle \underline{s}_{\mathcal{P}}, [\alpha, I] \rangle\}$

4: **while** $Open \neq \emptyset$ **do**

    - $\langle \bar{s}, [\alpha, I] \rangle \leftarrow Open$; $Open \leftarrow Open \setminus \{\langle \bar{s}, [\alpha, I] \rangle\}$

6:    **for all** $\langle a, \bar{s}' \rangle \in \text{OUT}(\bar{s})$ **do**

      if $\bar{s}' = \alpha$ **then**

8:        **return false**

      $I' \leftarrow \{i \mid (L_i, K_i) \in \mathcal{F} \wedge \bar{s}'_{n+1} \notin L_i \wedge i \in I\}$

10:     **if** $I' = \emptyset$ **then**

        $\alpha \leftarrow \bullet$; $I' \leftarrow \{i \mid (L_i, K_i) \in \mathcal{F} \wedge \bar{s}'_{n+1} \in K_i\}$

12:      **if** $I' \neq \emptyset$ **then**

        $\alpha \leftarrow \bar{s}'$

14:    **if** $\neg \exists \beta, J. \langle \bar{s}', [\beta, J] \rangle \in Closed$ **then**

      - $Closed \leftarrow Closed \cup \{\langle \bar{s}', [\alpha, I'] \rangle\}$

16:     - $Open \leftarrow Open \cup \{\langle \bar{s}', [\alpha, I'] \rangle\}$

    else if $\alpha \neq \bullet$ **then**

18:     **if** $\beta = \bullet$ **then**

      - $Closed \leftarrow (Closed \setminus \{\langle \bar{s}', [\beta, J] \rangle\}) \cup \{\langle \bar{s}', [\alpha, I'] \rangle\}$

20:      - $Open \leftarrow Open \cup \{\langle \bar{s}', [\alpha, I'] \rangle\}$

     else

22:      Mark blocking occurrence in $\bar{s}'$

  Post-process blocking occurrences; **return false** if cycle detected, else **true**

This observation is the basis for the *piggyback* algorithm in [16], which was initially designed to perform bounded liveness checking, and improved in [13] to handle liveness properties with a bounded suffix (i.e. the cycle in the state space is bounded in size, as opposed to the cycle in the property automaton). In Algorithm 1, we present a version of the piggyback algorithm tailored for the use of Rabin automata, which is, to the best of our knowledge, the first time this is done. At lines 1, 9 and 12, the acceptance condition for Rabin automata is checked, and the results of those checks are, where applicable, piggybacked along with the piggybacked state. This is the key difference between this and previous versions of the piggyback algorithm.

In Algorithm 1, α refers to the state that is piggybacked along with the state being visited or explored. The notation • refers to a value representing 'no state'. At lines 1–2, the initial state of $\mathcal{P}_\mathcal{G}$ is selected as a piggyback value if the initial state of $\mathcal{R}_{\neg\varphi}$ is in at least one K_i (indicated by I), i.e. potentially makes a cycle involving that state accepting. State α, together with the indices in I of the involved (L_i, K_i) are combined with the state. The combination is added to sets *Open* and *Closed* (line 3), where *Open* is the set of states that have been visited, but not yet explored, and *Closed* is the set of explored states.

Next, while *Open* is not empty, states are taken from that set, to be explored (lines 4–5). At line 6, the OUT function returns the outgoing transitions of $\bar{s}$, i.e. $\text{OUT}(\bar{s}) = \{\langle a, \bar{s}' \rangle \mid \bar{s} \xrightarrow{a} \bar{s}'\}$. At line 7, the early termination condition of the algorithm is checked: if at any time, one of the successors of a state is the state being piggybacked, we have clearly detected a cycle. At lines 9–10, it is checked whether successor $\bar{s}'$ can still be in an accepting cycle. This is the case if for at least one of the $(L_i, K_i) \in \mathcal{F}$ relevant for the piggybacked state, $\bar{s}'$ is not in L_i. If such an $(L_i.K_i)$ no longer exists, we remove the current piggybacked state, and consider $\bar{s}'$ as a new piggybacked value (lines 11–13). At line 14, the presence of $\bar{s}'$ in *Closed* is checked. If it is not present, $\bar{s}'$ is added to *Open* and *Closed* with the updated piggybacked information (lines 15–16). Else, if currently a state is being piggybacked, we have to consider re-exploration of $\bar{s}'$: if the piggybacked value of $\bar{s}'$ encountered in *Closed* is •, we reopen the state and update its information (lines 19–20). Else, we indicate at line 22 that a so-called *blocking situation* has occurred (which we discuss next). In the end, these situations are further analysed at lines 23–24. Note that re-exploration of a state can be done at most once: if it is in *Closed* without a piggybacked value, and it is reached from a state with a piggybacked value, it will be explored again, and added to *Closed* with the piggybacked value. Hence, the complexity of the algorithm is $O(|\mathcal{S}_\mathcal{P}|)$.

Unfortunately, the piggyback algorithm is not complete; in many situations, it fails to detect accepting cycles. Figure 2 illustrates two types of problems, where, for convenience, we consider one pair of state sets $(L, K) \in \mathcal{F}$. In the figure, double-lined states are in K, while no states are in L. Piggybacked states are listed between square brackets, and the search enters via incoming transitions. In Fig. 2a, when reaching $\bar{s}_1 \in K$, this state cannot be piggybacked, since $\bar{s}_0$ already is. This may cause a situation called *shadowing* [13]: the accepting cycle $\bar{s}_1 \rightarrow^+ \bar{s}_1$ is not recognised due to a different state being piggybacked.

Figure 2b illustrates a problem called *blocking* [13]. The search enters the cycle from $\bar{s}_0$ and $\bar{s}_1$, and piggybacks both. This means that when exploring $\bar{s}_2$, $\bar{s}_0$ is encountered with a different piggybacked value, and hence, the search is blocked (line 22 of Algorithm 1), i.e. it cannot continue along that path. Similarly, the search from $\bar{s}_0$ is blocked. The result is that the cycle is not detected.

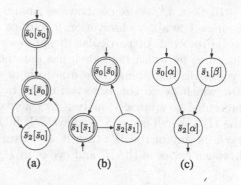

(a)   (b)   (c)

Fig. 2. Shadowing and blocking

However, the occurrence of blocking does not necessarily indicate the presence of cycles. Another cause for blocking is due to the confluence of paths, which tends to occur very frequently in state spaces, due to the interleaving semantics of the input models [27]. This is illustrated in Fig. 2c: from $\bar{s}_0$, value α is piggybacked to $\bar{s}_2$, due to which a search from $\bar{s}_1$ with value $\beta \neq \alpha$ is blocked.

In a way, one can interpret shadowing as a specific form of blocking; in Fig. 2a, the search is blocked at $\bar{s}_2$ due to reaching state $\bar{s}_1$ which already has a piggybacked value not equal to $\bar{s}_1$ itself. In [13], it is proposed to keep track of blocking occurrences during piggybacking, and post-processing those occurrences by starting a DFS with depth-bound b is launched from every point in the state space where blocking occurs, to determine whether or not a cycle of at most size b exists. However, not all blocking occurrences require further analysis. We observe the following, which is formalised in a lemma.

Lemma 1. *Consider an accepting cycle $\pi = s_1 \rightarrow^* s_2 \rightarrow s_3 \rightarrow^* s_1$ with, for some $(L_i, K_i) \in \mathcal{F}$, $S(\pi) \cap K_i \neq \emptyset$ and $S(\pi) \cap L_i = \emptyset$. Say that a search enters π via s_1, and piggybacks a value α along π, but is being blocked at s_3, because the latter already has a piggyback value β. Then, eventually, blocking will also occur at s_1, or an accepting cycle containing s_1 is discovered.*

Proof. By induction on the length m of $s_3 \rightarrow^* s_1$.

- $m = 0$: we have $s_3 = s_1$, therefore blocking at s_1 happened when considering the successors of s_2.
- $m = 1$: s_1 is a successor of s_3. We either have $\beta = s_1$, in which case an accepting cycle containing s_1 is discovered (line 7 of Algorithm 1), or the search is blocked at s_1, since s_1 is in *Closed*, $\beta \neq \bullet$, and $\alpha \neq \bullet$ (line 22 of Algorithm 1).
- $m = m' + 1$: let s_4 be the successor of s_3 in π. There are now two possibilities:
  1. either s_4 has no piggyback value, in which case s_4 will be added with piggyback value β to *Open*, either at line 16 or 20 of Algorithm 1, and by the induction hypothesis, eventually blocking will occur at s_1, or another accepting cycle through s_1 is discovered.
  2. or s_4 has a piggyback value $\gamma \neq \beta$. Then, another search along $s_4 \rightarrow^* s_1$ (with length m') is being conducted with piggyback value γ. By the induction hypothesis, either blocking will occur at s_1, or, in case $\gamma = s_1$ and exploration continues to s_1, an accepting cycle containing s_1 and s_4 will be discovered. □

In Sect. 4, we discuss how we analyse blocking occurrences on the GPU. Lemma 1 is a key observation to reduce the number of occurrences that need to be resolved. In particular, it suffices to look at those blocking occurrences at states by which the search has entered a cycle and has closed process-local cycles. Distinguishing these from others depends on knowing where the cycles are, which we do not. However, in the next section, several new algorithms are presented to statically analyse LTS networks to determine via which states in the Π_i' a search enters a local cycle. If in $\mathcal{P}_\mathcal{G}$ a given state does not enter a local cycle in any of the Π_i', then it also cannot enter a cycle in $\mathcal{P}_\mathcal{G}$. This relation between cycles in the Π_i' and cycles in $\mathcal{P}_\mathcal{G}$ is discussed next.

3.2   Static Analysis of Lts Networks

In this section, we present several algorithms to statically analyse networks under analysis, with the goal to extract information that can improve the effectiveness of the piggyback algorithm. These algorithms analyse the different Π_i' in isolation, and have a complexity which is at most quadratic in the size of an individual Π_i'. This is often much lower than the complexity of computing $\mathcal{P}_\mathcal{G}$, which is $O(|\mathcal{S}_1| \times \cdots \times |\mathcal{S}_{n+1}|)$. Lemma 2 serves as the starting point for our reasoning.

Lemma 2. *Consider an* LTS *network* $\mathcal{P} = \langle \Pi', \mathcal{V}' \rangle$. *For every cycle* $\pi = \bar{s} \rightarrow^+ \bar{s}$ *in* $\mathcal{P}_\mathcal{G}$, *the following holds for each of the* Π_i' *($i \in 1..n+1$):*

1. *either* $\forall \bar{s}' \in S(\pi).\bar{s}_i' = \bar{s}_i$
2. *or* $\exists \pi_i = \bar{s}_i \rightarrow^+ \bar{s}_i.\forall s \in S(\pi_i).\exists \langle \bar{s}', s \rangle \in S(\pi)$

Furthermore, for at least one Π_i', *case 2 holds.*

Lemma 2 follows from the following observation. Consider a state vector $\bar{s} = \langle s_0, \ldots, s_n \rangle \in \mathcal{S}_\mathcal{P}$ that is part of a cycle π. If we traverse π all the way back to $\bar{s}$, then locally in each Π_i', we have moved from s_i to s_i, meaning that either we did not move at all (case 1) or we have traversed a local cycle in Π_i' (case 2). Of course, for at least one of the Π_i', case 2 must hold, otherwise π would not contain any transitions, and hence not be a cycle.

Independent Cycles. Lemma 2 implies that if for at least one of the Π_i, s_i is contained in a *non-trivial, independent strongly connected component* (SCC), then $\bar{s}$ (and, in fact, any state vector containing s_i) is part of a cycle in $\mathcal{N}_\mathcal{G}$. An *SCC* is a subgraph in which every state is reachable from every other state in the SCC. It is *non-trivial* if it contains at least one transition.[2] Finally, it is *independent* if it consists of transitions that require no synchronisation with other transitions in the network. Since we avoid the need to synchronise with the property automaton whenever possible (see Sect. 2), there can be SCCs in a

---

[2] Alternatively, an SCC is called trivial if it contains exactly one state, but here we use the criterion that an SCC is trivial if it contains no transitions.

process LTS that require no synchronisation with any other process LTS, including the property automaton. Being aware of reaching independent cycles during model checking can be very helpful: if we ever reach a state vector containing at least one state in an independent cycle, and an accepting property state, then we immediately know that there is an accepting cycle.

Independent SCCs can be detected in each Π_i' by employing a variant of the well-known SCC algorithm of Tarjan [31], in which we limit ourselves to the exploration of independent transitions, and we launch Tarjan's algorithm once from each of the states $s_i \in \mathcal{S}_i'$, while never reexploring those states that were visited during previous explorations.

This approach runs in a time linear to the number of states, since Tarjan's algorithm runs in linear time, and each state is explored at most once. In the end, trivial SCCs are removed from the results.

Cycle Entry States. From Lemma 2, we know that during a search, a cycle in $\mathcal{P}_{\mathcal{G}}$ can only have been completely traversed as soon as at least one local cycle in one of the Π_i' is traversed. Because of that fact, we would like to analyse the Π_i' to determine which states are possible entry points to cycles (and therefore points where a cycle can also be closed).

There exist algorithms to identify all elementary cycles, i.e. cycles in which no state is present more than once, in a directed graph, for instance [18,31]. However, these algorithms have a time complexity which is exponential in the number of vertices, and therefore larger than we can allow, i.e. larger than computing $\mathcal{P}_{\mathcal{G}}$. Because of this, we propose a new algorithm (Algorithm 2), which does not identify all elementary cycles individually, but instead identifies all states by which at least one elementary cycle can be entered via some path from the initial state. Besides this, for every such state, it keeps track of the transition labels that require synchronisation in $\mathcal{P}$ and are associated to at least one transition of a cycle entered via that state. These labels are elements of what we call the *action dependency set* associated with a state. The algorithm has a worst case complexity of $O(n^2)$, with n the number of states.

As an example, consider the LTS in Fig. 3. The cycle entry states are marked black. If a search starts from s_0, then s_1, s_4, and s_3 are entry states: path $s_0 \rightarrow s_1$ leads to cycles $s_1 \rightarrow s_2 \rightarrow s_3 \rightarrow s_1$ and $s_1 \rightarrow s_2 \rightarrow s_4 \rightarrow s_3 \rightarrow s_1$, path $s_0 \rightarrow s_4$ leads to $s_4 \rightarrow s_3 \rightarrow s_1 \rightarrow s_2 \rightarrow s_4$, and path $s_0 \rightarrow s_4 \rightarrow s_3$ leads to $s_3 \rightarrow s_1 \rightarrow s_2 \rightarrow s_3$. The action dependency sets are $\{a,b,c,d,e\}$ for s_1, $\{e,c,a,d\}$ for s_4, and $\{c,a,b\}$ for s_3. Note that an SCC detection algorithm does not provide us the desired result. For instance, Tarjan's algorithm will identify $s_1, \ldots, s_4$ as an SCC, with either s_1 or s_4 as root state, depending on the DFS-order, but it will not distinguish s_2 from the other states.

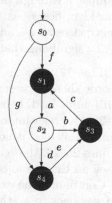

Fig. 3. Cycle entries

The DFS-based algorithm is described in procedure DFSCHECKENTRIES (line 5), which is applied to each of the initial states in $\mathcal{P}$ (line 6), after some global sets have been initialised. There are three *Closed* sets, i.e. sets consisting of fully explored states: $Closed_{co}$, containing closed states that are in a cycle which is currently open, i.e. partially on the DFS stack, $Closed_{cc}$, containing states that are on a closed cycle, and *Closed*, containing states not on a cycle. Furthermore, for each of the Π_i', there are several sets:

- *cycleentries*$_i$ contains the states in S_i' that have been identified as cycle entry states;
- *creps*$_i$ contains a subset of *cycleentries*$_i$ of so-called *representatives*. For each cycle in Π_i', at least one of its states is representative;
- *sdeps*$_i$ records prioritised connections between states and representatives, to keep track of which states are directly connected via a transition to a representative, and which states are indirectly connected via states that are directly connected;
- *asets*$_i$ contains the action dependency sets of the cycle entry states, i.e. states in *cycleentries*$_i$.

Finally, *cclosing* contains cycle entry states of open cycles, and *curdeps* contains the currently recorded connections between the state at the top of the DFS stack and representatives.

For each transition $s \xrightarrow{a} s'$ of state s for which DFSCHECKENTRIES is called, i.e. which is at the top of the DFS stack, a number of distinct situations is considered (we refer to the DFS stack as *stack* in Algorithm 2):

1: (Line 10): if s' is on the DFS stack ($s' \in stack$), then s' is clearly a cycle entry state, since $\underline{s}_i \rightarrow^* s \rightarrow s'$ leads to cycle $s' \rightarrow^+ s'$. Hence, we add s' to *cclosing* (the cycle is still open) and *cycleentries*$_i$. We record in *curdeps* that s relates to (representative) s' with priority 1, indicating a direct connection.

2: (Line 13): if s' is in $Closed_{co}$, then we relate s to all representatives that have been related to s', but now with an incremented priority, representing an indirect connection ($sdeps_i(s)(t) = \perp$ at line 15 means that $sdeps_i(s)(t)$ is undefined). For example, if through the LTS of Fig. 3, the algorithm first explores $s_0 \rightarrow s_1 \rightarrow s_2 \rightarrow s_3$, then identifies s_1 as cycle entry, records $\langle s_1, 1 \rangle$ as a direct connection for s_3, backtracks over s_3, and then reaches s_3 again via s_4, then s_4 gets the connection $\langle s_1, 2 \rangle$, signifying that s_4 relates to s_1 via s_3.

3: (Line 17): if s' is in $Closed_{cc}$, then s' is a cycle entry state. At line 19, D records those representatives to which s' has a more direct connection than s (with 'undefined' being the weakest connection). If D is not empty, then at lines 21–22, the relevant representatives get connected to s'. If any of the involved connections of s' is not direct, then reopening of s' is required (line 24). Finally, at lines 25–26, those connections are set to 1, by which repeated reopening of s' based on those connections is prevented.

Continuing the example from the previous item, if the search backtracks all the way back to s_0, then $s_1, \ldots, s_4$ are all in $Closed_{cc}$. If then, s_4 is reached again from s_0, s_4 is identified as cycle entry. However, the path $s_0 \rightarrow s_4$ can be extended such that s_3 is cycle entry, but this still needs to be detected. Since $\langle s_1, 2 \rangle$ is an indirect connection of s_4, it will be reexplored. This leads us to s_3, which will now be identified as cycle entry, at which point the search backtracks, since s_3 has no indirect connections.

4: (Line 27): if s' is neither on the stack, nor in any *Closed* set, then the search continues via s', and the connections of s' are connections for s as well.

Once s' has been explored, a is added to the action dependency set of the states in *curdeps*, if a-transitions require synchronisation (lines 30–31). Finally, *curdeps* is used to update $sdeps_i(s)$: for every representative in either of the two sets, we keep the strongest recorded connection in $sdeps_i(s)$.

When s is fully explored, s is added to *Closed* if there are no connections, i.e. s is not part of a cycle (lines 33–34). Otherwise, s is part of an open cycle (lines 35–36), and hence added to $Closed_{co}$. Finally, if s represents at least one open cycle, we move s to the set of representatives $creps_i$. Backtracking over s means that the associated open cycles are now closed. All states no longer related to an open cycle are moved to $Closed_{cc}$ (lines 37–41).

Essential Cycle Entries.
Finally, having detected all cycle entry states for each of the Π_i', we can consider

---

Algorithm 2. Cycle entry detection

Require: network $\mathcal{P} = \langle \Pi', \mathcal{V}' \rangle$
    procedure IDENTIFYCYCLEENTRIES($\mathcal{P}$):
2:    **for all** $i \in 1..n + 1$ **do**
        - $Closed, Closed_{co}, Closed_{cc}, cycleentries_i \leftarrow \emptyset$
4:      - $sdeps_i, asets_i, creps_i \leftarrow \emptyset$
        - $cclosing, curdeps \leftarrow \emptyset$
6:      - DFSCHECKENTRIES($\underline{s}_i, i$)
    procedure DFSCHECKENTRIES(s, i):
8:    **for all** $\langle a, s' \rangle \in$ OUT(s) **do**
        - $curdeps \leftarrow \emptyset$
10:    **if** $s' \in stack$ **then**
        - add s' to $cclosing$ and $cycleentries_i$
12:      - add $\langle s', 1 \rangle$ to $curdeps$
    else if $s' \in Closed_{co}$ **then**
14:      **for all** $\langle t, c \rangle \in sdeps_i(s')$ **do**
        if $sdeps_i(s)(t) = \perp$ **then**
16:        - add $\langle t, c + 1 \rangle$ to $curdeps$
    else if $s' \in Closed_{cc}$ **then**
18:      - add s' to $cycleentries_i$
        - $D \leftarrow \{t \mid \langle sdeps_i(s')(t) < sdeps_i(s)(t)\}$
20:    **if** $D \neq \emptyset$ **then**
        for all $t \in D$ **do**
22:        - $sdeps_i(t)(s') \leftarrow 1$
        if $\exists t \in D.sdeps_i(s')(t) > 1$ **then**
24:        - DFSCHECKENTRIES(s', i)
        for all $t \in D$ **do**
26:        - set $curdeps(t)$ and $sdeps_i(s')(t)$ to 1
    else if $s' \notin Closed$ **then**
28:      - DFSCHECKENTRIES(s', i)
        - $curdeps \leftarrow sdeps_i(s')$
30:    **if** a requires synchr. **then**
        - add a to $asets_i$ of the states in $curdeps$
32:    - update $sdeps_i(s)$ with $curdeps$
    if $sdeps_i(s) = \emptyset$ **then**
34:    - add s to $Closed$
    else if $s \notin Closed_{cc}$ **then**
36:    - add s to $Closed_{co}$
    if $s \in cclosing$ **then**
38:    - move s from $cclosing$ to $creps_i$
        for all $t \in Closed_{co}$ **do**
40:      **if** no states in $sdeps_i(t)$ are in $cclosing$ **then**
        - move t from $Closed_{co}$ to $Closed_{cc}$

how the Π_i' may synchronise. For instance, if a local cycle $\pi = s_0 \xrightarrow{a} s_0$ exists in Π_1', and a requires synchronisation, and there is only one other cycle π' containing an a-transition in Π_2', then any cycle containing a in $\mathcal{P}_{\mathcal{G}}$ must be the result of combining π and π'. Therefore, to be aware of the possibility of a cycle occurring in $\mathcal{P}_{\mathcal{G}}$ during a search, it suffices to keep track of only one of the two cycles π and π', i.e. only the cycle entry states of one of the two.

Algorithm 3 selects among the cycle entry states a subset containing what we call the *essential* cycle entry states, or essential states. At lines 1–2, we construct an integrated and sorted version of all the $creps_i$, in which the representatives of all Π_i' are sorted by the number of actions in their action dependency set,

---

Algorithm 3. Selecting essential states

Require: *creps, sdeps, asets,* $\mathcal{V}'$
- *sorted-creps* $\leftarrow \{\langle i, s \rangle \mid i \in 1..n+1 \land s \in creps_i\}$
2: - sort the $\langle i, s \rangle$ in *sorted-creps* on $|asets_i(s)|$
    for all $i \in 1..n+1$ **do**
4:      - *essential$_i$* $\leftarrow creps_i$
        - *removed$_i$* $\leftarrow \emptyset$
6: **for all** $\langle i, s \rangle \in$ *sorted-creps* **do**
        if $\forall a \in asets_i(s).\exists \langle a, T \rangle \in \mathcal{V}', j \in T \setminus \{i\}.a \notin removed_j$ **then**
8:          - move s from *essential$_i$* to *removed$_i$*
        for all $i \in 1..n+1, s \in essential_i$ **do**
10:         - add the states in *sdeps$_i$*(s) to *essential$_i$*

---

from small to large. Then, all representatives are at first selected (lines 3–5). The selection procedure is covered at lines 6–8: if for a representative s of Π_i', none of its actions is shared with a removed representative from some other Π_j', then s can be safely removed. Finally, at lines 9–10, all cycle entry states with connections to essential representatives are marked as being essential as well.

Note that the approach suggested here only approximates the real relation between elementary cycles in the network, since multiple cycles may share cycle entry states, and in those cases, their synchronising actions may be lumped together in one action dependency set. However, improving on this would involve the detection of all individual elementary cycles, which is too time-consuming.

3.3   Using the Static Analysis Results in the Piggyback Algorithm

The algorithms described in Sect. 3.2 can be used in a pre-processing phase to provide additional structural information for the piggyback algorithm. We describe here how and when that information can be used, referring back to Algorithm 1.

First of all, detecting independent cycles in the process LTSs results in a set of states C_i, for each Π_i', consisting of all the states that are in at least one independent cycle. Whenever the piggyback algorithm reaches a state vector $\bar{s}'$ for which 1) there exists at least one $i \in 1..n$ such that $\bar{s}_i' \in C_i$ and 2) $\{j \mid (L_j, K_j) \in \mathcal{F} \land \bar{s}_{n+1}' \in K_j\} \neq \emptyset$, then an accepting cycle has been found, since one can construct from $\bar{s}'$ a cycle by following the transitions in the independent cycle in Π_i'. This can be checked directly after line 6 in Algorithm 1.

Second of all, knowing the cycle entry states for each Π_i' can help to distinguish blocking situations occurring due to the confluence of paths from situations occurring due to the closing of a cycle. When blocking occurs on a state $\bar{s}$ in which no process state enters a process-local cycle, i.e. no state is a cycle entry state, we can conclude that the blocking cannot have been caused by closing a global (system-level) cycle. This check can be added to Algorithm 1 at line 21. Only if the check evaluates to true, will the blocking occurrence be marked. This can be even further improved if we also keep track of when we are closing process-local cycles, starting from the moment when the current piggyback value was picked up. Only in those cases where at least one such cycle is closed, is it possible that we are also closing a cycle in $\mathcal{P}_\mathcal{G}$. Besides this advantage, one can as well improve the selection of piggyback values in those cases where the Rabin automaton only contains cycles in which the cycle entry states are all in some K_i $(1 \leq i \leq |\mathcal{F}|)$: only when a state $\bar{s}$ contains an accepting property state *and* has at least one cycle entry state should it be selected for piggybacking. This can be used as an additional condition in Algorithm 1 at lines 2 and 12.

Finally, knowing the essential states for each Π_i' helps us to further distinguish promising from unpromising situations: only blocking situations involving essential states are interesting for post-processing, since a cycle in $\mathcal{P}_\mathcal{G}$ must be closed by revisiting a state $\bar{s}$ containing an essential state. Furthermore, under the same assumption about the Rabin automaton as described above, information on the essential states can help to make more informed decisions regarding the selection of piggyback values. This affects Algorithm 1 at the same lines as the ones mentioned above for cycle entry information.

4 GPU Model Checking

GPUEXPLORE [35,36] is an explicit-state model checker that practically runs entirely on a GPU (only the general progress is checked on the host side, i.e. by a thread running on the Central Processing Unit (CPU)). It is written in CUDA C, an extension of C offered by NVIDIA. It provides the Compute Unified Device Architecture interface to write applications for NVIDIA's GPUs. GPU-EXPLORE takes an LTS network as input, and can construct the system LTS using many threads in a BFS-based exploration, while checking on-the-fly for the presence of deadlocks and violations of safety properties. A safety property can be added as an automaton to the network. The general approach of GPU-EXPLORE is discussed here, leaving out many of the details that are not relevant for understanding the current work. The interested reader is referred to [35,36].

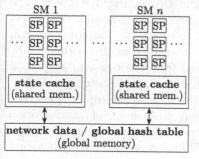

Fig. 4. GPUEXPLORE overview

In a CUDA program, the host launches CUDA functions called *kernels*, that are to be executed many times in parallel by a specified number of GPU threads. Usually, all threads run the same kernel using different parts of the input data, although some GPUs allow multiple different kernels to be executed simultaneously (GPUEXPLORE does not use this feature). Each thread is executed by a streaming processor (SP), see Fig. 4. Threads are grouped in *blocks* of a predefined size. Each block is assigned to a streaming multiprocessor (SM).

Each thread has a number of on-chip registers that allow fast access. The threads in a block together share memory to exchange data, which is located in the (on-chip) *shared memory* of an SM. Finally, the blocks can share data using the *global memory* of the GPU, which is relatively large, but slow, since it is off-chip. The global memory is used to exchange data between the host and the kernel. The GTX TITAN X, which we used for our experiments, has 12 GB global memory and 24 SMs, each having 128 SPs, which is in total 3,072 SPs.

Writing well-performing GPU applications is challenging, due to the execution model of GPUs, which is *Single Instruction Multiple Threads*. Threads are partitioned in groups of 32 called *warps*. The threads in a warp run in lock-step, sharing a program counter, so they always execute the same program instruction. Hence, thread divergence, i.e. the phenomenon of threads being forced to execute different instructions (e.g., due to if-then-else constructions) or to access physically distant parts of the global memory, negatively affects performance.

Model checking tends to introduce divergences frequently, as it requires combining the behaviour of the processes in the network, and accessing and storing state vectors of the system state space in the global memory. In GPUEXPLORE, this is mitigated by combining relevant network information as much as possible in 32-bit integers, and storing these as textures, that only allow read access and use a dedicated cache to speed up random accesses. Furthermore, in the global memory, a hash table is used to store state vectors (Fig. 4). The hash table has been designed to optimise accesses of entire warps: the space is partitioned into buckets consisting of 32 integers, precisely enough for one warp to fetch a bucket with one combined memory access. State vectors are hashed to buckets, and placed within a bucket in an available slot. If the bucket is full, another hash function is used to find a new bucket. Each block accesses the global hash table to collect vectors that still require exploration. To each state vector with n process states, a *group* of n threads is assigned to construct its successors using fine-grained parallelism. Since access to the global memory is slow, each block uses a dedicated state cache (Fig. 4). It serves to collect newly produced state vectors, that are subsequently stored in the global hash table in batches. With the cache, block-local duplicates can be detected. The approach allows to work with vectors that require any number of integers smaller than 32 to be stored.

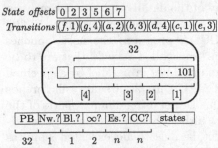

Fig. 5. Encodings of an LTS and a state vector with bookkeeping

The data structures used are illustrated in Fig. 5. At the top, an encoding of the LTS in Fig. 3 is given. The *State offsets* array contains the offsets needed to read the outgoing transitions of a state i in *Transitions*: they are stored from position *State offsets*[i] up to (not including) *State offsets*[$i+1$]. A transition is a pair of integers, the first being the (index of) a transition label, and the second being the target state. When possible, multiple target states are listed in one entry (in the case of non-determinism). Transitions are stored as compactly as possible: for a transition of Π_i', the $\log_2(|\mathcal{A}_i|)$ bits needed to store the label index are combined with the $\log_2(|\mathcal{S}_i|)$ bits needed to store the target state in one 32-bit integer.

Below the LTS encoding, the encoding of a state vector can be seen. The top part corresponds to how GPUEXPLORE originally used to encode state vectors: the state ID's for the individual process LTSs are concatenated. For each of the Π_i', $\log_2(|\mathcal{S}_i|)$ bits are reserved in the vector. If required, multiple 32-bit integers are used to store a vector. At the bottom of Fig. 5, the structure of a state vector extended with bookkeeping bits is displayed. Besides the states of the Π_i':

- n bits are reserved to indicate which of the processes have already fully traversed a local cycle since the last piggyback value was picked up (CC?);
- n bits are reserved to indicate which of the states are essential (Es.?);
- Two bits are reserved to indicate whether the property automaton is in a state that requires infinite visits, finite visits, or neither (∞?);
- One bit is used to indicate whether blocking occurred on the vector (Bl.?);
- One bit indicates whether the vector is new, i.e. requires exploration (Nw.?);
- Thirty-two bits are reserved to store a piggyback value (PB).

Instead of piggybacking vectors, which is costly space-wise, pointers to the global hash table are piggybacked. One 32-bit integer suffices: in 27 bits, we store the index of a bucket (in 12 GB, about 100 million buckets can be stored), and with the remaining 5 bits, the position of a vector within the bucket is given.

GPUEXPLORE is extended as follows to support the checking of linear-time properties. First of all, the network data contains the information we obtained through static analysis, plus the status of the property states (requires infinite visits, finite visits, or neither). The current implementation supports the use of Rabin automata in which $\mathcal{F}$ is a singleton; this can be straightforwardly extended by increasing the number of bookkeeping bits. Furthermore, transitions that lead to a cycle entry state and close a cycle are marked, and essential states are marked. Second of all, using that information, we mark state vectors in the obvious way, i.e. the status of the individual process states is kept in the vector. To do this correctly, it is important that these markings are at times merged; different groups may construct the same successor state with different markings. Both when storing states in the local state cache, and in the global hash table, this merging is performed.

The overall approach follows Algorithm 1 and the extensions discussed in Sect. 3.3. If all cycles in the Rabin automaton can only be entered via states in K ($\mathcal{F} = \{(L, K)\}$), then visiting a vector state with a property state in K is only selected as a piggyback value if at least one state in the vector is essential. This can avoid some of the issues of standard piggybacking, in particular shadowing such as in Fig. 2a, since $\bar{s}_0$ will not be selected as a piggyback value if no state in it is essential.

When blocking occurs on a state vector $\bar{s}$, this is marked (in Bl.?) *only* if $\bar{s}$ contains an essential state (Es.?) and at least one local cycle has been traversed (CC?). By Lemma 1, this is sufficient. Once the state space has been completely explored without detection of a counter-example, post-processing of the blocking occurrences must be conducted. Since DFSs cannot be performed efficiently on a GPU, we need to perform this post-processing in a way different from the technique in [13]. Instead, we launch up to sixteen parallel BFSs at a time, each performed by several thread blocks from one of the marked states. During each BFS, visited and explored states are marked in the global hash table using two bits. The space previously occupied to store a piggyback value pointer can be reused for this purpose, hence the space for 32/2 parallel BFSs. Each BFS is bounded by the fact that the global hash table is scanned completely for open states up to a predefined number of times. The search in each BFS can be limited to those processes for which it was indicated that they fully traversed a local cycle (in the CC? bits). The sixteen groups of thread blocks process all marked states in this way, until either none are left, or an accepting cycle has been detected.

5   Experimental Results

GPUEXPLORE is equipped with a separate preprocessor, written in PYTHON. It can read LTS networks and produces an output file that configures the GPU model checker. To the preprocessor, we added the ability to read Rabin automata, which are stored as normal LTSs with some additional information regarding $\mathcal{F}$. Also, we implemented the algorithms explained in Sect. 3. Results on cycle entry states and essential states is added to the configuration file, while results in independent SCCs are added by adapting the LTSs in the network: any state appearing in such an SCC is equipped with an independent selfloop. This allows the model checker to efficiently determine whether a state is in an independent SCC or not, just by looking at the outgoing transitions of that state.

We conducted experiments using input models from various sources, namely the BEEM database [26], the VLTS benchmark suite[3], the MCRL2 website[4], and two models (ABP and broadcast) designed by us.

To conduct the experiments, a machine with an AMD A6-3670 CPU, 16 GB memory, and an NVIDIA GEFORCE TITAN X GPU, running Linux Mint 17.2 was used. GPUEXPLORE used 3120 blocks, 512 threads per block, which turned out to be optimal for reachability analysis [35,36]. Table 1 provides the runtime results in seconds. Besides reachability analysis (**Rch.**) and standard piggybacking (**PB**), several variants of the algorithm have been used, namely:

- **+iSCC**: A version using only the information on independent SCCs;
- **+SPB**: +iSCC plus smart piggyback value selection based on essential states;
- **+SBR**: +SPB with smart blocking resolution, i.e. only blockings with essential states and the closing of a local cycle are considered.

---

[3] http://cadp.inria.fr/resources/vlts.
[4] http://www.mcrl2.org.

Table 1. GPU runtimes (in seconds) for various piggyback variants

Model	Prop.	$|\mathcal{S}_{\mathcal{P}_G}|$	Rch.	PB		+iSCC		+SPB		+SBR	
				Time	?	Time	?	Time	?	Time	?
1394	request-response	200K	2.68	5.01	✓	5.05	✓	4.10	✓	**3.02**	✓
1394.1	request-response	36.9M	10.42	16.39	✓	16.37	✓	13.20	✓	**12.11**	✓
acs	lock eventually freed	4.8K	1.61	0.40	✗	0.37	✗	0.38	✗	**0.35**	✗
acs.1	lock eventually freed	200K	2.14	0.45	✗	0.45	✗	0.46	✗	**0.43**	✗
wafer stepper.1	$\Box\Diamond$ all wafers exposed	3.8M	6.61	35.34	✓	35.32	✓	23.51	✓	**12.63**	✓
ABP	request-response	481.8M	968.44	253.57	✗	258.21	✗	230.58	✗	**180.35**	✗
broadcast	$\Box\Diamond$ communication succeeds	105.4M	151.05	53.43	✗	57.36	✗	48.35	✗	**47.36**	✗
transit	$\Box\Diamond$ message sent or buffered	4.4M	9.06	0.99	✗	**0.81**	✗	t.o.p.	-	t.o.p.	-
asyn3	$\Box\Diamond$ leader announced or reset	17.2M	49.65	2.84	✗	2.75	✗	2.75	✗	**2.70**	✗
asyn3.1	$\Box\Diamond$ leader announced or reset	215.4M	472.43	**2.39**	✗	2.52	✗	2.40	✗	2.43	✗
ODP	$\Box\Diamond$ WORK executed	178K	4.65	1.14	✗	**1.11**	✗	**1.11**	✗	1.12	✗
ODP.1	$\Box\Diamond$ WORK executed	10.1M	13.49	1.99	✗	2.02	✗	2.03	✗	**1.91**	✗
lamport.8	$\Box\Diamond P0@CS$	35.1M	35.89	2.33	✗	2.32	✗	**2.26**	✗	2.27	✗
lann.6	$\Box\Diamond P0@CS$	144M	136.23	**1.62**	✗	1.64	✗	4.03	✗	1.64	✗
lann.7	$\Box\Diamond P0@CS$	160M	202.46	1.56	✗	**1.50**	✗	1.51	✗	1.51	✗
peterson.7	$\Box P0$ wait $\implies \Diamond P0@CS$	142.5M	4223.36	**368.30**	✗	384.12	✗	502.53	✗	712.63	✗
szymanski.5	$\Box P0$ wait $\implies \Diamond P0@CS$	79.5M	323.34	**91.30**	✗	102.27	✗	165.52	✗	181.54	✗

In Table 1, for each model, a brief description of the property is given, where '$\Box$' and '$\Diamond$' are shorthand for 'always' and 'eventually', in line with the LTL operators. For each experiment, its result is reported, where ✓ indicates that the property is satisfied, and ✗ means that it is not.

We do not compare the GPUEXPLORE runtimes with those of a standard CPU model checker. It has been established that on the same benchmarks, GPU-EXPLORE outperforms state-of-the-art (single-core) explicit-state model checkers by one to two orders of magnitude [35, 36]. If we can establish that the checking of linear-time properties can be done in comparable runtimes, then we can safely conclude that the GPU can be effectively applied for this as well.

Table 1 does not provide the runtimes of the preprocessing steps for each experiment, which involve the relevant algorithms described in Sect. 3. In practically all the cases, preprocessing took only a fraction of the subsequent exploration time. An exception to this is the transit model, for which the detection of cycle entry states and essential states caused a time-out (t.o.p. = time-out during preprocessing in Table 1). In that model, one process LTS is much larger than the others, making it costly to analyse it in comparison to directly exploring the system LTS.

First of all, we experienced that for most of the analysed models, the standard piggyback algorithm is already very efficient, and we can conclude that it is suitable to check liveness properties with a GPU. Concerning the proposed extensions, there are two types of situations where we experienced improved run-times. The first situation is when post-processing has to be performed. In the cases 1394, 1394.1, and wafer stepper.1, the extensions were more efficient, due to being less prone to mark blocking occurrences. The second situation is when the infinitely visitable states in the Rabin automaton are not immediately reached in the state space search. More precisely, in those cases where there is a non-empty prefix in the property automaton before the suffix expressing the infinite behaviour part, the extensions made more informed decisions. This was the case for acs and broadcast. The ability to identify independent SCCs was also helpful in some cases: for transit, ODP, and lann.7, +iSCC was the most efficient option.

Finally, it should be noted that for peterson.7 and szymanski.5, two cases from the BEEM database, the extensions actually lead to worse results. It turns out that the infinitely visitable states of the Rabin automata are reachable already very early on during the state space search, leading to many possible candidates for piggybacking. This holds for all the extensions. In general, on the GPU, the extensions have one major drawback compared to standard piggybacking, which is the fact that vector markings have to be maintained in the global hash table. This means that additional writes to the global memory must be done frequently. In case this additional marking work does not productively contribute to finding a counter-example, the runtime only increases. It would be interesting to investigate whether the same can be observed when model checking is done on the CPU.

Concluding, the piggyback algorithm is very suitable to efficiently check liveness properties with a GPU. Under certain circumstances, the suggested extensions improve on these results, in particular when post-processing needs to be performed, and when the property has a non-empty prefix. In several cases, however, applying the extensions actually negatively influenced the runtimes. To overcome this, it seems that a good strategy would be to first run the standard piggyback algorithm, and stop it if post-processing would be required. Instead of post-processing, one could then launch the most informed variant (+SBR), to try to find a counter-example in that way. In case the latter is also not successful, post-processing is still possible.

6   Conclusions

We presented a method to check linear-time properties using a BFS-based search technique. It employs the piggybacking algorithm, adapted to take new insights regarding blocking into account. Furthermore, it uses structural information of the input model obtained by applying new preprocessing algorithms. Like standard piggybacking, it is complete for bounded-suffix model checking, i.e. for finding counter-examples involving cycles no longer than a given bound.

We demonstrated that both the original piggyback algorithm and the proposed extensions generally work effectively in a GPU model checker, but we expect that the extensions also work well in other settings where BFS-based techniques need to be applied.

Future Work. We plan to involve fairness constraints, to rule out specific counter-examples, and reduction techniques, such as partial order reduction [2].

References

1. Alpern, B., Schneider, F.: Defining liveness. Inform. Process. Lett. **21**(4), 181–185 (1985)
2. Baier, C., Katoen, J.P.: Principles of Model Checking. The MIT Press, Cambridge (2008)
3. Barnat, J., Bauch, P., Brim, L., Češka, M.: Designing fast LTL model checking algorithms for many-core GPUs. J. Parall. Distrib. Comput. **72**, 1083–1097 (2012)
4. Barnat, J., Brim, L., Ročkai, P.: A time-optimal on-the-fly parallel algorithm for model checking of weak LTL properties. In: Breitman, K., Cavalcanti, A. (eds.) ICFEM 2009. LNCS, vol. 5885, pp. 407–425. Springer, Heidelberg (2009)
5. Barnat, J., Brim, L., Stříbrná, J.: Distributed LTL model-checking in SPIN. In: Dwyer, M.B. (ed.) SPIN 2001. LNCS, vol. 2057, pp. 200–216. Springer, Heidelberg (2001)
6. Bartocci, E., DeFrancisco, R., Smolka, S.: Towards a GPGPU-parallel SPIN model checker. In: SPIN, pp. 87–96. ACM (2014)
7. Blom, S., van de Pol, J., Weber, M.: LTSMIN: distributed and symbolic reachability. In: Touili, T., Cook, B., Jackson, P. (eds.) CAV 2010. LNCS, vol. 6174, pp. 354–359. Springer, Heidelberg (2010)
8. Bošnački, D., Edelkamp, S., Sulewski, D., Wijs, A.: Parallel probabilistic model checking on general purpose graphic processors. STTT **13**(1), 21–35 (2011)
9. Češka, M., Pilar, P., Paoletti, N., Brim, L., Kwiatkowska, M.: PRISM-PSY: precise GPU-accelerated parameter synthesis for stochastic systems. In: Chechik, M., Raskin, J.-F. (eds.) TACAS 2016. LNCS, vol. 9636, pp. 367–384. Springer, Heidelberg (2016). doi:10.1007/978-3-662-49674-9_21
10. Courcoubetis, C., Vardi, M., Wolper, P., Yannakakis, M.: Memory efficient algorithms for the verification of temporal properties. In: Clarke, E.M., Kurshan, R.P. (eds.) CAV 1990. LNCS, vol. 531, pp. 233–242. Springer, Heidelberg (1990)
11. Dill, D.: The murphi verification system. In: Alur, R., Henzinger, T.A. (eds.) CAV 1996. LNCS, vol. 1102, pp. 390–393. Springer, Heidelberg (1996)
12. Evangelista, S., Laarman, A., Petrucci, L., van de Pol, J.: Improved multi-core nested depth-first search. In: Chakraborty, S., Mukund, M. (eds.) ATVA 2012. LNCS, vol. 7561, pp. 269–283. Springer, Heidelberg (2012)
13. Filippidis, I., Holzmann, G.: An improvement of the piggyback algorithm for parallel model checking. In: SPIN, pp. 48–57. ACM (2014)
14. Geldenhuys, J., Valmari, A.: Tarjan's algorithm makes on-the-Fly LTL verification more efficient. In: Jensen, K., Podelski, A. (eds.) TACAS 2004. LNCS, vol. 2988, pp. 205–219. Springer, Heidelberg (2004)
15. Grädel, E., Thomas, W., Wilke, T. (eds.): Automata, Logics, and Infinite Games. LNCS, vol. 2500. Springer, Heidelberg (2002)
16. Holzmann, G.J.: Parallelizing the spin model checker. In: Donaldson, A., Parker, D. (eds.) SPIN 2012. LNCS, vol. 7385, pp. 155–171. Springer, Heidelberg (2012)
17. Holzmann, G., Peled, D., Yannakakis, M.: On nested depth first search. In: SPIN, pp. 23–32. American Mathematical Society (1996)
18. Johnson, D.: Finding all the elementary circuits of a directed graph. SIAM J. Comput. **4**(1), 77–84 (1975)

19. Kahn, A.: Topological sorting of large networks. Commun. ACM **5**(11), 558–562 (1962)
20. Klein, J., Baier, C.: Experiments with deterministic ω-automata for formulas of linear temporal logic. TCS **363**(2), 182–195 (2006)
21. Kupferman, O.: Automata theory and model checking. In: Clarke, E.M., Henzinger, T.A., Veith, H. (eds.) Handbook of Model Checking. Springer, New York (2015)
22. Kurshan, R.P., Levin, V., Minea, M., Peled, D.A., Yenigün, H.: Static partial order reduction. In: Steffen, B. (ed.) TACAS 1998. LNCS, vol. 1384, pp. 345–357. Springer, Heidelberg (1998)
23. Laarman, A., Langerak, R., van de Pol, J., Weber, M., Wijs, A.: Multi-core nested depth-first search. In: Bultan, T., Hsiung, P.-A. (eds.) ATVA 2011. LNCS, vol. 6996, pp. 321–335. Springer, Heidelberg (2011)
24. Lang, F.: Refined interfaces for compositional verification. In: Najm, E., Pradat-Peyre, J.-F., Donzeau-Gouge, V.V. (eds.) FORTE 2006. LNCS, vol. 4229, pp. 159–174. Springer, Heidelberg (2006)
25. Molnár, V., Darvas, D., Vörös, A., Bartha, T.: Saturation-based incremental LTL model checking with inductive proofs. In: Baier, C., Tinelli, C. (eds.) TACAS 2015. LNCS, vol. 9035, pp. 643–657. Springer, Heidelberg (2015)
26. Pelánek, R.: BEEM: benchmarks for explicit model checkers. In: Bošnački, D., Edelkamp, S. (eds.) SPIN 2007. LNCS, vol. 4595, pp. 263–267. Springer, Heidelberg (2007)
27. Pelánek, R.: Properties of state spaces and their applications. STTT **10**(5), 443–454 (2008)
28. Rabin, M.: Decidability of second order theories and automata on infinite trees. Trans. AMS **141**, 1–35 (1969)
29. Schwoon, S., Esparza, J.: A note on on-the-fly verification algorithms. In: Halbwachs, N., Zuck, L.D. (eds.) TACAS 2005. LNCS, vol. 3440, pp. 174–190. Springer, Heidelberg (2005)
30. Sun, J., Liu, Y., Dong, J.S., Wang, H.H.: Specifying and verifying event-based fairness enhanced systems. In: Liu, S., Araki, K. (eds.) ICFEM 2008. LNCS, vol. 5256, pp. 5–24. Springer, Heidelberg (2008)
31. Tarjan, R.: Depth-first search and linear graph algorithms. SIAM J. Comput. **1**(2), 146–160 (1972)
32. Vardi, M., Wolper, P.: An automata-theoretic approach to automatic program verification. In: LICS, pp. 332–344. IEEE (1986)
33. Wijs, A.: GPU accelerated strong and branching bisimilarity checking. In: Baier, C., Tinelli, C. (eds.) TACAS 2015. LNCS, vol. 9035, pp. 368–383. Springer, Heidelberg (2015)
34. Wijs, A.J., Bošnački, D.: Improving GPU sparse matrix-vector multiplication for probabilistic model checking. In: Donaldson, A., Parker, D. (eds.) SPIN 2012. LNCS, vol. 7385, pp. 98–116. Springer, Heidelberg (2012)
35. Wijs, A., Bošnački, D.: GPUexplore: many-core on-the-fly state space exploration using GPUs. In: Ábrahám, E., Havelund, K. (eds.) TACAS 2014 (ETAPS). LNCS, vol. 8413, pp. 233–247. Springer, Heidelberg (2014)
36. Wijs, A., Bošnački, D.: Many-Core On-The-Fly Model Checking of Safety Properties Using GPUs. STTT (2016)
37. Wijs, A., Katoen, J.-P., Bošnački, D.: GPU-based graph decomposition into strongly connected and maximal end components. In: Biere, A., Bloem, R. (eds.) CAV 2014. LNCS, vol. 8559, pp. 310–326. Springer, Heidelberg (2014)

38. Wu, Z., Liu, Y., Liang, Y., Sun, J.: GPU accelerated counterexample generation in LTL model checking. In: Merz, S., Pang, J. (eds.) ICFEM 2014. LNCS, vol. 8829, pp. 413–429. Springer, Heidelberg (2014)
39. Wu, Z., Liu, Y., Sun, J., Shi, J., Qin, S.: GPU accelerated on-the-fly reachability checking. In: ICECCS, pp. 100–109. IEEE (2015)

BigraphER: Rewriting and Analysis Engine for Bigraphs

Michele Sevegnani[✉] and Muffy Calder

School of Computing Science, University of Glasgow,
Glasgow, UK
michele.sevegnani@glasgow.ac.uk

Abstract. BigraphER is a suite of open-source tools providing an efficient implementation of rewriting, simulation, and visualisation for bigraphs, a universal formalism for modelling interacting systems that evolve in time and space and first introduced by Milner. BigraphER consists of an OCaml library that provides programming interfaces for the manipulation of bigraphs, their constituents and reaction rules, and a command-line tool capable of simulating Bigraphical Reactive Systems (BRSs) and computing their transition systems. Other features are native support for both bigraphs and bigraphs with sharing, stochastic reaction rules, rule priorities, instantiation maps, parameterised controls, predicate checking, graphical output and integration with the probabilistic model checker PRISM.

1 Introduction

Bigraphs were first introduced by Robin Milner as a universal mathematical model for representing the spatial configuration of physical or virtual objects, their interaction capabilities and temporal evolution. They were subsequently extended to stochastic bigraphs [11] and bigraphs with sharing [16], and have been applied in areas such as wireless protocols, home network management, mixed reality systems, cloud computing, security and as meta-models to encode process calculi (*e.g.* Mobile Ambients, CSS).

BigraphER is a modelling and reasoning environment for bigraphs consisting of an OCaml library and a command-line tool. The functionality includes:

- native support for both bigraphs and bigraphs with sharing;
- a rewrite engine with support for stochastic reaction rules, rules with instantiation maps, rule priorities (stochastic) simulation and exhaustive state space exploration;
- predicate checking;
- efficient matching engine based on SAT (used to implement rewriting and predicate checking);
- support for parameterised controls and parameterised reaction rules;
- export labelled transition systems to probabilistic model checker PRISM [12];
- graphical output of bigraphs, reaction rules and transition systems (see Fig. 1 (right) for an example bigraph and graphical layout).

© Springer International Publishing Switzerland 2016
S. Chaudhuri and A. Farzan (Eds.): CAV 2016, Part II, LNCS 9780, pp. 494–501, 2016.
DOI: 10.1007/978-3-319-41540-6_27

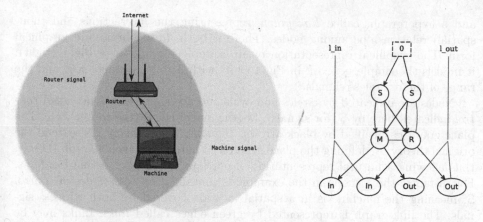

Fig. 1. Left: wireless network with a router and a machine; signal coverage is represented by coloured circles. Right: corresponding bigraphical representation automatically generated by BigraphER (S = signal, R = router, M = machine). (Color figure online)

Example Applications. While many early applications of bigraphs have been to meta-modelling, *e.g.* for encodings of the π-calculus, λ-calculus, and CCS (Calculus of Communicating Systems), applications in other domains are recently beginning to emerge. Some examples are: security for cyber-physical systems [18], quantitative analysis of biological processes [11], cloud computing [19], and a framework to control systems of networked mobile robotic systems [14]. BigraphER has been used to specify and analyse a wide range of case studies in many different application domains: wireless network protocols [6], wireless mesh networks [4], run-time policy management for domestic networks [5], and human-computer interaction in mixed-reality systems [2]. Example analysis has ranged from detecting basic "programming" errors (*e.g.* through type checking) in [2], to generation of example state spaces, and run-time checking of invariants (*i.e.* predicates), implemented on a router in [5].

Related Tools. BigMC [15] is an explicit-state model checking tool for BRSs based on the BPL matching engine [3]. Currently, it does not support stochastic bigraphs nor bigraphs with sharing and can only check reachability properties. Big Red [9] is a visual editor for bigraphs and bigraphical reaction rules implemented as an Eclipse plugin; it does not implement rewriting. DBtk [1] is an implementation of matching for directed bigraphs, a variant of bigraphs with a directed link structure; there is no support for rewriting and BRS execution.

2   Bigraphical Reactive Systems – Overview

A *bigraph* [13] is a pair of relations over the same set of *nodes*: a directed forest, called *place graph*, representing topological space in terms of node containment and a hypergraph, called *link graph*, representing the interactions and (non-spatial) relationships among nodes. There is both an algebraic and graphical form. The graphical representation of an example bigraph is in Fig. 1 (right); it models the simple network in Fig. 1 (left) with a router, a machine, and the range of their wireless signals.

Nodes are indicated by circles and ovals and are assigned a type called *control* indicated here by S (for signals), M (the machine), R (the router), *etc.* The place graph is specified by black arrows. *Bigraphs with sharing* [16] extend the original theory by defining the place graph as a Directed Acyclic Graph (DAG), thus allowing a natural representation of overlapping or intersecting locations. For instance, the M-node in the example is contained by *both* nodes of control S, meaning the machine is in a spatial location covered by both wireless signals. The link graph is represented by green edges called *links*. Links may be only partially specified, in which case they connect a *name*. Names are links (or potential links) to other bigraphs representing the external environment or context. By convention, names are drawn above the bigraph. In the example, names l_in and l_out are used to name incoming and outgoing (potential) links to remote resources. The number of links of a node, also called *arity*, depends on its control, *i.e.* entities with the same control have the same number of links. Dashed rectangles denote *regions* of adjacent parts of the system and *sites* are used to model parts of the model that have been abstracted away (see Fig. 3 (top)). A bigraph with node identifiers is said to be *concrete*. When all the identifiers are ignored, we obtain an *abstract* bigraph which can be interpreted as an equivalence class of bigraphs with the same structure.

A BRS consists of a set of *reaction rules* together with an initial bigraph on which the rules operate. In *stochastic bigraphs* [11], a rate is associated with each rule.

3   BigraphER Specification Language

The BigraphER specification language almost corresponds to the standard algebraic notation for bigraphical expressions [13, 16]. In the following, we highlight some of the distinctive features of the BigraphER language by presenting a simple model for wireless networks inspired by [5]. The model is specified by the code in Fig. 2. A valid BRS model consists of four separate blocks of definitions: a *signature* containing all the controls in the model, a set of bigraphs, a set of reaction rules and a *reactive system* specifying the initial state of the BRS, the priority hierarchy among reaction rules and a set of predicates.

Controls are defined in lines 1–2 by using keyword `ctrl`. The integer on the right-hand side of each definition indicates the arity of each control. The keyword `atomic` specifies that a node may not contain other nodes. Bigraph definitions are in lines 4–8. Line 5 defines bigraph s0. Expression M{w,s} denotes a node of control M with names w and s. Operators . and | denote nesting and merge product, respectively. Nesting is the operation allowing to place a bigraph inside another one; merge product is the operation placing two bigraphs

```
1  ctrl M = 2; ctrl R = 2; ctrl S = 1;
2  atomic ctrl In = 1; atomic ctrl Out = 1; atomic ctrl Block = 1;
3
4  big links = In{l_in} | Out{l_out};
5  big s0 = /s0 /s1 (share (/w (M{w,s0}.links || R{w,s1}.links))
6                   by ([{0,1}, {0,1}], 2)
7                   in (id{s0,s1,l_in,l_out} | S{s0} | S{s1}));
8  big is_in_blocked = M{w,s}.(In{l} |~Block{l} | id);
9
10 react block_in =
11   M{w,s}.(In{l} | id) --> M{w,s}.(In{l} | Block{l} | id);
12
13 react leave_net =
14   /s (share (M{w,s} || id) by ([{0, 1}, {1}], 2) in (id(1,{w,s}) || S{s}))
15   --> ({w} || 1 || 1 || 0 || 0);
16
17 brs
18   init s0;
19   rules = [ { block_in, leave_net } ];
20   preds = { is_in_blocked };
21 endbrs
```

Fig. 2. Specification of a BRS in the BigraphER language.

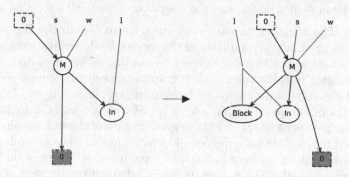

Fig. 3. Reaction rule block_in for blocking a machine's incoming traffic.

side-by-side inside the same region. Closures like /s0 indicate that a link has no names (see link between M and S). Sharing is introduced by ternary operator share ... by ... in .... The first argument specifies the entities to be shared, *e.g.* machine M and router R. The second argument specifies how they are shared: {0, 1} indicates that M is shared by the first and the second signals (counting from left to right). The third argument specifies the entities containing the shared entities, *e.g.* signals Ss0 and Ss1. The graphical representation of s0, automatically generated by BigraphER is shown in Fig. 1 (right).

The code in lines 10–11 defines reaction rule block_in. Operator --> is used to separate the left-hand side from the right-hand side of the rule. Expression id indicates the identity bigraph, *i.e.* the bigraph with one site inside one region. This reaction rule models a firewall rule blocking a machine's incoming traffic. The corresponding graphical representation is in Fig. 3. Reaction rule leave_net defined in lines 13–15 models a machine leaving the network.

Finally, lines 17–21 contain the reactive system definition. A BRS is defined by construct `brs ... endbrs`. Keyword `init` specifies the initial state of the system. In the example, this is bigraph `s0`. Construct `rules = [...]` defines a list of priority classes in descending order of priority. A priority class is specified by construct `{...}` and may only contain reaction rules identifiers. Construct `preds = {...}` defines a set of predicates. Predicate `is_in_blocked` (defined in line 8) can be used to tag states in which there are machines with blocked incoming traffic. In a more extensive model like in [5], this predicate can be used to verify network invariants after network policies are enforced by users.

This simple example highlights the main features; more complex examples including stochastic reaction rules, reducible priority classes and instantiation maps can be accessed at http://www.dcs.gla.ac.uk/~michele/bigrapher.html.

4   Components and Features

The BigraphER command-line tool is composed of three distinct modules: the compiler, the matching engine and the rewriting engine. All are coded in OCaml.

Compiler. The compiler translates an input source file in the BigraphER language into a run-time representation of the model. Each declaration specifies the binding of an identifier to a data type representing either a control, a bigraph or a (stochastic) reaction rule. Each bigraph is stored in memory as a pair of specialised data structures: a sparse boolean matrix encoding the DAG's adjacency matrix of the place graph, and a set of hyperedges (*i.e.* multisets with nodes and names as elements) for the representation of the link graph. Although the BigraphER language only defines abstract bigraphs, the compiler operates on the corresponding concrete bigraphs by assigning arbitrary node labellings. This is required to allow the enumeration of all distinct occurrences of a reaction rule and thus to compute *exit rates* in stochastic BRSs. Additional features are: type-checking of parameterised definitions, combinatorial generation of parametric reaction rules, graphical representation of all the bigraph defined in the input model (useful for debugging).

Matching Engine. The bigraph matching problem determines whether a bigraph, called *pattern*, occurs in another bigraph, called *target*. The BigraphER matching engine implements the algorithm introduced in [16]: a SAT encoding of a specialisation of the sub-graph isomorphism problem. For each instance of the problem, the matching engine generates a set of *constraints* (formulas in Conjunctive Normal Form (CNF)) encoding the instance. Solutions are then obtained by passing all the constraints through the OCaml bindings for the MiniSat solver [7]. Solutions are expressed as total maps from the nodes of the pattern to sub-sets of the nodes of target. Because the matching problem is **NP**-complete, two techniques to optimise performance have been adopted in the implementation. The first is to reduce the size of the SAT instances by applying Tseitin transformation [17] to constraints. The second is to minimise instances by exploiting the symmetries in the structure of the pattern: when enumerating all the occurrences, the automorphisms of the pattern are used to generate all the symmetric solutions starting from a computed solution. The matching engine also implements specialised constraints to support bigraph equality and predicate checking.

Rewrite Engine. This component computes the dynamic evolution of the (stochastic) BRS specified in the input file by iteratively applying all the reaction rules to each bigraph (state) until either a fixpoint or a user-defined bound on the number of states is reached.[1] The transition system generated by a BRS is represented internally by BigraphER as a directed graph; the Continuous Time Markov Chain resulting from a stochastic BRS as a labelled directed graph. Rule application consists of two steps: first the matching engine is queried for occurrences of the left-hand side of a reaction rule, then, for each distinct occurrence, a new state is computed by replacing the occurrence with the right-hand side of the rule (see Fig. 3). BigraphER also supports reaction rules with *instantiation maps*[2] allowing to easily duplicate or discard parts of a bigraph when a reaction rule is applied. The rewriting engine incrementally builds the state space in a breadth-first search (BFS). Support for simulation is obtained by computing only one random path of the transition system. Simulation for stochastic BRSs implements Gillespie's Stochastic Simulation Algorithm (SSA) [10]. Besides standard rule priorities, BigraphER admits *reducible classes*[3] *i.e.* priority classes in which rules are treated like rewriting within an equivalence class. This means that after applying all possible rules in an arbitrary order only a canonical form is stored. This feature allows, for instance, to reduce the number of intermediate states generated by the application of instantaneous stochastic reaction rules. Predicates expressed as matches are checked during the generation of the transition system: every time a new state is discovered, all the predicates specified in the input model are checked against it and the labelling function is updated. The rewriting engine can return either a textual or a graphical representation of the (labelled) transition system and its states. Graphical output is computed by the open-source graph layout generator Graphviz [8]. Textual output is compatible with the PRISM probabilistic model checker, thus enabling quantitative verification for BRSs.

OCaml Library. This component provides programming interfaces for the data structures used internally by the BigraphER command-line tool. For instance, it allows manipulation of bigraphs and their constituents by providing implementation for the following operations: composition, tensor product, parallel product, merge product and nesting. The library also provides APIs to check predicates, construct reaction rules and apply them to rewrite bigraphs. The full library documentation can be accessed at http://www.dcs.gla.ac.uk/~michele/docs/bigraph/index.html.

---

[1] Note that a model may have an infinite state space.

[2] An instantiation map is a function associating each site in the right-hand side to sites in the left-hand side.

[3] The reaction rules belonging to a reducible class are assumed confluent *i.e.* they yield the same result regardless of the order in which they are applied.

Technical Details and Availability. BigraphER is free and open source (BSD) and runs on all major operating systems. It is available for download from http://www.dcs.gla.ac.uk/~michele/bigrapher.html.

Acknowledgments. This work was supported by EPSRC project Homework (EP/F064225/1) and an EPSRC Doctoral Prize Research Fellowship.

References

1. Bacci, G., Grohmann, D., Miculan, M.: DBtk: a toolkit for directed bigraphs. In: Kurz, A., Lenisa, M., Tarlecki, A. (eds.) CALCO 2009. LNCS, vol. 5728, pp. 413–422. Springer, Heidelberg (2009)
2. Benford, S., Rodden, T., Calder, M., Sevegnani, M.: On lions, impala, and bigraphs: modelling interactions in physical/virtual spaces. ACM Trans. Comput. Hum. Interact. (2016, in press)
3. Birkedal, L., Damgaard, T.C., Glenstrup, A.J., Milner, R.: Matching of bigraphs. ENTCS **175**(4), 3–19 (2007)
4. Boucebsi, R., Belala, F.: Towards a channels allocation scheme model for WMNs based on SBRS with sharing. In: Proceedings of MeMo 2015, p. 5 (2015)
5. Calder, M., Koliousis, A., Sevegnani, M., Sventek, J.: Real-time verification of wireless home networks using bigraphs with sharing. Sci. Comput. Program. **80**(Pt. B), 288–310 (2014)
6. Calder, M., Sevegnani, M.: Modelling IEEE 802.11 CSMA/CA RTS/CTS with stochastic bigraphs with sharing. Formal Aspects Comput. Sci. **26**, 537–561 (2014)
7. Eén, N., Sörensson, N.: An extensible SAT-solver. In: Giunchiglia, E., Tacchella, A. (eds.) SAT 2003. LNCS, vol. 2919, pp. 502–518. Springer, Heidelberg (2004)
8. Ellson, J., Gansner, E.R., Koutsofios, L., North, S.C., Woodhull, G.: Graphviz - open source graph drawing tools. In: Mutzel, P., Jünger, M., Leipert, S. (eds.) GD 2001. LNCS, vol. 2265, p. 483. Springer, Heidelberg (2002)
9. Faithfull, A., Perrone, G., Hildebrandt, T.T.: Big Red: a development environment for bigraphs. In: Proceedings of GCM 2012, vol. 61 (2013)
10. Gillespie, D.T.: Exact stochastic simulation of coupled chemical reactions. J. Phys. Chem. **81**(25), 2340–2361 (1977)
11. Krivine, J., Milner, R., Troina, A.: Stochastic bigraphs. ENTCS **218**, 73–96 (2008)
12. Kwiatkowska, M., Norman, G., Parker, D.: PRISM 4.0: verification of probabilistic real-time systems. In: Gopalakrishnan, G., Qadeer, S. (eds.) CAV 2011. LNCS, vol. 6806, pp. 585–591. Springer, Heidelberg (2011)
13. Milner, R.: The Space and Motion of Communicating Agents. Cambridge University Press, Cambridge (2009)
14. Pereira, E., Kirsch, C., Sengupta, R., Sousa, J.: BigActors - a model for structure-aware computation. In: 4th International Conference on Cyber-Physical Systems, pp. 199–208. ACM/IEEE (2013)
15. Perrone, G., Debois, S., Hildebrandt, T.T.: A model checker for bigraphs. In: Proceedings of SAC 2012, pp. 1320–1325. ACM (2012)
16. Sevegnani, M., Calder, M.: Bigraphs with sharing. Theoret. Comput. Sci. **577**, 43–73 (2015)
17. Tseitin, G.S.: On the complexity of derivation in propositional calculus. Stud. Constr. Math. Math. Logic **2**(115–125), 10–13 (1968)

18. Tsigkanos, C., Pasquale, L., Ghezzi, C., Nuseibeh, B.: Ariadne: topology aware adaptive security for cyber-physical systems. In: ICSE 2015, vol. 2, pp. 729–732 (2015)
19. Yu, L., Tsai, W.T., Wei, X., Gao, J., Hildebrandt, T., Guo, X.Q.: Modeling and analysis of mobile cloud computing based on bigraph theory. MobileCloud **2014**, 67–76 (2014)

Verification-Aided Debugging: An Interactive Web-Service for Exploring Error Witnesses

Dirk Beyer and Matthias Dangl

University of Passau, Passau, Germany

Abstract. Traditionally, a verification task is considered solved as soon as a property violation or a correctness proof is found. In practice, this is where the actual work starts: Is it just a false alarm? Is the error reproducible? Can the error report later be re-used for bug fixing or regression testing? The advent of *exchangeable witnesses* is a paradigm shift in verification, from simple answers *true* and *false* towards qualitatively more valuable information about the reason for the property violation. This paper explains a convenient web-based toolchain that can be used to answer the above questions. We consider as example application the verification of C programs. Our first component collects witnesses and stores them for later re-use; for example, if the bug is fixed, the witness can be tried once again and should now be rejected, or, if the bug was not scheduled for fixing, the database can later provide the witnesses in case an engineer wants to start fixing the bug. Our second component is a web service that takes as input a witness for the property violation and (re-)validates it, i.e., it re-plays the witness on the system in order to re-explore the state-space in question. The third component is a web service that continues from the second step by offering an interactive visualization that interconnects the error path, the system's sources, the values on the path (test vectors), and the reachability graph. We evaluated the feasibility of our approach on a large benchmark of verification tasks.

1 Introduction

The answer of a verification tool to a given verification task (consisting of a specification and a system) is either that the system satisfies the specification or that the system violates the specification (or the answer 'unknown' is returned) [9]. If a violation of the specification is detected, an error path through the system is reported that exhibits the problem, such that the user can understand the problem and fix the bug: counterexamples to verification have been described as invaluable to debugging complex systems and have been a common feature of model checkers for several decades [7]. In particular, the successful technique of counterexample-guided abstraction refinement (CEGAR) [8] is based on analyzing error paths through the system.

© Springer International Publishing Switzerland 2016
S. Chaudhuri and A. Farzan (Eds.): CAV 2016, Part II, LNCS 9780, pp. 502–509, 2016.
DOI: 10.1007/978-3-319-41540-6_28

In the past few years, there was a strong focus in the community on using common exchange formats and reproducing errors described by previously computed counterexamples. ESBMC was extended to reproduce errors via instantiated code [11], and CPACHECKER was used to re-check previously computed error paths by interpreting them as automata that control the state-space search [6]. While these internal approaches to witness validation can reduce the amount of false alarms reported by a tool, they establish no additional trust in a report produced and validated by an untrusted verifier. The advantages of considering error witnesses as a valuable verification artifact were explained and supported by two completely different implementations of witness validators [4], namely CPACHECKER and AUTOMIZER. Also, competitions in the community required exchangeable witnesses: the competition on termination uses a certification-problem format (CPF)[1] and the competition on software verification uses a machine-readable, exchangeable format for error witnesses[2]. Our toolchain is based on the common exchange format that was used in SV-COMP [2,4], which allows specifying counterexample traces using control-flow paths and data values. Previous efforts towards helping users understand the counterexamples have lead to interactive trace visualizations [1,5,10], but the user was locked-in to a certain toolchain. The introduction of machine-readable error witnesses has opened up new possibilities for collecting, accumulating, and validating counterexample traces from different verifiers [4]. A wide range of software verifiers already supports a common exchange format, as shown by the competition on software verification[3], which has adopted error-witness validation already two years ago.

Error witnesses support traditional debugging very well: the test values that a witness might contain can direct a classic debugger through the system to the problematic part of the implementation or model. But the exchangeable witnesses support even a more abstract form of debugging, based on a graphical visualization of error paths and reachability graphs.

Figure 1 gives an overview over the components involved in our toolchain. There are three subsystems that the user interacts with: (1) We developed a *witness store* for persistently keeping error witnesses that different verification tools have produced. The database enables the user to select and retrieve specific witnesses for a given set of verification tasks. One possible use case is to fetch all witnesses that document a bug in a specific C program, to help the developer better understand the issue. (2) We offer an *online witness validator* with a convenient web-service API that enables validation without the need to install software. A bug report that a verifier returns can potentially be a false alarm, so it is convenient for the user to first automatically cross-examine the report, before manual effort is invested (and perhaps wasted). To validate an error witness, the user can send the validation task, which consists of the source-code file, the property, and a corresponding error witness (potentially obtained from the

---

[1] http://cl-informatik.uibk.ac.at/software/cpf

[2] http://sv-comp.sosy-lab.org/2016/witnesses/

[3] For example, see the list of systems in SV-COMP 2016 http://sv-comp.sosy-lab.org/2016/systems.php.

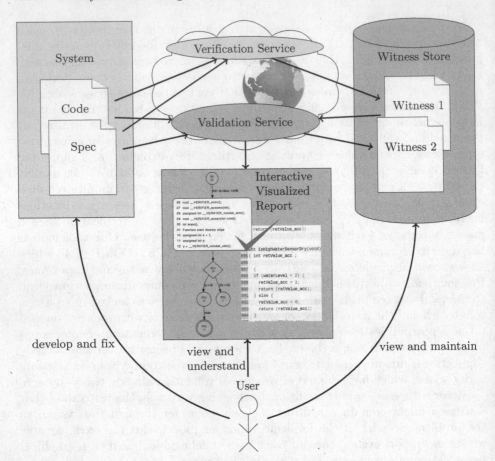

Fig. 1. System overview, blue parts are discussed in this paper (Color figure online)

witness database), to the validation service. The service then validates the error witness. If the witness is rejected, the user is advised to prioritize other tasks, because the specific error path that the witness describes has been declared as infeasible. If, instead, the witness is validated, the validation service feeds all information gained about the bug into the third component, the interactive report. (3) Successful witness validations produce a detailed and interactive web-based bug report. The report contains a debugger-like feature for stepping through the error path, while providing several context-sensitive representations of the buggy program. The report also encompasses all information required to reproduce the validation externally.

Application Example. Our application example is the verification of system programs written in the language C. While the concepts of our toolchain can be applied to other programming languages, we restrict our tools to C. The web service that we describe is available on the internet, and our primary target is to support open-source projects. Organizations that develop proprietary software can still benefit from our system, because it is easily installed on a local web server that is restricted to the organization's intranet.

Data to Experiment. As part of our evaluation, we ran several verification tools that participated in the competition on software verification (because those tools are known to generate useful witnesses) and fed the witnesses into our database. For the reader to assess our toolchain, we have compiled an archive with witnesses, validation results and error-path visualizations for offline use. The archive is available as supplement, and the validation results and visualization results can be reproduced via our live web service or offline using the CPACHECKER-based witness validator[4] The archive contains reports for a total of 1 382 witnesses for 26 verification tasks that contain a bug. The average number of witnesses that we collected is 53 witnesses per verification task, the program with the fewest has 4, the program with the most has 114 witnesses in our database.

2   Collection of Error-Paths in a Witness Store

We consider witnesses as a prime-value verification artifact, because they can make it (a) efficient to re-run a partial verification to explore the bug again and (b) easy to use different verification tools for validation.

Permanently storing witnesses opens many new practical applications to let verification technology have a larger impact on system development. Our witness store provides a means to take advantage of the various beneficial properties of machine-readable witnesses in a common exchange format:

- Witness Validation: Imprecise verifiers may sometimes produce false alarms and thus waste valuable developer time. With witness validation, users no longer need to trust the answer FALSE. Instead, they can concentrate on paying attention to witnesses that are confirmed by an automatic witness validator. Each validation run that confirms a witness can increase the user's confidence in the bug report.
- Witness Inspection: Witness validators with complementing strategies can be applied to a witness, each leveraging its strengths to add diagnostic information that the others may be incapable to derive. Therefore, witness validation can be understood as a chain of ever refining details for identifying, understanding, and fixing the bug.
- Bug Reports: In bug reports, attached witnesses can be used to provide a precise description of the erroneous behavior, including test-vector values.
- Re-Verification: Working with error witnesses is cheap in terms of resources, because the verification result can often be re-established with reduced effort.

---

[4] The URL to our supplementary web page, which includes the live web service, the archive for offline use, and a virtual machine set up for validating the witnesses and reproducing the results using CPACHECKER 1.6, is: https://www.sosy-lab.org/~dbeyer/witness-based-debugging/.

This is not only beneficial for validating a given witness, but also when checking for regressions: If the witness is still valid for a changed version of the system, the bug has been reintroduced or was not yet fixed [6].

3   Convenient Witness Validation

A witness validator is a verifier that analyzes the synchronized product of the system with the witness automaton, where transitions are synchronized using system operations and transition annotations. This means that the witness automaton observes the system paths that the verifier wants to explore: if the operation on the system path does not match the transition of the witness automaton, then the verifier is forbidden to explore that path further; if the operation on the path matches, then the witness automaton and the system proceed to the next state, possibly restricting the system's state such that the assumptions given in the data annotation are satisfied. Implementations of witness validators are available, see for example CPACHECKER and AUTOMIZER [4]. Our validation service uses the CPACHECKER witness validator as back-end. CPACHECKER supports and combines many different verification strategies, for example value analysis, predicate abstraction, CEGAR, bounded model checking, k-induction, and concrete memory graphs. The specific configuration that is effectively used to validate the witnesses via our web service is bit-accurate and combines value analysis and predicate abstraction. Our web service does not yet support arrays, concurrency, and termination analysis.

Conceptually, an *error-witness automaton* is a protocol automaton, and an *error-witness analysis* is a protocol analysis for an error-witness automaton [4], which runs as a component of a composite program analysis. Unlike observer automata [3], which can be used to represent the specification the analyzed program is verified with, error-witness automata not only observe the state-space exploration of the program analysis, but also *restrict* it to those successor states that lead the exploration toward a specification violation, whereas an observer automaton follows all abstract successor states. Therefore, the program analysis is *guided* by the error-witness automaton to explore the state space that violates the specification.

The process of determining if it is possible to independently re-establish a verification result, given the program, specification, result, and witness, is called *witness validation*. One way of implementing error-witness validation is by constructing a composite program analysis that has both a witness analysis and a specification analysis as components, which simultaneously restrict and observe the state-space exploration: the specification analysis checks if an analyzed path actually violates the specification, and the search of the composite program analysis is restricted by the witness validation such that only paths that the error-witness automaton can match are explored. For example, the analysis stops exploring a path, if, during the analysis of that path, the witness automaton takes a transition to a sink state. An error witness is confirmed by the witness validator if both, the witness automaton and the specification automaton, take a transition to their respective (accepting) error state [4].

4   Visualizing and Interactively Exploring Error-Paths

Figure 2 shows a screenshot of an interactive counterexample report. The screen is divided into two columns: The left column provides detailed information that is specific to the error path, namely the source code on the path to the property violation, and, like in a debugger, the program locations are decorated with test values that were computed by the witness validator. The right column embeds the specific information from the left column into the general context of the system and the analysis. It contains control-flow automata (CFA) for each of the functions, the abstract reachability graph (ARG) of the verification, full source code of the verification task, the verification log, statistics, and configuration parameters of the validation run. In all CFA and the ARG, the states on the path to the property violation are marked in red. Double clicking on a control-flow state that precedes a function call displays the CFA of the called function. Both columns, however, are not only useful in isolation: clicking on a line of code in the left column while viewing the ARG or CFA will navigate to the state corresponding to the clicked line of source code.

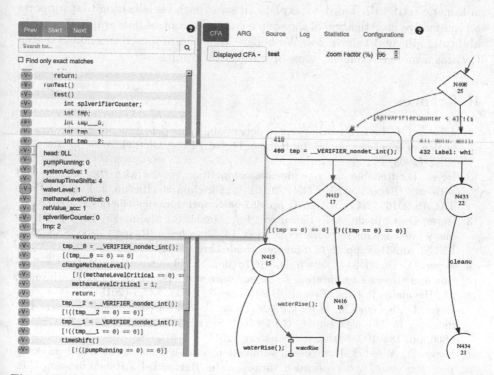

Fig. 2. Typical view of the error-path visualizer: program source code with violating test vector (left, green) and CFA with violating path (right, red); left view top shows the menu for debugger-like step-through, right view top shows the display options: CFA, ARG, Source, Log, Statistics, Configurations (Color figure online)

The visualization is built upon the JavaScript framework ANGLUARJS and the JQUERY and BOOTSTRAP web-development libraries. The layout of the graphs is computed using GraphViz and exchanged in SVG format. The complete data for one such error-path visualization takes on average 120 kB of memory.

5   Conclusion

Over the past decades, the algorithmic abilities of verification tools were considerably increased, but in practice, verification technology is still not as popular as testing. Why? Because it is inconvenient to use. Our work contributes to closing this gap, by considering not only the true/false answers as value, but actively using other results of the verification process, most prominently the error witnesses. We have presented a toolchain that supports engineers in understanding the error reports of verification systems. First, we archive verification witnesses permanently in a database. Second, we provide a convenient web service for witness validation, i.e., a verification task together with a witness can be given as input, and the results are presented via the web API (for manual inspection or automatic retrieval). Third, we explain an error-path visualization that supports an interactive investigation of the source code, the control-flow graph, the reachability graph, and test values. We believe that the proposed method is a step towards a more convenient usage of verification results.

References

1. Aljazzar, H., Leue, S.: Debugging of dependability models using interactive visualization of counterexamples. In: Rubino, G. (ed.) Proc. QUEST 2008, pp. 189–198. IEEE (2008)
2. Beyer, D.: Reliable and reproducible competition results with BENCHEXEC and witnesses (Report on SV-COMP 2016). In: Chechik, M., Raskin, J.-F. (eds.) Proc. TACAS 2016. LNCS, vol. 9636, pp. 887–904. Springer, Heidelberg (2016)
3. Beyer, D., Chlipala, A.J., Henzinger, T.A., Jhala, R., Majumdar, R.: The BLAST query language for software verification. In: Giacobazzi, R. (ed.) Proc. SAS 2004. LNCS, vol. 3148, pp. 2–18. Springer, Heidelberg (2004)
4. Beyer, D., Dangl, M., Dietsch, D., Heizmann, M., Stahlbauer, A.: Witness validation and stepwise testification across software verifiers. In: Di Nitto, E., Harman, M., Heymans, P. (eds.) Proc. FSE 2015, pp. 721–733. ACM (2015)
5. Beyer, D., Keremoglu, M.E.: CPACHECKER: A tool for configurable software verification. In: Gopalakrishnan, G., Qadeer, S. (eds.) Proc. CAV 2011. LNCS, vol. 6806, pp. 184–190. Springer, Heidelberg (2011)
6. Beyer, D., Wendler, P.: Reuse of verification results: Conditional model checking, precision reuse, and verification witnesses. In: Bartocci, E., Ramakrishnan, C.R. (eds.) Proc. SPIN 2013. LNCS, vol. 7976, pp. 1–17. Springer, Heidelberg (2013)
7. Clarke, E.M., Emerson, E.A., Sifakis, J.: Model checking: Algorithmic verification and debugging. Commun. ACM 52(11), 74–84 (2009)
8. Clarke, E.M., Grumberg, O., Jha, S., Lu, Y., Veith, H.: Counterexample-guided abstraction refinement for symbolic model checking. J. ACM 50(5), 752–794 (2003)

9. Clarke, E.M., Grumberg, O., Peled, D.: Model Checking. MIT Press, Cambridge (1999)
10. Groce, A., Kröning, D., Lerda, F.: Understanding counterexamples with explain. In: Alur, R., Peled, D.A. (eds.) Proc. CAV 2004. LNCS, vol. 3114, pp. 453–456. Springer, Heidelberg (2004)
11. Rocha, H., Barreto, R., Cordeiro, L., Neto, A.D.: Understanding programming bugs in ANSI-C software using bounded model checking counter-examples. In: Derrick, J., Gnesi, S., Latella, D., Treharne, H. (eds.) Proc. IFM 2012. LNCS, vol. 7321, pp. 128–142. Springer, Heidelberg (2012)

The KIND 2 Model Checker

Adrien Champion(✉), Alain Mebsout, Christoph Sticksel, and Cesare Tinelli

The University of Iowa, Iowa City, USA
adrien.champion@email.com

Abstract. KIND 2 is an open-source, multi-engine, SMT-based model checker for safety properties of finite- and infinite-state synchronous reactive systems. It takes as input models written in an extension of the Lustre language that allows the specification of assume-guarantee-style contracts for system components. KIND 2 was implemented from scratch based on techniques used by its predecessor, the PKIND model checker. This paper discusses a number of improvements over PKIND in terms of invariant generation. It also introduces two main features: contract-based compositional reasoning and certificate generation.

1 Introduction

KIND 2 is an SMT-based model checker for synchronous reactive systems. It relies on off-the-shelf SMT solvers to prove or disprove quantifier-free regular safety properties of models written in an extension of the synchronous dataflow language Lustre [11]. These properties can be expressed, in a separate annotation language, as invariants or as assume-guarantee-style contracts. KIND 2 is inspired by its predecessor PKIND [14] and uses several of the same techniques. However, it was engineered and implemented from scratch. Both checkers have several model checking engines, based on various techniques, which run concurrently and in cooperation, with the goal of proving or disproving properties and contracts.

KIND 2 is open-source and distributed in binary and source-code form under a liberal license at http://kind.cs.uiowa.edu. This paper focuses on its novel features, in particular, powerful invariant generation techniques, contract-based compositional reasoning, and proof certificate generation.

2 Functionality and Main Features

We start with a summary of KIND 2's basic functionality, *i.e.*, (dis)proving safety properties of reactive systems, and then describe KIND 2's distinguishing features.

The development of KIND 2 was partially funded by AFRL grant FA8750-13-C-0051, NASA grants NNA13AA21C, NNX14AI09G, and NNL14AA06C, and by Rockwell-Collins.

© Springer International Publishing Switzerland 2016
S. Chaudhuri and A. Farzan (Eds.): CAV 2016, Part II, LNCS 9780, pp. 510–517, 2016.
DOI: 10.1007/978-3-319-41540-6_29

Safety Analysis. Lustre is a dataflow language that allows one to define system components as *nodes*, each of which maps a continuous flow of inputs (of various basic types) to continuous flows of outputs based on both current input values and previous input and output values (see Fig. 1 for a simple example). Bigger components can be built by parallel composition of smaller ones, achieved syntactically with *node calls*. Through the use of observers [12], any (LTL) regular safety property can be expressed in Lustre as an invariant property, hence KIND 2 focuses on checking just invariant properties.

After various transformations and slicing, KIND 2 encodes Lustre nodes internally as state transition systems $\langle \mathbf{s}, I(\mathbf{s}), T(\mathbf{s}, \mathbf{s}') \rangle$ where $\mathbf{s}$ is the vector of typed state variables, I the initial state predicate, and T is a two-state transition predicate (with $\mathbf{s}'$ being a renamed version of $\mathbf{s}$). An *invariant property* P for such a system is a predicate over the variables $\mathbf{s}$ that must hold in every reachable state of

```
node sofar (x:bool) returns (p:bool);
let p = (true -> pre p) and x; tel

node sum (x:int) returns (s:int);
let s = x + (0 -> pre s);
--! PROPERTY sofar(x > 0) => s > 0;  tel
```

Fig. 1. Example of annotated Lustre. Node `sofar` encodes the "always in the past" operator of pLTL.

the system. Instances of I, T and P are quantifier-free first-order formulas over the theories of equality with uninterpreted functions and linear integer and real arithmetic.

The node construct allows one to specify modular and hierarchical systems. KIND 2 takes advantage of this by performing *modular reasoning* over nodes. Each node can be assigned its own properties and verified individually. The results of the verification process (*e.g.*, proven properties and auxiliary invariants) can be reused in the analysis of other components calling that node. KIND 2 takes this approach further by allowing the user to specify assume-guarantee-style contracts for each node, effectively enabling *compositional reasoning* by fine-grained abstraction of sub-components.

At the component level, given an encoding $S \triangleq \langle \mathbf{s}, I(\mathbf{s}), T(\mathbf{s}, \mathbf{s}') \rangle$ of a Lustre node and a property P, KIND 2 tries to verify that P is invariant for S using a combination (described in Sect. 2) of different induction-based model checking engines: k-induction [16], IC3 [3] and various auxiliary invariant generation methods. K-induction is a generalization of standard induction and consists in finding a value k for which P holds in all reachable states within $k - 1$ steps (base case), and is preserved by transition chains of length k (step case). IC3 is a popular directed reachability approach that iteratively strengthens the given property until it becomes inductive. We use an extension of IC3 to infinite-state systems which is based on an efficient form of approximate quantifier elimination. In our experience, IC3 is often complementary to k-induction as it can prove properties that are not k-inductive for any k while k-induction can handle properties that IC3 finds hard to strengthen to an inductive one. The invariant generation engines of KIND 2 produce on the fly auxiliary invariants that are used to incrementally strengthen the transition relation T, increasing the chances of proving the step case of k-induction and facilitating the job of IC3.

Incremental and Modular Invariant Generation. PKIND introduced an invariant generation technique parameterized by a partial order $\preceq$ over some (equality) type τ [13]. It starts from a set of candidate terms $\mathbb{C}$ of type τ over a system S and heuristically produces invariants of the form $c \preceq c'$ and $c = c'$ where $c, c' \in \mathbb{C}$. For the bool type, used in Lustre both for Boolean state variables and for properties, $\preceq$ is implication and $\mathbb{C}$ is constructed by mining the initial state predicate and the transition relation of S for Boolean terms. The approach maintains an index k and a directed acyclic graph (DAG), whose vertices are sets of terms from a partition of $\mathbb{C}$. A vertex $V = \{c_1, c_2, \ldots, c_n\}$ denotes the chain of equalities $c_1 = c_2 = \cdots = c_n$. An edge from node V to V' denotes the inequality $c \preceq c'$ for any term c in V and c' in V'. The DAG is a compact representation of a set of invariant conjectures about S. Initially, $k = 0$ and the DAG has a single node $\mathbb{C}$, conjecturing that all the terms in $\mathbb{C}$ are equivalent in every reachable state of S. This conjecture is tested with a Bounded Model Checking-style query to an SMT solver for a counterexample k states away from an initial state. If none is found, the conjecture is correct for states reachable in up to k steps from an initial one, and k is incremented. Otherwise, the DAG is modified by removing edges or splitting nodes so that its refined conjecture is consistent with the latest counterexample and all previous ones. The algorithm refines its DAG and increments k until k reaches a user-specified upper bound d. It then performs a multi-property $(d+1)$-induction step check over each element of the conjecture. Any equality or inequality between two candidate terms in the conjecture that is i-inductive for $i \leq d$ will be proved and communicated as invariant.

We have modified this technique so that it progresses in *lockstep*. When the conjecture is correct at depth k, the invariant generation engine of KIND 2 performs the $(k + 1)$-induction step check right away. This allows it to output invariants that are k-inductive for a small k faster. An additional benefit is that there is no need for a user-defined upper bound d, whose value can vastly influence runtimes—for instance on large systems, where unrolling the transition predicate several times can be extremely expensive.

Furthermore, KIND 2 can execute this invariant generation technique *modularly* when the input system is defined as the composition of two or more nodes. In that case, the subsystem hierarchy is traversed bottom-up. For each subsystem S, a set of $(k+1)$-inductive invariants (with k initially 0) is obtained as discussed above. Those invariants are then instantiated in every subsystem that has S as a direct subcomponent, recursively. Once the process reaches the top-level system, any invariants discovered at that level are communicated to the other reasoning engines of KIND 2. At that point a new bottom-up traversal starts with a greater value of k. This approach has two significant advantages with respect to running invariant generation on the full system monolithically: (*i*) it discovers invariants for subsystems more easily and quickly; (*ii*) it is self-reinforcing since instances of the invariants discovered for a subsystem of a component S can be used to help prove invariant conjectures for S.

Compositional Reasoning. *Compositional reasoning* is a popular technique to improve the scalability of verification tools on systems defined as hierarchies of components.[1] Components have *contracts* enforcing their use in a certain context in order for them to guarantee certain properties (Fig. 2 for an example). Analyzing a component consists in checking that its contract holds after abstracting at call-site all of its (possibly complex) sub-components by their own contract. A contract for a system $S \triangleq \langle s, I(s), T(s, s') \rangle$ is a pair $C \triangleq \langle A(s), G(s) \rangle$ where, informally, the *assumption* predicate A describes properties that S expects its inputs to have, while the *guarantee* predicate G expresses how the component behaves when A holds at all times. A contract can introduce local variables (streams), refer to previous values of streams, and call arbitrary Lustre nodes.

This makes KIND 2's contract language expressive enough to represent any regular safety properties, once they are recast in terms of past temporal logic (see [6] for more details on the contract language and its use). In KIND 2, verifying that S satisfies its contract reduces to verifying that $G(s)$ is an invariant for the system $S_A = \langle s, I(s) \wedge A(s), A(s) \wedge T(s, s') \wedge A(s') \rangle$. If S is a component of some larger system S', which provides it with input values, then S can be abstracted by its guarantee G at call-site in S' as long as the assumption A at call-site is an invariant for S'. If it is, we say the call is *safe*. If the call is unsafe, then so is S' since it does not respect the

```
node max (x:real) returns (m:real);
let m = x -> if x > pre x then x
             else pre x; tel

node avg (x,y:real) returns (a:real);
(*@contract
    assume x <= y;
    guarantee x <= a and a <= y; *)
let a = (x + y) / 2.0; tel

node sav (x:real) returns (s:real);
(*@contract
    assume x > 0.0 and x > pre x;
    guarantee s <= max(x); *)
let s = avg(x -> pre s, x); tel
```

Fig. 2. Lustre nodes with contracts.

contract of S. If all components of a system verify their contract and make only safe calls then the overall system is safe. KIND 2 can construct this argument via a *modular* analysis, where system components are analyzed bottom-up in the subsystem hierarchy with a process similar to modular invariant generation.

Refinement. KIND 2's modular and compositional analysis of multi-component systems resorts to contract refinement when needed. Consider a system S_1 with contract $C_1 = \langle A_1(s_1), G_1(s_1) \rangle$ that uses a subsystem S_2 with contract $C_2 = \langle A_2(s_2), G_2(s_2) \rangle$. Suppose that KIND 2 cannot prove S_1's contract compositionally, that is, by abstracting S_2 by its contract. A reason for this might be that the abstraction provided by C_2 is too weak. KIND 2 will then *refine* S_1 in the analysis by replacing S_2's contract with S_2 itself, provided, however, that the following conditions are met: *(i)* S_2 is safe (i.e., it verifies its contract and does not make unsafe calls), and *(ii)* all calls to S_2 in S_1 are provably safe. If

---

[1] For simplicity, we describe here only the case of asymmetric parallel composition, where there are no feedback loops between components, although KIND 2 can deal with the general case.

the new analysis succeeds, the user is notified of the specific contract abstraction under which the result was obtained. Otherwise, the refinement process continues recursively until no more contract refinement is possible. When a system like S_2 is used instead of its contract C_2 it is because it provably admits a smaller set of execution traces than C_2. Because of this, when analyzing a newly refined system, KIND 2 retains any invariant/property already proved and any information on properties that are still unproven or falsified. This means that when the analysis restarts after refinement, KIND 2 will only check the proof obligations that were not previously discharged, in effect restarting precisely from where the previous analysis had stopped.

Certification. Having to trust the results of complex model checkers like KIND 2 is a source of concern for some users. To address this problem, KIND 2 can produce an independently checkable *proof certificate* for the properties that it claims to have proven for a (sub)system.[2] This certificate is in the form of a *k-inductive invariant* (expressed as a formula together with a specific value of k) that implies all the proven properties. This form is general enough that it can be effectively produced by all the model checking engines described previously. Certificates coming from these engines are combined conjunctively thanks to the fact that a k-inductive invariant is also k'-inductive for any $k' \geq k$. Individual certificates are initially generated by single engines based on their deductions regarding some set of properties and invariants. The combined certificate is then simplified along two dimensions, the value of k and the size and complexity of the invariant itself, using various fixpoint-based heuristics relying on unsat cores and counterexamples to induction. The final certificate output by KIND 2 is written in SMT-LIB 2 format and embedded in an SMT-LIB 2 script that checks that the certificate is k-inductive and implies the proven input properties. As a first approximation, any SMT-LIB 2-compliant solver can then be used as a *certificate checker*. This essentially shifts the burden of trust from KIND 2 to the SMT solver, reducing the trusted core to the latter. In our initial empirical evaluation, this approach allows Kind 2 to *generate* and *check* certificates, with an SMT solver, with a reasonable overhead (in all cases, less than an order of magnitude). We are currently working on eliminating the SMT solver as well from the trusted core by capitalizing on the proof-producing capabilities of certain SMT solvers. Specifically, in collaboration with the developers of the CVC4 solver [2], we are instrumenting Kind 2 to generate from CVC4 a final certificate in the LFSC language [17]. This way, the trusted core will reduce even further, to the much simpler LFSC proof checker.

Architecture. KIND 2 is written in OCaml and has a concurrent architecture similar to that of PKIND. Its various engines (base case and inductive step of k-induction, IC3, invariant generation, and so on) run simultaneously and in cooperation. They exchange information, mostly about properties proved or disproved to be invariant, through a message passing interface implemented on

---

[2] Currently, certificate generation is available only for monolithic analyses. An extension to compositional ones is planned as future work.

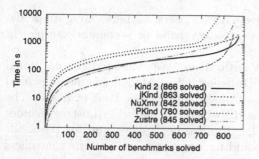

Fig. 3. Comparison between KIND 2 and other infinite-state model checkers. (Colour figure online)

Table 1. Techniques implemented in the tools.

Tool	k-induction	IC3
PKIND	yes+ig	no
ZUSTRE	no	yes+i
KIND 2	yes+m+ig	yes
JKIND	yes+ig	yes+ia
nuXMV	no	yes+ia

top of the ZeroMQ library. The concurrent execution of the base (BMC) of k-induction with the step case makes KIND 2 efficient at disproving properties. This architecture provides superior support for systems with multiple components and properties since it allows KIND 2 to check several properties per component at the same time and output counterexamples or proven properties incrementally, as it discovers them. Various off-the-shelf SMT solvers (currently, CVC4 [2], Yices [9], and Z3 [8]) are used as backend reasoning engines.

3 Experimental Evaluation

Compositionality and certificate generation make KIND 2's internal architecture more complex, and with a higher potential overhead, than comparable model checkers. So we provide an evaluation of KIND 2's performance as a monolithic model-checker first (without certificate generation), before discussing the performance of its compositional reasoning features.

Comparison with Other Tools. We compared KIND 2 with a number of recent model checkers for infinite-state systems: PKIND [14]; JKIND [10], a model checker similar to PKIND developed in Java by Rockwell-Collins; ZUSTRE, a Lustre front end for the Z3-based model checker Spacer [15]; and nuXMV [5], a general purpose model checker for synchronous finite-state and infinite-state systems. Table 1 shows the techniques implemented by each tool among a modular version (**m**) of k-induction with or without invariant generation (**ig**), and IC3 possibly augmented with interpolation (**i**) or implicit predicate abstraction [7] (**ia**). We ran each tool on a Linux machine with two 12-core 64-bit AMD Opteron processors and 32GB of memory on a set of single-property benchmarks that includes those discussed in [14].[3] nuXMV was given encoded versions of the original Lustre problems in its own input language, which were provided to use by its developers. We gave a timeout of five minutes for each problem. Figure 3

---

[3] The set is publicly available at https://github.com/kind2-mc/kind2-benchmarks.

shows that KIND 2 is very competitive with its peers, outperforming its predecessor PKIND and providing an answer (either *valid* or a counterexample) in more cases than any other tool.

Compositional vs. Monolithic Verification. We evaluated compositional reasoning in KIND 2 on the TCM (Transport Class Model) for medium-sized aircraft discussed and verified compositionally *by hand* by Brat et al. [4]. The subsystem of the TCM we had access to, which is modeled in Lustre, includes components for the latitudinal and longitudinal controllers, and for the mode logic that decides which controller should be active at any time. The controllers are heavily numerical and contain non-linear expressions, which are problematic for current SMT solvers. We wrote contracts corresponding to Federal Aviations Regulations [4] for most of the components of the subsystem. We also abstracted non-linear expressions by components with a linear contract.

The runtime to verify *every component* of the system bottom-up, *including* the abstractions of non-linear expressions, is about 400 s on a 2014 i7 CPU running OSX. A comparison with a purely monolithic approach is not possible because of the presence of non-linearity. All SMT solvers we tried would return *unknown*, even for checks dealing with a single, relatively simple component. As a consequence, we did a monolithic analysis of a modified TCM system where the non-linear expressions are replaced by their linear contract but otherwise nothing else is abstracted. In this setting, the analysis of the top level of the system ran for two hours without reaching a conclusion. We refer the interested reader to Champion *el al.* [6] for a more in-depth discussion.

4   Applications

KIND 2 is used in academia and in a variety of industrial settings. For the latter, it is for instance one of the backend model checkers in the AGREE framework for compositional verification of AADL models [1] at Rockwell-Collins. It has been used at General Electric for model-based test case generation. It is also used in an open-source model-checking plugin for Simulink developed by NASA Ames and CMU, which relies on Lustre model checkers and produces user feedback at the Simulink block level. KIND 2's proof certificates are leveraged as an innovative way to approach tool qualification with respect to DO-178C requirements in a NASA and FAA funded project.

References

1. Backes, J., Cofer, D., Miller, S., Whalen, M.W.: Requirements analysis of a quad-redundant flight control system. In: Havelund, K., Holzmann, G., Joshi, R. (eds.) NFM 2015. LNCS, vol. 9058, pp. 82–96. Springer, Heidelberg (2015)
2. Barrett, C., et al.: CVC4. In: Gopalakrishnan, G., Qadeer, S. (eds.) CAV 2011. LNCS, vol. 6806, pp. 171–177. Springer, Heidelberg (2011)
3. Bradley, A.R.: SAT-based model checking without unrolling. In: Jhala, R., Schmidt, D. (eds.) VMCAI 2011. LNCS, vol. 6538, pp. 70–87. Springer, Heidelberg (2011)

4. Brat, G., Bushnell, D., Davies, M., Giannakopoulou, D., Howar, F., Kahsai, T.: Verifying the safety of a flight-critical system. In: Bjørner, N., de Boer, F. (eds.) FM 2015. LNCS, vol. 9109, pp. 308–324. Springer, Heidelberg (2015)
5. Cavada, R., Cimatti, A., Dorigatti, M., Griggio, A., Mariotti, A., Micheli, A., Mover, S., Roveri, M., Tonetta, S.: The NUXMV symbolic model checker. In: Biere, A., Bloem, R. (eds.) CAV 2014. LNCS, vol. 8559, pp. 334–342. Springer, Heidelberg (2014)
6. Champion, A., Gurfinkel, A., Kahsai, T., Tinelli, C.: CoCoSpec: a mode-aware contract language for reactive systems. In: De Nicola, R., Kühn, E. (eds.) Proceedings of 14th International Conference, SEFM 2016, Held as Part of STAF 2016, Vienna, Austria, July 4–8, vol. 9763. Springer (2016)
7. Cimatti, A., Griggio, A., Mover, S., Tonetta, S.: IC3 modulo theories via implicit predicate abstraction. In: Ábrahám, E., Havelund, K. (eds.) TACAS 2014 (ETAPS). LNCS, vol. 8413, pp. 46–61. Springer, Heidelberg (2014)
8. de Moura, L., Bjørner, N.S.: Z3: an efficient SMT solver. In: Ramakrishnan, C.R., Rehof, J. (eds.) TACAS 2008. LNCS, vol. 4963, pp. 337–340. Springer, Heidelberg (2008)
9. Dutertre, B.: Yices 2.2. In: Biere, A., Bloem, R. (eds.) CAV 2014. LNCS, vol. 8559, pp. 737–744. Springer, Heidelberg (2014)
10. Gacek, A., Katis, A., Whalen, M.W., Backes, J., Cofer, D.: Towards realizability checking of contracts using theories. In: Havelund, K., Holzmann, G., Joshi, R. (eds.) NFM 2015. LNCS, vol. 9058, pp. 173–187. Springer, Heidelberg (2015)
11. Halbwachs, N., Caspi, P., Raymond, P., Pilaud, D.: The synchronous data-flow programming language LUSTRE. Proc. IEEE **79**(9), 1305–1320 (1991)
12. Halbwachs, N., Lagnier, F., Raymond, P.: Synchronous observers and the verification of reactive systems. In: Nivat, M., et al. (eds.) Algebraic Methodology and Software Technology, AMAST 1993. Workshops in Computing, pp. 83–96. Springer, Heidelberg (1993)
13. Kahsai, T., Ge, Y., Tinelli, C.: Instantiation-based invariant discovery. In: Bobaru, M., Havelund, K., Holzmann, G.J., Joshi, R. (eds.) NFM 2011. LNCS, vol. 6617, pp. 192–206. Springer, Heidelberg (2011)
14. Kahsai, T., Tinelli, C.: Pkind: a parallel k-induction based model checker. In: Proceedings 10th International Workshop on Parallel and Distributed Methods in verification, PDMC 2011, EPTCS, vol. 72, pp. 55–62 (2011)
15. Komuravelli, A., Gurfinkel, A., Chaki, S.: SMT-based model checking for recursive programs. In: Biere, A., Bloem, R. (eds.) CAV 2014. LNCS, vol. 8559, pp. 17–34. Springer, Heidelberg (2014)
16. Sheeran, M., Singh, S., Stålmarck, G.: Checking safety properties using induction and a SAT-solver. In: Johnson, S.D., Hunt Jr., W.A. (eds.) FMCAD 2000. LNCS, vol. 1954, pp. 108–125. Springer, Heidelberg (2000)
17. Stump, A., Oe, D., Reynolds, A., Hadarean, L., Tinelli, C.: SMT proof checking using a logical framework. Formal Methods Syst. Des. **41**(1), 91–118 (2013)

Author Index

Abd Elkader, Karam   I-329
Abdulla, Parosh Aziz   II-134
Albarghouthi, Aws   II-210
Alur, Rajeev   II-251
Atig, Mohamed Faouzi   II-134

Baier, Christel   I-23
Barthe, Gilles   I-43
Bayless, Sam   I-136
Benerecetti, Massimo   II-270
Beyer, Dirk   II-502
Biere, Armin   I-199
Bloem, Roderick   I-157
Bouyer, Patricia   I-513
Braud-Santoni, Nicolas   I-157

Calder, Muffy   II-494
Champion, Adrien   II-510
Chatterjee, Krishnendu   I-3
Chen, Rick   II-42
Chen, Yu-Fang   II-91
Cheng, Chih Hong   I-95
Chin, Wei-Ngan   I-382
Chistikov, Dmitry   II-157
Chu, Duc-Hiep   I-218
Cimatti, Alessandro   I-271, II-3
Colange, Maximilien   I-513
Cristiá, Maximiliano   I-179

D'Antoni, Loris   II-383
Daca, Przemysław   II-230
Dangl, Matthias   II-502
Daniel, Jakub   I-271
Deligiannis, Anastasios   II-42
Dell'Erba, Daniele   II-270
Dogadov, Boris   I-426
Dooley, Michael   I-292
Drechsler, Rolf   II-177
Drews, Samuel   II-210
Duggirala, Parasara Sridhar   I-477, I-531

Easwaran, Arvind   I-457
Ehlers, Rüdiger   II-333

Eldib, Hassan   II-343
Ernst, Michael D.   II-23
Esparza, Javier   II-312
Espitau, Thomas   I-43

Fan, Chuchu   I-531
Fedyukovich, Grigory   II-433
Feng, Xinyu   II-59
Ferrer Fioriti, Luis María   I-43
Finkbeiner, Bernd   I-118
Fiterău-Broştean, Paul   II-454
Fried, Dror   II-402
Fu, Hongfei   I-3
Fu, Ming   II-59
Fu, Zhoulai   II-187

Gallagher, John P.   I-261
Gario, Marco   II-3
Gehr, Timon   I-62
Gilday, David   II-42
Goharshady, Amir Kafshdar   I-3
Griggio, Alberto   I-271
Große, Daniel   II-177
Grumberg, Orna   I-329
Gurfinkel, Arie   II-433
Guth, Dwight   I-447

Hahn, Ernst Moritz   II-291
Hamza, Yassine   I-95
Hathhorn, Chris   I-447
He, Fei   I-310
Henzinger, Thomas A.   II-230
Herdt, Vladimir   II-177
Hoyes, David   II-42
Hsu, Justin   I-43
Hu, Alan J.   I-136

Jaax, Stefan   II-312
Jacky, Jonathan   II-23
Jacobs, Swen   I-157
Jaffar, Joxan   I-218
Janssen, Ramon   II-454
Jiang, Jie-Hong R.   I-241

Joloboff, Vania   I-84
Jonsson, Bengt   II-134
Jordan, Herbert   II-422

Kafle, Bishoksan   I-261
Kahsai, Temesghen   I-352
Keen, Will   II-42
Kiefer, Stefan   I-23
Klein, Felix   I-118
Klein, Joachim   I-23
Klenze, Tobias   I-136
Klüppelholz, Sascha   I-23
Křetínský, Jan   II-312
Kupriyanov, Andrey   II-230

Le, Hoang M.   II-177
Le, Quang Loc   I-382
Legay, Axel   I-84
Legg, Alexander   II-364
Leino, K.R.M.   I-361
Leonardsson, Carl   II-134
Li, Zhaohui   II-59
Lin, Anthony W.   II-112
Lin, Chun-Han   I-241
Loncaric, Calvin   II-23

Majumdar, Rupak   II-157
Manevich, Roman   I-426
Mao, Shu   I-310
Markey, Nicolas   I-513
Mattarei, Cristian   II-3
Mebsout, Alain   II-510
Misailovic, Sasa   I-62
Mitra, Sayan   I-531
Moarref, Salar   II-251
Mogavero, Fabio   II-270
Morales, José F.   I-261
Mover, Sergio   I-271
Müller, David   I-23
Müller, Peter   I-405

Narodytska, Nina   II-364
Ngo, Van Chan   I-84
Niemetz, Aina   I-199
Niksic, Filip   II-157

Păsăreanu, Corina S.   I-329
Pathirane, Ashan   II-42
Pernsteiner, Stuart   II-23

Piskac, Ruzica   II-80
Pit-Claudel, Clément   I-361
Prabhakar, Pavithra   I-495
Preiner, Mathias   I-199

Qi, Bolun   I-531

Raman, Vasumathi   II-333
Reid, Alastair   II-42
Rinetzky, Noam   I-426
Rossi, Gianfranco   I-179
Roşu, Grigore   I-447
Rozier, Kristin Yvonne   II-3
Ruess, Harald   I-95
Rümmer, Philipp   I-352, II-112
Ryzhyk, Leonid   II-364

Samanta, Roopsha   II-383
Sanchez, Huascar   I-352
Santolucito, Mark   II-80
Saxena, Manasvi   I-447
Schäf, Martin   I-352
Schewe, Sven   II-291
Scholz, Bernhard   II-422
Schwerhoff, Malte   I-405
Sevegnani, Michele   II-494
Sharygina, Natasha   II-433
She, Zhikun   I-457
Shepherd, Owen   II-42
Shoham, Sharon   I-329
Sickert, Salomon   II-312
Singh, Rishabh   II-383
Somenzi, Fabio   I-292
Song, Lei   II-91
Soto, Miriam García   I-495
Sticksel, Christoph   II-510
Su, Zhendong   II-187
Subotić, Pavle   II-422
Summers, Alexander J.   I-405
Sun, Jun   I-382

Tabajara, Lucas M.   II-402
Tatlock, Zachary   II-23
Tinelli, Cesare   II-510
Tonetta, Stefano   I-271, II-3
Topcu, Ufuk   II-251
Torlak, Emina   II-23
Trinh, Minh-Thai   I-218

Tsai, Tzung-Lin   I-241
Turrini, Andrea   II-291

Vaandrager, Frits   II-454
Vardi, Moshe Y.   II-402
Vechev, Martin   I-62
Viswanathan, Mahesh   I-477, I-531
Vrabel, Peter   II-42

Wang, Bow-Yaw   I-310
Wang, Chao   II-343
Wang, Hung-En   I-241
Wang, Xi   II-23
Wijs, Anton   II-472

Worrell, James   I-23
Wu, Meng   II-343
Wu, Zhilin   II-91

Xu, Fengwei   II-59
Xue, Bai   I-457

Yu, Fang   I-241

Zaidi, Ali   II-42
Zhai, Ennan   II-80
Zhang, Hui   II-59
Zhang, Lijun   II-291
Zhang, Xiaoran   II-59

Printed in the United States
By Bookmasters